Anonymous

Aids to Common Worship

services of Holy Scripture from the revised version

Anonymous

Aids to Common Worship
services of Holy Scripture from the revised version

ISBN/EAN: 9783337285524

Printed in Europe, USA, Canada, Australia, Japan

Cover: Foto ©Lupo / pixelio.de

More available books at **www.hansebooks.com**

Aids to Common Worship

Services of Holy Scripture

FROM THE REVISED VERSION

IN THE READINGS AND RENDERINGS PREFERRED
BY THE AMERICAN REVISERS

The Century Co.
New York

THE DE VINNE PRESS.

✢ PREFACE ✢

THERE is a rising call for aids in public Divine Service beyond those supplied by Hymn-books — those liturgies only of song. The Hymn-books used in all Churches, even in those that oppose stated forms of prayer, are really Prayer-books, since many favorite hymns are prayers. Indeed, these books show signs of a somewhat "advanced ritual"; for the forms of prayer which they furnish are not in plain and simple speech, but are highly artificial with meter and elaborate with rhyme, and are artistically wreathed with a fourfold chain of harmony. We all are praying out of a book; we are even singing our prayers.

In a multitude of congregations the reasonable demand has arisen that, since aids in one department of Public Service may, with universal approval, go to this length, such aids should also take on some breadth, supplying needs now evident in other departments. With an attempt at some such completeness, and for the sake of unity of plan, the aids which this Book offers are arranged as an organic system; yet any congregation may easily select and use only such materials as are edifying, while giving the system more or less regard or none at all.

THE FORMS LARGELY SCRIPTURAL

No attempt has been made at compilation on the broad field of Liturgies, ancient or modern, since several books of distinguished merit offer on that field a supply adequate for pulpit use. For the most part, the plan of the work set the humble but pleasant task of seeking out and systematically assigning, on a monthly and a yearly calendar, portions of Holy Scripture for the various uses of worship and instruction. Of the more than two thousand three hundred portions, above four hundred are given in full, and the remainder by reference to the Bible. A few usages, traditional from ages almost apostolic, have been added, on the principle that the heritage from the whole past of Christ's Church is neither to be refused in an attempted independence nor abused in a servile imitation, but *used* according to our own liberty in Christ Jesus, in such manner and extent as meet the wants of this new day.

THREE CHARACTERISTICS: SCRIPTURAL, CONGREGATIONAL, WORSHIPFUL

Three cardinal purposes may be said to have shaped this compilation: To gather and assign on a yearly scheme a reasonably full and balanced presentation of those portions of *Holy Scripture* most fitted for public worship and instruction: To bring *all the congregation*, young and old, into large and active participation — a common worship: To provide in every Service the *direct offering up of praise and prayer* to the living God, who in Christ makes Himself known to us as the Father and the Son and the Spirit.

THE CALENDAR: AN ANNUAL GOSPEL HISTORY

In any large presentation of the Bible, some method is requisite. Since God in His progressive revelation in the Scriptures saw fit to adopt the historical method, that method is certainly open to our Christian liberty, and seems commended to our Christian wisdom in preference to any method dictated by some doctrinal system that men have devised. To reproduce in grand outline the simple story of the Son of God — is not this, of all methods, the most natural to faith and love, the most impressive on feeling and on memory? Is it not, as against unbelief, the method most strongly assertive of the Gospel as being not wise opinion or logical argument, but historical fact? For the Gospel fundamentally is the record of the manifestation of God in the flesh: all the great doctrines of grace move in a procession of actual historic events. When this line of facts is set forth in that observance of *anniversaries* which is natural to man, some sort of Christian calendar for the year is the result. The Calendar here provided commemorates no apostle or saint, and further limits itself to the few cardinal facts in the work of our Lord as the Victim and the Victor Savior; adding, however, an observance of the New Year, and a general Fast Day and Thanksgiving Day.

USE OF THE REVISED VERSION

The selections of Holy Scripture are from the Revised Version, with the readings and renderings preferred by the American Committee of Revision as published by the English Revisers. The question of Versions, however, has here no practical reference to the New Testament; since with few exceptions the selections printed in full are from the Old Testament — those from the New being shown mostly by reference. Whatever may be the reserve in the general Christian verdict in this country regarding the New Testament Revision, it is undeniable that the Old Testament gains in the Revision a distinct approach to the Word as originally given from the Holy Spirit. To reject such gain might make void a chief claim of this book, since its fundamental principle pledges it against holding "the traditions of men" above the Word for which we all proclaim our reverence.

As to the further question of adopting the recorded preferences of the *American Committee*, it was, and it is, occasion of regret that such a sweeping innovation should be added to the number of which this work may already be accused. Involving change in a familiar rendering of the Divine Name in the Old Testament, it might seem to pass the limits set by modesty and reverence. Yet hesitancy was precluded, first of all, by the imperative principle above referred to; for in the Old Testament, evidently, the renderings of the American Committee are less bound by mere tradition, especially as concerns the Divine Name; moreover, the avoidance by the American Revisers of expressions needlessly obscure or offensive to modern ears, renders larger portions of the Word available for a public use.

Wherever in the Hebrew text the Divine *Name* "Jehovah," in its Hebrew form, occurs, the Name, Jehovah, is here given instead of "the LORD" and "GOD" of the English Versions — a change which nothing but custom will reconcile us to, but which brings us nearer the inspired utterance in the Old Testament. For the Hebrew word for "Jehovah" is, like "Jesus," a proper Name; and no more than "Jesus" is it to be changed *by us* to Lord or God: it was the Name chosen and expressly revealed by God Himself, who also declared it to be His "Memorial Name" by which He would be known "unto all generations" [Ex, iii, 15; vi, 2, 3]. In a few passages the English Revision preserves this great Name; but in about five thousand passages it follows the English Version of 1611 in setting aside God's own revealed, personal, covenant Name for a word ("LORD") which is not a Name, and which is used as the translation of not less than ten other Hebrew words; of which ten words rendered "Lord," four are applied to God, and the others to men, heathen idols, etc. Then in about three hundred other passages the English Revision changes the same proper name "Jehovah" into yet another word, the general term "GOD," which also is used as the translation of several other Hebrew words. All this confusion is avoided when we accept the Divine Name which Divine Inspiration chose to reveal. Also, it may be no slight gain when we thus permit to the Old Covenant its individuality, its proper flavor distinct from the New.

PREFACE   V

The compiler has not taken the liberty to vary from the suggestions of the American Committee except in rare instances. Beside a few slight adaptations for the introductory sentences, there are probably scarcely a dozen noticeable variations. To these must be added the Lord's Prayer, whose form in the Revised Version is so unfamiliar that the time for change from the words so precious by long devotional use seems not quite yet come — especially as the long-used words are not out of accord with the Revised Version, and are fully in line with all Biblical teachings. However, the word "Lead" (in "Lead us not into temptation"), not showing a clear agreement with New Testament teaching, is here changed to "Bring," as in the Revised Version.

VARIOUS PARTS OF THE SERVICE

The Introductory Sentences are selected from the Scriptures and assigned to each Service, Morning and Evening, as giving the key-note to a worshiping assembly more promptly and surely than the average "Invocation," or than the musical attempt known as the "Opening Piece."

The Responsive Lessons consist of the Psalter in its main portions, and of all extended Psalm-like passages from the Books of the Law and the Prophets, that seemed desirable for public use, — in all, one hundred and thirty-seven Lessons, about one-half from the Psalter. These are assigned to each Service, Morning and Evening, on all Lord's Days, etc., on the yearly Calendar. The attempt at fullness in this presentation of Holy Scripture has given the Book its size, which, however, is below that of the average Books of Hymns merely. The principle of the Hebrew parallelism — the echo-principle — one strophe taking up in repetition, or amplification, or confirmation, or by contrast, the sentiment of the other — has controlled both the selection for Responsive Lessons and the arrangement of the leading and the answering strophes. The antiphonal or responsive mode is not fitting for passages that are not (in the main, at least) antiphonal or echoing, either in verbal structure or in sentiment. Such passages, including the New Testament, with a few specific exceptions, are more impressively rendered by a single voice in calm, continuous flow. What avails it to force an echoing utterance when there is no echo to be uttered? In exceptional cases in which the parallelisms are not facile to modern use, our Christian liberty to vary from them is evident; but since, in the main, they mark out for us the old Scriptural path, it is probably our wisdom to reform our taste to the pattern showed us on the Hebrew temple-mount rather than to conform the Divine pattern to our taste.

The Prayers for the Day may be read at the end of the general prayer, or their use may be merely for suggestions. Indebted to the ancient Collects for their general style, they yet show many changes in material. All are framed after one mode — each prayer usually in three paragraphs, yet all comprised in one sentence. No two prayers begin with the same phrase. All have for nucleus the Scriptural formula of the Father and the Son and the Holy Spirit [Matt. xxviii, 19; II Cor. xiii, 14], while also addressing God as ONE: all specify the Lord Jesus as the Son of God, and offer through Him, as the Savior, their plea; all ascribe to God eternity, supremacy, and glory. Thus each presents in outline the essential and universal faith of the Church of Christ.

THE SONGS OF PRAISE

The Songs and the Music in this book are, with a few exceptions, restricted in range by a single purpose — that in every Service *certain parts* shall consist of *direct praise to God* by the *whole assembly in song*. Beyond this narrow range are many important applications of lyric art and of Church-music; but they are abundantly provided in the Hymn-books now in use.

The Praise-songs are arranged on the principle that *congregational praise* (unlike instruction or exhortation) gains but little help from novelty, and is even hindered or distracted by thoughts or words elaborately new or strange, and moves toward God most easily on paths so often traveled as to be familiar — the habitudes of the soul. The same Introductory Responses, Psalm Chants, and Hymns of Praise (words and music) recur in successive months, soon growing familiar to the congregation. If the Calendar be used, this monthly order is interrupted by similar Praise-songs assigned to the "Signal Days," such as Christmas, etc.; and these also, year by year the same, will gather power by use.

As the Psalm Chants end with *Gloria Patri* — the voices of worship from the Old Covenant merging in the praise of God as manifested in Christ — so in each Service the one metrical Hymn of general *Praise* by the congregation completes its offering with a Doxology to God as the Father and the Son and the Spirit. It was found that, of the usual Doxologies, many are not in the form of direct praise, but rather *calls* to praise; some are preaching rather than worship; some lack clear assertion of the Divine Oneness; some are more metaphysical or arithmetical than is the fashion of Scripture; others are too general; while for some hymns of less usual meters no Doxologies were found. Accordingly, those requisite were composed for this work; they are marked (Dox. added) that the authors of the hymns of which they seem to be a part may not be held chargeable for them. An inspection will show that while they can claim no originality — being, in large part, echoes from other productions — and while their limited scope, causing the same words to recur, combined with their metric and rhymic restrictions, may almost exclude them from consideration as poetry, they yet are in substance *Christian ascriptions;* they do not fail to offer to God, as the Father and the Son and the Spirit, and yet as ONE, the glory of His supremacy, eternity, and grace.

In the metrical Hymns such slight changes in personal pronouns, etc., as might conduce to directness in praise have been made, and are not noted. More serious alterations which in a few cases seemed necessary, are noted.

Some further explanations and suggestions may be found in notes preceding "The Service in the Lord's House," and preceding the "Offices for the Year," etc.

MUSICAL EDITORSHIP

The musical settings in this book were intrusted to WALDO S. PRATT, Associate Professor of Ecclesiastical Music and Hymnology in Hartford Theological Seminary. Professor Pratt's devout sentiment and discriminating taste, with his experience as a teacher of the philosophy and history of Church Music, and as a conductor of singers, have been applied to select and adapt from a wide field the musical settings here presented. Having the highest appreciation of the worshipful uses of music, with a sincere belief in the right and the duty of the Christian congregation at the proper times in every Service to unite all its voices in Divine praise, he has wrought in entire sympathy with the chief aim of this book. The compiler gratefully recognizes the result as giving the musical development most helpful to his own humble attempt in these Aids to Common Worship.

RICHARD GLEASON GREENE.

April 10, 1887.

(Note as to Table of Daily Scripture Lessons.)

IN this Table, pp. viii-xiii, the Bible as a whole, to the extent deemed appropriate for household or public reading, is presented in four series of daily Lessons, which advance together through the year. Each series follows the order of the Books in the Bible, taking no note of "Signal Days," except that special Lessons are assigned to four Days—Dec. 24, 25, 31, Jan. 1. These series may, for convenience, be stated thus:

FIRST SERIES—Law and History;   *Genesis*, through *Esther:*
SECOND "   —Psalm and Prophecy;   *Job*, through *Malachi:*
THIRD "   —Gospel of the Lord Jesus;   *The Four Evangelists:*
FOURTH "   —Apostolic Word;   *Acts, Epistles, Revelation.*

Of the four Lessons for each day, two from the Old Covenant, two from the New, all may be read, or any, at discretion; and a part of any may be omitted. A few of the Lessons are not commended for public reading in full except in the use of the renderings preferred by the American Revisers.

The Table is fitted for extension through two years if desired; one mode being to read, in a year whose date is "odd" (1, 3, etc.), from only the First and Third Series above; and in a year whose date is "even" (2, 4, etc.), from only the Second and Fourth Series; and the two Lessons may be divided between Morning and Evening.

All references to the Bible by chapter and verse are inclusive.

(Note as to the Form of an Ancient Creed.)

The traditional form of the venerable symbol commonly called the "Nicene Creed" (though indeed its origin is not known) has these words in the section that refers to Christ:

"The Only begotten Son of God,
"Begotten of His Father before all worlds,
"God of God, Light of Light, Very God of Very God;
"Begotten, not made;
"Being of one substance with the Father;
"By whom," etc.

There are many churches in which this creed—majestic echo of the common Christian faith from far antiquity—is never heard. Possibly, some such churches may find less repetition, and less remoteness from their usual thought concerning Christ, if for the above quoted phrases there are substituted the following even more ancient words, very words of our Lord and His apostles:

" The Only begotten Son of God,"
(*a*) Glorified with the Father before the world was—
(*b*) The same was the Word that was in the beginning with God, and was God—
(*c*) Through whom, etc.

(*a*) John, xvii, 5.   (*b*) John, i, 1, 2.   (*c*) John, i, 3-10; Col. i, 16; Heb. i, 3.

Contents

	PAGE
PREFACE	iii
NOTES	vii
TABLE OF DAILY SCRIPTURE LESSONS	x
CALENDAR FOR THE YEAR	xvi
TABLE OF OCCURRENCE OF MOVABLE DAYS	xviii
THE SERVICE — Note	xix
ORDER OF THE SERVICE, AS SHORTENED	xx
ORDER OF THE SERVICE	xxi
THE SERVICE IN THE LORD'S HOUSE	xxii—xxviii
THE GENERAL CALL TO PRAISE	xxii
CHRIST'S SUMMARY OF THE LAW	xxii
THE BEATITUDES OF THE GOSPEL	xxiii
AN ANCIENT CREED	xxiv
THE LORD'S PRAYER	xxvi
BENEDICTIONS	xxvii
OFFICES OF WORSHIP AND INSTRUCTION FOR THE YEAR	1—314
Introductory — Sentence and Response	
Scripture Lessons	
Responsive Lesson	
Psalm Chant	
Prayer of the Day	
Hymn of Praise	
MONTHLY SONGS OF PRAISE	315—351
Introductory Responses	
Psalm Chants	
Hymns of Praise	
ASCRIPTIONS AND OTHER SONGS	352—367
No. 1 TE DEUM LAUDAMUS (Chant)	352
TE DEUM LAUDAMUS (Anthem)	354
No. 2 GLORIA IN EXCELSIS DEO (In two Chants)	358
GLORIA IN EXCELSIS DEO (In three Chants — Old)	358
No. 3 GLORIA PATRI	359
No. 4 ALL HOLY	360
No. 5 SANCTUS (Chant)	360
SANCTUS (Anthem)	360
No. 6 BENEDICTUS	361
No. 7 DOXOLOGY OF ISRAEL	362
No. 8 THOU FATHER — (Metrical)	362

CONTENTS ix

	PAGE
No. 9 AGES UNTO AGES — (Metrical)	363
No. 10 GLORY, THANKS — (Metrical)	363
No. 11 BENEDICITE OMNIA	364
No. 12 SONG OF DANIEL	365

VENITE EXULTEMUS DEO 365
CANTATE DOMINO 366
BENEDIC ANIMA MEA 366

[For a list of fifteen other notable Scriptural Songs, occurring in various Services — see at end of ASCRIPTIONS, ETC.] 367

THE CHURCH — Note 368
ACTS AND USAGES IN CHURCH FELLOWSHIP .... 368—406

  ACT OF ORGANIZATION — RECOGNITION OF THE CHURCH FELLOWSHIP ...... 369—372
  RECOGNITION OF NEW MEMBERS ON TRANSFER FROM OTHER CHURCHES ... 373—376
  RECOGNITION OF NEW MEMBERS ON CONFESSION OF CHRIST 376
    — With observance of Christ's Ordinance of Baptism 379

  THE COMMUNION AT THE LORD'S TABLE — with its connected Service ...... 383—400
    AN ANCIENT CREED 385
    ANCIENT LITANY 386
    THE LORD'S PRAYER 388
    OFFERTORY 389
    SPECIAL SCRIPTURE PREFACES 393
    HALLELUJAH OF THE HEAVENLY HOST 395

  MINISTRATION OF THE BAPTISM OF LITTLE CHILDREN .... 401—406

INDEXES .... 407—413
  THE PSALM CHANTS 407
  VARIOUS SCRIPTURE PORTIONS IN MUSIC 407
  COMPOSERS OF CHANTS 408
  COMPOSERS OF MUSIC FOR ANTHEMS, ETC. 410

  METERS 410
  METRICAL TUNES 411
  METRICAL HYMNS 412

Table of Daily Scripture Lessons Through the Year

Jan.	OLD COVENANT Law and Hist'y	OLD COVENANT Psalm and Proph'y	NEW COVENANT Gospel	NEW COVENANT Apostolic Word
1	Gen. i, 1-19	Ecc. iii	Luke, xii, 22-40	Tit. ii, 11-14
2	i, 20-31	Job, i	Matt. i, 18-23	Acts, i, 1-21
3	ii, 1-17	ii	ii, 1-12	i, 12-26
4	ii, 18-25; iii, 1-8	iii, 1-9, 13-26	ii, 13-23	ii, 1-13
5	iii, 8-24	iv	iii, 1-10	ii, 14-21
6	iv, 3-15	v	iii, 11-17	ii, 22-36
7	iv, 16-26; v, 1-5	vi	iv, 1-11	ii, 37-47
8	vi, 5-22	vii	iv, 12-17	iii, 1-10
9	vii, 1-12	viii	iv, 18-25	iii, 11-18
10	vii, 13-24	ix	v, 1-12	iii, 19-26
11	viii, 1-14	x	v, 13-20	iv, 1-12
12	viii, 15-22; ix, 1-7	xi	v, 21-26	iv, 13-22
13	ix, 8-19	xii	v, 27-32	iv, 23-31
14	xi, 1-9, 27-32	xiii	v, 33-42	iv, 32-37
15	xii, 1-10	xiv	v, 43-48; vi, 1-4	v, 1-11
16	xiii	xv	vi, 5-15	v, 12-16
17	xiv	xvi, xvii	vi, 16-23	v, 17-32
18	xv, 1-18	xviii	vi, 24-34	v, 33-42
19	xvii, 1-9, 15-22	xix	vii, 1-12	vi, 1-8
20	xviii, 17-33	xx, 1-6, 8-29	vii, 13-20	vi, 8-15
21	xix, 12-29	xxi	vii, 21-29	vii, 1-14
22	xxi, 1-19	xxii	viii, 1-13	vii, 15-34
23	xxiii, 1-19	xxiii	viii, 14-22	vii, 35-43
24	xxiv, 1-28	xxiv	viii, 23-34	vii, 44-53
25	xxiv, 29-49	xxv, xxvi	ix, 1-8	vii, 54-60; viii, 1-4
26	xxiv, 50-67	xxvii	ix, 9-17	viii, 5-13
27	xxvii, 30-45	xxviii	ix, 18-26	viii, 14-25
28	xxvii, 46; xxviii, 1-9	xxix	ix, 27-38; x, 1	viii, 26-40
29	xxviii, 10-22	xxx	x, 1-15	ix, 1-9
30	xxix, 1-14	xxxi	x, 16-23	ix, 8-13
31	—	xxxii	—	ix, 19-31

Feb.	OLD COVENANT Law and Hist'y	OLD COVENANT Psalm and Prophy	NEW COVENANT Gospel	NEW COVENANT Apostolic Word
1	Gen. xxxii, 1-21	Job, xxxiii	Matt. x, 24-33	Acts, ix, 32-43
2	xxxii, 22-32	xxxiv	x, 34-42	x, 1-16
3	xxxiii, 1-17	xxxv, xxxvi, 1-19	xi, 1-10	x, 17-33
4	xxxv, 1-15	xxxvi, 20-33; xxxvii	xi, 11-19	x, 34-48
5	xxxvii, 1-17	xxxvii, 1-38	xi, 20-24	xi, 1-18
6	xxxvii, 18-36	xxxviii, 39-41; xxxix	xi, 25-30	xi, 19-30
7	xli, 14-37	xl	xii, 1-8	xii, 1-19
8	xli, 38-57	xli	xii, 9-21	xii, 20-25; xiii, 1-4
9	xlii, 1-28	xlii	xii, 22-30	xiii, 4-13
10	xlii, 29-38	Ps. i, ii, iii	xii, 31-37	xiii, 13-26
11	xliii, 1-14	iv, v	xii, 38-45	xiii, 27-37
12	xliii, 15-34	vi, vii	xii, 46-50	xiii, 38-52
13	xliv, 1-17	viii, ix	xiii, 1-9	xiv, 1-7
14	xliv, 16-34	x, xi	xiii, 10-17	xiv, 8-18
15	xlv, 1-15	xii, xiii, xiv, xv	xiii, 18-23	xiv, 19-28
16	xlv, 16-28	xvi, xvii	xiii, 24-30	xv, 1-11
17	xlvi, 1-7, 26-34	xviii	xiii, 31-35	xv, 12-21
18	xlvii, 1-12	xix, xx, xxi	xiii, 36-43	xv, 22-35
19	{xlvii, 28-31; xlviii, 1-7}	xxiii	xiii, 44-58	xv, 36-41; xvi, 1-5
20	xlviii, 8-22	xxiii, xxiv, xv	xiii, 53-58	xvi, 6-15
21	{xlix, 8-10, 22-26, 29-33}	xxvi, xxvii	xiv, 1-12	xvi, 16-24
22	l, 1-13	xxviii, xxix, xxx	xiv, 13-21	xvi, 25-40
23	l, 14-26	xxxi	xiv, 22-33	xvii, 1-9
24	Ex. i, 6-14, 22; ii, 1-10	xxxii, xxxiii	xiv, 34-36; xv, 1-9	xvii, 10-15
25	ii, 11-22	xxxiv	xv, 1, 2, 10-20	xvii, 16-34
26	ii, 23-25; iii, 1-12	xxxv	xv, 21-28	xviii, 1-11
27	iii, 13-22; iv, 1-9	xxxvi	xv, 29-39	xviii, 12-23
28	iv, 10-23	xxxvii	xvi, 1-12	{xviii, 24-28; xix, 1-7}
29	iv, 27-31; v, 1-13	xxxix, xl	xvi, 13-20	xix, 8-22

Table of Daily Scripture Lessons Through the Year

Mar.	OLD COVENANT Law and Hist'y	OLD COVENANT Psalm and Proph'y	NEW COVENANT Gospel	NEW COVENANT Apostolic Word
1	Ex. v, 14-23; vi, 1	Ps. xii, xiii	Matt. xvi, 21-28	Acts. xix, 23-41
2	vi, 2-13	xliii, xliv	xvii, 1-8	xx, 1-16
3	vi, 28-30; vii, 1-13	xiv, xlvi, xlvii	xvii, 9-20	xx, 17-27
4	vii, 14-25	xlviii, xlix	xvii, 22-27	xx, 28-38
5	viii, 1-15	l	xviii, 1-9	xxi, 1-16
6	viii, 16-32	li	xviii, 10-14	xxi, 17-26
7	ix, 1-17	lii, liii, liv	xviii, 15-20	xxi, 27-40; xxii, 1
8	ix, 13-35	lv	xviii, 21-35	xxii, 2-16
9	x, 1-11	lvi, lvii	xix, 1-9	xxii, 17-30
10	x, 12-29	lviii, lix	xix, 13-24	xxiii, 1-11
11	xi	lx, lxi	xix, 27-30	xxiii, 12-30
12	xii, 1-20	lxii, lxiii	xix, 30; xx, 1-16	xxiii, 31-35; xxiv, 1-9
13	xii, 21-28	lxiv, lxv	xx, 17-28	xxiv, 10-27
14	xii, 29-42	lxvi, lxvii	xx, 29-34	xxv, 1-5, 6-12
15	xiii, 1-10, 17-22	lxviii	xxi, 1-11	xxv, 13-27
16	xiv, 1-14	lxix	xxi, 12-17	xxvi, 1-19
17	xiv, 15-31	lxx, lxxi	xxi, 17-22	xxvi, 19-32
18	xv, 1-21	lxxii	xxi, 23-32	xxvii, 1-26
19	xv, 22-26; xvi, 1-8	lxxiii	xxi, 33-46	xxvii, 27-44
20	xvi, 9-27	lxxiv	xxii, 1-14	xxviii, 1-15
21	xvi, 23-35	lxxvi, lxxv	xxii, 15-22	xxviii, 16-31
22	xvii	lxxviii, 1-39	xxii, 23-33	Rom. i, 1-7
23	xviii, 1-12	lxxviii, 40-72	xxii, 31-46	i, 8-15
24	xviii, 13-27	lxxix, lxxx	xxiii, 1-12	i, 16-25, 28-32
25	xix, 1-14	lxxxi, lxxxii	xxiii, 13-22	ii, 1-16
26	xix, 16-25	lxxxiii, lxxxiv	xxiii, 23-28	ii, 17-29
27	xx, 1-21	lxxxv, lxxxvi	xxiii, 29-39; xxiv, 1-14	iii, 1-18
28	xxiii, 20-27; xxiii, 1-13	lxxxvii, lxxxviii	xxiv, 15-28	iii, 19-31
29	xxiii, 20-33	lxxxix	xxiv, 29-42	iv, 1-13
30	xxiv	xc, xci	xxiv, 14-30	iv, 13-25
31	xxv, 1-2	xcii, xciii		v, 1-11

Apr.	OLD COVENANT Law and Hist'y	OLD COVENANT Psalm and Proph'y	NEW COVENANT Gospel	NEW COVENANT Apostolic Word
1	Ex. xxvi, 1-13	Ps. xciv, xcv	Matt. xxv, 1-13	Rom. v, 12-21
2	xxxii, 1-14	xcvi, xcvii, xcviii	xxv, 1-13	vi, 1-14
3	xxxiii, 15-28 (or -35)	xcix, c, ci	xxvi, 14-25	vi, 15-23
4	xxxiii, 1-11	cii	xxvi, 26-35	vii, 1-6
5	xxxiii, 12-23	ciii	xxvi, 36-46	vii, 7-25
6	xxxiv, 1-14, 27-35	civ	xxvi, 47-56	viii, 1-11
7	{xxxv, 30-35; xxxvi, 1-7}	cv	xxvi, 57-68	viii, 12-17
8	xl, 17-38	cvi	xxvi, 69-75	viii, 18-25
9	Lev. xvi, 5-22	cvii	xxvii, 1-10	viii, 26-30
10	xix, 1-19	cviii, cix	xxvii, 11-26	viii, 31-39
11	xix, 30-37; xx, 6-8	cx, cxi, cxii	xxvii, 27-44	ix, 1-8
12	xxv, 1-24	cxiii, cxiv, cxv	xxvii, 45-56	ix, 14-24
13	xxv, 25-26, 35-43	cxvi, cxvii	xxvii, 57-66	ix, 25-33; x, 1-4
14	xxvi, 1-13	cxviii	xxviii, 1-15	x, 1-13
15	xxvi, 14-26	cxix, 1-40	xxviii, 16-20	x, 14-21
16	xxvi, 27-46	cxix, 41-80	Mk. i, 1-13	xi, 1-12
17	Num. x, 28-36	cxix, 81-128	i, 14-20	xi, 13-24
18	xi, 21-35	cxix, 129-176	i, 21-28	xi, 25-36
19	xii, 1-13	cxx-cxxiii	i, 29-39	xii, 1-9
20	xiii, 17-33	cxxiv-cxxviii	i, 40-45	xii, 10-21
21	xiv, 1-25	cxxix-cxxxii	ii, 1-12	xiii, 1-7
22	xiv, 26-45	cxxxiii-cxxxv	ii, 13-28	xiii, 8-14
23	xvi, 1-19	cxxxvi-cxxxviii	ii, 23-28; iii, 1-6	xiv, 1-11
24	xvi, 20-35	cxxxix, cxl	iii, 7-19	xiv, 12-23; xv, 1-3
25	xvi, 41-50	cxli-cxliii	iii, 20-30	xv, 4-13
26	xx, 1-13	cxliv, cxlv	iii, 31-35	xv, 14-21
27	xx, 14-29	cxlvi, cxlvii	iv, 1-9	xv, 22-33
28	xxi, 1-9	cxlviii-cl	iv, 10-20	xvi, 1-16
29	xxiii, 1-20	Prov. i	iv, 21-25	xvi, 17-27
30	xxiii, 21-35	ii	iv, 26-34	1 Cor. i, 1-9

Table of Daily Scripture Lessons Through the Year

May	OLD COVENANT Law and Hist'y	OLD COVENANT Psalm and Proph'y	NEW COVENANT Gospel	NEW COVENANT Apostolic Word
1	Num. xvii, 16-41; xxiii, 1-10	Prov. iii	Mk. iv, 35-41	1 Cor. i, 10-17
2	xviii, 11-26	iv	v, 1-20	i, 18-25
3	xxiii, 27-30; xxiv, 1-9	vi, 1-7	v, 21-34	i, 26-31
4	xxiv, 10-25	viii	v, 35-43	ii, 1-5
5	xxvii, 12-23	ix	vi, 1-6	iii, 6-16
6	xxxv, 19-34	x	vi, 7-13	iii, 1-10
7	Deut. i, 19-45	xi	vi, 14-29	iii, 11-17; iv, 1-5
8	iii, 18-29	xii	vi, 30-44	iv, 6-13
9	iv, 1-40	xiii	vi, 45-52	iv, 14-21
10	iv, 1-24	xiv	vi, 53-56	v, 3-13
11	iv, 25-40	xv	vii, 1-13	v, 1-8, 18-20
12	v, 1-33	xvi	vii, 5, 14-30	vi, 1-8, 18-20
13	vi, 1-15	xvii	vii, 24-30	vii, 16-24
14	vi, 16-25	xviii	vii, 31-37	viii
15	viii, 1-11	xix	viii, 1-10	ix, 1-12
16	viii, 12-26	xx	viii, 11-21	ix, 13-18
17	viii	xxi	viii, 22-26	ix, 19-27
18	ix, 1-20	xxii	viii, 27-33	x, 1-13
19	x, 12-22	xxiii	viii, 31-ix, 1; ix, 1	x, 14-22
20	xi, 1-12	xxiv	ix, 2-13	x, 23-33; xi, 1
21	xi, 13-28	xxv	ix, 14-29	xi, 3-11, 12, 16-22
22	xii, 1-28	xxvi	ix, 30-37	xi, 23-34
23	xii, 1-12	Ecc. ii, 1-11	ix, 38-50	xii, 1-12
24	xv, 20-31; xiii, 1-4	xxviii	x, 1-12	xiii
25	xv, 7-25	xxix	x, 13-16	xiv, 1-12
26	xvii, 14-20	xxx	x, 17-23	xiv, 13-25
27	xviii, 9-20	xxxi	x, 23-31	xiv, 26-40
28	xix, 1-15	Ecc. iii, 1-11	x, 32-45	Lk. i, 1-17 (or 1-23)
29	xx, 1-17	iii, 12-26	x, 46-52	i, 24-55
30	xxiv, 10-22	iv, 1-7	xi, 1-11	i, 39-66
31	xxviii, 1-14	v, 8-20; vi	xi, 12-14, 19-25	i, 67-80

June	OLD COVENANT Law and Hist'y	OLD COVENANT Psalm and Proph'y	NEW COVENANT Gospel	NEW COVENANT Apostolic Word
1	Deut. xxviii, 15-25	Ecc. vii, 1-18	Mk. xi, 15-18	1 Cor. xv, 35-49
2	xxviii, 45-52	viii, 1-15	xi, 27-33	xv, 50-58
3	xxviii, 59-68	viii, 16, 17; ix, 1-10	xii, 1-12	xvi, 1-9
4	xxix, 10-21	{ix, 17, 18; x, 1-18; xi, 1-8}	xii, 13-17	xvi, 10-24
5	xxx, 15-29	xi, 9, 10; xii	xii, 18-27	II Cor. i, 1-11
6	xxx, 11-20	i, 1-20	xii, 28-34	i, 12-22
7	xxx, 11-20	i, 21-31; ii, 1-9	xii, 35-44	i, 23, 24; ii, 1-11
8	xxxi, 1-8	ii, 10-22; iii, 1-15	xiii, 1-13	ii, 12-17
9	xxxi, 1-15	iv, 5, 6; v, 1-17	xiii, 14-23	iii, 1-11
10	xxxi, 16-28	v, 18-30	xiii, 24-31	iii, 12-18
11	xxxi, 29-43	vi; vii, 1-9	xiii, 32-37	iv, 1-6
12	{xxxii, 45-52; xxxiii, 1-5}	viii, 9-22; ix, 1-7	xiv, 1-11	iv, 7-15
13	xxxiii, 10-29; 26-29	ix, 8-21; x, 1-4	xiv, 12-26	v, 1-13
14	xxxiv	x, 5-27	xiv, 16-21	vi, 1-10
15	Josh. i, 1-9	x, 33, 34; xi, 1-10	xiv, 22-31	vi, 11-18; vii, 1
16	ii, 10-24	ii, 11-16; iii	xiv, 32-42	vii, 2-16
17	iii, 5-17	{xiii, 1-13, 17-22; xiv, 1, 2}	xiv, 43-50	viii, 1-9
18	v, 13-15; vi, 1-7	xiv, 3-27, 3, 2	xiv, 53-65	viii, 9-15
19	vi, 12-20	xvii, 7-14; xviii, 1-3	xiv, 66-72	viii, 16-24
20	vii, 1-13	xix, 1-12	xv, 1-15	ix, 1-6
21	viii, 1-9	xxiv, 1-20	xv, 15-22	ix, 7-15
22	viii, 10-29	xxiv, 21-23; xxv, 1-9	xv, 22-32	x, 1-6
23	ix, 3-27	xxvi, 1-15, 19-21	xv, 33-41	x, 7-18
24	x, 1-14	xxviii, 5-22	xv, 42-47	xi, 1-15
25	xi, 1-20	xxix, 1-12	xvi, 1-8	xi, 16-33
26	xxiii	xxix, 13-24	xvi, 9-20	xii, 1-10
27	xxiv, 1-25	xxx, 1-18	Lk. i, 1-17 (or 1-23)	xii, 11-21
28	xxiv, 25-33	xxx, 19-33	i, 46-55	xiii
29	Judg. ii, 1-10	xxxii; xxxiii, 1-8	i, 59-66	Gal. i, 1-10
30	ii, 11-23	{xxxiii, 13-20; xxxiii, 1-6, 15-24}	i, 67-80	i, 11-24

Table of Daily Scripture Lessons Through the Year

July

July	OLD COVENANT Law and Hist'y	Psalm and Proph'y	NEW COVENANT Gospel	Apostolic Word
1	Judg. iii, 5-14	Is. xxxiv	Lk. ii, 25-39	Gal. ii, 1-10
2	iv, 1-16	xxxv	ii, 40-52	ii, 11-21
3	v, 1-12	xxxviii, 9-21	iii, 1-6, 13-17	iii, 1-14
4	v, 13-31 (pt.)	xl, 1-17	iii, 7-14, 18-22	iii, 15-22
5	vi, 1-10	xl, 18-31; xli, 1-4	iv, 1-13	iii, 23-29
6	vi, 11-24	xlii, 8-29	iv, 14-21	iv, 8-20
7	vi, 25-40	xliii, 1-17	iv, 22-31	iv, 21-31
8	vii, 1-8	xliii, 18-25; xliii, 1-13	iv, 31-37	v, 1-12
9	ix, 9-35	xliii, 14-28; xliv, 1-5	iv, 38-44	v, 13-26
10	viii, 1-17	xliv, 6-20	v, 1-11	vi, 1-10
11	x, 1-16	xliv, 21-28; xlv, 1-9	v, 12-16	vi, 11-18
12	xi, 12-28	xlv, 11-25	v, 17-26	Eph. i, 1-14
13	xii, 1-6	xlvi, 11-13; xlviii, 4-13	v, 27-39	i, 15-23
14	xv, 9-20	xlviii	vi, 1-11	ii, 1-10
15	xv, 29-31		vi, 12-19	ii, 11-22
16	Ruth, i, 1-9, 14-22	xlix, 14-26	vi, 20-26	iii, 1-13
17	ii	l	vi, 27-38	iii, 14-21
18	I Sam. ii, 1-11	li, 1-16	vi, 39-49	iv, 1-7
19	ii, 27-35	li, 17-23; lii, 1-12	vii, 1-10	iv, 7-16
20	iii	liii, 13-15; liii	vii, 11-17	iv, 17-24
21	iv, 1-18	liv, 2-17	vii, 18-23	iv, 25-32
22	v	lv	vii, 24-35	v, 1-14
23	vii, 3-17	lvi; lvii, 1, 2, 15-21	vii, 36-50	v, 15-33
24	viii	lviii	viii, 1-8	vi, 1-9
25	ix, 14-27	lix	viii, 9-15	vi, 10-24
26	ix, 25-27; x, 1-9	lx	viii, 16-21	Phil. i, 1-11
27	x, 17-27	lxi	viii, 22-25	i, 12-21
28	xii	lxii; lxiii, 1-6	viii, 26-39	i, 21-30
29	xiii	lxiii, 7-19; lxiv	viii, 40-48	ii, 1-11
30	xiii, 1-14	lxv, 7-16	viii, 49-56	ii, 12-18
31	xiv, 1-16	lxv, 17-25; lxvi, 1-4	ix, 1-9	ii, 19-30

August

Aug.	OLD COVENANT Law and Hist'y	Psalm and Proph'y	NEW COVENANT Gospel	Apostolic Word
1	I Sam. xv, 10-31	Jer. i, 6-19	Lk. ix, 10-17	Phil. iii, 1-12
2	xvi, 1-13	ii, 1-13	ix, 18-27	iii, 12-16
3	xvi, 1-16	ii, 1-19, 28-35	ix, 28-36	iii, 17-21; iv, 1
4	xvii, 17-38	iii, 12-25	ix, 37-43	iv, 2-9
5	xvii, 39-54	iv, 1-18, 20-26	ix, 43-49	iv, 10-23
6	xvii, 55-58; xviii, 1-9	v, 1-6, 9-31	ix, 51-62	Col. i, 1-8
7	xix, 1-12	vi, 1-15	x, 1-9	i, 9-20
8	xx, 12-23	vii, 1-28	x, 1, 2, 10-26	i, 21-29
9	xx, 24-34	viii, 4-22	x, 17-24	ii, 1-7
10	xxiii, 19-29	ix, 1-16	x, 25-37	ii, 8-15
11	xxiv, 1-22	ix, 17-26; x, 1-10	x, 38-42	ii, 16-23
12	xxvi	x, 11-25; xi, 1-8	xi, 1-13	iii, 1-11
13	xxviii, 3-20	xii	xi, 14-26	iii, 12-25; iv, 1
14	xxxi, 1-24	xiii, 15-25	xi, 29-36	iv, 2-9
15	I Chr. x, 1-14	xiv	xi, 37-44	iv, 10-18
16	II Sam. i, 1-16	xv, 1-6, 10-21	xi, 45-54	I Thess. i
17	i, 17-27; ii, 1-6	xvii, 1-17	xii, 1-12	ii, 1-12
18	iii, 17-39	xvi, 19-27; xviii, 1-12	xii, 13-21	ii, 13-20
19	iv, 5-12	xix, 14, 15; xx, 1-13	xii, 22-34	iii, 1-13
20	v, 1-12	xxi	xii, 35-48	iii, 14-18
21	vi, 17-25	xxiii, 1-19	xii, 41-48	iv, 1-8
22	vi, 1-18	xxiii, 1-15	xiii, 1-9	iv, 9-18
23	I Chr. xvii, 1-15	xxiii, 16-32	xiii, 10-17	v, 1-11
24	xvii, 16-27	xxv, 1-14	xiii, 18-22	v, 12-28
25	I Sam. viii, 1-15	xxvi, 1-15	xiii, 23-30	II Thess. i
26	ix, 1-13	xxvii, 1-17	xiii, 31-35	ii, 1-12
27	x, 6-19	xxviii	xiv, 1-6	ii, 13-17; iii, 1-5
28	xi, 14-27	xix, 4-14	xiv, 7-14	iii, 6-18
29	xii, 1-14	xxx, 8-24	xiv, 15-24	I Tim. i, 1-8
30	xiii, 15-25	xxxi, 1-17	xv, 1-10	ii, 1-7
31	xv, 1-12	xxxi, 23-37	xv, 11-24	iii, 1-7

Table of Daily Scripture Lessons Through the Year

Sep.	OLD COVENANT Law and Hist'y	OLD COVENANT Psalm and Proph'y	NEW COVENANT Gospel	NEW COVENANT Apostolic Word
1	II Sam. xv, 13-30	Jer. xxvii, 13-17	Lk. xv, 25-32	I Tim. iii, 8-16
2	xvi, 5-14	xxiii, 28-44	xvi, 1-13	iv, 1-16
3	xviii, 1-8	xxxiii, 1-13	xvi, 17-28	v, 1-8
4	xviii, 19-33	xxxiii, 14-26	xvi, 19-31	v, 17-25
5	xix, 1-15	xxxiv, 8-17	xvii, 1-10	vi, 1-10
6	xix, 16-23	xxv	xvii, 11-19	vi, 11-16
7	xx, 13-22	xxxv, 1-26	xvii, 20-37	vi, 17-21
8	xxi, 15-22	{xxxvi, 7-9; xxxvii, 1-10}	xviii, 1-8	II Tim. i, 1-8
9	xxiii, 1-17	xxxvii, 11-29	xviii, 9-17	i, 8-18
10	II Chr. xxi, 16-27	xxxviii, 1-13	xviii, 18-30	ii, 1-13
11	xxii, 7-16	xxxix	xviii, 31-43	iii, 1-12
12	xxviii, 1-10	xliii	xix, 1-10	iii, 12-17
13	xxix, 1-9	xliv, 1-11, 15-28	xix, 11-27	iv, 1-8
14	xxix, 9-35	xlv; xlvi, 1-12, 27, 28	xix, 28-40	iv, 9-22
15	I K. iii, 4-15	l, 1-20	xix, 41-48	Tit. i, 1-16
16	iv, 7-34	l, 21-40	xx, 1-8	ii, 1-10
17	II Chr. i, 14-17; ii, 1-6	li, 1-13, 24-33	xx, 9-19	iii
18	I K. viii, 1-11	li, 47-66	xx, 19-26	Philemon
19	viii, 12-21	Lam. i, 1-7, 12-29	xx, 27-40	Heb. i
20	viii, 22-34	ii, 1-9, 13-19	xx, 41-47; xxi, 1-4	ii
21	II Chr. vi, 26-33	iii, 1-36	xxi, 5-19	iii
22	vi, 34-42; vii, 1-3	iii, 37-66	xxi, 20-28	iv, 1-10
23	I K. viii, 54-63	iv, 11-20; v	xxi, 29-38	iv, 11-16
24	II Chr. vii, 11-22	Ezki. i, 1-5, 11-28	xxii, 1-6	v
25	I K. x, 1-21	ii; iii, 4-15	xxii, 7-14	vi, 1-12
26	xi, 26-40	iii, 16-27	xxii, 11-23	vi, 13-20
27	xii, 1-20	v, 5-17; vi, 1-8	xxii, 24-34	vii, 13-20
28	xii, 25-33; xiii, 1-10	vii	xxii, 35-46	vii, 1-10
29	xiv, 1-18	viii	xxii, 47-53	vii, 11-25
30	II Chr. xii, 1-9	ix; x, 1-8	xxii, 54-62	vii, 26-28; viii, 1-6

Oct.	OLD COVENANT Law and Hist'y	OLD COVENANT Psalm and Proph'y	NEW COVENANT Gospel	NEW COVENANT Apostolic Word
1	II Chr. xiv, 1-13	Ezkl. xi, 5-25	Lk. xxii, 63-71	Heb. viii, 7-13
2	xv, 1-15	xii, 21-28; xiii, 1-16	xxiii, 1-12	ix, 1-10
3	xvi, 1-10	xiv, 1-8, 12-23	xxiii, 13-24	ix, 11-22
4	xviii, 3-13	xvii	xxiii, 24-38	ix, 23-28
5	I K. xvii, 1-6	xviii, 14-32	xxiii, 39-48	x, 1-10
6	xvii, 7-16	xix	xxiii, 49-56	x, 11-25
7	xvii, 17-24	xx, 1-25	xxiv, 1-12	x, 26-31
8	xviii, 17-29	xx, 33-49	xxiv, 13-35	x, 32-39
9	xviii, 30-46	{xxi, 1-7, 24-27; xxii, 1-8}	xxiv, 33-43	xi, 1-10
10	xix, 1-8	xxii, 17-31	xxiv, 44-53	xi, 13-22
11	xix, 9-21	xxvi	Jn. i, 1-18	xii, 1-13
12	xx, 1-12	xxvii, 1-11, 23-36	i, 19-28	xii, 14-29
13	xx, 23-33	xxviii, 1-19, 25, 26	i, 29-34	xiii, 1-13
14	xx, 35-43	xxix, 1-16	i, 35-42	Jas. i, 1-11
15	xxi, 1-16	{xxix, 17-21; xxx, 1-3}	i, 43-51	i, 12-18
16	xxi, 17-29	xxxi	ii, 1-12	i, 19-27
17	xxii, 1-16	{II Chr. xviii, 28; 34; xix, 1-7}	ii, 13-25	ii, 1-13
18	xxii, 1-13	xxxiii, 1-20	iii, 1-13	ii, 14-26
19	II K. i, 1-17	xxxiii, 21-33	iii, 14-21	iii, 1-12
20	ii, 1-15	xxxiv, 1-16, 22-31	iii, 22-36	iii, 13-18
21	iii, 5-24	xxxv	iv, 1-6	iv, 1-6
22	iv, 1-10	xxxvi, 1-15	iv, 7-8	iv, 7-17
23	iv, 18-37	xxxvi, 18-38	iv, 39-45	iv, 7-17
24	v, 1-9	xxxvii, 1-14	iv, 46-54	v, 1-11
25	v, 10-19	xxxviii	v, 1-9	v, 12-20
26	v, 1-19	{xxxix, 1-10, 17-29}	v, 14-23	I Pet. i, 1-12
27	v, 20-27; vi, 1-7	xlvii, 1-7	v, 30-47	i, 13-25
28	vi, 1-23	Dan. i	vi, 1-10	ii, 1-10
29	vii, 3-20	ii, 1-24	vi, 1-15	ii, 11-17
30	viii, 7-15	ii, 25-49	vi, 15-21	ii, 18-25

Table of Daily Scripture Lessons Through the Year

Nov.	OLD COVENANT Law and Hist'y	Psalm and Proph'y	NEW COVENANT Gospel	Apostolic Word
1	II K. ix, 1-26	Dan. iii	Jn. vi, 22-29	I Pet. iii, 1-7
2	ix, 17-8	iv, 1-18	vi, 28-40	iii, 8-16
3	ix, 30-37	iv, 19-37	vi, 41-51	iii, 17-22
4	x, 15-29	v	vi, 51-66	iv, 1-11
5	II Chr. xxiv, 1-14	vi	vi, 60-71	iv, 12-19
6	xxiv, 15-25	vii	vii, 1-13	v
7	xxv, 1-11	viii	vii, 14-24	II Pet. i, 1-11
8	II K. xiii, 14-25	ix	vii, 25-36	i, 12-21
9	xiii, 6-23	x; xl, 1	vii, 37-44	ii, 1-9
10	xvii, 24-41	xi, 1-19	vii, 45-52	ii, 9-22
11	II Chr. xxvi, 13-21	xi, 20-39	vii, 53; viii, 1-11	iii, 1-9
12	xxviii, 1-21	xi, 40-45; xii	viii, 12-20	iii, 10-18
13	xxix, 1-21	Hos. ii, 15-23; iv, 1-9	viii, 21-30	I Jn. i
14	xxx, 1-12	v, 8-15; vi, 1-7	viii, 30-47	ii, 1-11
15	xxx, 13-27	xi, 1-9	viii, 48-59	ii, 12-20
16	xxxi, 1-8	xi, 12; xii, 1-10	ix, 1-12	ii, 21-29
17	II K. xviii, 17-22, 28-37; xix, 1	xiii, 1-12, 14; xiv	ix, 13-25	iii, 1-12
18	xix, 1-19	Joel, i, 14-20; ii, 1-14	ix, 26-38	iii, 13-24
19	xix, 20-37	ii, 15-27	ix, 39-41; x, 1-6	iv, 1-12
20	xx, 1-11	ii, 28-32; iii	x, 7-21	iv, 12-21
21	xx, 12-21	Am. i, 1-12	x, 22-42	v, 1-12
22	II Chr. xxviii, 1-17	iii	xi, 1-26	v, 13-21
23	xxxiv, 1-13	iv, 4-13; v, 1-9	xi, 14-31	III Jn.
24	xxxiv, 14-28	v, 10-17; vi, 1-8	xi, 32-46	Jude, 1-16
25	II K. xviii, 1-11	vii, 10-17; viii, 14	xi, 47-57	17-25
26	xviii, 12-20	ix	xii, 1-11	Rev. i, 1-8
27	xxiii, 36; xxiv, 1-7; Obad. 1-17		xii, 12-19	i, 9-20
28	II K. xviii, 1-11	Jonah, i	xii, 20-36	ii, 1-11
29	xxv, 8-17; 9-21	ii	xii, 37-43	ii, 12-17
30	Ezra, i, 1-8	iii, iv	xii, 37-50	ii, 18-29

Dec.	OLD COVENANT Law and Hist'y	Psalm and Proph'y	NEW COVENANT Gospel	Apostolic Word
1	Ezra, iii, 8-13	Mic. i, 1-6; ii	Jn. xiii, 1-11	Rev. iii, 1-6
2	vii, 6-13, 33-28	iii; iv, 1-5	xiii, 1-29	iii, 7-13
3	viii, 35, 36; ix, 1-4	vi	xiii, 21-30	iii, 14-22
4	ix, 5-15	vii	xiii, 31-38	iv
5	x, 1-8	Nahum, i	xiv, 1-14	v
6	x, 9-26	ii	xiv, 15-24	vi, 9-17
7	Neh. l	iii	xiv, 25-31	vii, 9-17
8	ii, 1-19	Hab. i	xv, 1-8	viii, 1-6
9	ii, 11-20	ii	xv, 9-16	viii, 7-13
10	iv, 1-23	iii	xv, 17-27	x, 1-7
11	v, 1-13	Zeph. i	xvi, 1-15	xi, 1-14
12	vi, 1-16	ii	xvi, 16-24	xi, 15-19; xii, 1-6
13	viii, 1-12 (Omit in 4 and 7)	iii	xvi, 25-33	xii, 7-17
14	ix, 1-5; 5-15	Hag. I	xvii, 1-19	xiii, 1-10
15	ix, 16-27	ii	xvii, 20-26	xiii, 11-18
16	ix, 28-38	Zech. i, 1-17	xviii, 1-11	xiv, 6-13
17	xiii, 1-13	ii	xviii, 15-27	xiv, 14-20
18	xiii, 15-22	iv	xviii, 28-40	xv
19	Esth. i	vi, 9-15; vii	xix, 1-11	xvii
20	ii, 5-11	viii	xix, 12-22	xviii, 1-8, 21-24
21	ii, 15-23	ix, 1-14	xix, 23-30	xix, 1-10
22	iii, 1-15	xi	xix, 31-42	xix, 11-21
23	iv	xii; xiii, 1, 2	xx, 1-10	xx, 1-10
24	Deut. xviii, 13-19	Mic. iv, 6-13; v, 1-9	Lk. i, 26-33	Gal. iv, 1-7
25	Gen. iii, 8-15	Ezkl. xxxvi, 25-28	ii, 1-20	{ Jn. iv, 1-15
26	Esth. v	{ Zech. xiii, 7-9; xiv, 1-11 }	Jn. xx, 11-18	Rev. xx, 11-15; xxi, 1
27	vi		Mal. i, 1-13	xx, 19-23	xxi, 1-8
28	vii	ii, 4-16	xxi, 24-31	xxi, 9-16, 22-27
29	viii	ii, 17; iii, 1-12	xxi, 1-14	xxii, 1-9
30	ix, 20-32; x, 1-3	iii, 13-18; iv	Matt. xxiv, 4-51; xxv, 1-13	xxii, 10-21
31	Deut. viii, 1-6	Ecc. i		I Cor. iv, 16-18; v, 1-10

CALENDAR FOR THE YEAR

LORD'S DAYS, AND OTHER DAYS OF ANNUAL OBSERVANCE

The Lord's Days here shown — all that can occur in a series of years — are more than occur in any one year. The Lord's Days in the common Monthly Order have their titles set in a little to the right; while the Signal Days, which, like "Easter," etc., interrupt the Monthly Order for the sake of some special observance, have their titles, beginning fully to the left.
Days with titles still further to the right are omitted from the Monthly Order in some years.

DAY NO. *DAYS* *OCCURRENCE, ETC.*

1 NEW-YEAR DAY ....Jan. 1, M'rg. When a Lord's Day, this yields to Day
2 LORD'S DAY OF THE NEW YEAR... ... Jan. 1-7 [No. 2

3   LORD'S DAY SECOND IN JANUARY
4   LORD'S DAY THIRD IN JANUARY
5   LORD'S DAY FOURTH IN JANUARY
6   LORD'S DAY FIFTH IN JANUARY

7   LORD'S DAY FIRST IN FEBRUARY
8   LORD'S DAY SECOND IN FEBRUARY
9   LORD'S DAY THIRD IN FEBRUARY
10   LORD'S DAY FOURTH IN FEBRUARY
11   LORD'S DAY FIFTH IN FEBRUARY

12   LORD'S DAY FIRST IN MARCH
13   LORD'S DAY SECOND IN MARCH
14   LORD'S DAY THIRD IN MARCH   ⎫ Some or all of these five Lord's Days (Nos. 14–18) are
15   LORD'S DAY FOURTH IN MARCH   ⎬ omitted from the Monthly Order, according as they
16   LORD'S DAY FIFTH IN MARCH   ⎪ may be displaced in any year by the earlier date of
                                                                ⎪ Day No. 20, "Lord's Day Before the Crucifixion";
17   LORD'S DAY FIRST IN APRIL   ⎪ which date is shown in the first column of the
18   LORD'S DAY SECOND IN APRIL   ⎭ "Table of Occurrence"

19 FAST DAY (Friday before Good Friday) ..... Mar. 13–Apr. 16   Or other date, as appointed

20 LORD'S DAY BEFORE THE CRUCIFIXION Mar. 15–Apr. 18
21 THE CRUCIFIXION DAY (Good Friday). ...Mar. 20–Apr. 23   Friday before The Resurrection Day
22 THE RESURRECTION EVE (Easter Eve)...Mar. 21–Apr. 24, Evening: Saturday

23 THE RESURRECTION DAY (Easter) ...... Mar. 22–Apr. 25   "The Resurrection Day" is the
24 LORD'S DAY FIRST AFTER THE RESURRECTION   Lord's Day first after the full
25 LORD'S DAY SECOND AFTER THE RESURRECTION   moon that occurs on, or next
                                                                                       after, Mar. 21: if the full moon
26 LORD'S DAY THIRD AFTER THE RESURRECTION   occur on a Lord's Day, then
27 LORD'S DAY FOURTH AFTER THE RESURRECTION   "The Resurrection Day" is
28 LORD'S DAY FIFTH AFTER THE RESURRECTION   the Lord's Day following

29 THE ASCENSION DAY ....Apr. 30–June 3, M'rg: Thurs., 40th day after "The
30 LORD'S DAY AFTER THE ASCENSION ...May 3–June 6   [Resurrection Day"

31 THE PENTECOST DAY (Whitsunday) ......May 10–June 13: 50th day after "The Resurrection
32 LORD'S DAY AFTER THE PENTECOST...May 17–June 20   ("Trinity Sunday")   [Day"

CALENDAR FOR THE YEAR.

DAY NO.	DAYS	OCCURRENCE, ETC.
33	LORD'S DAY FOURTH IN MAY	Some or all of these five Lord's Days (Nos. 33–37) are omitted from the Monthly Order, according as they may be displaced in any year by the later date of No. 32, "Lord's Day After the Pentecost"; and on the Lord's Day which follows that date the Monthly Order is resumed
34	LORD'S DAY FIFTH IN MAY	
35	LORD'S DAY FIRST IN JUNE	
36	LORD'S DAY SECOND IN JUNE	
37	LORD'S DAY THIRD IN JUNE	
38	LORD'S DAY FOURTH IN JUNE	
39	LORD'S DAY FIFTH IN JUNE	
40	LORD'S DAY FIRST IN JULY	
41	LORD'S DAY SECOND IN JULY	
42	LORD'S DAY THIRD IN JULY	
43	LORD'S DAY FOURTH IN JULY	
44	LORD'S DAY FIFTH IN JULY	
45	LORD'S DAY FIRST IN AUGUST	
46	LORD'S DAY SECOND IN AUGUST	
47	LORD'S DAY THIRD IN AUGUST	
48	LORD'S DAY FOURTH IN AUGUST	
49	LORD'S DAY FIFTH IN AUGUST	
50	LORD'S DAY FIRST IN SEPTEMBER	
51	LORD'S DAY SECOND IN SEPTEMBER	
52	LORD'S DAY THIRD IN SEPTEMBER	
53	LORD'S DAY FOURTH IN SEPTEMBER	
54	LORD'S DAY FIFTH IN SEPTEMBER	
55	LORD'S DAY FIRST IN OCTOBER	
56	LORD'S DAY SECOND IN OCTOBER	
57	LORD'S DAY THIRD IN OCTOBER	
58	LORD'S DAY FOURTH IN OCTOBER	
59	LORD'S DAY FIFTH IN OCTOBER	
60	LORD'S DAY FIRST IN NOVEMBER	
61	LORD'S DAY SECOND IN NOVEMBER	
62	LORD'S DAY THIRD IN NOVEMBER	On Nov. 27 or 28, this is omitted from the Monthly Order — yielding to Day No. 65
63	LORD'S DAY FOURTH IN NOVEMBER	
64	THANKSGIVING DAY (Thursday last in Nov.) Nov. 24–30	Or other date, as appointed
65	LORD'S DAY FIRST IN ADVENT ....Nov. 27–Dec. 3	Lord's Day fourth before "The Nativity Day"
66	LORD'S DAY SECOND IN ADVENT.......Dec. 4–10	
67	LORD'S DAY THIRD IN ADVENT........Dec. 11–17	
68	LORD'S DAY FOURTH IN ADVENT ......Dec. 18–24	On Dec. 24, Ev'g, this yields to Day No. 69
69	THE NATIVITY EVE (Christmas Eve) ..... Dec. 24, Evening	
70	THE NATIVITY DAY (Christmas Day) ......Dec. 25, Mr'g	When a Lord's Day, this yields to Day No. 71
71	LORD'S DAY OF THE NATIVITY....... ..Dec. 25–31	Lord's Day on, or after, "The Nativity Day." On Dec. 31, Evening, this yields to Day No. 72
72	NEW-YEAR EVE .... Dec. 31, Evening	

TABLE OF OCCURRENCE OF MOVABLE DAYS

SHOWING THEIR DATES IN EACH YEAR THROUGH A HALF CENTURY

[The five *Lord's Days After the Resurrection* (Nos. 24–28), and the last three *Lord's Days in Advent* (Nos. 66–68), are not shown in this Table, as their place is evident]

Year of our Lord	Day No. 20 Lord's Day Before the Crucifixion (Palm Sunday)	Day No. 21 The Crucifixion Day (Good Friday)	Day No. 22 The Resurrection Eve	Day No. 23 The Resurrection Day (Easter)	Day No. 29 The Ascension Day	Day No. 30 Lord's Day After the Ascension	Day No. 31 The Pentecost Day (Whitsunday)	Day No. 32 Lord's Day After the Pentecost	Day No. 65 Lord's Day First in Advent	Year of our Lord
1887	Apr. 3	Apr. 8	Apr. 9	Apr. 10	May 19	May 22	May 29	June 5	Nov. 27	1887
1888	Mar. 25	Mar. 30	Mar. 31	— 1	— 10	— 13	— 20	May 27	Dec. 2	1888
1889	Apr. 14	Apr. 19	Apr. 20	— 21	— 30	June 2	June 9	June 16	— 1	1889
1890	Mar. 30	— 4	— 5	— 6	— 15	May 18	May 25	— 1	Nov. 30	1890
1891	— 22	Mar. 27	Mar. 28	Mar. 29	— 7	— 10	— 17	May 24	— 29	1891
1892	Apr. 10	Apr. 15	Apr. 16	Apr. 17	— 26	— 29	June 5	June 12	— 27	1892
1893	Mar. 26	Mar. 31	— 1	— 2	— 11	— 14	May 21	May 28	Dec. 3	1893
1894	— 18	— 23	Mar. 24	Mar. 25	— 3	— 6	— 13	— 20	— 2	1894
1895	Apr. 7	Apr. 12	Apr. 13	Apr. 14	— 23	— 26	June 2	June 9	— 1	1895
1896	Mar. 29	— 3	— 4	— 5	— 14	— 17	May 24	May 31	Nov. 29	1896
1897	Apr. 11	— 16	— 17	— 18	— 27	— 30	June 6	June 13	— 28	1897
1898	— 3	— 8	— 9	— 10	— 19	— 22	May 29	— 5	— 27	1898
1899	Mar. 26	Mar. 31	— 1	— 2	— 11	— 14	— 21	May 28	Dec. 3	1899
1900	Apr. 8	Apr. 13	— 14	— 15	— 24	— 27	June 3	June 10	— 2	1900
1901	Mar. 31	— 5	— 6	— 7	— 16	— 19	May 26	— 2	— 1	1901
1902	— 23	— 28	Mar. 29	Mar. 30	— 8	— 11	— 18	May 25	Nov. 30	1902
1903	Apr. 5	Apr. 10	Apr. 11	Apr. 12	— 21	— 24	— 31	June 7	— 29	1903
1904	Mar. 27	— 1	— 2	— 3	— 12	— 15	— 22	May 29	— 27	1904
1905	Apr. 16	— 21	— 22	— 23	June 1	June 4	June 11	June 18	Dec. 3	1905
1906	— 8	— 13	— 14	— 15	May 24	May 27	— 3	— 10	— 2	1906
1907	Mar. 24	Mar. 29	Mar. 30	Mar. 31	— 9	— 12	May 19	May 26	— 1	1907
1908	Apr. 12	Apr. 17	Apr. 18	Apr. 19	— 28	— 31	June 7	June 14	Nov. 29	1908
1909	— 4	— 9	— 10	— 11	— 20	— 23	May 30	— 6	— 28	1909
1910	Mar. 20	Mar. 25	Mar. 26	Mar. 27	— 5	— 8	— 15	May 22	— 27	1910
1911	Apr. 9	Apr. 14	Apr. 15	Apr. 16	— 25	— 28	June 4	June 11	Dec. 3	1911
1912	Mar. 31	— 5	— 6	— 7	— 16	— 19	May 26	— 2	— 1	1912
1913	— 16	Mar. 21	Mar. 22	Mar. 23	— 1	— 4	— 11	May 18	Nov. 30	1913
1914	Apr. 5	Apr. 10	Apr. 11	Apr. 12	— 21	— 24	— 31	June 7	— 29	1914
1915	Mar. 28	— 2	— 3	— 4	— 13	— 16	— 23	May 30	— 28	1915
1916	Apr. 16	— 21	— 22	— 23	June 1	June 4	June 11	June 18	Dec. 3	1916
1917	— 1	— 6	— 7	— 8	May 17	May 20	May 27	— 3	— 2	1917
1918	Mar. 24	Mar. 29	Mar. 30	Mar. 31	— 9	— 12	— 19	May 26	— 1	1918
1919	Apr. 13	Apr. 18	Apr. 19	Apr. 20	— 29	June 1	June 8	June 15	Nov. 30	1919
1920	Mar. 28	— 2	— 3	— 4	— 13	May 16	May 23	May 30	— 28	1920
1921	— 20	Mar. 25	Mar. 26	Mar. 27	— 5	— 8	— 15	— 22	— 27	1921
1922	Apr. 9	Apr. 14	Apr. 15	Apr. 16	— 25	— 28	June 4	June 11	Dec. 3	1922
1923	Mar. 25	Mar. 30	Mar. 31	— 1	— 10	— 13	May 20	May 27	— 2	1923
1924	Apr. 13	Apr. 18	Apr. 19	— 20	— 29	June 1	June 8	June 15	Nov. 30	1924
1925	— 5	— 10	— 11	— 12	— 21	May 24	May 31	— 7	— 29	1925
1926	Mar. 28	— 2	— 3	— 4	— 13	— 16	— 23	May 30	— 28	1926
1927	Apr. 10	— 15	— 16	— 17	— 26	— 29	June 5	June 12	— 27	1927
1928	— 1	— 6	— 7	— 8	— 17	— 20	May 27	— 3	Dec. 2	1928
1929	Mar. 24	Mar. 29	Mar. 30	Mar. 31	— 9	— 12	— 19	May 26	— 1	1929
1930	Apr. 13	Apr. 18	Apr. 19	Apr. 20	— 29	June 1	June 8	June 15	Nov. 30	1930
1931	Mar. 29	— 3	— 4	— 5	— 14	May 17	May 24	May 31	— 29	1931
1932	— 20	Mar. 25	Mar. 26	Mar. 27	— 5	— 8	— 15	— 22	— 27	1932
1933	Apr. 9	Apr. 14	Apr. 15	Apr. 16	— 25	— 28	June 4	June 11	Dec. 3	1933
1934	Mar. 25	Mar. 30	Mar. 31	— 1	— 10	— 13	May 20	May 27	— 2	1934
1935	Apr. 14	Apr. 19	Apr. 20	— 21	— 30	June 2	June 9	June 16	— 1	1935
1936	— 5	— 10	— 11	— 12	— 21	May 24	May 31	— 7	Nov. 29	1936
1937	Mar. 21	Mar. 26	Mar. 27	Mar. 28	— 6	— 9	— 16	May 23	— 28	1937
1938	Apr. 10	Apr. 15	Apr. 16	Apr. 17	— 26	— 29	June 5	June 12	— 27	1938
1939	— 2	— 7	— 8	— 9	— 18	— 21	May 28	— 4	Dec. 3	1939
1940	Mar. 17	Mar. 22	Mar. 23	Mar. 24	— 2	— 5	— 12	May 19	— 1	1940

THE SERVICE

Note

THIS form includes all the parts of a fully extended Service, from which various Congregations can select as they may deem edifying. To aid in such construction of a desired Service from this general scheme, here are indicated several modes, shorter and more simple in varying degrees according as the many Alternatives and Omissions may be observed; and the most simple form, which would be reached if *all* were observed, is shown in the Order which first follows these notes.

The Service is mainly the same for Morning and for Evening; though variations are suggested for Evening (any hour after the noon), and for a Service with the Communion. For the Communion and its connected Service, see the latter part of the book.

"Signal Days," referred to below, are Days which, like Easter, etc., interrupt with their special observance the common Monthly Order of Lord's Days: they may be found noted on the CALENDAR FOR THE YEAR.

Songs additional to those here indicated—such as Anthem by a choir, etc.—may be assigned by the Minister; to be introduced after IV, Scripture of the Old Covenant; or after VII, Scripture of the New Covenant; or after X, The Lord's Prayer. The Service may have Organ Prelude and Postlude: also there may be Organ Response (if so appointed) instantly after X, The Lord's Prayer; with Organ Voluntary during a Contribution (XI) when the Offertory is not used. Interludes between the stanzas of a *congregational* song are interruptions sometimes necessary, but whose frequency is not desirable.

The number and name of the "Day," also any parts of the Service, may be announced as may be requisite, orally, or by notices conspicuously posted.

At the end of every Prayer, "let all the people say AMEN" [Neh. viii, 6: I Cor. xiv, 15, 16]; likewise after the Benediction: and usually AMEN, by All, should end every song of direct praise or worship, especially every Doxology [I Chron. xvi, 36: Ps. cvi, 48].

It is fitting that All rise promptly with the Minister, in I, Introductory—standing till the end of III, Hymn. Standing is proper in song usually, especially in songs of worship (VI, IX, XII); also in VIII, Confession of Christian Faith; in the Short Prayer and Blessing at the end of XI, Offertory; and in XVI, Benediction. There appears no imperative reason for the Congregation to stand in the Responsive Lessons; since in large part the materials of these are not distinctively the direct address of worship to God. In Prayers (X, XIV) it is fitting that all kneel or bow down.

Words in brackets are to be omitted at discretion: portions in small capitals are for utterance by All—Congregation with Minister: portions in italics by Congregation alone.

ORDER OF THE SERVICE

AS IT MAY BE SHORTENED BY ALL THE OMISSIONS

[Omitting from the full Form on next page, Nos. II, IV, VIII, IX, XI]

Introductory
SENTENCE } Minister reads *both* — Congregation joining to say the *Response;* after which
RESPONSE } All sing the Call to Praise — "Praise God from whom all blessings flow."
— Tune, *Old Hundredth*

Hymn

Responsive Lesson OF MINISTER AND CONGREGATION
[This and the Psalm Chant are from the Old Covenant]

Psalm Chant OF CONGREGATIONAL PRAISE [Sung or said by All]
[Omitted at discretion when New Members are to be recognized in the Church]

Scripture of the New Covenant
[Either or both of the Lessons]

The Prayers
GENERAL PRAYERS
THE LORD'S PRAYER [By All]

Hymn of Praise BY CONGREGATION
Ending with DOXOLOGY

NOTICES }
CONTRIBUTION } As requisite

Sermon
[Shortened or omitted when the Communion is to follow]

Prayer

Hymn

Benediction

The Recognition of New Members in the Church, also the Baptism of Little Children, may follow the Scripture of the New Covenant

The Communion at the Lord's Table may take the place of all after the Sermon

ORDER OF THE SERVICE

At ANY Service the following may be omitted — II, IV, VII (part), X (parts 2, 3), XI (parts 2, 3). See preceding page.
Further SPECIAL omissions at discretion — the following:
  At Evening — VIII, IX, XIV;   With the Recognition of New Members — VI, XII
  With the Communion — IV, VII (part), XIII; also, all after XIII is set aside

Songs additional (Anthem, etc., by a choir) may be assigned to follow IV, or VII, or X

[ORGAN PRELUDE]

I **Introductory** [All rising with the Minister]
   SENTENCE, MINISTER   *See in "Offices for the Year," pages 1—314*
   RESPONSE, CONGREGATION   *See as above; or in "Monthly Songs," pages 315—351*

II **Christian Summary** [All still standing]
   CHRIST'S SUMMARY OF THE LAW; OR, THE BEATITUDES OF THE GOSPEL

III **Hymn**   FROM THE USUAL HYMNAL   [All still standing]

IV **Scripture of the Old Covenant**   *In "Offices for the Year"*

V **Responsive Lesson**   *In "Offices for the Year"*

VI **Psalm Chant** [By All, standing]   *In "Offices for the Year"; or, in "Monthly Songs"*

VII **Scripture of the New Covenant**   *In "Offices for the Year"*
   1 GOSPEL OF OUR LORD JESUS
   2 APOSTOLIC WORD   } Either, or both

VIII **Confession of Christian Faith** — THE CREED [By All, standing]
   INSTEAD OF CREED, MAY BE THE BAPTISM OF LITTLE CHILDREN, (See page 401)
   OR, THE RECOGNITION OF NEW MEMBERS, (See page 373 or 376)

IX **Song of Ascription** [By All, still standing]   *In "Ascriptions, etc.," pages 352—367*
   [NOT ANNOUNCED]

X **The Prayers** — 1, GENERAL PRAYERS: 2, PRAYER OF THE DAY:
   3, THE SILENT MOMENT OF PRAYER: 4, THE LORD'S PRAYER [By All]
   [ORGAN RESPONSE]

XI **Offertory**   *See in "Service with the Communion," page 389*
   1, SENTENCES: 2, PRAYER [All rising]: 3, BLESSING [By All, standing]
   (AFTER EACH SENTENCE, A PAUSE, OR SHORT MUSICAL RESPONSE)
   [IF A CONTRIBUTION FOR CURRENT EXPENSES ALONE, THE OFFERTORY IS NOT USED]

XII **Hymn of Praise** [By All, standing]   *In "Offices for the Year"; or, in "Monthly Songs"*

   [NOTICES, AS REQUISITE]

XIII **Sermon**

XIV **Prayer**

XV **Hymn**   FROM THE USUAL HYMNAL   [All standing]

XVI **Benediction**   [All still standing]   [ORGAN POSTLUDE]

xxi

The Service in the Lord's House

I Introductory

All rise — Congregation with Minister

1 SENTENCE from Minister
For each Day— see that Day (Morning, Evening) in OFFICES FOR THE YEAR

2 RESPONSE Sung by All, or said in unison by All (Cong. with Minister)
For each Day—see as above, in OFFICES FOR THE YEAR; or, in MONTHLY SONGS OF PRAISE, pages 315-351.

[*Alternative:* The *Response*, if not sung, may be *said* in unison by All; after which may be sung this Call to Praise: Tune, " Old Hundredth," L. M., page 317]

> PRAISE GOD, FROM WHOM ALL BLESSINGS FLOW!
> PRAISE HIM, ALL CREATURES HERE BELOW!
> PRAISE HIM ABOVE, YE HEAVENLY HOST!
> PRAISE FATHER, SON, AND HOLY GHOST!
>
> THOMAS KEN, D. D., 1697

II Christian Summary [Omitted at discretion] [All still standing]

Either, The Summary of the Law of God, by our Lord Jesus Christ, Matt. xxii. 37-40; Mark, xii. 29-31; compare Deut. vi, 4, 5 [Preferably at morning]

Or, The Beatitudes of our Lord Jesus Christ, Matt. v, 1-10 [Preferably at evening]

[Responses and Petitions, omitted at discretion]

Christ's Summary of the Law

Our Lord Jesus Christ saith:

THE first commandment in the Law is:
The Lord our God, the Lord, is One:
And thou shalt love the Lord thy God with all thy heart, and with
    all thy soul, and with all thy mind, and with all thy strength:
This is the great and first commandment.

    BLESSED LORD GOD, BE MERCIFUL TO US SINNERS. [Lk. xviii, 13]

And a second like unto it is this:
Thou shalt love thy neighbor as thyself.
    BLESSED LORD GOD, BE MERCIFUL TO US SINNERS.

There is none other commandment greater than these:
On these two commandments hangeth the whole Law, and the prophets.
    BLESSED LORD GOD, WE BESEECH THEE,
    WRITE THIS WHOLE LAW OF THY LOVE WITHIN OUR HEARTS.

THE SERVICE IN THE LORD'S HOUSE   xxiii

Or this —
THE BEATITUDES OF THE GOSPEL
OUR Lord Jesus Christ saith:

1 BLESSED are the poor in spirit: for theirs is the kingdom of heaven.
   GRACIOUS FATHER, GRANT US TO BE PARTAKERS IN THIS SPIRIT.
2 Blessed are they that mourn: for they shall be comforted.
   GRACIOUS FATHER, GRANT US TO BE PARTAKERS IN SUCH BLESSED MOURNING.
3 Blessed are the meek: for they shall inherit the earth.
   GRACIOUS FATHER, GRANT US TO BE PARTAKERS IN THIS MEEKNESS.
4 Blessed are they that hunger and thirst after righteousness: for they shall be filled.
   GRACIOUS FATHER, GRANT US TO BE PARTAKERS IN THIS HUNGER AND THIRST.
5 Blessed are the merciful: for they shall obtain mercy.
   GRACIOUS FATHER, GRANT US TO BE PARTAKERS IN THIS TWOFOLD MERCY.
6 Blessed are the pure in heart: for they shall see God.
   GRACIOUS FATHER, GRANT US TO BE PARTAKERS IN THIS PURENESS.
7 Blessed are the peacemakers: for they shall be called sons of God.
   GRACIOUS FATHER, GRANT US TO BE PARTAKERS IN THY WORK OF PEACE.
8 Blessed are they that have been persecuted for righteousness' sake: for theirs is the kingdom of heaven.
   GRACIOUS FATHER, GRANT US TO BE PARTAKERS IN ALL THINGS WHATSOEVER THAT PERTAIN TO GODLINESS:
   AND LET ALL THESE BLESSINGS COME UNTO US; EVEN THY FULL SALVATION ACCORDING TO THY WORD. [Ps. cxix, 41]

III **Hymn**   From the Hymnal used in the church   [All still standing]

IV **Scripture of the Old Covenant**   FROM MINISTER
For each Day — see that Day (Morning, Evening) in OFFICES FOR THE YEAR

SCRIPTURE OF THE OLD COVENANT — IN [Mention Book, Chapter, etc.]
A few words of introduction or explanation may be given with any Scripture Lesson

[*Alternative:* The Lesson may be any of those from the Old Covenant assigned to the same Day (or to any day in the same Week), in the TABLE OF DAILY SCRIPTURE LESSONS: And similarly with the New Covenant in VII, below]

[*Omissions:* When the Minister deems the Old Covenant sufficiently presented in V. Responsive Lesson, and VI, Psalm Chant: Also, at discretion, when the Communion is to follow]

——[Here may be introduced additional Song, at discretion]

V **Responsive Lesson**   OF MINISTER AND CONGREGATION
For each Day — see that Day (Morning, Evening) in OFFICES FOR THE YEAR
Lesson announced by number and name of the Day, or by page

THE SERVICE IN THE LORD'S HOUSE

VI **Psalm Chant**   OF THE CONGREGATION   [All rising]

   For a Signal Day—see that Day in OFFICES FOR THE YEAR
   For a Lord's Day in the common Monthly Order—see that Day (Morning, Evening)
   in MONTHLY SONGS OF PRAISE, pages 315-351; announced by page if requisite
   If this Psalm may not conveniently be sung, it may be said in unison, by All
   At the end, the ancient Doxology, *Gloria Patri*, may be sung, or said in unison, by All
   [*Omission:* Psalm Chant, at discretion, when New Members are to be recognized in the Church]

VII **Scripture of the New Covenant**   FROM MINISTER

   For each Day—see that Day (Morning, Evening) in OFFICES FOR THE YEAR
   1 GOSPEL OF OUR LORD JESUS—ACCORDING TO [Mention Book, Chapter, etc.]
   2 APOSTOLIC WORD—IN [Mention Book, Chapter, etc.]
   [*Alternative:* Similar to the Old Covenant in IV, above]
   [*Omissions:* One of these Lessons, at discretion, especially at Evening, or when the Communion is to follow]

——[Here may be introduced additional Song, at discretion]

VIII **Confession of Christian Faith**   BY ALL CHRISTIAN DISCIPLES

   Without announcement—this ancient creed, or any other brief form of Christian Confession which the Church may appoint

   AN ANCIENT CREED   [All Christian disciples rising]
   [Of unknown origin; but, doubtless, from formulas used at Baptism in the early Church; traceable in a rudimentary form at Rome in the third century; date of (nearly) its present form, about 500, in Gaul]

   I BELIEVE IN GOD THE FATHER ALMIGHTY,
   MAKER OF HEAVEN AND EARTH:

   AND IN JESUS CHRIST HIS ONLY SON OUR LORD:
   WHO WAS CONCEIVED BY THE HOLY GHOST,
   BORN OF THE VIRGIN MARY:
   SUFFERED UNDER PONTIUS PILATE,
   WAS CRUCIFIED, DEAD, AND BURIED:
   HE DESCENDED INTO HADES:
   THE THIRD DAY HE ROSE AGAIN FROM THE DEAD;
   HE ASCENDED INTO HEAVEN,
   AND SITTETH AT THE RIGHT HAND OF GOD THE FATHER ALMIGHTY:
   FROM THENCE HE SHALL COME TO JUDGE THE QUICK AND THE DEAD.

   I BELIEVE IN THE HOLY GHOST:
   THE HOLY CATHOLIC CHURCH, THE COMMUNION OF SAINTS:
   THE FORGIVENESS OF SINS:
   THE RESURRECTION OF THE BODY:
   AND THE LIFE EVERLASTING. AMEN.

   [*Alternative:* For another ancient creed, see in the Service with the Communion. When little children are to be baptized, or New Members to be recognized in the Church, such special Usage (see last part of Book) takes the place of the creed]

   [*Omission:* The Creed, at discretion; yet its use once in the Day is commended]

THE SERVICE IN THE LORD'S HOUSE   xxv

IX **Song of Ascription**   BY THE CONGREGATION   [All still standing]

Announced, if requisite, by page and first line
One of the following ancient Doxologies sung, or said in unison, by All: see these
numbers in ASCRIPTIONS AND OTHER SONGS, pages 352-367

TE DEUM LAUDAMUS (A Chief Song of the Church)......... No. 1, Page 352
GLORIA IN EXCELSIS DEO (The Great Doxology).......... " 2, " 358
GLORIA PATRI (The Less Doxology)...................... " 3, " 359
ALL HOLY (An Ascription of the New Covenant).......... " 4, " 360
SANCTUS (The Seraphic Hymn), Is. vi, 3: Rev. iv, 8...... " 5, " 360
BENEDICTUS (Song of Zacharias), Lk. i, 68–79.......... " 6, " 361
DOXOLOGY OF ISRAEL, Ps. lxxii, 18, 19.................. " 7, " 362
Or, A DOXOLOGY in meter.........................Nos. 8, 9, 10, " 362, 3

Or one of these Praise-songs — not at Morning—

BENEDICITE OMNIA (Ancient Hebrew Canticle) .... No. 11, Page 364
SONG OF DANIEL, Dan. ii, 20-23 ....,.................. " 12, " 365

The Ascriptions may be used promiscuously, or assigned as follows:

Te Deum, as a song of high praise, is appropriate at Morning Service on Day No. 2, Lord's Day of the New Year: 29, The Resurrection Day: 30, Lord's Day After the Ascension: 31, The Pentecost Day: 32, Lord's Day After the Pentecost: 64, Thanksgiving Day: 71, Lord's Day of the Nativity. If *Te Deum* may not conveniently be sung, *Gloria in Excelsis* is appropriate

Te Deum is the preferable Ascription also as an instant response of joy and praise at the end of Recognition of New Members in the Church on Confession of Christ; but if for any reason *Te Deum* be not convenient, *Gloria in Excelsis* is appropriate; or No. 4, "*All Holy*"; or No. 10, "*Glory, thanks*" (metrical)

Gloria in Excelsis is commended for Lord's Day First in the Month, at Morning Service; also at Evening Service when *Te Deum* has been used at Morning

Benedictus, in its full form, is an appropriate Ascription on Day No. 65, Lord's Day First in Advent: 69, The Nativity Eve: 70, The Nativity Day

[*Omission:* The Ascription, at discretion: yet its use is commended]

X **The Prayers**   [All kneeling or bowed down]

[Minister] Let us pray.

1 GENERAL PRAYERS:

[Not all these parts, as below, are requisite in every Service—particularly not in a second Service; and all except 5 and 6 may be brief: the *order* may be varied]

(1) Adoration: (2) Thanksgiving: (3) Confession of Sin: (4) Vow: (5) General Supplication: (6) General Intercession: (7) Plea, through Christ: (8) Ascription to God, the Father and the Son and the Holy Spirit [omitted when Prayer of the Day is used]   [All] AMEN.

2 PRAYER OF THE DAY   [All] AMEN.

. For each Day—see that Day (Morning) in OFFICES FOR THE YEAR

3 SILENT MOMENT OF PRAYER

[Minister]   O THOU that seest the heart!
   We lift up our hearts in silence unto Thee —

           *   *   *   *   *   *   *

THE SERVICE IN THE LORD'S HOUSE

4 THE LORD'S PRAYER by All   [Matt. vi, 9-13; Lk. xi, 2-4]

OUR FATHER WHO ART IN HEAVEN,
HALLOWED BE THY NAME.
THY KINGDOM COME.
THY WILL BE DONE ON EARTH, AS IT IS IN HEAVEN.

GIVE US THIS DAY OUR DAILY BREAD.
AND FORGIVE US OUR TRESPASSES,
AS WE FORGIVE THOSE WHO TRESPASS AGAINST US.
AND BRING US NOT INTO TEMPTATION,
BUT DELIVER US FROM EVIL.

•   FOR THINE IS THE KINGDOM, AND THE POWER AND THE GLORY,
FOR EVER AND EVER. AMEN.

Alternatives and Omissions: The order of the General Prayers may be changed, or any parts shortened or omitted, at discretion — particularly in a second Service; and instead of the General Prayers, at a Service with the Communion, the Litany — if acceptable to the Church — may be used : see in that Service. Prayer of the Day, and Silent Moment, omitted at discretion]

——[Here may be introduced additional Song, at discretion]

XI Offertory   On the Days and at the Services assigned

Preceded by requisite announcement of the object. Delayed till after Sermon, if expedient. For the Usage — see Service with the Communion, in last part of Book

[Contribution for ordinary expenses of the Church (not announced) may be at this time; but for such contribution alone the Offertory is not used]

XII Hymn of Praise   OF CONGREGATION   [All standing]

For a Signal Day — see that Day (Morning, Evening) in OFFICES FOR THE YEAR
For a Lord's Day in the common Monthly Order — see that Day (Morning, Evening) in MONTHLY SONGS OF PRAISE, pages 315-351 ; announced by page if requisite

Doxology in meter ends this Hymn

[*Omission:* At discretion, when New Members have been recognized in the Church]

——[Here may be Notices, as requisite]

XIII Sermon

[With the Communion, the Sermon may be shortened or omitted]

The Communion at the Lord's Table

On the Days appointed ; beginning at this point occupies the remainder of the Service: see "Service with the Communion, etc.," in last part of Book

XIV Prayer   [All kneeling or bowed down]

[*Omission:* At discretion, in Evening]   [All]   AMEN.

THE SERVICE IN THE LORD'S HOUSE　　　xxvii

XV **Hymn**　　From the Hymnal used in the Church　　[All standing]

XVI **Benediction**　　FROM MINISTER　　[All still standing]

[*Alternative:* If preferred, the *order* after the Sermon may be the following —
XIV, Hymn;
XV, Prayer and Benediction combined (All kneeling or bowed down); in which case Minister changes "you" to *us* in Benedictions below]

Before Benediction, Minister may, at discretion, utter one of the following —

ASCRIPTIONS

1. Rom. xi, 36
OF God, and through Him, and unto Him, are all things:
To Him be the glory forever:　　[All] AMEN.

2. I Tim. i, 17
NOW unto the King eternal, incorruptible, invisible, the only God, be honor and glory for ever and ever:　　AMEN.

3. From I Tim. vi, 15, 16
UNTO the blessed and only Potentate, the King of kings and Lord of lords —
Who only hath immortality, dwelling in light unapproachable —
Whom no man hath seen, nor can see —
To Him be honor and power eternal:　　AMEN.

4. Phil. iv, 20
NOW unto our God and Father be the glory for ever and ever:　　AMEN.

5. *Special:* II Cor. ix, 15
THANKS be to God for His unspeakable gift:　　AMEN.

6. *Special:* I Cor. xv, 57
THANKS be to God, who giveth us the victory through our Lord Jesus Christ:　　AMEN.

OLD COVENANT BENEDICTIONS

Minister may, at discretion, begin the Benediction with one or more of these:

1 BELOVED: let your going forth be in the Name of the Lord.

2 THE blessing of Jehovah be upon you.　　[Ps. cxxix, 8]

3 JEHOVAH bless you out of Zion;
Even He that made heaven and earth.　　[Ps. cxxxiv, 3]

4 JEHOVAH bless you, and keep you:
Jehovah make His face to shine upon you, and be gracious unto you:
Jehovah lift up His countenance upon you, and give you peace.　　[Num. vi, 24-26]

Minister then utters one of the following —

APOSTOLIC BENEDICTIONS

[Other Benedictions, with Ascriptions, are at the end of the various Usages in Church Fellowship — The Communion, etc. — in last part of Book. See also: Rom. xv, 33; I Tim. i, 2; I Pet. v, 14; II Jn. i, 3]

1. From II Cor. xiii, 14
THE grace of the Lord Jesus Christ, and the love of God, and the communion of the Holy Spirit, be with you all evermore:　　[All] AMEN.

2. From 1 Tim. 1, 2: Rom. i, 7: II Cor. xiii, 14
   GRACE, mercy, and peace, from God our Father and the Lord Jesus Christ, with the communion of the Holy Spirit, be with you all now and for evermore: AMEN.

3. From Rom. xv, 33: and from II Cor. xiii, 14
   Now the God of peace — the Father and the Son and the Holy Spirit — be with you all evermore: AMEN.

4. From II Thess. iii, 17
   THE grace of our Lord Jesus Christ be with you all forever: AMEN.

   [The following are appropriate in Church Fellowship]

5. Rom. xv, 13: and from II Thess. iii, 17
   Now the God of hope fill you with all joy and peace in believing, that you may abound in hope, in the power of the Holy Spirit:
   The grace of our Lord Jesus Christ be with you all forever: AMEN.

6. From II Thess. ii, 16, 17
   Now our Lord Jesus Christ Himself, and God our Father who loved us and gave us eternal comfort and good hope through grace, comfort your hearts and establish them in every good work and word, by His Holy Spirit, now and ever: AMEN.

7. II Thess. iii, 5: with No. 3 above
   THE Lord direct your hearts into the love of God, and into the patience of Christ:
   Grace, mercy, and peace, from God our Father and the Lord Jesus Christ, with the communion of the Holy Spirit, be with you all now and for evermore: AMEN.

8. II Pet. i, 2: and from II Cor. xiii, 14
   GRACE to you and peace be multiplied in the knowledge of God and of Jesus our Lord, with the communion of the Holy Spirit, evermore: AMEN.

9. I Pet. v, 14: and from II Cor. xiii, 14
   PEACE be unto you all that are in Christ:
   The grace of the Lord Jesus Christ, and the love of God, and the communion of the Holy Spirit, be with you all evermore: AMEN.

10. From Eph. vi, 23: and from II Cor. xiii, 14
    PEACE be to you, Brethren, and love with faith, from God the Father and the Lord Jesus Christ, with the communion of the Holy Spirit, evermore:
    AMEN.

[After the AMEN has been said, this may instantly be sung — at discretion]

W. S. P., 1887.

Offices of Worship and Instruction For the Year

Offices for the Year

For an Index to all Lord's Days, and other Days of Annual Observance, for which these Offices are provided, see in preceding pages — CALENDAR FOR THE YEAR. The ORDER OF SERVICE also is in preceding pages.

The following parts are here either given in full, or indicated by reference, for each Service — Morning and Evening — on every several Day.

INTRODUCTORY SENTENCE. A special Sentence for each Service.

INTRODUCTORY RESPONSE. The proper Response is here given for each Service; and for every *Signal Day* the music also. But for Lord's Days in the common *Monthly Order*, the same INTRODUCTORY RESPONSES (one for Morning, one for Evening) serve for the same Lord's Days in every month through the year; and the music for *these* is to be found at the end of these Offices, in the MONTHLY SONGS OF PRAISE. For example: the same words and music serve for the Lord's Day Evening, Second, in January — in February — in March, etc. [The same arrangement in general for the PSALM CHANT and for the HYMN OF PRAISE — below.] If preferred, instead of singing the Response, it may be *said* in unison by All — Congregation with Minister; after which may be sung "Praise God from whom all blessings flow."

SCRIPTURE LESSONS. Three Lessons for each Service are here indicated by reference to their places in the Bible: one Lesson from the Old Covenant, with one from the Gospels, and one from the history or words of the Apostles. But if in any service the Minister deem the Old Covenant sufficiently presented in the Responsive Reading and the Psalm of Praise, which follow, he may omit *this* Lesson from the Old Covenant. Though these Readings are recommended as carefully selected to bring into weekly prominence the most significant portions of Holy Scripture, yet the Minister may sometimes find occasion to use instead the Lessons appointed in the TABLE OF DAILY SCRIPTURE LESSONS in preceding pages; or he may select outside of any prescribed course. The abrupt beginning of some of the Lessons, due to necessary brevity, may make desirable a few prefatory words as to persons, time, place, etc. These Lessons are from the Revised Version, with the readings and renderings preferred by the American Revisers: in a few of the Lessons, in public reading from any other Version, small portions may be omitted. All references to the Bible by chapter and verse are *inclusive*.

RESPONSIVE LESSON. A special Lesson is here given for each Service. Lines printed in Roman letter, and not indented (or set in), are to be read by the Minister; lines indented and in *italics*, by the Congregation; lines in SMALL CAPITALS by All — Minister and Congregation.

PSALM CHANT. One for each *Signal Day*: but for Days in the common *Monthly Order* (Morning, Evening), see in MONTHLY SONGS OF PRAISE.

PRAYER OF THE DAY. A short Prayer is here given for every Day — the same for Morning and Evening, but omitted at discretion in Evening.

HYMN OF PRAISE. Two Hymns (Morning, Evening) for each *Signal Day*: but for Days in the common *Monthly Order*, see in MONTHLY SONGS OF PRAISE.

OFFICES OF WORSHIP AND INSTRUCTION FOR THE YEAR

1. NEW YEAR DAY

[When this is the Lord's Day, this observance is set aside—yielding to Day No. 2]

Introductory

Sentence

NOW it is high time for us to awake out of sleep—
Redeeming the time because the days are evil:
For the fashion of this world passeth away;
But the word of the Lord abideth forever. [From Rom. xiii, 11: also Eph. v, 16: 1 Cor. vii, 31: 1 Pet. i, 25]

Response
[Tune, in Day No. 2]

JEHOVAH is good;
His lovingkindness en- | dureth for | ever;
And His faithfulness | un-to | all gener- | ations. [Ps. c, 5]

Scripture Lessons

Old Covenant   Ecc. iii, 9-17: xii, 13, 14.
Gospel   Luke, xii, 22-40.
Apostolic Word Titus, ii, 1-14.

Responsive Lesson

From Job ix, xii, xxvi. [Same for Day No. 35, Evg.]

HOW can man be just with God?
If He be pleased to contend with him,
He cannot answer Him one of a thousand.
2 He is wise in heart, and mighty in strength:
Who hath hardened himself against Him, and prospered?
3 Who removeth the mountains, and they know it not,
When He overturneth them in His anger:
4 Who shaketh the earth out of her place,
And the pillars thereof tremble:
5 Who commandeth the sun, and it riseth not;
And sealeth up the stars:
6 Who alone stretcheth out the heavens,
And treadeth upon the waves of the sea:
7 Who maketh the Bear, Orion, and the Pleiades,
And the chambers of the south:
8 Who doeth great things past finding out;
Yea, marvelous things without number.
9 Lo, He goeth by me, and I see Him not;
He passeth on also, but I perceive Him not.

10 ASK now the beasts, and they shall teach thee;
And the fowls of the air, and they shall tell thee;
11 Or speak to the earth, and it shall teach thee;
And the fishes of the sea shall declare unto thee.

I. NEW YEAR DAY

12 Who knoweth not in all these,
That the hand of Jehovah hath wrought this?
13 In whose hand is the soul of every living thing,
And the breath of all mankind.
14 With Him is wisdom and might;
He hath counsel and understanding.
15 Behold, He breaketh down, and it cannot be built again;
He shutteth up a man, and there can be no opening.
16 Behold, He withholdeth the waters, and they dry up;
Again He sendeth them out, and they overturn the earth.
17 With Him is strength and wisdom;
The deceived and the deceiver are His.
18 He leadeth counselors away spoiled,
And judges maketh He fools.
19 He looseth the bond of kings,
And bindeth their loins with a girdle.
20 He leadeth priests away spoiled,
And overthroweth the mighty.
21 He removeth the speech of the trusty,
And taketh away the understanding of the elders.
22 He poureth contempt upon princes,
And looseth the belt of the strong.
23 He discovereth deep things out of darkness,
And bringeth out to light the shadow of death.
24 He increaseth the nations, and He destroyeth them:
He enlargeth the nations, and He leadeth them captive.
25 He taketh away understanding from the chiefs of the people of the earth,
And causeth them to wander in a wilderness where there is no way.
26 They grope in the dark without light,
And He maketh them to stagger like a drunken man.

---

27 HE stretcheth out the north over empty space,
And hangeth the earth upon nothing.
28 He bindeth up the waters in His thick clouds;
And the cloud is not rent under them.
29 He closeth in the face of His throne,
And spreadeth His cloud upon it.
30 He hath described a boundary upon the face of the waters,
Unto the confines of light and darkness.
31 The pillars of heaven tremble,
And are astonished at His rebuke.
32 He stirreth up the sea with His power,
And by His understanding He smiteth through arrogancy.
33 By His spirit the heavens are garnished;
His hand hath pierced the swift serpent.
34 Lo, these are but the outskirts of His ways:
And how small a whisper do we hear of Him!
BUT THE THUNDER OF HIS POWER WHO CAN UNDERSTAND?

Psalm Chant   Same as for Day No. 2

I. NEW YEAR DAY

Prayer of the Day

ETERNAL God, who of old hast laid the foundation of the earth, and whose Word is forever settled in the heavens; whose mercy is from everlasting, and rises anew in the morning of another year:

Give us grace to awake and arise into Christ Thy Son who is our Morning Light; and grant that in all the years of our pilgrimage, walking by faith in Him we may put on strength, and be enabled to endure in the way of life with joy unto the end:

Through Him who came a Wayfarer with us on the earth, our Savior, to whom with the Father and the Spirit — one God — be glory through eternal years: AMEN.

Hymn of Praise

EDWARD HENRY BICKERSTETH, D. D., 1862. (Dox. added.)

O GOD, the Rock of Ages!
  Who evermore hast been,
What time the tempest rages,
  Our dwelling-place serene:
Before Thy first creations,
  O Lord, the same as now,
To endless generations,
  The Everlasting, Thou!

2 Our years are like the shadows
  On sunny hills that lie,
Or grasses in the meadows
  That blossom but to die:
A sleep, a dream, a story,
  By strangers quickly told,
An unremaining glory
  Of things that soon are old.

3 O Thou who canst not slumber,
  Whose light grows never pale,
Teach us aright to number
  Our years before they fail!
On us Thy mercy lighten,
  On us Thy goodness rest,
And let Thy Spirit brighten
  The hearts Thyself hast blessed!

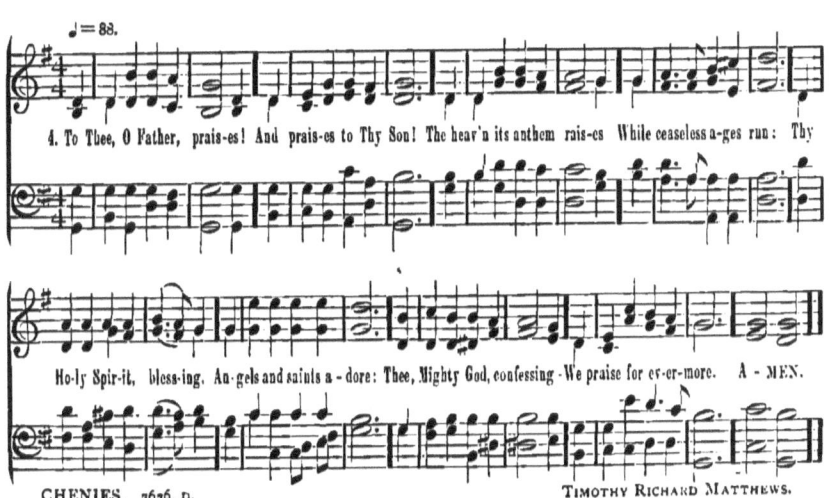

CHENIES. 7676, D. TIMOTHY RICHARD MATTHEWS.

2. LORD'S DAY OF THE NEW YEAR

Introductory
MORNING

Sentence BLESS Jehovah, O my soul;
And forget not all His benefits:
Who redeemeth thy life from destruction;
Who crowneth thee with lovingkindness and tender mercies. [Ps. ciii. 2, 4]

Response JEHOVAH is good;
His lovingkindness en- | dureth for | ever;
And His faithfulness | un-to | all gener- | ations. [Ps. c, 5]

F. G. Edwards.

[On this Day especially it is appropriate that the Ten Commandments be read (Exodus, xx, 1–17). They may precede the usual Summary of the Law of God by our Lord Jesus Christ, as given in THE SERVICE.]

Scripture Lessons
Old Covenant — Gen. i, 1–13.
Gospel — John, i, 1–5.
Apostolic Word — I Pet. i, 13–25.

Responsive Lesson
A PSALM OF DAVID, Ps. ciii. [Same for Day No. 40, Mng.]

BLESS Jehovah, O my soul;
  And all that is within me, bless His holy Name.
2 Bless Jehovah, O my soul,
  And forget not all His benefits:
3 Who forgiveth all thine iniquities;
  Who healeth all thy diseases;
4 Who redeemeth thy life from destruction;
  Who crowneth thee with lovingkindness and tender mercies:
5 Who satisfieth thy desire with good things;
  So that thy youth is renewed like the eagle.
6 Jehovah executeth righteous acts,
  And judgments for all that are oppressed.
7 He made known His ways unto Moses,
  His doings unto the children of Israel.
8 Jehovah is merciful and gracious,
  Slow to anger, and abundant in lovingkindness.
9 He will not always chide;
  Neither will He keep His anger forever.
10 He hath not dealt with us after our sins,
  Nor rewarded us after our iniquities.
11 For as the heaven is high above the earth,
  So great is His lovingkindness toward them that fear Him.
12 As far as the east is from the west,
  So far hath He removed our transgressions from us.

2. LORD'S DAY OF THE NEW YEAR—MORNING 5

13 Like as a father pitieth his children,
  So Jehovah pitieth them that fear Him.
14 For He knoweth our frame;
  He remembereth that we are dust.
15 As for man, his days are as grass;
  As a flower of the field, so he flourisheth.
16 For the wind passeth over it, and it is gone;
  And the place thereof shall know it no more.
17 But the lovingkindness of Jehovah is from everlasting to everlasting upon them that fear Him,
  And His righteousness unto children's children;
18 To such as keep His covenant,
  And to those that remember His precepts to do them.
19 Jehovah hath established His throne in the heavens;
  And His kingdom ruleth over all.
20 Bless Jehovah, ye angels of His:
  Ye mighty in strength, that fulfill His word,
  Hearkening unto the voice of His word.
21 Bless Jehovah, all ye His hosts;
  Ye ministers of His, that do His pleasure.
22 Bless Jehovah, all ye His works,
  In all places of His dominion:
  BLESS JEHOVAH, O MY SOUL.

Psalm Chant

From Psalm civ. [Same for Evg., and for Day No. 1]

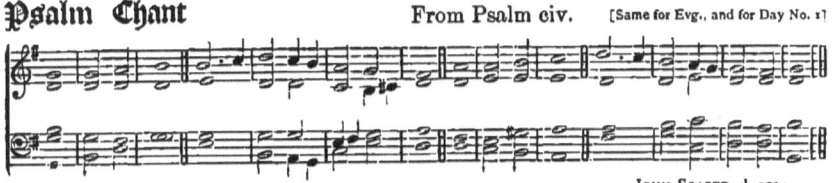

JOHN SOAPER, d. 1794.

B LESS Jehovah, | O my | soul.
  O Jehovah, my God, | Thou art | ver-y | great:
2 Thou art cloth'd with | honor and | majesty:
  Who coverest Thyself with | light as | with a | garment;
3 Who stretchest out the | heav'ns · like a | curtain;
  Who layeth the beams of His | cham-bers | in the | waters;
4 Who maketh the | clouds His | chariot;
  Who walketh upon the | wings | of the | wind:
5 Who maketh winds His messengers;
  Flames of | fire His | ministers:
  Who laid the foundations of the earth,
  That it should | not be | mov'd for | ever.
6 O Jehovah, how manifold | are Thy | works!
  In wisdom hast Thou made them all:
  The | earth is | full · of Thy | riches.
7 Let the glory of Jehovah en- | dure for | ever;
  Let Jehovah re- | joice | in His | works:
8 Who looketh on the | earth,· and it | trembleth;
  He toucheth the | moun-tains, | and they | smoke. *[Continued, next page]*

2. LORD'S DAY OF THE NEW YEAR — MORNING

9 I will sing unto Jehovah as | long • as I | live :
 I will sing praise to my God | while I | have any | being.
10 Let my meditation be sweet unto Him :
 I will re- | joice • in Je- | hovah.
 Bless Jehovah, O my soul. | Hal-le- | lu- | jah !
11 GLORY be to the Father | and • to the | Son
 And | to the | Ho-ly | Ghost :
12 As it was in the beginning, is now, and | ev-er | shall be,
 World | with-out | end. A- | MEN.

Prayer of the Day

LORD Jehovah, who inhabitest eternity, and whose lovingkindness leads us through our years; we beseech Thee, grant now in all Thy Church on earth a year of the right hand of the Most High:

And so assist us, creatures of a day, to arise in faith and redeem the time, that, freed from all our sins by Thy mercy in Thy Son Christ Jesus, we may overcome all things in His Name who for our sakes sojourned also in these mortal years:

Till, after these changing times we be brought to the unchanging glory of His presence, where He liveth and reigneth with the Father and the Holy Spirit — one God — to ages without end : AMEN.

Hymn of Praise

PHILIP DODDRIDGE, D. D. (Dox. added.)

OUR Helper, God ! we bless Thy name,
Whose love forever is the same :
The tokens of Thy gracious care
Open, and crown, and close the year.

2 Amid ten thousand snares we stand,
Supported by Thy guardian hand ;
And see, when we review our ways,
Ten thousand monuments of praise.

3 Thus far Thine arm has led us on ;
Thus far we make Thy mercy known ;
And while we tread this desert land,
New mercies shall new songs demand.

4 Our grateful souls, on Jordan's shore,
Shall raise one sacred pillar more ;
Then bear, in Thy bright courts above,
Inscriptions of immortal love.

DUKE STREET. L. M.   JOHN HATTON, 1790.

2. EVENING
LORD'S DAY OF THE NEW YEAR

Introductory

Sentence   JEHOVAH shall reign forever:
           Thy God, O Zion, unto all generations.
           Praise ye Jehovah.   [Ps. cxlvi, 10]

Response   JEHOVAH is good;
[Tune, in Morning]   His lovingkindness en- | dureth for | ever.
           And His faithfulness | un-to | all gener- | ations.   [Ps. c, 5]

Scripture Lessons   Old Covenant   Ecc. xi, 1–8: xii, 13, 14.
                            Gospel   Luke, xiii, 6–9.
                            Apostolic Word   Eph. v, 6–21.

Responsive Lesson   SONG OF DANIEL, Dan. ii, 20–23: Psalm xxxiii.

BLESSED be the Name of God forever and ever:
     For wisdom and might are His:
2 And He changeth the times and the seasons:
     He removeth kings, and setteth up kings:
3 He giveth wisdom unto the wise,
     And knowledge to them that know understanding:
4 He revealeth the deep and secret things:
     He knoweth what is in the darkness,
     And the light dwelleth with Him.
5 We thank Thee, and praise Thee,
     O Thou God of our fathers.

---

6 REJOICE in Jehovah, O ye righteous:
     Praise is comely for the upright.
7 Give thanks unto Jehovah with harp:
     Sing praises unto Him with the psaltery of ten strings.
8 Sing unto Him a new song;
     Play skillfully with a loud noise.
9 For the word of Jehovah is right,
     And all His work is done in faithfulness.
10 He loveth righteousness and justice:
     The earth is full of the lovingkindness of Jehovah.
11 By the word of Jehovah were the heavens made;
     And all the host of them by the breath of His mouth.
12 He gathereth the waters of the sea together as a heap:
     He layeth up the deeps in storehouses.
13 Let all the earth fear Jehovah:
     Let all the inhabitants of the world stand in awe of Him.
14 For He spake, and it was done;
     He commanded, and it stood fast.
15 Jehovah bringeth the counsel of the nations to nought:
     He maketh the thoughts of the peoples to be of none effect.
16 The counsel of Jehovah standeth fast forever,
     The thoughts of His heart to all generations.

2. LORD'S DAY OF THE NEW YEAR—EVENING

17 Blessed is the nation whose God is Jehovah;
The people whom He hath chosen for His own inheritance.
18 Jehovah looketh from heaven;
He beholdeth all the sons of men;
19 From the place of His habitation He looketh forth
Upon all the inhabitants of the earth —
20 He that fashioneth the hearts of them all,
That considereth all their works.
21 There is no king saved by the multitude of a host:
A mighty man is not delivered by great strength.
22 A horse is a vain thing for safety;
Neither shall he deliver any by his great power.
23 Behold, the eye of Jehovah is upon them that fear Him,
Upon them that hope in His lovingkindness;
24 To deliver their soul from death,
And to keep them alive in famine.
25 Our soul hath waited for Jehovah:
He is our help and our shield.
26 For our heart shall rejoice in Him,
Because we have trusted in His holy Name.
27 Let Thy lovingkindness, O Jehovah, be upon us,
According as we have hoped in Thee.

Psalm Chant   Same as for Morning

Hymn of Praise

PHILIP DODDRIDGE, D. D.   (Dox. added.)

GREAT God! we sing that mighty hand
By which supported still we stand;
The opening year Thy mercy shows;
Let mercy crown it till it close.

2 By day, by night, at home, abroad,
Still we are guarded by our God;
By Thine incessant bounty fed,
By Thine unerring counsel led.

3 With grateful hearts the past we own;
The future, all to us unknown,
We to Thy guardian care commit,
And peaceful leave before Thy feet.

4 In scenes exalted or depressed,
Be Thou our joy, and Thou our rest;
Thy goodness all our hopes shall raise,
Adored through all our changing days.

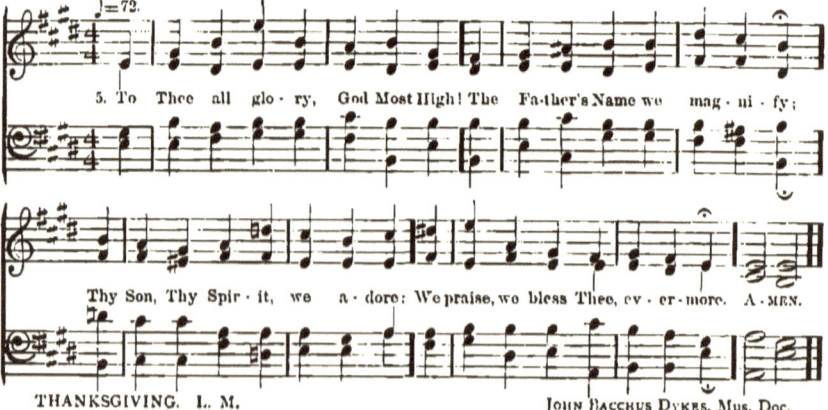

5. To Thee all glo-ry, God Most High! The Fa-ther's Name we mag-ni-fy;
Thy Son, Thy Spir-it, we a-dore: We praise, we bless Thee, ev-er-more. A-MEN.

THANKSGIVING. L. M.   JOHN BACCHUS DYKES, MUS. DOC.

3. LORD'S DAY SECOND IN JANUARY

Introductory
MORNING

Sentence IN the abundance of Thy lovingkindness will I come into Thy house, O Jehovah:
In Thy fear will I worship toward Thy holy temple. [Ps. v, 7]

Response
[Tune in
MONTHLY SONGS]

JEHOVAH send thee help from the | sanc-tu- | ary,
And | strength-en | thee · out of | Zion!
Remember | all thine | offerings,
And ac- | cept thy | sac-ri- | fice! [Ps. xx, 1-3]

Scripture Lessons

Old Covenant   Gen. i, 14–23.
Gospel   Matt. ii, 1–12.
Apostolic Word 1 John, i.

Responsive Lesson   Isaiah, lxi.

THE spirit of the Lord Jehovah is upon me;
  Because Jehovah hath anointed me to preach good tidings unto the meek;
2 He hath sent me to bind up the brokenhearted,
  To proclaim liberty to the captives,
  And the opening of the prison to them that are bound;
3 To proclaim the year of Jehovah's favor,
  And the day of vengeance of our God;
4 To comfort all that mourn;
  To appoint unto them that mourn in Zion,
5 To give unto them a garland for ashes,
  The oil of joy for mourning,
  The garment of praise for the spirit of heaviness;
6 That they might be called trees of righteousness,
  The planting of Jehovah, that He might be glorified.
7 And they shall build the old wastes,
  They shall raise up the former desolations,
8 And they shall repair the waste cities,
  The desolations of many generations.
9 And strangers shall stand and feed your flocks,
  And aliens shall be your plowmen and your vinedressers.
10 But ye shall be named the priests of Jehovah;
  Men shall call you the ministers of our God:
11 Ye shall eat the wealth of the nations,
  And in their glory shall ye boast yourselves.
12 Instead of your shame ye shall have double;
  And instead of dishonor they shall rejoice in their portion:
13 Therefore in their land they shall possess double:
  Everlasting joy shall be unto them.
14 For I Jehovah love justice,
  I hate robbery with iniquity;
15 And I will give them their recompense in truth,
  And I will make an everlasting covenant with them.

3. LORD'S DAY SECOND IN JANUARY—MORNING

16 And their seed shall be known among the nations,
  And their offspring among the peoples:
17 All that see them shall acknowledge them,
  That they are the seed which Jehovah hath blessed.
18 I will greatly rejoice in Jehovah,
  My soul shall be joyful in my God;
19 For He hath clothed me with the garments of salvation,
  He hath covered me with the robe of righteousness,
20 As a bridegroom decketh himself with a garland,
  And as a bride adorneth herself with her jewels.
21 For as the earth bringeth forth her bud,
  And as the garden causeth the things that are sown in it to spring forth;
22 So the Lord Jehovah will cause righteousness and praise to spring forth
  Before all the nations.

Psalm Chant See MONTHLY SONGS: Lord's Day Second—Morning.

Prayer of the Day

FATHER of Lights, who by the leading of a star didst manifest Thine only-begotten Son to the Gentiles:

Mercifully grant for His sake, that we beholding afar His rising light, may so know and follow Him here by faith, that we shall be brought to the full vision of His glory hereafter in the heavens:

Where He liveth in light eternal with Thee and Thy Spirit—one God: AMEN.

Hymn of Praise See MONTHLY SONGS: Lord's Day Second—Morning.

---

3. EVENING
LORD'S DAY SECOND IN JANUARY

Introductory

Sentence

BEHOLD, bless ye Jehovah, all ye servants of Jehovah,
[Who by night stand in the house of Jehovah:]
Lift up your hands to the sanctuary,
And bless ye Jehovah. [Ps. cxxxiv. 1. 2]

Response [Tune in MONTHLY SONGS]

LIFT up your hands to the | sanc-tu- | ary,
And | bless | ye Je- | hovah.
Jehovah bless Thee | out of | Zion!
Even He that | made | heav'n and | earth. [Ps. cxxxiv. 2, 3]

Scripture Lessons

Old Covenant   Jer. iii, 12–23.
Gospel   Mark, v, 21–34.
Apostolic Word Acts, ii, 36–47.

Responsive Lesson
Psalms, cxiv, cxv.

WHEN Israel went forth out of Egypt,
The house of Jacob from a people of strange language;
2 Judah became His sanctuary,
Israel His dominion.
3 The sea saw it, and fled;
Jordan was driven back.
4 The mountains skipped like rams,
The little hills like young sheep.
5 What aileth thee, O thou sea, that thou fleest?
Thou Jordan, that thou turnest back?
6 Ye mountains, that ye skip like rams;
Ye little hills, like young sheep?
7 Tremble, thou earth, at the presence of the Lord,
At the presence of the God of Jacob;
8 Who turned the rock into a pool of water,
The flint into a fountain of waters.

---

9 NOT unto us, O Jehovah,
Not unto us,
10 But unto Thy Name give glory,
For Thy lovingkindness,
11 And for Thy truth's sake.
Wherefore should the nations say, Where is now their God?
12 But our God is in the heavens:
He hath done whatsoever He pleased.
13 Their idols are silver and gold,
The work of men's hands.
14 They have mouths, but they speak not;
Eyes have they, but they see not;
15 They have ears, but they hear not;
Noses have they, but they smell not;
16 They have hands, but they handle not;
Feet have they, but they walk not;
Neither speak they through their throat.
17 They that make them shall be like unto them;
Yea, every one that trusteth in them.
18 O Israel, trust thou in Jehovah:
He is their help and their shield.
19 O house of Aaron, trust ye in Jehovah:
He is their help and their shield.
20 Ye that fear Jehovah, trust in Jehovah:
He is their help and their shield.
21 Jehovah hath been mindful of us; He will bless us:
He will bless the house of Israel;
22 He will bless the house of Aaron.
He will bless them that fear Jehovah,
Both small and great.
23 Jehovah increase you more and more,
You and your children.

3. LORD'S DAY SECOND IN JANUARY—EVENING

24 Blessed are ye of Jehovah,
   Who made heaven and earth.
25 The heavens are the heavens of Jehovah;
   But the earth hath He given to the children of men.
26 The dead praise not Jehovah,
   Neither any that go down into silence;
27 But we will bless Jehovah
   From this time forth and for evermore.
   PRAISE YE JEHOVAH.

Psalm Chant See MONTHLY SONGS: Lord's Day Second—Evening.

Hymn of Praise See MONTHLY SONGS: Lord's Day Second—Evening.

---

4. LORD'S DAY THIRD IN JANUARY
MORNING

Introductory

Sentence

I KNOW the thoughts that I think toward you, saith Jehovah,
Thoughts of peace and not of evil.
And ye shall seek Me and find Me,
When ye shall search for Me with all your heart.   [Jer. xxix, 11, 13]

Response
[Tune in
MONTHLY SONGS]

THOU hast said, | Seek ye • My | face :
My heart saith unto Thee,
Thy face, O Je- | ho-vah, | will I | seek.   [Ps. xxvii, 8]

Scripture Lessons   Old Covenant Gen. i, 24–31 ; ii, 1–3.
                        Gospel   Luke, iv, 1–15.
                        Apostolic Word Rom. i, 14–25.

Responsive Lesson   PSALMS OF DAVID, Ps. xix, liii.

THE heavens declare the glory of God;
   And the firmament showeth His handiwork.
2 Day unto day uttereth speech,
   And night unto night showeth knowledge.
3 There is no speech nor language;
   Their voice cannot be heard.
4 Their line is gone out through all the earth,
   And their words to the end of the world.
5 In them hath He set a tabernacle for the sun,
   Which is as a bridegroom coming out of his chamber,
   And rejoiceth as a strong man to run his course.
6 His going forth is from the end of the heaven,
   And his circuit unto the ends of it:
   And there is nothing hid from the heat thereof.

4. LORD'S DAY THIRD IN JANUARY—MORNING

7 The law of Jehovah is perfect, restoring the soul:
The testimony of Jehovah is sure, making wise the simple.
8 The precepts of Jehovah are right, rejoicing the heart:
The commandment of Jehovah is pure, enlightening the eyes.
9 The fear of Jehovah is clean, enduring forever:
The judgments of Jehovah are true, and righteous altogether.
10 More to be desired are they than gold, yea, than much fine gold:
Sweeter also than honey and the honeycomb.
11 Moreover by them is Thy servant warned:
In keeping of them there is great reward.
12 Who can discern his errors?
Clear Thou me from hidden faults.
13 Keep back Thy servant also from presumptuous sins;
Let them not have dominion over me:
14 Then shall I be perfect,
And I shall be clear from great transgression.
15 Let the words of my mouth
And the meditation of my heart
16 Be acceptable in Thy sight,
O Jehovah, my rock, and my redeemer.

---

17 THE fool hath said in his heart, There is no God.
Corrupt are they, and have done abominable iniquity;
THERE IS NONE THAT DOETH GOOD.
18 God looked down from heaven
Upon the children of men,
19 To see if there were any that did understand,
That did seek after God.
20 Every one of them is gone back; they are together become filthy;
There is none that doeth good, no, not one.
21 Have the workers of iniquity no knowledge?
Who eat up my people as they eat bread,
And call not upon God.
22 There were they in great fear, where no fear was:
For God hath scattered the bones of him that encampeth against thee;
23 Thou hast put them to shame,
Because God hath rejected them.
24 Oh that the salvation of Israel were come out of Zion!
When God bringeth back the captivity of His people,
25 Then shall Jacob rejoice,
And Israel shall be glad.

Psalm Chant
See MONTHLY SONGS: Lord's Day Third—Morning.

Prayer of the Day

O GOD, the Fountain of all truth and grace, who hast called us out of darkness into Thy marvelous light by the gracious coming of Thy Son, the Brightness of Thy Glory:

4. LORD'S DAY THIRD IN JANUARY—MORNING

Grant that we may be so illumined and led in Him who is the Way and the Truth and the Life, that our way may be peace, and our work righteousness, and the end everlasting Life:

Through Him, who with the Father and the Holy Spirit is glorified—one God in light for evermore: AMEN.

Hymn of Praise   See MONTHLY SONGS: Lord's Day Third—Morning.

---

4. EVENING
LORD'S DAY THIRD IN JANUARY

Introductory

Sentence

GOD, who said, Light shall shine out of darkness, hath shined in our hearts,
To give the light of the knowledge of the glory of God in the face of Jesus Christ. [II Cor. iv, 6]

Response
[Tune in
MONTHLY SONGS]

IT shall come to pass that at evening time there | shall be | light.
And it shall come to pass in that day,
That living waters shall go | out · from Je- | ru-sa- | lem.
[Zech. xiv, 7, 8]

Scripture Lessons

Old Covenant   Ezkl. xxxiii, 1-9.
Gospel   Luke, v, 1-11.
Apostolic Word   I Cor. i, 10-25.

Responsive Lesson   SONG OF MOSES AND MIRIAM AT THE RED SEA, from Ex. xv.

I WILL sing unto Jehovah, for He hath triumphed gloriously:
   The horse and his rider hath He thrown into the sea.
2 Jehovah is my strength and song,
   And He is become my salvation:
3 This is my God, and I will praise Him;
   My father's God, and I will exalt Him.
4 Jehovah is a man of war:
   Jehovah is His Name.
5 Pharaoh's chariots and his host hath He cast into the sea:
   And his chosen captains are sunk in the Red Sea.
6 The deeps cover them:
   They went down into the depths like a stone.
7 Thy right hand, O Jehovah, is glorious in power,
   Thy right hand, O Jehovah, dasheth in pieces the enemy;
8 And in the greatness of Thine excellency
   Thou overthrowest them that rise up against Thee:
9 Thou sendest forth Thy wrath,
   It consumeth them as stubble.

4. LORD'S DAY THIRD IN JANUARY — EVENING

10 And with the blast of Thy nostrils the waters were piled up,
   The floods stood upright as a heap;
   The deeps were congealed in the heart of the sea.
11 The enemy said, I will pursue, I will overtake, I will divide the spoil:
   My desire shall be satisfied upon them;
12 I will draw my sword,
   My hand shall destroy them.
13 Thou didst blow with Thy wind, the sea covered them:
   They sank as lead in the mighty waters.
14 Who is like unto Thee, O Jehovah, among the gods?
   Who is like Thee, glorious in holiness,
   FEARFUL IN PRAISES, DOING WONDERS?
15 Thou stretchedst out Thy right hand,
   The earth swallowed them.
16 Thou in Thy mercy hast led the people which Thou hast redeemed:
   Thou hast guided them in Thy strength to Thy holy habitation.
17 The peoples have heard, they tremble:
   Pangs have taken hold on the inhabitants of Philistia.
18 Then were the chiefs of Edom dismayed;
   The mighty men of Moab, trembling taketh hold upon them:
19 All the inhabitants of Canaan are melted away.
   Terror and dread falleth upon them:
   By the greatness of Thine arm they are as still as a stone;
20 Till Thy people pass over, O Jehovah,
   Till the people pass over that Thou hast purchased.
21 Thou shalt bring them in,
   And plant them in the mountain of Thine inheritance,
22 The place, O Jehovah, which Thou hast made for Thee to dwell in,
   The sanctuary, O Jehovah, which Thy hands have established.
   JEHOVAH SHALL REIGN FOREVER AND EVER.

23 Sing ye to Jehovah, for He hath triumphed gloriously;
   The horse and his rider hath He thrown into the sea.
   JEHOVAH SHALL REIGN FOREVER AND EVER.

Psalm Chant See MONTHLY SONGS: Lord's Day Third — Evening.

Hymn of Praise See MONTHLY SONGS: Lord's Day Third — Evening.

---

5. LORD'S DAY FOURTH IN JANUARY
MORNING

Introductory

Sentence I WAS glad when they said unto me,
   Let us go into the house of Jehovah.
   Our feet are standing within thy gates, O Jerusalem: [Ps. cxxii, 1, 2, 4]
   Whither the tribes go up, to give thanks unto the Name of Jehovah.

5. LORD'S DAY FOURTH IN JANUARY — MORNING

Response
[Tune in
MONTHLY SONGS]

I HAVE set watchmen upon thy walls, O Je- | ru-sa- | lem ;
They shall never hold their | peace | day nor | night :
Ye that are Jehovah's remembrancers, | keep not | silence,
Till He make Jerusalem a | praise | in the | earth. [Is. lxii, 6, 7]

Scripture Lessons

Old Covenant   Gen. ii, 4–17.
Gospel   John, iii, 1–13.
Apostolic Word   1 Cor. i, 26–31 : ii, 1–5.

Responsive Lesson

From the PROPHECY OF BALAAM, Num. xxiii, xxiv.

FROM the top of the rocks I see Him,
   And from the hills I behold Him:
2 Lo, it is a people that dwell alone,
   And shall not be reckoned among the nations.
3 Who can count the dust of Jacob,
   Or number the fourth part of Israel?
4 Let me die the death of the righteous,
   And let my last end be like His!

5 God is not a man, that He should lie ;
   Neither the son of man, that He should repent:
6 Hath He said, and shall He not do it ?
   Or hath He spoken, and shall He not make it good ?
7 Behold, I have received commandment to bless :
   And He hath blessed, and I cannot reverse it.
8 He hath not beheld iniquity in Jacob,
   Neither hath He seen perverseness in Israel:
9 Jehovah his God is with him,
   And the shout of a king is among them.
10 God bringeth them forth out of Egypt;
   He hath as it were the strength of the wild ox.
11 Surely there is no enchantment with Jacob,
   Neither is there any divination with Israel:
12 Now shall it be said of Jacob and of Israel,
   What hath God wrought!
13 Behold, the people riseth up as a lioness,
   And as a lion doth he lift himself up :

14 He saith, who heareth the words of God,
Who seeth the vision of the Almighty,
   Falling down, and having his eyes open:
15 How goodly are Thy tents, O Jacob,
   Thy tabernacles, O Israel!
16 As valleys are they spread forth,
   As gardens by the river side.
17 As lign-aloes which Jehovah hath planted,
   As cedar trees beside the waters.

18 God bringeth him forth out of Egypt;
He hath as it were the strength of the wild ox :
   He shall eat up the nations his adversaries,

5. LORD'S DAY FOURTH IN JANUARY—MORNING

19 And shall break their bones in pieces,
    And smite them through with his arrows.
20 He couched, he lay down as a lion,
    And as a lioness; who shall rouse him up?
21 Blessed be every one that blesseth thee,
    And cursed be every one that curseth thee.
22 He saith, who heareth the words of God,
    And knoweth the knowledge of the Most High,
23 Who seeth the vision of the Almighty,
    Falling down, and having his eyes open:
24 I see him, but not now:
    I behold him, but not nigh:
25 There shall come forth a Star out of Jacob,
    And a scepter shall rise out of Israel,
26 And shall smite through the corners of Moab,
    And break down all the sons of tumult.
27 And Edom shall be a possession,
    Seir also shall be a possession, who were His enemies;
28 While Israel doeth valiantly,
    And out of Jacob shall One have dominion.

Psalm Chant
See MONTHLY SONGS: Lord's Day Fourth—Morning.

Prayer of the Day
O LORD, we beseech Thee, of Thy Fatherly goodness keep Thy household continually in the true faith of Thy Son made flesh:
That we, resting only on the blessed hope of Thy redeeming grace, may evermore be upheld by Thy saving power, in Him,
Who is glorified with the Father and the Spirit—eternally one God: AMEN.

Hymn of Praise
See MONTHLY SONGS: Lord's Day Fourth—Morning.

---

5. EVENING
LORD'S DAY FOURTH IN JANUARY

Introductory

Sentence

DWELLING in the secret place of the Most High,
Abiding under the shadow of the Almighty—
I will say of Jehovah, He is my refuge and my fortress;
My God, in whom I trust.   [Ps. xci, 1, 2]

Response
[Tune in MONTHLY SONGS]

THERE is a river, the streams whereof make glad the | city of | God,
The holy place of the | taber-nacles | of the • Most | High.
Jehovah of | Hosts is | with us;
The God of | Ja-cob | is our | refuge.   [Ps. xlvi, 4, 7]

Scripture Lessons

Old Covenant   Jer. xxvi, 1–15.
Gospel   Matt. v, 13–20.
Apostolic Word   Rev. ii, 1–11.

Responsive Lesson

A PSALM OF ASAPH, Ps. lxxxi:
The MAGISTRATE'S PSALM (of David), ci.

SING aloud unto God our strength:
  Make a joyful noise unto the God of Jacob.
2 Take up the psalm, and bring hither the timbrel,
  The pleasant harp with the psaltery.
3 Blow the trumpet in the new moon,
  At the full moon, on our solemn feast day.
4 For it is a statute for Israel,
  An ordinance of the God of Jacob.
5 He appointed it in Joseph for a testimony,
When He went out over the land of Egypt:
  Where I heard a language that I knew not.
6 I removed his shoulder from the burden:
  His hands were freed from the basket.
7 Thou calledst in trouble,
  And I delivered thee;
8 I answered thee in the secret place of thunder;
  I proved thee at the waters of Meribah.
9 Hear, O My people, and I will testify unto thee:
  O Israel, if thou wouldst hearken unto Me!
10 There shall no strange god be in thee;
  Neither shalt thou worship any strange god.
11 I am Jehovah thy God,
Who brought thee up out of the land of Egypt:
  Open thy mouth wide, and I will fill it.
12 But My people hearkened not to My voice;
  And Israel would none of Me.
13 So I let them go after the stubbornness of their heart,
  That they might walk in their own counsels.
14 Oh that My people would hearken unto Me,
  That Israel would walk in My ways!
15 I should soon subdue their enemies,
  And turn My hand against their adversaries.
16 The haters of Jehovah should submit themselves unto Him:
  But their time should endure forever.
17 He should feed them also with the finest of the wheat:
  And with honey out of the rock should I satisfy thee.

---

18 I WILL sing of lovingkindness and judgment:
  Unto Thee, O Jehovah, will I sing praises.
19 I will behave myself wisely in a perfect way:
  Oh when wilt Thou come unto me?
20 I will walk within my house with a perfect heart.
  I will set no base thing before mine eyes:
21 I hate the work of them that turn aside;
  It shall not cleave unto me.

5. LORD'S DAY FOURTH IN JANUARY—EVENING

22 A perverse heart shall depart from me:
 I will know no evil thing.
23 Whoso privily slandereth his neighbor, him will I destroy:
 Him that hath a high look and a proud heart will I not suffer.
24 Mine eyes shall be upon the faithful of the land, that they may dwell with me:
 He that walketh in a perfect way, he shall minister unto me.
25 He that worketh deceit shall not dwell within my house:
 He that speaketh falsehood shall not be established before mine eyes.
26 Morning by morning will I destroy all the wicked of the land;
 To cut off all the workers of iniquity from the city of Jehovah.

Psalm Chant See MONTHLY SONGS: Lord's Day Fourth — Evening.

Hymn of Praise See MONTHLY SONGS: Lord's Day Fourth — Evening.

[NOT IN EVERY YEAR]

6. LORD'S DAY FIFTH IN JANUARY
MORNING

Introductory
Sentence

OUR soul hath waited for Jehovah;
 He is our help and our shield:
For our heart shall rejoice in Him,
 Because we have trusted in His holy Name. [Ps. xxxiii, 20, 21]

Response
[Tune in
MONTHLY SONGS]

THEY that know Thy Name will put their | trust in | Thee;
 For Thou, Jehovah, hast not forsaken | them that | seek | Thee. [Ps. ix, 10]

Scripture Lessons Old Covenant Gen. ii, 18–24.
  Gospel Luke, v, 17–26.
  Apostolic Word II Cor. v, 14–21.

Responsive Lesson Psalm, cxix, 1–32.

BLESSED are they that are perfect in the way,
 Who walk in the law of Jehovah.
2 Blessed are they that keep His testimonies,
 That seek Him with the whole heart.
3 Yea, they do no unrighteousness;
 They walk in His ways.
4 Thou hast commanded us Thy precepts,
 That we should observe them diligently.
5 Oh that my ways were established
 To observe Thy statutes!

6. LORD'S DAY FIFTH IN JANUARY—MORNING

6 Then shall I not be ashamed,
When I have respect unto all Thy commandments.
7 I will give thanks unto Thee with uprightness of heart,
When I learn Thy righteous judgments.
8 I will observe Thy statutes:
O forsake me not utterly.

9 Wherewithal shall a young man cleanse his way?
By taking heed thereto according to Thy word.
10 With my whole heart have I sought Thee:
O let me not wander from Thy commandments.
11 Thy word have I laid up in mine heart,
That I might not sin against Thee.
12 Blessed art Thou, Jehovah:
Teach me Thy statutes.
With my lips have I declared all the judgments of Thy mouth.
13 I have rejoiced in the way of Thy testimonies,
As much as in all riches.
14 I will meditate in Thy precepts,
And have respect unto Thy ways.
15 I will delight myself in Thy statutes:
I will not forget Thy word.

16 Deal bountifully with Thy servant, that I may live;
So will I observe Thy word.
17 Open Thou mine eyes,
That I may behold wondrous things out of Thy law.
18 I am a sojourner in the earth:
Hide not Thy commandments from me.
19 My soul breaketh for the longing
That it hath unto Thy judgments at all times.
20 Thou hast rebuked the proud that are cursed,
Who do wander from Thy commandments.
21 Take away from me reproach and contempt;
For I have kept Thy testimonies.
22 Princes also sat and talked against me:
But Thy servant did meditate in Thy statutes.
23 Thy testimonies also are my delight
And my counselors.

24 My soul cleaveth unto the dust:
Quicken Thou me according to Thy word.
25 I declared my ways, and Thou answeredst me:
Teach me Thy statutes.
26 Make me to understand the way of Thy precepts:
So shall I meditate of Thy wondrous works.
27 My soul melteth for heaviness:
Strengthen Thou me according unto Thy word.

6. LORD'S DAY FIFTH IN JANUARY—MORNING

28 Remove from me the way of falsehood:
 And grant me Thy law graciously.
29 I have chosen the way of faithfulness:
 Thy judgments have I set before me.
30 I cleave unto Thy testimonies:
 O Jehovah, put me not to shame.
31 I will run the way of Thy commandments,
 When Thou shalt enlarge my heart.

Psalm Chant   See MONTHLY SONGS: Lord's Day Fifth — Morning.

Prayer of the Day

GOD of Eternal Might, who drawest near in the person of Thy Son Jesus, giving help to them that have no strength:
 Look mercifully on our low estate, and cause Thy grace to triumph in our weakness and over our sinfulness; that we, arising, may follow those who through faith already inherit Thy promises in Christ our Savior,
 Who with the Father and the Holy Spirit liveth and reigneth—one God in glory without end: AMEN.

Hymn of Praise   See MONTHLY SONGS: Lord's Day Fifth — Morning.

---

6. EVENING
LORD'S DAY FIFTH IN JANUARY

Introductory Sentence

O GOD, Thou art my God; earnestly will I seek Thee:
My soul thirsteth for Thee, my flesh longeth for Thee.
So have I looked upon Thee in the sanctuary,
To see Thy power and Thy glory.
For Thy lovingkindness is better than life.   [Ps. lxiii, 1-3]

Response [Tune in MONTHLY SONGS]

WITH Thee, O God, is the | fountain of | life:
In Thy | light shall | we see | light.   [Ps. xxxvi, 9]

Scripture Lessons
 Old Covenant   Judg. ii, 11–23.
 Gospel   John, iii, 14–21.
 Apostolic Word   Rev. iii, 1–13.

Responsive Lesson   From the BLESSING OF THE TRIBES BY MOSES,
                       Deut. xxxiii.

JEHOVAH came from Sinai,
 And rose from Seir unto them;
2 He shined forth from mount Paran,
 And He came from the ten thousands of holy ones:

6. LORD'S DAY FIFTH IN JANUARY — EVENING

3 At His right hand was a fiery law unto them.
  Yea, He loveth the people;
   All His saints are in thy hand:
4 And they sat down at thy feet;
   Every one shall receive of thy words.
5 Moses commanded us a law,
   An inheritance for the assembly of Jacob.
6 And he was king in Jeshurun,
  When the heads of the people were gathered,
   All the tribes of Israel together.

7 The beloved of Jehovah shall dwell in safety by Him;
   *He covereth him all the day long,
   And he dwelleth between His shoulders.*

8 Blessed of Jehovah be his land;
  For the precious things of heaven, for the dew,
   And for the deep that coucheth beneath,
9 And for the precious things of the fruits of the sun,
   And for the precious things of the growth of the moons,
10 And for the chief things of the ancient mountains,
   And for the precious things of the everlasting hills,
11 And for the precious things of the earth and the fullness thereof,
   And the good will of Him that dwelt in the bush:
12 Let the blessing come upon the head of Joseph,
   And upon the crown of the head of him that was separate from his brethren.

13 Thy bars shall be iron and brass;
   And as thy days, so shall thy strength be.

14 There is none like unto God, O Jeshurun,
  Who rideth upon the heaven for thy help,
   And in His excellency on the skies.
15 The eternal God is thy dwelling place,
   And underneath are the everlasting arms:
16 And He thrust out the enemy from before thee,
   And said, Destroy.
17 And Israel dwelleth in safety,
   The fountain of Jacob alone,
18 In a land of grain and new wine;
   Yea, his heavens drop down dew.
19 Happy art thou, O Israel:
   Who is like unto thee, a people saved by Jehovah,
20 The shield of thy help,
   And that is the sword of thine excellency!
21 And thine enemies shall submit themselves unto thee:
   And thou shalt tread upon their high places.

Psalm Chant   See MONTHLY SONGS: Lord's Day Fifth — Evening.

Hymn of Praise   See MONTHLY SONGS: Lord's Day Fifth — Evening.

7. LORD'S DAY FIRST IN FEBRUARY

MORNING

Introductory

Sentence

FROM the rising of the sun even unto the going down of the same,
My Name shall be great among the Gentiles;
And in every place incense shall be offered unto My Name,
And a pure offering — saith Jehovah of Hosts.   [Mal. i, 11]

Response
[Tune in
Monthly Songs]

THE Mighty One, God Je- | hovah,* hath | spoken,
And called the earth from the rising of the sun unto the |
go-ing | down there- | of.
Out of Zion, the per- | fection of | beauty,
God | hath | shin-ed | forth.   [Ps. l, 1, 2]

Scripture Lessons Old Covenant   Isaiah, xxxi.
Gospel   Mark, v, 35–43.
Apostolic Word   Gal. iii, 23–29: iv, 1–7.

Responsive Lesson   Isaiah, xl, 27–31: xli, 1–5, 8–20.

WHY sayest Thou, O Jacob,
 And speakest, O Israel,
2 My way is hid from Jehovah,
 And my judgment is passed away from my God?
3 Hast thou not known?
 Hast thou not heard?
4 The everlasting God, Jehovah,
 The Creator of the ends of the earth,
5 Fainteth not, neither is weary;
 There is no searching of His understanding.
6 He giveth power to the faint;
 And to him that hath no might He increaseth strength.
7 Even the youths shall faint and be weary,
 And the young men shall utterly fall;
8 But they that wait for Jehovah shall renew their strength:
 They shall mount up with wings as eagles;
9 They shall run, and not be weary;
 They shall walk, and not faint.

10 Keep silence before Me, O islands;
 And let the peoples renew their strength:
11 Let them come near; then let them speak:
 Let us come near together to judgment.
12 Who hath raised up one from the east,
 Whom He calleth in righteousness to His foot?
13 He giveth nations before him,
 And maketh him rule over kings;
14 He giveth them as the dust to his sword,
 As the driven stubble to his bow.
15 He pursueth them, and passeth on safely;
 Even by a way that he had not gone with his feet.

16 Who hath wrought and done it, calling the generations from the beginning?
I Jehovah, the first, and with the last, I am He.
17 The isles saw, and feared;
The ends of the earth trembled: they drew near, and came.

18 But thou, Israel, My servant,
Jacob whom I have chosen,
The seed of Abraham My friend;
19 Thou whom I have taken hold of from the ends of the earth,
And called thee from the corners thereof,
20 And said unto thee, Thou art My servant,
I have chosen thee and not cast thee away;
21 Fear thou not, for I am with thee;
Be not dismayed, for I am thy God:
22 I will strengthen thee; yea, I will help thee;
Yea, I will uphold thee with the right hand of My righteousness.
23 Behold, all they that are incensed against thee shall be ashamed and confounded:
They that strive with thee shall be as nothing, and shall perish.
24 Thou shalt seek them, and shalt not find them,
Even them that contend with thee:
25 They that war against thee shall be as nothing,
And as a thing of nought.
26 For I Jehovah thy God will hold thy right hand,
Saying unto thee, Fear not; I will help thee.
27 Fear not, thou worm Jacob,
And ye men of Israel;
28 I will help thee, saith Jehovah,
And thy redeemer is the Holy One of Israel.
29 Behold, I will make thee a new sharp threshing instrument having teeth:
Thou shalt thresh the mountains, and beat them small,
And shalt make the hills as chaff.
30 Thou shalt fan them, and the wind shall carry them away,
And the whirlwind shall scatter them:
31 And thou shalt rejoice in Jehovah,
Thou shalt glory in the Holy One of Israel.
32 The poor and needy seek water and there is none,
And their tongue faileth for thirst;
33 I Jehovah will answer them,
I the God of Israel will not forsake them.
34 I will open rivers on the bare heights,
And fountains in the midst of the valleys:
35 I will make the wilderness a pool of water,
And the dry land springs of water.
36 I will plant in the wilderness the cedar, the acacia tree, and the myrtle, and the oil tree;
I will set in the desert the fir tree, the pine, and the box tree together:
37 That they may see, and know,
And consider, and understand together,
38 That the hand of Jehovah hath done this,
And the Holy One of Israel hath created it.

7. LORD'S DAY FIRST IN FEBRUARY — MORNING

Psalm Chant See MONTHLY SONGS: Lord's Day First -- Morning.

Prayer of the Day

ALMIGHTY Father, who hast been mindful of our low estate, and hast sent Thine only-begotten Son Christ Jesus, in whom Thou hast made a covenant of unspeakable grace with us sinners, making sure to us therein a heavenly inheritance:

Cause us evermore to rejoice in this Thy Gift, and to walk worthy of our holy calling; and, we beseech Thee, make known to all mankind Thy grace:

Through the same our Lord and Savior, who is glorified with Thee and the blessed Spirit — one eternal God: AMEN.

Hymn of Praise See MONTHLY SONGS: Lord's Day First — Morning.

---

7. EVENING
LORD'S DAY FIRST IN FEBRUARY

Introductory

Sentence

THUS saith Jehovah who created the heavens —
He is God that formed the earth and made it:
I said not unto the seed of Jacob, Seek ye Me in vain.
Look unto Me, and be ye saved, all the ends of the earth:
For I am God, and there is none else. [Is. xlv, 18, 19, 22]

Response
[Tune in
MONTHLY SONGS]

LOOK unto Me, and | be ye | sav'd,
    All the | ends | of the | earth.
Unto Me every | knee shall | bow,
    And every | tongue · shall con- | fess unto | God.
[Is. xlv, 22, 23 (Rom. xiv, 11)]

Scripture Lessons
Old Covenant   Gen. iii, 1-8.
Gospel   Luke, vi, 37-45.
Apostolic Word Rev. iii, 14-22.

Responsive Lesson From Ezkl. xxxvi.

YE mountains of Israel,
    Hear the word of Jehovah.
2 I have lifted up My hand, saying,
   Surely the heathen that are round about you,
    They shall bear their shame.
3 But ye, O mountains of Israel, ye shall shoot forth your branches,
    And yield your fruit to My people Israel;
    FOR THEY ARE AT HAND TO COME.
4 For, behold, I am for you, and I will turn unto you,
    And ye shall be tilled and sown:
5 And I will multiply men upon you,
    All the house of Israel, even all of it:

7. LORD'S DAY FIRST IN FEBRUARY—EVENING

6 And the cities shall be inhabited,
And the waste places shall be builded:
7 And I will multiply upon you man and beast;
And they shall increase and be fruitful:
8 And I will cause you to be inhabited after your former estate,
And will do better unto you than at your beginnings:
AND YE SHALL KNOW THAT I AM JEHOVAH.

9 Thus saith the Lord Jehovah:
I do not this for your sake, O house of Israel, but for My holy Name,
Which ye have profaned among the nations, whither ye went.
10 And I will sanctify My great Name, which hath been profaned among the nations,
Which ye have profaned in the midst of them;
11 And the nations shall know that I am Jehovah, saith the Lord Jehovah,
When I shall be sanctified in you before their eyes.
12 For I will take you from among the nations,
And gather you out of all the countries,
And will bring you into your own land.
13 And I will sprinkle clean water upon you,
And ye shall be clean:
14 From all your filthiness, and from all your idols,
Will I cleanse you.
15 A new heart also will I give you,
And a new spirit will I put within you:
16 And I will take away the stony heart out of your flesh,
And I will give you a heart of flesh.
17 And I will put My Spirit within you,
And cause you to walk in My statutes,
18 And ye shall keep My judgments,
And do them.
19 And ye shall dwell in the land that I gave to your fathers;
And ye shall be My people, and I will be your God.
20 Then shall ye remember your evil ways,
And your doings that were not good;
21 And ye shall loathe yourselves in your own sight for your iniquities
And for your abominations.
22 Not for your sake do I this, saith the Lord Jehovah, be it known unto you:
Be ashamed and confounded for your ways, O house of Israel.

23 Thus saith the Lord Jehovah:
For this moreover will I be inquired of by the house of Israel,
To do it for them.

Psalm Chant   See MONTHLY SONGS: Lord's Day First—Evening.

Hymn of Praise   See MONTHLY SONGS: Lord's Day First—Evening.

8. LORD'S DAY SECOND IN FEBRUARY

Introductory
MORNING

Sentence

SEND out Thy light and Thy truth, O God; let them lead me:
Let them bring me unto Thy holy hill,
And to Thy tabernacles.
Then will I go unto the altar of God,
Unto God, my exceeding joy.   [Ps. xliii, 3, 4]

Response
[Tune in
MONTHLY SONGS]

JEHOVAH send thee help from the | sanc-tu- | ary,
  And | strength-en | thee • out of | Zion !
Remember | all thine | offerings,
  And ac- | cept thy | sac-ri- | fice !   [Ps. xx, 1-3]

Scripture Lessons

Old Covenant   Prov. iii, 1–20.
Gospel   Matt. v, 33–42.
Apostolic Word Eph. ii, 1–10.

Responsive Lesson
From Is. xliii.

BUT now thus saith Jehovah that created thee, O Jacob,
    And He that formed thee, O Israel:
2 Fear not, for I have redeemed thee;
    I have called thee by thy name, thou art Mine.
3 When thou passest through the waters, I will be with thee;
    And through the rivers, they shall not overflow thee:
4 When thou walkest through the fire, thou shalt not be burned;
    Neither shall the flame kindle upon thee.
5 For I am Jehovah thy God,
    The Holy One of Israel, thy Savior;
6 I have given Egypt as thy ransom,
    Ethiopia and Seba for thee.
7 Since thou hast been precious in My sight, and honorable,
    And I have loved thee;
8 Therefore will I give men for thee,
    And peoples for thy life.
9 Fear not; for I am with thee:
I will bring thy seed from the east,
    And gather thee from the west;
10 I will say to the north, Give up;
    And to the south, Keep not back;
11 Bring My sons from far,
    And My daughters from the end of the earth;
12 Every one that is called by My Name, and whom I have created
    for My glory;
    I have formed him; yea, I have made him.
13 Bring forth the blind people that have eyes,
    And the deaf that have ears.
14 Let all the nations be gathered together,
    And let the peoples be assembled.

8. LORD'S DAY SECOND IN FEBRUARY—MORNING

15 Ye are My witnesses, saith Jehovah,
  And My servant whom I have chosen:
16 That ye may know and believe Me,
  And understand that I am He;
17 Before Me there was no God formed,
  Neither shall there be after Me.
18 I, even I, am Jehovah;
  And beside Me there is no savior.

19 Thus saith Jehovah, your Redeemer,
  The Holy One of Israel:
20 I am Jehovah, your Holy One,
  The Creator of Israel, your King.
21 Thus saith Jehovah, who maketh a way in the sea,
  And a path in the mighty waters;
22 Who bringeth forth the chariot and horse,
  The army and the power;
23 They lie down together, they shall not rise;
  They are extinct, they are quenched as flax:
24 Remember ye not the former things,
  Neither consider the things of old.
25 Behold, I will do a new thing;
  Now shall it spring forth; shall ye not know it?
26 I will even make a way in the wilderness,
  And rivers in the desert.
27 The beasts of the field shall honor me:
  Because I give waters in the wilderness,
  And rivers in the desert, to give drink to My people, My chosen:
28 The people which I formed for Myself,
  That they might set forth My praise.
29 Yet thou hast not called upon Me, O Jacob;
  But thou hast been weary of Me, O Israel.
30 Thou hast burdened Me with thy sins,
  Thou hast wearied Me with thine iniquities.
31 I, even I, am He that blotteth out thy transgressions for Mine own sake;
  And I will not remember thy sins.

Psalm Chant
See MONTHLY SONGS: Lord's Day Second—Morning.

Prayer of the Day

ARISE, O Lord, we beseech Thee; and with the glorious might of Thy salvation in Christ Jesus, succor us:

That, whereas by our sins we are sorely hindered in running the race set before us, Thy grace may always abound for our speedy help:

Through Thy Son, our Lord and Savior, to whom with the Father and the Holy Spirit—one God—be glory and dominion without end: AMEN.

Hymn of Praise
See MONTHLY SONGS: Lord's Day Second—Morning.

8. EVENING
LORD'S DAY SECOND IN FEBRUARY

Introductory

Sentence

PRAISE ye Jehovah.
Praise ye Jehovah from the heavens:
Praise Him in the heights.
Praise ye Him, all His angels;
Praise ye Him, all His host.
Praise ye Jehovah. [Ps. cxlviii, 1, 2, 14]

Response
[Tune in
MONTHLY SONGS]

LIFT up your hands to the | sanc-tu- | ary,
And | bless | ye Je- | hovah.
Jehovah bless thee | out of | Zion!
Even He that | made | heaven and | earth. [Ps. cxxxiv, 2, 3]

Scripture Lessons

Old Covenant   Gen. iii, 9-24.
Gospel   John, iii, 25-36.
Apostolic Word   Acts, xxvi, 9-20.

Responsive Lesson   PSALMS OF DAVID, Ps. xxxii, xxvi.

BLESSED is he whose transgression is forgiven,
   Whose sin is covered.
2 Blessed is the man unto whom Jehovah imputeth not iniquity,
   And in whose spirit there is no guile.
3 When I kept silence, my bones waxed old
   Through my groaning all the day long.
4 For day and night Thy hand was heavy upon me:
   My moisture was changed as with the drought of summer.
5 I acknowledged my sin unto Thee,
   And mine iniquity have I not hid:
6 I said, I will confess my transgressions unto Jehovah;
   And Thou forgavest the iniquity of my sin.
7 For this let every one that is godly pray unto Thee
   In a time when Thou mayst be found:
8 Surely when the great waters overflow
   They shall not reach unto him.
9 Thou art my hiding place; Thou wilt preserve me from trouble;
   Thou wilt compass me about with songs of deliverance.
10 I will instruct thee and teach thee in the way which thou shalt go:
   I will counsel thee with Mine eye upon thee.
11 Be ye not as the horse, or as the mule,
   Which have no understanding:
12 Whose trappings must be bit and bridle to hold them in,
   Else they will not come near unto thee.
13 Many sorrows shall be to the wicked:
   But he that trusteth in Jehovah, lovingkindness shall compass him about.
14 Be glad in Jehovah, and rejoice, ye righteous:
   And shout for joy, all ye that are upright in heart.

8. LORD'S DAY SECOND IN FEBRUARY—EVENING

15 JUDGE me, O Jehovah, for I have walked in mine integrity:
I have trusted also in Jehovah without wavering.
16 Examine me, O Jehovah, and prove me;
Try my reins and my heart.
17 For Thy lovingkindness is before mine eyes;
And I have walked in Thy truth.
18 I have not sat with men of falsehood;
Neither will I go in with dissemblers.
19 I hate the congregation of evil-doers,
And will not sit with the wicked.
20 I will wash mine hands in innocency;
So will I compass Thine altar, O Jehovah:
21 That I may make the voice of thanksgiving to be heard,
And tell of all Thy wondrous works.
22 O Jehovah, I love the habitation of Thy house,
And the place where Thy glory dwelleth.
23 Gather not my soul with sinners,
Nor my life with men of blood:
24 In whose hands is mischief,
And their right hand is full of bribes.
25 But as for me, I will walk in mine integrity:
Redeem me, and be merciful unto me.
26 My foot standeth in an even place:
In the congregations will I bless Jehovah.

Psalm Chant   See MONTHLY SONGS: Lord's Day Second—Evening.

Hymn of Praise   See MONTHLY SONGS: Lord's Day Second—Evening.

---

9. LORD'S DAY THIRD IN FEBRUARY
MORNING

Introductory

Sentence
GIVE ear, O Shepherd of Israel,
Thou that leadest Joseph like a flock;
Thou that sittest above the cherubim, shine forth.   [Ps. lxxx, 1]

Response
[Tune in
MONTHLY SONGS]
THOU hast said, | Seek ye · My | face:
My heart saith unto Thee,
Thy face, O Je- | ho-vah, | will I | seek.   [Ps. xxvii, 8]

Scripture Lessons   Old Covenant   Jer. vii, 1–15.
Gospel   Matt. vi, 19–34.
Apostolic Word   Eph. ii, 13–22.

9. LORD'S DAY THIRD IN FEBRUARY — MORNING

Responsive Lesson Ps. xlii, xliii: (of DAVID) from Ps. xl.

AS the hart panteth after the water brooks,
 So panteth my soul after Thee, O God.
2 My soul thirsteth for God, for the living God:
 When shall I come and appear before God?
3 My tears have been my meat day and night,
 While they continually say unto me, Where is thy God?
4 These things I remember,
 And pour out my soul within me,
5 How I went with the throng,
 And led them to the house of God,
6 With the voice of joy and praise,
 A multitude keeping holyday.
7 Why art thou cast down, O my soul?
 And why art thou disquieted within me?
8 Hope thou in God: for I shall yet praise Him
 For the help of His countenance.

9 O my God, my soul is cast down within me:
 Therefore do I remember Thee
10 From the land of Jordan, and the Hermons,
 From the hill Mizar.
11 Deep calleth unto deep at the noise of Thy waterspouts:
 All Thy waves and Thy billows are gone over me.
12 Yet Jehovah will command His lovingkindness in the day-time,
 And in the night His song shall be with me,
 EVEN A PRAYER UNTO THE GOD OF MY LIFE.
13 I will say unto God my Rock, Why hast Thou forgotten me?
 Why go I mourning because of the oppression of the enemy?
14 As with a sword in my bones, mine adversaries reproach me;
 While they continually say unto me, Where is thy God?
15 Why art thou cast down, O my soul?
 And why art thou disquieted within me?
16 Hope thou in God: for I shall yet praise Him,
 Who is the help of my countenance, and my God.

---

17 JUDGE me, O God, and plead my cause against an ungodly nation:
 O deliver me from the deceitful and unjust man.
18 For Thou art the God of my strength; why hast Thou cast me off?
 Why go I mourning because of the oppression of the enemy?
19 O send out Thy light and Thy truth;
 Let them lead me:
20 Let them bring me unto Thy holy hill,
 And to Thy tabernacles.
21 Then will I go unto the altar of God,
 Unto God my exceeding joy:
 And upon the harp will I praise Thee, O God, my God.
22 Why art thou cast down, O my soul?
 And why art thou disquieted within me?

9. LORD'S DAY THIRD IN FEBRUARY—MORNING

23 Hope thou in God: for I shall yet praise Him,
Who is the help of my countenance, and my God.

---

24 I WAITED patiently for Jehovah;
And He inclined unto me, and heard my cry.
25 He brought me up also out of a horrible pit,
Out of the miry clay;
26 And He set my feet upon a rock,
And established my goings.
27 And He hath put a new song in my mouth,
Even praise unto our God:
28 Many shall see it, and fear,
And shall trust in Jehovah.
29 Blessed is the man that maketh Jehovah his trust,
And respecteth not the proud, nor such as turn aside to lies.
30 Many, O Jehovah my God, are the wonderful works which Thou hast done,
And Thy thoughts which are to us-ward:
31 They cannot be set in order unto Thee;
If I would declare and speak of them,
They are more than can be numbered.
32 Let all those that seek Thee rejoice and be glad in Thee:
Let such as love Thy salvation say continually,
JEHOVAH BE MAGNIFIED.
33 But I am poor and needy;
Yet the Lord thinketh upon me:
34 Thou art my help and my deliverer;
Make no tarrying, O my God.

Psalm Chant
See MONTHLY SONGS: Lord's Day Third—Morning.

Prayer of the Day

WE beseech Thee, O Lord, hear the prayers of Thy people, which we offer only in Thy Son Christ Jesus:
That we who might justly suffer for our offenses, may mercifully be delivered for the glory of Thy grace in Him,
Who, of Thee, is made unto us salvation, and with the Father and the Spirit is glorified — one God, throughout all ages: AMEN.

Hymn of Praise
See MONTHLY SONGS: Lord's Day Third — Morning.

9. EVENING
LORD'S DAY THIRD IN FEBRUARY

Introductory

Sentence

JEHOVAH will hear when we call unto Him.
O Jehovah, lift Thou up the light of Thy countenance upon us.
[Ps. iv, 3, 6]

Response
[Tune in
MONTHLY SONGS]

IT shall come to pass that at evening time there | shall be | light.
And it shall come to pass in that day,
That living waters shall go | out • from Je- | ru-sa- | lem.
[Zech. xiv, 7, 8]

Scripture Lessons   Old Covenant   Gen. vi, 9–22; vii, 1.
Gospel   Luke, vii, 11–17.
Apostolic Word   Acts, ix, 10–19.

Responsive Lesson   From Mic. i, ii, iii.

HEAR, ye peoples, all of you;
   Hearken, O earth, and all that therein is:
2 And let the Lord Jehovah be witness against you,
   The Lord from His holy temple.
3 For, behold, Jehovah cometh forth out of His place,
   And will come down, and tread upon the high places of the earth.
4 And the mountains shall be melted under Him,
   And the valleys shall be cleft,
5 As wax before the fire,
   As waters that are poured down a steep place.
6 For the transgression of Jacob is all this,
   And for the sins of the house of Israel.
7 Woe to them that devise iniquity
   And work evil upon their beds!
8 When the morning is light, they practice it,
   Because it is in the power of their hand.
9 And they covet fields, and seize them;
   And houses, and take them away:
10 And they oppress a man and his house,
   Even a man and his heritage.
11 Shall it be said, O house of Jacob, Is the spirit of Jehovah straitened?
   Are these His doings?
   Do not My words do good to him that walketh uprightly?
12 Arise ye, and depart;
   For this is not your rest:
13 Because of uncleanness that destroyeth,
   Even with a grievous destruction.
14 If a man walking in the spirit of falsehood do lie,
   Saying, I will prophesy unto thee of wine and of strong drink;
   He shall even be the prophet of this people.
15 Hear, I pray you, ye heads of Jacob,
   And rulers of the house of Israel:

9. LORD'S DAY THIRD IN FEBRUARY — EVENING

16 Is it not for you to know judgment?
  Who hate the good, and love the evil;
17 Then shall they cry unto Jehovah,
  But He will not answer them:
18 Yea, He will hide His face from them at that time,
  According as they have wrought evil in their doings.
19 Therefore it shall be night unto you, that ye shall have no vision;
  And it shall be dark unto you, that ye shall not divine;
20 And the sun shall go down upon the prophets,
  And the day shall be black over them.
21 And the seers shall be ashamed,
  And the diviners confounded;
22 Yea, they all shall cover their lips:
  For there is no answer of God.
23 But I truly am full of power by the spirit of Jehovah,
  And of judgment, and of might,
24 To declare unto Jacob his transgression,
  And to Israel his sin.
25 Hear this, I pray you, ye heads of the house of Jacob,
  And rulers of the house of Israel,
26 That abhor judgment,
  And pervert all equity.
27 They build up Zion with blood,
  And Jerusalem with iniquity.
28 The heads thereof judge for reward,
  And the priests thereof teach for hire,
  And the prophets thereof divine for money:
29 Yet will they lean upon Jehovah, and say, Is not Jehovah in the midst of us?
  No evil shall come upon us.
30 Therefore shall Zion for your sake be plowed as a field,
  And Jerusalem shall become heaps,
  And the mountain of the house as the high places of a forest.

Psalm Chant   See MONTHLY SONGS: Lord's Day Third — Evening.

Hymn of Praise   See MONTHLY SONGS: Lord's Day Third — Evening.

---

10. LORD'S DAY FOURTH IN FEBRUARY
MORNING

Introductory

Sentence

JEHOVAH hath chosen Zion;
He hath desired it for His habitation, saying —
This is My resting-place forever;
Here will I dwell; for I have desired it.   [Ps. cxxxii. 13, 14]

10. LORD'S DAY FOURTH IN FEBRUARY—MORNING

Response
[Tune in
MONTHLY SONGS]

I HAVE set watchmen upon thy walls, O Je- | ru-sa- | lem :
They shall never hold their | peace | day nor | night :
Ye that are Jehovah's remembrancers, | keep not | silence,
Till He make Jerusalem a | praise | in the | earth.   [Is. lxii, 6, 7]

Scripture Lessons

Old Covenant   Hos. v, 13–15 : vi, 1–6.
Gospel   John, vi, 28–40.
Apostolic Word   Heb. iii, 1–14.

Responsive Lesson

Ps. xci : (of DAVID) cviii, 1–5.

HE that dwelleth in the secret place of the Most High
    Shall abide under the shadow of the Almighty.
2 I will say of Jehovah, He is my refuge and my fortress;
    My God, in whom I trust.
3 For He shall deliver thee from the snare of the fowler,
    And from the noisome pestilence.
4 He shall cover thee with His pinions,
    And under His wings shalt thou take refuge:
5 His truth is a shield
    And a buckler.
6 Thou shalt not be afraid for the terror by night,
    Nor for the arrow that flieth by day;
7 For the pestilence that walketh in darkness,
    Nor for the destruction that wasteth at noonday.
8 A thousand shall fall at thy side,
    And ten thousand at thy right hand;
9 But it shall not come nigh thee.
    Only with thine eyes shalt thou behold,
    And see the reward of the wicked.
10 Because thou hast said, Jehovah is my refuge;
    Thou hast made the Most High thy habitation;
11 There shall no evil befall thee,
    Neither shall any plague come nigh thy tent.
12 For He shall give His angels charge over thee,
    To keep thee in all thy ways.
13 They shall bear thee up in their hands,
    Lest thou dash thy foot against a stone.
14 Thou shalt tread upon the lion and adder :
    The young lion and the serpent shalt thou trample under feet.
15 Because he hath set his love upon Me,
    Therefore will I deliver him:
16 I will set him on high,
    Because he hath known My Name.
17 He shall call upon Me,
    And I will answer him;
18 I will be with him in trouble :
    I will deliver him, and honor him.
19 With long life will I satisfy him,
    And show him My salvation.

10. LORD'S DAY FOURTH IN FEBRUARY — MORNING

20 My heart is fixed, O God; I will sing,
Yea, I will sing praises, even with my glory.
21 Awake, psaltery and harp:
I myself will awake right early.
22 I will give thanks unto Thee, O Jehovah, among the peoples:
And I will sing praises unto Thee among the nations.
23 For Thy lovingkindness is great above the heavens,
And Thy truth reacheth unto the skies.
24 Be Thou exalted, O God, above the heavens:
And Thy glory above all the earth.

Psalm Chant   See MONTHLY SONGS: Lord's Day Fourth — Morning.

Prayer of the Day

O THOU, our Father, who art manifested in Thine only-begotten Son, the Prince of Peace, through whom Thou dost govern all things in the heavens and the earth:

Let Thy grace in Him both guide us and rule in us, so that we may know what we ought to do, and be strong to fulfill the same; and doing all things as unto the Lord in our several plans and relations, may dwell in Thy peace all the days of our life:

Through Him who is our Peace, who dwelleth in eternal glory with the Father and the Holy Spirit — the God of Peace: AMEN.

Hymn of Praise   See MONTHLY SONGS: Lord's Day Fourth — Morning.

---

10. EVENING
LORD'S DAY FOURTH IN FEBRUARY

Introductory

Sentence

O JEHOVAH, I love the habitation of Thy house,
And the place where Thy glory dwelleth.
In the congregation will I bless Jehovah.   [Ps. xxvi, 8, 12]

Response
[Tune in
MONTHLY SONGS]

THERE is a river, the streams whereof make glad the | city
    of | God,
The holy place of the | taber-nacles | of the • Most | High.
Jehovah of | Hosts is | with us;
The God of | Ja-cob | is our | refuge.   [Ps. xlvi, 4, 7]

Scripture Lessons   Old Covenant Gen. xii, 1-9.
                      Gospel   Matt. vii, 6-20.
                      Apostolic Word Rom. v, 1-11.

10. LORD'S DAY FOURTH IN FEBRUARY — EVENING 37

Responsive Lesson Job, xl, 2-14: xlii, 1-6.

JEHOVAH answered Job, and said,
Shall he that cavileth contend with the Almighty?
He that argueth with God, let him answer it.

2 Then Job answered Jehovah, and said,
Behold, I am of small account; what shall I answer thee?
I lay my hand upon my mouth.
3 Once have I spoken, and I will not answer;
Yea twice, but I will proceed no further.

4 Then Jehovah answered Job out of the whirlwind, and said,
Gird up thy loins now like a man:
I will demand of thee, and declare thou unto Me.
5 Wilt thou even annul My judgment?
Wilt thou condemn Me, that thou mayst be justified?
6 Or hast thou an arm like God?
And canst thou thunder with a voice like Him?
7 Deck thyself now with excellency and dignity;
And array thyself with honor and majesty.
8 Pour forth the overflowings of thine anger:
And look upon every one that is proud, and abase him.
9 Look on every one that is proud, and bring him low;
And tread down the wicked where they stand.
10 Hide them in the dust together;
Bind their faces in the hidden place.
11 Then will I also confess of thee
That thine own right hand can save thee.

12 Then Job answered Jehovah, and said,
I know that Thou canst do all things,
And that no purpose of Thine can be restrained.
13 Who is this that hideth counsel without knowledge?
Therefore have I uttered that which I understood not,
14 Things too wonderful for me,
Which I knew not.
15 Hear, I beseech Thee, and I will speak;
I will demand of Thee, and declare Thou unto me.
16 I had heard of Thee by the hearing of the ear;
But now mine eye seeth Thee,
17 Wherefore I abhor myself,
And repent in dust and ashes.

Psalm Chant   See MONTHLY SONGS: Lord's Day Fourth — Evening.

Hymn of Praise See MONTHLY SONGS: Lord's Day Fourth — Evening.

[RARELY OCCURRING]

11. LORD'S DAY FIFTH IN FEBRUARY

Introductory
MORNING

Sentence

HOW amiable are Thy tabernacles, O Jehovah of Hosts!
My soul longeth, yea, even fainteth for the courts of Jehovah:
My heart and my flesh cry out unto the living God. [Ps. lxxxiv, 1, 2]

Response
[Tune in
MONTHLY SONGS]

THEY that know Thy Name will put their | trust in | Thee;
For Thou, Jehovah, hast not forsaken | them that | seek | Thee. [Ps. ix, 10]

Scripture Lessons

Old Covenant   Ruth, i, 14–22.
Gospel   Luke, vii, 18–23.
Apostolic Word   James, i, 1–11.

Responsive Lesson

[Same in part as *Psalm Chants* for Days Nos. 27–30]

A PSALM OF DAVID, Ps. cxxxviii: A SONG OF LOVES, Ps. xlv.

1 I WILL give Thee thanks with my whole heart:
    Before the gods will I sing praises unto Thee.
2 I will worship toward Thy holy temple,
    And give thanks unto Thy Name for Thy lovingkindness
3 And for Thy truth:
    For Thou hast magnified Thy word above all Thy Name.
4 In the day that I called Thou answeredst me,
    Thou didst encourage me with strength in my soul.
5 All the kings of the earth shall give Thee thanks, O Jehovah,
    For they have heard the words of Thy mouth.
6 Yea, they shall sing of the ways of Jehovah;
    For great is the glory of Jehovah.
7 For though Jehovah be high, yet hath He respect unto the lowly:
    But the haughty He knoweth from afar.
8 Though I walk in the midst of trouble,
    Thou wilt revive me;
9 Thou shalt stretch forth Thine hand against the wrath of mine enemies,
    And Thy right hand shall save me.
10 Jehovah will perfect that which concerneth me:
    Thy mercy, O Jehovah, endureth forever;
    FORSAKE NOT THE WORKS OF THINE OWN HANDS.

---

11 My heart overfloweth with a goodly matter:
    I speak the things which I have made touching the King:
    My tongue is the pen of a ready writer.
12 Thou art fairer than the children of men;
    Grace is poured into thy lips:
    THEREFORE GOD HATH BLESSED THEE FOREVER.
13 Gird thy sword upon thy thigh, O mighty one,
    Thy glory and thy majesty.
    And in thy majesty ride on prosperously,

11. LORD'S DAY FIFTH IN FEBRUARY — MORNING

14 Because of truth and meekness and righteousness:
    And thy right hand shall teach thee terrible things.
15 Thine arrows are sharp;
    The peoples fall under thee;
    They are in the heart of the king's enemies.
16 Thy throne, O God, is forever and ever:
    A scepter of equity is the scepter of thy kingdom.
17 Thou hast loved righteousness,
    And hated wickedness:
18 Therefore God, thy God, hath anointed Thee
    With the oil of gladness above thy fellows.
19 All thy garments smell of myrrh, and aloes, and cassia;
    Out of ivory palaces stringed instruments have made Thee glad.
20 Kings' daughters are among thy honorable women:
    At thy right hand doth stand the queen in gold of Ophir.
21 Hearken, O daughter, and consider,
    And incline thine ear;
22 Forget also thine own people,
    And thy father's house;
23 So shall the king desire thy beauty:
    For He is thy Lord; and worship thou Him.
24 And the daughter of Tyre shall be there with a gift;
    Even the rich among the people shall entreat thy favor.
25 The king's daughter within the palace is all glorious:
    Her clothing is inwrought with gold.
26 She shall be led unto the king in broidered work:
    The virgins her companions that follow her shall be brought unto thee.
27 With gladness and rejoicing shall they be led:
    They shall enter into the king's palace.
28 Instead of thy fathers shall be thy children,
    Whom thou shalt make princes in all the earth.
29 I will make thy name to be remembered in all generations:
    Therefore shall the peoples give thee thanks forever and ever.

Psalm Chant

See MONTHLY SONGS: Lord's Day Fifth — Morning.

Prayer of the Day

GOD Almighty, whose never-failing providence ordereth all our way: In Thy tender mercy put away from us all hurtful things, even though we may desire them; and give unto us those things which are profitable for us according to Thy holy will in Thy Son Christ Jesus,
    Whom Thou, O Father, glorifiest with Thyself and the blessed Spirit — one God — now and ever: AMEN.

Hymn of Praise

See MONTHLY SONGS: Lord's Day Fifth — Morning.

11. EVENING
LORD'S DAY FIFTH IN FEBRUARY

Introductory

Sentence COME ye, and let us walk in the light of Jehovah. [Is. ii, 5]

Response
[Tune in
Monthly Songs]

WITH Thee, O God, is the | fountain of | life :
In Thy | light shall | we see | light. [Ps. xxxvi, 9]

Scripture Lessons

Old Covenant — Est. v, 9–14; vi, 1–12.
Gospel — Matt. viii, 5–13.
Apostolic Word — I Cor. vi, 1–8.

Responsive Lesson From a Psalm of David, Ps. xxxviii.

1 O JEHOVAH, rebuke me not in Thy wrath:
   Neither chasten me in Thy hot displeasure.
2 For Thine arrows stick fast in me,
   And Thy hand presseth me sore.
3 There is no soundness in my flesh because of Thine indignation;
   Neither is there any health in my bones because of my sin.
4 For mine iniquities are gone over my head:
   As a heavy burden they are too heavy for me.
5 I am faint and sore bruised:
   I have groaned by reason of the disquietness of my heart.
6 Lord, all my desire is before Thee;
   And my groaning is not hid from Thee.
7 My heart throbbeth, my strength faileth me:
   As for the light of mine eyes, it also is gone from me.
8 My lovers and my friends stand aloof from my plague;
   And my kinsmen stand afar off.
9 They also that seek after my life lay snares for me;
   And they that seek my hurt speak mischievous things,
   And meditate deceits all the day long.
10 But I, as a deaf man, hear not:
   And I am as a dumb man that openeth not his mouth.
11 Yea, I am as a man that heareth not,
   And in whose mouth are no reproofs.
12 For in Thee, O Jehovah, do I hope:
   Thou wilt answer, O Lord my God.
13 For I said, Lest they rejoice over me:
   When my foot slippeth, they magnify themselves against me.
14 For I am ready to fall,
   And my sorrow is continually before me.
15 For I will declare mine iniquity;
   I will be sorry for my sin.
16 But mine enemies are lively, and are strong:
   And they that hate me wrongfully are multiplied.
17 They also that render evil for good
   Are adversaries unto me, because I follow the thing that is good.

11. LORD'S DAY FIFTH IN FEBRUARY—EVENING   41

18 Forsake me not, O Jehovah:
  O my God, be not far from me.
19 Make haste to help me,
  O Lord my salvation.

Psalm Chant See MONTHLY SONGS: Lord's Day Fifth—Evening.

Hymn of Praise See MONTHLY SONGS: Lord's Day Fifth—Evening.

---

12. LORD'S DAY FIRST IN MARCH
MORNING

Introductory

Sentence STRONG is Thy hand, O Jehovah, and high is Thy right hand.
Righteousness and justice are the foundation of Thy throne:
Lovingkindness and truth go before Thy face.   [Ps. lxxxix, 13, 14]

Response
[Tune in
MONTHLY SONGS]

THE Mighty One, God Je- | hovah, hath | spoken,
And called the earth from the rising of the sun unto the |
  go-ing | down there- | of.
Out of Zion, the per- | fection of | beauty,
God | hath | shined | forth.   [Ps. l, 1, 2]

Scripture Lessons Old Covenant Gen. xv, 1-16.
Gospel Matt. vii, 21-29.
Apostolic Word Rom. vi, 12-23.

Responsive Lesson From Jer. xxxi.

JEHOVAH appeared of old unto me, saying,
Yea, I have loved thee with an everlasting love:
  Therefore with lovingkindness have I drawn thee.
2 Again will I build thee,
  And thou shalt be built, O virgin of Israel:
3 Again shalt thou be adorned with thy tabrets,
  And shalt go forth in the dances of them that make merry.
4 For there shall be a day, that the watchmen upon the hills of
  Ephraim shall cry, Arise ye,
  And let us go up to Zion unto Jehovah our God.
5 For thus saith Jehovah, Sing with gladness for Jacob,
  And shout for the chief of the nations:
6 Publish ye, praise ye, and say, O Jehovah, save Thy people,
  The remnant of Israel.
7 Behold, I will bring them from the north country,
  And gather them from the uttermost parts of the earth;

12. LORD'S DAY FIRST IN MARCH—MORNING

8 And with them the blind and the lame:
   A great company shall they return hither.
9 They shall come with weeping,
   And with supplications will I lead them:
10 I will cause them to walk by rivers of waters,
   In a straight way wherein they shall not stumble:
11 For I am a father to Israel,
   And Ephraim is My firstborn.

12 Hear the word of Jehovah, O ye nations,
   And declare it in the isles afar off;
13 And say, He that scattered Israel will gather him,
   And keep him, as a shepherd doth his flock.
14 For Jehovah hath ransomed Jacob,
   And redeemed him from the hand of him that was stronger than he.
15 And they shall come and sing in the height of Zion,
   And shall flow together unto the goodness of Jehovah:
16 And their soul shall be as a watered garden;
   And they shall not sorrow any more at all.

17 Thus saith Jehovah: A voice is heard in Ramah, lamentation,
      and bitter weeping,
   Rachel weeping for her children;
18 She refuseth to be comforted for her children,
   Because they are not.
19 Thus saith Jehovah: Refrain thy voice from weeping,
   And thine eyes from tears:
20 For thy work shall be rewarded, saith Jehovah;
   And they shall come again from the land of the enemy.
21 And there is hope for thy latter end, saith Jehovah;
   And thy children shall come again to their own border.

22 Behold, the days come, saith Jehovah,
   That I will make a new covenant with the house of Israel,
   And with the house of Judah:
23 Not according to the covenant that I made with their fathers
   In the day that I took them by the hand to bring them out of the land of Egypt;
24 Which My covenant they brake,
   Although I was a husband unto them, saith Jehovah.
25 But this is the covenant that I will make with the house of Israel
   After those days, saith Jehovah;
26 I will put My law in their inward parts,
   And in their heart will I write it;
27 And I will be their God,
   And they shall be My people:
28 And they shall teach no more every man his neighbor,
   And every man his brother,
29 Saying, Know Jehovah:
   For they all shall know Me,
   From the least of them unto the greatest of them, saith Jehovah:
30 For I will forgive their iniquity,
   And their sin will I remember no more.

12. LORD'S DAY FIRST IN MARCH — MORNING

31 Thus saith Jehovah, who giveth the sun for a light by day,
And the ordinances of the moon and of the stars for a light by night,
32 Who stirreth up the sea,
That the waves thereof roar;
JEHOVAH OF HOSTS IS HIS NAME:
33 If these ordinances depart from before Me, saith Jehovah,
Then the seed of Israel also shall cease from being a nation before Me forever.

Psalm Chant   See MONTHLY SONGS: Lord's Day First — Morning.

Prayer of the Day

IN the Name of the Lamb of God, we beseech Thee, Heavenly Father, that as we, by Thy Spirit, through faith, have heard the voice of prophets and the message of angels and the testimony of apostles, whereby we have known the incarnation of Thy Son Jesus Christ,

So we may inwardly know His cross and sacrifice, and be brought unto the glory of His resurrection;

Who hath ascended above all heavens, and with Thee and the Holy Spirit is worshiped — one ever-glorious God: AMEN.

Hymn of Praise   See MONTHLY SONGS: Lord's Day First — Morning.

---

12. EVENING
LORD'S DAY FIRST IN MARCH

Introductory Sentence

THE earth is Jehovah's, and the fullness thereof;
The world, and they that dwell therein.
For He hath founded it upon the seas,
And established it upon the floods.   [Ps. xxiv, 1, 2]

Response [Tune in MONTHLY SONGS]

LOOK unto Me, and | be ye | sav'd,
   All the | ends | of the | earth.
Unto Me every | knee shall | bow,
   And every | tongue shall con- | fess unto | God.
   [Is. xlv, 22, 23 (Rom. xiv, 11)]

Scripture Lessons
Old Covenant   Ezkl. xxvi, 1-14.
Gospel   Mark, vi, 14-28.
Apostolic Word   II Cor. xi, 21-33.

Responsive Lesson   Psalm lxxiv.

O GOD, why hast Thou cast us off forever?
   Why doth Thine anger smoke against the sheep of Thy pasture?
2 Remember Thy congregation,
   Which Thou hast purchased of old,

12. LORD'S DAY FIRST IN MARCH — EVENING

3 Which Thou hast redeemed to be the tribe of Thine inheritance;
And mount Zion, wherein Thou hast dwelt.
4 Lift up Thy feet unto the perpetual ruins,
All the evil that the enemy hath done in the sanctuary.
5 Thine adversaries have roared in the midst of Thine assembly;
They have set up their ensigns for signs.
6 They seemed as men that lifted up axes upon a thicket of trees.
And now all the carved work thereof they break down with hatchet and hammers.
7 They have set Thy sanctuary on fire;
They have profaned the dwelling-place of Thy Name even to the ground.
8 They said in their heart, Let us make havoc of them altogether:
They have burned up all the synagogues of God in the land.
9 We see not our signs:
There is no more any prophet;
Neither is there among us any that knoweth how long.
10 How long, O God, shall the adversary reproach?
Shall the enemy blaspheme Thy Name forever?
11 Why drawest Thou back Thy hand, even Thy right hand?
Pluck it out of Thy bosom and consume them.
12 Yet God is my King of old,
Working salvation in the midst of the earth.
13 Thou didst divide the sea by Thy strength:
Thou brakest the heads of the dragons in the waters.
14 Thou brakest the heads of leviathan in pieces,
Thou gavest him to be food to the people inhabiting the wilderness.
15 Thou didst cleave fountain and flood:
Thou driedst up mighty rivers.
16 The day is Thine, the night also is Thine:
Thou hast prepared the light and the sun.
17 Thou hast set all the borders of the earth:
Thou hast made summer and winter.
18 Remember this, that the enemy hath reproached, O Jehovah,
And that a foolish people have blasphemed Thy Name.
19 O deliver not the soul of Thy turtledove unto the wild beast:
Forget not the life of Thy poor forever.
20 Have respect unto the covenant:
For the dark places of the earth are full of the habitations of violence.
21 O let not the oppressed return put to shame:
Let the poor and needy praise Thy Name.
22 Arise, O God, plead Thine own cause:
Remember how the foolish man reproacheth Thee all the day.
23 Forget not the voice of Thine adversaries:
The tumult of those that rise up against Thee ascendeth continually.

Psalm Chant See MONTHLY SONGS: Lord's Day First — Evening.

Hymn of Praise See MONTHLY SONGS: Lord's Day First — Evening.

13. LORD'S DAY SECOND IN MARCH
MORNING

Introductory

Sentence

BLESSED is the man, O God, whom Thou choosest, and causest
to approach unto Thee,
That he may dwell in Thy courts.
We shall be satisfied with the goodness of Thy house,
Thy holy temple.   [Ps. lxv, 4]

Response
[Tune in
Monthly Songs]

JEHOVAH send thee help from the | sanc-tu- | ary,
And | strength-en | thee • out of | Zion!
Remember | all thine | offerings,
And ac- | cept thy | sac-ri- | fice!   [Ps. xx, 1-3]

Scripture Lessons   Old Covenant   Gen. xiv, 13-24.
Gospel   Matt. ix, 9-13, 27-34.
Apostolic Word   Rom. viii, 1-11.

Responsive Lesson   Answer of Jehovah, Job, xxxviii, 1-36.

JEHOVAH answered Job out of the whirlwind, and said:
Who is this that darkeneth counsel
By words without knowledge?
2 Gird up now thy loins like a man;
For I will demand of thee,
And declare thou unto Me.
3 Where wast thou when I laid the foundations of the earth?
Declare, if thou hast understanding.
4 Who determined the measures thereof, if thou knowest?
Or who stretched the line upon it?
5 Whereupon were the foundations thereof fastened?
Or who laid the corner-stone thereof;
6 When the morning stars sang together,
And all the sons of God shouted for joy?
7 Or who shut up the sea with doors,
When it brake forth, as if it had issued out of the womb;
8 When I made the cloud the garment thereof,
And thick darkness a swaddlingband for it,
9 And marked out for it My bound,
And set bars and doors,
10 And said, Hitherto shalt thou come, but no further;
And here shall thy proud waves be stayed?
11 Hast thou commandeth the morning since thy days began,
And caused the dayspring to know its place;
12 That it might take hold of the ends of the earth,
And the wicked be shaken out of it?
13 It is changed as clay under the seal;
And all things stand forth as a garment:
14 And from the wicked their light is withholden,
And the high arm is broken.

13. LORD'S DAY SECOND IN MARCH — MORNING

15 Hast thou entered into the springs of the sea?
   Or hast thou walked in the recesses of the deep?
16 Have the gates of death been revealed unto thee?
   Or hast thou seen the gates of the shadow of death?
17 Hast thou comprehended the earth in its breadth?
   Declare, if thou knowest it all.
18 Where is the way to the dwelling of light,
   And as for darkness, where is the place thereof;
19 That thou shouldest take it to the bound thereof,
   And that thou shouldest discern the paths to the house thereof?
20 Doubtless, thou knowest, for thou wast then born,
   And the number of thy days is great!
21 Hast thou entered the treasuries of the snow,
   Or hast thou seen the treasuries of the hail,
22 Which I have reserved against the time of trouble,
   Against the day of battle and war?
23 By what way is the light parted,
   Or the east wind scattered upon the earth?
24 Who hath cleft a channel for the waterflood,
   Or a way for the lightning of the thunder;
25 To cause it to rain on a land where no man is;
   On the wilderness, wherein there is no man;
26 To satisfy the waste and desolate ground;
   And to cause the tender grass to spring forth?
27 Hath the rain a father?
   Or who hath begotten the drops of dew?
28 Out of whose womb came the ice?
   And the hoary frost of heaven, who hath gendered it?
29 The waters hide themselves and become like stone,
   And the face of the deep is frozen.
30 Canst thou bind the cluster of the Pleiades,
   Or loose the bands of Orion?
31 Canst thou lead forth the Mazzaroth in their season?
   Or canst thou guide the Bear with her train?
32 Knowest thou the ordinances of the heavens?
   Canst thou establish the dominion thereof in the earth?
33 Canst thou lift up thy voice to the clouds,
   That abundance of waters may cover thee?
34 Canst thou send forth lightnings, that they may go,
   And say unto thee, Here we are?
35 Who hath put wisdom in the inward parts?
   Or who hath given understanding to the mind?

Psalm Chant

See MONTHLY SONGS: Lord's Day Second — Morning.

Prayer of the Day

GOD, the Father Almighty, who through the suffering and sacrifice of Thy Son, the Lamb of God, dost take away the sin of the world, and cause all those who are penitent to receive Thy forgiving love;

13. LORD'S DAY SECOND IN MARCH—MORNING

Create in us new and contrite hearts; that we, humbly lamenting our sins and acknowledging our wretchedness therein, may obtain of Thee, the God of all mercy, perfect forgiveness:
Through the same Thy Son Christ Jesus, to whom with Thee and the Spirit — one God — be glory without end: AMEN.

Hymn of Praise   See MONTHLY SONGS: Lord's Day Second — Morning.

---

13. EVENING
LORD'S DAY SECOND IN MARCH

Introductory

Sentence
THY lovingkindness, O God, is better than life;
My lips shall praise Thee.
So will I bless Thee while I live:
I will lift up my hands in Thy Name.   [Ps. lxiii, 3, 4]

Response
[Tune in MONTHLY SONGS]
LIFT up your hands to the | sanc-tu- | ary,
And | bless | ye Je- | hovah.
Jehovah bless Thee | out of | Zion!
Even He that | made | heav'n and | earth.   [Ps. cxxxiv, 2, 3]

Scripture Lessons
Old Covenant   Isaiah, i, 10–20.
Gospel   John, vi, 41–51.
Apostolic Word   Heb. iv, 14–16; v, 1–9.

Responsive Lesson   Psalm cxix, 33–64.

TEACH me, O Jehovah, the way of Thy statutes;
   And I shall keep it unto the end.
2 Give me understanding, and I shall keep Thy law;
   Yea, I shall observe it with my whole heart.
3 Make me to go in the path of Thy commandments;
   For therein do I delight.
4 Incline my heart unto Thy testimonies,
   And not to covetousness.
5 Turn away mine eyes from beholding vanity,
   And quicken me in Thy ways.
6 Confirm unto Thy servant Thy word,
   Which is in order unto the fear of Thee.
7 Turn away my reproach whereof I am afraid;
   For Thy judgments are good.
8 Behold, I have longed after Thy precepts:
   Quicken me in Thy righteousness.
9 Let Thy lovingkindnesses also come unto me, O Jehovah,
   Even Thy salvation, according to Thy word.
10 So shall I have an answer for him that reproacheth me;
   For I trust in Thy word.

13. LORD'S DAY SECOND IN MARCH — EVENING

11 And take not the word of truth utterly out of my mouth;
For I have hoped in Thy judgments.
12 So shall I observe Thy law continually
For ever and ever.
13 And I will walk at liberty;
For I have sought Thy precepts.
14 I will also speak of Thy testimonies before kings,
And will not be put to shame.
15 And I will delight myself in Thy commandments,
Which I have loved.
16 I will lift up my hands also unto Thy commandments, which I have loved;
And I will meditate in Thy statutes.
17 Remember the word unto Thy servant,
Because Thou hast made me to hope.
18 This is my comfort in my affliction:
For Thy word hath quickened me.
19 The proud have had me greatly in derision:
Yet have I not swerved from Thy law.
20 I have remembered Thy judgments of old, O Jehovah,
And have comforted myself.
21 Hot indignation hath taken hold upon me,
Because of the wicked that forsake Thy law.
22 Thy statutes have been my songs
In the house of my pilgrimage.
23 I have remembered Thy Name, O Jehovah, in the night,
And have observed Thy law.
24 This I have had,
Because I kept Thy precepts.
25 Jehovah is my portion:
I have said that I would observe Thy words.
26 I entreated Thy favor with my whole heart:
Be merciful unto me according to Thy word.
27 I thought on my ways,
And turned my feet unto Thy testimonies.
28 I made haste, and delayed not,
To observe Thy commandments.
29 The cords of the wicked have wrapped me round;
But I have not forgotten Thy law.
30 At midnight I will rise to give thanks unto Thee
Because of Thy righteous judgments.
31 I am a companion of all them that fear Thee,
And of them that observe Thy precepts.
32 The earth, O Jehovah, is full of Thy lovingkindness:
Teach me Thy statutes.

Psalm Chant See MONTHLY SONGS: Lord's Day Second — Evening.

Hymn of Praise See MONTHLY SONGS: Lord's Day Second — Evening.

[Some or all of the Days Nos. 14–18 are omitted from the *Monthly Order*, in various years, as may be required by the variable date of Easter: see in preceding pages, CALENDAR FOR THE YEAR.]

14. LORD'S DAY THIRD IN MARCH

Introductory
MORNING

Sentence

THUS saith the high and lofty One that inhabiteth eternity,
Whose Name is Holy:
I dwell in the high and holy place,
With him also that is of a contrite and humble spirit,
To revive the spirit of the humble,
And to revive the heart of the contrite ones. [Is. lvii, 15]

Response
[Tune in
MONTHLY SONGS]

THOU hast said, | Seek ye • My | face:
My heart saith unto Thee,
Thy face, O Je- | ho-vah, | will I | seek. [Ps. xxvii, 8]

Scripture Lessons
Old Covenant   Jer. xxiii, 16–29.
Gospel   John, viii, 28–37, 56–59.
Apostolic Word Acts, iii, 1–10.

Responsive Lesson
Psalms, xlix, xv.

HEAR this, all ye peoples;
Give ear, all ye inhabitants of the world:
2 Both low and high,
Rich and poor together.
3 My mouth shall speak wisdom;
And the meditation of my heart shall be of understanding.
4 I will incline mine ear to a parable:
I will open my dark saying upon the harp.
5 Wherefore should I fear in the days of evil,
When iniquity at my heels compasseth me about?
6 They that trust in their wealth,
And boast themselves in the multitude of their riches;
7 None of them can by any means redeem his brother,
Nor give to God a ransom for him:
8 (For the redemption of their life is costly,
And it faileth forever:)
9 That he should still live alway,
That he should not see corruption.
10 For he seeth that wise men die,
The fool and the brutish alike perish,
And leave their wealth to others.
11 Their inward thought is, that their houses shall continue forever,
And their dwelling-places to all generations;
They call their lands after their own names.
12 But man being in honor abideth not:
He is like the beasts that perish.

14. LORD'S DAY THIRD IN MARCH—MORNING

13 This their way is their folly:
Yet after them men approve their sayings.
14 They are appointed, as a flock, for Sheol;
Death shall be their shepherd:
15 And the upright shall have dominion over them in the morning;
And their beauty shall be for Sheol to consume, that there be no habitation for it.
16 But God will redeem my soul from the power of Sheol:
For He shall receive me.
17 Be not thou afraid when one is made rich,
When the glory of his house is increased:
18 For when he dieth he shall carry nothing away;
His glory shall not descend after him.
19 Though while he lived he blessed his soul,
And men praise thee, when thou doest well to thyself,
20 He shall go to the generation of his fathers;
They shall never see the light.
21 Man that is in honor, and understandeth not,
Is like the beasts that perish.

---

22 O JEHOVAH, who shall sojourn in Thy tabernacle?
Who shall dwell in Thy holy hill?
23 He that walketh uprightly,
And worketh righteousness,
24 And speaketh truth in his heart.
He that slandereth not with his tongue,
25 Nor doeth evil to his friend,
Nor taketh up a reproach against his neighbor.
26 In whose eyes a reprobate is despised;
But he honoreth them that fear Jehovah.
27 He that sweareth to his own hurt, and changeth not.
He that putteth not out his money to usury,
28 Nor taketh reward against the innocent.
He that doeth these things shall never be moved.

Psalm Chant
See MONTHLY SONGS: Lord's Day Third—Morning.

Prayer of the Day

HEAVENLY Father, whose Son Jesus fasted and was tempted in the wilderness; we beseech Thee arm us with the same mind that was in Him against all sin: And for His sake—the Lamb of God—who suffered in our behalf, give us grace to keep both our bodies and our souls in such holy discipline that we may be ready always to resist Satan, and to obey the motions of Thy blessed Spirit, Who with Thy blessed Son is glorified with Thee—one God, for evermore:
AMEN.

Hymn of Praise
See MONTHLY SONGS: Lord's Day Third—Morning.

14. EVENING
LORD'S DAY THIRD IN MARCH

Introductory

Sentence

JEHOVAH hath comforted Zion:
Joy and gladness shall be found therein,
Thanksgiving, and the voice of melody. [Is. li, 3]

Response
[Tune in
MONTHLY SONGS]

IT shall come to pass that at evening time there | shall be | light.
And it shall come to pass in that day
That living waters shall go | out • from Je- | ru-sa- | lem.
[Zech. xiv, 7, 8]

Scripture Lessons

Old Covenant — Ecc. xi, 9, 10; xii, 1-8.
Gospel — Matt. ix, 35-38; x, 1.
Apostolic Word — Heb. x, 11-25.

Responsive Lesson Job, xxviii.

SURELY there is a mine for silver,
And a place for gold which they refine.
2 Iron is taken out of the earth,
And brass is melted out of the stone.
3 Man setteth an end to darkness,
And searcheth out to the furthest bound
4 The stones of thick darkness
And of the shadow of death.
5 He breaketh open a shaft away from where men sojourn;
They are forgotten of the foot;
6 They hang afar from men,
They swing to and fro.
7 As for the earth, out of it cometh bread:
And underneath it is turned up as it were by fire.
8 The stones thereof are the place of sapphires,
And it hath dust of gold.
9 That path no bird of prey knoweth,
Neither hath the falcon's eye seen it:
10 The proud beasts have not trodden it,
Nor hath the fierce lion passed thereby.
11 He putteth forth his hand upon the flinty rock;
He overturneth the mountains by the roots.
12 He cutteth out channels among the rocks;
And his eye seeth every precious thing.
13 He bindeth the streams that they trickle not;
And the thing that is hid bringeth he forth to light.
14 But where shall wisdom be found?
And where is the place of understanding?
15 Man knoweth not the price thereof;
Neither is it found in the land of the living.
16 The deep saith, It is not in me:
And the sea saith, It is not with me.
17 It cannot be gotten for gold,
Neither shall silver be weighed for the price thereof.

14. LORD'S DAY THIRD IN MARCH — EVENING

18 It cannot be valued with the gold of Ophir,
  With the precious onyx, or the sapphire.
19 Gold and glass cannot equal it:
  Neither shall it be exchanged for jewels of fine gold.
20 No mention shall be made of coral or of crystal:
  Yea, the price of wisdom is above rubies.
21 The topaz of Ethiopia shall not equal it,
  Neither shall it be valued with pure gold.
22 Whence then cometh wisdom?
  And where is the place of understanding?
23 Seeing it is hid from the eyes of all living,
  And kept close from the fowls of the air.
24 Destruction and Death say,
  We have heard a rumor thereof with our ears.
25 God understandeth the way thereof,
  And He knoweth the place thereof.
26 For He looketh to the ends of the earth,
  And seeth under the whole heaven;
27 To make a weight for the wind;
  Yea, He meteth out the waters by measure.
28 When He made a decree for the rain,
  And a way for the lightning of the thunder:
29 Then did He see it, and declare it;
  He established it, yea, and searched it out.
30 And unto man He said,
  Behold, the fear of the Lord, that is wisdom;
  And to depart from evil is understanding.

Psalm Chant See MONTHLY SONGS: Lord's Day Third — Evening.

Hymn of Praise See MONTHLY SONGS: Lord's Day Third — Evening.

[See Note, Day No. 14, Morning]

15. LORD'S DAY FOURTH IN MARCH
MORNING

Introductory

Sentence
HEAR my cry, O God;
Attend unto my prayer.
I will dwell in Thy tabernacle for ever:
I will take refuge in the covert of Thy wings. [Ps. lxi, 1, 4]

Response
[Tune in
MONTHLY SONGS]
I HAVE set watchmen upon thy walls, O Je- | ru-sa- | lem ;
They shall never hold their | peace | day nor | night :
Ye that are Jehovah's remembrancers, | keep not | silence,
Till He make Jerusalem a | praise | in the | earth. [Is. lxii, 6, 7]

Scripture Lessons

Old Covenant II Kings, iv, 18–37.
Gospel Luke, ix, 28–36.
Apostolic Word Acts, iv, 1–12.

Responsive Lesson

PSALMS OF DAVID, Ps. ix, xi.

1 I WILL give thanks unto Jehovah with my whole heart;
I will show forth all Thy marvelous works.
2 I will be glad and exult in Thee:
I will sing praise to Thy Name, O Thou Most High.
3 When mine enemies turn back,
They stumble and perish at Thy presence.
4 For Thou hast maintained my right and my cause;
Thou satest in the throne judging righteously.
5 Thou hast rebuked the nations,
Thou hast destroyed the wicked,
6 Thou hast blotted out their name forever and ever.
The enemy are come to an end, they are desolate forever;
7 And the cities which Thou hast overthrown,
Their very memorial is perished.
8 But Jehovah sitteth as King forever:
He hath prepared His throne for judgment.
9 And He shall judge the world in righteousness,
He shall minister judgment to the peoples in uprightness.
10 Jehovah also will be a high tower for the oppressed,
A high tower in times of trouble;
11 And they that know Thy Name will put their trust in Thee;
For Thou, Jehovah, hast not forsaken them that seek Thee.
12 Sing praises to Jehovah, who dwelleth in Zion:
Declare among the people His doings.
13 For He that maketh inquisition for blood remembereth them:
He forgetteth not the cry of the poor.
14 Have mercy upon me, O Jehovah;
Behold my affliction which I suffer of them that hate me,
15 Thou that liftest me up from the gates of death;
That I may show forth all Thy praise:
16 In the gates of the daughter of Zion,
I will rejoice in Thy salvation.
17 The nations are sunk down in the pit that they made:
In the net which they hid is their own foot taken.
18 Jehovah hath made Himself known, He hath executed judgment:
The wicked is snared in the work of his own hands.
19 The wicked shall be turned back unto Sheol,
Even all the nations that forget God.
20 For the needy shall not alway be forgotten,
Nor the expectation of the poor perish forever.
21 Arise, O Jehovah; let not man prevail:
Let the nations be judged in Thy sight.
22 Put them in fear, O Jehovah:
Let the nations know themselves to be but men.

23 In Jehovah do I take refuge:
    How say ye to my soul, Flee as a bird to your mountain?
24 For, lo, the wicked bend the bow,
    They make ready their arrow upon the string,
25 That they may shoot in darkness at the upright in heart.
    If the foundations be destroyed, what can the righteous do?
26 Jehovah is in His holy temple,
    Jehovah, His throne is in heaven;
27 His eyes behold,
    His eyelids try, the children of men.
28 Jehovah trieth the righteous:
    But the wicked and him that loveth violence His soul hateth.
29 Upon the wicked He shall rain snares;
    Fire and brimstone and burning wind shall be the portion of their cup.
30 For Jehovah is righteous; He loveth righteousness:
    The upright shall behold His face.

Psalm Chant   See MONTHLY SONGS: Lord's Day Fourth—Morning.

Prayer of the Day

GOD of all grace, who hast given Thy holy Son, the Lamb of God, to die for our sins:
    For the merit of this spotless Sacrifice, and by its working in us, we beseech Thee, cleanse our consciences from dead works, that we may serve the living God, and receive through faith the eternal inheritance in Christ Jesus our Lord;
    To whom with the Father and the Holy Spirit—one God—be all honor and glory, world without end: AMEN.

Hymn of Praise   See MONTHLY SONGS: Lord's Day Fourth—Morning.

---

15. EVENING
LORD'S DAY FOURTH IN MARCH

Introductory

Sentence   JEHOVAH hath brought forth our righteousness:
    Come, and let us declare in Zion the work of Jehovah our God.
        [Jer. li, 10]

Response
[Tune in MONTHLY SONGS]

THERE is a river, the streams whereof make glad the | city of | God,
    The holy place of the | taber-nacles | of the • Most | High.
Jehovah of | Hosts is | with us;
    The God of | Ja-cob | is our | refuge.   [Ps. xlvi, 4, 7]

Scripture Lessons   Old Covenant Prov. ix, 1–12.
                                 Gospel   Matt. x, 1, 5–15.
                                 Apostolic Word Jas. i, 12–18.

15. LORD'S DAY FOURTH IN MARCH—EVENING   55

Responsive Lesson
Ezkl. xxviii, 2-19.

SON of man, say unto the prince of Tyre,
   Thus saith the Lord Jehovah:
2 Because thine heart is lifted up, and thou hast said, I am a god,
   I sit in the seat of God, in the midst of the seas;
3 Yet thou art man, and not God,
   Though thou didst set thine heart as the heart of God:
4 Behold, thou art wiser than Daniel;
   There is no secret that is hidden from thee:
5 By thy wisdom and by thine understanding thou hast gotten thee riches,
   And hast gotten gold and silver into thy treasures:
6 By thy great wisdom and by thy traffic hast thou increased thy riches,
   And thine heart is lifted up because of thy riches:
7 Therefore thus saith the Lord Jehovah:
   Because thou hast set thine heart as the heart of God;
8 Therefore behold, I will bring strangers upon thee,
   The terrible of the nations:
9 And they shall draw their swords against the beauty of thy wisdom,
   And they shall defile thy brightness.
10 They shall bring thee down to the pit;
   And thou shalt die the deaths of them that are slain, in the heart of the seas.
11 Wilt thou yet say before him that slayeth thee, I am God?
   But thou art man, and not God,
   In the hand of him that woundeth thee.
12 Thou shalt die the deaths of the uncircumcised by the hand of strangers;
   For I have spoken it, saith the Lord Jehovah.

13 Son of man, take up a lamentation for the king of Tyre,
   And say unto him, Thus saith the Lord Jehovah:
14 Thou sealest up the sum,
   Full of wisdom, and perfect in beauty.
15 Thou wast in Eden the garden of God;
   Every precious stone was thy covering.
16 The sardius, the topaz, and the diamond, the beryl, the onyx, and the jasper,
   The sapphire, the emerald, and the carbuncle, and gold:
17 The workmanship of thy tabrets and of thy pipes was in thee;
   In the day that thou wast created they were prepared.
18 Thou wast the anointed cherub that covereth:
   And I set thee,
19 So that thou wast upon the holy mountain of God;
   Thou hast walked up and down in the midst of the stones of fire.
20 Thou wast perfect in thy ways from the day that thou wast created.
   Till unrighteousness was found in thee.
21 By the abundance of thy traffic they filled the midst of thee with violence,
   And thou hast sinned:

15. LORD'S DAY FOURTH IN MARCH — EVENING

22 Therefore have I cast thee as profane
   Out of the mountain of God;
23 And I have destroyed thee, O covering cherub,
   From the midst of the stones of fire.
24 Thine heart was lifted up because of thy beauty,
   Thou hast corrupted thy wisdom by reason of thy brightness:
25 I have cast thee to the ground,
   I have laid thee before kings, that they may behold thee.
26 By the multitude of thine iniquities, in the unrighteousness of thy traffic,
   Thou hast profaned thy sanctuaries;
27 Therefore have I brought forth a fire from the midst of thee,
   It hath devoured thee,
28 And I have turned thee to ashes upon the earth
   In the sight of all them that behold thee.
29 All they that know thee among the peoples shall be astonished at thee:
   Thou art become a terror,
   And thou shalt never be any more.

Psalm Chant   See MONTHLY SONGS: Lord's Day Fourth — Evening.

Hymn of Praise   See MONTHLY SONGS: Lord's Day Fourth — Evening.

[*See Note, Day No.* 14, *Morning*]

16. LORD'S DAY FIFTH IN MARCH

Introductory

MORNING

Sentence

OFFER unto God the sacrifice of thanksgiving;
And pay thy vows unto the Most High.   [Ps. l, 14]

Response [Tune in MONTHLY SONGS]

THEY that know Thy Name will put their | trust in | Thee;
For Thou, Jehovah, hast not forsaken | them that | seek | Thee.   [Ps. ix, 10]

Scripture Lessons

Old Covenant   Hos. ii, 18–23.
Gospel   Mark, vi, 1–6.
Apostolic Word   Acts, iv, 13–22.

Responsive Lesson

PSALMS OF DAVID, Ps. xii, xiii: A PRAYER OF DAVID, xvii.

HELP, O Jehovah; for the godly man ceaseth;
   For the faithful fail from among the children of men.
2 They speak falsehood every one with his neighbor:
   With flattering lip, and with a double heart, do they speak.
3 Jehovah shall cut off all flattering lips,
   The tongue that speaketh great things:

16. LORD'S DAY FIFTH IN MARCH — MORNING

4 Who have said, With our tongue will we prevail;
    Our lips are our own: who is lord over us?
5 Because of the spoiling of the poor,
    Because of the sighing of the needy,
6 Now will I arise, saith Jehovah;
    I will set him in safety at whom they puff.
7 The words of Jehovah are pure words;
    As silver tried in a furnace on the earth,
    Purified seven times.
8 Thou shalt keep them, O Jehovah,
    Thou shalt preserve them from this generation forever.
9 The wicked walk on every side,
    When vileness is exalted among the sons of men.

10 How long, O Jehovah, wilt Thou forget me forever?
    How long wilt Thou hide Thy face from me?
11 How long shall I take counsel in my soul,
Having sorrow in my heart all the day?
    How long shall mine enemy be exalted over me?
12 Consider and answer me, O Jehovah my God:
    Lighten mine eyes, lest I sleep the sleep of death:
13 Lest mine enemy say, I have prevailed against him;
    Lest mine adversaries rejoice when I am moved.
14 But I have trusted in Thy mercy:
    My heart shall rejoice in Thy salvation:
15 I will sing unto Jehovah,
    Because He hath dealt bountifully with me.

16 HEAR the right, O Jehovah, attend unto my cry:
    Give ear unto my prayer, that goeth not out of feigned lips.
17 Let my sentence come forth from Thy presence;
    Let Thine eyes look upon equity.
18 Thou hast proved mine heart;
    Thou hast visited me in the night;
19 Thou hast tried me, and findest nothing;
    I am purposed that my mouth shall not transgress.
20 As for the works of men, by the word of Thy lips
    I have kept me from the ways of the violent.
21 My steps have held fast to Thy paths,
    My feet have not slipped.
22 I have called upon Thee, for Thou wilt answer me, O God:
    Incline Thine ear unto me, and hear my speech.
23 Show Thy marvelous lovingkindness,
    O Thou that savest by Thy right hand
24 Them that take refuge in Thee
    From those that rise up against them.
25 Keep me as the apple of the eye,
    Hide me under the shadow of Thy wings,
26 From the wicked that oppress me,
    My deadly enemies, that compass me about.

16. LORD'S DAY FIFTH IN MARCH—MORNING

27 They are inclosed in their own fat:
   With their mouth they speak proudly.
28 They have now compassed us in our steps:
   They set their eyes to cast us down to the earth.
29 He is like a lion that is greedy of his prey,
   And as it were a young lion lurking in secret places.
30 Arise, O Jehovah,
   Confront him, cast him down:
31 Deliver my soul from the wicked by Thy sword;
   From men, by Thy hand, O Jehovah,
32 From men of the world, whose portion is in this life,
   And whose belly Thou fillest with Thy treasure:
33 They are satisfied with children,
   And leave the rest of their substance to their babes.
34 As for me, I shall behold Thy face in righteousness:
   I shall be satisfied, when I awake, with beholding Thy form.

Psalm Chant
See MONTHLY SONGS: Lord's Day Fifth—Morning.

Prayer of the Day

O GOD Most High, who in all ages art the hope and confidence of Thy people: Mercifully regard the prayer with which, out of the depths, we cry unto Thee; and stretch forth the right hand of Thy majesty for our help, making our hearts glad in Thy full salvation:

Through the suffering and sacrifice of Christ Thy Son, the Lamb of God, who liveth and reigneth with the Father and the Spirit—one God, in glory everlasting: AMEN.

Hymn of Praise
See MONTHLY SONGS: Lord's Day Fifth—Morning.

---

16. EVENING
LORD'S DAY FIFTH IN MARCH

Introductory

Sentence
IN the way of Thy judgments, O Jehovah, have we waited for Thee; To Thy Name, even to Thy memorial Name, is the desire of our soul. [Is. xxvi, 8]

Response
[Tune in MONTHLY SONGS]
WITH Thee, O God, is the | fountain of | life:
In Thy | light shall | we see | light. [Ps. xxxvi, 9]

Scripture Lessons
Old Covenant Ezkl. xiv, 1–8.
Gospel Luke, viii, 26–39.
Apostolic Word 1 Peter, i, 1–12.

16. LORD'S DAY FIFTH IN MARCH — EVENING

Responsive Lesson   Psalms of David, Ps. lxiv, lxx: of Asaph, lxxvi.

HEAR my voice, O God, in my complaint:
    Preserve my life from fear of the enemy.
2 Hide me from the secret counsel of evil-doers;
    From the tumult of the workers of iniquity:
3 Who have whet their tongue like a sword,
    And have aimed their arrows, even bitter words:
4 That they may shoot in secret places at the perfect:
    Suddenly do they shoot at him, and fear not.
5 They encourage themselves in an evil purpose;
    They commune of laying snares privily;
6 They say, Who shall see them?
    They search out iniquities;
7 We have accomplished, say they, a diligent search:
    And the inward thought of every one, and the heart, is deep.
8 But God shall shoot at them;
    With an arrow suddenly shall they be wounded.
9 So they shall be made to stumble,
    Their own tongue being against them:
10 All that see them shall wag the head.
    And all men shall fear;
11 And they shall declare the work of God,
    And shall wisely consider of His doing.
12 The righteous shall be glad in Jehovah, and shall take refuge in Him;
    And all the upright in heart shall glory.

---

13 MAKE haste, O God, to deliver me;
    Make haste to help me, O Jehovah.
14 Let them be ashamed and confounded
    That seek after my soul:
15 Let them be turned backward and brought to dishonor
    That delight in my hurt.
16 Let them be turned back by reason of their shame
    That say, Aha, Aha.
17 Let all those that seek Thee rejoice and be glad in Thee;
    And let such as love Thy salvation say continually,
    LET GOD BE MAGNIFIED.
18 But I am poor and needy;
    Make haste unto me, O God:
19 Thou art my help and my deliverer;
    O Jehovah, make no tarrying.

---

20 IN Judah is God known:
    His name is great in Israel.
21 In Salem also is His tabernacle,
    And His dwelling-place in Zion.
22 There He brake the arrows of the bow;
    The shield, and the sword, and the battle.

16. LORD'S DAY FIFTH IN MARCH — EVENING

23 Glorious art Thou and excellent,
From the mountains of prey.
24 The stouthearted are become a spoil, they have slept their sleep;
And none of the men of might have found their hands.
25 At Thy rebuke, O God of Jacob,
Both chariot and horse are cast into a dead sleep.
26 Thou, even Thou, art to be feared:
And who may stand in Thy sight when once Thou art angry?
27 Thou didst cause sentence to be heard from heaven;
The earth feared, and was still,
28 When God arose to judgment,
To save all the meek of the earth.
29 Surely the wrath of man shall praise Thee:
The residue of wrath shalt Thou gird upon Thee.
30 Vow, and pay unto Jehovah your God:
Let all that be round about Him bring presents unto Him that ought to be feared.
31 He shall cut off the spirit of princes:
He is terrible to the kings of the earth.

Psalm Chant   See MONTHLY SONGS: Lord's Day Fifth — Evening.

Hymn of Praise   See MONTHLY SONGS: Lord's Day Fifth — Evening.

[*See Note, Day No. 14, Morning*]

17. LORD'S DAY FIRST IN APRIL

MORNING

Introductory

Sentence
GREAT is Jehovah, and highly to be praised;
And His greatness is unsearchable.
All Thy works shall give thanks unto Thee, O Jehovah;
And Thy saints shall bless Thee.   [Ps. cxlv, 3, 10]

Response
(Tune in
MONTHLY SONGS)
THE Mighty One, God Je- | hovah, hath | spoken,
And called the earth from the rising of the sun unto the | go-ing | down there- | of.
Out of Zion, the per- | fection of | beauty,
God | hath | shi-ned | forth.   [Ps. l, 1, 2]

Scripture Lessons
Old Covenant   Job, xi, 7–20.
Gospel   Luke, ix, 51–62.
Apostolic Word   I Cor. iii, 1–15.

Responsive Lesson

Psalm cxix, 65–104.

THOU hast dealt well with Thy servant,
O Jehovah, according unto Thy word.
2 Teach me good judgment and knowledge;
For I have believed in Thy commandments.
3 Before I was afflicted I went astray;
But now I observe Thy word.
4 Thou art good, and doest good;
Teach me Thy statutes.
5 The proud have forged a lie against me:
With my whole heart will I keep Thy precepts.
6 Their heart is as fat as grease;
But I delight in Thy law.
7 It is good for me that I have been afflicted;
That I might learn Thy statutes.
8 The law of Thy mouth is better unto me
Than thousands of gold and silver.

9 Thy hands have made me and fashioned me:
Give me understanding, that I may learn Thy commandments.
10 They that fear Thee shall see me and be glad;
Because I have hoped in Thy word.
11 I know, O Jehovah, that Thy judgments are righteous,
And that in faithfulness Thou hast afflicted me.
12 Let, I pray Thee, Thy lovingkindness be for my comfort,
According to Thy word unto Thy servant.
13 Let Thy tender mercies come unto me, that I may live:
For Thy law is my delight.
14 Let the proud be put to shame; for they have overthrown me wrongfully:
But I will meditate in Thy precepts.
15 Let those that fear Thee turn unto me,
And they shall know Thy testimonies.
16 Let my heart be perfect in Thy statutes;
That I be not put to shame.

17 My soul fainteth for Thy salvation:
But I hope in Thy word.
18 Mine eyes fail for Thy word,
While I say, When wilt Thou comfort me?
19 For I am become like a bottle in the smoke;
Yet do I not forget Thy statutes.
20 How many are the days of Thy servant?
When wilt Thou execute judgment on them that persecute me?
21 The proud have digged pits for me,
Who are not after Thy law.
22 All Thy commandments are faithful:
They persecute me wrongfully; help Thou me.
23 They had almost consumed me upon earth;
But I forsook not Thy precepts.

17. LORD'S DAY FIRST IN APRIL — MORNING

24 Quicken me after Thy lovingkindness;
  So shall I observe the testimony of Thy mouth.
25 Forever, O Jehovah,
  Thy word is settled in heaven.
26 Thy faithfulness is unto all generations:
  Thou hast established the earth, and it abideth.
27 They abide this day according to Thine ordinances;
  For all things are Thy servants.
28 Unless Thy law had been my delight,
  I should then have perished in mine affliction.
29 I will never forget Thy precepts;
  For with them Thou hast quickened me.
30 I am Thine, save me;
  For I have sought Thy precepts.
31 The wicked have waited for me to destroy me;
  But I will consider Thy testimonies.
32 I have seen an end of all perfection;
  But Thy commandment is exceeding broad.
33 Oh, how love I Thy law!
  It is my meditation all the day.
34 Thy commandments make me wiser than mine enemies;
  For they are ever with me.
35 I have more understanding than all my teachers;
  For Thy testimonies are my meditation.
36 I understand more than the aged,
  Because I have kept Thy precepts.
37 I have refrained my feet from every evil way,
  That I might observe Thy word.
38 I have not turned aside from Thy judgments;
  For Thou hast taught me.
39 How sweet are Thy words unto my taste!
  Yea, sweeter than honey to my mouth!
40 Through Thy precepts I get understanding:
  Therefore I hate every false way.

Psalm Chant
See MONTHLY SONGS: Lord's Day First — Morning.

Prayer of the Day

GOD of Power, who seest the helpless misery of man's fallen life: Vouchsafe unto us, we humbly beseech Thee, both the outward and the inward defense of Thy guardian care; shielding us from all bodily evils save those which Thy wisdom doth appoint in love, and keeping us pure from all thoughts that harm and pollute the soul:

For the sake of the Lamb of God, Thy Son, our suffering Savior, who is forever glorified with the Father and the Holy Spirit — one God: AMEN.

Hymn of Praise
See MONTHLY SONGS: Lord's Day First — Morning.

17. EVENING

LORD'S DAY FIRST IN APRIL

Introductory

Sentence   SING praises to God, sing praises.
For God is the King of all the earth:
Sing ye praises with understanding.   [Ps. xlvii, 6, 7]

Response
[Tune in
Monthly Songs]   LOOK unto Me, and | be ye | sav'd,
All the | ends | of the | earth.
Unto Me every | knee shall | bow,
And every | tongue * shall con- | fess unto | God.
[Is. xlv, 22, 23 (Rom. xiv, 11)]

Scripture Lessons   Old Covenant   Jer. xxii, 1-9.
Gospel   Luke, xiv, 7-14.
Apostolic Word Eph. iii, 14-21.

Responsive Lesson   PSALMS OF DAVID, Ps. cxl, cxli.

DELIVER me, O Jehovah, from the evil man;
  Preserve me from the violent man:
2 Which devise mischiefs in their heart;
  Continually do they gather themselves together for war.
3 They have sharpened their tongue like a serpent;
  Adders' poison is under their lips.
4 Keep me, O Jehovah, from the hands of the wicked;
  Preserve me from the violent man:
5 Who have purposed to thrust aside my steps.
  The proud have hid a snare for me, and cords;
6 They have spread a net by the way-side;
  They have set gins for me.
7 I said unto Jehovah, Thou art my God:
  Give ear unto the voice of my supplications, O Jehovah.
8 O Jehovah the Lord, the strength of my salvation,
  Thou hast covered my head in the day of battle.
9 Grant not, O Jehovah, the desires of the wicked;
  Further not his evil device; lest they exalt themselves.
10 As for the head of those that compass me about,
  Let the mischief of their own lips cover them.
11 Let burning coals fall upon them:
  Let them be cast into the fire;
12 Into deep pits,
  That they rise not up again.
13 An evil speaker shall not be established in the earth:
  Evil shall hunt the violent man to overthrow him.
14 I know that Jehovah will maintain the cause of the afflicted,
  And the right of the needy.
15 Surely the righteous shall give thanks unto Thy Name:
  The upright shall dwell in Thy presence.

16 O JEHOVAH, I have called upon Thee; make haste unto me:
  Give ear unto my voice, when I call unto Thee.

17. LORD'S DAY FIRST IN APRIL—EVENING

17 Let my prayer be set forth as incense before Thee;
The lifting up of my hands as the evening sacrifice.
18 Set a watch, O Jehovah, before my mouth;
Keep the door of my lips.
19 Incline not my heart to any evil thing,
To be occupied in deeds of wickedness
20 With men that work iniquity:
And let me not eat of their dainties.
21 Let the righteous smite me, it shall be a kindness;
And let Him reprove me, it shall be as oil upon the head;
22 Let not my head refuse it:
For even in their wickedness shall my prayer continue.
23 Their judges are thrown down by the sides of the rock;
And they shall hear my words; for they are sweet.
24 As when one ploweth and cleaveth the earth,
Our bones are scattered at the grave's mouth.
25 For mine eyes are unto Thee, O Jehovah the Lord:
In Thee do I take refuge;
Leave not my soul destitute.
26 Keep me from the snare which they have laid for me,
And from the gins of the workers of iniquity.
27 Let the wicked fall into their own nets,
While that I withal escape.

Psalm Chant — See MONTHLY SONGS: Lord's Day First—Evening.

Hymn of Praise — See MONTHLY SONGS: Lord's Day First—Evening.

[*See Note, Day No.* 14, *Morning*]

18. LORD'S DAY SECOND IN APRIL

MORNING

Introductory

Sentence

PRAY for the peace of Jerusalem:
They shall prosper that love thee.
Peace be within thy walls,
And prosperity within thy palaces. [Ps. cxxii, 6, 7]

Response
[Tune in
MONTHLY SONGS]

JEHOVAH send thee help from the | sanc-tu- | ary,
And | strength-en | thee • out of | Zion !
Remember | all thine | offerings,
And ac- | cept thy | sac-ri- | fice ! [Ps. xx, 1–3]

Scripture Lessons

Old Covenant   Ezkl. ii, 3–10.
Gospel   Matt. x, 34–42.
Apostolic Word Heb. xi, 13–20.

18. LORD'S DAY SECOND IN APRIL — MORNING

Responsive Lesson
Psalm cxxxvi.

O GIVE thanks unto Jehovah; for He is good:
   For His lovingkindness endureth forever.
2 O give thanks unto the God of gods:
   For His lovingkindness endureth forever.
3 O give thanks unto the Lord of lords:
   For His lovingkindness endureth forever.
4 To Him who alone doeth great wonders:
   For His lovingkindness endureth forever.
5 To Him that by understanding made the heavens:
   For His lovingkindness endureth forever.
6 To Him that spread forth the earth above the waters:
   For His lovingkindness endureth forever.
7 To Him that made great lights:
   For His lovingkindness endureth forever:
8 The sun to rule by day:
   For His lovingkindness endureth forever:
9 The moon and stars to rule by night:
   For His lovingkindness endureth forever.
10 To Him that smote Egypt in their firstborn:
   For His lovingkindness endureth forever:
11 And brought out Israel from among them:
   For His lovingkindness endureth forever:
12 With a strong hand, and with a stretched out arm:
   For His lovingkindness endureth forever.
13 To Him which divided the Red Sea in sunder:
   For His lovingkindness endureth forever:
14 And made Israel to pass through the midst of it:
   For His lovingkindness endureth forever:
15 But overthrew Pharaoh and his host in the Red Sea:
   For His lovingkindness endureth forever.
16 To Him which led His people through the wilderness:
   For His lovingkindness endureth forever.
17 To Him which smote great kings:
   For His lovingkindness endureth forever:
18 And slew famous kings:
   For His lovingkindness endureth forever:
19 Sihon king of the Amorites:
   For His lovingkindness endureth forever:
20 And Og king of Bashan:
   For His lovingkindness endureth forever:
21 And gave their land for an heritage:
   For His lovingkindness endureth forever:
22 Even an heritage unto Israel His servant:
   For His lovingkindness endureth forever.
23 Who remembered us in our low estate:
   For His lovingkindness endureth forever:
24 And hath delivered us from our adversaries:
   For His lovingkindness endureth forever.

18. LORD'S DAY SECOND IN APRIL—MORNING

25 He giveth food to all flesh:
For His lovingkindness endureth forever.
26 O give thanks unto the God of heaven:
For His lovingkindness endureth forever.

Psalm Chant
See MONTHLY SONGS: Lord's Day Second—Morning.

Prayer of the Day
MERCIFULLY regard our feebleness, Almighty God; And in the midst of the manifold temptations and dangers which on all sides beset us, be Thou our keeper: For the sake of the Lamb of God, Thy Son, our Sacrifice, who is exalted with the Father and the Spirit—one ever-blessed God. AMEN.

Hymn of Praise
See MONTHLY SONGS: Lord's Day Second—Morning.

---

18. EVENING
LORD'S DAY SECOND IN APRIL

Introductory
Sentence

THY way, O God, is in the sanctuary.
Thou art the God that doest wonders:
Thou hast made known Thy strength among the peoples. [Ps. lxxvii, 13, 14]

Response
[Tune in MONTHLY SONGS]

LIFT up your hands to the | sanc-tu- | ary,
And | bless | ye Je- | hovah.
Jehovah bless thee | out of | Zion!
Even He that | made | heav'n and | earth. [Ps. cxxxiv, 2, 3]

Scripture Lessons
Old Covenant Nahum, i, 1–10.
Gospel Matt. xii, 1–8.
Apostolic Word Jude, 17–25.

Responsive Lesson
From Psalm cv.

O GIVE thanks unto Jehovah, call upon His Name;
Make known His doings among the peoples.
2 Sing unto Him, sing praises unto Him;
Talk ye of all His marvelous works.
3 Glory ye in His holy Name:
Let the heart of them rejoice that seek Jehovah.
4 Seek ye Jehovah and His strength;
Seek His face evermore.
5 Remember His marvelous works that He hath done;
His wonders, and the judgments of His mouth;

18. LORD'S DAY SECOND IN APRIL—EVENING

6 O ye seed of Abraham His servant,
Ye children of Jacob, His chosen ones.
7 He is Jehovah our God:
His judgments are in all the earth.
8 He hath remembered His covenant forever,
The word which He commanded to a thousand generations;
9 The covenant which He made with Abraham,
And His oath unto Isaac;
10 And confirmed the same unto Jacob for a statute,
To Israel for an everlasting covenant:
11 Saying, Unto thee will I give the land of Canaan,
The lot of your inheritance:
12 When they were but a few men in number;
Yea, very few, and sojourners in it;
13 And they went about from nation to nation,
From one kingdom to another people.
14 He suffered no man to do them wrong;
Yea, He reproved kings for their sakes;
15 Saying, Touch not Mine anointed ones,
And do My prophets no harm.
16 And He called for a famine upon the land;
He brake the whole staff of bread.

17 Israel also came into Egypt;
And Jacob sojourned in the land of Ham.
18 And He increased His people greatly,
And made them stronger than their adversaries.
19 He turned their heart to hate His people,
To deal subtilly with His servants.
20 He sent Moses His servant,
And Aaron whom He had chosen.
21 They set among them His signs,
And wonders in the land of Ham.

22 He smote also all the firstborn in their land,
The chief of all their strength.
23 And He brought them forth with silver and gold:
And there was not one feeble person among His tribes.
24 Egypt was glad when they departed;
For the fear of them had fallen upon them.
25 He spread a cloud for a covering;
And fire to give light in the night.
26 They asked, and He brought quails,
And satisfied them with the bread of heaven.
27 He opened the rock, and waters gushed out;
They ran in the dry places like a river.
28 For He remembered His holy word,
And Abraham His servant.
29 And He brought forth His people with joy,
And His chosen with singing.

18. LORD'S DAY SECOND IN APRIL—EVENING

30 And He gave them the lands of the nations;
    And they took the labor of the peoples in possession:
31 That they might keep His statutes,
    And observe His laws.
        PRAISE YE JEHOVAH.

Psalm Chant   See MONTHLY SONGS: Lord's Day Second—Evening.

Hymn of Praise   See MONTHLY SONGS: Lord's Day Second—Evening.

---

19. FAST DAY
MORNING
[OFFICES FOR THIS DAY MAY BE USED FOR ANY PENITENTIAL SERVICE]

Introductory

Sentence   ENTER not, O Jehovah, into judgment with Thy servants;
    For in Thy sight no man living is righteous.   [Ps. cxliii, 2]

Response   THE sacrifices of God are a | bro-ken | spirit:
    A broken and a contrite heart, O God, | Thou wilt | not
    de- | spise.   [Ps. li, 17]

WILLIAM DIXON, bef. 1825.

Scripture Lessons   Old Covenant Ezkl. xviii, 20–32.
    Gospel Matt. vi, 16–23.
    Apostolic Word Jas. iv, 6 ("God")–10.

Responsive Lesson   Is. lvii, 14–16, 19–21; lviii.   [Same for Day No. 49, Mrg.]

CAST ye up, cast ye up, prepare the way,
    Take up the stumbling-block out of the way of My people.
2 For thus saith the high and lofty One that inhabiteth eternity,
    Whose Name is Holy:
3 I dwell in the high and holy place,
    With him also that is of a contrite and humble spirit,
4 To revive the spirit of the humble,
    And to revive the heart of the contrite ones.
5 For I will not contend forever,
    Neither will I be always wroth:
6 For the spirit should fail before Me,
    And the souls that I have made.

19. FAST DAY—MORNING

7 I create the fruit of the lips: Peace, peace, to him that is far off
    And to him that is near, saith Jehovah; and I will heal him.
8 But the wicked are like the troubled sea; for it cannot rest,
    And its waters cast up mire and dirt.
    THERE IS NO PEACE, SAITH MY GOD, TO THE WICKED.

9 Cry aloud, spare not,
    Lift up thy voice like a trumpet,
10 And declare unto My people their transgression,
    And to the house of Jacob their sins.
11 Yet they seek Me daily,
    And delight to know My ways:
12 As a nation that did righteousness,
    And forsook not the ordinance of their God,
13 They ask of Me righteous ordinances,
    They delight to draw near unto God.
14 Wherefore have we fasted, say they, and Thou seest not?
    Wherefore have we afflicted our soul, and Thou takest no knowledge?
15 Behold, in the day of your fast ye find your own pleasure,
    And exact all your labors.
16 Behold ye fast for strife and contention,
    And to smite with the fist of wickedness:
    Ye fast not this day so as to make your voice to be heard on high.
17 Is such the fast that I have chosen?
    The day for a man to afflict his soul?
18 Is it to bow down his head as a rush,
    And to spread sackcloth and ashes under him?
19 Wilt thou call this a fast,
    And an acceptable day to Jehovah?
20 Is not this the fast that I have chosen?
    To loose the bonds of wickedness,
    To undo the bands of the yoke,
21 And to let the oppressed go free,
    And that ye break every yoke?
22 Is it not to deal thy bread to the hungry,
    And that thou bring the poor that are cast out to thy house?
23 When thou seest the naked, that thou cover him;
    And that thou hide not thyself from thine own flesh?
24 Then shall thy light break forth as the morning,
    And thy healing shall spring forth speedily:
25 And thy righteousness shall go before thee;
    The glory of Jehovah shall be thy rearward.
26 Then shalt thou call, and Jehovah shall answer;
    Thou shalt cry, and He shall say, Here I am.
27 If thou take away from the midst of thee the yoke,
    The putting forth of the finger, and speaking wickedly;
28 And if thou draw out thy soul to the hungry,
    And satisfy the afflicted soul;
29 Then shall thy light rise in darkness,
    And thine obscurity be as the noonday:
30 And Jehovah shall guide thee continually,
    And satisfy thy soul in dry places, and make strong thy bones;

19. FAST DAY — MORNING

31 And thou shalt be like a watered garden,
   And like a spring of water, whose waters fail not.
32 And they that shall be of thee shall build the old waste places:
   Thou shalt raise up the foundations of many generations;
33 And thou shalt be called, The repairer of the breach,
   The restorer of paths to dwell in.
34 If thou turn away thy foot from the Sabbath,
   From doing thy pleasure on My holy day;
35 And call the Sabbath a delight,
   And the holy of Jehovah honorable;
36 And shalt honor it, not doing thine own ways,
   Nor finding thine own pleasure, nor speaking thine own words:
37 Then shalt thou delight thyself in Jehovah;
   And I will make thee to ride upon the high places of the earth;
38 And I will feed thee with the heritage of Jacob thy father:
   For the mouth of Jehovah hath spoken it.

Psalm Chant

A SONG OF ASCENTS, Psalm cxxx. [Same for Evg.]

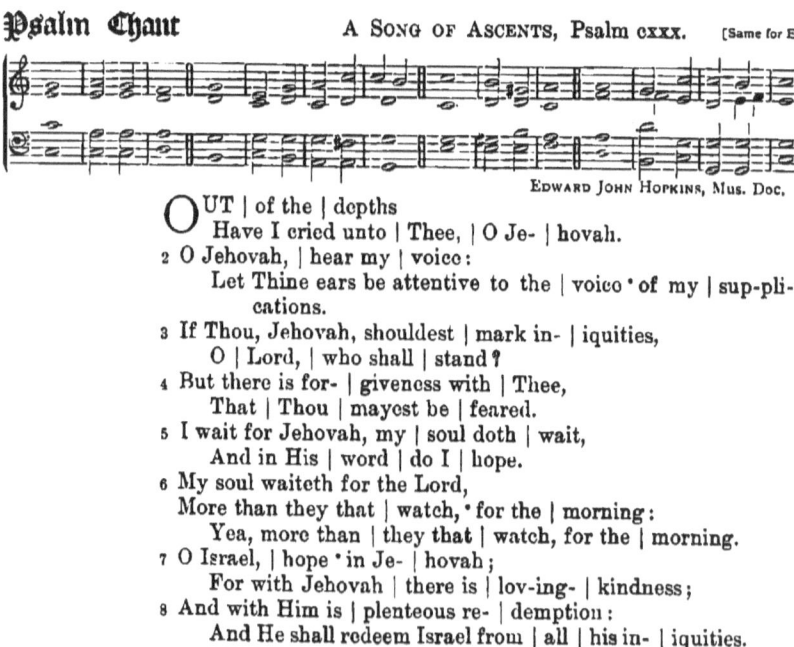

EDWARD JOHN HOPKINS, Mus. Doc.

O UT | of the | depths
   Have I cried unto | Thee, | O Je- | hovah.
2 O Jehovah, | hear my | voice:
   Let Thine ears be attentive to the | voice · of my | sup-pli- | cations.
3 If Thou, Jehovah, shouldest | mark in- | iquities,
   O | Lord, | who shall | stand?
4 But there is for- | giveness with | Thee,
   That | Thou | mayest be | feared.
5 I wait for Jehovah, my | soul doth | wait,
   And in His | word | do I | hope.
6 My soul waiteth for the Lord,
   More than they that | watch, · for the | morning:
   Yea, more than | they that | watch, for the | morning.
7 O Israel, | hope · in Je- | hovah;
   For with Jehovah | there is | lov-ing- | kindness;
8 And with Him is | plenteous re- | demption:
   And He shall redeem Israel from | all | his in- | iquities.
9 GLORY be to the Father, etc.

Prayer of the Day

MIGHTY Jehovah, merciful and gracious, long-suffering and abundant in goodness and truth; enter not into judgment with us Thy servants, nor let Thine anger come upon our state and nation for our many iniquities therein; but in Thy great compassion work in us, and in all the people, true repentance:

And grant that we who now might justly be afflicted, and are bowed down confessing our sins, may be refreshed with Thy forgiveness and lifted up in the joy of Thy strong salvation: Through the Lamb of God, Thy Son who suffered for all men, and who is enthroned with the Father and the Holy Spirit—one Almighty and Ever-living God: AMEN.

Hymn of Praise

JOHN SAMUEL BEWLEY MONSELL, LL. D. Pub. 1881.
(Dox. slightly alt.)

HOLY offerings, rich and rare,
Offerings of praise and prayer,
Purer life and purpose high,
Claspéd hands, uplifted eye,
Lowly acts of adoration
To the God of our salvation—
On His altar laid we leave them;
Christ, present them! God, receive them!

2 Promises in sorrow made,
Left, alas! too long unpaid;
Fervent wishes, earnest thought,
Never into action wrought—
Long withheld, we now restore them,
On Thy holy altar pour them:
There in trembling faith to leave them:
Christ, present them! God, receive them!

3 Vows and longings, hopes and fears,
Broken-hearted sighs and tears,
Dreams of what we yet might be
Could we cling more close to Thee,
Which, despite of faults and failings,
Help Thy grace in its prevailings—
On Thine altar laid we leave them:
Christ, present them! God, receive them!

4 Sinful thoughts and willful ways,
Love of self and human praise,
Pride of life and lust of eye,
Worldly pomp and vanity—
Faults that bind and will not leave us,
Though their staying sorely grieve us,
Help, oh, help us to outlive them:
Christ, atone for! God, forgive them!

5. God, the Father and the Son And the Spir-it— ev-er One! Though our mortal weakness raise Off'rings of im-per-fect praise, Yet with hearts bow'd down most lowly, Crying, Holy! Ho-ly! Ho-ly! On Thine al-tar laid we leave them; Christ present them! God receive them! A-MEN.

HOLY OFFERINGS. P. M.   RICHARD REDHEAD.

19. FAST DAY—MORNING

Or this Hymn
ANON. (Dox. added)

DREAD Jehovah! God of nations!
From Thy temple in the skies,
Hear Thy people's supplications,
Now for their deliverance rise;—
Lo! with deep contrition turning,
In Thy holy place we bend;
Hear us, fasting, praying, mourning;
Hear us, spare us, and defend.

2 Though our sins, our hearts confounding,
Long and loud for vengeance call,
Thou hast mercy more abounding,
Jesus' blood can cleanse them all;
Let that mercy vail transgression,
Let that blood our guilt efface;
Save Thy people from oppression,
Save from spoil Thy holy place.

LOVE DIVINE. 8787, D.   JOHN ZUNDEL, 1870.

19. EVENING
FAST DAY

Introductory

Sentence OUR transgressions are multiplied before Thee, O God,
And our sins testify against us:
For our transgressions are with us,
And as for our iniquities, we know them. [Is. lix, 12]

Response
[Tune, in Morning]
THE sacrifices of God are a | bro-ken | spirit:
A broken and a contrite heart, O God, | Thou wilt | not
de- | spise. [Ps. li, 17]

Scripture Lessons Old Covenant Lam. iii, 19–41.
Gospel Mark, ix, 43–49.
Apostolic Word Heb. iv, 11–16.

Responsive Lesson A PSALM OF DAVID, Ps. li : Ps. lxxx. [li, also for Day No. 51, Evg.]

HAVE mercy upon me, O God,
According to Thy lovingkindness:
2 According to the multitude of Thy tender mercies
Blot out my transgressions.
3 Wash me thoroughly from mine iniquity,
And cleanse me from my sin.
4 For I acknowledge my transgressions:
And my sin is ever before me.
5 Against Thee, Thee only, have I sinned,
And done that which is evil in Thy sight:
6 That Thou mayst be justified when Thou speakest,
And be clear when Thou judgest.
7 Behold, I was shapen in iniquity;
And in sin did my mother conceive me.
8 Behold, Thou desirest truth in the inward parts:
And in the hidden part Thou shalt make me to know wisdom.
9 Purge me with hyssop, and I shall be clean:
Wash me, and I shall be whiter than snow.
10 Make me to hear joy and gladness;
That the bones which Thou hast broken may rejoice.
11 Hide Thy face from my sins,
And blot out all mine iniquities.
12 Create in me a clean heart, O God;
And renew a right spirit within me.
13 Cast me not away from Thy presence;
And take not Thy holy Spirit from me.
14 Restore unto me the joy of Thy salvation:
And uphold me with a willing spirit.
15 Then will I teach transgressors Thy ways;
And sinners shall be converted unto Thee.
16 Deliver me from bloodguiltiness, O God, Thou God of my salvation;
And my tongue shall sing aloud of Thy righteousness.

19. FAST DAY—EVENING

17 O Lord, open Thou my lips;
  And my mouth shall show forth Thy praise.
18 For Thou delightest not in sacrifice; else would I give it:
  Thou hast no pleasure in burnt offering.
19 The sacrifices of God are a broken spirit:
  A broken and a contrite heart, O God, Thou wilt not despise.

20 Do good in Thy good pleasure unto Zion:
  Build Thou the walls of Jerusalem.
21 Then shalt Thou delight in the sacrifices of righteousness,
  In burnt offering and whole burnt offering:
  Then shall they offer bullocks upon Thine altar.

---

22 GIVE ear, O Shepherd of Israel,
  Thou that leadest Joseph like a flock;
    THOU THAT SITTEST ABOVE THE CHERUBIM, SHINE FORTH.
23 Before Ephraim and Benjamin and Manasseh, stir up Thy might,
  And come to save us.
24 Turn us again, O God;
  And cause Thy face to shine, and we shall be saved.

25 O Jehovah, God of hosts,
  How long wilt Thou be angry against the prayer of Thy people?
26 Thou hast fed them with the bread of tears,
  And given them tears to drink in large measure.
27 Thou makest us a strife unto our neighbors:
  And our enemies laugh among themselves.
28 Turn us again, O God of hosts;
  And cause Thy face to shine, and we shall be saved.

29 Thou broughtest a vine out of Egypt:
  Thou didst drive out the nations, and plantedst it.
30 Thou preparedst room before it,
  And it took deep root, and filled the land.
31 The mountains were covered with the shadow of it,
  And the boughs thereof were like cedars of God.
32 She sent out her branches unto the sea,
  And her shoots unto the River.
33 Why hast Thou broken down her fences,
  So that all they who pass by the way do pluck her?
34 The boar out of the wood doth ravage it,
  And the wild beasts of the field feed on it.
35 Turn again, we beseech Thee, O God of hosts;
  Look down from heaven,
  And behold and visit this vine,
36 And the stock which Thy right hand hath planted,
  And the branch that Thou madest strong for Thyself.
37 It is burned with fire, it is cut down:
  They perish at the rebuke of Thy countenance.
38 Let Thy hand be upon the man of Thy right hand,
  Upon the son of man whom Thou madest strong for Thyself.

19. FAST DAY—EVENING 75

39 So shall we not go back from Thee:
Quicken Thou us, and we will call upon Thy Name.
40 Turn us again, O Jehovah, God of hosts;
Cause Thy face to shine, and we shall be saved.

Psalm Chant   Same as for Morning

Hymn of Praise

Isaac Watts, D. D.   (Dox.—Author unknown.)

Mine eyes and my desire
 Are ever to the Lord;
I love to plead His promises,
 And rest upon His word.

2 Lord, turn to Thee my soul;
 Bring Thy salvation near:
When will Thy hand release my feet
 From sin's destructive snare?

3 When shall the sovereign grace
 Of my forgiving God

Restore me from those dangerous ways
 My wandering feet have trod?

4 Oh, keep my soul from death,
 Nor put my hope to shame!
For I have placed my only trust
 In my Redeemer's Name.

5 With humble faith I wait
 To see Thy face again;
Of Israel it shall ne'er be said,
 He sought the Lord in vain.

O, The Father and the Son And Spirit, we adore: We glorify, we worship Thee, One God for ev-er-more. A-MEN.

THATCHER. S. M.   Georg Friedrich Händel, 1743.

20. LORD'S DAY BEFORE THE CRUCIFIXION
MORNING

[THE OFFICES FOR THIS DAY ARE APPROPRIATE FOR ANY DAY BEFORE FRIDAY IN THIS WEEK]

Introductory

Sentence

THOU, Jehovah, spakest in vision to Thy saints,
And saidst, I have laid help upon One that is mighty. [Ps. lxxxix, 19]

Response

BEHOLD, I lay in Zion | for a · foun- | dation,
A | Stone, a | tried | Stone,
A precious Corner-stone of | sure foun- | dation:
And he that believeth on Him shall | not be | put to | shame.
[Is. xxviii, 16 (1 Pet. ii, 6)]

Sir GEORGE ALEXANDER MACFARREN, Mus. Doc.

Scripture Lessons

Old Covenant — Dan. ix, 20–27.
Gospel — John, xii, 20–33.
Apostolic Word — Heb. ix, 11–16.

Responsive Lesson

From ZECH. vi, ix, xii, xiii, xiv.

THUS speaketh Jehovah of hosts, saying,
Behold the man whose name is the Branch;
And he shall grow up out of his place,
And he shall build the temple of Jehovah;
Even he shall build the temple of Jehovah;
3 And he shall bear the glory,
And shall sit and rule upon his throne;
AND HE SHALL BE A PRIEST UPON HIS THRONE:
4 And the counsel of peace shall be between them both.
And they that are far off shall come and build in the temple of Jehovah.
5 Rejoice greatly, O daughter of Zion;
Shout, O daughter of Jerusalem:
6 Behold, thy King cometh unto thee:
He is just, and having salvation;
7 Lowly, and riding upon an ass,
Even upon a colt, the foal of an ass.
8 And I will cut off the chariot from Ephraim,
And the horse from Jerusalem;
9 And the battle bow shall be cut off;
And he shall speak peace unto the nations:
10 And his dominion shall be from sea to sea,
And from the River to the ends of the earth.
11 As for thee also, because of the blood of thy covenant,
I have sent forth thy prisoners out of the pit wherein is no water.
12 Turn you to the stronghold, ye prisoners of hope:
Even to-day do I declare that I will render double unto thee.

20. LORD'S DAY BEFORE THE CRUCIFIXION — MORNING

13 Thus saith Jehovah: I will pour upon the house of David,
   And upon the inhabitants of Jerusalem,
14 The spirit of grace and of supplication;
   And they shall look unto Me whom they have pierced:
15 And they shall mourn for him,
   As one mourneth for his only son;
16 And shall be in bitterness for him,
   As one that is in bitterness for his firstborn.
17 In that day there shall be a fountain opened to the house of David
   And to the inhabitants of Jerusalem,
   For sin and for uncleanness.
18 Awake, O sword, against My shepherd,
   And against the Man that is My fellow, saith Jehovah of hosts:
19 Smite the shepherd, and the sheep shall be scattered;
   And I will turn My hand upon the little ones.
20 And it shall come to pass, that in all the land, saith Jehovah,
   Two parts therein shall be cut off and die;
   But the third shall be left therein.
21 And I will bring the third part through the fire,
   And will refine them as silver is refined;
   And will try them as gold is tried:
22 They shall call on My Name,
   And I will hear them:
23 I will say, it is My people;
   And they shall say, Jehovah is my God.
24 It shall come to pass in that day,
   That the light shall be not with brightness and with gloom:
   But it shall be one day which is known unto Jehovah;
25 Not day, and not night:
   But it shall come to pass, that at evening-time there shall be light.
26 And it shall come to pass in that day,
   That living waters shall go out from Jerusalem;
27 Half of them toward the eastern sea,
   And half of them toward the western sea:
   IN SUMMER AND IN WINTER SHALL IT BE.
28 And Jehovah shall be King over all the earth:
   In that day shall Jehovah be One, and His Name one.

Psalm Chant

From a PSALM OF DAVID, Ps. xl. [Same for Evg.]

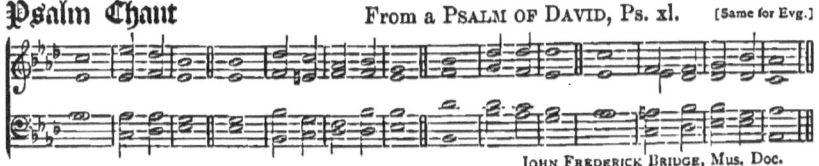

JOHN FREDERICK BRIDGE, Mus. Doc.

I WAITED patiently | for Je- | hovah:
   And He inclin'd unto | me, and | heard my | cry.
2 Sacrifice and offering Thou hast no delight in;
   Mine | ears · hast Thou | open'd:
   Burnt offering and sin-offering | hast Thou | not re- | quir'd.

20. LORD'S DAY BEFORE THE CRUCIFIXION — MORNING

3 Then said I, | Lo, • I am | come;
   In the roll of the | book • it is | written of | me:
4 I delight to do Thy will, | O my | God;
   Yea, Thy | law • is with- | in my | heart.
5 I have publish'd righteousness in the great | con-gre- | gation;
   Lo, I will not refrain my lips, | O Je- | hovah, Thou | knowest.
6 I have not hid Thy righteousness with- | in my | heart;
   I have declar'd Thy faithful- | ness and | Thy sal- | vation:
7 I have not conceal'd Thy lovingkindness and Thy truth from the great | con-gre- | gation.
   Withhold not Thou Thy tender | mercies from | me, • O Je- | hovah:
8 Let Thy lovingkindness and Thy truth continually pre- | serve | me.
   For innumerable evils have | com-pass'd | me a- | bout.
9 Be pleas'd, O Jehovah, | to de- | liver me:
   Make haste to | help me, | O Je- | hovah.
10 Let all those that seek Thee rejoice and be | glad in | Thee:
    Let such as love Thy salvation say continually,
    Je- | hovah be | magni- | fied.
11 GLORY be to the Father, etc.

Prayer of the Day

FATHER of an Infinite Majesty, who of Thy tender love toward mankind, hast given Thy Son Christ Jesus to take upon Him our flesh, and, as the Lamb of God, to suffer death upon the cross that He might take away our sins:

Mercifully grant us to have fellowship both in His sufferings, and in the glorious power of His resurrection, ascension, and kingdom;

To whom with Thee and the Spirit — one God — be all blessing and praise, from everlasting to everlasting: AMEN.

Hymn of Praise

ANON. From Latin Hymn ("Gloria in Excelsis") of fourth century or earlier.

LET glory be to God on high:
Peace be on earth as in the sky;
Good will to men! We bow the knee,
We praise, we bless, we worship Thee;
We give Thee thanks, Thy name we sing,
Almighty Father! Heavenly King!

2 O Lord, the sole begotten Son,
Who bore the crimes which we had done;
Son of the Father, who wast slain
To take away the sins of men;
O Lamb of God, whose blood was spilt
For all the world, and all its guilt; —

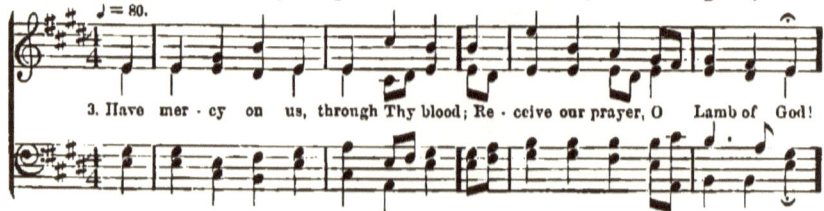

3. Have mercy on us, through Thy blood; Receive our prayer, O Lamb of God!

ST. WERBERGH. L. M. 6 l.   JOHN BACCHUS DYKES, Mus. Doc.

20. EVENING
LORD'S DAY BEFORE THE CRUCIFIXION

Introductory

Sentence

BE not Thou far off, O Jehovah:
O Thou, My Succor, haste Thee to help Me.
I will declare Thy Name unto My brethren;
In the midst of the congregation will I sing Thy praise.
[Ps. xxii, 19, 22 (Heb. ii, 12)]

Response
[Tune, in Morning]

BEHOLD, I lay in Zion | for a * foun- | dation,
A | Stone, a | tried | Stone,
A precious Corner-stone of | sure foun- | dation:
And he that believeth on Him shall | not be | put to | shame.
[Is. xxviii, 16 (1 Pet. ii,6)]

Scripture Lessons   Old Covenant   Jer. ix, 1–11.
Gospel   Matt. xxi, 1–11.
Apostolic Word   Heb. ix, 23–28.

Responsive Lesson   PSALMS OF DAVID, Ps. xxxi, xvi.

IN Thee, O Jehovah, do I take refuge;
Let me never be put to shame.
2 Deliver me in Thy righteousness.
Bow down Thine ear unto me; deliver me speedily:

20. LORD'S DAY BEFORE THE CRUCIFIXION — EVENING

3 Be Thou to me a strong rock,
A house of defense to save me.
4 For Thou art my rock and my fortress;
Therefore for Thy Name's sake lead me and guide me.
5 Pluck me out of the net that they have laid privily for me;
For Thou art my stronghold.
6 Into Thy hand I commend my spirit:
Thou hast redeemed me, O Jehovah, Thou God of truth.
7 I hate them that regard lying vanities:
But I trust in Jehovah.
8 I will be glad and rejoice in Thy lovingkindness:
For Thou hast seen my affliction;
Thou hast known my soul in adversities.
9 And Thou hast not shut me up into the hand of the enemy;
Thou hast set my feet in a large place.
10 Have mercy upon me, O Jehovah,
For I am in distress:
11 Mine eye wasteth away with grief,
Yea, my soul and my body.
12 For my life is spent with sorrow,
And my years with sighing:
13 My strength faileth because of mine iniquity,
And my bones are wasted away.
14 Because of all mine adversaries I am become a reproach,
Yea, unto my neighbors exceedingly,
15 And a fear to mine acquaintance:
They that did see me without fled from me.
16 I am forgotten as a dead man out of mind:
I am like a broken vessel.
17 For I have heard the defaming of many,
Terror on every side:
18 While they took counsel together against me,
They devised to take away my life.
19 But I trusted in Thee, O Jehovah:
I said, Thou art my God.
   MY TIMES ARE IN THY HAND:
20 Deliver me from the hand of mine enemies,
And from them that persecute me.
21 Make Thy face to shine upon Thy servant:
Save me in Thy lovingkindness.
22 Let me not be put to shame, O Jehovah;
For I have called upon Thee:
23 Let the wicked be put to shame,
Let them be silent in Sheol.
24 Let the lying lips be dumb, which speak against the righteous insolently,
With pride and contempt.
25 Oh, how great is Thy goodness,
Which Thou hast laid up for them that fear Thee,
26 Which Thou hast wrought for them that take refuge in Thee,
Before the sons of men!

20. LORD'S DAY BEFORE THE CRUCIFIXION — EVENING

27 In the covert of Thy presence shalt Thou hide them from the plottings of man:
   Thou shalt keep them secretly in a pavilion from the strife of tongues.
28 Blessed be Jehovah:
   For He hath showed me His marvelous lovingkindness, in a strong city.
29 As for me, I said in my haste, I am cut off from before Thine eyes:
   Nevertheless Thou heardest the voice of my supplications when I cried unto Thee.
   O LOVE JEHOVAH, ALL YE HIS SAINTS:
30 Jehovah preserveth the faithful,
   And plentifully rewardeth the proud doer.
31 Be strong, and let your heart take courage,
   All ye that hope in Jehovah.

---

32 PRESERVE me, O God:
   For in Thee do I take refuge.
33 O my soul, thou hast said unto Jehovah, Thou art my Lord:
   I have no good beyond Thee.
34 As for the saints that are in the earth,
   They are the excellent in whom is all my delight.
35 Their sorrows shall be multiplied
   That give gifts for another god:
36 Their drink offerings of blood will I not offer,
   Nor take their names upon my lips.
37 Jehovah is the portion of mine inheritance and of my cup:
   Thou maintainest my lot.
38 The lines are fallen unto me in pleasant places;
   Yea, I have a goodly heritage.
39 I will bless Jehovah, who hath given me counsel:
   Yea, my reins instruct me in the night seasons.
40 I have set Jehovah always before me:
   Because He is at my right hand, I shall not be moved.
41 Therefore my heart is glad and my glory rejoiceth:
   My flesh also shall dwell in safety.
42 For Thou wilt not leave my soul to Sheol;
   Neither wilt Thou suffer Thy holy one to see corruption.
43 Thou wilt show me the path of life:
   In Thy presence is fullness of joy;
   In Thy right hand there are pleasures forevermore.

[The last portion (40-43) may be used also on Day No. 22.]

Psalm Chant   Same as for Morning

[*Hymn of Praise — see next page*]

20. LORD'S DAY BEFORE THE CRUCIFIXION — EVENING

Hymn of Praise

FRANCES RIDLEY HAVERGAL, 1870. (Last stanza, added.)
LANCASHIRE. 7676, D. HENRY SMART.

1. O Savior, precious Savior! Whom yet unseen we love,
O Name of might and favor, All other names above:

REFRAIN. *In the last stanza, use the* DOXOLOGY *instead.*
We worship Thee, we bless Thee, To Thee alone we sing;
We praise Thee and confess Thee, Our holy Lord and King.

2 O Bringer of Salvation,
  Who wondrously hast wrought—
Thyself the revelation
Of love beyond our thought:
REF'N] We worship Thee, we bless Thee,
  To Thee alone we sing;
  We praise Thee and confess Thee,
  Our holy Lord and King.

3 In Thee all fullness dwelleth,
  All grace and power divine;
The glory that excelleth,
O Son of God, is Thine:
REFRAIN] We worship Thee —

4 O, grant the consummation
Of this our song above,
In endless adoration
And everlasting love:
REFRAIN] We worship Thee —

5 Jehovah, High and Holy!
Who from Thy dwelling-place
Dost come unto the lowly,
To dwell with them in grace:
[Dox. O Glorious God, we bless Thee —
The Father and the Son
And Spirit: we confess Thee
Eternal God alone.

A-MEN.

21. THE CRUCIFIXION DAY

MORNING *(Good Friday)*

Introductory

Sentence BEHOLD, the Lamb of God, that taketh away the sin of the world.
He was oppressed, yet when He was afflicted
He opened not His mouth:
As a lamb that is led to the slaughter,
And as a sheep that before her shearers is dumb,
So He opened not His mouth. [Jn. i, 29: Is. liii, 7]

Response WORTHY art Thou, the Lamb;
For | Thou wast | slain,
And didst purchase | un-to | God • with Thy | blood,
Men of every tribe and tongue and | people and | nation,
And madest them to be | unto our | God a | Kingdom.
[Rev. v, 9, 10]

EDWARD JOHN HOPKINS, Mus. Doc.

Scripture Lessons

Old Covenant Ex. xii, 21-27.

Gospel From Matt. xxvi, xxvii; and Luke, xxiii.

AND they that had taken Jesus led Him away to the house of Caiaphas the high priest, where the scribes and the elders were gathered together. But Peter followed Him afar off, unto the court of the high priest, and entered in, and sat with the officers, to see the end. Now the chief priests and the whole council sought false witness against Jesus, that they might put Him to death; and they found it not, though many false witnesses came. But afterward came two, and said, This man said, I am able to destroy the temple of God, and to build it in three days. And the high priest stood up, and said unto Him, Answerest thou nothing? what is it which these witness against thee? But Jesus held His peace. And the high priest said unto Him, I adjure thee by the living God, that thou tell us whether thou be the Christ, the Son of God. Jesus saith unto him, Thou hast said: nevertheless I say unto you, Henceforth ye shall see the Son of Man sitting at the right hand of power, and coming on the clouds of heaven. Then the high priest rent his garments, saying, He hath spoken blasphemy: what further need have we of witnesses? behold, now ye have heard the blasphemy: what think ye? They answered and said, He is worthy of death. Then did they spit in His face and buffet Him: and some smote Him with the palms of their hands, saying, Prophesy unto us, thou Christ: who is he that struck thee?

Now when morning was come, all the chief priests and the elders of the people took counsel against Jesus to put Him to death: and they bound Him, and led Him away, and delivered Him up to Pilate the governor.

Now Jesus stood before the governor: and the governor asked Him, saying, Art thou the King of the Jews? And Jesus said unto him, Thou sayest. And when He was accused by the chief priests and elders, He answered nothing. Then saith Pilate unto Him, Hearest thou not how many things they witness against thee? And He gave him no answer, not even to one word: insomuch that the governor marveled greatly.

And Pilate called together the chief priests and the rulers and the people, and said unto them, Ye brought unto me this man, as one that perverteth the people: and behold, I, having examined him before you, found no fault in this man touching those things whereof ye accuse him: no, nor yet Herod: for he sent him back unto us; and behold, nothing worthy of death hath been done by him. I will therefore chastise him, and release him. But they cried out all together, saying, Away with this man, and release unto us Barabbas: one who for a certain insurrection made in the city, and for murder, was cast into prison. And Pilate spake unto them again, desiring to release Jesus; but they shouted, saying, Crucify, crucify him. And he said unto them the third time, Why, what evil hath this man done? I have found no cause of death in him: I will therefore chastise him, and release him. But they were urgent with loud voices, asking that he might be crucified. And their voices prevailed.

So when Pilate saw that he prevailed nothing, but rather that a tumult was arising, he took water, and washed his hands before the multitude, saying, I am innocent of the blood of this righteous man: see ye to it. And all the people answered and said, His blood be on us, and on our children. Then released he unto them Barabbas: but Jesus he scourged and delivered to be crucified.

Then the soldiers of the governor took Jesus into the Prætorium, and gathered unto Him the whole band. And they stripped Him, and put on Him a scarlet robe. And they plaited a crown of thorns and put it upon His head, and a reed in His right hand; and they kneeled down before Him, and mocked Him, saying, Hail, King of the Jews! And they spat upon Him, and took the reed and smote Him on the head. And when they had mocked Him, they took off from Him the robe, and put on Him His garments, and led Him away to crucify Him.

And there were also two others, malefactors, led with Him to be put to death.

And when they came unto the place which is called The Skull, there they crucified Him, and the malefactors, one on the right and the other on the left. And when they had crucified Him, they parted His garments among them, casting lots; and they sat and watched Him there. And they set up over His head His accusation written, THIS IS JESUS THE KING OF THE JEWS.

And Jesus said, Father, forgive them; for they know not what they do.

And they that passed by railed on Him, wagging their heads, and saying, Thou that destroyest the temple, and buildest it in three days, save thyself: if thou art the Son of God, come down from the cross. In like manner also the chief priests mocking Him, with the scribes and elders, said, He saved others; himself he cannot save. He is the King of Israel; let him now come down from the cross, and we will believe on him. He trusted on God; let Him deliver him now, if He desireth him: for he said, I am the Son of God. And the soldiers also mocked Him, coming to Him, offering Him vinegar, and saying, If thou art the King of the Jews, save thyself.

And one of the malefactors that were hanged railed on Him, saying, Art not thou the Christ? save thyself and us. But the other answered, and rebuking him said, Dost thou not even fear God, seeing thou art in the same condemnation? And we indeed justly; for we receive the due reward of our deeds: but this man hath done nothing amiss. And he said, Jesus, remember me when Thou comest in Thy kingdom. And He said unto him, Verily I say unto thee, To-day shalt thou be with Me in paradise.

And it was now about the sixth hour, and a darkness came over the whole land

21. THE CRUCIFIXION DAY—MORNING

until the ninth hour, the sun's light failing: and the veil of the temple was rent in the midst. And Jesus, crying with a loud voice, said, Father, into Thy hands I commend My spirit: and having said this, He gave up the ghost.

Apostolic Word Heb. x, 1–18.

Responsive Lesson Isaiah, lii, 13–15; liii. [Also for the Evening, at discretion]

BEHOLD, My Servant shall deal wisely,
He shall be exalted and lifted up,
And shall be very high.
2 Like as many were astonished at thee
(His visage was so marred more than any man,
And his form more than the sons of men),
3 So shall he sprinkle many nations;
Kings shall shut their mouths because of him:
4 For that which had not been told them shall they see,
And that which they had not heard shall they understand.

5 Who hath believed our report?
And to whom hath the arm of Jehovah been revealed?
6 For he grew up before Him as a tender plant,
And as a root out of a dry ground:
7 He hath no form nor comeliness;
And when we see him there is no beauty that we should desire him.
8 He was despised, and rejected of men;
A man of sorrows, and acquainted with grief:
9 And as one from whom men hide their face he was despised,
And we esteemed him not.

10 Surely he hath borne our griefs
And carried our sorrows:
11 Yet we did esteem him stricken,
Smitten of God, and afflicted.
12 But he was wounded for our transgressions,
He was bruised for our iniquities:
13 The chastisement of our peace was upon him;
And with his stripes we are healed.
14 All we like sheep have gone astray;
We have turned every one to his own way:
AND JEHOVAH HATH LAID ON HIM THE INIQUITY OF US ALL.

15 He was oppressed, yet when he was afflicted
He opened not his mouth:
16 As a lamb that is led to the slaughter,
And as a sheep that before her shearers is dumb,
17 So he opened not his mouth.
By oppression and judgment he was taken away;
18 And as for his generation,
Who among them considered
19 That he was cut off out of the land of the living
For the transgression of my people
To whom the stroke was due?

21. THE CRUCIFIXION DAY — MORNING

20 And they made his grave with the wicked,
  And with a rich man in his death;
21 Although he had done no violence,
  Neither was any deceit in his mouth.
22 Yet it pleased Jehovah to bruise him;
  He hath put him to grief:
23 When Thou shalt make his soul an offering for sin,
  He shall see his seed,
24 He shall prolong his days,
  And the pleasure of Jehovah shall prosper in his hand.
25 He shall see of the travail of his soul,
  And shall be satisfied:
26 By the knowledge of himself shall My righteous Servant justify many:
  And he shall bear their iniquities.
27 Therefore will I divide him a portion with the great,
  And he shall divide the spoil with the strong:
28 Because he poured out his soul unto death,
  And was numbered with the transgressors:
29 Yet he bare the sin of many,
  And made intercession for the transgressors.

Psalm Chant From a PSALM OF DAVID, Ps. xxii. [Same for Ev'g. and for Day No. 22.]

BENJAMIN ST. JOHN BAPTIST JOULE.

M Y God, my God, why hast | Thou for- | saken me ?
  Why art Thou so far from helping me,
  And from the | words | of my | groaning ?
2 All they that see me | laugh • me to | scorn;
  They shoot out the | lip, they | shake the | head,
3 Saying, Commit thyself unto Jehovah; let | Him de- | liver him :
  Let Him rescue him, seeing | He de- | lighteth | in him.
4 The assembly of evil-doers have inclos'd me;
  They pierc'd my | hands • and my | feet;
5 They part my garments among them,
  And upon my | vesture do | they cast | lots.
6 But be not Thou far off, | O Je- | hovah :
  O Thou my | Succor! haste | Thee to | help me.
7 I will declare Thy Name | unto my | brethren :
  In the midst of the congre- | ga-tion | will I | praise Thee.
8 All the ends of the earth shall remember and turn | unto Je- | hovah :
  And all the kindreds of the | nations shall | worship be- | fore Thee.
9 A seed shall | serve | Him;
  It shall be told of the Lord | unto the | next gener- | ation.

21. THE CRUCIFIXION DAY—MORNING

10 They shall come and shall declare His | right-eous- | ness
Unto a people that shall be | born, that | He hath | done it.

11 GLORY be to the Father, etc.

Prayer of the Day

HOLY Father, who from the foundation of the world redeemest it unto Thyself in the blood of the Lamb of God, Thine only-begotten Son, manifesting to us sinners Thine unfathomable love: HEAR US IN HIS NAME.

WE humbly beseech Thee, by the awful mystery of His cross and Thy sacrifice in Him, to have mercy on us and on all men; and to make known this, Thy great salvation unto all nations, that He may see of the travail of His soul and be satisfied: HEAR US IN HIS NAME.

WE beseech Thee, that Thou, who hast loved Thy Church with an everlasting love, wouldst by Thy blessed Spirit rule the whole estate thereof, and graciously guide and keep every member of the same in true faith and all good works according to Christ Jesus: HEAR US IN HIS NAME.

WE beseech Thee, that Thou, who of old didst call forth from among idolaters Thy servant Abraham and madest him the Friend of God, wouldst remember the mercy of Thy covenant with him, and show compassion on his children, Thine ancient people, and take away the blindness of their heart, so that they may behold their Christ and King: HEAR US IN HIS NAME.

WE beseech Thee, that Thou who hast made all men and hatest nothing that Thou hast made, and desirest not the death of a sinner, wouldst show mercy in Christ Jesus on all Pagans, Moslems, and Infidels, and on all hearers of the gospel who obey not Thy Son—taking away from them their ignorance, or their hardness of heart and contempt of Thy word: HEAR US IN HIS NAME.

AND so—since Thou hast given Thy Son for all mankind—bring them all, Blessed Lord, whatsoever Thou hast given Him, home to Thy fold, that they all may be saved among the remnant of Thy true Israel, and be made one flock under one Shepherd, Thy Son Jesus Christ: HEAR US IN HIS NAME:

IN His Name who was dead, and is alive forevermore, and reigneth with Thee. O Father, and the Holy Spirit—one God—in the glory of a kingdom without end:
AMEN.

[*Hymn of praise—see next page*]

21. THE CRUCIFIXION DAY — MORNING

Hymn of Praise

RAY PALMER, D. D. 1858. (Dox. added.)
From Latin Hymn of Gregory the Great, sixth cen.

O CHRIST! our King, Creator, Lord!
Savior of all who trust Thy word!
To them who seek Thee ever near,
Now to our praises bend Thine ear.

2 In Thy dear cross a grace is found —
It flows from every streaming wound —
Whose power our inbred sin controls,
Breaks the firm bond, and frees our souls.

3 Thou didst create the stars of night;
Yet Thou hast vailed in flesh Thy light,
Hast deigned a mortal form to wear,
A mortal's painful lot to bear.

4 When Thou didst hang upon the tree,
The quaking earth acknowledged Thee;
When Thou didst there yield up Thy breath,
The world grew dark as shades of death.

5 Now in the Father's glory high,
Great Conqueror! never more to die,
Us by Thy mighty power defend,
And reign through ages without end.

6 To Thee, all glo - ry, God Most High! — The Father's Name we mag - ni - fy;
Thy Son, Thy Spir - it, we a - dore: We praise, we bless Thee, ev - er - more. A-MEN.

GERMANY. L. M.   LUDWIG VAN BEETHOVEN, d. 1827.

---

21. EVENING

Introductory   THE CRUCIFIXION DAY   *(Good Friday)*

Sentence THE assembly of evil-doers have inclosed Me:
There is none to help.
Father! into Thy hands I commend My Spirit.
[Ps. xxii, 16, 11: xxxi, 5 (Lk. xxiii, 46)]

Response
[Tune, in Morning]

WORTHY art Thou, the Lamb;
For | Thou wast | slain, |
And didst purchase | un-to | God · with Thy | blood,
Men of every tribe and tongue and | people and | nation,
And madest them to be | unto our | God a | Kingdom.
[Rev. v, 9, 10]

21. THE CRUCIFIXION DAY— EVENING

Scripture Lessons
Old Covenant   Zech. xi, 4-14.
Gospel   Matt. xxvii, 45-56.
Apostolic Word   Heb. x, 19-25.

Responsive Lesson   A PSALM OF DAVID, Ps. lv.
[Or the lesson for the Morning may be used]

GIVE ear to my prayer, O God,
    And hide not Thyself from my supplication.
2 Attend unto me, and answer me:
    I am restless in my complaint, and moan;
3 Because of the voice of the enemy,
    Because of the oppression of the wicked;
4 For they cast iniquity upon me,
    And in anger they persecute me.
5 My heart is sore pained within me:
    And the terrors of death are fallen upon me.
6 Fearfulness and trembling are come upon me,
    And horror hath overwhelmed me.
7 And I said, Oh, that I had wings like a dove!
    Then would I fly away, and be at rest.
8 Lo, then would I wander far off,
    I would lodge in the wilderness.
9 I would haste me to a shelter
    From the stormy wind and tempest.
10 Destroy, O Lord, and divide their tongue:
    For I have seen violence and strife in the city.
11 Day and night they go about it upon the walls thereof:
    Iniquity also and mischief are in the midst of it.
12 Wickedness is in the midst thereof:
    Oppression and guile depart not from her streets.
13 For it was not an enemy that reproached me;
    Then I could have borne it:
14 Neither was it he that hated me that did magnify himself against me;
    Then I would have hid myself from him:
15 But it was thou, a man mine equal,
    My companion, and my familiar friend.
16 We took sweet counsel together,
    We walked in the house of God with the throng.
17 Let death come suddenly upon them,
    Let them go down alive into Sheol:
18 For wickedness is in their dwelling,
    In the midst of them.
19 As for me, I will call upon God;
    And Jehovah shall save me.
20 Evening, and morning, and at noonday, will I complain and moan;
    And He shall hear my voice.
21 He hath redeemed my soul in peace from the battle that was against me:
    For they were many that strove with me.

21. THE CRUCIFIXION DAY — EVENING

22 God shall hear, and answer them — even He that abideth of old —
The men who have no changes, and who fear not God.
23 He hath put forth his hands against such as were at peace with him:
He hath profaned his covenant.
24 His mouth was smooth as butter,
But his heart was war:
25 His words were softer than oil,
Yet were they drawn swords.
26 Cast thy burden upon Jehovah, and He shall sustain thee:
He shall never suffer the righteous one to be moved.
27 But Thou, O God, shalt bring them down into the pit of destruction:
Bloodthirsty and deceitful men shall not live out half their days;
BUT I WILL TRUST IN THEE.

[At discretion may be added a section (13-23) from the Responsive Lesson for Day No. 20, M'rg.]

Psalm Chant   Same as for Morning

Hymn of Praise
ANONYMOUS. From Latin Hymn "Te Deum," ascribed to AMBROSE, Bishop of Milan, A. D. 390. (Dox. added.)

THOU art the everlasting Son,
O Christ! and, high upon Thy throne,
Thou art at the right hand of God,
And hast redeemed us by Thy blood;
And heaven and earth are full of Thee,—
The glory of Thy Majesty!

2 When all the sharpness of our death
Was overcome in Thy last breath,
Then didst Thou open wide heaven's door

To all believers evermore:
O Lamb of God! and Thou wilt come,
To be our Judge, and take us home.

3 In Thee we trust: we pray Thee, Lord,
Remember Thy most precious blood!
In honor may we numbered be
With all the noble company,
Who bow before Thy Mercy-seat,
And cast their treasures at Thy feet.

4. Let glo-ry be to God on high: Thy ho-ly Name we mag-ni-fy,
E-ter-nal o'er the heav'n-ly host— Thou Fa-ther, Son, and Ho-ly Ghost!

21. THE CRUCIFIXION DAY — EVENING 91

We praise, we bless, we wor-ship Thee Who art and hast been and shalt be. A - MEN.

MELITA. L. M. 6l.   JOHN BACCHUS DYKES, Mus. Doc.

22. THE RESURRECTION EVE *(Easter Even)*

Introductory

Sentence

FATHER! into Thy hands I commend My spirit:
My flesh also shall dwell in hope:
Because Thou wilt not leave My soul in Hades,
Neither wilt Thou give Thy holy One to see corruption.
Thou wilt shew Me the path of life.

[Ps. xxxi, 5 (Lk. xxiii, 46): Ps. xvi, 9-11 (Acts, ii, 26-28; xiii, 35)]

Response
[Tune in Day No. 21]

WORTHY art Thou, the Lamb;
For | thou wast | slain,
And didst purchase | un-to | God · with Thy | blood,
Men of every tribe and tongue and | people and | nation,
And madest them to be | unto our | God a | kingdom.

[Rev. v, 9, 10]

Scripture Lessons

Old Covenant   Isaiah, l, 4-11.
Gospel   John, xix, 31-42: Matt. xxvii, 61-66.
Apostolic Word   I Pet. iii, 17-22: Rom. vi, 1-14.

Responsive Lesson

Psalm, lxxxviii: PSALMS OF DAVID, iii, iv:
SONG OF JONAH, Jon. ii, 2-9 (Matt. xii, 40).

O JEHOVAH, the God of my salvation,
  I have cried day and night before Thee:
2 Let my prayer enter into Thy presence;
  Incline Thine ear unto my cry;
3 For my soul is full of troubles,
  And my life draweth nigh unto Sheol.
4 I am counted with them that go down into the pit;
  I am as a man that hath no help:
5 Cast off among the dead,
  Like the slain that lie in the grave,
6 Whom Thou rememberest no more;
  And they are cut off from Thy hand.
7 Thou hast laid me in the lowest pit,
  In dark places, in the deeps.

22. THE RESURRECTION EVE

8 Thy wrath lieth hard upon me,
And Thou hast afflicted me with all Thy waves.
9 Thou hast put mine acquaintance far from me;
Thou hast made me an abomination unto them:
10 I am shut up, and I cannot come forth.
Mine eye wasteth away by reason of affliction:
11 I have called daily upon Thee, O Jehovah,
I have spread forth my hands unto Thee.
12 Wilt Thou show wonders to the dead?
Shall they that are deceased arise and praise Thee?
13 Shall Thy lovingkindness be declared in the grave?
Or Thy faithfulness in Destruction?
14 Shall Thy wonders be known in the dark?
And Thy righteousness in the land of forgetfulness?
15 But unto Thee, O Jehovah, have I cried,
And in the morning shall my prayer come before Thee.
16 O Jehovah, why castest Thou off my soul?
Why hidest Thou Thy face from me?
17 I am afflicted and ready to die from my youth up:
While I suffer Thy terrors I am distracted.
18 Thy fierce wrath has gone over me;
Thy terrors have cut me off.
19 They came round about me like water all the day long;
They compassed me about together.
20 Lover and friend hast Thou put far from me,
And mine acquaintance into darkness.

---

21 O JEHOVAH, how are mine adversaries increased!
Many are they that rise up against me.
22 Many there are who say of my soul,
There is no help for him in God.
23 But Thou, Jehovah, art a shield about me;
My glory, and the lifter up of my head.
24 I cry unto Jehovah, with my voice,
And He answereth me out of His holy hill.
25 I laid me down and slept; I awaked;
For Jehovah sustaineth me.
26 I will not be afraid of ten thousands of the people,
That have set themselves against me round about.
27 Arise, O Jehovah;
Save me, O my God:
28 For Thou hast smitten all mine enemies upon the cheek bone;
Thou hast broken the teeth of the wicked.
29 Salvation belongeth unto Jehovah:
Thy blessing be upon Thy people.

---

30 ANSWER me when I call, O God of my righteousness;
Thou hast set me at large when I was in distress:
31 Have mercy upon me,
And hear my prayer.

22. THE RESURRECTION EVE

32 O ye sons of men, how long shall my glory be turned into dishonor?
  How long will ye love vanity, and seek after falsehood?
33 But know that Jehovah hath set apart him that is godly for Himself:
  Jehovah will hear when I call unto Him.
34 Stand in awe, and sin not:
  Commune with your own heart upon your bed, and be still.
35 Offer the sacrifices of righteousness,
  And put your trust in Jehovah.
36 Many there are that say, Who will show us any good?
  O Jehovah, lift Thou up the light of Thy countenance upon us.
37 Thou hast put gladness in my heart,
  More than they have when their grain and their new wine are increased.
38 In peace will I both lay me down and sleep:
  For Thou, Jehovah, alone makest me dwell in safety.

---

39 I CALLED by reason of mine affliction unto Jehovah,
  And He answered me;
40 Out of the belly of Sheol cried I,
  And Thou heardest my voice.
41 For Thou didst cast me into the depth,
  In the heart of the seas.
42 And the flood was round about me:
  All Thy waves and Thy billows passed over me.
43 And I said, I am cast out from before Thine eyes;
  Yet I will look again toward Thy holy temple.
44 The waters compassed me about,
  Even to the soul;
45 The deep was round about me;
  The weeds were wrapped about my head.
46 I went down to the bottoms of the mountains;
  The earth with her bars closed upon me forever:
47 Yet hast thou brought up my life from Sheol, O Jehovah my God.
  When my soul fainted within me, I remembered Jehovah:
48 And my prayer came in unto Thee,
  Into Thy holy temple.
49 They that regard lying vanities forsake their own lovingkindness.
  But I will sacrifice unto Thee with the voice of thanksgiving.
50 I will pay that which I have vowed.
  Salvation is of Jehovah.

[At discretion may be added (or used instead of a part of the above) a portion (40-43) of the Responsive Lesson for Day No. 20, Ev'g.]

Psalm Chant   Same as for Day No. 21

22. THE RESURRECTION EVE

Prayer of the Day

LORD of Eternal Life and Light, whose only begotten Son, the Lamb of God, hath tasted death for every man, that He might lead us sinners forth who were captives therein, and might bring us on high, O Father, to Thee:

We humbly beseech Thee, baptize us into the dying of our Lord Jesus, and bury us with Him in renouncing all the evil of our fleshly mind; that we may also now be made alive together with Christ:

So that at last through the grave, and gate of death, we with all Thy ransomed flock may pass to our perfect resurrection in Him, who died and was buried and rose again, and is alive forevermore and reigneth with the Father and the Spirit— one glorious God: AMEN.

Hymn of Praise

EDWARD WILTON EDDIS, 1863.

OUR sins, our sorrows, Lord, were laid on Thee;
Thy stripes have healed, Thy bonds have set us free;
And now Thy toil is o'er, Thy grief and pain
Have passed away; the vail is rent in twain.

2 Ev'n now our place is with Thee on the throne,
For Thou abidest ever with Thine own;
Yet in the tomb with Thee, we watch for day;
O, let Thine angel roll the stone away!

3. O, by Thy life with · in us, set us free! Re · veal the glo · ry that is hid with Thee!

Glo · ry to God the Father, God the Son, And God the Ho · ly Spir · it— ev · er One. A · MEN.

TOULON. 10s.　　　　　CLAUDE GOUDIMEL, 1551.

23. THE RESURRECTION DAY
MORNING *(Easter Day)*

Introductory

Sentence I HEARD a voice of many angels round about the throne;
And the number of them was ten-thousand times ten-thousand,
and thousands of thousands;
Saying with a great voice — Worthy is the Lamb that hath been slain
To receive the power and riches and wisdom and might and honor and
glory and blessing. [Rev. v, 11, 12]

Response WORTHY is the Lamb that | hath been | slain
To receive the power and riches and wisdom and might
and | honor and | glory and | blessing. [Rev. v, 12]

Henry Hiles, Mus. Doc.

Scripture Lessons
Old Covenant Isaiah, lii, 13–15; liii, 10–12.
Gospel Matt. xxviii, 1–10.
Apostolic Word I Cor. xv, 1–11.

Responsive Lesson Isaiah, xlix, 1–13 : Psalm ii.

LISTEN, O isles, unto me;
And hearken, ye peoples, from far:
2 Jehovah hath called me from the womb;
From before my birth hath He made mention of my name:
3 And He hath made my mouth like a sharp sword,
In the shadow of His hand hath He hid me;
4 And He hath made me a polished shaft,
In His quiver hath He kept me close:
5 And He said unto me, Thou art My servant;
Israel, in whom I will be glorified.
6 But I said, I have labored in vain:
I have spent my strength for nought and vanity.
7 Yet surely my judgment is with Jehovah,
And my recompense with my God.
8 And now, saith Jehovah that formed me from the womb to be
His servant,
To bring Jacob again to Him,
And that Israel be gathered unto Him:
9 (For I am honorable in the eyes of Jehovah,
And my God is become my strength:)
0 Yea, He saith, It is too light a thing
That thou shouldest be My servant to raise up the tribes of Jacob,
And to restore the preserved of Israel:
11 I will also give thee for a light to the Gentiles,
That thou mayest be My salvation unto the end of the earth.

23. THE RESURRECTION DAY—MORNING

12 Thus saith Jehovah, the redeemer of Israel, and his Holy One,
  To him whom man despiseth,
13 To him whom the nation abhorreth,
  To a servant of rulers:
14 Kings shall see and arise;
  Princes, and they shall worship;
15 Because of Jehovah that is faithful,
  Even the Holy One of Israel who hath chosen thee.
16 Thus saith Jehovah, In an acceptable time have I answered thee,
  And in a day of salvation have I helped thee:
17 And I will preserve thee,
  And give thee for a covenant of the people,
18 To raise up the land,
  To make them inherit the desolate heritages;
19 Saying to them that are bound, Go forth;
  To them that are in darkness, Show yourselves.
20 They shall feed in the ways,
  And on all bare heights shall be their pasture.
21 They shall not hunger nor thirst;
  Neither shall the heat nor sun smite them;
22 For He that hath mercy on them shall lead them,
  Even by the springs of water shall He guide them.
23 And I will make all My mountains away,
  And My highways shall be exalted.
24 Lo, these shall come from far:
  And, lo, these from the north and from the west;
  And these from the land of Sinim.
25 Sing, O heavens; and be joyful, O earth;
  And break forth into singing, O mountains:
26 For Jehovah hath comforted His people,
  And will have compassion upon His afflicted.

---

27 WHY do the nations rage,
  And the peoples meditate a vain thing?
28 The kings of the earth set themselves,
  And the rulers take counsel together,
29 Against Jehovah,
  And against His Anointed,
30 Saying, Let us break their bonds asunder,
  And cast away their cords from us.
31 He that sitteth in the heavens shall laugh:
  The Lord shall have them in derision.
32 Then shall He speak unto them in His wrath,
  And vex them in His sore displeasure:—
  YET HAVE I SET MY KING UPON MY HOLY HILL OF ZION.
33 I will tell of the decree:
  Jehovah said unto me, Thou art My Son;
  This day have I begotten thee.
34 Ask of Me, and I will give thee the nations for thine inheritance
  And the uttermost parts of the earth for thy possession.

23. THE RESURRECTION DAY—MORNING 97

35 Thou shalt break them with a rod of iron;
Thou shalt dash them in pieces like a potter's vessel.
36 Now therefore be wise, O ye kings:
Be instructed, ye judges of the earth.
37 Serve Jehovah with fear,
And rejoice with trembling.
38 Kiss the Son, lest He be angry, and ye perish in the way,
For His wrath will soon be kindled.
BLESSED ARE ALL THEY THAT TAKE REFUGE IN HIM.

Psalm Chant

From Psalm cxviii. [Same for Ev'g. and for Day No. 24]

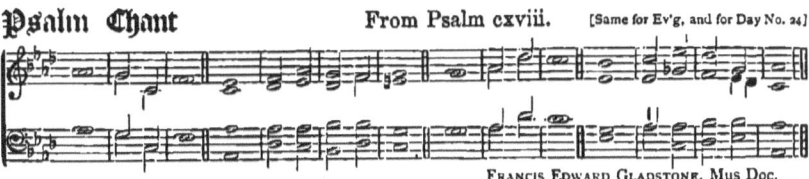

FRANCIS EDWARD GLADSTONE, Mus Doc.

O GIVE thanks unto Jehovah, for | He is | good:
For His loving- | kindness en- | dureth for | ever.
2 Jehovah is my strength and song,
And He is be- | come • my sal- | vation.
The voice of rejoicing and salvation | is • in the | tents • of the | righteous.
3 The right hand of Jehovah | do-eth | valiantly.
The right hand of Jehovah is exalted:
The right hand of Je- | ho-vah | do-eth | valiantly.
4 Jehovah hath | chasten'd me | sore:
But he hath not given me | o-ver | un-to | death.
5 Open unto me the gates of righteousness:
I will enter into them, I will give thanks | un-to Je- | hovah.
This is the gate of Jehovah;
The righteous shall | en-ter | into | it.
6 I will give thanks unto Thee, for Thou hast answer'd me,
And art be- | come • my sal- | vation.
The stone which the builders rejected,
Is be- | come the | head • of the | corner.
7 This is Jehovah's doing;
It is marvelous | in our | eyes.
This is the day which Jehovah hath made;
We will re- | joice • and be | glad in | it.
8 O give thanks unto Jehovah, for | He is | good:
For His loving- | kindness en- | dureth for | ever,
9 GLORY be to the Father, etc.

Prayer of the Day

ETERNAL Father, the fountain of life, who hast brought again from the dead with everlasting victory Thy Son Jesus, the glorious Prince of Salvation:
Create and support in us by Thy Holy Spirit, the aspirations of faith which are the breathings of the life eternal; that we may now be raised from sin, and daily more and more may put on the Lord Jesus Christ who is the Resurrection and the Life:

7

23. THE RESURRECTION DAY—MORNING

So that we with Thy whole redeemed Church may triumph over death at last, in the full image of our risen Lord the mighty Conqueror; to whom, with Thee, O Living Father, and Thy Life-giving Spirit — one God — be all glory and blessing, now and in the ages of the life eternal: AMEN.

Hymn of Praise — JOHN ELLERTON: From Latin Hymn of VENANTIUS HONORIUS CLEMENTIANUS FORTUNATUS, Bishop of Poictiers, sixth cen. (Dox. added.)

PRAGUE. 6565, D. JOHN BAPTISTE CALKIN.

1. Welcome, happy morning! Age to age shall say; Hell to-day is vanquish'd, Heav'n is won to-day:
Lo! the dead is liv-ing, Lord for ev-er-more! Him, their true Creator, All His works a-dore!

REFRAIN. *In the last stanza, use the* DOXOLOGY *instead.*

Welcome, happy morn-ing! Age to age shall say; Hell to-day is vanquish'd, Heav'n is won to-day:
Lo! the dead is liv-ing, Lord for ev-er-more! Him, their true Crea-tor, All His works a-dore!

WELCOME, happy morning!
  Age to age shall say:
Hell to-day is vanquished,
  Heaven is won to-day!
Lo! the dead is living,
  Lord forevermore!
Him, their true Creator,
  All His works adore!
REFRAIN] Welcome —

2 Months in due succession,
  Days of lengthening light,
Hours and passing moments,
  Praise Thee in their flight;
Brightness of the morning,
  Sky and fields and sea,
Vanquisher of darkness,
  Bring their praise to Thee.
REFRAIN] Welcome —

23. THE RESURRECTION DAY — MORNING

3 Maker and Redeemer,
   Life and health of all,
Thou from heaven beholding
   Human nature's fall,
Of the Father's Godhead
   True and only Son,
Manhood to deliver,
   Manhood didst put on.
REFRAIN] Welcome —

4 Thou, of life the author,
   Death didst undergo,
Tread the path of darkness,
   Saving strength to show;
Come, then, True and Faithful!
   Now fulfill Thy word;
'T is Thine own third morning;
   Rise, my buried Lord!
REFRAIN] Welcome —

5 Loose the hearts long prisoned,
   Bound with Satan's chain;
All that now is fallen
   Raise to life again;
Show Thy face in brightness,
   Bid the nations see;
Bring again our daylight;
   Day returns with Thee.
DOX.] Blest be Thou our Father,
   With Thy Son our Lord,
And Thy Holy Spirit,—
   God of Grace adored;
Life is Thine forever;
   Light in Thee we see:
Thou most high in glory
   Evermore shalt be.

Or this Hymn. ELIZABETH SCOTT, d. 1776. (Dox. added.)

ALL hail! Triumphant Lord!
Heaven with hosannas rings;
While earth in humbler strains,
Thy praise responsive sings:
Worthy, Thou Lamb who once wast slain,
Through endless years to live and reign!

ST. GODRIC. H. M.   JOHN BACCHUS DYKES, Mus. Doc., 1861.

23. EVENING
THE RESURRECTION DAY   *(Easter Day)*

Introductory

Sentence

WHO is This that cometh from Edom,
With crimsoned garments from Bozrah?
This that is glorious in His apparel,
Marching in the greatness of His strength?
I that speak in righteousness,
Mighty to save.   [Is. lxiii, 1]

Response
[Tune, in Morning.]

WORTHY is the Lamb that | hath been | slain
To receive the power and riches and wisdom and might
and | honor and | glory and | blessing.   [Rev. v, 12]

Scripture Lessons

Old Covenant   Zeph. iii, 14-20.
Gospel   John, xx, 1-10.
Apostolic Word   Acts, x, 34-43.

Responsive Lesson   From A SONG OF DAVID, Psalm xviii.

1 LOVE Thee, O Jehovah, my strength.
  Jehovah is my rock and my fortress and my deliverer:
2 My God, my strong rock, in Him will I take refuge;
  My shield and the horn of my salvation, my high tower.
3 I will call upon Jehovah, who is worthy to be praised:
  So shall I be saved from mine enemies.
4 The cords of death compassed me,
  And the floods of ungodliness made me afraid.
5 The cords of Sheol were round about me.
  The snares of death came upon me.
6 In my distress I called upon Jehovah,
  And cried unto my God:
7 He heard my voice out of His temple,
  And my cry before Him came into His ears.
8 Then the earth shook and trembled,
  The foundations also of the mountains quaked,
  And were shaken, because He was wroth.
9 There went up a smoke out of His nostrils,
  And fire out of His mouth devoured:
  Coals were kindled by it.
10 He bowed the heavens also, and came down;
  And thick darkness was under His feet.
11 And He rode upon a cherub, and did fly;
  Yea, He flew swiftly upon the wings of the wind.
12 He made darkness His hiding place,
  His pavilion round about Him;
13 Darkness of waters,
  Thick clouds of the skies.
14 At the brightness before Him, His thick clouds passed,
  Hailstones and coals of fire.
15 And He sent out His arrows, and scattered them:
  Yea, lightnings manifold, and discomfited them.

23. THE RESURRECTION DAY—EVENING

16 Then the channels of waters appeared,
   And the foundations of the world were laid bare,
17 At Thy rebuke, O Jehovah,
   At the blast of the breath of Thy nostrils.
18 He sent from on high, He took me;
   He drew me out of many waters.
19 He delivered me from my strong enemy,
   And from them that hated me, for they were too mighty for me.
20 They came upon me in the day of my calamity:
   But Jehovah was my stay.
21 He brought me forth also into a large place;
   He delivered me, because He delighted in me.
22 For all His judgments were before me,
   And I put not away His statutes from me.
23 Therefore hath Jehovah recompensed me according to my righteousness,
   According to the cleanness of my hands in His eyesight.
24 With the merciful Thou wilt show Thyself merciful;
   With the perfect man Thou wilt show Thyself perfect;
25 As for God, His way is perfect:
   The word of Jehovah is tried;
   He is a shield unto all them that take refuge in Him.
26 For who is God, save Jehovah?
   And who is a rock, beside our God?—
27 The God that girdeth me with strength,
   And maketh my way perfect.
28 Thou hast also given me the shield of Thy salvation:
   And Thy right hand hath holden me up;
   AND THY GENTLENESS HATH MADE ME GREAT.
29 Thou hast enlarged my steps under me,
   And my feet have not slipped.
30 Thou hast delivered me from the strivings of the people;
   Thou hast made me the head of the nations:
   A people whom I have not known shall serve me.
31 As soon as they hear of me they shall obey me:
   The strangers shall submit themselves unto me.
32 The strangers shall fade away,
   And shall come trembling out of their close places.
33 Jehovah liveth; and blessed be my rock;
   And exalted be the God of my salvation:
34 Even the God that executeth vengeance for me,
   And subdueth peoples under me.
   He rescueth me from mine enemies:
35 Yea, Thou liftest me up above them that rise up against me:
   Thou deliverest me from the violent man.
36 Therefore I will give thanks unto Thee, O Jehovah, among the nations,
   And will sing praises unto Thy Name.
37 Great deliverance giveth He to His king;
   And showeth lovingkindness to His anointed,
   To David and to his seed, for evermore.

23. THE RESURRECTION DAY—EVENING

Psalm Chant Same as for Morning

Hymn of Praise JOHN MASON NEALE, D. D., tr. From Latin Hymn of AMBROSE, Bishop of Milan, fourth cen. (Dox. added.)

O LORD Most High, eternal King,
By Thee redeemed Thy praise we sing;
The bonds of death are burst by Thee,
And grace has won the victory.

2 Ascending to the Father's throne
Thou claim'st the kingdom as Thine own;
Thy days of mortal weakness o'er,
All power is Thine for evermore.

3 To Thee the whole creation now
Shall, in its threefold order, bow,
Of things on earth, and things on high,
And things that underneath us lie.

4 Be Thou our joy, O mighty Lord,
As Thou wilt be our great reward;
Let all our glory be in Thee,
Both now and through eternity.

5. To Thee, all glo-ry, God Most High!—The Fa-ther's Name we mag-ni-fy; Thy Son, Thy Spir-it, we a-dore: We praise, we bless Thee, ev-er-more. A-MEN.

OCTAVIUS. L. M. JOSEPH EMERSON SWEETZER, 1849.

---

24. LORD'S DAY FIRST AFTER THE RESURRECTION

MORNING

Introductory

Sentence EVERY created thing that is in the heaven and on the earth and
under the earth and on the sea,
And all things that are in them, heard I saying—
Unto Him that sitteth on the throne,
And unto the Lamb,
Be the blessing and the honor and the glory and the dominion,
For ever and ever.
[Rev. v. 13]

24. LORD'S DAY FIRST AFTER THE RESURRECTION — MORNING

Response

UNTO Him that sitteth on the throne,
And | unto the | Lamb, [dominion,
Be the blessing and the honor and the glory and the
For | ever and | ever: A- | MEN. [Rev. v, 13, 14]

PYMAR.

Scripture Lessons

Old Covenant Job. xix, 25-27: Dan. xii, 2, 3.
Gospel Luke, xxiii, 54-56; xxiv, 1-12.
Apostolic Word I Cor. xv, 12-20.

Responsive Lesson

From ISAIAH, xxv, xxvi.

O JEHOVAH, Thou art my God; I will exalt Thee;
  I will praise Thy Name;
2 For Thou hast done wonderful things,
  Even counsels of old, in faithfulness and truth.
3 For Thou hast made of a city a heap;
  Of a fortified city a ruin:
4 A palace of strangers to be no city;
  It shall never be built.
5 Therefore shall the strong people glorify Thee,
  The city of the terrible nations shall fear Thee.
6 For Thou hast been a stronghold to the poor,
  A stronghold to the needy in his distress,
7 A refuge from the storm, a shadow from the heat,
  When the blast of the terrible ones is as a storm against the wall.
8 And in this mountain shall Jehovah of hosts make unto all peoples a feast of fat things,
  A feast of wines on the lees,
9 Of fat things full of marrow,
  Of wines on the lees well refined.
10 And He will destroy in this mountain the face of the covering that is cast over all peoples,
  And the veil that is spread over all nations.
11 He hath swallowed up death forever;
  And the Lord Jehovah will wipe away tears from off all faces;
12 And the reproach of His people shall he take away from off all the earth:
  For Jehovah hath spoken it.
13 And it shall be said in that day, Lo, this is our God;
  We have waited for Him, and He will save us:
14 This is Jehovah; we have waited for Him,
  We will be glad and rejoice in His salvation.
15 In that day shall this song be sung in the land of Judah:
  We have a strong city;
  Salvation will He appoint for walls and bulwarks.

24. LORD'S DAY FIRST AFTER THE RESURRECTION—MORNING

16 Open ye the gates,
That the righteous nation that keepeth faith may enter in.
17 Thou wilt keep him in perfect peace, whose mind is stayed on Thee:
Because he trusteth in Thee.
18 Trust ye in Jehovah forever:
For in Jehovah, even Jehovah, is an everlasting rock.
19 The way of the just is uprightness:
Thou that art upright dost direct the path of the just.
20 Yea, in the way of Thy judgments, O Jehovah, have we waited for Thee;
To Thy Name, even to Thy memorial Name, is the desire of our soul.
21 With my soul have I desired Thee in the night;
Yea, with my spirit within me will I seek Thee earnestly.
22 For when Thy judgments are in the earth,
The inhabitants of the world learn righteousness.
23 O Jehovah, Thou wilt ordain peace for us:
For Thou hast also wrought all our works for us.
24 Thy dead shall live;
My dead bodies shall arise.
25 Awake and sing, ye that dwell in the dust:
For thy dew is as the dew of herbs,
AND THE EARTH SHALL CAST FORTH THE DEAD.
26 Come, my people, enter into thy chambers,
And shut thy doors about thee:
27 Hide thyself for a little moment,
Until the indignation be overpast.
28 For, behold, Jehovah cometh out of His place
To punish the inhabitants of the earth for their iniquity:
29 The earth also shall disclose her blood,
And shall no more cover her slain.

Psalm Chant   Same as for Day No. 23

Prayer of the Day

GLORIOUS Lord God, who through the Resurrection of Thy Son Jesus hast overcome death and opened unto us the gate of everlasting life:

Make us daily to rise from sin and live anew in Him, and continually to overcome the world in the victory of faith:

That we may have part at last in the resurrection of the just when they shall appear in glory with Him who is the Prince of Salvation, and who with the Father and the Spirit — one God — is exalted above all heavens throughout all ages:

AMEN.

24. LORD'S DAY FIRST AFTER THE RESURRECTION — MORNING

Hymn of Praise
The Rev. Isaac Watts, D. D., 1707, alt. (Dox. added.)

WORTHY art Thou who once wast slain —
Thou Prince of Peace, who groaned and died —
Worthy to rise and live and reign
At Thine almighty Father's side.

2 Honor immortal must be paid,
Instead of scandal and of scorn;
While glory shines around Thy head,
And a bright crown without a thorn.

3 Blessings forever on the Lamb,
Who bore the curse for wretched men;
Let angels sound Thy sacred Name,
And every creature say, Amen.

4. O Father, Son, and Ho-ly Ghost—Thou God Most High! Thee we a-dore: From earth and all the heavenly host, To Thee, all glo-ry ev-er-more! To Thee, all glo-ry ev-er-more! A-MEN.

PARK STREET. L. M.   FREDERIC MARC ANTOINE VENUA, abt. 1810.

---

24. EVENING
LORD'S DAY FIRST AFTER THE RESURRECTION

Introductory

Sentence

THE voice of thy watchmen, O Zion!
They lift up the voice, together do they sing.
Break forth into joy, sing together:
For Jehovah hath comforted His people,
He hath redeemed Jerusalem.   [Is. lii, 8, 9]

Response
[Tune, in Morning]

UNTO Him that sitteth on the throne,
And | unto the | Lamb,   [dominion,
Be the blessing and the honor and the glory and the
For | ever and | ever: A- | MEN.   [Rev. v, 13. 14]

Scripture Lessons
Old Covenant   Ezkl. xxxix, 25–29.
Gospel   Mark, xvi, 1–8.
Apostolic Word   1 Cor. xv, 20–34.

24. LORD'S DAY FIRST AFTER THE RESURRECTION — EVENING

Responsive Lesson Songs of Ascents, Ps. cxxiv, cxxv, cxxvi : cxvii.

IF it had not been Jehovah who was on our side,
   Let Israel now say;
2 If it had not been Jehovah who was on our side,
   When men rose up against us:
3 Then they had swallowed us up alive,
   When their wrath was kindled against us:
4 Then the waters had overwhelmed us,
   The stream had gone over our soul:
   Then the proud waters had gone over our soul.
5 Blessed be Jehovah,
   Who hath not given us as a prey to their teeth.
6 Our soul is escaped as a bird out of the snare of the fowlers:
   The snare is broken, and we are escaped.
7 Our help is in the Name of Jehovah,
   Who made heaven and earth.

---

8 THEY that trust in Jehovah
   Are as Mount Zion, which cannot be moved,
   But abideth forever.
9 As the mountains are round about Jerusalem,
   So Jehovah is round about His people,
   FROM THIS TIME FORTH AND FOREVERMORE.
10 For the scepter of wickedness shall not rest upon the lot of the righteous;
   That the righteous put not forth their hands unto iniquity.
11 Do good, O Jehovah, unto those that are good,
   And to them that are upright in their hearts.
12 But as for such as turn aside unto their crooked ways,
   Jehovah shall lead them forth with the workers of iniquity.
   PEACE BE UPON ISRAEL.

---

13 WHEN Jehovah brought back those that returned to Zion,
   We were like unto them that dream.
14 Then was our mouth filled with laughter,
   And our tongue with singing:
15 Then said they among the nations, Jehovah hath done great things for them.
   Jehovah hath done great things for us; whereof we are glad.
16 Turn again our captivity, O Jehovah,
   As the streams in the South.
   THEY THAT SOW IN TEARS SHALL REAP IN JOY.
17 Though he goeth on his way weeping,
   Bearing forth the seed;
18 He shall come again with joy,
   Bringing his sheaves with him.

---

19 O PRAISE Jehovah, all ye nations;
   Laud Him, all ye peoples.
20 For His lovingkindness is great toward us;
   And the truth of Jehovah endureth forever.
   PRAISE YE JEHOVAH.

24. LORD'S DAY FIRST AFTER THE RESURRECTION — EVENING 107

Psalm Chant Same as for Day No. 23

Hymn of Praise CHARITIE LEES BANCROFT, 1860. (Dox. added.)

HE comes in blood-stained garments;
Upon His brow a crown;
The gates of brass fly open,
The iron bands drop down;
From off the fettered captive
The chains of Satan fall,
While angels shout triumphant,
That Christ is Lord of all.

2 Oh, Christ, Thy love is mighty!
Long-suffering is Thy grace;
And glorious is the splendor
That beameth from Thy face.
Our hearts up-leap in gladness
When we behold that love,
As we go singing onward
To dwell with Thee above.

3. O Might-y God and Ho-ly! High is Thy dwelling-place: Yet thence Thy mercy shin-eth—The brightness of Thy face: To Thee all praise and glo-ry, God of e-ter-nal might!—O Fa-ther, Son, and Spir-it; Thou un-cre-at-ed Light! A-MEN.

DAY OF REST. 7676, D.

JAMES WILLIAM ELLIOTT.

25. LORD'S DAY SECOND AFTER THE RESURRECTION

𝔍ntroductory

MORNING

Sentence

I SAW, and Behold, a great multitude which no man could number,
Out of every nation, and of all tribes and peoples and tongues,
Standing before the throne and before the Lamb,
Arrayed in white robes, and palms in their hands; and they cry with a great voice, saying —
Salvation unto our God who sitteth on the throne, and unto the Lamb!
[Rev. vii, 9, 10]

Response

AMEN: Blessing and glory and wisdom and thanksgiving and honor and | power and | might,
Be unto our God for | ever and | ever: A- | MEN. [Rev. vii. 12]

JOHN FRECKLETON BURROWES, d. 1852.

Scripture Lessons

Old Covenant   Zech. iii, 1–8; iv, 6, 7.
Gospel   John, xx, 11–18.
Apostolic Word I Cor. xv, 35–49.

Responsive Lesson

Isaiah, li, 3–16: lii, 7–10.

JEHOVAH hath comforted Zion:
　He hath comforted all her waste places,
2 And hath made her wilderness like Eden,
　And her desert like the garden of Jehovah;
3 Joy and gladness shall be found therein,
　Thanksgiving, and the voice of melody.

4 Attend unto Me, O My people;
　And give ear unto Me, O My nation:
5 For a law shall go forth from Me,
　And I will establish My judgment for a light of the peoples.
6 My righteousness is near,
　My salvation is gone forth,
　And Mine arms shall judge the peoples;
7 The isles shall wait for Me,
　And on Mine arm shall they trust.
8 Lift up your eyes to the heavens,
　And look upon the earth beneath:
9 For the heavens shall vanish away like smoke,
　And the earth shall wax old like a garment;
　And they that dwell upon it shall die in like manner:
10 But My salvation shall be forever,
　And My righteousness shall not be abolished.

11 Hearken unto Me, ye that know righteousness,
　The people in whose heart is My law;

25. LORD'S DAY SECOND AFTER THE RESURRECTION—MORNING

12 Fear ye not the reproach of men,
   Neither be ye dismayed at their revilings.
13 For the moth shall eat them up like a garment,
   And the worm shall eat them like wool:
14 But My righteousness shall be forever,
   And My salvation unto all generations.

15 Awake, awake, put on strength,
   O arm of Jehovah;
16 Awake, as in the days of old,
   The generations of ancient times.
17 Art thou not it that cut Rahab in pieces,
   That pierced the dragon?
18 Art thou not it which dried up the sea,
   The waters of the great deep;
19 That made the depths of the sea a way
   For the redeemed to pass over?
20 And the ransomed of Jehovah shall return, and come with singing unto Zion;
   And everlasting joy shall be upon their heads:
21 They shall obtain gladness and joy,
   And sorrow and sighing shall flee away.

22 I, even I, am He that comforteth you:
   Who art thou, that thou art afraid of man that shall die,
   And of the son of man who shall be made as grass;
23 And hast forgotten Jehovah thy Maker,
   That stretched forth the heavens,
   And laid the foundations of the earth;
24 And fearest continually all the day
   Because of the fury of the oppressor,
   When he maketh ready to destroy?
25 And where is the fury of the oppressor?
   The captive exile shall speedily be loosed;
26 And he shall not die and go down into the pit,
   Neither shall his bread fail.
27 For I am Jehovah thy God,
   Who stirreth up the sea, that the waves thereof roar:
   JEHOVAH OF HOSTS IS HIS NAME.
28 And I have put My words in thy mouth,
   And have covered thee in the shadow of My hand,
29 That I may plant the heavens,
   And lay the foundations of the earth;
   AND SAY UNTO ZION, THOU ART MY PEOPLE.

30 How beautiful upon the mountains
   Are the feet of him that bringeth good tidings,
   That publisheth peace.
31 That bringeth good tidings of good,
   That publisheth salvation;
   THAT SAITH UNTO ZION, THY GOD REIGNETH.

110 25. LORD'S DAY SECOND AFTER THE RESURRECTION—MORNING

32 The voice of thy watchmen! they lift up the voice,
Together do they sing;
33 For they shall see, eye to eye,
When Jehovah returneth to Zion.
34 Break forth into joy, sing together,
Ye waste places of Jerusalem:
35 For Jehovah hath comforted His people,
He hath redeemed Jerusalem.
36 Jehovah hath made bare His holy arm in the eyes of all the nations;
And all the ends of the earth have seen the salvation of our God.

Psalm Chant   From a SONG OF DAVID, Psalm xviii.   [Same for Ev'g, and for Day No. 26]

WILLIAM HAWES, d. 1846.

I LOVE Thee, O Je- | hovah my | Strength!
  Jehovah is my rock and my | fortress and | my de- | liverer.
2 The cords of death compass'd me,
  And the floods of ungodliness | made • me a- | fraid.
  The cords of Sheol were round about me;
  The snares of | death | came up- | on me.
3 In my distress I call'd upon Jehovah,
  And cried | unto my | God:
  He heard my voice out of His temple,
  And my cry before | Him came | into His | ears.
4 He bow'd the heavens also, and came down,
  And thick darkness was | under His | feet.
  The foundations of the world were laid bare,
  At | Thy re- | buke, O Je- | hovah.
5 He deliver'd me from my | strong | enemy,
  And from them that hated me, for | they • were too | might-y | for me.
6 Thou hast also given me the shield of | Thy sal- | vation:
  And Thy right hand hath holden me up,
  And Thy gentle- | ness hath | made me | great.
7 Thou hast deliver'd me from the strivings | of the | people;
  Thou hast made | me the | head • of the | nations:
8 A people whom I have not known shall | serve | me.
  Thou liftest me up above | them that | rise • up a- | gainst me.
9 Therefore I will give thanks unto Thee, O Jehovah, a- | mong the | nations,
  And will sing | prais-es | unto Thy | Name.
10 Great deliverance giveth | He • to His | King;
  And showeth lovingkindness to His Anointed,
  To David and to his | seed, for | ev-er- | more.
11 GLORY be to the Father, etc.

25. LORD'S DAY SECOND AFTER THE RESURRECTION — MORNING 111

Prayer of the Day

O LORD our Righteousness, who of Thine abundant mercy hast awakened us who were dead in sin, to a glorious and immortal hope by the Resurrection of Thy Son Jesus our Savior:

Let Thy great love constrain us, we beseech Thee; that we who have been redeemed through His death may walk after the example of His holy life, and be joined evermore with Him, the Shepherd and Bishop of our souls:

And blessed be the Father and the Son and the Holy Spirit — one God over all for ever: AMEN.

Hymn of Praise

The Rev. ISAAC WATTS, D. D., 1709.
(Dox. added.)

COME, let us join our cheerful songs
  With angels round the throne;
Ten thousand thousand are their tongues,
  But all their joys are one.

2 "Worthy the Lamb that died," they cry,
  "To be exalted thus!"
"Worthy the Lamb!" our lips reply,
  "For He was slain for us."

3 Jesus is worthy to receive
  Honor and power divine;
And blessings more than we can give,
  Be, Lord, forever Thine!

4 Let all that dwell above the sky,
  And air, and earth, and seas,
Conspire to lift Thy glories high,
  And speak Thine endless praise.

5 The whole creation join in one
  To bless the sacred Name
Of Him who sits upon the throne,
  And to adore the Lamb!

6. O Ho-ly, Bless-ed, Might-y One! Thou God whom we a-dore;
To Thee be glo-ry— Fa-ther, Son, And Spir-it— ev-er-more! A-MEN.

NOTTINGHAM. C. M.   JEREMIAH CLARKE, 1700.

25. EVENING
LORD'S DAY SECOND AFTER THE RESURRECTION

Introductory

Sentence   JEHOVAH hath made bare His holy arm in the eyes of all the nations. And all the ends of the earth have seen the salvation of our God.
[Is. lii. 10]

Response
[Tune, in Morning]
   AMEN: Blessing and glory and wisdom and thanksgiving and honor and | power and | might,
Be unto our God for | ever and | ever: A- | MEN.   [Rev. vii, 12]

Scripture Lessons   Old Covenant   Jer. xxxii, 36–44.
Gospel   John, xx, 19–23.
Apostolic Word   1 Cor. xv, 50–58.

Responsive Lesson   Psalm lxvi: A PSALM OF DAVID, XX.

MAKE a joyful noise unto God, all the earth:
Sing forth the glory of His Name:
Make His praise glorious.
2 Say unto God, How terrible are Thy works!
Through the greatness of Thy power
Shall Thine enemies submit themselves unto Thee.
3 All the earth shall worship Thee,
And shall sing unto Thee;
They shall sing to Thy Name.
4 Come, and see the works of God;
He is terrible in His doing toward the children of men.
5 He turned the sea into dry land:
They went through the river on foot:
There did we rejoice in Him.
6 He ruleth by His might forever;
His eyes observe the nations:
Let not the rebellious exalt themselves.
7 O bless our God, ye peoples,
And make the voice of His praise to be heard:
8 Who holdeth our soul in life,
And suffereth not our feet to be moved.
9 For Thou, O God, hast proved us:
Thou hast tried us, as silver is tried.
10 Thou broughtest us into the net;
Thou layedst a sore burden upon our loins.
11 Thou hast caused men to ride over our heads;
We went through fire and through water;
But Thou broughtest us out into a wealthy place.
12 I will come into Thy house with burnt offerings,
I will pay Thee my vows,
13 Which my lips have uttered,
And my mouth hath spoken, when I was in distress.

25. LORD'S DAY SECOND AFTER THE RESURRECTION—EVENING

14 I will offer unto Thee burnt offerings of fatlings,
   With the incense of rams;
   I will offer bullocks with goats.
15 Come and hear, all ye that fear God,
   And I will declare what He hath done for my soul.
16 I cried unto Him with my mouth,
   And He was extolled with my tongue.
17 If I regard iniquity in my heart,
   The Lord will not hear:
18 But verily God hath heard;
   He hath attended to the voice of my prayer.
19 Blessed be God, who hath not turned away my prayer,
   Nor His lovingkindness from me.

20 JEHOVAH answer thee in the day of trouble;
   The name of the God of Jacob set thee up on high;
21 Send thee help from the sanctuary,
   And strengthen thee out of Zion;
22 Remember all thine offerings,
   And accept thy burnt sacrifice;
23 Grant thee thy heart's desire,
   And fulfill all thy counsel.
24 We will triumph in thy salvation,
   And in the name of our God we will set up our banners:
   JEHOVAH FULFILL ALL THY PETITIONS.
25 Now know I that Jehovah saveth His anointed;
   He will answer him from His holy heaven
   With the saving strength of His right hand.
26 Some trust in chariots, and some in horses:
   But we will make mention of the Name of Jehovah our God.
27 They are bowed down and fallen:
   But we are risen, and stand upright.
28 Save, O Jehovah:
   Let the King answer us when we call.

Psalm Chant
Same as for Morning

Hymn of Praise
The Rev. JOHN CHANDLER, tr. 1837. From Latin Hymn of ninth or tenth cen. (Dox. added.)

O CHRIST! our hope, our heart's desire,
   Redemption's only spring!
Creator of the world art Thou,
   Its Savior and its King.

2 How vast the mercy and the love,
   Which laid our sins on Thee,
And led Thee to a cruel death
   To set Thy people free!

3 But now the bonds of death are burst,
   The ransom has been paid:
And Thou art on Thy Father's throne,
   In glorious robes arrayed.

4 Oh, may Thy mighty love prevail,
   Our sinful souls to spare!
Oh, may we come before Thy throne
   And find acceptance there!

[*Tune — on next page*]

114 25. LORD'S DAY SECOND AFTER THE RESURRECTION — EVENING

DENFIELD. C. M.   CARL GOTTHELF GLÄSER, 1828.

26. LORD'S DAY THIRD AFTER THE RESURRECTION

Introductory   MORNING

Sentence   AWAKE, awake, put on thy strength, O Zion.
How beautiful upon the mountains are the feet of him that bringeth good tidings,
That publisheth peace,
That bringeth good tidings of good,
That publisheth salvation,
That saith unto Zion, Thy God reigneth!   [Is. lii, 1, 7]

Response   UNTO Him that loveth us, and loosed us from our | sins • by His | blood;
And He made us to be a kingdom,
To be priests | unto His | God and | Father;
To Him be the glory | and the • do- | minion,
For | ever and | ever: A- | MEN.   [Rev. i, 5, 6]

JOSEPH BARNBY.

Scripture Lessons
Old Covenant   Isaiah, xlviii, 12-17.
Gospel   Luke, xxiv, 13-32.
Apostolic Word Acts, ii, 22-32.

Responsive Lesson   PSALMS OF DAVID, Ps. xxxiv, xxxvi.

I WILL bless Jehovah at all times:
His praise shall continually be in my mouth.

26. LORD'S DAY THIRD AFTER THE RESURRECTION—MORNING

2 My soul shall make her boast in Jehovah:
The meek shall hear thereof, and be glad.
3 O magnify Jehovah with me,
And let us exalt His Name together.
4 I sought Jehovah, and He answered me,
And delivered me from all my fears.
5 They looked unto Him, and were lightened:
And their faces shall never be confounded.
6 This poor man cried, and Jehovah heard him,
And saved him out of all his troubles.
7 The angel of Jehovah encampeth round about them that fear Him,
And delivereth them.
8 O taste and see that Jehovah is good:
Blessed is the man that taketh refuge in Him.
9 O fear Jehovah, ye His saints;
For there is no want to them that fear Him.
10 The young lions do lack, and suffer hunger:
But they that seek Jehovah shall not want any good thing.
11 Come, ye children, hearken unto me:
I will teach you the fear of Jehovah.
12 What man is he that desireth life,
And loveth many days that he may see good?
13 Keep thy tongue from evil,
And thy lips from speaking guile.
14 Depart from evil, and do good;
Seek peace, and pursue it.
15 The eyes of Jehovah are toward the righteous,
And His ears are open unto their cry.
16 The face of Jehovah is against them that do evil,
To cut off the remembrance of them from the earth.
17 The righteous cried, and Jehovah heard,
And delivered them out of all their troubles.
18 Jehovah is nigh unto them that are of a broken heart,
And saveth such as are of a contrite spirit.
19 Many are the afflictions of the righteous:
But Jehovah delivereth him out of them all.
20 He keepeth all his bones:
Not one of them is broken.
21 Evil shall slay the wicked:
And they that hate the righteous shall be condemned.
22 Jehovah redeemeth the soul of His servants:
And none of them that take refuge in Him shall be condemned.

---

23 THE transgression of the wicked saith within my heart,
There is no fear of God before his eyes.
24 For he flattereth himself in his own eyes,
That his iniquity shall not be found out and be hated.
25 The words of his mouth are iniquity and deceit:
He hath left off to be wise and to do good.

116 26. LORD'S DAY THIRD AFTER THE RESURRECTION — MORNING

26 He deviseth iniquity upon his bed;
He setteth himself in a way that is not good;
He abhorreth not evil.
27 Thy lovingkindness, O Jehovah, is in the heavens;
Thy faithfulness reacheth unto the skies.
28 Thy righteousness is like the mountains of God;
Thy judgments are a great deep:
29 O Jehovah, Thou preservest man and beast.
How precious is Thy lovingkindness, O God!
30 And the children of men take refuge
Under the shadow of Thy wings.
31 They shall be abundantly satisfied with the fatness of Thy house;
And Thou shalt make them drink of the river of Thy pleasures.
32 For with Thee is the fountain of life:
In Thy light shall we see light.
33 O continue Thy lovingkindness unto them that know Thee;
And Thy righteousness to the upright in heart.
34 Let not the foot of pride come against me,
And let not the hand of the wicked drive me away.
35 There are the workers of iniquity fallen:
They are thrust down, and shall not be able to rise.

Psalm Chant
Same as for Day No. 25

Prayer of the Day

GOD of all Truth and Grace, who in bringing Thy Holy One forth from the grave hast caused the Sun of righteousness to rise fully upon the world:

Be pleased so to illumine our souls with the beams of Thy heavenly wisdom in Jesus Christ Thy Son, that we, continually walking in His light, may be wise to avoid evil and to follow that which is good:

Through Him, who overcame all the power of darkness, and is glorified with the Father and the Spirit — one living God, world without end: AMEN.

Hymn of Praise
RAY PALMER, D. D., 1867. (Dox. added.)
[Sing the Refrain with each stanza.]

1 O CHRIST, the Lord of heaven! to thee,
Clothed with all majesty divine,
Eternal power and glory be!
Eternal praise of right is Thine.

2 Reign, Prince of life! that once Thy brow
Didst yield to wear the wounding thorn;
Reign, throned beside the Father now,
Adored the Son of God first-born.

3 To Thee, the Lamb, our mortal songs,
Born of deep fervent love, shall rise;
All honor to Thy Name belongs,
Our lips would sound it to the skies.

4 "Jesus!" — all earth shall speak the word;
"Jesus!" — all heaven resound it still:
Immanuel, Savior, Conqueror, Lord!
Thy praise the universe shall fill.

5. O Fa - ther, Son, and Ho - ly Ghost— Thou God Most High! Thee we a - dore:

26. LORD'S DAY THIRD AFTER THE RESURRECTION—MORNING 117

HOSANNA. L. M.   John Bacchus Dykes, Mus. Doc.

---

26. EVENING
LORD'S DAY THIRD AFTER THE RESURRECTION

Introductory

Sentence

THE Stone which the builders rejected, the same is become the head of the corner.
This is Jehovah's doing:
It is marvelous in our eyes.
This is the day which Jehovah hath made;
We will rejoice and be glad in it.   [Ps. cxviii. 22-24 (1 Pet. ii. 7)]

Response
[Tune, in Morning]

UNTO Him that loveth us, and loosed us from our | sins * by His | blood;
And he made us to be a kingdom,
To be priests | unto His | God and | Father;
To Him be the glory | and the * do- | minion,
For | ever and | ever: A- | MEN.   [Rev. i. 5, 6]

Scripture Lessons
   Old Covenant   Exodus, v, 19-23; vi, 1-8.
   Gospel   Luke, xxiv, 33-43.
   Apostolic Word   Acts, xiii, 27-38.

Responsive Lesson   A Psalm of Asaph, Ps. lxxiii.

SURELY God is good to Israel,
   Even to such as are pure in heart.
2 But as for me, my feet were almost gone;
   My steps had well-nigh slipped.
3 For I was envious at the arrogant,
   When I saw the prosperity of the wicked.

26. LORD'S DAY THIRD AFTER THE RESURRECTION—EVENING

4 For there are no bands in their death:
    But their strength is firm.
5 They are not in trouble as other men;
    Neither are they plagued like other men.
6 Therefore pride is a chain about their neck;
    Violence covereth them as a garment.
7 Their eyes stand out with fatness:
    They have more than heart could wish.
8 They scoff, and in wickedness utter oppression:
    They speak loftily.
9 They have set their mouth in the heavens,
    And their tongue walketh through the earth.
10 Therefore His people return hither:
    And waters of a full cup are drained by them.
11 And they say, How doth God know?
    And is there knowledge in the Most High?
12 Behold, these are the wicked;
    And, being alway at ease, they increase in riches.
13 Surely in vain have I cleansed my heart,
    And washed my hands in innocency;
14 For all the day long have I been plagued,
    And chastened every morning.
15 If I had said, I will speak thus;
    Behold, I had dealt treacherously with the generation of Thy children.
16 When I thought how I might know this,
    It was too painful for me;
17 Until I went into the sanctuary of God,
    And considered their latter end.
18 Surely Thou settest them in slippery places:
    Thou castest them down to destruction.
19 How are they become a desolation in a moment!
    They are utterly consumed with terrors.
20 As a dream when one awaketh;
    So, O Lord, when Thou awakest, Thou shalt despise their image.
21 For my heart was grieved,
    And I was pricked in my reins:
22 So brutish was I, and ignorant;
    I was as a beast before Thee.
23 Nevertheless, I am continually with Thee:
    Thou hast holden my right hand.
24 Thou shalt guide me with Thy counsel,
    And afterward receive me to glory.
25 Whom have I in heaven but Thee?
    And there is none upon earth that I desire beside Thee.
26 My flesh and my heart faileth:
    But God is the strength of my heart and my portion forever.
27 For, lo, they that are far from Thee shall perish:
    Thou hast destroyed all them that play the harlot departing from Thee.

26. LORD'S DAY THIRD AFTER THE RESURRECTION — EVENING

28 But it is good for me to draw near unto God:
I have made the Lord Jehovah my refuge,
That I may tell of all Thy works.

Psalm Chant   Same as for Day 25

Hymn of Praise   JAMES MONTGOMERY, pub. 1853. (Dox. added.)

COME, let us sing the song of songs,—
The saints in heaven began the strain—
The homage which to Christ belongs:
"Worthy the Lamb, for Thou wast slain!"

2 Slain to redeem us by His blood,
To cleanse from every sinful stain,
And make us kings and priests to God—
"Worthy the Lamb, for Thou wast slain!"

3 To Him, enthroned by filial right,
All power in heaven and earth proclaim,
Honor, and majesty, and might:
"Worthy the Lamb, for Thou wast slain!"

4 Long as we live, and when we die,
And while in heaven with Him we reign:
This song, our song of songs shall be:
"Worthy the Lamb, for Thou wast slain!"

5. O Father, Son, and Holy Ghost— Thou God Most High! Thee we adore:
From earth and all the heavenly host, To Thee, all glory evermore! A-MEN.

CALKIN. L. M.   JOHN BAPTISTE CALKIN, 1872.

---

27. LORD'S DAY FOURTH AFTER THE RESURRECTION

MORNING

Introductory

Sentence   THEY that stand upon the glassy sea mingled with fire, having harps of God,
Are singing the song of Moses the servant of God,
And the song of the Lamb,
Saying, Great and marvelous are Thy works, O Lord, God the Almighty;
Righteous and true are Thy ways, Thou King of the ages.   [Rev. xv. 2, 3]

120 27. LORD'S DAY FOURTH AFTER THE RESURRECTION — MORNING

Response

WHO shall not fear, O Lord, and glori- | fy Thy | Name ?
For Thou | on-ly | art | holy ;
For all the nations shall come and | worship be- | fore Thee ;
For Thy righteous acts | have been • made | mani- | fest.
[Rev. xv. 4]

HENRY SMART.

Scripture Lessons

Old Covenant   Exodus, xiv, 5–16.
Gospel   John, xx, 24–31.
Apostolic Word   Col. ii, 8–15.

Responsive Lesson

A PSALM OF DAVID, Ps. xxxvii.

FRET not thyself because of evil doers,
    Neither be thou envious against them that work unrighteousness.
2 For they shall soon be cut down like the grass,
    And wither as the green herb.
3 Trust in Jehovah, and do good :
    Dwell in the land, and feed on His faithfulness.
4 Delight thyself also in Jehovah ;
    And He shall give thee the desires of thine heart.
5 Commit thy way unto Jehovah ;
    Trust also in Him, and He shall bring it to pass.
6 And He shall make thy righteousness to go forth as the light,
    And thy judgment as the noonday.
7 Rest in Jehovah,
    And wait patiently for Him.
8 Fret not thyself because of him who prospereth in his way,
    Because of the man who bringeth wicked devices to pass.
9 Cease from anger, and forsake wrath :
    Fret not thyself, it tendeth only to evil-doing.
10 For evil-doers shall be cut off :
    But those that wait for Jehovah, they shall inherit the land.
11 For yet a little while, and the wicked shall not be :
    Yea, thou shalt diligently consider his place, and he shall not be.
12 But the meek shall inherit the land ;
    And shall delight themselves in the abundance of peace.
13 The wicked plotteth against the just,
    And gnasheth upon him with his teeth.
14 The Lord shall laugh at him :
    For He seeth that his day is coming.
15 The wicked have drawn out the sword,
    And have bent their bow ;
16 To cast down the poor and needy,
    To slay such as be upright in the way :
17 Their sword shall enter into their own heart,
    And their bows shall be broken.

27. LORD'S DAY FOURTH AFTER THE RESURRECTION—MORNING

18 Better is a little that the righteous hath
   Than the abundance of many wicked.
19 For the arms of the wicked shall be broken:
   But Jehovah upholdeth the righteous.
20 Jehovah knoweth the days of the perfect:
   And their inheritance shall be forever.
21 They shall not be put to shame in the time of evil;
   And in the days of famine they shall be satisfied.
22 But the wicked shall perish,
   And the enemies of Jehovah shall be as the fat of lambs:
23 They shall consume;
   In smoke shall they consume away.
24 The wicked borroweth, and payeth not again:
   But the righteous dealeth graciously, and giveth.
25 For such as be blessed of Him shall inherit the land;
   And they that be cursed of Him shall be cut off.
26 A man's goings are established of Jehovah;
   And He delighteth in his way.
27 Though he fall, he shall not be utterly cast down:
   For Jehovah upholdeth him with His hand.
28 I have been young, and now am old:
   Yet have I not seen the righteous forsaken,
   Nor his seed begging their bread.
29 All the day long he dealeth graciously, and lendeth;
   And his seed is blessed.
30 Depart from evil, and do good;
   And dwell forevermore.
31 For Jehovah loveth judgment,
   And forsaketh not His saints;
32 They are preserved forever:
   But the seed of the wicked shall be cut off.
33 The righteous shall inherit the land,
   And dwell therein forever.
34 The mouth of the righteous talketh of wisdom,
   And his tongue speaketh judgment.
35 The law of his God is in his heart;
   None of his steps shall slide.
36 The wicked watcheth the righteous,
   And seeketh to slay him.
37 Jehovah will not leave him in his hand,
   Nor condemn him when he is judged.
38 Wait for Jehovah,
   And keep His way,
39 And He shall exalt thee to inherit the land;
   When the wicked are cut off, thou shalt see it.
40 I have seen the wicked in great power,
   And spreading himself like a green tree in its native soil.
41 But one passed by, and, lo, he was not:
   Yea, I sought him, but he could not be found.
42 Mark the perfect man, and behold the upright:
   For there is a happy end to the man of peace.

27. LORD'S DAY FOURTH AFTER THE RESURRECTION — MORNING

43 As for transgressors, they shall be destroyed together:
The end of the wicked shall be cut off.
44 But the salvation of the righteous is of Jehovah:
He is their strong hold in the time of trouble.
45 And Jehovah helpeth them,
And rescueth them:
46 He rescueth them from the wicked, and saveth them,
Because they have taken refuge in Him.

Psalm Chant   A PSALM OF DAVID, Ps. cxxxviii.   [Same for Ev'g, and for Day No. 28]

JOSEPH BARNBY.

I WILL give Thee thanks | with my · whole | heart:
Before the gods will I sing | prais-es | un-to | Thee.
2 I will worship toward Thy holy temple,
And give thanks unto Thy Name for Thy lovingkindness | and for · Thy | truth:
For Thou hast magnified Thy | word a- | bove · all Thy | Name.
3 In the day that I call'd Thou |˙answer- · edst | me,
Thou didst encourage | me with | strength · in my | soul.
4 All the kings of the earth shall give Thee thanks, | O Je- | hovah,
For they have | heard the | words · of Thy | mouth.
5 Yea, they shall sing of the | ways · of Je- | hovah,
For great is the | glo-ry | of Je- | hovah.
6 For though Je-hovah be high, yet hath He respect | unto the | lowly:
But the haughty He | knoweth | from a- | far.
7 Though I walk in the midst of trouble, | Thou · wilt re- | vive me;
Thou shalt stretch forth Thine hand against the wrath of mine enemies,
And Thy right | hand shall | save | me.
8 Jehovah will perfect that which con- | cern-eth | me:
Thy lovingkindness, O Jehovah, endureth for ever;
Forsake not the | work of | Thine own | hands.
9 GLORY be to the Father, etc.

Prayer of the Day

FATHER of Mercies, who hast given us cause of perpetual joy in the victory of Thy Son Jesus for us over death:

Possess us with such sense of Thy wonderful love and Thy redeeming power in Him, that casting away both the desire of sin and the fear of death, we may triumph always in all things, through this adorable Savior:

To the eternal glory of the Father and the Son and the Holy Spirit — one God of our salvation: AMEN.

27. LORD'S DAY FOURTH AFTER THE RESURRECTION — MORNING 123

Hymn of Praise
ROBERT ROBINSON, pub. 1786. (Dox. added.)

LORD of every land and nation!
Ancient of eternal days!
Sounded through the wide creation—
Be Thy just and awful praise.
  Alleluia! Amen.

2 For Thy rich, Thy free redemption,
Bright, though vailed in darkness long,
Thought is poor, and poor expression;
Who can sing that wondrous song?
  Alleluia! Amen.

3 Brightness of the Father's glory!
Shall Thy praise unuttered lie?
Break, my tongue! such guilty silence,
Sing the Lord who came to die:—
  Alleluia! Amen.

4 From the highest throne of glory,
To the cross of deepest woe,
Came to ransom guilty captives!—
Flow, my praise! for ever flow:
  Alleluia! Amen.

5 Re-ascend, immortal Savior!
Leave Thy footstool, take Thy throne;
Thence return and reign forever;—
Be the kingdom all Thine own!
  Alleluia! Amen.

LOWE. 8787. ALBERT LOWE.

27. EVENING
LORD'S DAY FOURTH AFTER THE RESURRECTION

Introductory

Sentence I HEARD, as it were the voice of a great multitude,
And as the voice of many waters, and as the voice of mighty thunders, saying —

27. LORD'S DAY FOURTH AFTER THE RESURRECTION — EVENING

Hallelujah! for the Lord our God, the Almighty reigneth.
Let us rejoice and be exceeding glad,
And let us give the glory unto Him. [Rev. xix, 6, 7]

Response
[Tune, in Morning]

WHO shall not fear, O Lord, and glori- | fy Thy | Name?
For Thou | on-ly | art | holy;
For all the nations shall come and | worship be- | fore Thee;
For Thy righteous acts | have been • made | man-i- | fest.
[Rev. xv, 4]

Scripture Lessons

Old Covenant   Exodus, xiv, 19–31.
Gospel   John, xxi, 1–14.
Apostolic Word   Col. ii, 16–23.

Responsive Lesson

PSALMS OF DAVID, Ps. xxix, xxx.

GIVE unto Jehovah, O ye sons of the mighty,
   Give unto Jehovah glory and strength.
2 Give unto Jehovah the glory due unto His Name;
   Worship Jehovah in the beauty of holiness.
3 The voice of Jehovah is upon the waters:
   The God of glory thundereth,
   Even Jehovah upon many waters.
4 The voice of Jehovah is powerful;
   The voice of Jehovah is full of majesty.
5 The voice of Jehovah breaketh the cedars;
   Yea, Jehovah breaketh in pieces the cedars of Lebanon.
6 He maketh them also to skip like a calf;
   Lebanon and Sirion like a young wild-ox,
   THE VOICE OF JEHOVAH CLEAVETH THE FLAMES OF FIRE,
7 The voice of Jehovah shaketh the wilderness;
   Jehovah shaketh the wilderness of Kadesh.
8 The voice of Jehovah maketh the hinds to calve,
   And strippeth the forest bare:
   AND IN HIS TEMPLE EVERY THING SAITH, GLORY.
9 Jehovah sat as king at the Flood;
   Yea, Jehovah sitteth as King forever.
10 Jehovah will give strength unto His people;
   Jehovah will bless His people with peace.

---

11 I WILL extol Thee, O Jehovah; for Thou hast raised me up,
   And hast not made my foes to rejoice over me.
12 O Jehovah my God, I cried unto Thee,
   And Thou hast healed me.
13 O Jehovah, Thou hast brought up my soul from Sheol:
   Thou hast kept me alive, that I should not go down to the pit.
14 Sing praise unto Jehovah, O ye saints of His,
   And give thanks to His holy memorial Name.
15 For His anger is but for a moment;
   His favor is for a lifetime.

27. LORD'S DAY FOURTH AFTER THE RESURRECTION — EVENING 125

16 Weeping may tarry for the night,
But joy cometh in the morning.
17 As for me, I said in my prosperity, I shall never be moved.
Thou, Jehovah, of Thy favor hadst made my mountain to stand strong:
18 Thou didst hide Thy face;
I was troubled.
19 I cried to Thee, O Jehovah;
And unto Jehovah I made supplication:
20 What profit is there in my blood,
When I go down to the pit?
21 Shall the dust praise Thee?
Shall it declare Thy truth?
22 Hear, O Jehovah, and have mercy upon me:
O Jehovah, be Thou my helper.
23 Thou hast turned for me my mourning into dancing;
Thou hast loosed my sackcloth, and girded me with gladness:
24 To the end that my glory may sing praise to Thee, and not be silent.
O Jehovah my God, I will give thanks unto Thee forever.

Psalm Chant   Same as for Morning

Hymn of Praise   Isaac Watts, D. D., 1696. (Dox. added.)

BEHOLD the glories of the Lamb,
Amid His Father's throne;
Prepare new honors for His Name,
And songs before unknown.

2 Now to the Lamb that once was slain,
Be endless blessings paid!

Salvation, glory, joy remain
Forever on Thy head!

3 Thou hast redeemed our souls with blood,
Hast set the prisoners free,
Hast made us kings and priests to God,
And we shall reign with Thee.

BEDFORD. C. M.   WILLIAM WHEALL, 1732.

28. LORD'S DAY FIFTH AFTER THE RESURRECTION

Introductory

MORNING

Sentence

THERE were great voices in heaven, and they said —
The kingdom of the world is become the Kingdom of our Lord and
    of His Christ:
And He shall reign for ever and ever. [Rev. xi. 15]

Response

THE kingdom of the world is become the Kingdom of our
    Lord | and of • His | Christ:
And He shall | reign for | ever and | ever.
We give Thee thanks, O Lord God the Almighty, who | art • and
    who | wast;
Because Thou hast taken Thy great | pow-er | and didst |
    reign. [Rev. xi. 15, 17]

JOHN STAINER, MUS. DOC.

Scripture Lessons

Old Covenant   Exodus, xvii, 1–7.
Gospel   John, xxi, 15–25.
Apostolic Word   Col. iii, 1–11.

Responsive Lesson

Isaiah, lxii; lxiii, 1–5.

FOR Zion's sake will I not hold my peace,
   And for Jerusalem's sake I will not rest,
2 Until her righteousness go forth as brightness,
   And her salvation as a lamp that burneth.
3 And the nations shall see thy righteousness,
   And all kings thy glory;
4 And thou shalt be called by a new name,
   Which the mouth of Jehovah shall name.
5 Thou shalt also be a crown of beauty in the hand of Jehovah,
   And a royal diadem in the hand of thy God.
6 Thou shalt no more be termed Forsaken;
   Neither shall thy land any more be termed Desolate:
7 But thou shalt be called Hephzi-bah:
   And thy land Beulah:
8 For Jehovah delighteth in thee,
   And thy land shall be married.
9 I have set watchmen upon thy walls, O Jerusalem;
   They shall never hold their peace day nor night:
10 Ye that are Jehovah's remembrancers,
   Take ye no rest,
11 And give Him no rest, till He establish,
   And till He make Jerusalem a praise in the earth.

28. LORD'S DAY FIFTH AFTER THE RESURRECTION—MORNING

12 Jehovah hath sworn by His right hand,
And by the arm of His strength,
13 Surely I will no more give thy grain to be food for thine enemies;
And strangers shall not drink thy new wine for which thou hast labored:
14 But they that have garnered it shall eat it, and praise Jehovah;
And they that have gathered it shall drink it in the courts of My sanctuary.

15 Go through, go through the gates;
Prepare ye the way of the people:
16 Cast up, cast up the high way; gather out the stones;
Lift up an ensign for the peoples.
17 Behold, Jehovah hath proclaimed unto the end of the earth,
Say ye to the daughter of Zion, Behold, thy Salvation cometh;
18 Behold His reward is with Him,
And His recompense before Him.
19 And they shall call them The holy people,
The redeemed of Jehovah:
20 And thou shalt be called Sought out,
A city not forsaken.

21 Who is this that cometh from Edom,
With crimsoned garments from Bozrah?
22 This that is glorious in his apparel,
Marching in the greatness of his strength?
23 I that speak in righteousness,
Mighty to save.
24 Wherefore art thou red in thine apparel,
And thy garments like him that treadeth in the wine-vat?
25 I have trodden the wine-press alone;
And of the peoples there was no man with me:
26 Yea, I trod them in mine anger,
And trampled them in my wrath;
27 And their lifeblood is sprinkled upon my garments,
And I have stained all my raiment.
28 For the day of vengeance was in my heart,
And the year of my redeemed is come.
29 And I looked, and there was none to help;
And I wondered that there was none to uphold:
30 Therefore mine own arm brought salvation unto me;
And my wrath, it upheld me.

Psalm Chant
Same as for Day No. 27

Prayer of the Day

GOD of our Salvation, who hast raised up for us a mighty Deliverer, the Lord our Righteousness:

Give us grace to enter into a good hope through the faith of the Resurrection of this, Thy Son Jesus; looking unto Him who keepeth the souls of His saints, and

28. LORD'S DAY FIFTH AFTER THE RESURRECTION — MORNING

who shall change the body of our humiliation, and shall fashion it after the likeness of the body of His glory wherein He appeareth as our Savior,
    Who with the Father and the Spirit is from eternity to eternity — one God:
AMEN.

Hymn of Praise

REGINALD HEBER, D. D., pub. 1811.   (Dox. added.)

HOSANNA to the living Lord!
Hosanna to the incarnate Word!
To Christ, Creator, Savior, King,
Let earth, let heaven, Hosanna sing.

2 Hosanna, Lord! Thine angels cry;
Hosanna, Lord! Thy saints reply:
Above, beneath us, and around,
The dead and living swell the sound.

3 O Savior, with protecting care
Return to this Thy house of prayer:

Assembled in Thy sacred Name,
Where we Thy parting promise claim.

4 But, chiefest, in our cleansèd breast,
Eternal! bid Thy Spirit rest;
And make our secret soul to be
A temple pure, and worthy Thee.

5 So in the last and dreadful day,
When earth and heaven shall melt away,
Thy flock, redeemed from sinful stain,
Shall swell the sound of praise again.

SCEPTER. L. M.   CHARLES STEGGALL, Mus. Doc., 1872.

28. EVENING

LORD'S DAY FIFTH AFTER THE RESURRECTION

Introductory

Sentence GREAT is the mystery of Godliness:—   [angels,
He who was manifested in the flesh, justified in the Spirit, seen of Preached among the nations, believed on in the world, received up into glory.   [1 Tim iii, 16]

28. LORD'S DAY FIFTH AFTER THE RESURRECTION — EVENING

Response
[Tune, in Morning]

THE kingdom of the world is become the Kingdom of our
Lord | and of * His | Christ :
And He shall | reign for | ever and | ever.
We give Thee thanks, O Lord God the Almighty, who | art * and
who | wast ;
Because Thou hast taken Thy great | pow-er, | and didst |
reign. [Rev. xi, 15, 17]

Scripture Lessons

Old Covenant Num. xxi, 4-9.
Gospel Mark, xvi, 9-20.
Apostolic Word Phil. ii, 1-11.

Responsive Lesson

PSALMS OF DAVID, Ps. xxvii, xxviii.

JEHOVAH is my light and my salvation;
Whom shall I fear?
2 Jehovah is the strength of my life;
Of whom shall I be afraid?
3 When evil doers came upon me to eat up my flesh,
Even mine adversaries and my foes, they stumbled and fell.
4 Though a host should encamp against me,
My heart shall not fear:
5 Though war should rise against me,
Even then will I be confident.
6 One thing have I asked of Jehovah, that will I seek after;
That I may dwell in the house of Jehovah all the days of my life.
7 To behold the beauty of Jehovah,
And to inquire in His temple.
8 For in the day of trouble He shall keep me secretly in His pavilion:
In the covert of His tabernacle shall He hide me;
9 He shall lift me up upon a rock.
And now shall my head be lifted up above mine enemies round about me;
10 And I will offer in His tabernacle sacrifices of joy;
I will sing, yea, I will sing praises unto Jehovah.
11 Hear, O Jehovah, when I cry with my voice:
Have mercy also upon me, and answer me.
12 When Thou saidst, Seek ye My face; my heart said unto Thee,
Thy face, O Jehovah, will I seek.
13 Hide not Thy face from me;
Put not Thy servant away in anger:
14 Thou hast been my help, cast me not off,
Neither forsake me, O God of my salvation.
15 For my father and my mother have forsaken me,
But Jehovah will take me up.
16 Teach me Thy way, O Jehovah;
And lead me in a plain path,
17 Because of mine enemies.
Deliver me not over unto the will of mine adversaries:

28. LORD'S DAY FIFTH AFTER THE RESURRECTION — EVENING

18 For false witnesses are risen up against me,
 And such as breathe out cruelty.
19 I had fainted, unless I had believed to see the goodness of Jehovah
 In the land of the living.
20 Wait for Jehovah:
 Be strong, and let thy heart take courage;
 YEA, WAIT THOU FOR JEHOVAH.

---

21 UNTO Thee, O Jehovah, will I call:
 My Rock, be not Thou deaf unto me:
22 Lest, if Thou be silent unto me,
 I become like them that go down into the pit.
23 Hear the voice of my supplications, when I cry unto Thee,
 When I lift up my hands toward Thy holy oracle.
24 Draw me not away with the wicked,
 And with the workers of iniquity;
25 Who speak peace with their neighbors,
 But mischief is in their hearts.
26 Give them according to their work,
 And according to the wickedness of their doings:
27 Give them after the operation of their hands;
 Render to them their desert.
28 Because they regard not the works of Jehovah,
 Nor the operation of His hands.
29 He shall break them down,
 And not build them up.

30 Blessed be Jehovah,
 Because He hath heard the voice of my supplications.
31 Jehovah is my strength and my shield;
 My heart hath trusted in Him, and I am helped:
32 Therefore, my heart greatly rejoiceth;
 And with my song will I praise Him.
33 Jehovah is their strength,
 And He is a stronghold of salvation to His anointed.
34 Save Thy people, and bless Thine inheritance:
 Be their Shepherd also, and bear them up forever.

Psalm Chant   Same as for Day No. 27

Hymn of Praise

JOHN BAKEWELL, pub. 1759. (Dox. added.)

HAIL, Thou once despiséd Jesus!
 Hail, Thou Galilean King!
Thou didst suffer to release us;
 Thou didst free salvation bring.
Hail, Thou agonizing Savior,
 Bearer of our sin and shame!
By Thy merits we find favor!
 Life is given through Thy Name.

2 Paschal Lamb, by God appointed,
 All our sins on Thee were laid;
By Almighty Love anointed,
 Thou hast full atonement made:
All Thy people are forgiven
 Through the virtue of Thy blood;
Opened is the gate of heaven,
 Peace is made 'twixt man and God.

28. LORD'S DAY FIFTH AFTER THE RESURRECTION — EVENING   131

3. God on high! let all a-dore Thee; Heav'n and earth Thy praises bring; We Thy people bend before Thee; Light doth from Thy presence spring. Father, Son, and Spir-it— glorious! Lord of all to endless days; To Thy Name, O God, vic-to-rious—Blessing, honor, love, and praise! A - MEN.

FABEN. 8787, D.   JOHN HENRY WILLCOX, Mus. Doc., 1849.

29. THE ASCENSION DAY

Introductory

Sentence LORD, Thou hast ascended on high,
Thou hast led away captives;
Thou hast received gifts among men.   [Ps. lxviii, 18]

Response LIFT up your heads, O ye gates;
[Tune, in Day No. 30] And be ye lifted up, ye ever- | last-ing | doors :
And the King of | glo-ry | shall come | in.   [Ps. xxiv, 7]

Scripture Lessons

Old Covenant Dan. vii, 9 – 14.   [Same as for Day No. 68, M'rg]
Gospel John, vi, 60 – 65.
Apostolic Word Acts iv, 23 – 31.

Responsive Lesson

PSALMS OF DAVID, Ps. xxi; from xxii; cx.
[cx, also for Day No. 68, Ev'g]

THE king shall joy in Thy strength, O Jehovah;
 And in Thy salvation how greatly shall he rejoice!
2 Thou hast given him his heart's desire,
 And hast not withholden the request of his lips.
3 For Thou meetest him with the blessings of goodness;
 Thou settest a crown of fine gold on his head.

29. THE ASCENSION DAY

4 He asked life of Thee, Thou gavest it him;
Even length of days for ever and ever.
5 His glory is great in Thy salvation:
Honor and majesty dost Thou lay upon him.
6 For Thou makest him most blessed forever:
Thou makest him glad with joy in Thy presence.
7 For the king trusteth in Jehovah,
And through the lovingkindness of the Most High he shall not be moved.
8 Thy hand shall find out all Thine enemies:
Thy right hand shall find out those that hate Thee.
9 Thou shalt make them as a fiery furnace
In the time of Thine anger.
10 Jehovah shall swallow them up in His wrath,
And the fire shall devour them.
11 Their fruit shalt Thou destroy from the earth,
And their seed from among the children of men.
12 For they intended evil against Thee:
They devised a device, which they are not able to perform.
13 For Thou shalt make them turn their back,
Thou shalt make ready with Thy bowstrings against the face of them.
14 Be Thou exalted, O Jehovah, in Thy strength:
So will we sing and praise Thy power.

---

15 I WILL declare Thy Name unto my brethren:
In the midst of the congregation will I praise Thee.
16 Ye that fear Jehovah, praise Him;
All ye the seed of Jacob, glorify Him.
17 For He hath not despised nor abhorred the affliction of the afflicted;
Neither hath He hid His face from him;
BUT WHEN HE CRIED UNTO HIM, HE HEARD.
18 Of Thee cometh my praise in the great congregation:
I will pay my vows before them that fear Him.
19 All the ends of the earth shall remember and turn unto Jehovah:
And all the kindreds of the nations shall worship before Thee.
20 For the kingdom is Jehovah's,
And He is the ruler over the nations.

---

21 JEHOVAH saith unto my Lord, Sit Thou at My right hand,
Until I make Thine enemies Thy footstool.
22 Jehovah shall send forth the rod of Thy strength out of Zion:
Rule Thou in the midst of Thine enemies.
23 Thy people offer themselves willingly in the day of Thy power, in holy attire;
Out of the womb of the morning, Thou hast the dew of Thy youth.
24 Jehovah hath sworn, and will not repent,
Thou art a priest forever
After the order of Melchizedek.
25 The Lord at Thy right hand
Shall strike through kings in the day of His wrath.
He shall judge among the nations.

29. THE ASCENSION DAY . 133

26 He shall fill the places with dead bodies;
  He shall strike through the head in many countries.
27 He shall drink of the brook in the way:
  Therefore shall He lift up the head.

Psalm Chant Same as for Day No. 30

Prayer of the Day

O GOD, the King of glory, who hast exalted Thy Son Jesus Christ with great triumph into Thy Kingdom above all heavens:
 In His Name we beseech Thee, leave not us comfortless in this mortal state; but evermore send down on us and Thy whole household, Thy Holy Spirit the Comforter, to reveal Christ within us:
 That we also may in heart and mind daily ascend whither our Master hath gone, and with Him may continually dwell, who dwelleth with the Father and the Comforter — one God, world without end: AMEN.

Hymn of Praise
JAMES RUSSELL WOODFORD, D. D. (Dox. added.)

CHRIST, above all glory seated!
King eternal, strong to save!
To Thee, Death, by death defeated,
Triumph high and glory gave.

2 Thou art gone where now is given
What no mortal might could gain,
On the eternal throne of heaven,
In Thy Father's power to reign,

3 There Thy kingdoms all adore Thee,
Heaven above and earth below,

While the depths of hell before Thee,
Trembling and defeated bow.

4 We, O Lord! with hearts adoring,
Follow Thee above the sky:
Hear our prayers Thy grace imploring,
Lift our souls to Thee on high.

5 So when Thou again in glory
On the clouds of heaven shalt shine,
We Thy flock shall stand before Thee,
Owned forevermore as Thine.

CARTHAGE. 8787. ALEXIS FEODOROVITCH VON LVOFF, 1830.

30. LORD'S DAY AFTER THE ASCENSION

Introductory
MORNING

Sentence

JEHOVAH saith unto my Lord, Sit Thou at My right hand,
Until I make Thine enemies Thy footstool.
Jehovah shall send forth the rod of Thy strength out of Zion:
Rule Thou in the midst of Thine enemies. [Ps. cx. 1, 2]

Response

LIFT up your heads, O ye gates;
And be ye lifted up, ye ever- | last-ing | doors:
And the King of | glo-ry | shall come | in. [Ps. xxiv. 7]

JONATHAN BATTISHILL, d. 1801.

Scripture Lessons

Old Covenant — Dan. ii, 31-45.
Gospel — Luke, xxiv, 44-53.
Apostolic Word — Acts, i, 1-11.

Responsive Lesson

A PSALM OF DAVID, Ps. xxiv:
A PSALM OF SOLOMON, lxxii.

THE earth is Jehovah's, and the fullness thereof;
The world, and they that dwell therein.
2 For He hath founded it upon the seas,
And established it upon the floods.
3 Who shall ascend into the hill of Jehovah?
And who shall stand in His holy place?
4 He that hath clean hands,
And a pure heart;
5 Who hath not lifted up his soul unto vanity,
And hath not sworn deceitfully.
6 He shall receive a blessing from Jehovah,
And righteousness from the God of his salvation.
7 This is the generation of them that seek after Him,
That seek Thy face,— even Jacob.
8 Lift up your heads, O ye gates;
And be ye lifted up, ye everlasting doors:
AND THE KING OF GLORY SHALL COME IN.
9 Who is the King of glory?
Jehovah strong and mighty,
JEHOVAH MIGHTY IN BATTLE.
10 Lift up your heads, O ye gates;
Yea, lift them up, ye everlasting doors:
AND THE KING OF GLORY SHALL COME IN.
11 Who is this King of glory?
Jehovah of hosts,
HE IS THE KING OF GLORY.

30. LORD'S DAY AFTER THE ASCENSION — MORNING

12 GIVE the king Thy judgments, O God,
  And Thy righteousness unto the king's son.
13 He shall judge Thy people with righteousness,
  And Thy poor with judgment.
14 The mountains shall bring peace to the people,
  And the hills, in righteousness.
15 He shall judge the poor of the people,
  He shall save the children of the needy,
  And shall break in pieces the oppressor.
16 They shall fear Thee while the sun endureth,
  And so long as the moon, throughout all generations.
17 He shall come down like rain upon the mown grass:
  As showers that water the earth.
18 In his days shall the righteous flourish;
  And abundance of peace, till the moon be no more.
19 He shall have dominion also from sea to sea,
  And from the River unto the ends of the earth.
20 They that dwell in the wilderness shall bow before him;
  And his enemies shall lick the dust.
21 The kings of Tarshish and of the isles shall bring presents:
  The kings of Sheba and Seba shall offer gifts.
22 Yea, all kings shall fall down before him:
  All nations shall serve him.
23 For he shall deliver the needy when he crieth;
  And the poor, that hath no helper.
24 He shall have pity on the poor and needy,
  And the souls of the needy he shall save.
25 He shall redeem their soul from oppression and violence;
  And precious shall their blood be in his sight; and they shall live;
26 And to him shall be given of the gold of Sheba:
  And men shall pray for him continually;
  They shall bless him all the day long,
27 There shall be abundance of grain in the earth,
  Upon the top of the mountains:
28 The fruit thereof shall shake like Lebanon:
  And they of the city shall flourish like grass of the earth.
29 His name shall endure forever;
  His name shall be continued as long as the sun:
30 And men shall be blessed in him;
  All nations shall call him happy.

31 Blessed be Jehovah God, the God of Israel,
  Who only doeth wondrous things:
32 And blessed be His glorious Name forever;
  And let the whole earth be filled with His glory.
  AMEN, AND AMEN.

30. LORD'S DAY AFTER THE ASCENSION — MORNING

Psalm Chant From A SONG OF LOVES — Ps. xlv. [Same for Ev'g, and for Day No. 29]

SAMUEL WESLEY.

MY heart overfloweth with a | good-ly | matter:
I speak the things which I have | made | touching the | King.
2 Thou art fairer than the children of men;
Grace is pour'd | into Thy | lips:
Therefore God hath | bless'd | thee, for | ever.
3 Gird Thy sword upon Thy thigh, O Mighty One,
Thy glory | and Thy | majesty.
And in Thy majesty | ride on | prosper-ous- | ly,
4 Because of truth and meekness and | right-eous- | ness:
And Thy right hand shall | teach Thee | terri-ble | things.
5 Thy throne, O God, is for | ever and | ever:
A scepter of equity is the | scep-ter | of Thy | kingdom.
6 Thou hast lov'd righteousness and | ha-ted | wickedness:
Therefore God, Thy God, hath anointed Thee with the oil of | gladness a- | bove Thy | fellows.
7 Kings' daughters are among Thine | honor-able | women:
At Thy right hand doth stand the | Queen in | gold of | Ophir.
8 I will make Thy Name to be remember'd in | all gener- | ations:
Therefore shall the peoples give Thee | thanks for | ever and | ever.

9 GLORY be to the Father, etc.

Prayer of the Day

LORD of Hosts, Thou King of Glory, whose Son Christ Jesus hath gone up on high through the everlasting doors into Thy heavenly Kingdom, where He reigneth with the Father and the Spirit — one God:

For the sake of this merciful and faithful High Priest, and according to His gracious promise, pour forth on us, and on all men, the plenteousness of Thy Spirit the Comforter;

That He may cause us now to be in Christ, and so may bring us hereafter to dwell where Christ is, through whom unto God be glory in the Church throughout all ages, world without end: AMEN.

Hymn of Praise

MATTHEW BRIDGES; pub. 1848. (Dox added.)

RISE, glorious Conqueror, rise;
Into Thy native skies, —
  Assume Thy right;
And where in many a fold
The clouds are backward rolled —
Pass through those gates of gold,
  And reign in light!

2 Victor o'er death and Hell!
Cherubic legions swell
  Thy radiant train:
Praises all heaven inspire;
Each angel sweeps his lyre,
And waves his wings of fire, —
  Thou Lamb once slain!

30. LORD'S DAY AFTER THE ASCENSION — MORNING

3 Enter, incarnate God! —
No feet but Thine, have trod
  The serpent down:
Blow the full trumpets, blow!
Wider yon portals throw!
Savior triumphant — go,
  And take Thy crown!

4 Lion of Judah — Hail!
And let Thy Name prevail
  From age to age;
Lord of the rolling years,
Claim for Thine own the spheres,
For Thou hast bought with tears
  Thy heritage!

5. O God! to Thee a - lone—The Father and the Son And Spir-it, blest—To Thee whom we a-dore; Who wast all worlds before, And shalt be ev - er-more; Be praise address'd. A - MEN.

ITALIAN HYMN. 6646664.   FELICE DE GIARDINI, 1760.

30. EVENING
LORD'S DAY AFTER THE ASCENSION

Introductory

Sentence

CHRIST hath entered not into a holy place made with hands, like in pattern to the true;
But into heaven itself, now to appear before the face of God for us.
Having then a great High Priest who hath passed through the heavens, Jesus the Son of God,
Let us therefore draw near with boldness unto the throne of grace, that we may receive mercy,
And may find grace to help us in time of need.
For our King of Glory hath gone in, even as it was written of Him.
        [Heb. ix, 24: iv, 14, 16 (Ps. xxiv, 7)]

Response
[Tune, in Morning]

LIFT up your heads, O ye gates;
And be ye lifted up, ye ever- | last-ing | doors:
And the King of | Glo-ry | shall come | in.   [Ps. xxiv, 7]

Scripture Lessons
  Old Covenant   II Kings, ii, 7–12.
  Gospel   John, xiv, 25–31.
  Apostolic Word   Eph. i, 15–23.

30. LORD'S DAY AFTER THE ASCENSION — EVENING

Responsive Lesson   A SONG OF ASCENTS, Ps. cxxxii: cxviii, 19-24.

O JEHOVAH, remember for David all his affliction;
How he sware unto Jehovah,
And vowed unto the Mighty One of Jacob:
2 Surely I will not come into the tabernacle of my house,
Nor go up into my bed;
3 I will not give sleep to mine eyes,
Or slumber to mine eyelids:
4 Until I find out a place for Jehovah,
A tabernacle for the Mighty One of Jacob.
5 Lo, we heard of it in Ephrathah:
We found it in the field of the wood.
6 We will go into His tabernacles;
We will worship at His footstool.
7 Arise, O Jehovah, into Thy resting-place;
Thou, and the ark of Thy strength.
8 Let Thy priests be clothed with righteousness;
And let Thy saints shout for joy.
9 For Thy servant David's sake
Turn not away the face of Thine anointed.
10 Jehovah hath sworn unto David in truth;
He will not turn from it:
Of the fruit of thy body will I set upon thy throne.
11 If thy children will keep My covenant
And My testimony that I shall teach them,
12 Their children also shall sit upon thy throne for evermore.
For Jehovah hath chosen Zion;
He hath desired it for His habitation.
13 This is My resting-place forever:
Here will I dwell; for I have desired it.
14 I will abundantly bless her provision:
I will satisfy her poor with bread.
15 Her priests also will I clothe with salvation:
And her saints shall shout aloud for joy.
16 There will I make the horn of David to bud:
I have ordained a lamp for Mine anointed.
17 His enemies will I clothe with shame:
But upon himself shall his crown flourish.

---

18 OPEN to me the gates of righteousness:
I will enter into them, I will give thanks unto Jehovah.
19 This is the gate of Jehovah;
The righteous shall enter into it.
20 I will give thanks unto Thee, for Thou hast answered me,
And art become my salvation.
21 The stone which the builders rejected
Is become the head of the corner.
22 This is Jehovah's doing;
It is marvelous in our eyes.
23 This is the day which Jehovah hath made;
We will rejoice and be glad in it.

30. LORD'S DAY AFTER THE ASCENSION — EVENING 139

Psalm Chant   Same as for Morning

Hymn of Praise   Christopher Wordsworth, D. D.; pub. 1862. (Dox. added.)

See, the Conqueror mounts in triumph !
  See the King in royal state,
Riding on the clouds, His chariot,
  To His heavenly palace gate !
Hark ! the choirs of angel voices
  Joyful hallelujahs sing,
And the portals high are lifted
  To receive their heavenly King.

2 Who is this that comes in glory,
  With the trump of jubilee ?
Lord of battles, God of armies,
  He has gained the victory;
He, who on the cross did suffer,
  He, who from the grave arose,
He has vanquished sin and Satan,
  He by death has spoiled His foes.

3 Thou hast raised our human nature,
  On the clouds to God's right hand;
There we sit in heavenly places,
  There with Thee in glory stand;

Jesus reigns, adored by angels;
  Man with God is on the throne;
Mighty Lord! in Thine ascension,
  We by faith behold our own.

4 Lift us up from earth to heaven,
  Give us wings of faith and love,
Gales of holy aspirations,
  Wafting us to realms above;
That, with hearts and minds uplifted,
  We with Christ our Lord may dwell,
Where He sits enthroned in glory,
  In the heavenly citadel.

5 So at last, when He appeareth,
  We from out our graves may spring,
With our youth renewed like eagles',
  Flocking round our heavenly King.
Caught up on the clouds of heaven,
  And may meet Him in the air —
Rise to realms where He is reigning,
  And may reign forever there.

6. Lord Jehovah! ev-er blessed; Maj-es-ty is Thine a-lone: Gird-ed with Thy ho-ly splendor, Thou hast made Thy grace Thy throne. Glory in the highest! Glo-ry Un-to God for ev-er-more— Father, Son, and Ho-ly Spir-it! Thee let earth and heav'n adore. A-men.

PROMISE. 8787, D.   Henry Smart.

31. THE PENTECOST DAY (*Whitsunday*)

MORNING

𝕴ntroductory

Sentence **B**EHOLD, the glory of the God of Israel came from the way of the east;
And His voice was like the sound of many waters:
And the earth shined with His glory.
And the Spirit took me up, and brought me into the inner court;
And behold, the glory of Jehovah filled the house. [Ezkl. xliii, 2, 5]

Response **W**ORTHY art Thou, our Lord and our God, to receive the glory and the | honor • and the | power:
For Thou didst create all things,
And because of Thy will they | were, and | were cre- | ated.
[Rev. iv, 11]

Thomas Kelway, d. 1749.

Scripture Lessons

Old Covenant Ezkl. xxxvii, 1–10.
Gospel John, xv, 26, 27: xvi, 1–15.
Apostolic Word Acts, ii, 1–12.

Responsive Lesson   Psalm civ.

BLESS Jehovah, O my soul.
  O Jehovah my God, Thou art very great:
2 Thou art clothed with honor and majesty.
  Who coverest Thyself with light as with a garment:
3 Who stretchest out the heavens like a curtain:
  Who layeth the beams of His chambers in the waters:
4 Who maketh the clouds His chariot;
  Who walketh upon the wings of the wind:
5 Who maketh winds His messengers;
  Flames of fire His ministers:
6 Who laid the foundations of the earth,
  That it should not be moved forever.
7 Thou coveredst it with the deep as with a vesture;
  The waters stood above the mountains.
8 At Thy rebuke they fled;
  At the voice of Thy thunder they hasted away;
9 (The mountains rose, the valleys sank;)
  Unto the place which Thou hadst founded for them.
10 Thou hast set a bound that they may not pass over;
  That they turn not again to cover the earth.
11 He sendeth forth springs into the valleys;
  They run among the mountains:
12 They give drink to every beast of the field;
  The wild asses quench their thirst.

31. THE PENTECOST DAY — MORNING

13 By them the fowl of the heaven have their habitation,
   They sing among the branches.
14 He watereth the mountains from His chambers:
   The earth is filled with the fruit of Thy works.
15 He causeth the grass to grow for the cattle,
   And herb for the service of man:
16 That he may bring forth food out of the earth:
   And wine that maketh glad the heart of man,
17 And oil to make his face to shine,
   And bread that strengtheneth man's heart.
18 The trees of Jehovah are filled with moisture;
   The cedars of Lebanon, which He hath planted;
19 Where the birds make their nests:
   As for the stork, the fir trees are her house.
20 The high mountains are for the wild goats;
   The rocks are a refuge for the conies.
21 He appointed the moon for seasons:
   The sun knoweth his going down.
22 Thou makest darkness, and it is night;
   Wherein all the beasts of the forest do creep forth.
23 The young lions roar after their prey,
   And seek their food from God.
24 The sun ariseth, they get them away,
   And lay them down in their dens.
25 Man goeth forth unto his work
   And to his labor until the evening.
26 O Jehovah, how manifold are Thy works!
   In wisdom hast Thou made them all:
27 The earth is full of Thy riches. There is the sea, great and wide,
   Wherein are things creeping innumerable, both small and great beasts.
28 There go the ships;
   There is leviathan, which Thou hast formed to take his pastime therein.
29 These all wait upon Thee,
   That Thou mayst give them their food in due season.
   That Thou givest unto them they gather;
30 Thou openest Thy hand, they are satisfied with good.
   Thou hidest Thy face, they are troubled;
31 Thou takest away their breath, they die,
   And return to their dust.
32 Thou sendest forth Thy spirit, they are created;
   And Thou renewest the face of the ground.
33 Let the glory of Jehovah endure forever;
   Let Jehovah rejoice in His works:
34 Who looketh on the earth, and it trembleth;
   He toucheth the mountains, and they smoke.
35 I will sing unto Jehovah as long as I live:
   I will sing praise to my God while I have any being.
36 Let my meditation be sweet unto Him:
   I will rejoice in Jehovah.

31. THE PENTECOST DAY—MORNING

37 Let sinners be consumed out of the earth.
And let the wicked be no more.
38 Bless Jehovah, O my soul.
PRAISE YE JEHOVAH.

Psalm Chant From A PSALM OF DAVID, Ps. lxviii. [Same for Ev'g]

JOHN JONES, d. 1796.

LET God arise, let His ene- | mies be | scatter'd.
But let the righteous be glad; let them ex- | ult be- | fore | God.
2 O God, when Thou wentest forth before Thy people,
When Thou didst march | through the | wilderness;
The earth trembled,
The heavens also | dropp'd • at the | presence of | God.
3 Thou, O God, didst send a | plenti-ful | rain, [weary.
Thou didst confirm Thine in- | heri-tance | when • it was |
4 Thy congregation | dwelt there- | in:
Thou, O God, didst prepare of Thy | good-ness | for the | poor.
5 Thou hast as- | scended on | high,
Thou hast led a- | way | captives;
6 Thou hast receiv'd gifts among men, yea, among the re- | bel-
lious | also,
That Jehovah | God might | dwell with | them.
7 They have seen Thy | goings, O· | God,
Even the goings of my God, my King, | into the | sanctu- | ary.
8 Thy God hath com- | manded thy | strength:
Strengthen, O God, that which | Thou hast | wrought for | us.
9 Princes shall come out of Egypt:
Ethiopia shall haste to stretch out her | hands unto | God.
Sing unto God, ye kingdoms of the earth;
O sing | prais-es | unto the | Lord.
10 Lo, He uttereth His voice, and that a | might-y | voice.
The God of Israel, He giveth strength and power unto His |
peo-ple. | Blessèd be | God.
11 GLORY be to the Father, etc.

Prayer of the Day

GOD of all strength and consolation, Thou only Creator, who didst gloriously fulfill the great promise of Thy Son Jesus, sending down Thy Holy Spirit on the Day of Pentecost to dwell continually in Thy Church, the power of a new creation:

For Christ's sake replenish us and the whole household of Thy Son, with the same blessed Spirit revealing Christ in us; that He may show us our sin, work in us faith, lead us into all truth, establish us in hope, make us fruitful in good works, and keep us ever in His holy comfort,

Who with the Father and the Son — one God, is glorified evermore: AMEN.

31. THE PENTECOST DAY—MORNING 143

Hymn of Praise
JAMES MONTGOMERY, 1825. (Dox. added.)

SPIRIT of power and might, behold
A world by sin destroyed!
Creator Spirit, as of old,
Move on the formless void.

2 Give Thou the word: that healing sound
Shall quell the deadly strife,
And earth again, like Eden crowned,
Produce the tree of life.

3 If sang the morning stars for joy
When nature rose to view,
What strains will angel harps employ
When Thou shalt all renew!

4 Lo! every kindred, tongue, and tribe,
Assembling round the throne,
The new creation shall ascribe
To sovereign love alone.

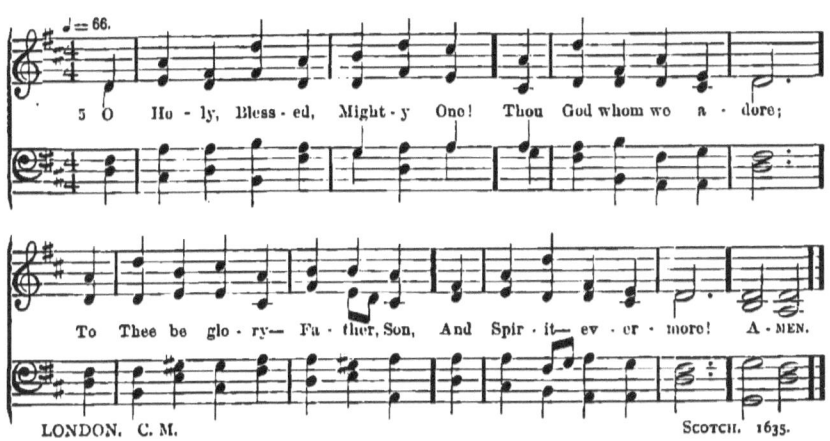

5 O Ho-ly, Bless-ed, Might-y One! Thou God whom we a-dore;
To Thee be glo-ry— Fa-ther, Son, And Spir-it— ev-er-more! A-MEN.

LONDON. C. M.   SCOTCH. 1635.

---

31. EVENING
THE PENTECOST DAY

Introductory
Sentence ACCORDING to God's mercy He saved us, through the washing of regeneration and renewing of the Holy Spirit,
Which He poured out upon us richly, through Jesus Christ our Savior.
[Tit. iii, 5, 6]

Response
[Tune, in Morning]
WORTHY art Thou, our Lord and our God, to receive the glory and the | honor • and the | power:
For Thou didst create all things,
And because of Thy will they | were, and | were cre- | ated.
[Rev. iv, 11]

Scripture Lessons
Old Covenant Ezkl. xlvii, 1-12.
Gospel   John, xiv, 15-24.
Apostolic Word Acts, ii, 32-39.

31. THE PENTECOST DAY — EVENING

Responsive Lesson   From Joel ii: Psalms, xlvi, xlvii.

BE glad, ye children of Zion,
   And rejoice in Jehovah your God:
2 For He giveth you the former rain in just measure,
   And He causeth to come down to you the rain,
   The former rain and the latter rain.
3 And it shall come to pass afterward, that I will pour out My Spirit upon all flesh;
   And your sons and your daughters shall prophesy,
4 Your old men shall dream dreams,
   Your young men shall see visions;
5 And also upon the servants and upon the handmaids in those days
   Will I pour out My Spirit.
6 And I will show wonders in the heavens and in the earth,
   Blood, and fire, and pillars of smoke.
7 The sun shall be turned into darkness,
   And the moon into blood,
8 Before the great and terrible day of Jehovah come.
   AND IT SHALL COME TO PASS, THAT WHOSOEVER SHALL CALL ON THE NAME OF JEHOVAH SHALL BE DELIVERED.

---

9 GOD is our refuge and strength,
   A very present help in trouble.
10 Therefore, will we not fear, though the earth do change,
   And though the mountains be moved in the heart of the seas;
11 Though the waters thereof roar and be troubled,
   Though the mountains shake with the swelling thereof.

12 There is a river, the streams whereof make glad the city of God,
   The holy place of the tabernacles of the Most High.
13 God is in the midst of her; she shall not be moved:
   God shall help her, and that right early.
14 The nations raged, the kingdoms were moved:
   He uttered His voice, the earth melted.
15 Jehovah of hosts is with us;
   The God of Jacob is our refuge.

16 Come, behold the works of Jehovah,
   What desolations He hath made in the earth.
   He maketh wars to cease unto the end of the earth;
17 He breaketh the bow, and cutteth the spear in sunder;
   He burneth the chariots in the fire.
18 Be still, and know that I am God:
   I will be exalted among the nations
   I will be exalted in the earth.
19 Jehovah of hosts is with us;
   The God of Jacob is our refuge.

---

20 O CLAP your hands, all ye peoples;
   Shout unto God with the voice of triumph.

31. THE PENTECOST DAY—EVENING

21 For Jehovah Most High is terrible;
 He is a great King over all the earth.
22 He shall subdue the peoples under us,
 And the nations under our feet.
23 He shall choose our inheritance for us,
 The glory of Jacob whom He loved.
24 God is gone up with a shout,
 Jehovah with the sound of a trumpet.
25 Sing praises to God, sing praises:
 Sing praises unto our King, sing praises.
26 For God is the King of all the earth:
 Sing ye praises with understanding.
27 God reigneth over the nations:
 God sitteth upon His holy throne.
28 The princes of the peoples are gathered together
 To be the people of the God of Abraham:
29 For the shields of the earth belong unto God;
 He is greatly exalted.

Psalm Chant   Same as for Morning

Hymn of Praise   JOHN DRYDEN, abt. 1690. From Latin Hymn, prob. of CHARLEMAGNE, A.D. 800; or of GREGORY the Great, sixth cen. (Dox. added.)

CREATOR Spirit, by whose aid
The world's foundations first were laid,
Come, visit every waiting mind;
Come, pour Thy joys on human-kind.

2 Thrice-holy Fount, thrice-holy Fire,
Our hearts with heavenly love inspire;
Come, and Thy sacred unction bring
To sanctify us, while we sing.

3 O source of uncreated light,
The Father's promised Paraclete,—
From sin and sorrow set us free,
And make us temples worthy Thee!

4 Chase from our minds th' infernal foe,
And peace, the fruit of love, bestow;
Give us Thyself, that we may see
The Father and the Son, by Thee.

4. To Thee, all glo-ry, God Most High!—The Fa-ther's Name we mag-ni-fy; Thy Son, Thy Spir-it, we a-dore; We praise, we bless Thee, ev-er-more. A-MEN.

DRYDEN. L. M.   JOHN BAPTISTE CALKIN, 1872.

32. LORD'S DAY AFTER THE PENTECOST
(Trinity Sunday)

Introductory
MORNING

Sentence ONE of the Seraphim cried unto another, and said —
Holy! Holy! Holy! Jehovah of Hosts:
The whole earth is full of His glory. [Is. vi, 3]

Response HOLY! Holy! Holy! the Lord | God, • the Al- | mighty,
Who was and who | is • and who | is to | come.
Glory and honor and thanks to Him that sitteth | on the | throne,
To Him that | liveth for | ever and | ever. [Rev. iv, 8, 9]

JOSEPH BARNBY.

Scripture Lessons
Old Covenant Isaiah, lix, 14–21.
Gospel Matt. iii, 11–17.
Apostolic Word I John, v, 1–12, 20, 21.

Responsive Lesson
From ISAIAH, xxxii, xxxiii : xxxv.

BEHOLD, a King shall reign in righteousness,
  And princes shall rule in justice.
2 And a Man shall be as an hiding-place from the wind,
  And a covert from the tempest;
3 As streams of water in a dry place,
  As the shade of a great rock in a weary land.
4 And the eyes of them that see shall not be dim,
  And the ears of them that hear shall hearken.
5 The heart also of the rash shall understand knowledge,
  And the tongue of the stammerers shall be ready to speak plainly.
6 The Spirit shall be poured upon us from on high,
  And the wilderness become a fruitful field,
  And the fruitful field be counted for a forest.
7 Then justice shall dwell in the wilderness,
  And righteousness shall abide in the fruitful field.
8 And the work of righteousness shall be peace;
  And the effect of righteousness quietness and confidence forever.
9 And my people shall abide in a peaceable habitation,
  And in sure dwellings, and in quiet resting-places.
10 Jehovah is exalted; for He dwelleth on high;
  He hath filled Zion with justice and righteousness.
11 And there shall be stability in thy times,
  Abundance of salvation, wisdom, and knowledge:
  THE FEAR OF JEHOVAH IS HIS TREASURE.
12 Now will I arise, saith Jehovah; now will I lift up Myself;
  Now will I be exalted.

13 Hear, ye that are far off, what I have done;
   And ye that are near, acknowledge My might.
14 Thine eyes shall see the King in His beauty:
   They shall behold a far stretching land.
15 Look upon Zion, the city of our solemnities:
   Thine eyes shall see Jerusalem a quiet habitation,
16 A tent that shall not be removed,
   The stakes whereof shall never be plucked up,
   Neither shall any of the cords thereof be broken.
17 But there Jehovah will be with us in majesty,
   A place of broad rivers and streams;
18 For Jehovah is our Judge, Jehovah is our lawgiver,
   Jehovah is our King; He will save us.
19 And the inhabitant shall not say, I am sick:
   The people that dwell therein shall be forgiven their iniquity.

---

20 THE wilderness and the solitary place shall be glad;
   And the desert shall rejoice, and blossom as the rose.
21 It shall blossom abundantly,
   And rejoice even with joy and singing;
22 The glory of Lebanon shall be given unto it,
   The excellency of Carmel and Sharon:
23 They shall see the glory of Jehovah,
   The excellency of our God.
24 Strengthen ye the weak hands,
   And confirm the feeble knees.
25 Say to them that are of a fearful heart, Be strong, fear not:
   Behold, your God will come with vengeance,
26 With the recompense of God;
   He will come and save you.
27 Then the eyes of the blind shall be opened,
   And the ears of the deaf shall be unstopped.
28 Then shall the lame man leap as an hart,
   And the tongue of the dumb shall sing:
29 For in the wilderness shall waters break out,
   And streams in the desert.
30 And the glowing sand shall become a pool,
   And the thirsty ground springs of water:
31 In the habitation of jackals, where they lay,
   Shall be grass with reeds and rushes.
32 And a highway shall be there, and a way,
   And it shall be called The way of holiness;
   The unclean shall not pass over it;
33 But it shall be for those:
   The wayfaring men, yea fools, shall not err therein.
34 No lion shall be there,
   Nor shall any ravenous beast go up thereon,
35 They shall not be found there;
   But the redeemed shall walk there:

32. LORD'S DAY AFTER THE PENTECOST — MORNING

36 And the ransomed of Jehovah shall return, and come with singing unto Zion;
And everlasting joy shall be upon their heads:
37 They shall obtain gladness and joy,
And sorrow and sighing shall flee away.

Psalm Chant

From Is. vi, 3: Ps. lxxii, 19; lvii, 11: Deut. vi, 4 (Mk. xii, 29): Is. xxxvii, 16: Ps. xlvii, 3; 1, 2; cxviii, 14; lxxxvi, 10: Is. xxxii, 15 (Joel, ii, 28): Ps. xli, 13: Also, Matt. xxviii, 18–20; II Cor. xiii, 14. [Same for Ev'g]

JAMES TURLE.

HOLY! Holy! Holy! Thou Je- | hovah of | Hosts:
Blessèd be Thy | glo-rious | Name for- | ever.
2 The whole earth is | full • of Thy | glory:
Be Thou exalted, O | God, a- | bove the | heavens.
3 Thou, Jehovah our | God, art | One:
O Jehovah of Hosts, | Thou art | God a- | lone.
4 Thou hast made Thyself known in Zion;
Out of Zion Thou hast | shi-ned | forth.
Thou, Jehovah, art our strength and song,
And Thou art be- | come | our Sal- | vation:
5 For Thou hast laid help upon | One • that is | mighty;
And Thy Spirit hast Thou pour'd up- | on us | from on | high.
6 Holy! Holy! Holy! the Name of the Father and the | Son • and
Holy! Holy! Holy! Thou One Jehovah,   [the | Spirit:
From everlasting to ever- | lasting: A- | men • and A- | men.

Prayer of the Day

HOLY! Holy! Holy! Jehovah, God Almighty! Who, by Thy Spirit in the hearts of Thy believing people, makest Thyself known as the Father through Thy gracious manifestation in the Son — according to the revelation of the mystery kept in silence from times eternal but now manifest in Christ Jesus:

In His Name we beseech Thee, establish us and Thy whole church in this vision by faith of the One God — the Father and the Son and the Holy Spirit:

And so increase us daily in this gracious knowledge, and in all godliness therein, that we may be brought unto life in the full glory of Thy presence; unto whom be all blessing, dominion, and majesty, to ages everlasting: AMEN.

Hymn of Praise

JAMES WALLIS EASTBURN, abt. 1819.

O HOLY! holy! holy! Lord!
  Bright in Thy deeds and in Thy Name,
Forever be Thy Name adored,
  Thy glories let the world proclaim!

2 O Jesus! Lamb once crucified
  To take our load of sins away,

Thine be the hymn that rolls its tide
  Along the realms of upper day!

3 O Holy Spirit! from above,
  In streams of light and glory given,
Thou source of ecstasy and love,
  Thy praises ring thro' earth and heaven!

32. LORD'S DAY AFTER THE PENTECOST — MORNING 149

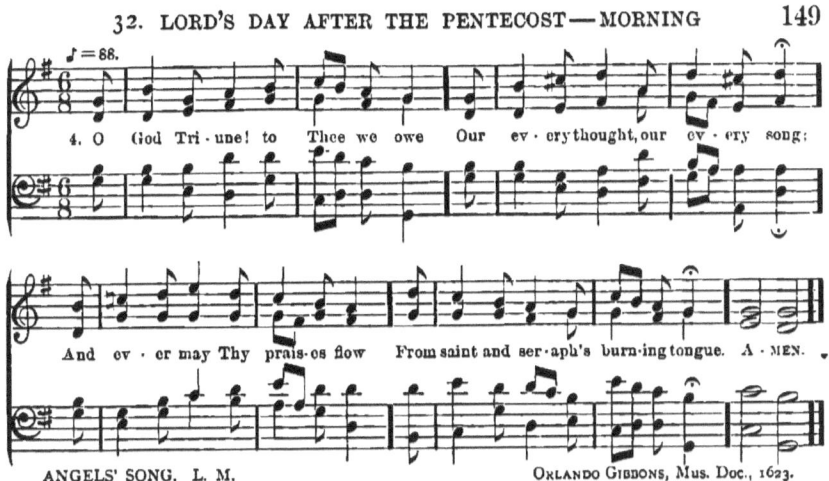

4. O God Tri-une! to Thee we owe Our ev-ery thought, our ev-ery song;
And ev-er may Thy prais-es flow From saint and ser-aph's burn-ing tongue. A-MEN.

ANGELS' SONG. L. M.   Orlando Gibbons, Mus. Doc., 1623.

32. EVENING
LORD'S DAY AFTER THE PENTECOST

Introductory

Sentence

KNOW ye not that ye are a temple of God,
And that the Spirit of God dwelleth in you?
In Christ Jesus ye are builded together for a habitation of God in the Spirit.
O Jehovah! holiness becometh Thine house forever.
[1 Cor. iii, 16: Eph. ii, 22: Ps. xciii, 5]

Response
[Tune, in Morning]

HOLY! Holy! Holy! the Lord | God,* the Al- | mighty,
Who was and who | is * and who | is to | come.
Glory and honor and thanks to Him that sitteth | on the | throne,
To Him that | liveth for | ever and | ever.   [Rev. iv, 8, 9]

Scripture Lessons   Old Covenant   Isaiah, vi, 1-8.
                             Gospel   Matt. xxviii, 16-20.
                             Apostolic Word   II Cor. iii, 2-8, 17, 18.

Responsive Lesson   Prov. viii.

DOTH not Wisdom cry,
    And Understanding put forth her voice?
2 In the top of high places by the way,
    Where the paths meet, she standeth;
3 Beside the gates at the entry of the city,
    At the coming in at the doors, she crieth aloud:
4 Unto you, O men, I call;
    And my voice is to the sons of men.
5 O ye simple, understand subtilty;
    And, ye fools, be ye of an understanding heart.

6 Hear, for I will speak excellent things;
   And the opening of my lips shall be right things.
7 For my mouth shall utter truth;
   And wickedness is an abomination to my lips.
8 All the words of my mouth are in righteousness;
   There is nothing crooked or perverse in them.
9 They are all plain to him that understandeth,
   And right to them that find knowledge.
10 Receive my instruction, and not silver;
   And knowledge rather than choice gold.
11 For wisdom is better than rubies; [unto her.
   And all the things that may be desired are not to be compared
12 I Wisdom have made subtilty my dwelling,
   And find out knowledge and discretion.
13 The fear of Jehovah is to hate evil:
   *Pride, and arrogancy, and the evil way,
   And the perverse mouth, do I hate.*
14 Counsel is mine, and sound knowledge:
   I am understanding; I have might.
15 By me kings reign,
   And princes decree justice.
16 By me princes rule,
   And nobles, even all the judges of the earth.
17 I love them that love me;
   And those that seek me diligently shall find me.
18 Riches and honor are with me;
   Yea, durable riches and righteousness.
19 My fruit is better than gold, yea, than fine gold;
   And my revenue than choice silver.
20 I walk in the way of righteousness,
   In the midst of the paths of judgment:
21 That I may cause those that love me to inherit substance,
   And that I may fill their treasuries.
22 Jehovah possessed me in the beginning of His way,
   Before His works of old.
23 I was set up from everlasting, from the beginning,
   Before the earth was.
24 When there were no depths, I was brought forth;
   When there were no fountains abounding with water.
25 Before the mountains were settled,
   Before the hills was I brought forth:
26 While as yet He had not made the earth, nor the fields,
   Nor the beginning of the dust of the world.
27 When He established the heavens, I was there:
   When He set a circle upon the face of the deep:
28 When He made firm the skies above:
   When the fountains of the deep became strong:
29 When He gave to the sea its bound,
   That the waters should not transgress His commandment:
30 When He marked out the foundations of the earth:
   Then I was by Him as a master workman:

32. LORD'S DAY AFTER THE PENTECOST — EVENING

31 And I was daily His delight,
  Rejoicing always before Him;
32 Rejoicing in His habitable earth;
  And my delight was with the sons of men.
33 Now therefore, my sons, hearken unto me:
  For blessed are they that keep my ways.
34 Hear instruction, and be wise,
  And refuse it not:
35 Blessed is the man that heareth me,
  Watching daily at my gates,
  Waiting at the posts of my doors.
36 For whoso findeth me findeth life,
  And shall obtain favor of Jehovah.
37 But he that sinneth against me wrongeth his own soul:
  All they that hate me love death.

Psalm Chant
Same as for Morning

Hymn of Praise
CHRISTOPHER WORDSWORTH, D. D., pub. 1862.
(Dox. alt.)

HOLY! holy! holy! Lord,
  God of hosts, eternal King,
By the heavens and earth adored!
  Angels and archangels sing,
Chanting everlastingly
To the blesséd Trinity.

2 Thousands, tens of thousands, stand,
  Spirits blest, before the throne,
Speeding thence at Thy command,
  And, when Thy commands are done,
Singing everlastingly
To the blesséd Trinity.

3 Cherubim and seraphim
  Vail their faces with their wings;
Eyes of angels are too dim
  To behold the King of kings,
While they sing eternally
To the blesséd Trinity.

4 Thee apostles, prophets Thee,
  Thee the noble martyr band,
Praise with solemn jubilee,
  Thee, the church in every land;
Singing everlastingly
To the blesséd Trinity.

5. Ho-ly! Ho-ly! Ho-ly! Lord; Fa-ther, Son, and Ho-ly Ghost—
   Ev-er-more One God a-dored! Join us with Thy heav'n-ly host,
Sing-ing ev-er-last-ing-ly To the bless-ed Trin-i-ty. A-MEN.

DIX. 7s, 6l.
KONRAD KOCHER, 1838.

[Some or all of the Days Nos. 33–37 are omitted from the *Monthly Order*, in various years, as may be required by the variable date of Easter: see in preceding pages, CALENDAR FOR THE YEAR.]

33. LORD'S DAY FOURTH IN MAY

Introductory   MORNING

Sentence O THAT the salvation of Israel were come out of Zion!
When God bringeth back the captivity of His people,
Then shall Jacob rejoice, and Israel shall be glad.   [Ps. liii, 6]

Response
[Tune in
MONTHLY SONGS]   I HAVE set watchmen upon thy walls, O Je- | ru-sa- | lem ;
They shall never hold their | peace | day nor | night :
Ye that are Jehovah's remembrancers, | keep not | silence,
Till He make Jerusalem a | praise | in the | earth.   [Is. lxii, 6, 7]

Scripture Lessons   Old Covenant   Lam. i, 1–7.
Gospel   Matt. xi, 20–30.
Apostolic Word   I Tim. vi, 1–10.

Responsive Lesson   A PSALM OF ASAPH, Ps. lxxx.   [Also, for Day No. 19, Ev'g]

G IVE ear, O Shepherd of Israel,
   Thou that leadest Joseph like a flock ;
      THOU THAT SITTEST ABOVE THE CHERUBIM, SHINE FORTH.
2 Before Ephraim and Benjamin and Manasseh, stir up Thy might,
   And come to save us.
3 Turn us again, O God ;
   And cause Thy face to shine, and we shall be saved.

4 O Jehovah, God of hosts,
   How long wilt Thou be angry against the prayer of Thy people?
5 Thou hast fed them with the bread of tears,
   And given them tears to drink in large measure.
6 Thou makest us a strife unto our neighbors :
   And our enemies laugh among themselves.
7 Turn us again, O God of hosts ;
   And cause Thy face to shine, and we shall be saved.

8 Thou broughtest a vine out of Egypt :
   Thou didst drive out the nations, and plantedst it.
9 Thou preparedst room before it,
   And it took deep root, and filled the land.
10 The mountains were covered with the shadow of it,
   And the boughs thereof were like cedars of God.
11 She sent out her branches unto the sea,
   And her shoots unto the River.
12 Why hast Thou broken down her fences,
   So that all they who pass by the way do pluck her ?
13 The boar out of the wood doth ravage it,
   And the wild beasts of the field feed on it.
14 Turn again, we beseech Thee, O God of hosts ;
Look down from heaven,
   And behold, and visit this vine,

33. LORD'S DAY FOURTH IN MAY—MORNING

15 And the stock which Thy right hand hath planted,
  And the branch that Thou madest strong for Thyself.
16 It is burned with fire, it is cut down:
  They perish at the rebuke of Thy countenance.
17 Let Thy hand be upon the man of Thy right hand,
  Upon the son of man whom Thou madest strong for Thyself.
18 So shall we not go back from Thee:
  Quicken Thou us, and we will call upon Thy Name.
19 Turn us again, O Jehovah, God of hosts;
  Cause Thy face to shine, and we shall be saved.

Psalm Chant — See MONTHLY SONGS: Lord's Day Fourth — Morning.

Prayer of the Day

EVER Blessed Jehovah! The strength of all them that take refuge in Thee: Because through the weakness of our nature we do no good thing without Thee, our eyes are unto Thee who art always ready to grant the indwelling of Thy Spirit to work in us both to will and to do for Thy good pleasure:
Grant this gift in all Thy Church, for Thy Son our Savior's sake, to whom with the Father and the same blessed Spirit — one God — be all honor and glory, world without end: AMEN.

Hymn of Praise — See MONTHLY SONGS: Lord's Day Fourth — Morning.

---

33. EVENING
LORD'S DAY FOURTH IN MAY

Introductory

Sentence

AS the hart panteth after the water brooks,
So panteth my soul after Thee, O God.
My soul thirsteth for God, for the living God.   [Ps. xlii, 1, 2]

Response [Tune in MONTHLY SONGS]

THERE is a river, the streams whereof make glad the | city of | God,
The holy place of the | taber-nacles | of the · Most | High.
Jehovah of | Hosts is | with us;
The God of | Ja-cob | is our | refuge.   [Ps. xlvi, 4, 7]

Scripture Lessons

Old Covenant — Exodus, xvi, 9-18, 31-35.
Gospel — Mark, vi, 30-44.
Apostolic Word — Acts, vii, 54-60; viii, 1-4.

Responsive Lesson

SONG OF HANNAH, from I Sam. ii: A DOXOLOGY from DAVID, Ps. xli, 13.

MY heart exulteth in Jehovah,
  My horn is exalted in Jehovah.
2 My mouth is enlarged over mine enemies,
  Because I rejoice in Thy salvation.

33. LORD'S DAY FOURTH IN MAY—EVENING

3 There is none holy as Jehovah;
   For there is none beside Thee:
   Neither is there any rock like our God.
4 Talk no more so exceeding proudly;
   Let not arrogancy come out of your mouth:
5 For Jehovah is a God of knowledge,
   And by Him actions are weighed.
6 The bows of the mighty men are broken,
   And they that stumbled are girded with strength.
7 They that were full have hired out themselves for bread;
   And they that were hungry have ceased:
8 Jehovah killeth, and maketh alive:
   He bringeth down to the grave, and bringeth up.
9 Jehovah maketh poor, and maketh rich:
   He bringeth low, He also lifteth up.
10 He raiseth up the poor out of the dust,
   He lifteth up the needy from the dunghill,
11 To make them sit with princes,
   And inherit the throne of glory:
12 For the pillars of the earth are Jehovah's,
   And He hath set the world upon them.
13 He will keep the feet of His holy ones,
   But the wicked shall be put to silence in darkness:
14 For by strength shall no man prevail.
   They that strive with Jehovah shall be broken to pieces;
15 Against them shall He thunder in heaven: .
   Jehovah shall judge the ends of the earth;
16 And He shall give strength unto His king,
   And exalt the horn of His anointed.

17 BLESSED be Jehovah, the God of Israel,
   From everlasting and to everlasting.
   AMEN, AND AMEN.

Psalm Chant See MONTHLY SONGS: Lord's Day Fourth — Evening.

Hymn of Praise See MONTHLY SONGS: Lord's Day Fourth — Evening.

[*See Note, Day No.* 33, *Morning*]

34. LORD'S DAY FIFTH IN MAY

Introductory   MORNING

Sentence

O MY soul, hope thou in God:
   For I shall yet praise Him for the help of His countenance. [Ps. xlii, 5]

Response
[Tune in
MONTHLY SONGS]

THEY that know Thy Name will put their | trust in | Thee;
   For Thou, Jehovah, hast not forsaken | them that | seek | Thee.   [Ps. ix, 10]

34. LORD'S DAY FIFTH IN MAY — MORNING

Scripture Lessons
Old Covenant II Sam. xvi, 5-14.
Gospel Matt. xii, 38-45.
Apostolic Word Rev. vii, 9-17.

Responsive Lesson From Job xxiii: xxiv, 1-13: xxv, 2-5.

O THAT I knew where I might find Him,
 That I might come even to His seat!
2 I would set my cause in order before Him,
 And fill my mouth with arguments.
3 I would know the words which He would answer me,
 And understand what He would say unto me.
4 Behold, I go forward, but He is not there;
 And backward, but I cannot perceive Him:
5 On the left hand, when He doth work, but I cannot behold Him:
 He hideth Himself on the right hand, that I cannot see Him.
6 But He knoweth the way that I take;
 When He hath tried me, I shall come forth as gold.
7 My foot hath held fast to His steps;
 His way have I kept, and turned not aside.
8 I have not gone back from the commandment of His lips:
 I have treasured up the words of His mouth more than my necessary food.
9 But He is in one mind, and who can turn Him?
 And what His soul desireth, even that He doeth.
10 Therefore am I troubled at His presence;
 When I consider, I am afraid of Him.
11 For God hath made my heart faint,
 And the Almighty hath troubled me:
12 Why are times not laid up by the Almighty?
 And why do not they which know Him see His days?
13 There are that remove the landmarks;
 They violently take away flocks, and feed them.
14 They drive away the ass of the fatherless,
 They take the widow's ox for a pledge.
15 They turn the needy out of the way:
 The poor of the earth all hide themselves.
16 Behold, as wild asses in the desert
 They go forth to their work, seeking diligently for food;
 The wilderness yieldeth them food for their children.
17 They cut their provender in the field;
 And they glean the vintage of the wicked.
18 They lie all night naked without clothing,
 And have no covering in the cold.
19 They are wet with the showers of the mountains,
 And embrace the rock for want of a shelter.
20 There are that pluck the fatherless from the breast,
 And take a pledge of the poor:
21 So that they go about naked without clothing,
 And being hungry they carry the sheaves;

34. LORD'S DAY FIFTH IN MAY — MORNING

22 They make oil within the walls of these men;
 They tread their wine-presses, and suffer thirst.
23 From out of the populous city men groan,
 And the soul of the wounded crieth out:
24 Yet God regardeth not the folly.
 These are of them that rebel against the light;
25 They know not the ways thereof,
 Nor abide in the paths thereof.

26 Then one answered and said:
 Dominion and fear are with God;
 He maketh peace in His high places.
27 Is there any number of His armies?
 And upon whom doth not His light arise?
28 How then can man be just with God?
 Or how can he be clean that is born of a woman?
29 Behold, even the moon hath no brightness,
 And the stars are not pure in His sight.

Psalm Chant   See MONTHLY SONGS: Lord's Day Fifth — Morning.

Prayer of the Day

OUR Heavenly Father! who never failest to help and govern Thy Church, the household of those whom Thou dost bring into Thy steadfast fear and love:
 Grant that we, to whom Thou hast given a justifying faith, may not lack a strong perseverance through the indwelling of Thy Holy Spirit:
 For the sake of Thy Son Christ Jesus, who with Thee and the same Spirit — one God — is glorified to ages everlasting: AMEN.

Hymn of Praise   See MONTHLY SONGS: Lord's Day Fifth — Morning.

---

34. EVENING
LORD'S DAY FIFTH IN MAY

Introductory

Sentence

UNTO Thee, O Jehovah, will I call.
 Hear the voice of my supplications when I cry unto Thee,
When I lift up my hands toward Thy holy oracle. [Ps. xxviii, 1, 2]

Response
[Tune in
MONTHLY SONGS]

WITH Thee, O God, is the | fountain of | life:
 In Thy | light shall | we see | light.

Scripture Lessons   Old Covenant   Obad. 1–15.
 Gospel   Mark, ix, 42–50.
 Apostolic Word   Tit. ii, 1–15.

34. LORD'S DAY FIFTH IN MAY—EVENING

Responsive Lesson Ps. cxlvii: A Psalm of David, lxv, 1, 8–13.
[Same for Day No 64]

PRAISE ye Jehovah;
  For it is good to sing praises unto our God;
  For it is pleasant, and praise is comely.
2 Jehovah doth build up Jerusalem;
  He gathereth together the outcasts of Israel.
3 He healeth the broken in heart,
  And bindeth up their wounds.
4 He counteth the number of the stars;
  He giveth them all their names.
5 Great is our Lord, and mighty in power;
  His understanding is infinite.
6 Jehovah upholdeth the meek:
  He bringeth the wicked down to the ground.
7 Sing unto Jehovah with thanksgiving;
  Sing praises upon the harp unto our God:
8 Who covereth the heaven with clouds,
  Who prepareth rain for the earth,
  Who maketh grass to grow upon the mountains.
9 He giveth to the beast his food,
  And to the young ravens which cry.
10 He delighteth not in the strength of the horse:
  He taketh no pleasure in the legs of a man.
11 Jehovah taketh pleasure in them that fear Him,
  In those that hope in His lovingkindness.
12 Praise Jehovah, O Jerusalem;
  Praise thy God, O Zion.
13 For He hath strengthened the bars of thy gates;
  He hath blessed thy children within thee.
14 He maketh peace in thy borders;
  He filleth thee with the finest of the wheat.
15 He sendeth out His commandment upon earth;
  His word runneth very swiftly.
16 He giveth snow like wool;
  He scattereth the hoar frost like ashes.
17 He casteth forth His ice like morsels:
  Who can stand before His cold?
18 He sendeth out His word, and melteth them:
  He causeth His wind to blow, and the waters flow.
19 He showeth His word unto Jacob,
  His statutes and His judgments unto Israel.
20 He hath not dealt so with any nation:
  And as for His judgments, they have not known them.
  PRAISE YE JEHOVAH.

---

21 PRAISE waiteth for Thee, O God, in Zion.
  Thou makest the outgoings of the morning and evening to rejoice.
22 Thou visitest the earth,
  And waterest it,

34. LORD'S DAY FIFTH IN MAY — EVENING

23 Thou greatly enrichest it;
   The river of God is full of water:
24 Thou providest them grain, when Thou hast so prepared the earth:
   Thou waterest her furrows abundantly;
25 Thou settlest the ridges thereof;
   Thou makest it soft with showers;
26 Thou blessest the springing thereof:
   Thou crownest the year with Thy goodness:
27 And Thy paths drop fatness;
   They drop upon the pastures of the wilderness:
28 And the hills are girded with joy;
   The pastures are clothed with flocks;
29 The valleys also are covered over with grain;
   They shout for joy, they also sing.
   PRAISE WAITETH FOR THEE, O GOD, IN ZION.

Psalm Chant See MONTHLY SONGS: Lord's Day Fifth — Evening.

Hymn of Praise See MONTHLY SONGS: Lord's Day Fifth — Evening.

[*See Note, Day No. 33, Morning*]

35. LORD'S DAY FIRST IN JUNE

Introductory   MORNING

Sentence   FROM the rising of the sun unto the going down of the same, Jehovah's Name is to be praised.
Praise ye Jehovah.   [Ps. cxiii, 3, 9]

Response
[Tune in
MONTHLY SONGS]

THE Mighty One, God Je- | hovah, hath | spoken,
   And called the earth from the rising of the sun unto the | go-ing | down there- | of.
Out of Zion, the per- | fection of | beauty,
   God | hath | shi-ned | forth.   [Ps. l, 1, 2]

Scripture Lessons   Old Covenant   Gen. 1, 14-26.
                       Gospel   Matt. xxv, 14-30.
                       Apostolic Word Rev. xix, 5-10.

Responsive Lesson   PSALMS OF DAVID, Psalms lii, liv, lvi.

WHY boastest thou thyself in mischief, O mighty man?
   The mercy of God endureth continually.
2 Thy tongue deviseth very wickedness;
   Like a sharp razor, working deceitfully.
3 Thou lovest evil more than good;
   And lying rather than to speak righteousness.

35. LORD'S DAY FIRST IN JUNE—MORNING

4 Thou lovest all devouring words,
O thou deceitful tongue.
God shall likewise destroy thee forever.
5 He shall take thee up, and pluck thee out of thy tent,
And root thee out of the land of the living.
6 The righteous also shall see it, and fear,
And shall laugh at him, saying,
Lo, this is the man that made not God his strength;
7 But trusted in the abundance of his riches,
And strengthened himself in his wickedness.
8 But as for me, I am like a green olive-tree in the house of God:
I trust in the lovingkindness of God for ever and ever.
9 I will give Thee thanks forever,
Because Thou hast done it:
10 And I will hope in Thy Name, for it is good,
In the presence of Thy saints.

---

11 SAVE me, O God, by Thy Name,
And judge me in Thy might.
12 Hear my prayer, O God;
Give ear to the words of my mouth.
13 For strangers are risen up against me,
And violent men have sought after my soul:
THEY HAVE NOT SET GOD BEFORE THEM.
14 Behold, God is my helper:
The Lord is of them that uphold my soul.
15 He shall requite the evil unto mine enemies:
Destroy Thou them in Thy truth.
16 With a freewill offering will I sacrifice unto Thee:
I will give thanks unto Thy Name, O Jehovah, for it is good.
17 For He hath delivered me out of all trouble;
And mine eye hath seen my desire upon mine enemies.

---

18 BE merciful unto me, O God; for man would swallow me up:
All the day long he fighting oppresseth me.
19 Mine enemies would swallow me up all the day long:
For they be many that fight proudly against me.
20 What time I am afraid,
I will put my trust in Thee.
21 In God (I will praise His word),
In God have I put my trust, I will not be afraid;
What can flesh do unto me?
22 All the day long they wrest my words:
All their thoughts are against me for evil.
23 They gather themselves together, they hide themselves,
They mark my steps, even as they have waited for my soul.
24 Shall they escape by iniquity?
In anger cast down the peoples, O God.
25 Thou tellest my wanderings:
Put Thou my tears into Thy bottle;
Are they not in Thy book?

35. LORD'S DAY FIRST IN JUNE—MORNING

26 Then shall mine enemies turn back in the day that I call:
This I know, that God is for me.
27 In God (I will praise His word),
In Jehovah (I will praise His word),
28 In God have I put my trust, I will not be afraid;
What can man do unto me?
29 Thy vows are upon me, O God:
I will render thank offerings unto Thee.
30 For Thou hast delivered my soul from death.
Hast Thou not delivered my feet from falling?
31 That I may walk before God
In the light of the living.

Psalm Chant   See MONTHLY SONGS: Lord's Day First—Morning.

Prayer of the Day

GRANT, O Lord, we beseech Thee, that the course of this world may be so peaceably ordered by Thy governance, that Thy Church may serve Thee in all godly quietness, and in the joyful stewardship and swift ministering of Thy gospel among all nations:

According to the power of Thy blessed Spirit, who is Thy gift through Thy Son Jesus our Savior,

And unto whom with the Father and the Son — one God — be everlasting praise: AMEN.

Hymn of Praise   See MONTHLY SONGS: Lord's Day First—Morning.

---

35. EVENING
LORD'S DAY FIRST IN JUNE

Introductory Sentence

EXALT ye Jehovah our God,
And worship at His holy hill:
For Jehovah our God is holy.   [Ps. xcix, 9]

Response [Tune in MONTHLY SONGS]

LOOK unto Me, and | be ye | sav'd,
All the | ends | of the | earth.
Unto Me every | knee shall | bow,
And every | tongue · shall con- | fess unto | God.
   [Is. xlv, 22, 23 (Rom. xiv, 11)]

Scripture Lessons
Old Covenant   Amos, ix, 11–15.
Gospel   John, xviii, 15–27.
Apostolic Word   Gal. v, 13–26.

Responsive Lesson   Job, ix, 2–12: from xii: xxvi, 7–14.   [Same for Day No. 1]

HOW can man be just with God?
If He be pleased to contend with him,
He cannot answer Him one of a thousand.

35. LORD'S DAY FIRST IN JUNE—EVENING

2 He is wise in heart, and mighty in strength:
Who hath hardened himself against Him, and prospered?
3 Who removeth the mountains, and they know it not,
When He overturneth them in His anger:
4 Who shaketh the earth out of her place,
And the pillars thereof tremble:
5 Who commandeth the sun, and it riseth not;
And sealeth up the stars:
6 Who alone stretcheth out the heavens,
And treadeth upon the waves of the sea:
7 Who maketh the Bear, Orion, and the Pleiades,
And the chambers of the south:
8 Who doeth great things past finding out;
Yea, marvelous things without number.
9 Lo, He goeth by me, and I see Him not:
He passeth on also, but I perceive Him not.

---

10 Ask now the beasts, and they shall teach thee;
And the fowls of the air, and they shall tell thee:
11 Or speak to the earth, and it shall teach thee;
And the fishes of the sea shall declare unto thee.
12 Who knoweth not in all these,
That the hand of Jehovah hath wrought this?
13 In whose hand is the soul of every living thing,
And the breath of all mankind.
14 With Him is wisdom and might;
He hath counsel and understanding.
15 Behold, He breaketh down, and it cannot be built again;
He shutteth up a man, and there can be no opening.
16 Behold, He withholdeth the waters, and they dry up;
Again, He sendeth them out, and they overturn the earth.
17 With Him is strength and wisdom;
The deceived and the deceiver are His.
18 He leadeth counselors away spoiled,
And judges maketh He fools.
19 He looseth the bond of kings,
And bindeth their loins with a girdle.
20 He leadeth priests away spoiled,
And overthroweth the mighty.
21 He removeth the speech of the trusty,
And taketh away the understanding of the elders.
22 He poureth contempt upon princes,
And looseth the belt of the strong.
23 He discovereth deep things out of darkness,
And bringeth out to light the shadow of death.
24 He increaseth the nations, and He destroyeth them:
He enlargeth the nations, and He leadeth them captive.
25 He taketh away understanding from the chiefs of the people of the earth,
And causeth them to wander in a wilderness where there is no way.

35. LORD'S DAY FIRST IN JUNE—EVENING

26 They grope in the dark without light,
   And He maketh them to stagger like a drunken man.

27 HE stretcheth out the north over empty space,
   And hangeth the earth upon nothing.
28 He bindeth up the waters in His thick clouds;
   And the cloud is not rent under them.
29 He closeth in the face of His throne,
   And spreadeth His cloud upon it.
30 He hath described a boundary upon the face of the waters,
   Unto the confines of light and darkness.
31 The pillars of heaven tremble
   And are astonished at His rebuke.
32 He stirreth up the sea with His power,
   And by His understanding He smiteth through arrogancy.
33 By His Spirit the heavens are garnished;
   His hand hath pierced the swift serpent.
34 Lo, these are but the outskirts of His ways:
   And how small a whisper do we hear of Him!
   BUT THE THUNDER OF HIS POWER WHO CAN UNDERSTAND?

Psalm Chant   See MONTHLY SONGS: Lord's Day First—Evening.

Hymn of Praise   See MONTHLY SONGS: Lord's Day First—Evening.

[See Note, Day No. 33, Morning]

36. LORD'S DAY SECOND IN JUNE

Introductory   MORNING

Sentence   BEAUTIFUL in elevation, the joy of the whole earth,
   Is Mount Zion, the city of the great King.
   God hath made Himself known in her palaces for a refuge.   [Ps. xlviii, 2, 3]

Response
[Tune in
MONTHLY SONGS]

JEHOVAH send thee help from the | sanc-tu- | ary,
   And | strength-en | thee • out of | Zion!
   Remember | all thine | offerings,
   And ac- | cept thy | sac-ri- | fice!   [Ps. xx, 1-3]

Scripture Lessons   Old Covenant   Jer. xvii, 19-27.
   Gospel   John, x, 7-18.
   Apostolic Word   Acts, v, 17-32.

Responsive Lesson   PSALMS OF DAVID, v, vi: A SONG OF ASCENTS, cxxi.

GIVE ear to my words, O Jehovah,
   Consider my meditation.
2 Hearken unto the voice of my cry, my King, and my God:
   For unto Thee do I pray.

36. LORD'S DAY SECOND IN JUNE — MORNING

3 O Jehovah, in the morning shalt Thou hear my voice;
   In the morning will I order my prayer unto Thee, and will keep watch.
4 For Thou art not a God that hath pleasure in wickedness:
   Evil shall not sojourn with Thee.
5 The arrogant shall not stand in Thy sight:
   Thou hatest all workers of iniquity.
6 Thou shalt destroy them that speak lies:
   Jehovah abhorreth the bloodthirsty and deceitful man.
7 But as for me, in the abundance of Thy lovingkindness will I come into Thy house:
   In Thy fear will I worship toward Thy holy temple.
8 Lead me, O Jehovah, in Thy righteousness because of mine enemies;
   Make Thy way straight before my face.
9 For there is no faithfulness in their mouth;
   Their inward part is very wickedness:
10 Their throat is an open sepulcher;
   They flatter with their tongue.
11 Hold them guilty, O God;
   Let them fall by their own counsels:
12 Thrust them out in the multitude of their transgressions;
   For they have rebelled against Thee.
13 But let all those that take refuge in Thee rejoice,
   Let them ever shout for joy, because Thou defendest them:
14 Let them also that love Thy Name be joyful in Thee.
   For Thou wilt bless the righteous;
15 O Jehovah, Thou wilt compass him with favor
   As with a shield.

---

16 O JEHOVAH, rebuke me not in Thine anger,
   Neither chasten me in Thy hot displeasure.
17 Have mercy upon me, O Jehovah; for I am withered away:
   O Jehovah, heal me; for my bones are vexed.
18 My soul also is sore vexed:
   And Thou, Jehovah, how long?
19 Return, O Jehovah, deliver my soul:
   Save me for Thy lovingkindness' sake.
20 For in death there is no remembrance of Thee:
   In Sheol who shall give Thee thanks?
21 I am weary with my groaning;
   Every night make I my bed to swim;
   I water my couch with my tears.
22 Mine eye wasteth away because of grief;
   It waxeth old because of all mine adversaries.
23 Depart from me, all ye workers of iniquity;
   For Jehovah hath heard the voice of my weeping.
24 Jehovah hath heard my supplication;
   Jehovah will receive my prayer.
25 All mine enemies shall be put to shame and sore vexed:
   They shall turn back, they shall suddenly be put to shame.

36. LORD'S DAY SECOND IN JUNE—MORNING

26 I WILL lift up mine eyes unto the mountains:
   Whence shall my help come?
27 My help cometh from Jehovah,
   Who made heaven and earth.
28 He will not suffer thy foot to be moved:
   He that keepeth thee will not slumber.
29 Behold, He that keepeth Israel
   Shall neither slumber nor sleep.
30 Jehovah is thy keeper:
   Jehovah is thy shade upon thy right hand.
31 The sun shall not smite thee by day,
   Nor the moon by night.
32 Jehovah shall keep thee from all evil;
   He shall keep thy soul.
33 Jehovah shall keep thy going out and thy coming in,
   From this time forth and forever more.

Psalm Chant   See MONTHLY SONGS: Lord's Day Second—Morning.

Prayer of the Day

L ORD God the Almighty, without whom nothing is strong, nothing is good:
    Increase and multiply in all Thy Church the gifts of Thy Holy Spirit, that Thou mayest be our perpetual Ruler and Guide while we pass through things temporal, till Thou bring us unto the everlasting possession:
   Grant this, O Father, for the sake of Jesus Christ Thy Son, who liveth and reigneth with Thee and the same Spirit—one God, in glory without end: AMEN.

Hymn of Praise   See MONTHLY SONGS: Lord's Day Second—Morning.

---

36. EVENING
LORD'S DAY SECOND IN JUNE

Introductory

Sentence   B EHOLD, how good and how pleasant it is for brethren to dwell
             together in unity!
   Like the dew of Hermon,
   That cometh down upon the mountains of Zion:
   For there Jehovah commanded the blessing,
   Even life for evermore.   [Ps. cxxxiii, 1, 3]

Response   L IFT up your hands to the | sanc-tu- | ary,
[Tune in   And | bless | ye Je- | hovah.
MONTHLY SONGS]   Jehovah bless thee | out of | Zion!
           Even He that | made | heav'n and | earth.   [Ps. cxxxiv, 2, 3]

36. LORD'S DAY SECOND IN JUNE—EVENING

Scripture Lessons
Old Covenant   Exodus, xxxii, 1-14.
Gospel   Matt. xiii, 16-23.
Apostolic Word   I Cor. iii, 16-23; iv, 1-5.

Responsive Lesson   Psalm cxix, 105-136.

THY word is a lamp unto my feet,
And light unto my path.
2 I have sworn, and have confirmed it,
That I will observe Thy righteous judgments.
3 I am afflicted very much:
Quicken me, O Jehovah, according unto Thy word.
4 Accept, I beseech Thee, the freewill offerings of my mouth, O Jehovah,
And teach me Thy judgments.
5 My soul is continually in my hand;
Yet do I not forget Thy law.
6 The wicked have laid a snare for me;
Yet went I not astray from Thy precepts.
7 Thy testimonies have I taken as a heritage forever;
For they are the rejoicing of my heart.
8 I have inclined my heart to perform Thy statutes forever,
Even unto the end.
9 I hate them that are of a double mind;
But Thy law do I love.
10 Thou art my hiding-place and my shield:
I hope in Thy word.
11 Depart from me, ye evil-doers;
That I may keep the commandments of my God.
12 Uphold me according unto Thy word, that I may live;
And let me not be put to shame in my hope.
13 Hold Thou me up, and I shall be safe,
And shall have respect unto Thy statutes continually.
14 Thou hast set at nought all them that err from Thy statutes;
For their deceit is falsehood.
15 Thou puttest away all the wicked of the earth like dross:
Therefore I love Thy testimonies.
16 My flesh trembleth for fear of Thee;
And I am afraid of Thy judgments.
17 I have done justice and righteousness:
Leave me not to mine oppressors.
18 Be surety for Thy servant for good:
Let not the proud oppress me.
19 Mine eyes fail for Thy salvation,
And for Thy righteous word.
20 Deal with Thy servant according unto Thy lovingkindness.
And teach me Thy statutes.
21 I am Thy servant, give me understanding;
That I may know Thy testimonies.

36. LORD'S DAY SECOND IN JUNE — EVENING

22 It is time for Jehovah to work;
  For they have made void Thy law.
23 Therefore I love Thy commandments above gold,
  Yea, above fine gold.
24 Therefore I esteem all Thy precepts concerning all things to be right;
  And I hate every false way.
25 Thy testimonies are wonderful:
  Therefore doth my soul keep them.
26 The opening of Thy words giveth light;
  It giveth understanding unto the simple.
27 I opened wide my mouth, and panted;
  For I longed for Thy commandments.
28 Turn Thee unto me, and have mercy upon me,
  As Thou usest to do unto those that love Thy Name.
29 Order my footsteps in Thy word;
  And let not any iniquity have dominion over me.
30 Redeem me from the oppression of man:
  So will I observe Thy precepts.
31 Make Thy face to shine upon Thy servant;
  And teach me Thy statutes.
32 Mine eyes run down with streams of water,
  Because they observe not Thy law.

Psalm Chant See MONTHLY SONGS: Lord's Day Second — Evening.

Hymn of Praise See MONTHLY SONGS: Lord's Day Second — Evening.

[See Note, Day No. 33, Morning]

37. LORD'S DAY THIRD IN JUNE

Introductory MORNING

Sentence SOW to yourselves in righteousness, reap according to loving-
  Break up your fallow ground: [kindness;
  For it is time to seek Jehovah,
  Till He come and rain righteousness upon you. [Hos. x, 12]

Response
[Tune in
MONTHLY SONGS]

THOU hast said, | Seek ye · My | face :
  My heart saith unto Thee,
  Thy face, O Je- | ho-vah, | will I | seek. [Ps. xxvii, 8]

Scripture Lessons

Old Covenant Prov. xvi, 1–12.
Gospel Luke, x, 25–37.
Apostolic Word Eph. iv, 1–16.

37. LORD'S DAY THIRD IN JUNE—MORNING

Responsive Lesson Job, iv, 12-21; v, 1, 6-18.

NOW a thing was secretly brought to me,
And mine ear received a whisper thereof.
2 In thoughts from the visions of the night,
When deep sleep falleth on men,
3 Fear came upon me, and trembling,
Which made all my bones to shake.
4 Then a spirit passed before my face;
The hair of my flesh stood up.
5 It stood still, but I could not discern the appearance thereof;
A form was before mine eyes:
6 There was silence,
And I heard a voice,
7 Saying, Shall mortal man be more just than God?
Shall a man be more pure than his Maker?
8 Behold, He putteth no trust in His servants;
And His angels He chargeth with folly:
9 How much more them that dwell in houses of clay,
*Whose foundation is in the dust,
Who are crushed before the moth!*
10 Betwixt morning and evening they are destroyed:
They perish forever without any regarding it.
11 Is not their tent-cord plucked up within them?
They die, and that without wisdom.
12 Call now; is there any that will answer thee?
And to which of the holy ones wilt thou turn?

13 For affliction cometh not forth of the dust,
Neither doth trouble spring out of the ground.
14 But man is born unto trouble,
As the sparks fly upward.
15 But as for me, I would seek unto God,
And unto God would I commit my cause:
16 Who doeth great things and unsearchable;
Marvelous things without number:
17 Who giveth rain upon the earth,
And sendeth waters upon the fields:
18 So that He setteth up on high those that are low;
And those who mourn are exalted to safety.
19 He frustrateth the devices of the crafty,
So that their hands cannot perform their enterprise.
20 He taketh the wise in their own craftiness:
And the counsel of the cunning is carried headlong.
21 They meet with darkness in the day-time,
And grope at noonday as in the night.
22 Behold, happy is the man whom God correcteth:
Therefore despise not thou the chastening of the Almighty.
23 For He maketh sore, and bindeth up;
He woundeth, and His hands make whole.

37. LORD'S DAY THIRD IN JUNE — MORNING

Psalm Chant   See MONTHLY SONGS: Lord's Day Third — Morning.

Prayer of the Day

JEHOVAH our Shepherd, who hast called Thy church unto Thine eternal glory by Christ Jesus:

So lead us that we who live through Thy Spirit may always walk in Thy Spirit; that, being sober and vigilant, clothed with humility, and casting all our care on Thee, we may overcome the world, withstand the flesh, resist the devil, and obtain the crown of life:

Through Thy Son our Savior, to whom with the Father and the Spirit — one God — be all honor and glory evermore: AMEN.

Hymn of Praise   See MONTHLY SONGS: Lord's Day Third — Morning.

---

37. EVENING
LORD'S DAY THIRD IN JUNE

Introductory

Sentence

HOW precious is Thy lovingkindness, O God!
And the children of men take refuge under the shadow of Thy wings.
They shall be abundantly satisfied with the fatness of Thy house;
And Thou shalt make them drink of the river of Thy pleasures.
[Ps. xxxvi, 7, 8]

Response
[Tune in MONTHLY SONGS]

IT shall come to pass that at evening time there | shall be | light.
And it shall come to pass in that day,
That living waters shall go | out * from Je- | ru-sa- | lem.
[Zech. xiv, 7, 8]

Scripture Lessons   Old Covenant   Exodus, xxxii, 15-26.
Gospel   John, x, 22-38.
Apostolic Word   Rom. x, 4-13.

Responsive Lesson   Psalm cvii.

O GIVE thanks unto Jehovah; for He is good:
For His lovingkindness endureth forever.
2 Let the redeemed of Jehovah say so,
Whom He hath redeemed from the hand of the adversary;
3 And gathered them out of the lands,
From the east and from the west,
From the north and from the south.

4 They wandered in the wilderness in a desert way;
They found no city of habitation.
5 Hungry and thirsty,
Their soul fainted in them.

37. LORD'S DAY THIRD IN JUNE—EVENING

6 Then they cried unto Jehovah in their trouble,
  And He delivered them out of their distresses.
7 He led them also by a straight way,
  That they might go to a city of habitation.
8 O that men would praise Jehovah for His lovingkindness,
  And for His wonderful works to the children of men!
9 For He satisfieth the longing soul,
  And the hungry soul He filleth with good.

10 Such as sat in darkness and in the shadow of death,
  Being bound in affliction and iron;
11 Because they rebelled against the words of God,
  And contemned the counsel of the Most High:
12 Therefore He brought down their heart with labor;
  They fell down, and there was none to help.
13 Then they cried unto Jehovah in their trouble,
  And He saved them out of their distresses.
14 He brought them out of darkness and the shadow of death,
  And brake their bonds in sunder.
15 O that men would praise Jehovah for His goodness,
  And for His wonderful works to the children of men!
16 For He hath broken the gates of brass,
  And cut the bars of iron in sunder.

17 Fools because of their transgression,
  And because of their iniquities, are afflicted.
18 Their soul abhorreth all manner of food;
  And they draw near unto the gates of death.
19 Then they cry unto Jehovah in their trouble,
  And He saveth them out of their distresses.
20 He sendeth His word, and healeth them,
  And delivereth them from their destructions.
21 O that men would praise Jehovah for His goodness,
  And for His wonderful works to the children of men!
22 And let them offer the sacrifices of thanksgiving,
  And declare His works with singing.

23 They that go down to the sea in ships,
  That do business in great waters;
24 These see the works of Jehovah,
  And His wonders in the deep,
25 For He commandeth, and raiseth the stormy wind,
  Which lifteth up the waves thereof.
26 They mount up to the heaven, they go down again to the depths:
  Their soul melteth away because of trouble.
27 They reel to and fro, and stagger like a drunken man,
  And are at their wits' end.
28 Then they cry unto Jehovah in their trouble,
  And He bringeth them out of their distresses.
29 He maketh the storm a calm,
  So that the waves thereof are still.

37. LORD'S DAY THIRD IN JUNE—EVENING

30 Then are they glad because they be quiet;
So He bringeth them unto their desired haven.
31 O that men would praise Jehovah for His goodness,
And for His wonderful works to the children of men!
32 Let them exalt Him also in the assembly of the people,
And praise Him in the seat of the elders.
33 He turneth rivers into a wilderness,
And water-springs into a thirsty ground;
34 A fruitful land into a salt desert,
For the wickedness of them that dwell therein.
35 He turneth a wilderness into a pool of water,
And a dry land into water-springs.
36 And there He maketh the hungry to dwell,
That they may prepare a city of habitation;
37 And sow fields, and plant vineyards,
And get them fruits of increase.
38 He blesseth them also, so that they are multiplied greatly;
And He suffereth not their cattle to decrease.
39 Again, they are diminished and bowed down
Through oppression, trouble, and sorrow.
40 He poureth contempt upon princes,
And causeth them to wander in the waste, where there is no way.
41 Yet setteth He the needy on high from affliction,
And maketh him families like a flock.
42 The upright shall see it, and be glad;
And all iniquity shall stop her mouth.
43 Whoso is wise shall give heed to these things;
And they shall consider the lovingkindnesses of Jehovah.

Psalm Chant　　See MONTHLY SONGS: Lord's Day Third — Evening.

Hymn of Praise　　See MONTHLY SONGS: Lord's Day Third — Evening.

---

38. LORD'S DAY FOURTH IN JUNE

Introductory　　MORNING

Sentence　JEHOVAH loveth the gates of Zion.
Glorious things are spoken of Thee, O city of God. [Ps. lxxxvii, 2, 3]

Response
[Tune in
MONTHLY SONGS]
I HAVE set watchmen upon thy walls, O Je- | ru-sa- | lem;
They shall never hold their | peace | day nor | night:
Ye that are Jehovah's remembrancers, | keep not | silence,
Till He make Jerusalem a | praise | in the | earth. [Is. lxii, 6, 7]

Scripture Lessons　　Old Covenant　Gen. xiii.
Gospel　John, xi, 21–35.
Apostolic Word　Eph. iv, 17–32; v, 1, 2.

Responsive Lesson

From Isaiah, v.

1. LET me sing for my wellbeloved
    A song of my beloved touching his vineyard.
2. My wellbeloved had a vineyard in a very fruitful hill:
    And he made a trench about it,
3. And gathered out the stones thereof,
    And planted it with the choicest vine,
4. And built a tower in the midst of it,
    And also hewed out a wine-press therein:
5. And he looked that it should bring forth grapes,
    And it brought forth wild grapes.
6. And now, O inhabitants of Jerusalem and men of Judah,
    Judge, I pray you, betwixt me and my vineyard.
7. What could have been done more to my vineyard, that I have not done in it?
    Wherefore, when I looked that it should bring forth grapes, brought it forth wild grapes?
8. And now go to: I will tell you what I will do to my vineyard: I will take away the hedge thereof,
    And it shall be eaten up;
9. I will break down the fence thereof,
    And it shall be trodden down:
10. And I will lay it waste; it shall not be pruned nor hoed;
    But there shall come up briers and thorns:
11. I will also command the clouds
    That they rain no rain upon it.
12. For the vineyard of Jehovah of hosts is the house of Israel,
    And the men of Judah His pleasant plant:
13. And He looked for justice, but behold oppression;
    For righteousness, but behold a cry.
14. Woe unto them that join house to house,
    That lay field to field,
15. Till there be no room,
    And ye be made to dwell alone in the midst of the land!
16. Woe unto them that rise up early in the morning, that they may follow strong drink;
    That tarry late into the night, till wine inflame them!
17. And the harp and the lute, the tabret and the pipe, and wine,
    Are in their feasts:
18. But they regard not the work of Jehovah,
    Neither have they considered the operation of His hands.
19. Therefore my people are gone into captivity,
    For lack of knowledge:
20. And their honorable men are famished,
    And their multitude are parched with thirst.
21. Therefore Sheol hath enlarged her desire,
    And opened her mouth without measure:
22. And their glory, and their multitude, and their pomp,
    And he that rejoiceth among them, descend into it.

38. LORD'S DAY FOURTH IN JUNE—MORNING

23 And the mean man is bowed down, and the great man is humbled,
   And the eyes of the lofty are humbled:
24 But Jehovah of hosts is exalted in judgment,
   And God the Holy One is sanctified in righteousness.

25 Woe unto them that draw iniquity with cords of vanity,
   And that draw sin as it were with a cart-rope:
26 That say, Let Him make speed,
   Let Him hasten His work, that we may see it:
27 And let the counsel of the Holy One of Israel draw nigh and come,
   That we may know it!

28 Woe unto them that call evil good, and good evil;
   That put darkness for light, and light for darkness;
   That put bitter for sweet, and sweet for bitter!

29 Woe unto them that are wise in their own eyes,
   And prudent in their own sight!

30 Woe unto them that are mighty to drink wine,
   And men of strength to mingle strong drink:
31 Who justify the wicked for a reward,
   And take away the righteousness of the righteous from him!
32 Therefore as the tongue of fire devoureth the stubble,
   And as the dry grass sinketh down in the flame,
33 So their root shall be as rottenness,
   And their blossom shall go up as dust:
34 Because they have rejected the law of Jehovah of hosts,
   And despised the word of the Holy One of Israel.

Psalm Chant
See MONTHLY SONGS: Lord's Day Fourth—Morning.

Prayer of the Day

GOD of Light, who by Thy Spirit hast given all Holy Scriptures as the revelation of Thy Son who is the Living Word:

Grant that through the same Spirit we, with Thy whole Church, may in such wise hear them, read, mark, learn, and inwardly digest them, that in patience and comfort of Thy holy word we may embrace and ever hold fast the blessed hope of eternal life in Christ,

Who with the Holy Spirit is glorified with the Father—ever one God: AMEN.

Hymn of Praise
See MONTHLY SONGS: Lord's Day Fourth—Morning.

38. EVENING
LORD'S DAY FOURTH IN JUNE

Introductory

Sentence

SAVE Thy people, O Jehovah,
And bless thine inheritance:
Be their Shepherd also,
And bear them up for ever. [Ps. xxviii, 9]

Response
[Tune in
MONTHLY SONGS]

THERE is a river, the streams whereof make glad the | city of |
God,
The holy place of the | taber-nacles | of the • Most | High.
Jehovah of | Hosts is | with us;
The God of | Ja-cob | is our | refuge. [Ps. xlvi, 4, 7]

Scripture Lessons

Old Covenant   Exodus, xxxiii, 12-23.
Gospel   Luke, xii, 1-12.
Apostolic Word   Rom. xi, 25-36.

Responsive Lesson

Psalm, cxxxvii, 1-6:   PSALMS OF DAVID, cxlii, cxliii.

BY the rivers of Babylon,
   There we sat down,
2 Yea, we wept, when we remembered Zion,
   Upon the willows in the midst thereof we hanged up our harps.
3 For there they that led us captive required of us songs,
   And they that wasted us required of us mirth,
4 Saying, Sing us one of the songs of Zion.
   How shall we sing the song of Jehovah in a strange land?
5 If I forget thee, O Jerusalem,
   Let my right hand forget her cunning.
6 Let my tongue cleave to the roof of my mouth, if I remember thee not;
   If I prefer not Jerusalem above my chief joy.

---

7 I CRY with my voice unto Jehovah;
   With my voice unto Jehovah do I make supplication.
8 I pour out my complaint before Him;
   I show before Him my trouble.
9 When my spirit was overwhelmed within me, Thou knewest my path.
   In the way wherein I walk have they hidden a snare for me.
10 Look on my right hand, and see;
   For there is no man that knoweth me:
11 Refuge hath failed me;
   No man careth for my soul.
12 I cried unto Thee, O Jehovah;
   I said, Thou art my refuge,
   My portion in the land of the living.
13 Attend unto my cry; for I am brought very low:
   Deliver me from my persecutors; for they are stronger than I.

38. LORD'S DAY FOURTH IN JUNE—EVENING

14 Bring my soul out of prison,
   That I may give thanks unto Thy Name.
15 The righteous shall compass me about;
   For Thou shalt deal bountifully with me.

16 HEAR my prayer, O Jehovah;
   Give ear to my supplications:
17 In Thy faithfulness answer me,
   And in Thy righteousness.
18 And enter not into judgment with Thy servant;
   For in Thy sight no man living is righteous.
19 For the enemy hath persecuted my soul:
   He hath smitten my life down to the ground:
20 He hath made me to dwell in dark places,
   As those that have been long dead.
21 Therefore is my spirit overwhelmed within me;
   My heart within me is desolate.
22 I remember the days of old;
   I meditate on all Thy doings:
   I muse on the work of Thy hands.
23 I spread forth my hands unto Thee:
   My soul thirsteth after Thee, as a weary land.
24 Make haste to answer me, O Jehovah;
   My spirit faileth:
25 Hide not Thy face from me;
   Lest I become like them that go down into the pit.
26 Cause me to hear Thy lovingkindness in the morning;
   For in Thee do I trust:
27 Cause me to know the way wherein I should walk;
   For I lift up my soul unto Thee.
28 Deliver me, O Jehovah, from mine enemies:
   I flee unto Thee to hide me.
29 Teach me to do Thy will; for Thou art my God:
   Thy Spirit is good: lead me in the land of uprightness.
30 Quicken me, O Jehovah, for Thy Name's sake:
   In Thy righteousness bring my soul out of trouble.
31 And in Thy lovingkindness cut off mine enemies,
   And destroy all them that afflict my soul;
   FOR I AM THY SERVANT.

Psalm Chant   See MONTHLY SONGS: Lord's Day Fourth—Evening.

Hymn of Praise   See MONTHLY SONGS: Lord's Day Fourth—Evening.

[NOT IN EVERY YEAR]

39. LORD'S DAY FIFTH IN JUNE
MORNING

Introductory

Sentence — LET Thy lovingkindness, O Jehovah, be upon us, According as we have hoped in Thee. [Ps. xxxiii, 22]

Response [Tune in MONTHLY SONGS] — THEY that know Thy Name will put their | trust in | Thee ; For Thou, Jehovah, hast not forsaken | them that | seek | Thee. [Ps. ix, 10]

Scripture Lessons

Old Covenant — I Kings, xi, 4-13.
Gospel — Luke, x, 17-24.
Apostolic Word — Philippians, iii, 7-16.

Responsive Lesson — From A PSALM OF DAVID : Ps. lxix.

SAVE me, O God ;
For the waters are come in unto my soul.
I sink in deep mire, where there is no standing :
2 I am come into deep waters,
Where the floods overflow me.
3 I am weary with my crying ; my throat is dried :
Mine eyes fail while I wait for my God.
4 They that hate me without a cause
Are more than the hairs of mine head :
5 They that would cut me off, being mine enemies wrongfully, are mighty :
Then I restored that which I took not away.
6 O God, Thou knowest my foolishness ;
And my sins are not hid from Thee.
7 Let not them that wait for Thee be put to shame through me, O Lord Jehovah of hosts :
Let not those that seek Thee be brought to dishonor through me, O God of Israel.
8 Because for Thy sake I have borne reproach :
Shame hath covered my face.
9 I am become a stranger unto my brethren,
And an alien unto my mother's children.
10 For the zeal of Thine house hath eaten me up ;
And the reproaches of them that reproach Thee are fallen upon me.
11 When I wept, and chastened my soul with fasting, that was to my reproach.
When I made sackcloth my clothing, I became a proverb unto them.
12 They that sit in the gate talk of me ;
And I am the song of the drunkards.
13 But as for me, my prayer is unto Thee, O Jehovah, in an acceptable time :
O God, in the abundance of Thy lovingkindness,
14 Answer me in the truth of Thy salvation.
Deliver me out of the mire, and let me not sink.
15 Let me be delivered from them that hate me, and out of the deep [waters.
Let not the waterflood overwhelm me,

39. LORD'S DAY FIFTH IN JUNE — MORNING

16 Neither let the deep swallow me up;
   And let not the pit shut her mouth upon me.
17 Answer me, O Jehovah; for Thy lovingkindness is good:
   According to the multitude of Thy tender mercies, turn Thou unto me.
18 And hide not Thy face from Thy servant;
   For I am in distress; answer me speedily.
19 Draw nigh unto my soul, and redeem it:
   Ransom me because of mine enemies.
20 Thou knowest my reproach, and my shame, and my dishonor:
   Mine adversaries all are before Thee.
21 Reproach hath broken my heart;
   And I am full of heaviness:
22 And I looked for some to take pity, but there was none;
   And for comforters, but I found none.
23 They gave me also gall for my food,
   And in my thirst they gave me vinegar to drink.
24 But I am poor and sorrowful:
   Let Thy salvation, O God, set me up on high.
25 I will praise the Name of God with a song,
   And will magnify Him with thanksgiving.
26 And it shall please Jehovah better than an ox,
   Or a bullock that hath horns and hoofs.
27 The meek have seen it, and are glad:
   Ye that seek after God, let your heart live.
28 For Jehovah heareth the needy,
   And despiseth not His prisoners.
29 Let heaven and earth praise Him,
   The seas, and every thing that moveth therein.
30 For God will save Zion, and build the cities of Judah;
   And they shall abide there, and have it in possession.
31 The seed also of His servants shall inherit it;
   And they that love His Name shall dwell therein.

Psalm Chant
See MONTHLY SONGS: Lord's Day Fifth — Morning.

Prayer of the Day
LORD of all Power and Might, the Author and Giver of all good things, who dwellest by Thy Spirit in Thy Church:
Graft in our hearts the love of Thee, increase in us faith toward Thy Son, nourish us with all goodness, and of Thy great mercy keep us in the same:
For the sake of Christ our Savior, who with the Father and the Spirit — one God, is glorified to ages everlasting: AMEN.

Hymn of Praise
See MONTHLY SONGS: Lord's Day Fifth — Morning.

39. EVENING
LORD'S DAY FIFTH IN JUNE

Introductory

Sentence
GRACIOUS is Jehovah, and righteous;
Yea, our God is merciful.
Return unto thy rest, O my soul,
For Jehovah hath dealt bountifully with thee. [Ps. cxvi, 5, 7]

Response
[Tune in
Monthly Songs]
WITH Thee, O God, is the | fountain of | life:
In Thy | light shall | we see | light. [Ps. xxxvi, 9]

Scripture Lessons

Old Covenant   Exodus, xxxiii, 1–11.
Gospel   Matt. xxv, 31–46.
Apostolic Word   Heb. xi, 23–40.

Responsive Lesson   Psalms, cxvii; cxviii, 1–18: cxiii, 1–8.

O PRAISE Jehovah, all ye nations;
   Laud Him, all ye peoples.
2 For His mercy is great toward us;
   And the truth of Jehovah endureth forever.
        PRAISE YE JEHOVAH.

3 O GIVE thanks unto Jehovah; for He is good:
   For His lovingkindness endureth forever.
4 Let Israel now say,
   That His lovingkindness endureth forever.
5 Let the house of Aaron now say,
   That His lovingkindness endureth forever.
6 Let them now that fear Jehovah say,
   That His lovingkindness endureth forever.
7 Out of my distress I called upon Jehovah:
   Jehovah answered me and set me in a large place.
8 Jehovah is on my side; I will not fear:
   What can man do unto me?
9 Jehovah is on my side among them that help me:
   Therefore shall I see my desire upon them that hate me.
10 It is better to trust in Jehovah than to put confidence in man.
   It is better to trust in Jehovah than to put confidence in princes.
11 All nations compassed me about:
   In the Name of Jehovah I will cut them off.
12 They compassed me about; yea, they compassed me about:
   In the Name of Jehovah I will cut them off.
13 They compassed me about like bees;
They are quenched as the fire of thorns:
   In the Name of Jehovah I will cut them off.
14 Thou didst thrust sore at me that I might fall:
   But Jehovah helped me.
15 Jehovah is my strength and song;
   And He is become my salvation.

39. LORD'S DAY FIFTH IN JUNE—EVENING

16 The voice of rejoicing and salvation is in the tents of the righteous:
    The right hand of Jehovah doeth valiantly.
17 The right hand of Jehovah is exalted:
    The right hand of Jehovah doeth valiantly.
18 I shall not die, but live,
    And declare the works of Jehovah.
19 Jehovah hath chastened me sore:
    But He hath not given me over unto death.

---

20 PRAISE ye Jehovah.
    Praise, O ye servants of Jehovah,
    Praise the Name of Jehovah.
21 Blessed be the Name of Jehovah
    From this time forth and for evermore.
22 From the rising of the sun unto the going down of the same
    Jehovah's Name is to be praised.
23 Jehovah is high above all nations,
    And His glory above the heavens.
24 Who is like unto Jehovah our God,
    That hath His seat on high,
    That humbleth Himself to behold the things that are in heaven and in the earth?
25 He raiseth up the poor out of the dust,
    And lifteth up the needy from the dunghill;
26 That He may set him with princes,
    Even with the princes of His people.

Psalm Chant   See MONTHLY SONGS: Lord's Day Fifth—Evening.

Hymn of Praise   See MONTHLY SONGS: Lord's Day Fifth—Evening.

---

40. LORD'S DAY FIRST IN JULY

MORNING

Introductory

Sentence

PRAISE waiteth for Thee, O God, in Zion:
    And unto Thee shall the vow be performed.
O Thou that hearest prayer,
    Unto Thee shall all flesh come.   [Ps. lxv, 1, 2]

Response
[Tune in MONTHLY SONGS]

THE Mighty One, God Je | hovah, hath | spoken,
    And called the earth from the rising of the sun unto the | go-ing | down there- | of.
Out of Zion, the per- | fection of | beauty,
    God | hath | shi-ned | forth.   [Ps. l, 1, 2]

40. LORD'S DAY FIRST IN JULY—MORNING

Scripture Lessons Old Covenant Zech. viii, 1-8.
Gospel Matt. xiii, 31-43.
Apostolic Word 1 Cor. ii, 6-16.

Responsive Lesson A PSALM OF DAVID, Ps. ciii. [Same for Day No. 2, M'ng]

[On the fourth day of July may be used instead, Responsive Lesson for Day No. 64; or for Day No. 3, Evening]

BLESS Jehovah, O my soul;
And all that is within me, bless His Holy Name.
2 Bless Jehovah, O my soul,
And forget not all His benefits:
3 Who forgiveth all thine iniquities;
Who healeth all thy diseases;
4 Who redeemeth thy life from destruction;
Who crowneth thee with lovingkindness and tender mercies:
5 Who satisfieth thy desire with good things;
So that thy youth is renewed like the eagle.
6 Jehovah executeth righteous acts,
And judgments for all that are oppressed.
7 He made known His ways unto Moses,
His doings unto the children of Israel.
8 Jehovah is merciful and gracious,
Slow to anger, and abundant in lovingkindness.
9 He will not always chide;
Neither will He keep His anger forever.
10 He hath not dealt with us after our sins,
Nor rewarded us after our iniquities.
11 For as the heaven is high above the earth,
So great is His lovingkindness toward them that fear Him.
12 As far as the east is from the west,
So far hath He removed our transgressions from us.
13 Like as a father pitieth his children,
So Jehovah pitieth them that fear Him.
14 For He knoweth our frame;
He remembereth that we are dust.
15 As for man, his days are as grass;
As a flower of the field, so he flourisheth.
16 For the wind passeth over it, and it is gone;
And the place thereof shall know it no more.
17 But the lovingkindness of Jehovah is from everlasting to everlasting upon them that fear Him,
And His righteousness unto children's children;
18 To such as keep His covenant,
And to those that remember His precepts to do them.
19 Jehovah hath established His throne in the heavens;
And His kingdom ruleth over all.
20 Bless Jehovah, ye angels of His:
Ye mighty in strength, that fulfill His word,
Hearkening unto the voice of His word.

180   40. LORD'S DAY FIRST IN JULY — MORNING

21 Bless Jehovah, all ye His hosts;
    Ye ministers of His, that do His pleasure.
22 Bless Jehovah, all ye His works,
    In all places of His dominion:
     BLESS JEHOVAH, O MY SOUL.

Psalm Chant

See MONTHLY SONGS: Lord's Day First — Morning.
[On the fourth day of July the Psalm Chant for Day No. 64 may be used instead, at discretion]

Prayer of the Day

GOD of Peace, we pray Thee replenish with Thy Spirit the church which Thou hast called in Thy Son; that we may love that which Thou dost command, and desire that which Thou dost promise; that so, in the midst of all worldly vanity and change, our hearts may be surely fixed where alone are true joys and everlasting peace:

And we beseech Thee, spread this Thy peace over all men, and gather the nations beneath Thy wings:

For Christ our Savior's sake, through whom Thou reconcilest all things unto Thyself who art the Father and the Son and the Holy Spirit — one ever glorious God: AMEN.

Hymn of Praise

See MONTHLY SONGS: Lord's Day First — Morning.
[On the fourth day of July, "Before Jehovah's Awful Throne"]

---

40. EVENING
LORD'S DAY FIRST IN JULY

Introductory

Sentence

LET us search and try our ways, and turn again to Jehovah.
Let us lift up our heart with our hands unto God in the heavens.
    [Lam. iii, 40, 41]

Response
Tune in
[MONTHLY SONGS]

LOOK unto Me, and | be ye | sav'd,
   All the | ends | of the | earth.
Unto Me every | knee shall | bow
   And every | tongue • shall con- | fess unto | God.
    [Is. xlv, 22, 23 (Rom. xiv, 11)]

Scripture Lessons

Old Covenant   Habk. ii, 1–14.
Gospel   John, xii, 44–50.
Apostolic Word   Rev. xx, 11–15.

Responsive Lesson

From Isaiah, lxv.
[On the fourth day of July may be used instead, Responsive Lesson for Day No. 6, Evening; or for Day No. 39, Evening]

I AM inquired of by them that asked not for Me;
   I am found of them that sought Me not:
2 I said, Behold Me, behold Me,
   Unto a nation that was not called by My Name.

40. LORD'S DAY FIRST IN JULY—EVENING

3 I have spread out My hands all the day unto a rebellious people,
   That walketh in a way that is not good,
4 After their own thoughts;
   A people that provoketh Me to My face continually:
5 Who say, Stand by thyself, come not near to me,
   For I am holier than thou.
6 Behold, it is written before Me:
   I will not keep silence, but will recompense,
7 Yea, I will recompense into their bosom, your own iniquities,
   And the iniquities of your fathers together, saith Jehovah,
8 And I will bring forth a seed out of Jacob,
   And out of Judah an inheritor of My mountains:
9 And My chosen shall inherit it,
   And My servants shall dwell there.
10 But ye that forsake Jehovah,
   That forget My holy mountain,
11 That prepare a table for Fortune,
   And that fill up mingled wine unto Destiny;
12 I will destine you to the sword,
   And ye all shall bow down to the slaughter:
13 Because when I called, ye did not answer;
   When I spake, ye did not hear;
14 But ye did that which was evil in Mine eyes,
   And chose that wherein I delighted not.
15 For, behold, I create new heavens,
   And a new earth:
16 And the former things shall not be remembered,
   Nor come into mind.
17 But be ye glad and rejoice forever in that which I create:
   For, behold, I create Jerusalem a rejoicing, and her people a joy.
18 And I will rejoice in Jerusalem,
   And joy in My people:
19 And the voice of weeping shall be no more heard in her,
   Nor the voice of crying.
20 They shall not labor in vain,
   Nor bring forth for calamity;
21 For they are the seed of the blessed of Jehovah,
   And their offspring with them.
22 And it shall come to pass that, before they call, I will answer;
   And while they are yet speaking, I will hear.
23 The wolf and the lamb shall feed together, and the lion shall eat straw like the ox:
   And dust shall be the serpent's food.
24 They shall not hurt nor destroy
   In all My holy mountain, saith Jehovah.

Psalm Chant   See MONTHLY SONGS: Lord's Day First — Evening.

Hymn of Praise   See MONTHLY SONGS: Lord's Day First — Evening.
[On the fourth day of July, "Blest be Thou, O God of Israel"]

41. LORD'S DAY SECOND IN JULY

MORNING

Introductory

Sentence

SERVE Jehovah with gladness;
Come before His presence with singing.
Enter into His gates with thanksgiving,
And into His courts with praise. [Ps. c, 2, 4]

Response
[Tune in
MONTHLY SONGS]

JEHOVAH send thee help from the | sanc-tu- | ary,
And | strength-en | thee • out of | Zion!
Remember | all thine | offerings,
And ac- | cept thy | sac-ri- | fice! [Ps. xx, 1-3]

Scripture Lessons

Old Covenant   1 Kings, xvii, 1-16.
Gospel   Matt. xiii, 44-52.
Apostolic Word   1 Cor. x, 23-33; xi, 1.

Responsive Lesson

From Micah, vi, vii.

HEAR ye now what Jehovah saith:
Arise, contend thou before the mountains,
    And let the hills hear thy voice.
2 Hear, O ye mountains, Jehovah's controversy,
    And ye enduring foundations of the earth:
3 For Jehovah hath a controversy with His people,
    And He will plead with Israel.
4 O My people, what have I done unto thee?
    And wherein have I wearied thee? testify against Me.
5 Wherewith shall I come before Jehovah,
    And bow myself before the high God?
6 Shall I come before Him with burnt offerings,
    With calves of a year old?
7 Will Jehovah be pleased with thousands of rams,
    Or with ten thousands of rivers of oil?
8 Shall I give my firstborn for my transgression,
    The fruit of my body for the sin of my soul?
9 He hath showed thee, O man, what is good;
    And what doth Jehovah require of thee,
10 But to do justly, and to love mercy,
    And to walk humbly with thy God.

11 The voice of Jehovah crieth unto the city,
    And the man of wisdom will see Thy Name:
12 Hear ye the rod,
    And who hath appointed it.
13 Are there yet the treasures of wickedness in the house of the wicked,
    And the scant measure that is abominable?
14 Shall I be pure with wicked balances,
    And with a bag of deceitful weights?

41. LORD'S DAY SECOND IN JULY—MORNING

15 For the rich men thereof are full of violence,
And the inhabitants thereof have spoken lies;
And their tongue is deceitful in their mouth.
16 Therefore I also have smitten thee with a grievous wound;
I have made thee desolate because of thy sins.
17 Thou shalt eat, but not be satisfied;
And thy humiliation shall be in the midst of thee:
18 And thou shalt remove, but shalt not carry away safe;
And that which thou carriest away will I give up to the sword.
19 Thou shalt sow, but shalt not reap:
Thou shalt tread the olives, but shalt not anoint thee with oil;
20 And the vintage,
But shalt not drink the new wine.

21 But as for me, I will look unto Jehovah;
I will wait for the God of my salvation:
MY GOD WILL HEAR ME.
22 Rejoice not against me, O mine enemy: when I fall, I shall arise:
When I sit in darkness, Jehovah shall be a light unto me.
23 I will bear the indignation of Jehovah,
Because I have sinned against Him;
24 Until He plead my cause,
And execute judgment for me:
25 He will bring me forth to the light,
And I shall behold His righteousness.

26 Who is a God like unto Thee, that pardoneth iniquity,
And passeth by the transgression of the remnant of His heritage?
27 He retaineth not His anger forever,
Because He delighteth in lovingkindness.
28 He will turn again,
And have compassion upon us;
29 He will tread our iniquities under foot:
And Thou wilt cast all their sins into the depths of the sea.

Psalm Chant
See MONTHLY SONGS: Lord's Day Second—Morning.

Prayer of the Day

ILLUMINE our minds, Thou Sun of Righteousness, with the pure wisdom, even the light of Thy Holy Spirit:
That we may walk before Thee, O God, in simplicity and godly sincerity all our days, not taking counsel of the world or of the flesh, but seeking only to know and do Thy will in Jesus Christ Thy Son,
Who is Head over all things to Thy Church, living and reigning with the Father and the Spirit—one God, in glory evermore: AMEN.

Hymn of Praise
See MONTHLY SONGS: Lord's Day Second—Morning.

41. EVENING
LORD'S DAY SECOND IN JULY

Introductory

Sentence

PRAISE ye the Name of Jehovah:
Ye that stand in the house of Jehovah,
In the courts of the house of our God.
Blessed be Jehovah out of Zion. [Ps. cxxxv, 1, 2, 21]

Response
[Tune in
MONTHLY SONGS]

LIFT up your hands to the | sanc-tu- | ary,
And | bless | ye Je- | hovah.
Jehovah bless thee | out of | Zion!
Even He that | made | heaven and | earth. [Ps. cxxxiv, 2, 3]

Scripture Lessons   Old Covenant   Prov. xxiii, 17-23, 29-35.
Gospel   Luke, xii, 13-21.
Apostolic Word   Acts, viii, 26-40.

Responsive Lesson   From Psalm lxxi.

IN Thee, O Jehovah, do I take refuge:
   Let me never be put to shame.
2 Deliver me in Thy righteousness, and rescue me:
   Bow down Thine ear unto me, and save me.
3 Be Thou to me a rock of habitation,
   Whereunto I may continually resort:
4 Thou hast given commandment to save me;
   For Thou art my rock and my fortress.
5 Rescue me, O my God, out of the hand of the wicked,
   Out of the hand of the unrighteous and cruel man.
6 For Thou art my hope, O Lord Jehovah:
   Thou art my trust from my youth.
7 By Thee have I been holden up from the womb:
   My praise shall be continually of Thee.
8 I am as a wonder unto many:
   But Thou art my strong refuge.
9 My mouth shall be filled with Thy praise,
   And with Thy honor all the day.
10 Cast me not off in the time of old age;
   Forsake me not when my strength faileth.
11 For mine enemies speak concerning me;
   And they that watch for my soul take counsel together,
12 Saying, God hath forsaken him:
   Pursue and take him; for there is none to deliver.
13 O God, be not far from me:
   O my God, make haste to help me.
14 Let them be put to shame and consumed that are adversaries to my soul;
   Let them be covered with reproach and dishonor that seek my hurt.
15 But I will hope continually,
   And will praise Thee yet more and more.

41. LORD'S DAY SECOND IN JULY—EVENING

16 My mouth shall tell of Thy righteousness,
And of Thy salvation all the day;
For I know not the numbers thereof.
17 I will come with the mighty acts of the Lord Jehovah:
I will make mention of Thy righteousness, even of Thine only.
18 O God, Thou hast taught me from my youth;
And hitherto have I declared Thy wondrous works.
19 Yea, even when I am old and grayheaded,
O God, forsake me not;
20 Until I have declared Thy strength unto the next generation,
Thy might to every one that is to come.
21 Thy righteousness, also, O God, is very high;
Thou who hast done great things,
O GOD, WHO IS LIKE UNTO THEE?
22 Thou, who hast showed us many and sore troubles,
Shalt quicken us again,
And shalt bring us up again from the depths of the earth.
23 Increase Thou my greatness,
And turn again and comfort me.
24 I will also praise Thee with the psaltery,
Even Thy truth, O my God:
25 Unto Thee will I sing praises with the harp,
O Thou Holy One of Israel.
26 My lips shall greatly rejoice when I sing praises unto Thee;
And my soul, which Thou hast redeemed.
27 My tongue also shall talk of Thy righteousness all the day long:
For they are put to shame, for they are confounded, that seek my hurt.

Psalm Chant   See MONTHLY SONGS: Lord's Day Second—Evening.

Hymn of Praise   See MONTHLY SONGS: Lord's Day Second—Evening.

---

42. LORD'S DAY THIRD IN JULY
MORNING

Introductory

Sentence   THE true worshipers shall worship the Father in spirit and truth:
For such doth the Father seek to be His worshipers.
God is a Spirit:
And they that worship Him must worship in spirit and truth.
[John iv, 23, 24]

Response
[Tune in
MONTHLY SONGS]   THOU hast said, | Seek ye • My | face:
My heart saith unto Thee,
Thy face, O Je- | ho-vah, | will I | seek.   [Ps. xxvii, 8]

Scripture Lessons   Old Covenant   Deut. xxx, 11–20.
Gospel   Mark, viii, 27–38.
Apostolic Word   Col. i, 9–20.

42. LORD'S DAY THIRD IN JULY—MORNING

Responsive Lesson Psalms, xcv, xcvii.

O COME, let us sing unto Jehovah:
   Let us make a joyful noise to the rock of our salvation.
2 Let us come before His presence with thanksgiving,
   Let us make a joyful noise unto Him with psalms.
3 For Jehovah is a great God,
   And a great King above all gods.
4 In His hand are the deep places of the earth;
   The heights of the mountains are His also.
5 The sea is His, and He made it;
   And His hands formed the dry land.
6 O come, let us worship and bow down;
   Let us kneel before Jehovah our Maker:
7 For He is our God,
   And we are the people of His pasture,
   And the sheep of His hand.
8 To-day, O that ye would hear His voice!
   Harden not your heart, as at Meribah.
   As in the day of Massah in the wilderness:
9 When your fathers tempted Me,
   Proved me, and saw My work.
10 Forty years long was I grieved with that generation,
   And said, It is a people that do err in their heart,
   And they have not known My ways:
11 Wherefore I sware in My wrath,
   That they should not enter into My rest.

---

12 JEHOVAH reigneth; let the earth rejoice;
   Let the multitude of isles be glad.
13 Clouds and darkness are round about Him:
   Righteousness and justice are the foundation of His throne.
14 A fire goeth before Him,
   And burneth up His adversaries round about.
15 His lightnings lightened the world:
   The earth saw, and trembled.
16 The mountains melted like wax at the presence of Jehovah,
   At the presence of the Lord of the whole earth.
17 The heavens declare His righteousness,
   And all the peoples have seen His glory.
18 Put to shame are all they that serve graven images,
   That boast themselves of idols:
   WORSHIP HIM, ALL YE GODS.
19 Zion heard and was glad,
   And the daughters of Judah rejoiced;
   Because of Thy judgments, O Jehovah.
20 For Thou, Jehovah, art most high above all the earth:
   Thou art exalted far above all gods.
      O YE THAT LOVE JEHOVAH, HATE EVIL:
21 He preserveth the souls of His saints;
   He delivereth them out of the hand of the wicked.

42. LORD'S DAY THIRD IN JULY—MORNING

22 Light is sown for the righteous,
  And gladness for the upright in heart.
23 Be glad in Jehovah, ye righteous;
  And give thanks to His holy memorial Name.

Psalm Chant See MONTHLY SONGS: Lord's Day Third—Morning.

Prayer of the Day

O GOD the Lord, strong to deliver and mighty to save; who in all generations art the dwelling-place of Thy people:
Fulfill in Thy church on earth, we beseech Thee, the work of Thy converting Spirit; that we, who have been called into the way of righteousness, may receive power to continue steadfastly therein until the day of Thy Son Christ Jesus:
For His sake, who with the Father and the Holy Spirit—one God, is worshiped and glorified, world without end: AMEN.

Hymn of Praise See MONTHLY SONGS: Lord's Day Third—Morning.

---

42. EVENING
LORD'S DAY THIRD IN JULY

Introductory

Sentence

I AM come a Light into the world—saith the Lord Jesus—
That whosoever believeth on Me may not abide in the darkness.
He that followeth Me shall have the light of life. [John, xii, 46; viii, 12]

Response
[Tune in
MONTHLY SONGS]

IT shall come to pass that at evening time there | shall be | light.
And it shall come to pass in that day,
That living waters shall go | out • from Je- | ru-sa- | lem.
[Zech. xiv, 7, 8]

Scripture Lessons   Old Covenant   Job, xxii, 12–22.
                        Gospel   Luke, xiii, 23–30.
                        Apostolic Word Acts, xiv, 8–18.

Responsive Lesson   From Isaiah, x, 1–27.

WOE unto them that decree unrighteous decrees,
  And to the writers that write perverseness:
2 To turn aside the needy from justice,
  And to take away the right of the poor of My people,
3 That widows may be their spoil,
  And that they may make the fatherless their prey!
4 And what will ye do in the day of visitation,
  And in the desolation which shall come from far?
5 To whom will ye flee for help?
  And where will ye leave your glory?

42. LORD'S DAY THIRD IN JULY—EVENING

6 Ho Assyrian, the rod of Mine anger,
  The staff in whose hand is My indignation !
7 I will send him against a profane nation,
  And against the people of My wrath will I give him a charge,
8 To take the spoil, and to take the prey,
  And to tread them down like the mire of the streets.
9 Howbeit he meaneth not so,
  Neither does his heart think so ;
10 But it is in his heart to destroy,
  And to cut off nations not a few.
11 For he saith, Are not my princes all of them kings ?
  Is not Calno as Carchemish ? is not Hamath as Arpad ?
  Is not Samaria as Damascus ?
12 As my hand hath found the kingdoms of the idols,
  Whose graven images did excel them of Jerusalem and of Samaria ;
13 Shall I not, as I have done unto Samaria and her idols,
  So do to Jerusalem and her idols ?
14 Wherefore it shall come to pass, that when the Lord hath performed His whole work upon Mount Zion
  And on Jerusalem,
15 I will punish the fruit of the stout heart of the king of Assyria,
  And the glory of his high looks.
16 For he hath said, By the strength of my hand I have done it,
  And by my wisdom ; for I have understanding:
17 And I have removed the bounds of the peoples,
  And have robbed their treasures,
18 And I have brought down as a valiant man them that sit on thrones:
  And my hand hath found as a nest the riches of the peoples ;
19 And as one gathereth eggs that are forsaken,
  Have I gathered all the earth :
20 And there was none that moved the wing,
  Or that opened the mouth, or chirped.
21 Shall the axe boast itself against him that heweth therewith ?
  Shall the saw magnify itself against him that wieldeth it ?
22 As if a rod should wield them that lift it up,
  Or as if a staff should lift up him that is not wood.
23 Therefore shall the Lord, Jehovah of hosts, send among his fat ones leanness ;
  And under his glory there shall be kindled a burning like the burning of fire.
24 And the light of Israel shall be for a fire,
  And his Holy One for a flame :
25 And it shall burn and devour his thorns and his briers in one day.
  And He shall consume the glory of his forest,
26 And of his fruitful field, both soul and body :
  And it shall be as when a standardbearer fainteth.
27 And it shall come to pass in that day, that the remnant of Israel,
  And they that are escaped of the house of Jacob,

42. LORD'S DAY THIRD IN JULY—EVENING

28 Shall no more again lean upon him that smote them;
But shall lean upon Jehovah, the Holy One of Israel, in truth.
29 A remnant shall return,
Even the remnant of Jacob, unto the mighty God.
30 For though thy people, O Israel, be as the sand of the sea,
Only a remnant of them shall return:
31 A consumption is determined,
Overflowing with righteousness.
32 For a consummation, and that determined, shall the Lord, Jehovah of hosts, make
In the midst of all the earth.
33 Therefore thus saith the Lord, Jehovah of hosts,
O My people that dwellest in Zion,
Be not afraid of the Assyrian:
34 Though he smite thee with the rod,
And lift up his staff against thee, after the manner of Egypt.
35 For yet a very little while, and the indignation shall be accomplished,
And Mine anger, in their destruction.
36 And it shall come to pass in that day, that his burden shall depart from off thy shoulder,
And his yoke from off thy neck,
AND THE YOKE SHALL BE DESTROYED BECAUSE OF THE ANOINTING.

Psalm Chant See MONTHLY SONGS: Lord's Day Third—Evening.

Hymn of Praise See MONTHLY SONGS: Lord's Day Third—Evening.

---

43. LORD'S DAY FOURTH IN JULY
MORNING

Introductory

Sentence OUR help is in the Name of Jehovah,
Who made heaven and earth.
Show us Thy lovingkindness, O Jehovah,
And grant us Thy salvation. [Ps. cxxiv, 8; lxxxv, 7]

Response
[Tune in
MONTHLY SONGS]
I HAVE set watchmen upon thy walls, O Je- | ru-sa- | lem;
They shall never hold their | peace | day nor | night:
Ye that are Jehovah's remembrancers, | keep not | silence,
Till He make Jerusalem a | praise | in the | earth. [Is. lxii, 6, 7]

Scripture Lessons Old Covenant 1 Kings, xix, 1–18.
Gospel John, xiv, 1–14.
Apostolic Word Rev. xxi, 1–8.

43. LORD'S DAY FOURTH IN JULY—MORNING

Responsive Lesson From A Psalm of David: Ps. cxxxix.

O JEHOVAH, Thou hast searched me and known me.
Thou knowest my downsitting and mine uprising,
THOU UNDERSTANDEST MY THOUGHT AFAR OFF.
2 Thou searchest out my path and my lying down,
And art acquainted with all my ways.
3 For there is not a word in my tongue,
But, lo, Jehovah, Thou knowest it altogether.
4 Thou hast beset me behind and before,
And laid Thy hand upon me.
5 Such knowledge is too wonderful for me;
It is high, I cannot attain unto it.
6 Whither shall I go from Thy Spirit?
Or whither shall I flee from Thy presence?
7 If I ascend up into heaven, Thou art there:
If I make my bed in Sheol, behold, Thou art there.
8 If I take the wings of the morning,
And dwell in the uttermost parts of the sea;
9 Even there shall Thy hand lead me,
And Thy right hand shall hold me.
10 If I say, Surely the darkness shall overwhelm me,
And the light about me shall be night;
11 Even the darkness hideth not from Thee,
But the night shineth as the day:
THE DARKNESS AND THE LIGHT ARE BOTH ALIKE TO THEE.
12 I will give thanks unto Thee;
For I am fearfully and wonderfully made:
13 Wonderful are Thy works;
And that my soul knoweth right well.
14 My frame was not hidden from Thee, when I was made in secret
And curiously wrought in the lowest parts of the earth.
15 Thine eyes did see mine unformed substance,
And in Thy book were all my members written,
16 Which day by day were fashioned,
When as yet there was none of them.
17 How precious also are Thy thoughts unto me, O God!
How great is the sum of them!
18 If I should count them, they are more in number than the sand:
When I am awake, I am still with Thee.
19 Surely Thou wilt slay the wicked, O God!
Depart from me therefore, ye bloodthirsty men.
20 For they speak against Thee wickedly,
And Thine enemies take Thy Name in vain.
21 Do not I hate them, O Jehovah, that hate Thee?
And am I not grieved against those that rise up against Thee?
22 I hate them with perfect hatred:
They are become mine enemies.
23 Search me, O God, and know my heart:
Try me and know my thoughts:
24 And see if there be any way of wickedness in me,
And lead me in the way everlasting.

43. LORD'S DAY FOURTH IN JULY—MORNING

Psalm Chant See MONTHLY SONGS: Lord's Day Fourth—Morning.

Prayer of the Day

GREAT God, who makest known Thine Almighty power chiefly in showing mercy: receive with fatherly tenderness us sinners who flee from Thy wrath unto Thyself:

And grant unto Thy Church such plenitude of Thy Spirit enlarging our heart, that we may run in the way of Thy commandments, and so may obtain Thy gracious promises and be made partakers of Thy heavenly treasure:

Through Thy Son, our Lord the Christ, to whom with the Father and the Spirit—one God, be glory everlasting: AMEN.

Hymn of Praise See MONTHLY SONGS: Lord's Day Fourth—Morning.

---

43. EVENING
LORD'S DAY FOURTH IN JULY

Introductory

Sentence

THY statutes, O Jehovah, have been my songs
In the house of my pilgrimage.
The opening of Thy words giveth light;
It giveth understanding unto the simple. [Ps. cxix, 54, 130]

Response
[Tune in
MONTHLY SONGS]

THERE is a river, the streams whereof make glad the | city of | God,
The holy place of the | taber-nacles | of the · Most | High.
Jehovah of | Hosts is | with us;
The God of | Ja-cob | is our | refuge. [Ps. xlvi, 4, 7]

Scripture Lessons Old Covenant Deut. xxxiv.
Gospel Matt. xiv, 22–33.
Apostolic Word I Pet. ii, 11–25.

Responsive Lesson From Isaiah, xiv.

THOU shalt take up this parable against the king of Babylon, and say,
How hath the oppressor ceased!
The golden city ceased!
2 Jehovah hath broken the staff of the wicked,
The scepter of the rulers;
3 That smote the peoples in wrath with a continual stroke,
That ruled the nations in anger, with a persecution that none restrained.
4 The whole earth is at rest, and is quiet:
They break forth into singing.

5 Sheol from beneath is moved for thee to meet thee at thy coming:
   It stirreth up the dead for thee,
6 Even all the chief ones of the earth:
   It hath raised up from their thrones all the kings of the nations.
7 All they shall answer and say unto thee,
   Art thou also become weak as we?
   Art thou become like unto us?
8 Thy pomp is brought down to Sheol,
   And the noise of thy viols:
9 The worm is spread under thee,
   And worms cover thee.
10 How art thou fallen from heaven, O day-star, son of the morning!
   How art thou cut down to the ground, who didst lay low the nations!
11 And thou saidst in thy heart, I will ascend into heaven,
   I will exalt my throne above the stars of God;
12 And I will sit upon the mount of congregation,
   In the uttermost parts of the north:
13 I will ascend above the heights of the clouds;
   I will be like the Most High.
14 Yet thou shalt be brought down to Sheol,
   To the uttermost parts of the pit.
15 They that see thee shall narrowly look upon thee,
   They shall consider thee,
16 Saying, Is this the man that made the earth to tremble,
   That did shake kingdoms;
17 That made the world as a wilderness, and overthrew the cities thereof:
   That let not loose his prisoners to their home?
18 All the kings of the nations, all of them, sleep in glory,
   Every one in his own house.
19 But thou art cast forth away from thy sepulcher,
   Like an abominable branch,
20 Clothed with the slain, that are thrust through with the sword,
   That go down to the stones of the pit:
   As a carcase trodden under foot.
21 Prepare ye slaughter for his children
   For the iniquity of their fathers;
22 That they rise not up, and possess the earth,
   And fill the face of the world with cities.
23 And I will rise up against them, saith Jehovah of hosts,
   And cut off from Babylon name and remnant,
   And son and son's son, saith Jehovah.
24 I will also make it a possession for the porcupine, and pools of water:
   And I will sweep it with the besom of destruction, saith Jehovah of hosts.
25 Jehovah of hosts hath sworn, saying,
   Surely as I have thought, so shall it come to pass;
   And as I have purposed, so shall it stand.
26 This is the purpose that is purposed upon the whole earth:
   And this is the hand that is stretched out upon all the nations.

43. LORD'S DAY FOURTH IN JULY—EVENING

27 For Jehovah of hosts hath purposed, and who shall annul it?
And His hand is stretched out, and who shall turn it back?

28 What then shall one answer the messengers of the nation?
That Jehovah hath founded Zion,
AND IN HER SHALL THE AFFLICTED OF HIS PEOPLE TAKE REFUGE.

Psalm Chant See MONTHLY SONGS: Lord's Day Fourth—Evening.

Hymn of Praise See MONTHLY SONGS: Lord's Day Fourth—Evening.

[*NOT IN EVERY YEAR*]

44. LORD'S DAY FIFTH IN JULY
MORNING

Introductory

Sentence

GOD be merciful unto us, and bless us,
And cause His face to shine upon us;
That Thy way may be known upon earth,
Thy salvation among all nations. (Ps. lxvii, 1, 2)

Response
[Tune in
MONTHLY SONGS]

THEY that know Thy Name will put their | trust in | Thee;
For Thou, Jehovah, hast not forsaken | them that | seek | Thee. (Ps. ix, 10)

Scripture Lessons   Old Covenant Num. xx, 1-13.
Gospel Luke, xiv, 15-24.
Apostolic Word II Cor. iv, 16-18; v, 1-10.

Responsive Lesson From Isaiah, lxiii, lxiv.

I WILL make mention of the lovingkindnesses of Jehovah,
And the praises of Jehovah,
2 According to all that Jehovah hath bestowed on us;
And the great goodness toward the house of Israel,
3 Which He hath bestowed on them according to His mercies,
And according to the multitude of His lovingkindnesses.
4 For He said, Surely, they are My people,
Children that will not deal falsely:
So He was their savior.
5 In all their affliction He was afflicted,
And the angel of His presence saved them:
6 In His love and in His pity He redeemed them;
And He bare them, and carried them all the days of old.
7 But they rebelled,
And grieved His holy Spirit:
8 Therefore He was turned to be their enemy,
And Himself fought against them.

44. LORD'S DAY FIFTH IN JULY — MORNING

    9 Then He remembered the days of old,
       Moses, and his people,
  10 Saying, Where is He that brought them up out of the sea with the shepherds of His flock?
       Where is He that put His holy Spirit in the midst of them?
  11 That caused His glorious arm to go at the right hand of Moses?
       That divided the water before them,
       To make Himself an everlasting name?
  12 That led them through the depths, as a horse in the wilderness,
       That they stumbled not?
  13 Look down from heaven,
       And behold from the habitation of Thy holiness and of Thy glory.
  14 For Thou art our Father, though Abraham knoweth us not,
       And Israel doth not acknowledge us:
  15 Thou, Jehovah, art our Father;
       Our Redeemer from everlasting is Thy Name.
  16 O that Thou wouldest rend the heavens,
       That Thou wouldest come down,
       That the mountains might flow down at Thy presence;
  17 As when fire kindleth the brushwood,
       And the fire causeth the waters to boil:
  18 To make Thy Name known to Thine adversaries,
       That the nations may tremble at Thy presence!
  19 When Thou didst terrible things which we looked not for, Thou camest down,
       The mountains flowed down at Thy presence.
  20 For from of old men have not heard,
       Nor perceived by the ear,
  21 Neither hath the eye seen a God beside Thee,
       Who worketh for him that waiteth for Him.
  22 Thou meetest him that rejoiceth and worketh righteousness,
       Those that remember Thee in Thy ways.
  23 For we are all become as one that is unclean,
       And all our righteousnesses are as a polluted garment:
  24 And we all do fade as a leaf;
       And our iniquities, like the wind, take us away.
  25 And there is none that calleth upon Thy Name,
       That stirreth up himself to take hold of Thee:
  26 For Thou hast hid Thy face from us,
       And hast consumed us by means of our iniquities.
  27 But now, O Jehovah, Thou art our Father;
       We are the clay, and Thou our potter:
       AND WE ALL ARE THE WORK OF THY HAND.

Psalm Chant

See MONTHLY SONGS: Lord's Day Fifth — Morning.

Prayer of the Day

GOD Only Wise, who art always more ready to hear than Thy church to pray, and givest more than we either know how to ask or can ever deserve:
Pour down on us the abundance of Thy Spirit, forgiving us those things where-

44. LORD'S DAY FIFTH IN JULY—MORNING

fore our consciences are afraid, and giving us those good things which we are not worthy to ask but through the merit and mediation of Christ Thy Son,
Who abideth in glory with the Father and the Holy Spirit—one God evermore: AMEN.

Hymn of Praise See MONTHLY SONGS: Lord's Day Fifth — Morning.

---

44. EVENING
LORD'S DAY FIFTH IN JULY

Introductory Sentence

LET not the wise man glory in his wisdom, saith Jehovah;
Neither let the mighty man glory in his might,
Let not the rich man glory in his riches;
But let him that glorieth glory in this,
That he understandeth and knoweth Me, that I am Jehovah,
Who exercise lovingkindness, justice, and righteousness in the earth.
[Jer. ix, 23, 24]

Response [Tune in MONTHLY SONGS]

WITH Thee, O God, is the | fountain of | life:
In Thy | light shall | we see | light. [Ps. xxxvi, 9]

Scripture Lessons
Old Covenant   I Sam. viii, 1-10, 19-22.
Gospel   Matt. xv, 29-39.
Apostolic Word   I Tim. vi, 11-21.

Responsive Lesson   PSALMS OF DAVID, Ps. lvii: from lx: lxi.

BE merciful unto me, O God, be merciful unto me;
For my soul taketh refuge in Thee:
2 Yea, in the shadow of Thy wings will I take refuge,
Until these calamities be overpast,
3 I will cry unto God Most High;
Unto God that performeth all things for me.
4 He shall send from heaven, and save me,
When he that would swallow me up reproacheth;
GOD SHALL SEND FORTH HIS LOVINGKINDNESS AND HIS TRUTH.
5 My soul is among lions;
I lie among them that are set on fire,
6 Even the sons of men, whose teeth are spears and arrows,
And their tongue a sharp sword.
7 Be Thou exalted, O God, above the heavens;
Let Thy glory be above all the earth.
8 They have prepared a net for my steps;
My soul is bowed down:
9 They have digged a pit before me;
They are fallen into the midst thereof themselves.

44. LORD'S DAY FIFTH IN JULY — EVENING

10 My heart is fixed, O God, my heart is fixed:
I will sing, yea, I will sing praises.
11 Awake up, my glory; awake, psaltery and harp:
I myself will awake right early.
12 I will give thanks unto Thee, O Lord, among the peoples:
I will sing praises unto Thee among the nations.
13 For Thy lovingkindness is great unto the heavens,
And Thy truth unto the skies.
14 Be Thou exalted, O God, above the heavens;
Let Thy glory be above all the earth.

---

15 O GOD, Thou hast cast us off, Thou hast broken us down;
Thou hast been angry; O restore us again.
16 Thou hast made the land to tremble; Thou hast rent it:
Heal the breaches thereof; for it shaketh.
17 Thou hast shewed Thy people hard things:
Thou hast made us to drink the wine of staggering.
18 Thou hast given a banner to them that fear Thee,
That it may be displayed because of the truth.
19 That Thy beloved may be delivered,
Save with Thy right hand, and answer us.
20 Hast not Thou, O God, cast us off?
And Thou goest not forth, O God, with our hosts.
21 Give us help against the adversary:
For vain is the help of man.
22 Through God we shall do valiantly:
For He it is that shall tread down our adversaries.

---

23 HEAR my cry, O God;
Attend unto my prayer.
24 From the end of the earth will I call unto Thee,
When my heart is overwhelmed:
  LEAD ME TO THE ROCK THAT IS HIGHER THAN I.
25 For Thou hast been a refuge for me,
A strong tower from the enemy.
26 I will dwell in Thy tabernacle forever:
I will take refuge in the covert of Thy wings.
27 For Thou, O God, hast heard my vows:
Thou hast given me the heritage of those that fear Thy Name.
28 Thou wilt prolong the king's life:
His years shall be as many generations.
29 He shall abide before God forever:
O prepare lovingkindness and truth, that they may preserve him.
30 So will I sing praise unto Thy Name forever,
That I may daily perform my vows.

Psalm Chant   See MONTHLY SONGS: Lord's Day Fifth — Evening.

Hymn of Praise   See MONTHLY SONGS: Lord's Day Fifth — Evening.

45. LORD'S DAY FIRST IN AUGUST

MORNING

Introductory

Sentence

PRAISE ye Jehovah.
Praise God in His sanctuary:
Praise Him in the firmament of His power.
Let everything that hath breath praise Jehovah.
Praise ye Jehovah. [Ps. cl, 1, 6]

Response
[Tune in
MONTHLY SONGS]

THE Mighty One, God Je- | hovah, hath | spoken,
And called the earth from the rising of the sun unto the | go-ing | down there- | of.
Out of Zion, the per- | fection of | beauty,
God | hath | shi-ned | forth. [Ps. l, 1, 2]

Scripture Lessons

Old Covenant   Exodus, ii, 23-25; iii, 1-8.
Gospel   John, xv, 1-16.
Apostolic Word   Rom. viii, 11-25.

Responsive Lesson

SONGS OF ASCENTS, OF DAVID, Ps. cxxxiii, cxxii:
OF ASCENTS, cxxiii; cxxxv, 1-7, 13-21.

BEHOLD, how good and how pleasant it is
For brethren to dwell together in unity!
It is like the precious oil upon the head,
2 That ran down upon the beard,
Even Aaron's beard;
That came down upon the skirt of his garments;
3 Like the dew of Hermon,
That cometh down upon the mountains of Zion:
4 For there Jehovah commanded the blessing,
Even life for evermore.

---

5 I WAS glad when they said unto me,
Let us go unto the house of Jehovah.
6 Our feet are standing within thy gates, O Jerusalem;
Jerusalem, that art builded as a city that is compact together:
7 Whither the tribes go up,
Even the tribes of Jehovah,
8 An ordinance for Israel,
To give thanks unto the Name of Jehovah.
9 For there are set thrones for judgment,
The thrones of the house of David.
10 Pray for the peace of Jerusalem:
They shall prosper that love thee.
11 Peace be within thy walls,
And prosperity within thy palaces.
12 For my brethren and companions' sakes,
I will now say, Peace be within thee.
13 For the sake of the house of Jehovah our God
I will seek thy good.

45. LORD'S DAY FIRST IN AUGUST—MORNING

14 Unto Thee do I lift up mine eyes,
O Thou that sittest in the heavens.
15 Behold, as the eyes of servants look unto the hand of their master,
As the eyes of a maiden unto the hand of her mistress ;
16 So our eyes look unto Jehovah our God,
Until He have mercy upon us.
17 Have mercy upon us, O Jehovah, have mercy upon us:
For we are exceedingly filled with contempt.
18 Our soul is exceedingly filled with the scorning of those that are at ease,
And with the contempt of the proud.

---

19 Praise ye Jehovah,
Praise ye the Name of Jehovah.
Praise Him, O ye servants of Jehovah:
20 Ye that stand in the house of Jehovah,
In the courts of the house of our God.
21 Praise ye Jehovah; for Jehovah is good:
Sing praises unto His Name ; for it is pleasant.
22 For Jehovah hath chosen Jacob unto Himself,
And Israel for His own possession.
23 For I know that Jehovah is great,
And that our Lord is above all gods.
24 Whatsoever Jehovah pleased, that hath He done,
In heaven and in earth, in the seas and in all deeps.
25 He causeth the vapors to ascend from the ends of the earth ;
He maketh lightnings for the rain :
He bringeth forth the wind out of His treasuries ;
26 Thy Name, O Jehovah, endureth forever;
Thy memorial Name, O Jehovah, throughout all generations.
27 For Jehovah shall judge His people,
And repent Himself concerning His servants.

28 The idols of the nations are silver and gold,
The work of men's hands.
29 They have mouths, but they speak not;
Eyes have they, but they see not ;
30 They have ears, but they hear not;
Neither is there any breath in their mouths.
31 They that make them shall be like unto them;
Yea, every one that trusteth in them.
32 O house of Israel, bless ye Jehovah :
O house of Aaron, bless ye Jehovah :
33 O house of Levi, bless ye Jehovah :
Ye that fear Jehovah, bless ye Jehovah.
34 Blessed be Jehovah out of Zion,
Who dwelleth at Jerusalem.
Praise ye Jehovah.

Psalm Chant   See Monthly Songs: Lord's Day First—Morning.

45. LORD'S DAY FIRST IN AUGUST — MORNING

Prayer of the Day

O GOD who dwellest in Zion, who through Thy Holy Spirit hast espoused Thy Church in one body to Thy Son:
Bestow on us a strong and steadfast faith in this great mystery of grace; that thus Thy Church, delivered from all sects and schisms, may keep the unity of Thy Spirit: and we beseech Thee, draw all men into this living Body:
And make all members therein to grow up in all things into Him who is the Head, even Christ; that they all may be one in Him, who is one with the Father and the Spirit — God over all, blessed forevermore: AMEN.

Hymn of Praise

See MONTHLY SONGS: Lord's Day First — Morning.

---

45. EVENING
LORD'S DAY FIRST IN AUGUST

Introductory

Sentence

JEHOVAH reigneth; let the peoples tremble:
He sitteth above the cherubim; let the earth be moved.
Jehovah is great in Zion;
And He is high above all the peoples. [Ps. xcix, 1, 2]

Response [Tune in MONTHLY SONGS]

LOOK unto Me, and | be ye | sav'd,
All the | ends | of the | earth.
Unto Me every | knee shall | bow,
And every | tongue • shall con- | fess unto | God.
[Is. xlv, 22, 23 (Rom. xiv, 11)]

Scripture Lessons

Old Covenant   Exodus, iii, 9-15.
Gospel   Luke, xv, 1-10.
Apostolic Word   1 John, ii, 1-11.

Responsive Lesson

From Isaiah, xliv.

HEAR, O Jacob, My servant;
   And Israel, whom I have chosen:
2 Thus saith Jehovah that made thee, and formed thee from the womb,
   Who will help thee:
3 Fear not, O Jacob, My servant;
   And thou, Jeshurun, whom I have chosen.
4 For I will pour water upon him that is thirsty,
   And streams upon the dry ground:
5 I will pour My Spirit upon thy seed,
   And My blessing upon thine offspring:
6 And they shall spring up among the grass,
   As willows by the water-courses.
7 One shall say, I am Jehovah's;
   And another shall call himself by the name of Jacob;

45. LORD'S DAY FIRST IN AUGUST—EVENING

8 And another shall subscribe with his hand unto Jehovah,
  And surname himself by the name of Israel.
9 Thus saith Jehovah, the King of Israel,
  And his Redeemer, Jehovah of hosts:
10 I am the First, and I am the Last;
  And beside Me there is no God.
11 They that fashion a graven image are all of them vanity;
  And their delectable things shall not profit:
12 And their own witnesses see not, nor know;
  That they may be put to shame.
13 He feedeth on ashes:
  A deceived heart hath turned him aside,
14 That he cannot deliver his soul,
  Nor say, Is there not a lie in my right hand?
15 Remember these things, O Jacob;
  And Israel, for thou art My servant:
16 I have formed thee; thou art My servant:
  O Israel, thou shalt not be forgotten of Me.
17 I have blotted out, as a thick cloud, thy transgressions,
  And as a cloud, thy sins:
18 Return unto Me;
  For I have redeemed thee.
19 Sing, O ye heavens, for Jehovah hath done it;
  Shout, ye lower parts of the earth;
20 Break forth into singing, ye mountains,
  O forest, and every tree therein:
21 For Jehovah hath redeemed Jacob,
  And will glorify Himself in Israel.
22 Thus saith Jehovah, thy Redeemer,
  And He that formed thee from the womb:
23 I am Jehovah, that maketh all things;
  That stretcheth forth the heavens alone;
  That spreadeth abroad the earth; who is with Me?
24 That frustrateth the tokens of the liars,
  And maketh diviners mad;
25 That turneth wise men backward,
  And maketh their knowledge foolish:
26 That confirmeth the word of His servant,
  And performeth the counsel of His messengers;
27 That saith of Jerusalem, She shall be inhabited;
  And of the cities of Judah, They shall be built,
  AND I WILL RAISE UP THE WASTE PLACES THEREOF:
28 That saith to the deep, Be dry,
  And I will dry up thy rivers:
29 Even saying of Jerusalem, She shall be built;
  And of the temple, Thy foundation shall be laid.

Psalm Chant   See MONTHLY SONGS: Lord's Day First—Evening.

Hymn of Praise   See MONTHLY SONGS: Lord's Day First—Evening.

46. LORD'S DAY SECOND IN AUGUST

Introductory
MORNING

Sentence

MY King and my God, Blessed are they that dwell in Thy house.
Blessed is the man whose strength is in Thee;
In whose heart are the high-ways to Zion. [Ps. lxxxiv, 3-5]

Response
[Tune in
Monthly Songs]

JEHOVAH send thee help from the | sanc-tu- | ary,
 And | strength-en | thee • out of | Zion!
Remember | all thine | offerings,
 And ac- | cept thy | sac-ri- | fice! [Ps. xx, 1-3]

Scripture Lessons
Old Covenant — Lev. xix, 9–18.
Gospel — John, xv, 17–27.
Apostolic Word — Rom. viii, 26–39.

Responsive Lesson
From Jeremiah, ix, x.

THUS saith Jehovah, Let not the wise man glory in his wisdom,
Neither let the mighty man glory in his might,
Let not the rich man glory in his riches:
2 But let him that glorieth glory in this,
That he understandeth, and knoweth Me,
3 That I am Jehovah who exercise lovingkindness, justice, and righteousness, in the earth:
For in these things I delight, saith Jehovah.
4 Thus saith Jehovah, Learn not the way of the nations,
And be not dismayed at the signs of heaven;
5 For the nations are dismayed at them.
For the customs of the peoples are vanity.
6 There is none like unto Thee, O Jehovah;
Thou art great, and Thy Name is great in might.
7 Who would not fear Thee, O King of the nations?
For to Thee doth it appertain:
8 Forasmuch as among all the wise men of the nations,
And in all their royal estate, there is none like unto Thee.
9 But they are together brutish and foolish:
The instruction of idols, it is but a stock.
10 But Jehovah is the true God;
He is the living God, and an everlasting King:
11 At His wrath the earth trembleth,
And the nations are not able to abide His indignation.
12 The gods that have not made the heavens and the earth,
These shall perish from the earth, and from under the heavens.
13 He hath made the earth by His power,
He hath established the world by His wisdom,
AND BY HIS UNDERSTANDING HATH HE STRETCHED OUT THE HEAVENS:
14 When He uttereth His voice, there is a tumult of waters in the heavens,
And He causeth the vapors to ascend from the ends of the earth;

46. LORD'S DAY SECOND IN AUGUST—MORNING

15 He maketh lightnings for the rain,
   And bringeth forth the wind out of His treasuries.
16 Every man is become brutish and is without knowledge;
   Every goldsmith is put to shame by his graven image:
17 For his molten image is falsehood,
   And there is no breath in them.
18 They are vanity, a work of delusion:
   In the time of their visitation they shall perish.
19 The portion of Jacob is not like these;
   For He is the former of all things;
20 And Israel is the tribe of His inheritance:
   Jehovah of Hosts is His Name.

21 Woe is me for my hurt! my wound is grievous:
   But I said, Truly this is my grief, and I must bear it:
22 My tent is despoiled, and all my cords are broken:
   My children are gone forth of me, and they are not.
23 There is none to stretch forth my tent any more,
   And to set up my curtains.
24 For the shepherds are become brutish,
   And have not inquired of Jehovah:
25 Therefore they have not prospered,
   And all their flocks are scattered.
26 The voice of tidings, behold it cometh,
   And a great commotion out of the north country,
27 To make the cities of Judah a desolation,
   A dwelling-place of jackals.
28 O Jehovah, I know that the way of man is not in himself:
   It is not in man that walketh to direct his steps.
29 O Jehovah, correct me, but in measure;
   Not in Thine anger, lest Thou bring me to nothing.

Psalm Chant
See MONTHLY SONGS: Lord's Day Second—Morning.

Prayer of the Day

GIVER of every good and perfect gift: we seek from Thee the increase of faith, hope, and love, by the grace of Thy Spirit in all Thy Church:

And, that we may obtain that which Thou dost promise, make us to love that which Thou dost require:

For the sake of Thy Son our Savior, who with the Father and the Holy Spirit is glorified—one God now and ever: AMEN.

Hymn of Praise
See MONTHLY SONGS: Lord's Day Second—Morning.

46. EVENING
LORD'S DAY SECOND IN AUGUST

Introductory

Sentence
O COME, let us worship and bow down:
Let us kneel before Jehovah our Maker.
For He is our God, and we are the people of His pasture,
And the sheep of His hand. [Ps. xcv, 6, 7]

Response
[Tune in Monthly Songs]
LIFT up your hands to the | sanc-tu- | ary,
And | bless | ye Je- | hovah.
Jehovah bless thee | out of | Zion!
Even He that | made | heav'n and | earth. [Ps. cxxxiv, 2, 3]

Scripture Lessons
Old Covenant II Kings, iv, 1-7.
Gospel Luke, xv, 11-24 (or -32).
Apostolic Word I John, ii, 15-25.

Responsive Lesson Psalm cii.

HEAR my prayer, O Jehovah,
And let my cry come unto Thee.
  Hide not Thy face from me in the day of my distress.
2 Incline Thine ear unto me;
  In the day when I call, answer me speedily.
3 For my days consume away like smoke,
  And my bones are burned as a firebrand.
4 My heart is smitten like grass, and withered;
  For I forget to eat my bread.
5 By reason of the voice of my groaning
  My bones cleave to my flesh.
6 I am like a pelican of the wilderness;
  I am become as an owl of the waste places.
7 I watch, and am become like a sparrow
  That is alone upon the housetop.
8 Mine enemies reproach me all the day;
  They that are mad against me do curse by me.
9 For I have eaten ashes like bread,
  And mingled my drink with weeping.
10 Because of Thine indignation and Thy wrath:
  For Thou hast taken me up, and cast me away.
11 My days are like a shadow that declineth;
  And I am withered like grass.
12 But Thou, Jehovah, shalt abide forever;
  And Thy memorial Name unto all generations.
13 Thou shalt arise, and have mercy upon Zion:
  For it is time to have pity upon her,
  Yea, the set time is come.
14 For Thy servants take pleasure in her stones,
  And have pity upon her dust.
15 So the nations shall fear the Name of Jehovah,
  And all the kings of the earth Thy glory:

46. LORD'S DAY SECOND IN AUGUST—EVENING

16 For Jehovah hath built up Zion,
   He hath appeared in His glory;
17 He hath regarded the prayer of the destitute,
   And hath not despised their prayer.
18 This shall be written for the generation to come:
   And a people which shall be created shall praise Jehovah.
19 For He hath looked down from the height of His sanctuary;
   From heaven did Jehovah behold the earth;
20 To hear the sighing of the prisoner;
   To loose those that are appointed to death;
21 That men may declare the Name of Jehovah in Zion,
   And His praise in Jerusalem;
22 When the peoples are gathered together,
   And the kingdoms, to serve Jehovah.

23 He weakened my strength in the way;
   He shortened my days.
24 I said, O my God, take me not away in the midst of my days:
   Thy years are throughout all generations.
25 Of old hast Thou laid the foundation of the earth;
   And the heavens are the work of Thy hands.
26 They shall perish, but Thou shalt endure:
   Yea, all of them shall wax old like a garment;
27 As a vesture shalt Thou change them,
   And they shall be changed:
28 But Thou art the same,
   And Thy years shall have no end.
29 The children of Thy servants shall continue,
   And their seed shall be established before Thee.

Psalm Chant See MONTHLY SONGS: Lord's Day Second — Evening.

Hymn of Praise See MONTHLY SONGS: Lord's Day Second — Evening.

---

47. LORD'S DAY THIRD IN AUGUST

Introductory MORNING

Sentence

SEEK ye Jehovah while He may be found,
Call ye upon Him while He is near:
Let the wicked forsake his way,
And the unrighteous man his thoughts:
And let him return unto Jehovah, and He will have mercy upon him,
And to our God, for He will abundantly pardon. [Is. lv, 6, 7]

Response
[Tune in
MONTHLY SONGS]

THOU hast said, | Seek ye • My | face :
   My heart saith unto Thee,
   Thy face, O Je- | ho-vah, | will I | seek. [Ps. xxvii, 8]

47. LORD'S DAY THIRD IN AUGUST — MORNING

Scripture Lessons Old Covenant Jer. xviii, 1-12.
　　　　　　　　　　Gospel   Matt. xvi, 13-20.
　　　　　　　　　　Apostolic Word Acts, xvi, 25-40.

Responsive Lesson   Psalm cxvi:
THE LAST WORDS OF THE PSALMIST DAVID, II Sam. xxiii, 1-5.

1 I LOVE Jehovah, because He heareth my voice
　　And my supplications.
2 Because He hath inclined His ear unto me,
　　Therefore will I call upon Him as long as I live
3 The cords of death compassed me.
　　And the pains of Sheol gat hold upon me:
4 I found trouble and sorrow.
　Then called I upon the Name of Jehovah:
　　O Jehovah, I beseech Thee, deliver my soul.
5 Gracious is Jehovah, and righteous;
　　Yea, our God is merciful.
6 Jehovah preserveth the simple:
　　I was brought low, and He saved me.
7 Return unto thy rest, O my soul;
　　For Jehovah hath dealt bountifully with thee.
8 For Thou hast delivered my soul from death,
　　Mine eyes from tears,
9 And my feet from falling.
　　I will walk before Jehovah in the land of the living.
10 I believe, for I will speak:
　I was greatly afflicted:
　　I said in my haste, all men are a lie.
11 What shall I render unto Jehovah for all His benefits toward me?
　　I will take the cup of salvation, and call upon the Name of Jehovah.
12 I will pay my vows unto Jehovah,
　　Yea, in the presence of all His people.
13 Precious in the sight of Jehovah is the death of His saints.
　　O Jehovah, truly I am Thy servant:
14 I am Thy servant, the son of Thine handmaid;
　　Thou hast loosed my bonds.
15 I will offer to Thee the sacrifice of thanksgiving,
　　And will call upon the Name of Jehovah.
16 I will pay my vows unto Jehovah,
　　Yea, in the presence of all His people ;
17 In the courts of Jehovah's house,
　　In the midst of thee, O Jerusalem,
　　PRAISE YE JEHOVAH.

---

18 DAVID the son of Jesse saith,
　　And the man who was raised on high saith,
19 The anointed of the God of Jacob,
　　And the sweet psalmist of Israel:
20 The Spirit of Jehovah spake by me,
　　And His word was upon my tongue.

47. LORD'S DAY THIRD IN AUGUST—MORNING

21 The God of Israel said,
The Rock of Israel spake to me:
22 One that ruleth over men righteously,
That ruleth in the fear of God,
23 He shall be as the light of the morning, when the sun riseth,
A morning without clouds;
24 When the tender grass springeth out of the earth.
Through clear shining after rain.
25 Verily my house is not so with God;
Yet He hath made with me an everlasting covenant,
26 Ordered in all things, and sure:
For it is all my salvation, and all my desire.

Psalm Chant
See MONTHLY SONGS: Lord's Day Third — Morning.

Prayer of the Day
O GOD, the High and Holy One, who inhabitest eternity:
Glorify Thy grace, we beseech Thee, in the midst of our manifold weakness and sin; and in all our temptations hold us up with Thy mighty hand, through the Holy Spirit, the Comforter and Keeper of Thy flock:
For the sake of Thy Son who loved the Church and gave Himself for it; unto whom with the Father and the Spirit — one God — be glory without end: AMEN.

Hymn of Praise
See MONTHLY SONGS: Lord's Day Third — Morning.

---

47. EVENING
LORD'S DAY THIRD IN AUGUST

Introductory

Sentence

GIVE ear unto my voice, O Jehovah, when I call unto Thee,
Let my prayer be set forth as incense before Thee;
The lifting up of my hands as the evening sacrifice. [Ps. cxli, 1, 2]

Response
[Tune in MONTHLY SONGS]

IT shall come to pass that at evening time there | shall be | light.
And it shall come to pass in that day,
That living waters shall go | out · from Je- | ru-sa- | lem.
[Zech. xiv, 7, 8]

Scripture Lessons
Old Covenant   II Kings, v, 1–16.
Gospel   Matt. xviii, 1–9.
Apostolic Word   Heb. xii, 1–13.

Responsive Lesson
Jeremiah, xvi, 19–21; xvii, 1, 3–14.

O JEHOVAH, my strength, and my strong hold,
And my refuge in the day of affliction,
2 Unto Thee shall the nations come
From the ends of the earth,

47. LORD'S DAY THIRD IN AUGUST—EVENING

3 And shall say, Our fathers have inherited nought but lies,
Even vanity and things wherein there is no profit.
4 Shall a man make unto himself gods,
Which yet are no gods?
5 Therefore, behold, I will cause them to know,
This once will I cause them to know Mine hand and My might;
AND THEY SHALL KNOW THAT MY NAME IS JEHOVAH.

6 The sin of Judah is written with a pen of iron,
And with the point of a diamond:
7 It is graven upon the table of their heart,
And upon the horns of your altars.
8 O My mountain in the field,
I will give thy substance and all thy treasures for a spoil,
And thy high places, because of sin, throughout all thy borders.
9 And thou, even of thyself, shalt discontinue from thine heritage
that I gave thee;
And I will cause thee to serve thine enemies in the land which thou knowest not:
10 For ye have kindled a fire in Mine anger
Which shall burn forever.

11 Thus saith Jehovah: Cursed is the man that trusteth in man,
And maketh flesh his arm,
And whose heart departeth from Jehovah.
12 For he shall be like the heath in the desert,
And shall not see when good cometh;
13 But shall inhabit the parched places in the wilderness,
A salt land and not inhabited.
14 Blessed is the man that trusteth in Jehovah,
And whose hope Jehovah is.
15 For he shall be as a tree planted by the waters,
And that spreadeth out his roots by the river,
16 And shall not fear when heat cometh,
But his leaf shall be green;
17 And shall not be careful in the year of drought,
Neither shall cease from yielding fruit.
18 The heart is deceitful above all things,
And it is desperately sick: who can know it?
19 I Jehovah search the heart,
I try the reins,
20 Even to give every man according to his ways,
According to the fruit of his doings.
21 As the partridge that sitteth on eggs which she hath not laid,
So is he that getteth riches, and not by right;
22 In the midst of his days they shall leave him,
And at his end he shall be a fool.

23 A glorious throne, set on high from the beginning, is the place of
our sanctuary,
O Jehovah, the Hope of Israel, all that forsake Thee shall be put to shame;

47. LORD'S DAY THIRD IN AUGUST — EVENING

24 They that depart from Me shall be written in the earth,
  Because they have forsaken Jehovah, the fountain of living waters.
25 Heal me, O Jehovah, and I shall be healed;
  Save me, and I shall be saved:
  FOR THOU ART MY PRAISE.

Psalm Chant See MONTHLY SONGS: Lord's Day Third — Evening.

Hymn of Praise See MONTHLY SONGS: Lord's Day Third — Evening.

---

48. LORD'S DAY FOURTH IN AUGUST
MORNING

Introductory

Sentence

LOOK down from heaven,
  And behold from the habitation of Thy holiness and of Thy glory.
Thou, Jehovah, art our Father;
Our Redeemer from everlasting, is Thy Name. [Is. lxiii, 15, 16]

Response
[Tune in
MONTHLY SONGS]

I HAVE set watchmen upon thy walls, O Je- | ru-sa- | lem ;
  They shall never hold their | peace | day nor | night :
Ye that are Jehovah's remembrancers, | keep not | silence,
  Till He make Jerusalem a | praise | in the | earth. [Is. lxii, 6, 7]

Scripture Lessons   Old Covenant Ezekiel, xxxiii, 10 – 20.
            Gospel   Matt. xviii, 10 – 22.
            Apostolic Word Acts, xvii, 22 – 31.

Responsive Lesson   From the FAREWELL SONG OF MOSES, Deut. xxxii.

GIVE ear, ye heavens, and I will speak;
  And let the earth hear the words of my mouth :
2 My doctrine shall drop as the rain,
  My speech shall distill as the dew ;
3 As the small rain upon the tender grass,
  And as the showers upon the herb :
4 For I will proclaim the Name of Jehovah :
  Ascribe ye greatness unto our God.
5 The Rock, His work, is perfect ;
  For all His ways are judgment :
6 A God of faithfulness and without iniquity,
  Just and right is He.
7 They have dealt corruptly with Him, they are not His children,
    it is their blemish ;
  They are a perverse and crooked generation.

48. LORD'S DAY FOURTH IN AUGUST — MORNING

8 Do ye thus requite Jehovah,
   O foolish people and unwise?
9 Remember the days of old,
   Consider the years of many generations.
10 Ask thy father, and he will show thee;
   Thine elders, and they will tell thee.
11 When the Most High gave to the nations their inheritance,
   When He separated the children of men,
12 He set the bounds of the peoples
   According to the number of the children of Israel.
13 For Jehovah's portion is His people:
   Jacob is the lot of His inheritance.
14 He found him in a desert land,
   And in the waste howling wilderness;
15 He compassed him about, He cared for him,
   He kept him as the apple of His eye:
16 As an eagle that stirreth up her nest,
   That fluttereth over her young,
17 He spread abroad His wings, He took them,
   He bare them on His pinions:
18 Jehovah alone did lead him,
   And there was no strange god with him.
19 He made him ride on the high places of the earth,
   And he did eat the increase of the field.

20 Then he forsook God who made him,
   And lightly esteemed the Rock of his salvation.
21 They moved Him to jealousy with strange gods,
   With abominations provoked they Him to anger.
22 Of the Rock that begat thee thou art unmindful,
   And hast forgotten God that gave thee birth.
23 And Jehovah saw it, and abhorred them,
   Because of the provocation of His sons and His daughters.
24 And He said, I will hide My face from them,
   I will see what their end shall be:
25 For they are a very perverse generation,
   Children in whom is no faith.
26 They have moved Me to jealousy with that which is not God;
   They have provoked Me to anger with their vanities:
27 And I will move them to jealousy with those who are not a people;
   I will provoke them to anger with a foolish nation.
28 For a fire is kindled in Mine anger,
   And burneth unto the lowest Sheol,
29 And devoureth the earth with her increase,
   And setteth on fire the foundations of the mountains.
30 For they are a nation void of counsel,
   And there is no understanding in them.
31 O that they were wise, that they understood this,
   That they would consider their latter end!
32 How should one chase a thousand,
   And two put ten thousand to flight,

48. LORD'S DAY FOURTH IN AUGUST — MORNING

33 Except their Rock had sold them,
And Jehovah had delivered them up?
34 For their rock is not as our Rock,
Even our enemies themselves being judges.

Psalm Chant
See MONTHLY SONGS: Lord's Day Fourth — Morning.

Prayer of the Day

GOD of Mercy, in Christ's Name we beseech Thee for ourselves, as for all whom the Lord our God doth call to be of His Church:
That we, being made obedient unto the calling of Thy Son Jesus Christ, may forsake all worldly affections; and denying covetousness and all lusts of the flesh, may evermore follow the motions of Thy Holy Spirit,
Who is one with the Father and the Son — God in glory everlasting: AMEN.

Hymn of Praise
See MONTHLY SONGS: Lord's Day Fourth — Morning.

---

48. EVENING
LORD'S DAY FOURTH IN AUGUST

Introductory

Sentence

I WILL wash my hands in innocency;
So will I compass Thine altar, O Jehovah:
That I may make the voice of thanksgiving to be heard,
And tell of all Thy wondrous works. [Ps. xxvi, 6, 7]

Response
[Tune in MONTHLY SONGS]

THERE is a river, the streams whereof make glad the | city of | God,
The holy place of the | taber-nacles | of the · Most | High.
Jehovah of | Hosts is | with us;
The God of | Ja-cob | is our | refuge. [Ps. xlvi, 4, 7]

Scripture Lessons

Old Covenant — II Kings, vi, 8 – 18.
Gospel — John, xvi, 16 – 24.
Apostolic Word — Eph. vi, 1 – 9.

Responsive Lesson
A PSALM OF ASAPH, Psalm lxxvii.

I WILL cry unto God with my voice;
Even unto God with my voice, and He will give ear unto me.
2 In the day of my trouble I sought Jehovah:
My hand was stretched out in the night, and slacked not;
My soul refused to be comforted.
3 I remember God, and am disquieted:
I complain, and my spirit is overwhelmed.

48. LORD'S DAY FOURTH IN AUGUST—EVENING

4 Thou holdest mine eyes watching:
   I am so troubled that I cannot speak.
5 I have considered the days of old,
   The years of ancient times.
6 I call to remembrance my song in the night:
   I commune with mine own heart;
   And my spirit made diligent search.
7 Will Jehovah cast off forever?
   And will He be favorable no more?
8 Is his lovingkindness clean gone forever?
   Doth His promise fail for evermore?
9 Hath God forgotten to be gracious?
   Hath He in anger shut up His tender mercies?
10 And I said, This is my infirmity;
   But I will remember the years of the right hand of the Most High.
11 I will make mention of the deeds of Jehovah;
   For I will remember Thy wonders of old.
12 I will meditate also upon all Thy work,
   And muse on Thy doings.
13 Thy way, O God, is in the sanctuary:
   Who is a great God like unto God?
14 Thou art the God that doest wonders:
   Thou hast made known Thy strength among the peoples.
15 Thou hast with Thine arm redeemed Thy people,
   The sons of Jacob and Joseph.
16 The waters saw Thee, O God;
   The waters saw Thee, they were afraid:
17 The depths also trembled.
   The clouds poured out water;
   The skies sent out a sound:
18 Thine arrows also went abroad.
   The voice of Thy thunder was in the whirlwind;
19 The lightnings lightened the world:
   The earth trembled and shook.
20 Thy way was in the sea,
   And Thy paths in the great waters,
   And Thy footsteps were not known.
21 Thou leddest Thy people like a flock,
   By the hand of Moses and Aaron.

Psalm Chant   See MONTHLY SONGS: Lord's Day Fourth — Evening.

Hymn of Praise   See MONTHLY SONGS: Lord's Day Fourth — Evening.

[*NOT IN EVERY YEAR*]

49. LORD'S DAY FIFTH IN AUGUST
MORNING

Introductory

Sentence   JEHOVAH sitteth as King forever.
Jehovah will give strength unto His people;
Jehovah will bless His people with peace.   [Ps. xxix, 10, 11]

Response
[Tune in
Monthly Songs]

THEY that know Thy Name will put their | trust in | Thee;
For Thou, Jehovah, hast not forsaken | them that | seek |
Thee.   [Ps. ix, 10]

Scripture Lessons   Old Covenant   Joshua, xxiv, 14–25.
Gospel   Matt. xviii, 21–35.
Apostolic Word   II Tim. iii, 14–17; iv, 1–8.

Responsive Lesson   Isaiah, lvii, 14–21; lviii.   [Same for Day No. 19, M'ng]

CAST ye up, cast ye up, prepare the way,
    Take up the stumbling-block out of the way of my people.
2 For thus saith the high and lofty One that inhabiteth eternity,
    Whose Name is Holy:
3 I dwell in the high and holy place,
    With him also that is of a contrite and humble spirit,
4 To revive the spirit of the humble,
    And to revive the heart of the contrite ones.
5 For I will not contend forever,
    Neither will I be always wroth:
6 For the spirit should fail before Me,
    And the souls that I have made.
7 I create the fruit of the lips: Peace, peace, to him that is far off
    And to him that is near, saith Jehovah; and I will heal him.
8 But the wicked are like the troubled sea; for it cannot rest,
    And its waters cast up mire and dirt.
       THERE IS NO PEACE, SAITH MY GOD, TO THE WICKED.

9 Cry aloud, spare not,
    Lift up thy voice like a trumpet,
10 And declare unto My people their transgression,
    And to the house of Jacob their sins.
11 Yet they seek Me daily,
    And delight to know My ways:
12 As a nation that did righteousness,
    And forsook not the ordinance of their God,
13 They ask of Me righteous ordinances,
    They delight to draw near unto God.
14 Wherefore have we fasted, say they, and Thou seest not?
    Wherefore have we afflicted our soul, and Thou takest no knowledge?
15 Behold, in the day of your fast ye find your own pleasure,
    And exact all your labors.

49. LORD'S DAY FIFTH IN AUGUST — MORNING

16 Behold, ye fast for strife and contention,
  And to smite with the fist of wickedness:
    Ye fast not this day so as to make your voice to be heard on high.
17 Is such the fast that I have chosen?
    The day for a man to afflict his soul?
18 Is it to bow down his head as a rush,
    And to spread sackcloth and ashes under him?
19 Wilt thou call this a fast,
    And an acceptable day to Jehovah?
20 Is not this the fast that I have chosen?
  To loose the bonds of wickedness,
    To undo the bands of the yoke,
21 And to let the oppressed go free,
    And that ye break every yoke?
22 Is it not to deal thy bread to the hungry,
    And that thou bring the poor that are cast out to thy house?
23 When thou seest the naked, that thou cover him;
    And that thou hide not thyself from thine own flesh?
24 Then shall thy light break forth as the morning,
    And thy healing shall spring forth speedily:
25 And thy righteousness shall go before thee;
    The glory of Jehovah shall be thy rearward.
26 Then shalt thou call, and Jehovah shall answer;
    Thou shalt cry, and He shall say, Here I am.
27 If thou take away from the midst of thee the yoke,
    The putting forth of the finger, and speaking wickedly;
28 And if thou draw out thy soul to the hungry,
    And satisfy the afflicted soul;
29 Then shall thy light rise in darkness,
    And thine obscurity be as the noonday:
30 And Jehovah shall guide thee continually,
    And satisfy thy soul in dry places, and make strong thy bones:
31 And thou shalt be like a watered garden,
    And like a spring of water, whose waters fail not.
32 And they that shall be of thee shall build the old waste places:
    Thou shalt raise up the foundations of many generations;
33 And thou shalt be called The repairer of the breach,
    The restorer of paths to dwell in.
34 If thou turn away thy foot from the Sabbath,
    From doing thy pleasure on My holy day;
35 And call the Sabbath a delight,
    And the holy of Jehovah honorable;
36 And shalt honor it, not doing thine own ways,
    Nor finding thine own pleasure, nor speaking thine own words:
37 Then shalt thou delight thyself in Jehovah;
    And I will make thee to ride upon the high places of the earth;
38 And I will feed thee with the heritage of Jacob thy father:
    For the mouth of Jehovah hath spoken it.

Psalm Chant   See MONTHLY SONGS: Lord's Day Fifth — Morning.

49. LORD'S DAY FIFTH IN AUGUST—MORNING

Prayer of the Day

LORD, who hast called Thy Church unto Thyself:
Make Thy grace always to go before us and to follow us; causing us to be given continually unto all good works, the fruits of faith;
Which are wrought in us only by Thy blessed Spirit through Christ Thy Son in oneness with Thee, O Father, the God of glory evermore: AMEN.

Hymn of Praise

See MONTHLY SONGS: Lord's Day Fifth —Morning.

---

49. EVENING
LORD'S DAY FIFTH IN AUGUST

Introductory

Sentence

NOT unto us, O Jehovah, not unto us,
But unto Thy Name, give glory,
For Thy lovingkindness and for Thy truth's sake. [Ps. cxv, 1]

Response
[Tune in
MONTHLY SONGS]

WITH Thee, O God, is the | fountain of | life:
In Thy | light shall | we see | light. [Ps. xxxvi, 9]

Scripture Lessons

Old Covenant — Jonah, iii; iv, 1-5.
Gospel — Mark, x, 46-52.
Apostolic Word — Gal. v, 25, 26; vi, 1-10.

Responsive Lesson

From ASAPH, Psalm lxxviii, 1-39.

GIVE ear, O my people, to my law:
Incline your ears to the words of my mouth.
2 I will open my mouth in a parable;
I will utter dark sayings of old:
3 Which we have heard and known,
And our fathers have told us.
4 We will not hide them from their children,
Telling to the generation to come the praises of Jehovah,
5 And His strength,
And His wondrous works that He hath done.
6 For He established a testimony in Jacob,
And appointed a law in Israel,
7 Which He commanded our fathers,
That they should make them known to their children:
8 That the generation to come might know them,
Even the children who should be born;
9 Who should arise and tell them to their children:
That they might set their hope in God,
10 And not forget the works of God,
But keep His commandments:

49. LORD'S DAY FIFTH IN AUGUST—EVENING

11 And might not be as their fathers,
   A stubborn and rebellious generation ;
12 A generation that set not their heart aright,
   And whose spirit was not steadfast with God.
13 The children of Ephraim, being armed and carrying bows,
   Turned back in the day of battle.
14 They kept not the covenant of God,
   And refused to walk in His law ;
15 And they forgat His doings,
   And His wondrous works that He had showed them.
16 Marvelous things did He in the sight of their fathers,
   In the land of Egypt, in the field of Zoan.
17 He clave the sea, and caused them to pass through ;
   And He made the waters to stand as a heap.
18 In the day-time also He led them with a cloud,
   And all the night with a light of fire.
19 He clave rocks in the wilderness,
   And gave them drink abundantly as out of the depths.
20 He brought streams also out of the rock,
   And caused waters to run down like rivers.
21 Yet went they on still to sin against Him,
   To rebel against the Most High in the desert.
22 And they tempted God in their heart
   By asking food for their lust.
23 Yea, they spake against God ;
   They said, Can God prepare a table in the wilderness ?
24 Behold, He smote the rock, that waters gushed out,
   And streams overflowed ;
25 Can He give bread also ?
   Will He provide flesh for His people ?
26 Therefore Jehovah heard, and was wroth :
   And a fire was kindled against Jacob,
   And anger also went up against Israel ;
27 Because they believed not in God,
   And trusted not in His salvation.
28 Yet He commanded the skies above,
   And opened the doors of heaven ;
29 And He rained down manna upon them to eat,
   And gave them of the grain of heaven.
30 Man did eat the bread of the mighty :
   He sent them food to the full.
31 He caused the east wind to blow in the heaven :
   And by His power He guided the south wind.
32 He rained flesh also upon them as the dust,
   And winged fowl as the sand of the seas :
33 And He let it fall in the midst of their camp,
   Round about their habitations.
34 So they did eat, and were well filled ;
   And He gave them that they lusted after.
35 They were not estranged from their lust,
   Their food was yet in their mouths,

49. LORD'S DAY FIFTH IN AUGUST—EVENING

36 When the anger of God went up against them,
And slew of the fattest of them,
And smote down the young men of Israel.
37 For all this they sinned still,
And believed not in His wondrous works.
38 Therefore their days did He consume in vanity,
And their years in terror.
39 When He slew them, then they inquired after Him:
And they returned and sought God early.
40 And they remembered that God was their rock,
And the Most High God their redeemer.
41 But they flattered Him with their mouth,
And lied unto Him with their tongue.
42 For their heart was not right with Him,
Neither were they faithful in His covenant.
43 But He, being merciful, forgave their iniquity,
And destroyed them not:
44 Yea, many a time turned He His anger away,
And did not stir up all His wrath.
45 And He remembered that they were but flesh;
A wind that passeth away, and cometh not again.

Psalm Chant   See MONTHLY SONGS: Lord's Day Fifth—Evening.

Hymn of Praise   See MONTHLY SONGS: Lord's Day Fifth—Evening.

---

50. LORD'S DAY FIRST IN SEPTEMBER
MORNING

Introductory

Sentence

SING unto Jehovah, all the earth.
Sing unto Jehovah, bless His Name;
Show forth His salvation from day to day.
Honor and majesty are before Him:
Strength and beauty are in His sanctuary.   [Ps. xcvi, 1, 2, 6]

Response
[Tune in
MONTHLY SONGS]

THE Mighty One, God Je- | hovah, hath | spoken,
And called the earth from the rising of the sun unto the | go-ing | down there- | of.
Out of Zion, the per- | fection of | beauty,
God | hath | shi-ned | forth.   [Ps. l, 1, 2]

Scripture Lessons   Old Covenant   I Chron. xxix, 6–19.
Gospel   Mark, xii, 35–44.
Apostolic Word   Rev. xxi, 9–14, 21–27.

Responsive Lesson

Psalms, cxlviii, cxlix, cl.

PRAISE ye Jehovah.
Praise ye Jehovah from the heavens:
Praise Him in the heights.
2 Praise ye Him, all His angels:
Praise ye Him, all His host.
3 Praise ye Him, sun and moon:
Praise Him, all ye stars of light.
4 Praise Him, ye heaven of heavens,
And ye waters that be above the heavens.
5 Let them praise the Name of Jehovah:
For He commanded, and they were created.
6 He hath also established them for ever and ever:
He hath made a decree which shall not pass away.
7 Praise Jehovah from the earth,
Ye dragons, and all deeps:
8 Fire and hail, snow and vapor;
Stormy wind, fulfilling His word:
9 Mountains and all hills;
Fruitful trees and all cedars:
10 Beasts and all cattle;
Creeping things and flying fowl:
11 Kings of the earth and all peoples;
Princes and all judges of the earth:
12 Both young men and maidens;
Old men and children:
13 Let them praise the Name of Jehovah;
For His Name alone is exalted:
14 His glory is above the earth and heaven.
And He hath lifted up the horn of His people,
15 The praise of all His saints;
Even of the children of Israel, a people near unto Him.
PRAISE YE JEHOVAH.

---

16 PRAISE ye Jehovah.
Sing unto Jehovah a new song,
And His praise in the assembly of the saints.
17 Let Israel rejoice in Him that made him:
Let the children of Zion be joyful in their King.
18 Let them praise His Name in the dance:
Let them sing praises unto Him with the timbrel and harp.
19 For Jehovah taketh pleasure in His people:
He will beautify the meek with salvation.
20 Let the saints exult in glory:
Let them sing for joy upon their beds.
21 Let the high praises of God be in their mouth,
And a two-edged sword in their hand;
22 To execute vengeance upon the nations,
And punishments upon the peoples;

50. LORD'S DAY FIRST IN SEPTEMBER—MORNING

23 To bind their kings with chains,.
   And their nobles with fetters of iron;
24 To execute upon them the judgment written:
   This honor have all His saints.
   PRAISE YE JEHOVAH.

---

25 PRAISE ye Jehovah.
   Praise God in His sanctuary:
   Praise Him in the firmament of His power.
26 Praise Him for His mighty acts:
   Praise Him according to His excellent greatness.
27 Praise Him with the sound of the trumpet:
   Praise Him with the psaltery and harp.
28 Praise Him with the timbrel and dance:
   Praise Him with stringed instruments and the pipe.
29 Praise Him upon the loud cymbals:
   Praise Him upon the high sounding cymbals.
30 Let everything that hath breath praise Jehovah.
   PRAISE YE JEHOVAH.

Psalm Chant   See MONTHLY SONGS: Lord's Day First—Morning.

Prayer of the Day

CAST Thy bright beams of light upon Thy Church, O God: That, bringing forth plenteously the fruit of good works from faith, we may be a people for Thy praise, and in the power of Thy Spirit may hasten the glory of His Kingdom, who is the Light of all nations,

Even Thy Son our Savior, who liveth and reigneth with the Father and the Holy Spirit—ever one God: AMEN.

Hymn of Praise   See MONTHLY SONGS: Lord's Day First—Morning.

---

50. EVENING
LORD'S DAY FIRST IN SEPTEMBER

Introductory

Sentence

O JEHOVAH, our Lord,
   How excellent is Thy Name in all the earth!
Who hast set Thy glory upon the heavens.   [Ps. viii, 1]

Response
Tune in
[MONTHLY SONGS]

LOOK unto Me, and | be ye | sav'd,
   All the | ends | of the | earth.
Unto Me every | knee shall | bow,
   And every | tongue • shall con- | fess unto | God.

[Is. xlv, 22, 23 (Rom. xiv, 11)]

50. LORD'S DAY FIRST IN SEPTEMBER — EVENING

Scripture Lessons
Old Covenant — Zech. viii, 9-23.
Gospel — John, xvi, 25-33.
Apostolic Word — James, i, 19-27.

Responsive Lesson Jer. xxix, 11-14; xxx, 10-24.

I KNOW the thoughts that I think toward you, saith Jehovah,
Thoughts of peace, and not of evil,
To give you hope in your latter end.
2 And ye shall call upon Me, and ye shall go and pray unto Me,
And I will hearken unto you.
3 And ye shall seek Me, and find Me,
When ye shall search for Me with all your heart.
4 And I will be found of you, saith Jehovah,
And I will turn again your captivity,
5 And I will gather you from all the nations,
And from all the places whither I have driven you, saith Jehovah;
6 And I will bring you again unto the place
Whence I caused you to be carried away captive.

7 Therefore fear thou not, O Jacob My servant, saith Jehovah;
Neither be dismayed, O Israel:
8 For, lo, I will save thee from afar,
And thy seed from the land of their captivity;
9 And Jacob shall return, and shall be quiet and at ease,
And none shall make him afraid.
10 For I am with thee, saith Jehovah, to save thee:
For I will make a full end of all the nations whither I have scattered thee,
But I will not make a full end of thee;
11 But I will correct thee in measure,
And will in no wise leave thee unpunished.

12 For thus saith Jehovah: Thy hurt is incurable,
And thy wound grievous.
13 There is none to plead thy cause, that thou mayest be bound up:
Thou hast no healing medicines.
14 All thy lovers have forgotten thee;
They seek thee not:
15 For I have wounded thee with the wound of an enemy,
With the chastisement of a cruel one;
16 For the greatness of thine iniquity,
Because thy sins were increased.
17 Why criest thou for thy hurt? thy pain is incurable.
For the greatness of thine iniquity,
Because thy sins were increased, I have done these things unto thee.
18 Therefore all they that devour thee shall be devoured;
And all thine adversaries, every one of them, shall go into captivity;
19 And they that spoil thee shall be a spoil,
And all that prey upon thee will I give for a prey.
20 For I will restore health unto thee,
And I will heal thee of thy wounds, saith Jehovah;

21 Because they have called thee an outcast,
   Saying, It is Zion, whom no man seeketh after.
22 Thus saith Jehovah: Behold, I will turn again the captivity of Jacob's tents,
   And have compassion on his dwelling-places;
23 And the city shall be builded upon her own heap,
   And the palace shall remain after the manner thereof.
24 And out of them shall proceed thanksgiving
   And the voice of them that make merry:
25 And I will multiply them, and they shall not be few;
   I will also glorify them, and they shall not be small.
26 Their children also shall be as aforetime,
   And their congregation shall be established before Me,
27 And I will punish all that oppress them.
   And their prince shall be of themselves,
   And their ruler shall proceed from the midst of them;
28 And I will cause him to draw near, and he shall approach unto Me:
   For who is he that hath had boldness to approach unto Me? saith Jehovah.
29 And ye shall be My people,
   And I will be your God.
30 Behold the tempest of Jehovah, even His wrath, is gone forth,
   A sweeping tempest: it shall burst upon the head of the wicked.
31 The fierce anger of Jehovah shall not return,
   Until He have executed,
32 And till He have performed the intents of His heart:
   In the latter days ye shall understand it.

Psalm Chant   See MONTHLY SONGS: Lord's Day First—Evening.

Hymn of Praise   See MONTHLY SONGS: Lord's Day First—Evening.

---

51. LORD'S DAY SECOND IN SEPTEMBER

Introductory

MORNING

Sentence

BLESSED is the man that trusteth in Jehovah,
   And whose hope Jehovah is.
A glorious throne, set on high from the beginning,
Is the place of our sanctuary.   [Jer. xvii, 7, 12]

Response
[Tune in
MONTHLY SONGS]

JEHOVAH send thee help from the | sanc-tu- | ary,
   And | strength-en | thee · out of | Zion!
Remember | all thine | offerings,
   And ac- | cept thy | sac-ri- | fice!   [Ps. xx, 1-3]

51. LORD'S DAY SECOND IN SEPTEMBER — MORNING

Scripture Lessons
Old Covenant   II Chron. vii, 11–22.
Gospel   Matt. xix, 1–9.
Apostolic Word   Eph. v, 22–33.

Responsive Lesson   A PSALM OF DAVID, Ps. li.   [Same for Day No. 19, Ev'g]

HAVE mercy upon me, O God,
  According to Thy lovingkindness:
2 According to the multitude of Thy tender mercies
  Blot out my transgressions.
3 Wash me thoroughly from mine iniquity,
  And cleanse me from my sin.
4 For I acknowledge my transgressions:
  And my sin is ever before me.
5 Against Thee, Thee only, have I sinned,
  And done that which is evil in Thy sight:
6 That Thou mayest be justified when Thou speakest,
  And be clear when Thou judgest.
7 Behold, I was shapen in iniquity;
  And in sin did my mother conceive me.
8 Behold, Thou desirest truth in the inward parts:
  And in the hidden part Thou shalt make me to know wisdom.
9 Purge me with hyssop, and I shall be clean:
  Wash me, and I shall be whiter than snow.
10 Make me to hear joy and gladness;
  That the bones which Thou hast broken may rejoice.
11 Hide Thy face from my sins,
  And blot out all mine iniquities.
12 Create in me a clean heart, O God;
  And renew a right spirit within me.
13 Cast me not away from Thy presence;
  And take not Thy holy Spirit from me.
14 Restore unto me the joy of Thy salvation:
  And uphold me with a willing spirit.
15 Then will I teach transgressors Thy ways;
  And sinners shall be converted unto Thee.
16 Deliver me from bloodguiltiness, O God, Thou God of my salvation;
  And my tongue shall sing aloud of Thy righteousness.
17 O Lord, open Thou my lips;
  And my mouth shall show forth Thy praise.
18 For Thou delightest not in sacrifice; else would I give it:
  Thou hast no pleasure in burnt offering.
19 The sacrifices of God are a broken spirit:
  A broken and a contrite heart, O God, Thou wilt not despise.

20 Do good in Thy good pleasure unto Zion:
  Build Thou the walls of Jerusalem.
21 Then shalt Thou delight in the sacrifices of righteousness,
  In burnt offering and whole burnt offering:
  Then shall they offer bullocks upon Thine altar.

51. LORD'S DAY SECOND IN SEPTEMBER — MORNING

Psalm Chant   See MONTHLY SONGS: Lord's Day Second — Morning.

Prayer of the Day

MERCIFUL Lord God, the Fountain of all wisdom, who knowest our necessities before we ask, and our ignorance in asking:

Have compassion on our infirmities; and those good things which, for our unworthiness we dare not, or for our blindness we cannot ask, vouchsafe to give us, with the grace of Thy Spirit and for the worthiness of our Savior Christ Thy Son:

And to God, the Father and the Son and the Spirit, be glory in the Church, throughout all ages: AMEN.

Hymn of Praise   See MONTHLY SONGS: Lord's Day Second — Morning.

---

51. EVENING
LORD'S DAY SECOND IN SEPTEMBER

Introductory

Sentence

STAND up and bless Jehovah your God from everlasting to everlasting:
And blessed be Thy glorious Name which is exalted above all blessing and praise. [Neh. ix, 5]

Response
[Tune in
MONTHLY SONGS]

LIFT up your hands to the | sanc-tu- | ary,
And | bless | ye Je- | hovah.
Jehovah bless thee | out of | Zion!
Even He that | made | heaven and | earth. [Ps. cxxxiv, 2, 3]

Scripture Lessons
Old Covenant   Jer. xxxiv, 8–17.
Gospel   Luke, xvii, 11–19.
Apostolic Word   Rom. xii, 1–9.

Responsive Lesson   From Hosea, x, xi, xii, xiii.

ISRAEL is a luxuriant vine,
   Which putteth forth his fruit:
2 According to the abundance of his fruit he hath multiplied his altars;
   According to the goodness of his land they have made goodly pillars.
3 Their heart is divided;
   Now shall they be found guilty:
4 He shall smite their altars,
   He shall spoil their pillars.
5 Sow to yourselves in righteousness,
   Reap according to lovingkindness;
6 Break up your fallow ground:
   For it is time to seek Jehovah,
   Till He come and rain righteousness upon you.

51. LORD'S DAY SECOND IN SEPTEMBER — EVENING

7 Ye have plowed wickedness, ye have reaped iniquity;
   Ye have eaten the fruit of lies:
8 For thou didst trust in thy way,
   In the multitude of thy mighty men.
9 Therefore shall a tumult arise among thy people,
   And all thy fortresses shall be spoiled.

10 When Israel was a child, then I loved him,
   And called My son out of Egypt.
11 I taught Ephraim to go;
   I took them on Mine arms:
   But they knew not that I healed them.
12 I drew them with cords of a man,
   With bands of love.
13 And My people are bent to backsliding from Me:
   Though they call them to Him that is on high,
   None at all will exalt Him.
14 How shall I give thee up, Ephraim?
   How shall I deliver thee, Israel?
15 How shall I make thee as Admah?
   How shall I set thee as Zeboim?
16 My heart is turned within Me,
   My compassions are kindled together.
17 I will not execute the fierceness of Mine anger,
   I will not return to destroy Ephraim:
18 For I am God, and not man;
   The Holy One in the midst of thee.

19 Ephraim feedeth on wind,
   And followeth after the east wind.
20 Jehovah hath also a controversy with Judah,
   And will punish Jacob according to his ways:
   According to his doings will He recompense him.
21 In his manhood he had power with God:
   Yea, he had power over the Angel, and prevailed:
22 He wept, and made supplication unto Him:
   He found Him at Beth-el, and there He spake with us;
23 Even Jehovah, the God of hosts;
   Jehovah is His memorial Name.
24 Therefore turn thou to thy God:
   Keep lovingkindness and judgment,
   And wait for thy God continually.

25 Ephraim said, Surely I have become rich, I have found me wealth:
   In all my labors they shall find in me none iniquity that were sin.
26 When Ephraim spake, there was trembling;
   He exalted himself in Israel:
   But when he offended in Baal, he died.
27 Therefore they shall be as the morning cloud,
   And as the dew that passeth early away,   [ing-floor,
28 As the chaff that is driven with the whirlwind out of the thresh-
   And as the smoke out of the chimney.

51. LORD'S DAY SECOND IN SEPTEMBER—EVENING

29 Yet I am Jehovah, thy God from the land of Egypt;
And thou shalt know no god but Me,
And beside Me there is no savior.
30 According to their pasture, so were they filled,
They were filled, and their heart was exalted:
Therefore have they forgotten Me.
31 It is thy destruction, O Israel, that thou art against Me,
Against thy help.
32 Where now is thy king, that he may save thee in all thy cities?
And thy judges, of whom thou saidst, Give me a king and princes?
33 I have given thee a king in Mine anger,
And have taken him away in My wrath.
34 I will ransom them from the power of the grave;
I will redeem them from death:
35 O death, where are thy plagues?
O grave, where is thy destruction?

Psalm Chant   See MONTHLY SONGS: Lord's Day Second—Evening.

Hymn of Praise   See MONTHLY SONGS: Lord's Day Second—Evening.

---

52. LORD'S DAY THIRD IN SEPTEMBER
MORNING

Introductory

Sentence

UNTO THEE do I lift up mine eyes,
O Thou that sittest in the heavens.
Our eyes look unto Jehovah our God,
Until He have mercy upon us.   [Ps. cxxiii, 1, 2]

Response
[Tune in
MONTHLY SONGS]

THOU hast said, | Seek ye • My | face:
My heart saith unto Thee,
Thy face, O Je- | ho-vah, | will I | seek.   [Ps. xxvii, 8]

Scripture Lessons   Old Covenant   II Chron. xxxvi, 11–21.
                             Gospel   John, xvii, 1–19.
                             Apostolic Word   I John, iii, 1–11.

Responsive Lesson   From Job, xxxiii, xxxiv.

GOD speaketh once,
Yea, twice, though man regardeth it not.
2 In a dream, in a vision of the night,
When deep sleep falleth upon men,
In slumberings upon the bed;
3 Then He openeth the ears of men,
And sealeth their instruction,

4 That He may withdraw man from his purpose,
   And hide pride from man;
5 He keepeth back his soul from the pit,
   And his life from perishing by the sword.
6 He is chastened also with pain upon his bed,
   And with continual strife in his bones:
7 So that his life abhorreth bread,
   And his soul dainty food.
8 His flesh is consumed away, that it cannot be seen;
   And his bones that were not seen stick out.
9 Yea, his soul draweth near unto the pit,
   And his life to the destroyers.

10 If there be with him an angel, an interpreter,
   One among a thousand, to show unto man what is right for him;
11 Then He is gracious unto him, and saith,
   Deliver him from going down to the pit,
   I have found a ransom.
12 His flesh shall be fresher than a child's;
   He returneth to the days of his youth:
13 He prayeth unto God, and He is favorable unto him;
   So that he seeth His face with joy:
   And He restoreth unto man his righteousness.
14 He singeth before men, and saith, I have sinned,
   And perverted that which was right, and it profited me not:
15 He hath redeemed my soul from going into the pit,
   And my life shall behold the light.
16 Lo, all these things doth God work,
   Twice, yea thrice, with a man,
17 To bring back his soul from the pit,
   That he may be enlightened with the light of the living.

18 For the work of a man shall He render unto him,
   And cause every man to find according to His ways.
19 Yea, of a surety, God will not do wickedly,
   Neither will the Almighty pervert judgment.
20 If He set His heart upon man,
   If He gather unto Himself his spirit and his breath;
21 All flesh shall perish together,
   And man shall turn again unto dust.

22 He respecteth not the persons of princes,
   Nor regardeth the rich more than the poor;
23 For they all are the work of His hands.
   In a moment they die, even at midnight;
24 The people are shaken and pass away,
   And the mighty are taken away without hand.
25 For His eyes are upon the ways of a man,
   And He seeth all his goings.
26 There is no darkness, nor shadow of death,
   Where the workers of iniquity may hide themselves.

52. LORD'S DAY THIRD IN SEPTEMBER — MORNING

27 For He needeth not further to consider a man,
   That he should go before God in judgment.
28 He breaketh in pieces mighty men in ways past finding out,
   And setteth others in their stead.
29 Therefore He taketh knowledge of their works;
   And He overturneth them in the night, so that they are destroyed.
30 He striketh them as wicked men
   In the open sight of others;
31 Because they turned aside from following Him,
   And would not have regard to any of His ways:
32 So that they caused the cry of the poor to come unto Him,
   And He heard the cry of the afflicted.
33 When He giveth quietness, who then can condemn?
   And when He hideth His face, who then can behold Him?
34 Alike, whether it be done unto a nation, or unto a man:
   That the godless man reign not,
   That there be none to ensnare the people.
35 For hath any said unto God, I have borne chastisement,
   I will not offend any more:
36 That which I see not teach Thou me:
   If I have done iniquity, I will do it no more?

Psalm Chant   See MONTHLY SONGS: Lord's Day Third — Morning.

Prayer of the Day

GOD of the Eternal Covenant, who by Thy Spirit dost build Thy Church upon the foundation of the apostles and prophets — Jesus Christ Himself being the chief Corner-Stone:

Grant that we and all who are baptized into the confession of Thy Son may stand fast in Thy covenant, keeping the unity of the Spirit in the bond of peace, and being joined evermore with Thy holy and universal Church, the Body of Christ:

Through His sacrifice who is the gracious Shepherd and Bishop of our souls, who is glorified with the Father and the Holy Spirit — one God for evermore: AMEN.

Hymn of Praise   See MONTHLY SONGS: Lord's Day Third — Morning.

---

52. EVENING
LORD'S DAY THIRD IN SEPTEMBER

Introductory
Sentence

LIGHT is sown for the righteous,
And gladness for the upright in heart.
Rejoice in Jehovah, ye righteous,
And give thanks to His holy memorial Name —
His memorial Name unto all generations.

[Ps. xcvii, 11, 12: Ex. iii, 15]

52. LORD'S DAY THIRD IN SEPTEMBER—EVENING

Response [Tune in MONTHLY SONGS]

IT shall come to pass that at evening time there | shall be | light. And it shall come to pass in that day, That living waters shall go | out • from Je- | ru-sa- | lem.
[Zech. xiv, 7, 8]

Scripture Lessons Old Covenant Prov. xxviii, 1-14.
Gospel Luke, xviii, 9-14 (or -17).
Apostolic Word Rom. xii, 10-21.

Responsive Lesson A PSALM OF DAVID: Ps. cxliv: SONG OF ASCENTS, OF SOLOMON, from Ps. cxxvii: from Ps. cxxviii.

BLESSED be Jehovah my Rock,
Who teacheth my hands to war,
  And my fingers to fight:
2 My Lovingkindness, and my Fortress,
  My High Tower, and my Deliverer;
3 My Shield, and He in whom I take refuge;
  Who subdueth my people under me.
4 O Jehovah, what is man, that Thou takest knowledge of him?
  Or the son of man, that Thou makest account of him?
5 Man is like to vanity:
  His days are as a shadow that passeth away.
6 Bow Thy heavens, O Jehovah, and come down:
  Touch the mountains, and they shall smoke.
7 Cast forth lightning, and scatter them;
  Send out Thine arrows, and discomfit them.
8 Stretch forth Thine hand from above; rescue me,
  And deliver me out of great waters,
9 Out of the hand of aliens, whose mouth speaketh deceit,
  And their right hand is a right hand of falsehood.
10 I will sing a new song unto Thee, O God:
  Upon a psaltery of ten strings will I sing praises unto Thee.
11 It is He that giveth salvation unto kings:
  Who rescueth David His servant from the hurtful sword.
12 Rescue me, and deliver me out of the hand of aliens,
Whose mouth speaketh deceit,
  And their right hand is a right hand of falsehood.
13 When our sons shall be as plants grown up in their youth;
  And our daughters as corner-stones hewn after the fashion of palace;
14 When our garners are full, affording all manner of store;
  And our sheep bring forth thousands and ten thousands in our fields;
15 When our oxen are well laden;
When there is no breaking in, and no going forth,
  And no outcry in our streets;
16 Happy is the people that is in such a case:
  Yea, happy is the people, whose God is Jehovah.

17 EXCEPT Jehovah build the house, they labor in vain that build it:
  Except Jehovah keep the city, the watchman waketh but in vain.

52. LORD'S DAY THIRD IN SEPTEMBER — EVENING

18 It is vain for you that ye rise up early, and so late take rest,
   And eat the bread of toil:
   FOR SO HE GIVETH UNTO HIS BELOVED SLEEP.
19 Lo, children are a heritage of Jehovah:
   As arrows in the hand of a mighty man,
   So are the children of youth.

---

20 BLESSED is every one that feareth Jehovah,
   That walketh in His ways.
21 For thou shalt eat the labor of thine hands:
   Happy shalt thou be, and it shall be well with thee.
22 Thy children shall be like olive plants, round about thy table.
   Behold, that thus shall the man be blessed that feareth Jehovah.
23 Jehovah shall bless thee out of Zion:
   And thou shalt see the good of Jerusalem all the days of thy life.
24 Yea, thou shalt see thy children's children.
   PEACE BE UPON ISRAEL.

Psalm Chant See MONTHLY SONGS: Lord's Day Third — Evening.

Hymn of Praise See MONTHLY SONGS: Lord's Day Third — Evening.

---

53. LORD'S DAY FOURTH IN SEPTEMBER
MORNING

Introductory

Sentence

THERE shall be a day, that the watchmen upon the hills shall cry —
Arise ye, and let us go up to Zion unto Jehovah our God.
And they shall come and sing in the height of Zion,
And shall flow together unto the goodness of Jehovah. [Jer. xxxi, 6, 12]

Response
[Tune in MONTHLY SONGS]

I HAVE set watchmen upon thy walls, O Je- | ru-sa- | lem;
  They shall never hold their | peace | day nor | night:
Ye that are Jehovah's remembrancers, | keep not | silence,
  Till He make Jerusalem a | praise | in the | earth. [Is. lxii, 6, 7]

Scripture Lessons
  Old Covenant Deut. xv, 7–15.
  Gospel   John, xvii, 20–26.
  Apostolic Word II Peter, i, 16–21.

Responsive Lesson   A PSALM OF DAVID, Ps. xxv.

UNTO Thee, O Jehovah, do I lift up my soul.
  O my God, in Thee have I trusted,
2 Let me not be put to shame:
  Let not mine enemies triumph over me.
3 Yea, none that wait for Thee shall be put to shame.
  They shall be put to shame that deal treacherously without cause.
4 Show me Thy ways, O Jehovah: teach me Thy paths.
  Guide me in Thy truth, and teach me;

53. LORD'S DAY FOURTH IN SEPTEMBER—MORNING

5 For Thou art the God of my salvation;
  For Thee do I wait all the day. [nesses:
6 Remember, O Jehovah, Thy tender mercies and Thy lovingkind-
  For they have been ever of old.
7 Remember not the sins of my youth,
  Nor my transgressions:
8 According to Thy lovingkindness remember Thou me,
  For Thy goodness' sake, O Jehovah.
9 Good and upright is Jehovah:
  Therefore will He instruct sinners in the way.
10 The meek will He guide in judgment:
  And the meek will He teach His way.
11 All the paths of Jehovah are lovingkindness and truth
  Unto such as keep His covenant and His testimonies.
12 For Thy Name's sake, O Jehovah,
  Pardon mine iniquity, for it is great.
13 What man is he that feareth Jehovah?
  Him shall He instruct in the way that he shall choose.
14 His soul shall dwell at ease;
  And his seed shall inherit the land.
15 The secret of Jehovah is with them that fear Him;
  And He will show them His covenant.
16 Mine eyes are ever toward Jehovah;
  For He shall pluck my feet out of the net.
17 Turn Thee unto me, and have mercy upon me:
  For I am desolate and afflicted.
  The troubles of my heart are enlarged:
18 O bring Thou me out of my distresses.
  Consider mine affliction and my travail;
  And forgive all my sins.
19 Consider mine enemies, for they are many;
  And they hate me with cruel hatred.
20 O keep my soul, and deliver me:
  Let me not be put to shame, for I take refuge in Thee.
21 Let integrity and uprightness preserve me,
  For I wait for Thee,
  Redeem Israel, O God, out of all his troubles.

Psalm Chant   See MONTHLY SONGS: Lord's Day Fourth—Morning.

Prayer of the Day

JEHOVAH Most Gracious, who seest that we put not our trust in anything that we are or can do:
  Mercifully defend us against all adversities, or, so mightily aid us therein by Thy Spirit that we faint not under them, but bring forth fruit with patience, in the Name of Thy Son our Savior;
  That in Thy Church Thou mayest be glorified, who art the eternal God—the Father and the Son and the Spirit: AMEN.

Hymn of Praise   See MONTHLY SONGS: Lord's Day Fourth—Morning.

53. EVENING
LORD'S DAY FOURTH IN SEPTEMBER

Introductory

Sentence

O COME, let us sing unto Jehovah:
Let us make a joyful noise to the Rock of our salvation.
Let us come before His presence with thanksgiving,
Let us make a joyful noise unto Him with psalms. [Ps. xcv, 1, 2]

Response
[Tune in
Monthly Songs]

THERE is a river, the streams whereof make glad the | city
of | God,
The holy place of the | taber-nacles | of the · Most | High.
Jehovah of | Hosts is | with us;
The God of | Ja-cob | is our | refuge. [Ps. xlvi, 4, 7]

Scripture Lessons

Old Covenant   Amos, v, 4-15.
Gospel   Matt. xx, 17-28.
Apostolic Word Acts, xix, 1-7.

Responsive Lesson   THE DOOM OF EGYPT, Ezekiel, xxxi, 2-16.

THUS saith Jehovah: Whom art thou like in thy greatness?
Behold, the Assyrian was a cedar in Lebanon with fair branches,
And with a shadowing shroud,
2 And of a high stature;
And his top was among the thick boughs.
3 The waters nourished him,
The deep made him to grow:
4 Her rivers ran round about her plantation;
And she sent out her channels unto all the trees of the field.
5 Therefore his stature was exalted above all the trees of the field;
And his boughs were multiplied,
6 And his branches became long by reason of many waters,
When he shot them forth.
7 All the fowls of heaven made their nests in his boughs,
And under his branches did all the beasts of the field bring forth
their young,
And under his shadow dwelt all great nations.
8 Thus was he fair in his greatness, in the length of his branches:
For his root was by many waters.
9 The cedars in the garden of God could not hide him:
The fir trees were not like his boughs,
10 And the plane trees were not as his branches;
Nor was any tree in the garden of God like unto him in his beauty.
11 I made him fair by the multitude of his branches:
So that all the trees of Eden, that were in the garden of God, envied him.
12 Therefore thus saith the Lord Jehovah:
Because thou art exalted in stature,
13 And he hath set his top among the thick boughs,
And his heart is lifted up in his height;

53. LORD'S DAY FOURTH IN SEPTEMBER — EVENING

14 I will even deliver him into the hand of the mighty one of the nations;
He shall surely deal with him:
I have driven him out for his wickedness.
15 And strangers, the terrible of the nations, have cut him off,
And have left him:
16 Upon the mountains and in all the valleys his branches are fallen,
And his boughs are broken by all the water-courses of the land;
17 And all the peoples of the earth are gone down from his shadow,
And have left him.
18 Upon his ruin all the fowls of the heaven shall dwell,
And all the beasts of the field shall be upon his branches:
19 To the end that none of all the trees by the waters exalt themselves in their stature,
Neither set their top among the thick boughs;
20 For they are all delivered unto death,
To the nether parts of the earth,
21 In the midst of the children of men,
With them that go down to the pit.

22 Thus saith the Lord Jehovah:
In the day when he went down to Sheol I caused a mourning:
I covered the deep for him,
23 And I restrained the rivers thereof,
And the great waters were stayed:
24 And I caused Lebanon to mourn for him,
And all the trees of the field fainted for him.
25 I made the nations to shake at the sound of his fall,
When I cast him down to Sheol with them that descend into the pit.

Psalm Chant See MONTHLY SONGS: Lord's Day Fourth — Evening.

Hymn of Praise See MONTHLY SONGS: Lord's Day Fourth — Evening.

[*NOT IN EVERY YEAR*]
54. LORD'S DAY FIFTH IN SEPTEMBER
MORNING

Introductory

Sentence — O JEHOVAH, open Thou my lips;
And my mouth shall show forth Thy praise. [Ps. li, 15]

Response
[Tune in
MONTHLY SONGS] — THEY that know Thy Name will put their | trust in | Thee;
For Thou, Jehovah, hast not forsaken | them that | seek | Thee. [Ps. ix, 10]

Scripture Lessons
Old Covenant — Ezra, ix, 5–15.
Gospel — Luke, xvi, 19–31.
Apostolic Word — Titus, iii, 1–11.

54. LORD'S DAY FIFTH IN SEPTEMBER—MORNING

Responsive Lesson THE DOOM OF TYRE, from Ezekiel, xxvii.

THE word of Jehovah:
O thou that dwellest at the entry of the sea,
Who art the merchant of the peoples unto many isles,
2 Thus saith the Lord Jehovah:
Thou, O Tyre, hast said, I am perfect in beauty.
Thy borders are in the heart of the seas,
3 Thy builders have perfected thy beauty.
They have made all thy planks of fir trees from Senir:
4 They have taken cedars from Lebanon to make a mast for thee.
Of the oaks of Bashan have they made thine oars;
5 They have made thy benches of ivory inlaid in boxwood,
From the isles of Kittim.
6 Of fine linen with broidered work from Egypt was thy sail,
That it might be to thee for an ensign.
7 All the ships of the sea with their mariners were in thee to deal in thy merchandise,
Persia and Lud and Put were in thine army, thy men of war:
8 They hanged the shield and helmet in thee;
They set forth thy comeliness.
9 The men of Arvad with thine army were upon thy walls round about,
And the Gammadim were in thy towers:
10 They hanged their shields upon thy walls round about;
They have perfected thy beauty.
11 Many isles were the mart of thy hand:
They brought thee in exchange horns of ivory and ebony.
12 Syria was thy merchant, by reason of the multitude of thy handiworks.
Judah, and the land of Israel, they were thy traffickers.
13 Damascus was thy merchant for the multitude of thy handiworks,
By reason of the multitude of all kinds of riches.
14 Arabia, and all the princes of Kedar,
They were the merchants of thy hand.
15 The ships of Tarshish were thy caravans for thy merchandise:
And thou wast replenished, and made very glorious in the heart of [the seas.
16 Thy rowers have brought thee into great waters:
The east wind hath broken thee in the heart of the seas.
17 Thy riches, and thy wares, thy merchandise, thy mariners, and thy pilots,
And the dealers in thy merchandise,
18 And all thy men of war, that are in thee,
With all thy company which is in the midst of thee,
19 Shall fall into the heart of the seas in the day of thy ruin.
At the sound of the cry of thy pilots the suburbs shall shake.
20 And all that handle the oar,
The mariners, and all the pilots of the sea,
21 Shall come down from their ships,
They shall stand upon the land,

54. LORD'S DAY FIFTH IN SEPTEMBER — MORNING

22 And shall cause their voice to be heard over thee,
And shall cry bitterly, and shall cast up dust upon their heads.
23 And in their wailing they shall take up a lamentation for thee,
And lament over thee,
24 Saying, Who is there like Tyre,
Like her that is brought to silence in the midst of the sea?
25 When thy wares went forth out of the seas,
Thou filledst many peoples;
26 Thou didst enrich the kings of the earth
With the multitude of thy riches and of thy merchandise.
27 In the time that thou wast broken by the seas in the depths of the waters,
Thy merchandise and all thy company did fall in the midst of thee.
28 All the inhabitants of the isles are astonished at thee;
Thou art become a terror, and thou shalt never be any more.

Psalm Chant   See MONTHLY SONGS: Lord's Day Fifth — Morning.

Prayer of the Day

SEND us Thy pardon and peace, O Lord, who preservest us by Thy chastening, and healest us by Thy pardoning:
   That being cleansed from all our sins by the renewing of Thy Spirit, we may serve Thee with a joyful mind:
   Through Jesus Christ Thy Son our Lord, who with the Father and the Holy Spirit — one God — dwelleth in Thy Church, and is worshiped and glorified in Thine everlasting Kingdom: AMEN.

Hymn of Praise   See MONTHLY SONGS: Lord's Day Fifth — Morning.

---

54. EVENING
LORD'S DAY FIFTH IN SEPTEMBER

Introductory

Sentence

JEHOVAH taketh pleasure in them that fear Him,
In those that hope in His lovingkindness.
Praise Thy God, O Zion.   [Ps. cxlvii, 11, 12]

Response
[Tune in
MONTHLY SONGS]

WITH Thee, O God, is the | fountain of | life:
In Thy | light shall | we see | light.   [Ps. xxxvi, 9]

Scripture Lessons
Old Covenant   1 Sam. iii, 1–10, 19–21.
Gospel   Matt. xix, 16–24.
Apostolic Word   Acts, xix, 8–20.

Responsive Lesson   PSALMS OF DAVID, Ps. lxii, lxiii.

MY soul waiteth in silence for God only:
From Him cometh my salvation.
2 He only is my rock and my salvation:
He is my high tower; I shall not be greatly moved.

54. LORD'S DAY FIFTH IN SEPTEMBER—EVENING

3 How long will ye set upon a man,
   That ye may slay him, all of you,
4 Like a leaning wall,
   Like a tottering fence?
5 They only consult to thrust him down from his dignity;
   They delight in lies:
6 They bless with their mouth,
   But they curse inwardly.
7 My soul, wait thou in silence for God only;
   For my expectation is from Him.
8 He only is my rock and my salvation:
   He is my high tower; I shall not be moved.
9 With God is my salvation and my glory:
   The rock of my strength, and my refuge, is in God.
10 Trust in Him at all times, ye people;
   Pour out your heart before Him:
   GOD IS A REFUGE FOR US.
11 Surely men of low degree are vanity,
   And men of high degree are a lie:
12 In the balances they will go up;
   They are together lighter than vanity.
13 Trust not in oppression,
   And become not vain in robbery:
   If riches increase, set not your heart thereon.
14 God hath spoken once,
   Twice have I heard this;
15 That power belongeth unto God:
   Also unto Thee, O Lord, belongeth lovingkindness:
   FOR THOU RENDEREST TO EVERY MAN ACCORDING TO HIS WORK.

---

16 O GOD, Thou art my God; earnestly will I seek Thee:
   My soul thirsteth for Thee;
17 My flesh longeth for Thee, in a dry and weary land,
   Where no water is.
18 So have I looked upon Thee in the sanctuary,
   To see Thy power and Thy glory.
   FOR THY LOVINGKINDNESS IS BETTER THAN LIFE;
19 My lips shall praise Thee.
   So will I bless Thee while I live:
   I will lift up my hands in Thy Name.
20 My soul shall be satisfied as with marrow and fatness;
   And my mouth shall praise Thee with joyful lips;
21 When I remember Thee upon my bed,
   And meditate on Thee in the night watches.
22 For Thou hast been my help,
   And in the shadow of Thy wings will I rejoice.
23 My soul followeth hard after Thee:
   Thy right hand upholdeth me.
24 But those that seek my soul, to destroy it,
   Shall go into the lower parts of the earth.

54. LORD'S DAY FIFTH IN SEPTEMBER — EVENING

25 They shall be given over to the power of the sword :
They shall be a portion for foxes.
26 But the king shall rejoice in God :
Every one that sweareth by Him shall glory ;
For the mouth of them that speak lies shall be stopped.

Psalm Chant   See MONTHLY SONGS: Lord's Day Fifth — Evening.

Hymn of Praise   See MONTHLY SONGS: Lord's Day Fifth — Evening.

---

55. LORD'S DAY FIRST IN OCTOBER
MORNING

Introductory

Sentence

GIVE unto Jehovah, ye kindreds of the peoples,
Give unto Jehovah glory and strength.
Bring an offering, and come into His courts.
O worship Jehovah in the beauty of holiness.   [Ps xcvi, 7-9]

Response
[Tune in
MONTHLY SONGS]

THE Mighty One, God Je- | hovah, hath | spoken,
And called the earth from the rising of the sun unto the |
go-ing | down there- | of.
Out of Zion, the per- | fection of | beauty,
God | hath | shi-ned | forth.   [Ps. l, 1, 2]

Scripture Lessons   Old Covenant   Jer. xxxiii, 1-11.
Gospel   Matt. xxi, 12-22.
Apostolic Word   Eph. vi, 10-24.

Responsive Lesson   Micah, iv, 1-8 : Hosea, xiv.

IN the latter days it shall come to pass,
That the mountain of Jehovah's house shall be established in the
top of the mountains,
And it shall be exalted above the hills ;
2 And peoples shall flow unto it.
And many nations shall go and say, Come ye,
3 And let us go up to the mountain of Jehovah,
And to the house of the God of Jacob ;
4 And He will teach us of His ways,
And we will walk in His paths :
5 For out of Zion shall go forth the law,
And the word of Jehovah from Jerusalem.
6 And He shall decide concerning many peoples,
And shall reprove strong nations afar off ;
7 And they shall beat their swords into plowshares,
And their spears into pruning-hooks :

8 Nation shall not lift up sword against nation,
Neither shall they learn war any more.
9 But they shall sit every man under his vine and under his fig tree;
And none shall make them afraid:
FOR THE MOUTH OF JEHOVAH OF HOSTS HATH SPOKEN IT.
10 For all the peoples will walk every one in the name of his god,
And we will walk in the Name of Jehovah our God for ever and ever.

11 In that day, saith Jehovah, will I assemble her that is lame,
And I will gather her that is driven away,
And her that I have afflicted;
12 And I will make her that was lame a remnant,
And her that was cast far off a strong nation:
13 And Jehovah shall reign over them in Mount Zion
From henceforth even forever.
14 And thou, O tower of the flock,
The hill of the daughter of Zion,
15 Unto thee shall it come; yea, the former dominion shall come,
The kingdom of the daughter of Jerusalem.

---

16 O ISRAEL, return unto Jehovah thy God;
For thou hast fallen by thine iniquity.
17 Take with you words,
And return unto Jehovah:
18 Say unto Him, Take away all iniquity, and accept that which is good:
So will we render as bullocks the offering of our lips.
19 Asshur shall not save us;
We will not ride upon horses:
20 Neither will we say any more to the work of our hands, Ye are our gods:
For in Thee the fatherless findeth mercy.
21 I will heal their backsliding, I will love them freely:
For Mine anger is turned away from him.
22 I will be as the dew unto Israel:
He shall blossom as the lily,
And cast forth his roots as Lebanon.
23 His branches shall spread, and his beauty shall be as the olive tree,
And his smell as Lebanon.
24 They that dwell under his shadow shall return;
They shall revive as the grain,
25 And blossom as the vine:
The scent thereof shall be as the wine of Lebanon.
26 Ephraim shall say, What have I to do any more with idols?
I have answered, and will regard him.
27 Who is wise, and he shall understand these things?
Prudent, and he shall know them?
28 For the ways of Jehovah are right, and the just shall walk in them;
But transgressors shall fall therein.

55. LORD'S DAY FIRST IN OCTOBER — MORNING

Psalm Chant See MONTHLY SONGS: Lord's Day First — Morning.

Prayer of the Day

JEHOVAH of Hosts, who hast set the services of angels and men in a wonderful order, in the unity of the Kingdom of Thy Son: grant that as Thy holy angels always do Thee service in the heavens, so we, Thy Church, praying always in the Holy Spirit, may serve Thee on the earth:

And since they all are ministering spirits sent forth to do service for the sake of them that shall inherit salvation, mercifully cause them, in Thy wisdom, to succor and defend us sojourning in the flesh:

For the sake of Christ Thy Son, the Lord of angels and the King of saints, who with the Father and the Spirit is exalted — one God of endless glory, majesty, and might: AMEN.

Hymn of Praise See MONTHLY SONGS: Lord's Day First — Morning.

---

55. EVENING
LORD'S DAY FIRST IN OCTOBER

Introductory

Sentence

DROP down, ye heavens, from above,
And let the skies pour down righteousness:
Let the earth open, and let her cause righteousness to spring up together:
I, Jehovah, have created it.   [Isaiah, xlv, 8]

Response
[Tune in
MONTHLY SONGS]

LOOK unto Me, and | be ye | sav'd,
All the | ends | of the | earth.
Unto Me every | knee shall | bow,
And every | tongue * shall con- | fess unto | God.
      [Is. xlv, 22, 23 (Rom. xiv, 11)]

Scripture Lessons
Old Covenant Nehemiah, vi, 1–13.
Gospel Luke, xx, 27–40.
Apostolic Word II Cor. xii, 1–10.

Responsive Lesson   Isaiah, liv, 2–8, 10–17.

ENLARGE the place of thy tent,
   And let them stretch forth the curtains of thine habitations;
2 Spare not: lengthen thy cords,
   And strengthen thy stakes.
3 For thou shalt spread abroad on the right hand
   And on the left:
4 And thy seed shall possess the nations,
   And make the desolate cities to be inhabited.

55. LORD'S DAY FIRST IN OCTOBER — EVENING

5 Fear not; for thou shalt not be put to shame:
Neither be thou confounded;
For thou shalt not be put to shame:
6 For thou shalt forget the shame of thy youth,
And the reproach of thy widowhood shalt thou remember no more.
7 For thy Maker is thine husband;
Jehovah of hosts is His Name:
8 And the Holy One of Israel is thy redeemer;
The God of the whole earth shall He be called.
9 For Jehovah hath called thee as a wife forsaken and grieved in spirit,
Even a wife of youth, when she is cast off, saith thy God.
10 For a small moment have I forsaken thee;
But with great mercies will I gather thee.
11 In overflowing wrath I hid My face from thee for a moment;
But with everlasting kindness will I have mercy on thee,
SAITH JEHOVAH THY REDEEMER.
12 For the mountains shall depart,
And the hills be removed;
13 But My kindness shall not depart from thee,
Neither shall My covenant of peace be removed,
SAITH JEHOVAH THAT HATH MERCY ON THEE.
14 O thou afflicted, tossed with tempest,
And not comforted,
15 Behold, I will set thy stones in fair colors,
And lay thy foundations with sapphires.
16 And I will make thy pinnacles of rubies, and thy gates of carbuncles,
And all thy border of precious stones.
17 And all thy children shall be taught of Jehovah;
And great shall be the peace of thy children.
18 In righteousness shalt thou be established:
Thou shalt be far from oppression, for thou shalt not fear;
And from terror, for it shall not come near thee.
19 Behold, they may gather together, but not by Me:
Whosoever shall gather together against thee shall fall because of thee.
20 Behold, I have created the smith that bloweth the fire of coals, and bringeth forth a weapon for his work;
And I have created the waster to destroy.
21 No weapon that is formed against thee shall prosper;
And every tongue that shall rise against thee in judgment thou shalt condemn.
22 This is the heritage of the servants of Jehovah,
And their righteousness which is of Me, saith Jehovah.

Psalm Chant See MONTHLY SONGS: Lord's Day First — Evening.

Hymn of Praise See MONTHLY SONGS: Lord's Day First — Evening.

56. LORD'S DAY SECOND IN OCTOBER
MORNING

Introductory

Sentence

WALK about Zion, and go round about her:
Number the towers thereof.
Mark ye well her bulwarks,
Consider her palaces.
We have thought on Thy lovingkindness, O God,
In the midst of Thy temple. [Ps. xlviii, 12, 13, 9]

Response
[Tune in
Monthly Songs]

JEHOVAH send thee help from the | sanc-tu- | ary,
And | strength-en | thee • out of | Zion!
Remember | all thine | offerings,
And ac- | cept thy | sac-ri- | fice! [Ps. xx, 1-3]

Scripture Lessons

Old Covenant   Job, xxxi, 24–40.
Gospel   Matt. xxii, 1–14.
Apostolic Word   Acts, xx, 17–32.

Responsive Lesson   Psalm, cxi, cxii.

PRAISE ye Jehovah.
I will give thanks unto Jehovah with my whole heart,
2 In the council of the upright,
And in the congregation.
3 The works of Jehovah are great,
Sought out of all them that have pleasure therein.
4 His work is honor and majesty:
And His righteousness endureth forever.
He hath made His wonderful works to be remembered:
5 Jehovah is gracious and merciful.
He hath given food unto them that fear Him:
He will ever be mindful of His covenant.
6 He hath showed His people the power of His works,
In giving them the heritage of the nations.
7 The works of His hands are truth and judgment;
All His precepts are sure.
8 They are established for ever and ever,
They are done in truth and uprightness.
9 He hath sent redemption unto His people;
He hath commanded His covenant forever:
HOLY AND REVEREND IS HIS NAME.
10 The fear of Jehovah is the beginning of wisdom;
A good understanding have all they that do His commandments:
HIS PRAISE ENDURETH FOREVER.

---

11 PRAISE ye Jehovah.
Blessed is the man that feareth Jehovah,
That delighteth greatly in His commandments.
12 His seed shall be mighty upon earth.
The generation of the upright shall be blessed.

13 Wealth and riches are in his house:
   And his righteousness endureth forever.
14 Unto the upright there ariseth light in the darkness:
   He is gracious and merciful and righteous.
15 Well is it with the man that dealeth graciously and lendeth;
   He shall maintain his cause in judgment.
16 For he shall never be moved;
   The righteous shall be had in everlasting remembrance.
17 He shall not be afraid of evil tidings:
   His heart is fixed, trusting in Jehovah.
18 His heart is established, he shall not be afraid,
   Until he see his desire upon his adversaries.
19 He hath dispersed,
   He hath given to the needy;
20 His righteousness endureth forever:
   His horn shall be exalted with honor.
21 The wicked shall see it, and be grieved;
   He shall gnash with his teeth, and melt away:
   The desire of the wicked shall perish.

Psalm Chant

See MONTHLY SONGS: Lord's Day Second — Morning.

Prayer of the Day

O GOD, our Refuge and Strength, Author of all goodness, Father of our Lord Jesus; hear us and the whole company of Thy suppliant people:

Granting us that by the inward motions of Thy Spirit, we may in such wise ask faithfully for the things which we need as effectually to obtain them, according to Thy blessed will in Christ our Savior:

And to God — the Father and the Son and the Holy Spirit — be glory now and ever: AMEN.

Hymn of Praise

See MONTHLY SONGS: Lord's Day Second — Morning.

---

56. EVENING
LORD'S DAY SECOND IN OCTOBER

Introductory Sentence

JEHOVAH is nigh unto all them that call upon Him,
To all that call upon Him in truth.
My mouth shall speak the praise of Jehovah:
And let all flesh bless His holy Name for ever and ever. [Ps. cxlv, 18, 21]

Response [Tune in MONTHLY SONGS]

LIFT up your hands to the | sanc-tu- | ary,
   And | bless | ye Je- | hovah.
Jehovah bless thee | out of | Zion!
   Even He that | made | heaven and | earth. [Ps. cxxxiv, 2, 3]

56. LORD'S DAY SECOND IN OCTOBER—EVENING

Scripture Lessons Old Covenant Daniel, iii, 8–18.
Gospel Matt. xxii, 15–22.
Apostolic Word Col. iii, 12–25; iv, 1.

Responsive Lesson SONGS OF ASCENTS, Ps. cxx, cxxix, cxxx.

IN my distress I cried unto Jehovah,
  And He answered me.
2 Deliver my soul, O Jehovah, from lying lips,
  And from a deceitful tongue.
3 What shall be given unto thee, and what shall be done more unto thee, thou deceitful tongue?
  Sharp arrows of the mighty, with coals of juniper.
4 Woe is me, that I sojourn in Meshech,
  That I dwell among the tents of Kedar!
5 My soul hath long had her dwelling with him that hateth peace.
  I am for peace:
  But when I speak, they are for war.

6 MANY a time have they afflicted me from my youth up,
  Let Israel now say;
7 Many a time have they afflicted me from my youth up:
  Yet they have not prevailed against me.
8 The plowers plowed upon my back;
  They made long their furrows.
9 Jehovah is righteous:
  He hath cut asunder the cords of the wicked.
10 Let them be put to shame and turned backward,
  All they that hate Zion.
11 Let them be as the grass upon the housetops,
  Which withereth before it groweth up:
12 Wherewith the reaper filleth not his hand,
  Nor he that bindeth sheaves his bosom.
13 Neither do they which go by say,
  The blessing of Jehovah be upon you;
  We bless you in the Name of Jehovah.

14 OUT of the depths have I cried unto Thee, O Jehovah.
  Lord, hear my voice.
15 Let Thine ears be attentive
  To the voice of my supplications.
16 If Thou, Jehovah, shouldest mark iniquities,
  O Lord, who shall stand?
17 But there is forgiveness with Thee,
  That Thou mayest be feared.
18 I wait for Jehovah, my soul doth wait,
  And in His word do I hope.
19 My soul waiteth for the Lord,
  More than they that watch, for the morning;
  Yea, more than they that watch, for the morning.

56. LORD'S DAY SECOND IN OCTOBER—EVENING

20 O Israel, hope in Jehovah;
  For with Jehovah there is lovingkindness,
21 And with Him is plenteous redemption.
  And He shall redeem Israel from all his iniquities.

Psalm Chant   See MONTHLY SONGS: Lord's Day Second — Evening.

Hymn of Praise See MONTHLY SONGS: Lord's Day Second — Evening.

---

57. LORD'S DAY THIRD IN OCTOBER

Introductory   MORNING

Sentence

GOD resisteth the proud, but giveth grace to the humble.
Draw nigh to God, and He will draw nigh to you.
Humble yourselves in the sight of the Lord, and He shall exalt you.
[Jas. iv, 6, 8, 10]

Response
[Tune in
MONTHLY SONGS]

THOU hast said, | Seek ye • My | face :
  My heart saith unto Thee,
  Thy face, O Je- | ho-vah, | will I | seek.   [Ps. xxvii, 8]

Scripture Lessons   Old Covenant   Gen. xviii, 22-33.
                        Gospel   Mark, xiv, 1-9.
                        Apostolic Word Rom. xiii, 1-7.

Responsive Lesson   Psalms, xcix; cvi, 1-5; cxlvi.

JEHOVAH reigneth :
  Let the peoples tremble:
2 He sitteth above the cherubim;
  Let the earth be moved.
3 Jehovah is great in Zion;
  And He is high above all the peoples.
4 Let them praise Thy great and terrible Name :
  HOLY IS HE.
5 The king's strength also loveth justice;
  Thou dost establish equity.
6 Thou executest justice,
  And righteousness in Jacob.
7 Exalt ye Jehovah our God,
  And worship at His footstool :
  HOLY IS HE.
8 Moses and Aaron among His priests,
  And Samuel among them that call upon His Name;
9 They called upon Jehovah, and He answered them.
  He spake unto them in the pillar of cloud :

57. LORD'S DAY THIRD IN OCTOBER—MORNING

10 They kept His testimonies, and the statute that He gave them.
Thou answeredst them, O Jehovah our God:
11 Thou wast a God that forgavest them,
Though Thou tookest vengeance of their doings.
12 Exalt ye Jehovah our God,
And worship at His holy hill.
FOR JEHOVAH OUR GOD IS HOLY.

---

13 PRAISE ye Jehovah.
O give thanks unto Jehovah;
14 For He is good:
For His mercy endureth forever.
15 Who can utter the mighty acts of Jehovah,
Or show forth all His praise?
16 Blessed are they that keep judgment,
And he that doeth righteousness at all times.
17 Remember me, O Jehovah, with the favor that Thou bearest unto Thy people:
O visit me with Thy salvation:
18 That I may see the prosperity of Thy chosen,
That I may rejoice in the gladness of Thy nation,
That I may glory with Thine inheritance.

---

19 PRAISE ye Jehovah.
Praise Jehovah, O my soul.
20 While I live will I praise Jehovah:
I will sing praises unto my God while I have any being.
21 Put not your trust in princes,
Nor in the son of man, in whom there is no help.
22 His breath goeth forth, he returneth to his earth;
In that very day his thoughts perish.
23 Happy is he that hath the God of Jacob for his help,
Whose hope is in Jehovah his God:
24 Who made heaven and earth,
The sea, and all that in them is:
25 Who keepeth truth forever:
Who executeth judgment for the oppressed;
26 Who giveth food to the hungry:
Jehovah looseth the prisoners;
27 Jehovah openeth the eyes of the blind;
Jehovah raiseth up them that are bowed down;
28 Jehovah loveth the righteous;
Jehovah preserveth the strangers;
29 He upholdeth the fatherless and widow;
But the way of the wicked He turneth upside down.
30 Jehovah shall reign forever,
Thy God, O Zion, unto all generations.
PRAISE YE JEHOVAH.

Psalm Chant See MONTHLY SONGS: Lord's Day Third—Morning.

57. LORD'S DAY THIRD IN OCTOBER — MORNING

Prayer of the Day

THOU Living God, who art the Eternal Love — who hast taught us that all our doings without love are nothing worth:

Send Thy Holy Spirit, and from Thine own fullness of life pour into our hearts and upon Thy whole Church, that most excellent gift of a holy love, which is humble, meek, kind, and long-suffering, the very bond of peace and of all perfectness:

This we ask in the Name of our Savior, the Son of Thy Love, who is forever blessed with the Father and the Spirit — one God: AMEN.

Hymn of Praise

See MONTHLY SONGS: Lord's Day Third — Morning.

---

57. EVENING
LORD'S DAY THIRD IN OCTOBER

Introductory

Sentence

JEHOVAH, even Jehovah, is my strength and song;
And He is become my salvation.
Therefore with joy shall ye draw water out of the wells of salvation.
[Is. xii, 2, 3]

Response
[Tune in
MONTHLY SONGS]

IT shall come to pass that at evening time there | shall be | light.
And it shall come to pass in that day,
That living waters shall go | out * from Je- | ru-sa- | lem.
[Zech. xiv, 7, 8]

Scripture Lessons

Old Covenant   Daniel, v, 17–31.
Gospel   Matt. xxii, 34–46.
Apostolic Word   1 Cor. xii, 1–14.

Responsive Lesson

From Job, xxxv, xxxvi.

LOOK unto the heavens and see;
   And behold the skies, which are higher than thou.
2 If thou hast sinned, what effectest thou against Him?
   And if thy transgressions be multiplied, what doest thou unto Him?
3 If thou be righteous, what givest thou Him?
   Or what receiveth He of thine hand?
4 Thy wickedness may hurt a man as thou art;
   And thy righteousness may profit a son of man.
5 By reason of the multitude of oppressions they cry out;
   They cry for help by reason of the arm of the mighty.
6 But none saith, Where is God my Maker,
   Who giveth songs in the night;
7 Who teacheth us more than the beasts of the earth,
   And maketh us wiser than the fowls of heaven?
8 There they cry, but none giveth answer,
   Because of the pride of evil men.

57. LORD'S DAY THIRD IN OCTOBER — EVENING

9 Surely God will not hear vanity,
   Neither will the Almighty regard it.
10 Behold, God is mighty, and despiseth not any:
   He is mighty in strength of understanding.
11 He preserveth not the life of the wicked:
   But giveth to the afflicted their right.
12 He withdraweth not His eyes from the righteous:
   But with kings upon the throne He setteth them forever,
   And they are exalted.
13 And if they be bound in fetters,
   And be taken in the cords of affliction;
14 Then He showeth them their work,
   And their transgressions, that they have behaved themselves proudly,
15 He openeth also their ear to instruction,
   And commandeth that they return from iniquity.
16 But if they hearken not, they shall perish by the sword,
   And they shall die without knowledge.
17 But they that are godless in heart lay up anger:
   They cry not for help when He bindeth them.
18 Behold, God doeth loftily in His power:
   Who is a teacher like unto Him?
19 Who hath enjoined Him His way?
   Or who can say, Thou hast wrought unrighteousness?
20 Behold, God is great, and we know Him not;
   The number of His years is unsearchable.
21 For He draweth up the drops of water,
   Which distill in rain from His vapor:
22 Which the skies pour down
   And drop upon man abundantly.
23 Yea, can any understand the spreadings of the clouds,
   The thunderings of His pavilion?

Psalm Chant   See MONTHLY SONGS: Lord's Day Third — Evening.

Hymn of Praise   See MONTHLY SONGS: Lord's Day Third — Evening.

---

58. LORD'S DAY FOURTH IN OCTOBER

MORNING

Introductory

Sentence   I WILL lift up mine eyes unto the mountains:
   Whence shall my help come?
   My help cometh from Jehovah,
   Who made heaven and earth.   [Ps. cxxi. 1, 2]

58. LORD'S DAY FOURTH IN OCTOBER — MORNING

Response [Tune in Monthly Songs]

I HAVE set watchmen upon thy walls, O Je- | ru-sa- | lem ;
They shall never hold their | peace | day nor | night :
Ye that are Jehovah's remembrancers, | keep not | silence,
Till He make Jerusalem a | praise | in the | earth. [Is. lxii. 6, 7]

Scripture Lessons

Old Covenant — Haggai, i, 1–13.
Gospel — Luke, xix, 11–27.
Apostolic Word — 1 Peter, v, 1–11.

Responsive Lesson

Isaiah, xlix, 13–26.

SING, O heavens ;
And be joyful, O earth ;
   And break forth into singing, O mountains ;
2 For Jehovah hath comforted His people,
   And will have compassion upon His afflicted.
3 But Zion said Jehovah hath forsaken me,
   And the Lord hath forgotten me.
4 Can a woman forget her sucking child,
   That she should not have compassion on the son of her womb?
5 Yea, these may forget,
   Yet will not I forget thee.
6 Behold, I have graven thee upon the palms of My hands ;
   Thy walls are continually before Me.
7 Thy children make haste ;
   Thy destroyers and they that made thee waste shall go forth of thee.
8 Lift up thine eyes round about, and behold :
   All these gather themselves together, and come to thee.
9 As I live, saith Jehovah, thou shalt surely clothe thee with them all as with an ornament,
   And gird thyself with them, like a bride.
10 For, as for thy waste and thy desolate places
   And thy land that hath been destroyed,
11 Surely now shalt thou be too strait for the inhabitants,
   And they that swallowed thee up shall be far away.
12 The children of thy bereavement shall yet say in thine ears,
The place is too strait for me :
   Give place to me that I may dwell.
13 Then shalt thou say in thine heart, Who hath begotten me these,
   Seeing I have been bereaved of my children,
14 And am solitary, an exile, and wandering to and fro ?
   And who hath brought up these?
15 Behold, I was left alone ;
   These, where were they?
16 Thus saith the Lord Jehovah,
Behold, I will lift up My hand to the nations,
   And set up Mine ensign to the peoples :
17 And they shall bring thy sons in their bosom,
   And thy daughters shall be carried upon their shoulders.
18 And kings shall be thy nursing fathers,
   And their queens thy nursing mothers :

58. LORD'S DAY FOURTH IN OCTOBER — MORNING

19 They shall bow down to thee with their faces to the earth,
 And lick the dust of thy feet;
20 And thou shalt know that I am Jehovah,
 And they that wait for Me shall not be put to shame.
21 Shall the prey be taken from the mighty,
 Or the lawful captives be delivered?
22 But thus saith Jehovah, Even the captives of the mighty shall be taken away,
 And the prey of the terrible shall be delivered:
23 For I will contend with him that contendeth with thee,
 And I will save thy children.
24 And I will feed them that oppress thee with their own flesh;
 And they shall be drunken with their own blood, as with sweet wine:
25 And all flesh shall know that I Jehovah am thy savior,
 And thy redeemer, the Mighty One of Jacob.

Psalm Chant   See MONTHLY SONGS: Lord's Day Fourth — Morning.

Prayer of the Day

LORD of all Light and Truth, who in the revelation of Thy Son by Thy Spirit hast given the perfect oracles of Thy Word, for the heritage of Thy Church and a heavenly treasure for all men:

Graciously enlighten our minds therein by the same Spirit, that we may give heed thereto as unto a light that shineth in a dark place, until the Day dawn and the Day Star arise in our hearts — even the Sun of Righteousness, the Living Word,

Who with the Father and the Holy Spirit was in the beginning, is now, and ever shall be — one glorious God: AMEN.

Hymn of Praise   See MONTHLY SONGS: Lord's Day Fourth — Morning.

---

58. EVENING
LORD'S DAY FOURTH IN OCTOBER

Introductory

Sentence   GREAT is Jehovah, and highly to be praised,
 In the city of our God, in His holy mountain.   [Ps. xlviii, 1]

Response
[Tune in MONTHLY SONGS]
  THERE is a river, the streams whereof make glad the | city of | God,
 The holy place of the | taber-nacles | of the • Most | High.
 Jehovah of | Hosts is | with us;
 The God of | Ja-cob | is our | refuge.   [Ps. xlvi, 4, 7]

Scripture Lessons
  Old Covenant   Daniel, vi, 1–10.
  Gospel   Matt. xxiii, 1–12.
  Apostolic Word   I Cor. xiii.

58. LORD'S DAY FOURTH IN OCTOBER—EVENING

Responsive Lesson
Ps. cxix, 137-176.

RIGHTEOUS art Thou, Jehovah,
And upright are Thy judgments.
2 Thou hast commanded Thy testimonies in righteousness
And very faithfulness.
3 My zeal hath consumed me,
Because mine adversaries have forgotten Thy words.
4 Thy word is very pure;
Therefore Thy servant loveth it.
5 I am small and despised:
Yet do not I forget Thy precepts.
6 Thy righteousness is an everlasting righteousness,
And Thy law is truth.
7 Trouble and anguish have taken hold on me:
Yet Thy commandments are my delight.
8 Thy testimonies are righteous forever:
Give me understanding, and I shall live.

9 I have called with my whole heart; answer me, O Jehovah:
I will keep Thy statutes.
10 I have called unto Thee; save me,
And I shall observe Thy testimonies.
11 I anticipated the dawning of the morning, and cried:
I hoped in Thy words.
12 Mine eyes anticipated the night watches,
That I might meditate in Thy word.
13 Hear my voice according unto Thy lovingkindness:
Quicken me, O Jehovah, according to Thy judgments.
14 They draw nigh that follow after wickedness;
They are far from Thy law.
15 Thou art nigh, O Jehovah;
And all Thy commandments are truth.
16 Of old have I known from Thy testimonies,
That Thou hast founded them forever.

17 Consider mine affliction, and deliver me;
For I do not forget Thy law.
18 Plead Thou my cause, and redeem me:
Quicken me according to Thy word.
19 Salvation is far from the wicked;
For they seek not Thy statutes.
20 Great are Thy tender mercies, O Jehovah:
Quicken me according to Thy judgments.
21 Many are my persecutors and mine adversaries;
Yet have I not swerved from Thy testimonies.
22 I beheld the treacherous, and was grieved;
Because they observe not Thy word.
23 Consider how I love Thy precepts:
Quicken me, O Jehovah, according to Thy lovingkindness.
24 The sum of Thy word is truth;
And every one of Thy righteous judgments endureth forever.

58. LORD'S DAY FOURTH IN OCTOBER—EVENING

25 Princes have persecuted me without a cause;
   But my heart standeth in awe of Thy words.
26 I rejoice at Thy word,
   As one that findeth great spoil.
27 I hate and abhor falsehood;
   But Thy law do I love.
28 Seven times a day do I praise Thee,
   Because of Thy righteous judgments.
29 Great peace have they who love Thy law;
   And they have none occasion of stumbling.
30 I have hoped for Thy salvation, O Jehovah,
   And have done Thy commandments.
31 My soul hath observed Thy testimonies;
   And I love them exceedingly.
32 I have observed Thy precepts and Thy testimonies;
   For all my ways are before Thee.
33 Let my cry come near before Thee, O Jehovah:
   Give me understanding according to Thy word.
34 Let my supplication come before Thee:
   Deliver me according to Thy word.
35 Let my lips utter praise;
   For Thou teachest me Thy statutes.
36 Let my tongue sing of Thy word;
   For all Thy commandments are righteousness.
37 Let Thy hand be ready to help me;
   For I have chosen Thy precepts.
38 I have longed for Thy salvation, O Jehovah;
   And Thy law is my delight.
39 Let my soul live, and it shall praise Thee;
   And let Thy judgments help me.
40 I have gone astray like a lost sheep; seek Thy servant;
   For I do not forget Thy commandments.

Psalm Chant   See MONTHLY SONGS: Lord's Day Fourth — Evening.

Hymn of Praise   See MONTHLY SONGS: Lord's Day Fourth — Evening.

[*NOT IN EVERY YEAR*]

59. LORD'S DAY FIFTH IN OCTOBER

Introductory   MORNING

Sentence

LET the heart of them rejoice that seek Jehovah.
Seek ye Jehovah and His strength;
Seek His face evermore. [Ps. cv, 3, 4]

Response
[Tune in
MONTHLY SONGS]

THEY that know Thy Name will put their | trust in | Thee;
For Thou, Jehovah, hast not forsaken | them that | seek | Thee. [Ps. ix, 10]

59. LORD'S DAY FIFTH IN OCTOBER—MORNING

Scripture Lessons Old Covenant I Sam. xxviii, 4-20.
  Gospel John, xviii, 28-37.
  Apostolic Word James, iii.

Responsive Lesson Job, xiv, 1-21; xix, 25-27.

M AN that is born of a woman
  Is of few days, and full of trouble.
2 He cometh forth like a flower, and is cut down:
  He fleeth also as a shadow, and continueth not.
3 And dost Thou open Thine eyes upon such an one,
  And bringest me into judgment with Thee?
4 Who can bring a clean thing out of an unclean?
  Not one.
5 Seeing his days are determined,
  The number of his months is with Thee,
6 And Thou hast appointed his bounds
  That he cannot pass;
7 Look away from him, that he may rest,
  Till he shall accomplish, as a hireling, his day.
8 For there is hope of a tree, if it be cut down, that it will sprout again,
  And that the tender branch thereof will not cease.
9 Though the root thereof wax old in the earth,
  And the stock thereof die in the ground;
10 Yet through the scent of water it will bud,
  And put forth boughs like a plant.
11 But man dieth, and is laid low:
  Yea, man giveth up the ghost, and where is he?
12 As the waters fail from the sea,
  And the river wasteth and drieth up;
13 So man lieth down and riseth not:
  Till the heavens be no more, they shall not awake,
  Nor be roused out of their sleep.
14 O that Thou wouldest hide me in Sheol,
  That Thou wouldest keep me secret, until Thy wrath be past,
15 That Thou wouldest appoint me a set time,
  And remember me!
16 If a man die, shall he live again?
  All the days of my warfare would I wait,
  Till my release should come.
17 Thou shouldest call, and I would answer Thee:
  Thou wouldest have a desire to the work of Thy hands.
18 But now Thou numberest my steps:
  Dost Thou not watch over my sin?
19 My transgression is sealed up in a bag,
  And Thou fastenest up mine iniquity.
20 And surely the mountain falling cometh to nought,
  And the rock is removed out of its place;
21 The waters wear the stones;
  The overflowings thereof wash away the dust of the earth:

59. LORD'S DAY FIFTH IN OCTOBER—MORNING

22 So Thou destroyest the hope of man.
Thou prevailest forever against him, and he passeth;
Thou changest his countenance, and sendest him away.
23 His sons come to honor, and he knoweth it not;
And they are brought low, but he perceiveth it not of them.

24 BUT as for me, I know that my redeemer liveth,
And at last He shall stand up upon the earth;
25 And after my skin, even this body, is destroyed,
Then without my flesh shall I see God:
26 Whom I, even I, shall see on my side,
And mine eyes shall behold, and not as a stranger.

Psalm Chant   See MONTHLY SONGS: Lord's Day Fifth — Morning.

Prayer of the Day

FATHER in Heaven, whom truly to know is everlasting life:
Grant us to know Thee in Christ Thy Son who is the Way and the Truth and the Life, and to be steadfast evermore in the faith and the confession of Him, with the whole company of Thy believing Church — being strengthened by Thy Spirit, To whom with Thee and Thy blessed Son — one God — be all glory forever:
AMEN.

Hymn of Praise   See MONTHLY SONGS: Lord's Day Fifth — Morning.

---

59. EVENING
LORD'S DAY FIFTH IN OCTOBER

Introductory

Sentence

CREATE in me a clean heart, O God;
And renew a right spirit within me.
Cast me not away from Thy presence;
And take not Thy Holy Spirit from me.   [Ps. li, 10, 11]

Response
[Tune in
MONTHLY SONGS]

WITH Thee, O God, is the | fountain of | life:
In Thy | light shall | we see | light.   [Ps. xxxvi, 9]

Scripture Lessons   Old Covenant   Lev. xix, 30-37.
Gospel   Luke, xix, 1-10.
Apostolic Word   Acts, xxiv, 10-27.

Responsive Lesson   From A PSALM OF ASAPH, Ps. lxxviii, 40-69.

HOW oft did Israel rebel against God in the wilderness,
And grieve Him in the desert!
2 And they turned again and tempted God,
And provoked the Holy One of Israel.

3 They remembered not His hand,
  Nor the day when He redeemed them from the adversary.
4 How He set His signs in Egypt,
  And His wonders in the field of Zoan:
5 And turned their rivers into blood,
  And their streams, that they could not drink.
6 He sent among them swarms of flies, which devoured them;
  And frogs, which destroyed them.
7 He gave also their increase unto the caterpillar,
  And their labor unto the locust.
8 He destroyed their vines with hail,
  And their sycamore trees with frost.
9 He gave over their cattle also to the hail,
  And their flocks to hot thunderbolts.
10 He cast upon them the fierceness of His anger,
  Wrath, and indignation, and trouble,
  A band of angels of evil.
11 He made a path for His anger;
  He spared not their soul from death,
  But gave their life over to the pestilence;
12 And smote all the firstborn in Egypt,
  The chief of their strength in the tents of Ham:
13 But He led forth His own people like sheep,
  And guided them in the wilderness like a flock.
14 And He led them safely, so that they feared not:
  But the sea overwhelmed their enemies.
15 And He brought them to the border of His sanctuary,
  To this mountain, which His right hand had purchased.
16 He drove out the nations also before them,
  And allotted them for an inheritance by line,
  And made the tribes of Israel to dwell in their tents.

17 Yet they tempted and rebelled against the Most High God,
  And kept not His testimonies;
18 But turned back, and dealt treacherously like their fathers:
  They were turned aside like a deceitful bow.
19 For they provoked Him to anger with their high places,
  And moved Him to jealousy with their graven images.
20 When God heard this, He was wroth,
  And greatly abhorred Israel:
21 So that He forsook the tabernacle of Shiloh,
  The tent which He placed among men;
22 And delivered his strength into captivity,
  And his glory into the adversary's hand.
23 He gave His people over also unto the sword;
  And was wroth with His inheritance.
24 Fire devoured their young men;
  And their maidens had no marriage-song.
25 Their priests fell by the sword;
  And their widows made no lamentation.

59. LORD'S DAY FIFTH IN OCTOBER—EVENING

26 Then the Lord awaked as one out of sleep,
And He smote His adversaries backward:
He put them to a perpetual reproach.
27 Moreover He refused the tent of Joseph,
And chose not the tribe of Ephraim;
28 But chose the tribe of Judah,
The mount Zion which He loved.
29 And He built His sanctuary like the heights,
Like the earth which He hath established forever.

Psalm Chant   See MONTHLY SONGS: Lord's Day Fifth—Evening.

Hymn of Praise   See MONTHLY SONGS: Lord's Day Fifth — Evening.

---

60. LORD'S DAY FIRST IN NOVEMBER
MORNING

Introductory

Sentence

COME ye, and let us go up to the mountain of Jehovah,
To the house of the God of Jacob;
And He will teach us of His ways,
And we will walk in His paths:
For out of Zion shall go forth the law,
And the word of Jehovah from Jerusalem.   [Is. ii, 3]

Response
[Tune in
MONTHLY SONGS]

THE Mighty One, God Je- | hovah, hath | spoken,
And called the earth from the rising of the sun unto the | go-ing | down there- | of.
Out of Zion, the per- | fection of | beauty,
God | hath | shi-ned | forth.   [Ps. l, 1, 2]

Scripture Lessons   Old Covenant   Gen. xvii, 1-9.
Gospel   Luke, xxii, 24-34.
Apostolic Word   Heb. xii, 18-29.

Responsive Lesson   Isaiah, lx.

ARISE, shine; for thy light is come,
And the glory of Jehovah is risen upon thee.
2 For, behold, darkness shall cover the earth,
And gross darkness the peoples:
3 But Jehovah shall arise upon thee,
And His glory shall be seen upon thee.
4 And nations shall come to thy light,
And kings to the brightness of thy rising.

5 Lift up thine eyes round about, and see:
   They all gather themselves together, they come to thee:
6 Thy sons shall come from far,
   And thy daughters shall be carried in the arms.
7 Then thou shalt see and be lightened,
   And thy heart shall tremble and be enlarged;
8 Because the abundance of the sea shall be turned unto thee,
   The wealth of the nations shall come unto thee.
9 The multitude of camels shall cover thee,
   The dromedaries of Midian and Ephah;
10 All they from Sheba shall come:
   They shall bring gold and frankincense,
   And shall proclaim the praises of Jehovah.
11 All the flocks of Kedar shall be gathered together unto thee,
   The rams of Nebaioth shall minister unto thee:
12 They shall come up with acceptance on Mine altar,
   And I will glorify the house of My glory.
13 Who are these that fly as a cloud,
   And as the doves to their windows?
14 Surely the isles shall wait for Me,
   And the ships of Tarshish first,
15 To bring thy sons from far,
   Their silver and their gold with them,
16 For the Name of Jehovah thy God,
   And for the Holy One of Israel,
   BECAUSE HE HATH GLORIFIED THEE.
17 And strangers shall build up thy walls,
   And their kings shall minister unto thee:
18 For in My wrath I smote thee,
   But in My favor have I had mercy on thee.
19 Thy gates also shall be open continually;
   They shall not be shut day nor night;
20 That men may bring unto thee the wealth of the nations,
   And their kings led with them.
21 For that nation and kingdom that will not serve thee shall perish;
   Yea, those nations shall be utterly wasted.
22 The glory of Lebanon shall come unto thee,
   The fir tree, the pine, and the box tree together;
23 To beautify the place of My sanctuary,
   And I will make the place of My feet glorious.
24 And the sons of them that afflicted thee shall come bending unto thee;
   And all they that despised thee shall bow themselves down at the soles of thy feet;
25 And they shall call thee The city of Jehovah,
   The Zion of the Holy One of Israel.
26 Whereas thou hast been forsaken and hated,
   So that no man passed through thee,
27 I will make thee an eternal excellency,
   A joy of many generations.

60. LORD'S DAY FIRST IN NOVEMBER—MORNING

28 And thou shalt know that I Jehovah am thy savior,
And thy redeemer, the Mighty One of Jacob.
29 For brass I will bring gold,
And for iron I will bring silver,
30 And for wood brass,
And for stones iron:
31 I will also make thine officers peace,
And thine exactors righteousness.
32 Violence shall no more be heard in thy land,
Desolation nor destruction within thy borders;
33 But thou shalt call thy walls Salvation,
And thy gates Praise.
34 The sun shall be no more thy light by day;
Neither for brightness shall the moon give light unto thee:
35 But Jehovah shall be unto thee an everlasting light,
And thy God thy glory.
36 Thy sun shall no more go down,
Neither shall thy moon withdraw itself:
37 For Jehovah shall be thine everlasting light,
And the days of thy mourning shall be ended.
38 Thy people also shall all be righteous,
They shall inherit the land forever;
39 The branch of My planting,
The work of My hands, that I may be glorified.
40 The little one shall become a thousand,
And the small one a strong nation:
  I JEHOVAH WILL HASTEN IT IN ITS TIME.

Psalm Chant
See MONTHLY SONGS: Lord's Day First—Morning.

Prayer of the Day

O GOD, the Light of Life, Thou Father of our spirits, and faithful Creator of our souls anew; whose Church on earth and in all heavens is knit together by Thy Spirit in one communion and fellowship, the Body of Thy Son:

We give Thee thanks for all those who, through faith in Him, having overcome the world have triumphed over death, and are now refreshed in the light of Christ's presence in the Church on high:

And we beseech Thee, keep us in their fellowship—even us in this short sojourn and pilgrimage; granting us likewise to overcome in life and in death, through the same victorious Son of God who is the Resurrection and the Life, who with the Father and the Holy Spirit—one God—liveth in one perpetual day: AMEN.

Hymn of Praise
See MONTHLY SONGS: Lord's Day First—Morning.

60. EVENING
LORD'S DAY FIRST IN NOVEMBER

Introductory

Sentence

JEHOVAH reigneth; He is clothed with majesty;
Jehovah is clothed with strength;
He hath girded Himself therewith.
Thy throne is established of old:
Thou art from everlasting. [Ps. xciii, 1, 2]

Response
Tune in
[MONTHLY SONGS]

LOOK unto Me, and | be ye | sav'd,
All the | ends | of the | earth.
Unto Me every | knee shall | bow,
And every | tongue • shall con- | fess unto | God.
[Is. xlv, 22, 23 (Rom. xiv, 11)]

Scripture Lessons

Old Covenant — Ezekiel, xi, 16–25.
Gospel — Matt. xxiii, 23–28.
Apostolic Word — Rom. xiii, 8–14.

Responsive Lesson A PRAYER OF DAVID, Ps. lxxxvi: lxxxvii.

BOW down Thine ear, O Jehovah, and answer me;
   For I am poor and needy.
2 Preserve my soul; for I am godly:
   O Thou my God, save Thy servant that trusteth in Thee.
3 Be merciful unto me, O Lord;
   For unto Thee do I cry all the day long.
4 Rejoice the soul of Thy servant;
   For unto Thee, O Lord, do I lift up my soul.
5 For Thou, Lord, art good, and ready to forgive,
   And abundant in lovingkindness unto all them that call upon Thee.
6 Give ear, O Jehovah, unto my prayer;
   And hearken unto the voice of my supplications.
7 In the day of my trouble I will call upon Thee;
   For Thou wilt answer me.
8 There is none like unto Thee among the gods, O Lord;
   Neither are there any works like unto Thy works.
9 All nations whom Thou hast made shall come and worship before
      Thee, O Lord;
   And they shall glorify Thy Name.
10 For Thou art great, and doest wondrous things:
   Thou art God alone.
11 Teach me Thy way, O Jehovah; I will walk in Thy truth:
   Unite my heart to fear Thy Name.
12 I will praise Thee, O Lord my God, with my whole heart;
   And I will glorify Thy Name for evermore.
13 For great is Thy lovingkindness toward me;
   And Thou hast delivered my soul from the lowest Sheol.
14 O God, the proud are risen up against me,
   And the congregation of violent men have sought after my soul,
   And have not set Thee before them.

60. LORD'S DAY FIRST IN NOVEMBER—EVENING

15 But Thou, O Lord, art a God merciful and gracious,
   Slow to anger, and abundant in lovingkindness and truth.
16 O turn unto me, and have mercy upon me;
   Give Thy strength unto Thy servant,
   And save the son of Thy handmaid.
17 Show me a token for good;
   That they which hate me may see it, and be put to shame,
   Because Thou, Jehovah, hast helped me, and comforted me.

---

18 His foundation is in the holy mountains.
   Jehovah loveth the gates of Zion
   More than all the dwellings of Jacob.
   GLORIOUS THINGS ARE SPOKEN OF THEE, O CITY OF GOD.
19 I will make mention of Egypt and Babylon as among them that know me;
   Behold Philistia, and Tyre, with Ethiopia; this one was born there.
20 Yea, of Zion it shall be said, This one and that one was born in her;
   And the Most High Himself shall establish her.
21 Jehovah shall count, when He writeth up the peoples,
   This one was born there.
22 They that sing as well as they that dance shall say,
   All my fountains are in thee.

Psalm Chant   See MONTHLY SONGS: Lord's Day First — Evening.

Hymn of Praise   See MONTHLY SONGS: Lord's Day First — Evening.

---

61. LORD'S DAY SECOND IN NOVEMBER

MORNING

Introductory

Sentence   JEHOVAH will create over the whole habitation of Mount Zion,
   And over her assemblies,
   A cloud and smoke by day, and the shining of a flaming fire by night:
   For over all the glory shall be spread a canopy.   [Is. iv, 5]

Response
[Tune in
MONTHLY SONGS]
   JEHOVAH send thee help from the | sanc-tu- | ary,
   And | strength-en | thee · out of | Zion!
   Remember | all thine | offerings,
   And ac- | cept thy | sac-ri- | fice!   [Ps. xx, 1-3]

Scripture Lessons   Old Covenant   Dan. x, 4-21; xi, 1.
       Gospel   Matt. xxv, 1-13.
       Apostolic Word   Rom. xiv, 1-12.

61. LORD'S DAY SECOND IN NOVEMBER—MORNING

Responsive Lesson From A PSALM OF DAVID, Ps. lxviii.

LET God arise,
Let His enemies be scattered;
2 Let them also that hate Him flee before Him.
As smoke is driven away, so drive them away:
3 As wax melteth before the fire,
So let the wicked perish at the presence of God.
4 But let the righteous be glad; let them exult before God:
Yea, let them rejoice with gladness.
5 Sing unto God,
Sing praises to His Name:
6 Cast up a highway for Him that rideth through the deserts;
His Name is Jehovah; and exult ye before Him.
7 A father of the fatherless, and a judge of the widows,
Is God in His holy habitation.
God setteth the solitary in families;
8 He bringeth out the prisoners into prosperity:
But the rebellious dwell in a parched land.

9 O God, when Thou wentest forth before Thy people,
When Thou didst march through the wilderness;
10 The earth trembled.
The heavens also dropped at the presence of God:
11 That Sinai trembled at the presence of God,
The God of Israel.
12 Thou, O God, didst send a plentiful rain,
Thou didst confirm Thine inheritance, when it was weary.
13 Thy congregation dwelt therein;
Thou, O God, didst prepare of Thy goodness for the poor.
14 The Lord giveth the word:
The women that publish the tidings are a great host.
15 Kings of armies flee, they flee:
And she that tarrieth at home divideth the spoil.
16 When the Almighty scattered kings therein,
It was as when it snoweth in Zalmon.
17 A mountain of God is the mountain of Bashan;
A high mountain is the mountain of Bashan.
18 Why look ye askance, ye high mountains,
At the mountain which God hath desired for His abode?
Yea, Jehovah will dwell in it forever.
19 Thou hast ascended on high,
Thou hast led away captives;
20 Thou hast received gifts among men,
Yea, among the rebellious also,
That Jehovah God might dwell with them.

21 Blessed be the Lord, who daily beareth our burden,
Even the God who is our salvation.
22 God is unto us a God of deliverances;
And unto Jehovah the Lord belongeth escape from death.

61. LORD'S DAY SECOND IN NOVEMBER — MORNING

23 They have seen Thy goings, O God,
  Even the goings of my God, my King, into the sanctuary.
24 The singers went before, the minstrels followed after,
  In the midst of the damsels playing with timbrels.
25 Bless ye God in the congregations,
  Even the Lord, ye that are of the fountain of Israel.
26 Thy God hath commanded thy strength:
  Strengthen, O God, that which Thou hast wrought for us.
27 Princes shall come out of Egypt;
  Ethiopia shall haste to stretch out her hands unto God.
28 Sing unto God, ye kingdoms of the earth;
  O sing praises unto the Lord;
29 To Him that rideth upon the heaven of heavens which are of old;
  Lo, He uttereth His voice, and that a mighty voice.
30 Ascribe ye strength unto God:
  His excellency is over Israel,
  And His strength is in the skies.
31 O God, Thou art terrible out of Thy holy places:
  The God of Israel, He giveth strength and power unto His people.
  BLESSED BE GOD.

Psalm Chant See MONTHLY SONGS: Lord's Day Second — Morning.

Prayer of the Day

GOD of all goodness:
 Graciously stir us up by Thy blessed Spirit in heart and mind to all good works, to which Thou callest Thy Church in one Body, which are the fruit of faith in Christ Thy Son, and whose end is everlasting life with Him,
  Who with the Father and the Spirit is glorified — one God, world without end:
                                            AMEN.

Hymn of Praise See MONTHLY SONGS: Lord's Day Second — Morning.

---

61. EVENING
LORD'S DAY SECOND IN NOVEMBER

Introductory

Sentence

LET the children of Zion be joyful in their King.
 For Jehovah taketh pleasure in His people:
He will beautify the meek with salvation.
Praise ye Jehovah.   [Ps. cxlix, 2, 4, 9.]

Response
[Tune in
MONTHLY SONGS]

LIFT up your hands to the | sanc-tu- | ary,
  And | bless | ye Je- | hovah.
Jehovah bless thee | out of | Zion!
  Even He that | made | heaven and | earth.   [Ps. cxxxiv, 2, 3]

Scripture Lessons
Old Covenant   Prov. xxx, 4-14; xxxi, 8, 9.
Gospel   John, xix, 5-16.
Apostolic Word   Acts, xxvi, 1-11.

Responsive Lesson
Job, xxxvii, 1-23.

YEA, at this my heart trembleth,
And is moved out of its place.
2 Hear, O hear the noise of His voice,
And the sound that goeth out of His mouth.
3 He sendeth it forth under the whole heaven,
And His lightning unto the ends of the earth.
4 After it a voice roareth;
He thundereth with the voice of His majesty:
And He stayeth them not when His voice is heard.
5 God thundereth marvelously with His voice;
Great things doeth He, which we cannot comprehend.
6 For He saith to the snow, Fall thou on the earth;
Likewise to the shower of rain,
And to the showers of His mighty rain.
7 He sealeth up the hand of every man;
That all men whom He hath made may know it.
8 Then the beasts go into coverts,
And remain in their dens.
9 Out of the chamber of the south cometh the storm:
And cold out of the north.
10 By the breath of God ice is given:
And the breadth of the waters is straitened.
11 Yea, He ladeth the thick cloud with moisture;
He spreadeth abroad the cloud of His lightning:
And it is turned round about by His guidance,
12 That they may do whatsoever He commandeth them
Upon the face of the habitable world:
13 Whether it be for correction, or for His land,
Or for mercy, that He cause it to come.
14 Hearken unto this: stand still,
And consider the wondrous works of God.
15 Dost thou know how God layeth His charge upon them,
And causeth the lightning of His cloud to shine?
16 Dost thou know the balancings of the clouds,
The wondrous works of Him who is perfect in knowledge?
17 How thy garments are warm,
When the earth is still by reason of the south wind?
18 Canst thou with Him spread out the sky,
Which is strong as a molten mirror?
19 Teach us what we shall say unto Him:
For we cannot order our speech by reason of darkness.
20 Shall it be told Him that I would speak?
Or should a man wish that he were swallowed up?
21 And now men see not the light
Which is bright in the skies:

61. LORD'S DAY SECOND IN NOVEMBER—EVENING

22 But the wind passeth, and cleareth them.
  Out of the north cometh golden splendor:
23 God hath upon Him terrible majesty.
  Touching the Almighty, we cannot find Him out;
24 He is excellent in power:
  And in judgment and plenteous justice.

Psalm Chant See MONTHLY SONGS: Lord's Day Second—Evening.

Hymn of Praise See MONTHLY SONGS: Lord's Day Second—Evening.

---

62. LORD'S DAY THIRD IN NOVEMBER
MORNING

Introductory

Sentence

OPEN Thou mine eyes, O Jehovah,
That I may behold wondrous things out of Thy law.
Make Thy face to shine upon Thy servant;
And teach me Thy statutes. [Ps. cxix, 18, 135]

Response
['Tune in
MONTHLY SONGS]

THOU hast said, | Seek ye • My | face :
My heart saith unto Thee,
Thy face, O Je- | ho-vah, | will I | seek. [Ps. xxvii, 8]

Scripture Lessons   Old Covenant   Mal. iii, 7–18.
  Gospel   Matt. xxvi, 36–46.
  Apostolic Word   1 John, iv, 7–21.

Responsive Lesson   Isaiah, lv: from lvi.

HO, every one that thirsteth,
Come ye to the waters,
  And he that hath no money;
  Come ye, buy, and eat;
2 Yea, come, buy wine and milk without money
  And without price.
3 Wherefore do ye spend money for that which is not bread?
  And your labor for that which satisfieth not?
4 Hearken diligently unto Me, and eat ye that which is good,
  And let your soul delight itself in fatness.
5 Incline your ear, and come unto Me;
  Hear, and your soul shall live:
6 And I will make an everlasting covenant with you,
  Even the sure lovingkindnesses of David.
7 Behold, I have given him for a witness to the peoples,
  A leader and commander to the peoples.

8 Behold, thou shalt call a nation that thou knowest not,
  And a nation that knew not thee shall run unto thee,
9 Because of Jehovah thy God,
  And for the Holy One of Israel;
  For He hath glorified thee.

10 Seek ye Jehovah while He may be found,
   Call ye upon Him while He is near:
11 Let the wicked forsake his way,
   And the unrighteous man his thoughts:
12 And let him return unto Jehovah, and He will have mercy upon him;
   And to our God, for He will abundantly pardon.
13 For My thoughts are not your thoughts,
   Neither are your ways My ways, saith Jehovah.
14 For as the heavens are higher than the earth,
   So are My ways higher than your ways,
   And My thoughts than your thoughts.
15 For as the rain cometh down and the snow from heaven,
   And returneth not thither, but watereth the earth,
16 And maketh it bring forth and bud,
   And giveth seed to the sower and bread to the eater;
17 So shall My word be that goeth forth out of My mouth:
   It shall not return unto Me void,
18 But it shall accomplish that which I please,
   And it shall prosper in the thing whereto I sent it.
19 For ye shall go out with joy,
   And be led forth with peace:
20 The mountains and the hills shall break forth before you into singing,
   And all the trees of the field shall clap their hands.
21 Instead of the thorn shall come up the fir tree,
   And instead of the brier shall come up the myrtle tree:
22 And it shall be to Jehovah for a name,
   For an everlasting sign that shall not be cut off.

23 Thus saith Jehovah, Keep ye judgment,
   And do righteousness:
24 For My salvation is near to come,
   And My righteousness to be revealed.
25 Blessed is the man that doeth this,
   And the son of man that holdeth fast by it;
26 That keepeth the sabbath from profaning it,
   And keepeth his hand from doing any evil.
27 Also the strangers, that join themselves to Jehovah,
   To minister unto Him, and to love the Name of Jehovah,
28 To be His servants, every one that keepeth the sabbath from profaning it,
   And holdeth fast by My covenant;
29 Even them will I bring to My holy mountain,
   And make them joyful in My house of prayer;

62. LORD'S DAY THIRD IN NOVEMBER — MORNING

30 Their burnt offerings and their sacrifices shall be accepted upon
Mine altar:
FOR MY HOUSE SHALL BE CALLED A HOUSE OF PRAYER
FOR ALL PEOPLES.

Psalm Chant   See MONTHLY SONGS: Lord's Day Third — Morning.

Prayer of the Day

VOUCHSAFE unto Thy believing Church, O God, that by the inspirations of Thy salutary grace we may know that which is right and think that which is good, and in the might of Thy Spirit may do the same:
Having our citizenship in the heavens whither Thy Son our Lord Jesus hath gone to prepare us a place —
Through whom Thou bringest many sons to the presence of Thine eternal glory, who art the Father and the Son and the Holy Spirit — one God: AMEN.

Hymn of Praise   See MONTHLY SONGS: Lord's Day Third — Morning.

---

62. EVENING
LORD'S DAY THIRD IN NOVEMBER

Introductory

Sentence

WE have the word of prophecy made more sure;
Whereunto ye do well that ye take heed,
As unto a lamp shining in a dark place, until the day dawn,
And the Day-star arise in your hearts.   [II Pet. i, 19]

Response
[Tune in
MONTHLY SONGS]

IT shall come to pass that at evening time there | shall be | light.
And it shall come to pass in that day,
That living waters shall go | out • from Je- | ru-sa- | lem.
[Zech. xiv. 7, 8]

Scripture Lessons   Old Covenant   Gen. xxviii, 10–22.
Gospel   Mark, xv, 1–15.
Apostolic Word   Rev. xxii, 1–9.

Responsive Lesson   From Isaiah, xlv.

THUS saith Jehovah to Cyrus,
Whose right hand I have holden, to subdue nations before him,
And I will loose the loins of kings;
2 To open the doors before him,
•   *And the gates shall not be shut;*
3 I will go before thee,
And make the rugged places plain:
4 I will break in pieces the doors of brass,
And cut in sunder the bars of iron:

62. LORD'S DAY THIRD IN NOVEMBER — EVENING

5 And I will give thee the treasures of darkness,
   And hidden riches of secret places,
6 That thou mayest know that it is I Jehovah who call thee by thy name,
   Even the God of Israel.
7 For Jacob My servant's sake,
   And Israel My chosen,
8 I have called thee by thy name:
   I have surnamed thee, though thou hast not known Me.
9 I am Jehovah, and there is none else;
   Beside Me there is no God:
10 I will gird thee, though thou hast not known Me:
    That they may know from the rising of the sun, and from the west,
    That there is none beside Me:
11 I am Jehovah, and there is none else.
    I form the light, and create darkness;
12 I make peace, and create evil;
    I am Jehovah, that doeth all these things.

13 Drop down, ye heavens, from above,
    And let the skies pour down righteousness:
14 Let the earth open,
    That they may bring forth salvation,
15 And let her cause righteousness to spring up together;
    I Jehovah have created it.

16 Woe unto him that striveth with his Maker!
    A potsherd among the potsherds of the earth!
17 Shall the clay say to him that fashioneth it, What makest thou?
    Or thy work, He hath no hands?
18 I have made the earth,
    And created man upon it:
19 I, even My hands, have stretched out the heavens,
    And all their host have I commanded.
20 I have raised him up in righteousness,
    And I will make straight all his ways:
21 He shall build My city, and he shall let My exiles go free,
    Not for price nor reward, saith Jehovah of hosts.

22 Verily Thou art a God that hidest Thyself,
    O God of Israel, the savior.
23 They shall be put to shame, yea, confounded all of them:
    They shall go into confusion together that are makers of idols.
24 But Israel shall be saved by Jehovah with an everlasting salvation:
    Ye shall not be put to shame nor confounded world without end.

25 For thus saith Jehovah that created the heavens;
    He is God; that formed the earth and made it;
26 He established it, He created it not a waste,
    He formed it to be inhabited:

62. LORD'S DAY THIRD IN NOVEMBER—EVENING

27 I am Jehovah; and there is none else.
I have not spoken in secret,
  In a place of the land of darkness;
28 I said not unto the seed of Jacob, Seek ye Me in vain:
I Jehovah speak righteousness,
  I declare things that are right.
29 Assemble yourselves and come;
  Draw near together, ye that are escaped of the nations.
30 There is no God else beside Me;
  A just God and a savior; there is none beside Me.
31 Look unto Me, and be ye saved, all the ends of the earth:
  For I am God, and there is none else.
32 By Myself have I sworn,
The word is gone forth from My mouth in righteousness,
  And shall not return,
33 That unto Me every knee shall bow,
  Every tongue shall swear.
34 Only in Jehovah, shall one say, have I righteousness and strength:
  Even to Him shall men come.
35 In Jehovah shall all the seed of Israel be justified,
  And shall glory.

Psalm Chant   See MONTHLY SONGS: Lord's Day Third — Evening.

Hymn of Praise   See MONTHLY SONGS: Lord's Day Third — Evening.

---

63. LORD'S DAY FOURTH IN NOVEMBER
[On Nov. 27 or 28, this observance is set aside—yielding to Day No. 65]

MORNING

Introductory

Sentence **T**HEREFORE will Jehovah wait, that He may be gracious unto you.
Blessed are all they that wait for Him.
He will surely be gracious unto thee at the voice of thy cry;
When He shall hear, He will answer thee.   [Is. xxx, 18, 19]

Response
[Tune in
MONTHLY SONGS]

I HAVE set watchmen upon thy walls, O Je- | ru-sa- | lem ;
They shall never hold their | peace | day nor | night :
Ye that are Jehovah's remembrancers, | keep not | silence,
Till He make Jerusalem a | praise | in the | earth.   [Is. lxii, 6, 7]

Scripture Lessons   Old Covenant   Joel, ii, 1-13.   [Partly the same as for Day No. 66, Mr'g]
Gospel   John, xix, 23-30.
Apostolic Word   II Thess. ii, 1-12.

63. LORD'S DAY FOURTH IN NOVEMBER—MORNING

Responsive Lesson From Isaiah, viii: xxix, 13-24.

1. MAKE an uproar, O ye peoples, and ye shall be broken in pieces;
    And give ear, all ye of far countries:
2. Gird yourselves, and ye shall be broken in pieces;
    Gird yourselves, and ye shall be broken in pieces.
3. Take counsel together, and it shall be brought to nought;
    Speak the word, and it shall not stand:
    FOR GOD IS WITH US.
4. For Jehovah spake thus to me with a strong hand,
    And instructed me that I should not walk in the way of this people,
5. Saying—Say ye not, A conspiracy, concerning all whereof this people shall say, A conspiracy;
    Neither fear ye their fear,
    Nor be in dread thereof.
6. Jehovah of hosts, Him shall ye sanctify; and let Him be your fear.
    And let Him be your dread.
7. And He shall be for a sanctuary; but for a stone of stumbling
    And for a rock of offense
8. To both the houses of Israel,
    For a gin and for a snare to the inhabitants of Jerusalem.
9. And many shall stumble thereon, and fall,
    And be broken, and be snared, and be taken.
10. Bind thou up the testimony,
    Seal the law among my disciples.
11. And I will wait for Jehovah, that hideth His face from the house of Jacob,
    And I will look for Him.
12. And when they shall say unto you, Seek unto them that have familiar spirits
    And unto the wizards, that chirp and that mutter:
13. Should not a people seek unto their God?
    On behalf of the living should they seek unto the dead?
14. To the law and to the testimony!
    If they speak not according to this word,
    Surely there is no morning for them.

---

15. AND the Lord said, Forasmuch as this people draw nigh unto Me,
    And with their mouth and with their lips do honor Me,
16. But have removed their heart far from Me,
    And their fear of Me is a commandment of men which hath been taught them:
17. Therefore, behold, I will proceed to do a marvelous work among this people,
    Even a marvelous work and a wonder:
18. And the wisdom of their wise men shall perish,
    And the understanding of their prudent men shall be hid.
19. Woe unto them that seek deep to hide their counsel from Jehovah,
    And their works are in the dark,

63. LORD'S DAY FOURTH IN NOVEMBER — MORNING

20 And they say, Who seeth us?
  And who knoweth us?
21 Ye turn things upside down! Shall the potter be counted as clay;
  That the thing made should say of him that made it, He made me not;
  Or the thing formed say of him that formed it, He hath no understanding?
22 Is it not yet a very little while, and Lebanon shall be turned into a fruitful field,
  And the fruitful field shall be counted for a forest?
23 And in that day shall the deaf hear the words of the book,
  And the eyes of the blind shall see out of obscurity and out of darkness.
24 The meek also shall increase their joy in Jehovah,
  And the poor among men shall rejoice in the Holy One of Israel.
25 For the terrible one is brought to nought,
  And the scorner ceaseth,
26 And all they that watch for iniquity are cut off:
  That make a man an offender in a cause,
27 And lay a snare for him that reproveth in the gate,
  And turn aside the just with a thing of nought.
28 Therefore thus saith Jehovah, who redeemed Abraham,
  Concerning the house of Jacob:
29 Jacob shall not now be ashamed,
  Neither shall his face now wax pale.
30 But when he seeth his children, the work of My hands, in the midst of him,
  They shall sanctify My Name;
31 Yea, they shall sanctify the Holy One of Jacob,
  And shall stand in awe of the God of Israel.
32 They also that err in spirit shall come to understanding,
  And they that murmur shall receive instruction.

Psalm Chant

See MONTHLY SONGS: Lord's Day Fourth — Morning.

Prayer of the Day

ETERNAL Jehovah, the Father of all men, whose are all souls, and who numberest Thy saints: grant Thy grace upon all men to bring them unto Thy Son our Savior:

And we beseech Thee, join us with Thy whole Church in one Body, by Thy Spirit with Thy Son; even as Thy Son and Spirit are in Thee — one God:

That when Thou bringest again them that sleep in Jesus — at His coming — Thou gather not our souls with the ungodly, but make us to be numbered with Thy saints in glory everlasting: For all glory, Lord, is Thine: AMEN.

Hymn of Praise

See MONTHLY SONGS: Lord's Day Fourth — Morning.

63. EVENING

LORD'S DAY FOURTH IN NOVEMBER

Introductory

Sentence

I WILL make mention of the lovingkindnesses of Jehovah,
And the praises of Jehovah,
According to all that Jehovah hath bestowed on us;
According to the multitude of His lovingkindnesses. [Is. lxiii, 7]

Response
[Tune in
Monthly Songs]

THERE is a river, the streams whereof make glad the | city of | God,
The holy place of the | taber-nacles | of the · Most | High.
Jehovah of | Hosts is | with us;
The God of | Ja-cob | is our | refuge. [Ps. xlvi, 4, 7]

Scripture Lessons   Old Covenant   Num. ix, 15-23.
Gospel   Luke, xxiii, 32, 33, 39-46.
Apostolic Word   Rev. xxii, 10-17.

Responsive Lesson   From Ezekiel, xxxiv.

THUS saith the Lord Jehovah:
Behold, I Myself, even I, will search for My sheep,
And will seek them out.
2 As a shepherd seeketh out his flock
In the day that he is among his sheep that are scattered abroad,
3 So will I seek out My sheep; and I will deliver them
Out of all places whither they have been scattered in the cloudy and dark day.
4 And I will bring them out from the peoples,
And gather them from the countries,
5 And will bring them into their own land;
And I will feed them upon the mountains of Israel,
6 By the water-courses,
And in all the inhabited places of the country.
7 I will feed them with good pasture,
And upon the mountains of the height of Israel shall their fold be:
8 There shall they lie down in a good fold,
And on fat pasture shall they feed upon the mountains of Israel.
9 I Myself will feed My sheep,
And I will cause them to lie down, saith the Lord Jehovah.
10 I will seek that which was lost,
And will bring again that which was driven away,
11 And will bind up that which was broken,
And will strengthen that which was sick.
12 And I will set up one shepherd over them,
And he shall feed them,
13 Even My servant David; he shall feed them,
And he shall be their shepherd.

63. LORD'S DAY FOURTH IN NOVEMBER—EVENING

14 And I Jehovah will be their God,
And My servant David prince among them;
I Jehovah have spoken it.
15 And I will make with them a covenant of peace,
And will cause evil beasts to cease out of the land;
16 And they shall dwell securely in the wilderness,
And sleep in the woods.
17 And I will make them and the places round about My hill a blessing;
And I will cause the shower to come down in its season;
THERE SHALL BE SHOWERS OF BLESSING.
18 And the tree of the field shall yield its fruit,
And the earth shall yield her increase,
19 And they shall be secure in their land;
And they shall know that I am Jehovah,
20 When I have broken the bars of their yoke,
And have delivered them out of the hand of those that served themselves of them.
21 And they shall no more be a prey to the heathen,
Neither shall the beast of the earth devour them;
22 But they shall dwell securely,
And none shall make them afraid.
23 And I will raise up unto them a plantation for renown,
And they shall be no more consumed with famine in the land,
Neither bear the shame of the heathen any more.
24 And they shall know that I Jehovah their God am with them,
And that they, the house of Israel, are my people, saith the Lord Jehovah.
25 And ye My sheep, the sheep of My pasture, are men,
And I am your God, saith the Lord Jehovah.

Psalm Chant   See MONTHLY SONGS: Lord's Day Fourth—Evening.

Hymn of Praise   See MONTHLY SONGS: Lord's Day Fourth—Evening.

---

64. THANKSGIVING DAY

Introductory

Sentence   WHAT shall I render unto Jehovah for all His benefits toward me?
I will offer to Thee the sacrifice of thanksgiving,
And will call upon the Name of Jehovah.
I will pay my vows unto Jehovah,
Yea, in the presence of all His people;
In the courts of the house of Jehovah.
Praise ye Jehovah.   [Ps. cxvi. 12, 17-19]

64. THANKSGIVING DAY

Response

O PRAISE Jehovah, | all ye | nations;
Laud | Him, | all ye | peoples.
For His lovingkindness is | great toward | us;
And the truth of Jehovah endureth forever. | Hal-le- | lu- | jah!   [Ps. cxvii]

William Crotch, Mus. Doc., d. 1847.

Thanksgiving Call   From Ps. cxxxvi.

[The second number in each couplet is a *suffrage*, sung (or said) by all]

O GIVE thanks unto Jehovah, for He is good;
   For His lovingkindness endureth forever:
2 O give thanks unto the Lord of-lords;
   For His lovingkindness endureth forever:
3 To Him who alone doeth great wonders;
   For His lovingkindness endureth forever:
4 To Him that by understanding made the heavens;
   For His lovingkindness endureth forever:
5 To Him that spread forth the earth above the waters;
   For His lovingkindness endureth forever:
6 To Him who led His people through the wilderness;
   For His lovingkindness endureth forever:
7 Who remembered us in our low estate;
   For His lovingkindness endureth forever:
8 And hath delivered us from our adversaries;
   For His lovingkindness endureth forever:
9 He giveth food to all flesh;
   For His lovingkindness endureth forever:
10 O give thanks unto the God of Heaven;
   For His lovingkindness endureth forever.

W. S. P.

Scripture Lessons

Old Covenant	Deut. viii, 6–20.
Gospel	Luke, xii, 24–31.
Apostolic Word	Acts, xvii, 24–28.

Additional: The Canticle, "Benedicite Omnia," may be introduced after IV, Scripture of the Old Covenant, or elsewhere. See in Ascriptions and Other Songs, No. 10.

64. THANKSGIVING DAY

Responsive Lesson   Ps. cxlvii: from A Psalm of David, lxv, 8–13.

[Same for Day No. 34, Ev'g]

PRAISE ye Jehovah;
  For it is good to sing praises unto our God;
  For it is pleasant, and praise is comely.
2 Jehovah doth build up Jerusalem;
  He gathereth together the outcasts of Israel.
3 He healeth the broken in heart,
  And bindeth up their wounds.
4 He counteth the number of the stars;
  He giveth them all their names.
5 Great is our Lord, and mighty in power;
  His understanding is infinite.
6 Jehovah upholdeth the meek:
  He bringeth the wicked down to the ground.
7 Sing unto Jehovah with thanksgiving;
  Sing praises upon the harp unto our God:
8 Who covereth the heaven with clouds,
Who prepareth rain for the earth,
  Who maketh grass to grow upon the mountains.
9 He giveth to the beast his food,
  And to the young ravens which cry.
10 He delighteth not in the strength of the horse:
  He taketh no pleasure in the legs of a man.
11 Jehovah taketh pleasure in them that fear Him,
  In those that hope in His lovingkindness.
12 Praise Jehovah, O Jerusalem;
  Praise thy God, O Zion.
13 For He hath strengthened the bars of thy gates;
  He hath blessed thy children within thee.
14 He maketh peace in thy borders;
  He filleth thee with the finest of the wheat.
15 He sendeth out His commandment upon earth;
  His word runneth very swiftly.
16 He giveth snow like wool;
  He scattereth the hoar frost like ashes.
17 He casteth forth His ice like morsels:
  Who can stand before His cold?
18 He sendeth out His word, and melteth them:
  He causeth His wind to blow, and the waters flow.
19 He showeth His word unto Jacob,
  His statutes and His judgments unto Israel.
20 He hath not dealt so with any nation:
  And as for His judgments, they have not known them.
  PRAISE YE JEHOVAH.

---

21 PRAISE waiteth for Thee, O God, in Zion.
  Thou makest the outgoings of the morning and evening to rejoice.
22 Thou visitest the earth, and waterest it.
  Thou greatly enrichest it; the river of God is full of water:

64. THANKSGIVING DAY

23 Thou providest them grain, when Thou hast so prepared the earth:
Thou waterest her furrows abundantly;
24 Thou settlest the ridges thereof;
Thou makest it soft with showers;
25 Thou blessest the springing thereof:
Thou crownest the year with Thy goodness:
26 And Thy paths drop fatness;
They drop upon the pastures of the wilderness:
27 And the hills are girded with joy;
The pastures are clothed with flocks;
28 The valleys also are covered over with grain;
They shout for joy, they also sing.
PRAISE WAITETH FOR THEE, O GOD, IN ZION.

Psalm Chant From Psalm, xliv: DOXOLOGY OF DAVID, 1 Chron. xxix, 10–19.
[May be used also on July 4 and Dec. 21]

THOMAS SAUNDERS DUPUIS, Mus. Doc., d. 1796.

WE have heard with our ears, O God, our | fathers have | told us,
What work Thou didst in their days, | in the | days of | old.
2 Thou didst drive out the nations with Thy hand, but | them • Thou didst | plant;
Thou didst afflict the peoples, but | them • Thou didst | spread a- | broad.
3 For they gat not the land in possession | by • their own | sword,
Neither did | their own | arm | save them:
4 But Thy right hand and Thine arm and the | light • of Thy | countenance,
Because Thou hadst a | fa-vor | un-to | them.
5 We will not trust in our bow,
Neither shall | our sword | save us.
But Thou hast sav'd us from our adversaries,
And hast put | them to | shame that | hate us.
6 In God have we made our boast | all the • day | long,
And we will give thanks | unto Thy | Name for | ever.

7 BLESSED be Thou Jehovah, the God of our fathers, for | ever and | ever.
Thine, O Jehovah, is the greatness and the power,
And the glory and the | victo-ry | and the | majesty:
8 For all that is in the heaven and in the | earth is | Thine:
Thine is the Kingdom, O Jehovah,
And Thou art ex- | alted as | Head a-bove | all.

64. THANKSGIVING DAY

9 Both riches and honor come of Thee, and Thou rulest | o-ver | all;
And in Thy hand is power and might;
And in Thy hand it is to make great, and to give | strength | unto | all.
10 Now therefore, our God, we thank Thee, and praise Thy | glorious | Name:
For all things come of Thee; and | all | is Thine | own.
11 For we are strangers before Thee,
And sojourners as all our | fathers | were:
Our days on the earth are as a shadow,
| And * there is | no a- | biding.
12 O Thou that triest the heart, and hast pleasure | in up- | rightness,
Jehovah, the God of our fathers;
Prepare our heart unto Thee, to | keep | Thy com- | mandments.
13 GLORY be to the Father, etc.

Song of Ascription
TE DEUM LAUDAMUS, or other Song: See in ASCRIPTIONS.

Prayer of the Day

SOVEREIGN Lord, who leadest forth upon the earth seed-time and harvest, and crownest the year with Thy goodness: We who live only by Thy bountiful word, give Thee thanks for the manifold mercies which Thou ordainest for us in the frame of nature and in the course of Thy providences: We testify to Thee with the voice of rejoicing, who hast comforted our homes and hast magnified Thy goodness unto our land:

And we beseech Thee, implant in us such gratitude for all Thy gifts, and for Thyself who art our God, as shall always spring forth and grow up in our lives and bear the fruits of godliness, to the glory of Thy grace in Thy Son Christ Jesus, by whose hand Thou holdest forth to us all blessings and all hopes:

Now therefore, O our God, we thank Thee, and we praise and bless Thy glorious Name — Father and Son and Holy Spirit, who art exalted above all blessing and all praise, yet dost condescend to inhabit the praises of Thy people, world without end:

AMEN.

[Hymn of Praise — see next page]

64. THANKSGIVING DAY

Hymn of Praise

ANNA LŒTITIA BARBAULD; pub. 1795. (Dox. added.)

PRAISE to God, immortal praise,
For the love that crowns our days!
Bounteous Source of every joy,
Let Thy praise our tongues employ.
For the blessings of the field,
For the stores the gardens yield;
For the joy which harvests bring,
Grateful praise to Thee we sing.

2 All that spring with bounteous hand
Scatters o'er the smiling land;
All that liberal autumn pours
From her rich, o'erflowing stores;
These, great God, to Thee we owe,
Source whence all our blessings flow;
And for these, our souls shall raise
Grateful vows and solemn praise.

3. Hal-le-lu-jah! Praise the Lord, Earth and heav'n with glad ac-cord. God of Blessing! hear our songs, Thou to whom all praise belongs: Thee, Eternal God, Most High—Thee we laud and mag-ni-fy: Glorious o'er the Heav'nly host— Fa-ther, Son, and Ho-ly Ghost. A - MEN.

ST. GEORGE. 7s, D. Sir GEORGE JOB ELVEY, Mus. Doc., 1860.

Or this Hymn —   LEONARD BACON, D. D., 1838. (Dox. added.)

O GOD, beneath Thy guiding hand,
Our exiled fathers crossed the sea,
And when they trod the wintry strand,
With prayer and psalm they worshiped Thee.

2 Thou heardst, well pleased, the song, the prayer—
Thy blessing came; and still its power
Shall onward through all ages bear
The memory of that holy hour.

3 Laws, freedom, truth, and faith in God
Came with those exiles o'er the waves,
And where their pilgrim feet have trod,
The God they trusted guards their graves.

4 And here Thy Name, O God of love,
Their children's children shall adore,
Till these eternal hills remove,
And spring adorns the earth no more.

64. THANKSGIVING DAY

5. O Father, Son, and Holy Ghost— Thou God Most High! Thee we adore:
From earth and all the heav'nly host, To Thee, all glory evermore! A-MEN.

WIMBORNE. L. M.   J. WHITTAKER, 1849.

65. LORD'S DAY FIRST IN ADVENT

𝕴ntroductory   MORNING

Sentence   THE voice of one that crieth —
Prepare ye in the wilderness the way of Jehovah:
Make straight in the desert a highway for our God. [Is. xl, 3]

Response   BEHOLD, the Lord Jehovah will come as a | might-y | One.
He shall feed His | flock | like a | shepherd.
And the glory of Jehovah shall be reveal'd,
And all flesh shall | see it ᐧ to- | gether:
For the mouth of Je- | hovah hath | spo-ken | it. [Is. xl, 10, 11, 5]

JONATHAN BATTISHILL, d. 1801.

𝕾cripture 𝕷essons
Old Covenant   Dan. xii.
Gospel   John, i, 19-28.
Apostolic Word   I Thess. iv, 13-18.

𝕽esponsive 𝕷esson   Isaiah, ii, 2-22; iv, 5, 6.

  IT shall come to pass in the latter days,
That the mountain of Jehovah's house shall be established in the top of the mountains,
And shall be exalted above the hills;
AND ALL NATIONS SHALL FLOW UNTO IT.

65. LORD'S DAY FIRST IN ADVENT — MORNING

2 And many peoples shall go and say,
   Come ye, and let us go up to the mountain of Jehovah,
   To the house of the God of Jacob;
3 And He will teach us of His ways,
   And we will walk in His paths:
4 For out of Zion shall go forth the law,
   And the word of Jehovah from Jerusalem.
5 And He shall judge between the nations,
   And shall decide concerning many peoples:
6 And they shall beat their swords into plowshares,
   And their spears into pruning-hooks:
7 Nation shall not lift up sword against nation,
   Neither shall they learn war any more.

8 O house of Jacob, come ye,
   And let us walk in the light of Jehovah.
9 For Thou hast forsaken Thy people the house of Jacob,
   Because they are filled with customs from the east,
10 And are soothsayers like the Philistines,
   And they strike hands with the children of strangers.
11 Their land also is full of silver and gold,
   Neither is there any end of their treasures;
12 Their land also is full of horses,
   Neither is there any end of their chariots.
13 Their land also is full of idols;
   They worship the work of their own hands,
   That which their own fingers have made,
14 And the mean man is bowed down, and the great man is brought low:
   Therefore forgive them not.
15 Enter into the rock,
   And hide thee in the dust,
16 From before the terror of Jehovah,
   And from the glory of His majesty.
17 The lofty looks of man shall be brought low,
   And the haughtiness of men shall be bowed down,
   AND JEHOVAH ALONE SHALL BE EXALTED IN THAT DAY.
18. For there shall be a day of Jehovah of hosts upon all that is proud and haughty,
   And upon all that is lifted up;
   AND IT SHALL BE BROUGHT LOW:
19 And upon all the cedars of Lebanon, that are high and lifted up,
   And upon all the oaks of Bashan;
20 And upon all the high mountains,
   And upon all the hills that are lifted up;
21 And upon every lofty tower,
   And upon every fortified wall;
22 And upon all the ships of Tarshish,
   And upon all pleasant imagery.
23 And the loftiness of man shall be bowed down,
   And the haughtiness of men shall be brought low:

65. LORD'S DAY FIRST IN ADVENT—MORNING

24 And Jehovah alone shall be exalted in that day.
And the idols shall utterly pass away.
25 And men shall go into the caves of the rocks,
And into the holes of the earth,
26 From before the terror of Jehovah,
And from the glory of His majesty,
WHEN HE ARISETH TO SHAKE MIGHTILY THE EARTH.
27 In that day a man shall cast away his idols of silver,
And his idols of gold,
28 Which they made for him to worship,
To the moles and to the bats;
29 To go into the caverns of the rocks,
And into the clefts of the ragged rocks,
30 From before the terror of Jehovah,
And from the glory of His majesty,
WHEN HE ARISETH TO SHAKE MIGHTILY THE EARTH.
31 Cease ye from man, whose breath is in his nostrils:
For wherein is he to be accounted of?

32 And Jehovah will create over the whole habitation of mount
And over her assemblies, [Zion,
33 A cloud and smoke by day, and the shining of a flaming fire by
For over all the glory shall be spread a canopy. [night:

Psalm Chant   From A PSALM OF DAVID, Ps. ix.   [Same for Ev'g, and for Day No. 66]

NORRIS, d. 1790.

I WILL give thanks unto Jehovah | with my · whole | heart;
  I will show forth | all Thy | marvel-ous | works.
2 I will be glad and ex- | ult in | Thee:
  I will sing praise to Thy | Name, O | Thou Most | High.
3 Jehovah sitteth as | King for | ever:
  He hath pre- | par'd His | throne for | judgment.
4 And He shall judge the world in | right-eous- | ness,
  He shall minister judgment to the | peo-ples | in up- | rightness.
5 For He that maketh inquisition for blood re- | mem-bereth | them:
  He forgetteth | not the | cry · of the | poor.
6 Jehovah hath made Himself known,
  He hath | exe-cuted | judgment:
  The wicked is snared in the | work of | his own | hands.
7 For the needy shall not alway | be for- | gotten,
  Nor the expectation of the | poor | perish for | ever.
8 Arise, O Jehovah, let not | man pre- | vail:
  Let the nations be | judg'd | in Thy | sight.

9 GLORY be to the Father, etc.

65. LORD'S DAY FIRST IN ADVENT — MORNING

Prayer of the Day

ALMIGHTY GOD, give us grace that we may cast away the works of darkness and put upon us the armor of light, now in the time of this mortal life in which Thy Son Jesus Christ came to visit us in great humility:

That in the last day, when He shall come again in His glorious majesty to judge both the quick and the dead, we may rise to the life immortal:

Through Him, who liveth and reigneth with the Father and the Holy Spirit — one God, now and ever: AMEN.

Hymn of Praise

MARCH. (Dox. added.)

ETERNAL God! Eternal King!
Ruler of heaven and earth beneath!
From Thee our hopes, our comforts spring;
In Thee we live and move and breathe.

2 Thy word brought forth the flaming sun,
The changeful moon, the starry host;
In Thine appointed course they run,
Till in the final ruin lost.

3 The final, awful hour is near,
Time paces on with ceaseless tread,
When opening graves that voice shall hear,
And render up the sleeping dead.

4 O, in that great decisive day,
May we be found in Christ, and stand,
While flaming worlds shall melt away,
Accepted, owned, at Thy right hand!

5. O Fa-ther, Son, and Ho-ly Ghost— Thou God Most High! Thee we a-dore: From earth and all the heav'nly host, To Thee, all glo-ry ev-er-more! A-MEN.

KENT. L. M.　　　　　　　　　　JOHANN FRIEDRICH LAMPE, 1746.

65. EVENING
LORD'S DAY FIRST IN ADVENT

Introductory

Sentence

THE night is far spent, and the day is at hand: Let us therefore cast off the works of darkness, And let us put on the armor of light. [Rom. xiii, 12]

Response
[Tune, in Morning]

BEHOLD, the Lord Jehovah will come as a | might-y | One.
He shall feed His | flock | like a | shepherd.
And the glory of Jehovah shall be reveal'd,
And all flesh shall | see it • to- | gether:
For the mouth of Je- | hovah hath | spo-ken | it. [Is. xl, 10, 11, 5]

Scripture Lessons   Old Covenant   Mal. iii, 1-6.
   Gospel   Matt. xxiv, 1-14.
   Apostolic Word   1 Thess. v, 1-11.

Responsive Lesson   A PSALM OF ASAPH, Ps. l.

THE Mighty One, God Jehovah, hath spoken,
   And called the earth from the rising of the sun unto the going down thereof.
2 Out of Zion, the perfection of beauty,
   God hath shined forth.
3 Our God shall come,
   And shall not keep silence:
4 A fire shall devour before Him,
   And it shall be very tempestuous round about Him.
5 He shall call to the heavens above,
   And to the earth, that He may judge His people:
6 Gather My saints together unto Me;
   Those that have made a covenant with Me by sacrifice.
7 And the heavens shall declare His righteousness;
   For God is judge Himself.
8 Hear, O My people, and I will speak;
   O Israel, and I will testify unto thee:
9 I am God, even thy God.
   I will not reprove thee for thy sacrifices;
   And thy burnt offerings are continually before Me.
10 I will take no bullock out of thy house,
   Nor he-goats out of thy folds.
11 For every beast of the forest is Mine,
   And the cattle upon a thousand hills.
12 I know all the fowls of the mountains:
   And the wild beasts of the field are Mine.
13 If I were hungry, I would not tell thee:
   For the world is Mine, and the fullness thereof.
14 Will I eat the flesh of bulls,
   Or drink the blood of goats?

65. LORD'S DAY FIRST IN ADVENT — EVENING

15 Offer unto God the sacrifice of thanksgiving;
  And pay thy vows unto the Most High:
16 And call upon Me in the day of trouble;
  I will deliver thee, and thou shalt glorify Me.

17 But unto the wicked God saith,
  What hast thou to do to declare My statutes,
  And that thou hast taken My covenant in thy mouth?
18 Seeing thou hatest instruction,
  And castest My words behind thee.
19 When thou sawest a thief, thou consentedst with him,
  And hast been partaker with adulterers.
20 Thou givest thy mouth to evil,
  And thy tongue frameth deceit.
21 Thou sittest and speakest against thy brother;
  Thou slanderest thine own mother's son.
22 These things hast thou done, and I kept silence;
  Thou thoughtest that I was altogether such a one as thyself:
23 But I will reprove thee,
  And set them in order before thine eyes.

24 Now consider this, ye that forget God, lest I tear you in pieces,
  And there be none to deliver:
25 Whoso offereth the sacrifice of thanksgiving glorifieth Me;
  And to him that ordereth his way aright will I show the salvation of God.

Psalm Chant Same as for Morning.

Hymn of Praise
JOHN ROSS MACDUFF, D. D., 1853. (Dox. added.)

CHRIST is coming! let creation
  Bid her groans and travail cease:
Let the glorious proclamation
  Hope restore and faith increase;
    Christ is coming!
  Come, Thou blessèd Prince of peace!

2 Earth can now but tell the story
  Of Thy bitter cross and pain;
She shall yet behold Thy glory
  When Thou comest back to reign;
    Christ is coming!
  Let each heart repeat the strain.

3 Long Thine exiles have been pining,
  Far from rest and home and Thee:
But, in heavenly vesture shining,
  Soon they shall Thy glory see;
    Christ is coming!
  Haste the joyous jubilee.

4 With that "blessèd hope" before us,
  Let no harp remain unstrung;
Let the mighty advent chorus
  Onward roll from tongue to tongue;
    Christ is coming!
  Come, Lord Jesus, quickly come.

5. God E-ter-nal! we a-dore Thee, Lord of all the heav'n-ly host:

65. LORD'S DAY FIRST IN ADVENT—EVENING

Earth and heav'n with joy be-fore Thee, Wor-ship give with praise ut-most: Thine be glo-ry!— Fa-ther, Son, and Ho-ly Ghost. A-MEN.

MADELAY. 878747.   SAMUEL REAY, 1876.

---

66. LORD'S DAY SECOND IN ADVENT
MORNING

Introductory

Sentence   YET a very little while, He that cometh shall come and shall not tarry.
Behold, He cometh with the clouds, and every eye shall see Him.
He who testifieth these things saith, Yea, I come quickly.
Amen! come Lord Jesus.   [Heb. x, 37; Rev. i, 7; xxii, 20]

Response   KEEP ye judgment, and do righteousness:
For My salvation is | near to | come,
And My righteous- | ness to | be re- | veal'd.   [Is. lvi, 1]

CHARLES STEGGALL, Mus. Doc.

Scripture Lessons   Old Covenant   Zeph. i, 14–18; ii, 1–3.
                          Gospel   Matt. xxiv, 29–36.
                          Apostolic Word   II Peter, iii, 1–10.

Responsive Lesson   From Joel, ii, iii: Mal. iv.

BLOW ye the trumpet in Zion,
     And sound an alarm in My holy mountain;
2 Let all the inhabitants of the land tremble:
     For the day of Jehovah cometh, for it is nigh at hand;

66. LORD'S DAY SECOND IN ADVENT—MORNING

3 A day of darkness and gloominess,
  A day of clouds and thick darkness, as the dawn spread upon the mountains;
4 A great people and a strong,
  There hath not been ever the like,
5 Neither shall be any more after them,
  Even to the years of many generations.
6 A fire devoureth before them;
  And behind them a flame burneth:
7 The land is as the garden of Eden before them, and behind them a desolate wilderness;
  Yea, and none hath escaped them.
8 The earth quaketh before them;
  The heavens tremble:
9 The sun and the moon are darkened,
  And the stars withdraw their shining:
10 And Jehovah uttereth His voice before His army; for His camp is very great;
  For He is strong that executeth His word:
11 For the day of Jehovah is great and very terrible;
  And who can abide it?
12 Yet even now, saith Jehovah, turn ye unto Me with all your heart,
  And with fasting, and with weeping, and with mourning:
13 And rend your heart, and not your garments, and turn unto Jehovah your God:
  For He is gracious and merciful,
14 Slow to anger, and abundant in lovingkindness,
  And repenteth Him of the evil.

15 For, behold, in those days, and in that time,
  When I shall bring again the captivity of Judah and Jerusalem,
16 I will gather all nations,
  And will bring them down into the valley of Jehoshaphat;
17 And I will execute judgment upon them there for My people
  And for My heritage Israel,
18 Whom they have scattered among the nations,
  And parted My land.

19 Proclaim ye this among the nations;
  Prepare war; stir up the mighty men;
  Let all the men of war draw near, let them come up.
20 Beat your plowshares into swords, and your pruning-hooks into spears:
  Let the weak say, I am strong.
21 Haste ye, and come, all ye nations round about,
  And gather yourselves together:
  Thither cause Thy mighty ones to come down, O Jehovah.
22 Let the nations bestir themselves, and come up to the valley of Jehoshaphat:
  For there will I sit to judge all the nations round about.

66. LORD'S DAY SECOND IN ADVENT — MORNING

23 Put ye in the sickle, for the harvest is ripe:
Come, tread ye; for the wine-press is full,
24 The vats overflow;
For their wickedness is great.
25 Multitudes, multitudes in the valley of decision!
For the day of Jehovah is near in the valley of decision.
26 The sun and the moon are darkened,
And the stars withdraw their shining.
27 And Jehovah shall roar from Zion,
And utter His voice from Jerusalem;
AND THE HEAVENS AND THE EARTH SHALL SHAKE:
28 But Jehovah will be a refuge unto His people,
And a strong hold to the children of Israel.
29 So shall ye know that I am Jehovah your God,
Dwelling in Zion, My holy mountain.

---

30 FOR, behold, the day cometh, it burneth as a furnace;
And all the proud, and all that work wickedness, shall be stubble:
31 And the day that cometh shall burn them up, saith Jehovah of hosts,
That it shall leave them neither root nor branch.
32 But unto you that fear My Name shall the sun of righteousness arise with healing in his wings;
And ye shall go forth, and gambol as calves of the stall.
33 And ye shall tread down the wicked;
For they shall be ashes under the soles of your feet
In the day that I do make, saith Jehovah of hosts.
34 Remember ye the law of Moses My servant,
Which I commanded unto him in Horeb for all Israel,
Even statutes and judgments.
35 Behold, I will send you Elijah the prophet
Before the great and terrible day of Jehovah come.
36 And he shall turn the heart of the fathers to the children,
And the heart of the children to their fathers;
Lest I come and smite the earth with a curse.

Psalm Chant

Same as for Day No. 65.

Prayer of the Day

CLEANSE our conscience, Almighty God, by the daily visitation of Thy grace in Christ Thy Son:
That when He who came in our flesh shall be manifested in His glory, He may find us fit for His appearing, and ready without spot, in the company of all His saints, to meet Him coming in the clouds of heaven;
Who in Thine everlasting Kingdom is glorified with the Father and the Spirit — one God: AMEN.

66. LORD'S DAY SECOND IN ADVENT — MORNING

Hymn of Praise

Sir EDWARD DENNY; 1839.   (Dox. added.)

LIGHT of the lonely pilgrim's heart!
Star of the coming day!
Arise, and with thy morning beams
Chase all our griefs away.

2 Come, blessèd Lord! let every shore
And answering island sing
The praises of Thy royal Name,
And own Thee as their King.

3 Jesus! Thy fair creation groans —
The air, the earth, the sea —
In unison with all our hearts,
And calls aloud for Thee.

4 Thine was the cross, with all its fruits
Of grace and peace divine;
Be Thine the crown of glory now,
The palm of victory Thine.

5. E-ter-nal glo-ry, bless-ing, praise, To Thee our God, Most High!
O Fa-ther, Son, and Ho-ly Ghost! — Thy Name we mag-ni-fy. A-MEN.

PILGRIM SONG. C. M.   SAMUEL SEBASTIAN WESLEY, Mus. Doc., 1872.

---

66. EVENING
LORD'S DAY SECOND IN ADVENT

Introductory

Sentence   I AM the Alpha and the Omega — saith the Lord God —
Who is and who was and who is to come, the Almighty.   [Rev. i, 8]

Response
[Tune, in Morning]
K EEP ye judgment, and do righteousness:
For My salvation is | near to | come,
And My righteous- | ness to | be re- | veal'd.   [Is. lvi, 1]

Scripture Lessons

Old Covenant   Isaiah, xiii, 2–13.
Gospel   Luke, xxi, 24, 33–36.
Apostolic Word   II Peter, iii, 10–18.

Responsive Lesson

Psalm i: PSALMS OF ASAPH, Ps. lxxv, lxxxii.

B LESSED is the man that walketh not in the counsel of the wicked,
Nor standeth in the way of sinners,
Nor sitteth in the seat of the scoffing.

66. LORD'S DAY SECOND IN ADVENT—EVENING

2 But his delight is in the law of Jehovah;
And in His law doth he meditate day and night.
3 And he shall be like a tree planted by the streams of water,
That bringeth forth its fruit in its season,
4 Whose leaf also doth not wither,
And whatsoever he doeth shall prosper.
5 The wicked are not so;
But are like the chaff which the wind driveth away.
6 Therefore the wicked shall not stand in the judgment,
Nor sinners in the congregation of the righteous.
7 For Jehovah knoweth the way of the righteous:
But the way of the wicked shall perish.

---

8 WE give thanks unto Thee, O God;
We give thanks,
9 For Thy Name is near:
Men tell of Thy wondrous works.
10 When I shall find the set time, I will judge uprightly.
The earth and all the inhabitants thereof are dissolved:
I have set up the pillars of it.
11 I said unto the arrogant, Deal not arrogantly:
And to the wicked, Lift not up the horn:
12 Lift not up your horn on high;
Speak not with a stiff neck.
13 For neither from the east, nor from the west,
Nor yet from the south, cometh lifting up.
14 But God is the judge:
He putteth down one, and lifteth up another.
15 For in the hand of Jehovah there is a cup, and the wine foameth;
It is full of mixture,
16 And He poureth out of the same:
Surely the dregs thereof, all the wicked of the earth shall drain them, and drink them.
17 But I will declare forever,
I will sing praises to the God of Jacob.
18 All the horns of the wicked also will I cut off;
But the horns of the righteous shall be lifted up.

---

19 GOD standeth in the congregation of God;
He judgeth among the gods.
20 How long will ye judge unjustly,
And respect the persons of the wicked?
21 Judge the poor and fatherless:
Do justice to the afflicted and destitute.
22 Rescue the poor and needy:
Deliver them out of the hand of the wicked.
23 They know not,
Neither do they understand;
24 They walk to and fro in darkness:
All the foundations of the earth are moved.

66. LORD'S DAY SECOND IN ADVENT—EVENING

²⁵ I said, Ye are gods,
And all of you sons of the Most High.
²⁶ Nevertheless ye shall die like men,
And fall like one of the princes.
²⁷ Arise, O God, judge the earth:
FOR THOU SHALT INHERIT ALL THE NATIONS.

Psalm Chant　　Same as for Day No. 65.

Hymn of Praise　　JOHN CENNICK, alt. by CHARLES WESLEY. Pub. 1752. (Dox. added.)

Lo! HE comes with clouds descending,
Once for favored sinners slain!
Thousand thousand saints attending,
Swell the triumph of His train!
Hallelujah!
Jesus comes, and comes to reign.

2 Yea, Amen! let all adore Thee,
High on Thine eternal throne!
Savior, take the power and glory;
Make Thy righteous sentence known!
Men and angels
Kneel and bow to Thee alone!

3. God E-ter-nal! we a-dore Thee, Lord of all the heav'n-ly host: Earth and heav'n with joy be-fore Thee Wor-ship give with praise ut-most: Thine be glo-ry!—Thine be glo-ry!— Fa-ther, Son, and Ho-ly Ghost. A-MEN.

REGENT SQUARE. 878747.　　　　HENRY SMART, 1868.

67. LORD'S DAY THIRD IN ADVENT
MORNING

Introductory

Sentence

BLOW ye the trumpet in Zion,
Sound an alarm in My holy mountain.
For the day of Jehovah cometh;
As the dawn spread upon the mountains. [Joel ii, 1, 2]

Response

JEHOVAH cometh; He cometh to | judge the | earth:
He shall judge the world with righteousness,
And the | peo-ples | with His | truth. [Ps. xcvi, 13]

THOMAS JACKSON, d. 1781.

Scripture Lessons Old Covenant Isaiah, xxiv, 1-8, 17-23.
Gospel Matt. xxiv, 36-44.
Apostolic Word Rev. i, 1-8.

Responsive Lesson A SONG OF DAVID, Ps. vii: x.

O JEHOVAH my God, in Thee do I take refuge:
  Save me from all them that pursue me,
2 And deliver me: lest he tear my soul like a lion,
  Rending it in pieces, while there is none to deliver.
3 O Jehovah my God, if I have done this;
  If there be iniquity in my hands;
4 If I have rewarded evil unto him that was at peace with me;
  (Yea, I have delivered him that without cause was mine adversary:)
5 Let the enemy pursue my soul,
  And overtake it;
6 Yea, let him tread my life down to the earth,
  And lay my glory in the dust.
7 Arise, O Jehovah, in Thine anger,
  Lift up Thyself against the rage of mine adversaries:
8 And awake for me;
  Thou hast commanded judgment.
9 And let the congregation of the peoples compass Thee about:
  And over them return Thou on high.
     JEHOVAH MINISTERETH JUDGMENT TO THE PEOPLES:
10 Judge me, O Jehovah, according to my righteousness,
  And to mine integrity that is in me.
11 O let the wickedness of the wicked come to an end,
  But establish Thou the righteous:
  For the righteous God trieth the hearts and reins.
12 My shield is with God,
  Who saveth the upright in heart.
13 God is a righteous judge,
  Yea, a God that hath indignation every day.

14 If a man turn not, He will whet His sword;
   He hath bent His bow, and made it ready.
15 He hath also prepared for him the instruments of death;
   He maketh His arrows fiery shafts.
16 Behold, he travaileth with iniquity;
   Yea, he hath conceived mischief, and brought forth falsehood.
17 He hath made a pit, and digged it,
   And is fallen into the ditch which he made.
18 His mischief shall return upon his own head,
   And his violence shall come down upon his own pate.
19 I will give thanks unto Jehovah according to His righteousness:
   And will sing praise to the Name of Jehovah Most High.

---

20 WHY standest Thou afar off, O Jehovah?
   Why hidest Thou Thyself in times of trouble?
21 In the pride of the wicked the poor is hotly pursued;
   Let them be taken in the devices that they have devised.
21 For the wicked boasteth of his heart's desire,
   And the covetous renounceth, yea, contemneth Jehovah.
23 The wicked, in the pride of his countenance, saith, He will not require it.
   All his thoughts are, There is no God.
24 His ways are firm at all times;
   Thy judgments are far above out of his sight:
25 As for all his adversaries, he puffeth at them.
   He saith in his heart, I shall not be moved:
   To all generations I shall not be in adversity.
26 His mouth is full of cursing and deceit and oppression:
   Under his tongue is mischief and iniquity.
27 He sitteth in the lurking-places of the villages:
   In the covert places doth he murder the innocent:
28 His eyes are privily set against the helpless.
   He lurketh in the covert as a lion in his den:
29 He lieth in wait to catch the poor:
   He doth catch the poor, when he draweth him in his net.
30 He croucheth, he boweth down,
   And the helpless fall by his strong ones.
31 He saith in his heart, God hath forgotten:
   He hideth His face; He will never see it.
32 Arise, O Jehovah; O God, lift up Thy hand:
   Forget not the poor.
33 Wherefore doth the wicked contemn God,
   And say in his heart, Thou wilt not require it?
34 Thou hast seen it; for Thou beholdest mischief and spite,
   To requite it with Thy hand.
35 The helpless committeth himself unto Thee;
   Thou hast been the helper of the fatherless.
36 Break Thou the arm of the wicked;
   And as for the evil man, seek out his wickedness till Thou find none.
37 Jehovah is King for ever and ever:
   The nations are perished out of His land.

67. LORD'S DAY THIRD IN ADVENT — MORNING

38 O Jehovah, Thou hast heard the desire of the meek:
Thou wilt prepare their heart, Thou wilt cause Thine ear to hear:
39 To judge the fatherless and the oppressed,
That man who is of the earth may be terrible no more.

Psalm Chant From a PRAYER OF HABAKKUK, Hab. iii. [Same for Ev'g, and for Day No. 68]

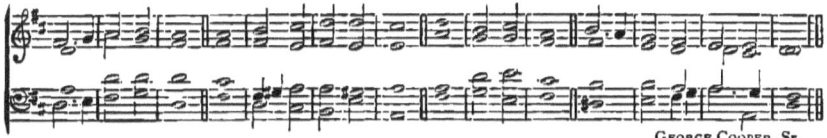

GEORGE COOPER, Sr.

O JEHOVAH, I have heard the report of Thee, and | am a- | fraid:
O Jehovah, revive Thy | work · in the | midst · of the | years:
2 In the midst of the years | make it | known;
In | wrath re- | mem-ber | mercy.
3 God, the Holy One, came: His glory | cover'd the | heavens,
And the earth was | full | of His | praise;
4 And His brightness was | as the | light:
He had rays coming out of His hand;
And there was the | hid-ing | of His | power.
5 Before Him | went the | pestilence,
And fiery | bolts went | forth · at His | feet.
6 He stood and | measur'd the | earth;
He beheld and | drove a- | sunder the | nations.
7 And the eternal | mountains were | scatter'd,
The ever- | last-ing | hills did | bow.
8 The mountains saw Thee and were afraid;
The tempest of waters | passed | by:
The deep uttered his voice,
And lifted | up his | hands on | high.
9 The sun and moon stood still in their | hab-i- | tation;
At the light of Thine arrows as they went,
At the | shining · of Thy | glit-tering | spear.
10 Thou wentest forth for the salvation | of Thy | people,
For the sal- | vation of | Thine an- | ointed.
11 GLORY be to the Father, etc.

Prayer of the Day

O LORD our God, whose blessed Son was manifested that He might destroy the works of the devil, and make us the sons of God, and who cometh the second time that He may glorify us with Himself:
Mercifully grant that we, having this hope in Him, may purify ourselves even as He is pure; that when He shall appear again in power and great glory, we may be made like unto Him in His eternal Kingdom,
Wherein He is exalted with the Father and the Spirit — one God: AMEN.

67. LORD'S DAY THIRD IN ADVENT—MORNING

Hymn of Praise
CHARLES WESLEY. Pub. 1782. (Dox. added.)

O THOU whom we adore!
To bless our earth again,
Assume Thine own almighty power,
And o'er the nations reign.

2 The world's Desire and Hope,
All power to Thee is given;
Now set the last great empire up,
Eternal Lord of Heaven!

3 A gracious Savior, Thou
Wilt all Thy creatures bless;
And every knee to Thee shall bow,
And every tongue confess.

4 According to Thy word,
Now be Thy grace revealed;
And with the knowledge of the Lord
Let all the earth be filled.

5. We join the heav'n-ly host, Thy glo-rious Name to praise; Thou Fa-ther, Son, and Ho-ly Ghost!—One God to end-less days. A-MEN.

FERGUSON. S. M.   GEORGE KINGSLEY, 1843.

---

67. EVENING
LORD'S DAY THIRD IN ADVENT

Introductory

Sentence

O WORSHIP Jehovah in the beauty of holiness:
Tremble before Him, all the earth.
Let the heavens be glad, and let the earth rejoice;
Let the sea roar and the fullness thereof;
Before Jehovah, for He cometh.   [Ps. xcvi, 9, 11, 13]

Response
(Tune, in Morning)

JEHOVAH cometh; He cometh to | judge the | earth:
He shall judge the world with righteousness,
And the | peo-ples | with His | truth.   [Ps. xcvi, 13]

Scripture Lessons

Old Covenant   Isaiah, xxx, 18–21, 25–30.
Gospel   Mark, xiii, 32–37.
Apostolic Word   Phil. iii, 20, 21; iv, 1–7.

67. LORD'S DAY THIRD IN ADVENT — EVENING

Responsive Lesson

Psalms xciv, xcviii.

O JEHOVAH, Thou God to whom vengeance belongeth,
Thou God to whom vengeance belongeth, shine forth.
2 Lift up Thyself, Thou judge of the earth:
Render to the proud their desert.
3 O Jehovah, how long shall the wicked,
How long shall the wicked triumph?
4 They prate, they speak arrogantly:
All the workers of iniquity boast themselves.
5 They break in pieces Thy people, O Jehovah,
And afflict Thy heritage.
6 They slay the widow and the stranger,
And murder the fatherless.
7 And they say, Jehovah shall not see,
Neither shall the God of Jacob consider.
8 Consider, ye brutish among the people:
And ye fools, when will ye be wise?
9 He that planted the ear, shall He not hear?
He that formed the eye, shall He not see?
10 He that chastiseth the nations, shall not He correct,
Even He that teacheth man knowledge?
11 Jehovah knoweth the thoughts of man,
That they are vanity.
12 Blessed is the man whom Thou chastenest, O Jehovah,
And teachest out of Thy law;
13 That Thou mayest give him rest from the days of adversity,
Until the pit be digged for the wicked.
14 For Jehovah will not cast off His people,
Neither will He forsake His inheritance.
15 For judgment shall return unto righteousness:
And all the upright in heart shall follow it.
16 Who will rise up for me against the evil-doers?
Who will stand up for me against the workers of iniquity?
17 Unless Jehovah had been my help,
My soul had soon dwelt in silence.
18 When I said, My foot slippeth;
Thy lovingkindness, O Jehovah, held me up.
19 In the multitude of my thoughts within me
Thy comforts delight my soul.
20 Shall the throne of wickedness have fellowship with Thee,
Which frameth mischief by statute?
21 They gather themselves together against the soul of the righteous,
And condemn the innocent blood.
22 But Jehovah hath been my high tower;
And my God the rock of my refuge.
And He hath brought upon them their own iniquity.
23 And shall cut them off in their own evil;
Jehovah our God shall cut them off.

67. LORD'S DAY THIRD IN ADVENT — EVENING

24 O SING unto Jehovah a new song;
   For He hath done marvelous things:
   His right hand, and His holy arm, hath wrought salvation for Him.
25 Jehovah hath made known His salvation:
   His righteousness hath He openly showed in the sight of the nations.
26 He hath remembered His lovingkindness and His faithfulness
      toward the house of Israel:
   All the ends of the earth have seen the salvation of our God.
27 Make a joyful noise unto Jehovah, all the earth:
   Break forth and sing for joy, yea, sing praises.
28 Sing praises unto Jehovah with the harp;
   With the harp and the voice of melody.
29 With trumpets and sound of cornet
   Make a joyful noise before the King Jehovah.
30 Let the sea roar, and the fullness thereof;
   The world, and they that dwell therein;
31 Let the floods clap their hands;
   Let the hills sing for joy together;
32 Before Jehovah, for He cometh to judge the earth:
   He shall judge the world with righteousness,
      And the peoples with equity.

Psalm Chant   Same as for Morning.

Hymn of Praise

JOSIAH CONDER, d. 1855. (Dox. added.)

SEE the ransomed millions stand —
Palms of conquest in their hands!
This before the throne their strain —
" Hell is vanquished — death is slain ! —
Blessing, honor, glory, might,
Are the Conqueror's native right!
Thrones and powers before Him fall —
Lamb of God, and Lord of all !"

2 Hasten, Lord! the promised hour;
Come in glory and in power!
Still Thy foes are unsubdued:
Nature sighs to be renewed:
Time has nearly reached its sum:
All things, with the Bride, say, " Come!"
Jesus! whom all worlds adore,
Come — and reign for evermore!

3. Hal - le - lu - jah! Praise the Lord, Earth and heav'n ! with glad ac - cord. God of blessing!

hear our songs, Thou to whom all praise be - longs: Thee, E - ternal God, Most High — Thee we laud and

67. LORD'S DAY THIRD IN ADVENT — EVENING

mag · ni · fy: Glorious o'er the heav'n·ly host— Father, Son, and Ho·ly Ghost. A·MEN.

COBURG. 7s, D.   ALBERT, Prince Consort.

68. LORD'S DAY FOURTH IN ADVENT
MORNING

Introductory

Sentence   BEHOLD, Jehovah hath proclaimed unto the end of the earth —
Say ye to the Daughter of Zion, Behold, thy Salvation cometh:
Behold, His reward is with Him,
And His recompense before Him.   [Is. lxii, 11]

Response   IT shall come to | pass • in that | day,
That the Root of Jesse which standeth for an | en-sign |
of the | peoples —
Unto Him shall the | na-tions | seek;
And His | rest-ing | place • shall be | glorious.   [Is. xi, 10]

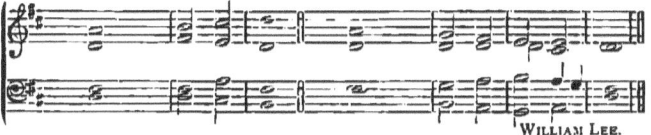

WILLIAM LEE.

Scripture Lessons   Old Covenant   Isaiah, xxviii, 14–22.
                               Gospel   Luke, iii, 1–6, 15–17.
                               Apostolic Word   Heb. x, 1–10.   [Same as part for Day No. 21]

Responsive Lesson   From Isaiah, xl.

COMFORT ye, comfort ye My people, saith your God,
   Speak ye comfortably to Jerusalem,
2 And cry unto her, that her warfare is accomplished,
That her iniquity is pardoned;
   That she hath received of Jehovah's hand double for all her sins.
3 The voice of one that crieth,
Prepare ye in the wilderness the way of Jehovah,
   Make straight in the desert a highway for our God.
4 Every valley shall be exalted,
   And every mountain and hill shall be made low:
5 And the crooked shall be made straight,
   And the rough places plain:
6 And the glory of Jehovah shall be revealed,
   And all flesh shall see it together:
   FOR THE MOUTH OF JEHOVAH HATH SPOKEN IT.

7 The voice of one saying, Cry.
  And one said, What shall I cry?
8 All flesh is grass,
  And all the goodliness thereof is as the flower of the field:
9 The grass withereth, the flower fadeth;
  Because the breath of Jehovah bloweth upon it:
  Surely the people is grass.
10 The grass withereth, the flower fadeth:
  BUT THE WORD OF OUR GOD SHALL STAND FOREVER.
11 O thou that tellest good tidings to Zion,
  Get thee up into the high mountain;
12 O thou that tellest good tidings to Jerusalem,
  Lift up thy voice with strength;
13 Lift it up, be not afraid;
  Say unto the cities of Judah, Behold, your God!
14 Behold, the Lord Jehovah will come as a mighty one,
  And His arm shall rule for Him:
15 Behold, His reward is with Him,
  And His recompense before Him.
16 He shall feed His flock like a shepherd,
  He shall gather the lambs in His arm,
17 And carry them in His bosom,
  And shall gently lead those that give suck.
18 Who hath measured the waters in the hollow of His hand,
  And meted out Heaven with the span,
19 And comprehended the dust of the earth in a measure,
  And weighed the mountains in scales,
  And the hills in a balance?
20 Who hath directed the Spirit of Jehovah,
  Or being His counselor hath taught Him?
21 With whom took He counsel, and who instructed Him,
  And taught Him in the path of judgment,
22 And taught Him knowledge,
  And showed to Him the way of understanding?
23 Behold, the nations are as a drop of a bucket,
  And are counted as the small dust of the balance:
24 Behold, He taketh up the isles as a very little thing.
  And Lebanon is not sufficient to burn,
  Nor the beasts thereof sufficient for a burnt offering.
25 All the nations are as nothing before Him;
  They are counted to Him less than nothing, and vanity.
26 To whom then will ye liken God?
  Or what likeness will ye compare unto Him?
27 It is He that sitteth upon the circle of the earth,
  And the inhabitants thereof are as grasshoppers;
28 That stretcheth out the heavens as a curtain,
  And spreadeth them out as a tent to dwell in:
29 That bringeth princes to nothing;
  He maketh the judges of the earth as vanity.
30 Moreover He bloweth upon them, and they wither,
  And the whirlwind taketh them away as stubble.

68. LORD'S DAY FOURTH IN ADVENT — MORNING

31 To whom then will ye liken Me,
   That I should be equal to him? saith the Holy One.
32 Lift up your eyes on high, and see who hath created these,
   That bringeth out their host by number:
33 He calleth them all by name; by the greatness of His might,
   And for that He is strong in power, not one is lacking.

Psalm Chant
Same as for Day No. 67.

[On Dec. 21, Morning or Evening, may be used, instead, Psalm Chant for Day No. 64]

Prayer of the Day

INCLINE Thine ear, O Lord, to our prayers through Christ Jesus; and visit the darkness of our mind with the Dayspring from on high:

That we may always make ready the way of our Lord Christ whether in His meekness or in His majesty:

So that at the final coming of Thy Son to judge the world, we may hasten with joy to meet Him who is most high in glory with the Father and the Holy Spirit — one God, to ages without end: AMEN.

Hymn of Praise

RALPH WARDLAW, D. D.   (Dox., unknown author.)

O LORD our God! arise;
The cause of truth maintain;
And wide o'er all the peopled world
Extend her blessed reign.

2 Thou Prince of life! arise,
Nor let Thy glory cease;
Far spread the conquests of Thy grace,
And bless the earth with peace.

3 Thou Holy Ghost! arise,
Extend Thy healing wing,
And, o'er a dark and ruined world,
Let light and order spring.

4 All on the earth! arise,
To God the Savior sing;
From shore to shore, from earth to heaven,
Let echoing anthems ring.

5. The Father and the Son And Spirit, we adore: We glorify, we worship Thee, One God for evermore. A-MEN.

SWABIA. S. M.   German, 1745.

On Dec. 21, Morning or Evening, may be used, instead, Hymn of Praise for Day No. 64, "O God, beneath Thy guiding hand"]

68. EVENING
LORD'S DAY FOURTH IN ADVENT
[On Dec. 24, Evening, this observance may be set aside—yielding to Day No. 69]

Introductory

Sentence

COME, and let us return unto Jehovah.
And let us know — let us follow on to know Jehovah;
His going forth is sure as the morning:
And He shall come unto us as the rain,
As the latter rain that watereth the earth.   [Hos. vi, 1, 3]

Response
[Tune, in Morning]

IT shall come to | pass • in that | day,
That the Root of Jesse which standeth for an | en-sign | of the | peoples —
Unto Him shall the | na-tions | seek;
And His | rest-ing | place • shall be | glorious.   [Is. xi, 10]

Scripture Lessons   Old Covenant   Dan. vii, 15–27.
Gospel   John, v, 21–29.
Apostolic Word   Rom. xv, 4–13.

Responsive Lesson   Psalms, xcvi, lxxxv: A PSALM OF DAVID, cx.
[cx, also for Day No. 29]

O SING unto Jehovah a new song:
  Sing unto Jehovah, all the earth.
2 Sing unto Jehovah, bless His Name;
  Show forth His salvation from day to day.
3 Declare His glory among the nations,
  His marvelous works among all the peoples.
4 For great is Jehovah, and highly to be praised:
  He is to be feared above all gods.
5 For all the gods of the peoples are idols:
  But Jehovah made the heavens.
6 Honor and majesty are before Him:
  Strength and beauty are in His sanctuary.
7 Give unto Jehovah, ye kindreds of the peoples,
  Give unto Jehovah glory and strength.
8 Give unto Jehovah the glory due unto His Name:
  Bring an offering, and come into His courts.
  O WORSHIP JEHOVAH IN THE BEAUTY OF HOLINESS:
9 Tremble before Him, all the earth.
  Say among the nations, Jehovah reigneth.
10 The world also is established that it cannot be moved:
  He shall judge the peoples with equity.
11 Let the heavens be glad,
  And let the earth rejoice;
12 Let the sea roar, and the fullness thereof;
  Let the field exult, and all that is therein;
13 Then shall all the trees of the wood sing for joy;
  Before Jehovah, for He cometh;
  FOR HE COMETH TO JUDGE THE EARTH:

68. LORD'S DAY FOURTH IN ADVENT — EVENING

14 He shall judge the world with righteousness,
   And the peoples with His truth.

---

15 O JEHOVAH, Thou hast been favorable unto Thy land:
   Thou hast brought back the captivity of Jacob.
16 Thou hast forgiven the iniquity of Thy people,
   Thou hast covered all their sin.
17 Thou hast taken away all Thy wrath:
   Thou hast turned Thyself from the fierceness of Thine anger.
18 Turn us, O God of our salvation,
   And cause Thine indignation toward us to cease.
19 Wilt Thou be angry with us forever?
   Wilt Thou draw out Thine anger to all generations?
20 Wilt Thou not quicken us again:
   That Thy people may rejoice in Thee?
21 Show us Thy lovingkindness, O Jehovah,
   And grant us Thy salvation.
22 I will hear what God Jehovah will speak:
   For He will speak peace unto His people, and to His saints:
   But let them not turn again to folly.
23 Surely His salvation is nigh them that fear Him;
   That glory may dwell in our land.
24 Lovingkindness and truth are met together;
   Righteousness and peace have kissed each other.
25 Truth springeth out of the earth;
   And righteousness hath looked down from heaven.
26 Yea, Jehovah shall give that which is good;
   And our land shall yield her increase.
27 Righteousness shall go before Him;
   And shall make His footsteps a way to walk in.

---

28 JEHOVAH saith unto my Lord, Sit Thou at My right hand,
   Until I make Thine enemies Thy footstool.
29 Jehovah shall send forth the rod of Thy strength out of Zion:
   Rule Thou in the midst of Thine enemies.
30 Thy people offer themselves willingly in the day of Thy power,
   In holy attire;
31 Out of the womb of the morning,
   Thou hast the dew of Thy youth.
32 Jehovah hath sworn, and will not repent,
   Thou art a priest forever,
   After the order of Melchizedek.
33 The Lord at Thy right hand
   Shalt strike through kings in the day of His wrath.
   He shall judge among the nations.
34 He shall fill the places with dead bodies;
   He shall strike through the head in many countries.
35 He shall drink of the brook in the way:
   THEREFORE SHALL HE LIFT UP THE HEAD.

Psalm Chant   Same as for Day No. 67.

68. LORD'S DAY FOURTH IN ADVENT—EVENING

Hymn of Praise
CHARLES WESLEY, before 1744. (Dox. added.)

COME, Thou long-expected Jesus,
  Born to set Thy people free;
From our fears and sins release us,
  Let us find our rest in Thee.

2 Israel's Strength and Consolation,
  Hope of all the saints Thou art;
Dear Desire of every nation,
  Joy of every longing heart.

3 Born, Thy people to deliver;
  Born a child, and yet a King;
Born to reign in us forever,
  Now Thy precious kingdom bring.

4 By Thine own eternal Spirit,
  Rule in all our hearts alone;
By Thine all-sufficient merit,
  Raise us to Thy glorious throne.

5. Father, Son, and Spirit— glorious! Lord of all to endless days;
To Thy Name, O God, victorious— Blessing, honor, love, and praise! A-MEN.

NEWTON FERNS. 8787.   SAMUEL SMITH.

69. THE NATIVITY EVE (Christmas Eve)

Introductory
Sentence

BECAUSE of the tender mercy of our God,
The dayspring from on high shall visit us,
To shine upon them that sit in darkness and the shadow of death;
To guide our feet into the way of peace.   [Luke, i, 78, 79]

Response
[Tune in Day No. 71]

GLORY to | God • in the | highest !
And on earth peace among men in | whom He | is well | pleased !   [Luke, ii, 14]

Scripture Lessons
Old Covenant   Deut. xviii, 13–19.
Gospel   Luke, i, 26–33.
Apostolic Word   Gal. iv, 1–7.

[After the Scripture of the New Covenant may be sung, if desired, *Magnificat* (The Song of the Virgin Mary), Luke, i, 46–55]

MAGNIFICAT

MY soul doth magni- | fy the | Lord,
  And my spirit hath re- | joic'd in | God my | Savior.
2 For He hath looked upon the low es- | tate • of His | handmaiden :
  For behold, henceforth all gener- | ations shall | call me | blessèd.

69. THE NATIVITY EVE

3 For He that is mighty hath done to me great things; and holy | is His | Name.
  And His mercy is unto generations and generations on | them that | fear | Him.
4 He hath show'd | strength • with His | arm;
  He hath scatter'd the proud in the imagin- | a-tion | of their | heart.
5 He hath put down princes | from their | thrones
  And hath exalted | them of | low de- | gree.
6 The hungry He hath | fill'd • with good | things;
  And the rich He hath | sent | empty a- | way.
7 He hath helped Isra- | el His | servant,
  That He | might re- | member | mercy
8 (As He spake | unto our | fathers)
  Toward Abraham | and his | seed for | ever. ‖ AMEN. ‖

Responsive Lesson From Micah, iv: v, 1-5: from Ps. lxxxix: A SONG OF ASCENTS, OF DAVID, Ps. cxxxi.

THOU, O tower of the flock,
  The hill of the daughter of Zion—
2 Unto thee shall it come; yea, the former dominion shall come,
  The kingdom of the daughter of Jerusalem.
3 Now why dost thou cry out aloud?
  Is there no king in thee?
  Is thy counselor perished?
4 And now many nations are assembled against thee, that say, Let her be defiled,
  And let our eye see its desire upon Zion.
5 But they know not the thoughts of Jehovah,
  Neither understand they His counsel:
6 For He hath gathered them
  As the sheaves to the threshing-floor.
7 Arise and thresh, O daughter of Zion:
  For I will make thy horn iron,
  And I will make thy hoofs brass:
8 And thou shalt beat in pieces many peoples:
  And I shall devote their gain unto Jehovah,
  And their substance unto the Lord of the whole earth.
9 Now shalt thou gather thyself in troops, O daughter of troops:
  He hath laid siege against us:
  They shall smite the judge of Israel with a rod upon the cheek.
10 But thou, Beth-lehem Ephrathah,
  Which art little to be among the thousands of Judah,
11 Out of thee shall One come forth unto Me that is to be ruler in Israel;
  Whose goings forth are from of old, from everlasting.
12 Therefore will He give them up, until the time that she which travaileth hath brought forth: [*Israel.*
  Then the residue of His brethren shall return unto the children of

69. THE NATIVITY EVE

13 And He shall stand, and shall feed His flock in the strength of Jehovah,
In the majesty of the Name of Jehovah His God:
14 And they shall abide;
For now shall He be great unto the ends of the earth.
AND THIS MAN SHALL BE OUR PEACE:

---

15 I HAVE made a covenant with My chosen,
I have sworn unto David My servant;
16 Thy seed will I establish forever,
And build up thy throne to all generations.
17 O Jehovah, God of hosts,
Who is a mighty one, like unto Thee, O Jehovah?
And Thy faithfulness is round about Thee.
18 Thou rulest the pride of the sea:
When the waves thereof arise, Thou stillest them.
19 Thou hast broken Egypt in pieces, as one that is slain;
Thou hast scattered Thine enemies with the arm of Thy strength.
20 The heavens are Thine, the earth also is Thine:
The world and the fullness thereof, Thou hast founded them.
21 The north and the south, Thou hast created them:
Tabor and Hermon rejoice in Thy Name.
22 Thou hast a mighty arm:
Strong is Thy hand, and high is Thy right hand.
23 Thou saidst, I have found David My servant;
With My holy oil have I anointed him:
24 With whom My hand shall be established;
Mine arm also shall strengthen him.
25 The enemy shall not exact upon him;
Nor the son of wickedness afflict him.
26 And I will beat down his adversaries before him,
And smite them that hate him.
27 But My faithfulness and My lovingkindness shall be with him;
And in My Name shall his horn be exalted.
28 My lovingkindness will I keep for him for evermore,
And My covenant shall stand fast with him.
29 His seed also will I make to endure forever,
And his throne as the days of heaven.
30 My covenant will I not break,
Nor alter the thing that is gone out of My lips.

---

31 O JEHOVAH, my heart is not haughty,
Nor mine eyes lofty;
32 Neither do I exercise myself in great matters,
Or in things too wonderful for me.
33 Surely I have stilled and quieted my soul;
Like a weaned child with his mother,
My soul is with me like a weaned child.
34 O Israel, hope in Jehovah,
FROM THIS TIME FORTH AND FOR EVERMORE.

69. THE NATIVITY EVE   301

Psalm Chant   Same as for Day No. 71.

Prayer of the Day

ALMIGHTY and Eternal God, who hast given us Thine adorable, true, and only begotten Son—the Brightness of Thy glory and the express Image of Thy Person—to come in our nature, being born of a virgin by the power of the Holy Spirit:
Grant that, by the same Spirit, we being born anew and made Thy children through adoption and grace in Christ Jesus, may daily be renewed after the image of this Thy Son:
Till in us He be perfectly formed who throughout all ages is in Thee, O Father, with Thy blessed Spirit—one God: AMEN.

Hymn of Praise   CATHERINE WINKWORTH, tr. Pub. 1855. From German Hymn of LAURENTIUS LAURENTI, 1700. (Dox. added.)

O THOU essential Word,
 Who wast from everlasting
With God, for Thou wast God;
 On Thee our burden casting,
O Savior of our race,
 Welcome indeed Thou art,
Redeemer, Fount of Grace,
 To this my longing heart.

2 Come, self-existent Word,
 And speak Thou in my spirit;
The soul where Thou art heard,
 Doth endless peace inherit.
Thou Light that lightenest all,
 Abide through faith in me,
Nor let me from Thee fall,
 Nor seek a guide but Thee.

3. { O God—the Father, Son, And spir-it!—we a-dore Thee; }
   { E-ter-nal, Glorious One! All heav'ns give praise before Thee: } In grace enthroned art Thou;
All blessing to Thy Name!—Who hast been, and art now, And e'er shalt be, the same. A-MEN.

ST. NICHOLAS. P. M.   JOHANN CRÜGER, 1648.

70. THE NATIVITY DAY (*Christmas*)

[When this is the Lord's Day, this observance is set aside — yielding to Day No. 71: or, parts from both may be combined]

Introductory

Sentence

BEHOLD, I bring you good tidings of great joy which shall be to all the people:
For there is born to you this day in the city of David, a Savior who is Christ the Lord. [Luke, ii, 10, 11]

Response
[Tune in Day No. 71]

GLORY to | God · in the | highest!
And on earth peace among men in | whom He | is well | pleas'd! [Luke, ii, 14]

Scripture Lessons

Old Covenant   Ezekiel, xxxvii, 21-27.
Gospel   Luke, ii, 1-20.
Apostolic Word   I John, iv, 1-15.

[After the Scripture of the New Covenant, may be sung, if desired, *Nunc Dimittis* (The Song of Simeon), Luke, ii, 29–32]

NUNC DIMITTIS.

NOW lettest Thou Thy servant de- | part, O | Lord,
According to Thy | word, | in | peace;
2 For mine eyes have seen | Thy sal- | vation,
Which Thou hast prepar'd before the | face of | all | peoples;
3 A light for revelation | to the | Gentiles,
And the glory of Thy people | Is-ra- | el. ‖ A- | MEN. ‖

Responsive Lesson

From Jeremiah, xxxiii, xxiii: Isaiah, ix, 1-7: Zechariah, ii, 10-13. [Is. ix, 1-7 also for Day No. 71, M'rg]

BEHOLD, the days come, saith Jehovah, that I will perform that good word
Which I have spoken concerning the house of Israel
And concerning the house of Judah.
2 Behold, the days come, saith Jehovah,
That I will raise unto David a righteous Branch,
3 And He shall reign as King and deal wisely,
And shall execute judgment and justice in the land.
4 In His days Judah shall be saved,
And Israel shall dwell safely:
5 And this is His Name whereby He shall be called,
JEHOVAH IS OUR RIGHTEOUSNESS.

6 THERE shall be no gloom to her that was in anguish.
In the former time He brought into contempt the land of Zebulun
And the land of Naphtali;
7 But in the latter time hath He made it glorious, by the way of the sea,
Beyond Jordan, Galilee of the nations.
8 The people that walked in darkness have seen a great light:
They that dwelt in the land of the shadow of death,
Upon them hath the light shined.

70. THE NATIVITY DAY

9 Thou hast multiplied the nation,
Thou hast increased their joy:
10 They joy before Thee according to the joy in harvest,
As men rejoice when they divide the spoil.
11 For the yoke of his burden, and the staff of his shoulder,
The rod of his oppressor,
THOU HAST BROKEN AS IN THE DAY OF MIDIAN.
12 For all the armor of the armed man in the tumult,
And the garments rolled in blood,
13 Shall be for burning,
For fuel of fire.
14 For unto us a Child is born,
Unto us a Son is given;
15 And the government shall be upon His shoulder:
And His Name shall be called
WONDERFUL, COUNSELOR, MIGHTY GOD, EVERLASTING FATHER, PRINCE OF PEACE.
16 Of the increase of His government and of peace there shall be Upon the throne of David, [no end,
And upon his kingdom,
17 To establish it, and to uphold it with judgment
And with righteousness henceforth even forever.
THE ZEAL OF JEHOVAH OF HOSTS SHALL PERFORM THIS.

---

18 SING and rejoice, O daughter of Zion:
For, lo, I come,
And I will dwell in the midst of thee, saith Jehovah.
19 And many nations shall join themselves to Jehovah in that day,
And shall be My people:
20 And I will dwell in the midst of thee,
And thou shalt know that Jehovah of hosts hath sent Me unto thee.
21 And Jehovah shall inherit Judah as His portion in the holy land,
And shall yet choose Jerusalem.
22 Be silent, all flesh, before Jehovah:
FOR HE IS WAKED UP OUT OF HIS HOLY HABITATION.

Psalm Chant Same as for Day No. 71.

Prayer of the Day

BLESSED Lord Jehovah—the Father and the Son and the Spirit; who hast lightened our darkness in the gracious manifestation of the only-begotten Son from the heavens, our Savior Jesus, born of a virgin:
　Grant us faith to know Thee who comest among us in such meekness; that with all angels we may hasten to worship and proclaim the Eternal Word made flesh:
　And of Thy grace grant us to be born anew in Him after the fashion of His great humility, who is our Life and Light and Hope, the Prince of Peace and Lord of Lords in the glory of a Kingdom without end: AMEN.

[After the Prayers, may be sung, if desired, *Magnificat* (Song of the Virgin Mary): see in Day No. 69]

70. THE NATIVITY DAY

Hymn of Praise JOHN MASON NEALE, D. D., and Sir HENRY WILLIAMS BAKER, tr. Pub. 1861
From Latin Hymn of AURELIUS CLEMENS PRUDENTIUS, about A. D. 410.
(Dox. slightly alt.)

OF the Father's love begotten,
Ere the worlds began to be,
He, the Alpha and Omega,
He the source, the ending He,
Of the things that are, that have been,
And that future years shall see,
Evermore and evermore!

2 At His word the worlds were framéd;
He commanded; it was done:
Heaven and earth and depths of ocean
In their threefold order one;
All that grows beneath the shining
Of the moon and burning sun,
Evermore and evermore!

3 He is found in human fashion,
Death and sorrow here to know,
That the race of Adam's children,
Doomed by law to endless woe,
May not henceforth die and perish
In the dreadful gulf below,
Evermore and evermore!

4 This is He whom seers in old time
Chanted of with one accord;
Whom the voices of the prophets
Promised in their faithful word;
Now He shines, the long-expected:
Let creation praise its Lord:
Evermore and evermore!

5 O ye heights of heav'n, adore Him!
Angel hosts His praises sing!
All dominions bow before Him
And extol our God and King!
Let no tongue on earth be silent,
Every voice in concert ring,
Evermore and evermore!

6. Christ, to Thee! to Thee, O Father! And, O Holy Ghost, to Thee!—
One and only God—thanksgiving And unwearied praises be, Honor, glory, and dominion, And eternal victory, Evermore and evermore! A-MEN.

EVERMORE. P. M.   JOHANN SEBASTIAN BACH, d. 1750.

71. LORD'S DAY OF THE NATIVITY

Introductory
MORNING

Sentence   I HEARD a great voice out of the throne, saying—
Behold the Tabernacle of God is with men,
And He shall dwell with them,
And they shall be His peoples,
And God Himself shall be with them, and be their God.   [Rev. xxi, 3]

Response   GLORY to | God • in the | highest!
And on earth peace among men in | whom He | is well |
pleas'd!   [Luke, ii, 14]

WILLIAM CROTCH, Mus. Doc., d. 1847.

Scripture Lessons   Old Covenant   Ezekiel, i, 26-28: ii, 1, 2.
Gospel   John, i, 6-18: (or Matt. i, 18-23).
Apostolic Word   Heb. i.

[For additional Songs, *Magnificat* and *Nunc Dimittis*, see in Days Nos. 69, 70]

Responsive Lesson   Isaiah, ix, 1-7: from Is. xlii. [Is. ix, 1-7 also for Day No. 70, M'rg]

THERE shall be no gloom to her that was in anguish.
In the former time He brought into contempt the land of
    And the land of Naphtali;   [Zebulun
2 But in the latter time hath He made it glorious, by the way of
    Beyond Jordan, Galilee of the nations.   [the sea,
3 The people that walked in darkness have seen a great light:
    They that dwelt in the land of the shadow of death,
    Upon them hath the light shined.
4 Thou hast multiplied the nation,
    Thou hast increased their joy:
5 They joy before Thee according to the joy in harvest,
    As men rejoice when they divide the spoil.
6 For the yoke of his burden, and the staff of his shoulder,
    The rod of his oppressor,
    THOU HAST BROKEN AS IN THE DAY OF MIDIAN.
7 For all the armor of the armed man in the tumult,
    And the garments rolled in blood,
8 Shall be for burning,
    For fuel of fire.
9 For unto us a Child is born,
    Unto us a Son is given;
10 And the government shall be upon His shoulder:
    And His Name shall be called
    WONDERFUL, COUNSELOR, MIGHTY GOD, EVERLASTING
    FATHER, PRINCE OF PEACE.

11 Of the increase of His government and of peace there shall be
Upon the throne of David, [no end,
And upon his kingdom,
12 To establish it, and to uphold it with judgment
And with righteousness henceforth even forever.
THE ZEAL OF JEHOVAH OF HOSTS SHALL PERFORM THIS.

13 BEHOLD My servant, whom I uphold;
My chosen, in whom My soul delighteth:
14 I have put My spirit upon Him;
He shall bring forth judgment to the Gentiles.
15 He shall not cry, nor lift up,
Nor cause his voice to be heard in the street.
16 A bruised reed shall He not break,
And the smoking flax shall He not quench:
HE SHALL BRING FORTH JUDGMENT IN TRUTH.
17 He shall not fail nor be discouraged,
Till He have set judgment in the earth;
And the isles shall wait for His law.
18 Thus saith God Jehovah, He that created the heavens,
And stretched them forth;
19 He that spread abroad the earth
And that which cometh out of it;
20 He that giveth breath unto the people upon it,
And spirit to them that walk therein:
21 I Jehovah have called Thee in righteousness,
And will hold Thy hand, and will keep Thee,
22 And give Thee for a covenant of the people,
For a light of the Gentiles;
23 To open the blind eyes,
To bring out the prisoners from the dungeon,
And them that sit in darkness out of the prison house.
24 I am Jehovah; that is My Name:
And My glory will I not give to another,
Neither My praise unto graven images.
25 Behold, the former things are come to pass,
And new things do I declare:
Before they spring forth I tell you of them.

26 Sing unto Jehovah a new song,
And His praise from the end of the earth;
27 Ye that go down to the sea, and all that is therein,
The isles, and the inhabitants thereof.
28 Let the wilderness and the cities thereof lift up their voice,
The villages that Kedar doth inhabit;
29 Let the inhabitants of Sela sing,
Let them shout from the top of the mountains.
30 Let them give glory unto Jehovah,
And declare His praise in the islands.
31 Jehovah shall go forth as a mighty man;
He shall stir up jealousy like a man of war:

71. LORD'S DAY OF THE NATIVITY — MORNING

32 He shall cry, yea, He shall shout aloud;
  He shall do mightily against His enemies.
33 I have long time holden My peace;
  I have been still, and refrained Myself.
34 I will lay waste mountains and hills,
  And dry up all their herbs;
35 And I will make the rivers islands,
  And will dry up the pools.
36 And I will bring the blind by a way that they know not;
  In paths that they know not will I lead them: [straight.
37 I will make darkness light before them, and crooked places
  These things will I do, and I will not forsake them.
38 Hear, ye deaf;
  And look, ye blind, that ye may see.
39 It pleased Jehovah, for His righteousness' sake,
  TO MAGNIFY THE LAW, AND MAKE IT HONORABLE.

   From Psalm, lxxxix.   [Same for Ev'g, and for Days Nos. 69, 70]

RICHARD WOODWARD, Mus. Doc., d. 1778.

I WILL sing of the lovingkindnesses of Je- | hovah for | ever:
  With my mouth will I make known Thy faithful- | ness to | all gener- | ations.
2 For I have said, Lovingkindness shall be built | up for | ever;
  Thy faithfulness shalt Thou es- | tablish * in the | ver-y | heavens.
3 And the heavens shall praise Thy wonders, | O Je- | hovah;
  Thy faithfulness also in the as- | sembly * of the | ho-ly | ones.
4 Righteousness and justice are the foun- | dation * of Thy | throne:
  Lovingkindness and truth | go be- | fore Thy | face.
5 Blessed is the people that know the | joy-ful | sound:
  They walk, O Jehovah, in the | light of | Thy | countenance.
6 Thou spakest in vision to Thy saints, and saidst —
  I have laid help upon | One * that is | mighty;
  I have exalted | One chos'n | out * of the | people.
7 I will set His hand also | on the | sea,
  And His | right hand | on the | rivers.
8 He shall cry unto Me, | Thou * art My | Father,
  My God, and the | Rock of | My sal- | vation.
9 I also will make Him | My First- | born,
  The highest of the | kings | of the | earth.
10 His throne — it shall be establish'd for ever as the moon,
  And as the faithful | witness * in the | sky.
    Blessed be Jehovah for evermore: A- | men, | and A- | men.
11 GLORY be to the Father, etc.

71. LORD'S DAY OF THE NATIVITY — MORNING

Prayer of the Day

HEAR us, Jehovah, Father of Eternal Majesty — who in the glory of Thy grace hast come among us in exceeding lowliness in the person of our blessed Lord Jesus:

Vouchsafe unto us the precious gift of faith whereby we may know that the Eternal Word is made flesh and that the Son of God is come; that we, through Thy Holy Spirit, may be born anew in Him who was born on earth for us a Savior,

To whom, with Thee, O Father, and the same Spirit — one God — be glory everlasting: AMEN.

Hymn of Praise

MARTIN LUTHER, tr., 1523. From Hymn of NOTTKER BALBULUS, d. 912.
(Dox. added.)

ALL praise to Thee, eternal Lord,
Clothed in a garb of flesh and blood;
Choosing a manger for Thy throne,
While worlds on worlds are Thine alone!

2 Once did the skies before Thee bow;
A virgin's arms contain Thee now;
Angels, who did in Thee rejoice,
Now listen for Thine infant voice.

3 A little child, Thou art our guest,
That weary ones in Thee may rest;
Forlorn and lowly is Thy birth,
That we may rise to heaven from earth.

4 Thou comest in the darksome night
To make us children of the light;
To make us, in the realms divine,
Like Thine own angels round Thee shine.

5. To Thee, all glo - ry, God Most High! — The Fa-ther's Name we mag - ni - fy;
Thy Son, Thy Spir - it, we a - dore: We praise, we bless Thee, ev - er - more. A-MEN.

GRACE CHURCH. L. M.　　　　　　　　　　　　　　　IGNAZ JOSEF PLEYEL, d. 1831.

---

71. EVENING
LORD'S DAY OF THE NATIVITY

[On Dec. 31, Evening, this observance may be set aside — yielding to Day No. 72]

Introductory

Sentence HEREIN was the love of God manifested in us —
That God hath sent His only begotten Son into the world,
That we might live through Him.　　　　　　　[1 John, iv, 9]

71. LORD'S DAY OF THE NATIVITY—EVENING

Response
[Tune, in Morning]

GLORY to | God • in the | highest!
And on earth peace among men in | whom He | is well | pleased! [Luke, ii, 14]

Scripture Lessons
Old Covenant — Isaiah, xii.
Gospel — Luke, ii, 25–35.
Apostolic Word — Heb. ii.

Responsive Lesson From Isaiah, xi: from Zech. vi. [From Zech. vi, also for Day No. 20, M'rg]

THERE shall come forth a shoot out of the stock of Jesse,
And a branch out of his roots shall bear fruit:
2 And the Spirit of Jehovah shall rest upon Him,
The spirit of wisdom and understanding,
3 The spirit of counsel and might,
The spirit of knowledge and of the fear of Jehovah;
4 And His delight shall be in the fear of Jehovah:
And He shall not judge after the sight of His eyes,
Neither decide after the hearing of His ears:
5 But with righteousness shall He judge the poor,
And decide with equity for the meek of the earth:
6 And He shall smite the earth with the rod of His mouth,
And with the breath of His lips shall He slay the wicked.
7 And righteousness shall be the girdle of His loins,
And faithfulness the girdle of His reins.
8 And the wolf shall dwell with the lamb,
And the leopard shall lie down with the kid;
9 And the calf and the young lion and the fatling together;
And a little child shall lead them.
10 And the cow and the bear shall feed;
Their young ones shall lie down together:
And the lion shall eat straw like the ox.
11 And the sucking child shall play on the hole of the asp,
And the weaned child shall put his hand on the adder's den.
12 They shall not hurt nor destroy in all My holy mountain:
For the earth shall be full of the knowledge of Jehovah, as the waters cover the sea.
13 And it shall come to pass in that day, that the root of Jesse,
Which standeth for an ensign of the peoples,
14 Unto Him shall the nations seek;
And His resting-place shall be glorious.
15 And it shall come to pass in that day, that the Lord shall set His hand again the second time
To recover the remnant of His people, which shall remain,
16 From Assyria, and from Egypt, and from Pathros, and from Cush, and from Elam, and from Shinar, and from Hamath,
And from the islands of the sea.
17 And He shall set up an ensign for the nations,
And shall assemble the outcasts of Israel,
18 And gather together the dispersed of Judah
From the four corners of the earth.

71. LORD'S DAY OF THE NATIVITY—EVENING

19 The envy also of Ephraim shall depart,
   And they that vex Judah shall be cut off:
20 Ephraim shall not envy Judah,
   And Judah shall not vex Ephraim.
21 And Jehovah shall utterly destroy the tongue of the Egyptian sea;
   And with His scorching wind shall He wave His hand over the River,
22 And shall smite it into seven streams,
   And cause men to march over dryshod.
23 And there shall be a highway for the remnant of His people,
   Which shall remain, from Assyria;
24 Like as there was for Israel
   In the day that he came up out of the land of Egypt.

---

25 THUS speaketh Jehovah of hosts, saying,
   Behold, the Man whose name is The Branch;
   And He shall grow up out of His place,
26 And He shall build the temple of Jehovah:
   Even He shall build the temple of Jehovah;
27 And He shall bear the glory,
   And shall sit and rule upon His throne;
   AND HE SHALL BE A PRIEST UPON HIS THRONE:
28 And the counsel of peace shall be between them both.
   AND THEY THAT ARE FAR OFF SHALL COME AND BUILD IN THE TEMPLE OF JEHOVAH.

Psalm Chant
Same as for Morning.

Hymn of Praise
WILLIAM WALSHAM HOW, D.D. (Dox. added.)

O ONE with God the Father
   In majesty and might,
The brightness of His glory,
   Eternal Light of light;
O'er this our home of darkness
   Thy rays are streaming now;
The shadows flee before Thee,
   The world's true Light art Thou.

2 Yet, Lord, we see but darkly:—
   O heavenly Light, arise,
Dispel these mists that shroud us,
   And hide Thee from our eyes!

We long to track the footprints
   That Thou Thyself hast trod;
We long to see the pathway
   That leads to Thee our God.

3 O Jesus, shine around us
   With radiance of Thy grace;
O Jesus, turn upon us
   The brightness of Thy face.
We need no star to guide us,
   As on our way we press,
If Thou Thy light vouchsafest,
   O Sun of righteousness!

4 O Mighty God and Ho-ly! High in Thy dwelling-place; Yet thence Thy mercy

71. LORD'S DAY OF THE NATIVITY—EVENING

shi-neth— The brightness of Thy face: To Thee, all praise and glo-ry, God of e-ter-nal might!—O Fa-ther, Son, and Spir-it; Thou un-cre-at-ed Light! A-MEN.

AURELIA. 7676, D.   SAMUEL SEBASTIAN WESLEY, Mus. Doc., 1864.

72. NEW-YEAR EVE

Introductory

Sentence

HEAR my prayer, O Jehovah,
And give ear unto my cry;
For I am a stranger with Thee,
A sojourner, as all my fathers were.   [Ps. xxxix, 12]

Response

A THOUSAND years in Thy sight are but as yesterday |
when * it is | past,
And as a | watch | in the | night.
So teach us to | number our | days,
That we may | get us * a | heart of | wisdom.   [Ps. xc, 4, 12]

EDWARD FRANCIS RIMBAULT, Ph.D., LL.D.

Scripture Lessons   Old Covenant   Ecc. i, 1–15: xii, 13, 14.
Gospel   Matt. xxiv, 42–51; xxv, 1–13.
Apostolic Word   II Cor. iv, 16–18; v, 1–10.

Responsive Lesson   From A PSALM OF DAVID, Ps. xxxix, 4–13;
A PRAYER OF MOSES, Ps. xc.

WHILE I was musing the fire kindled:
Then spake I with my tongue:
2 O Jehovah, make me to know mine end,
And the measure of my days, what it is;
Let me know how frail I am.

72. NEW-YEAR EVE

3 Behold, Thou hast made my days as handbreadths;
   And mine age is as nothing before Thee:
4 Surely every man at his best estate is altogether vanity.
   Surely every man walketh in a vain show:
5 Surely they are disquieted in vain:
   He heapeth up riches, and knoweth not who shall gather them.
6 And now, Lord, what wait I for?
   My hope is in Thee.
7 Deliver me from all my transgressions:
   Make me not the reproach of the foolish.
8 I was dumb, I opened not my mouth;
   Because Thou didst it.
9 Remove Thy stroke away from me:
   I am consumed by the blow of Thy hand.
10 When Thou with rebukes dost correct man for iniquity,
    Thou makest his beauty to consume away like a moth:
    SURELY EVERY MAN IS VANITY.
11 Hear my prayer, O Jehovah, and give ear unto my cry;
    Hold not Thy peace at my tears:
12 For I am a stranger with Thee,
    A sojourner, as all my fathers were.
13 O spare me, that I may recover strength,
    Before I go hence, and be no more.

---

14 LORD, Thou hast been our dwelling place
    In all generations.
15 Before the mountains were brought forth,
    Or ever Thou hadst formed the earth and the world,
      EVEN FROM EVERLASTING TO EVERLASTING, THOU ART
      GOD.
16 Thou turnest man to destruction;
    And sayest, Return, ye children of men.
17 For a thousand years in Thy sight are but as yesterday when it is past,
    And as a watch in the night.
18. Thou carriest them away as with a flood; they are as a sleep:
    In the morning they are like grass which groweth up.
19 In the morning it flourisheth, and groweth up;
    In the evening it is cut down, and withereth.
20 For we are consumed in Thine anger,
    And in Thy wrath are we troubled.
21 Thou hast set our iniquities before Thee,
    Our secret sins in the light of Thy countenance.
22 For all our days are passed away in Thy wrath:
    We bring our years to an end as a sigh.
23 The days of our years are threescore years and ten,
    Or even by reason of strength fourscore years;
24 Yet is their pride but labor and sorrow;
    For it is soon gone, and we fly away.
25 Who knoweth the power of Thine anger,
    And Thy wrath according to the fear that is due unto Thee?

72. NEW-YEAR EVE 313

26 So teach us to number our days,
That we may get us a heart of wisdom.
27 Return, O Jehovah; how long?
And let it repent Thee concerning Thy servants.
28 O satisfy us in the morning with Thy lovingkindness;
That we may rejoice and be glad all our days.
29 Make us glad according to the days wherein Thou hast afflicted us,
And the years wherein we have seen evil.
30 Let Thy work appear unto Thy servants,
And Thy glory upon their children.
31 And let the favor of Jehovah our God be upon us:
And establish Thou the work of our hands upon us;
YEA, THE WORK OF OUR HANDS ESTABLISH THOU IT.

Psalm Chant   From Psalm cii.

WILLIAM HENRY HAVERGAL.

HEAR my prayer, | O Je- | hovah,
 And let my | cry come | un-to | Thee.
2 My days are like a shadow | that de- | clineth,
 And | I am | wither'd like | grass.
3 But Thou, Jehovah, shalt a- | bide for- | ever,
 And Thy memorial Name | un-to | all gener- | ations.
4 Thou shalt arise, and have mercy | up-on | Zion:
 For it is time to have pity upon her,
 | Yea, the * set | time is | come.
5 O my God, take me not away in the | midst * of my | days:
 Thy years are through- | out all | gen-er- | ations.
6 Of old hast Thou laid the foun- | dation . of the | earth,
 And the heavens | are the | work * of Thy | hands.
7 They shall perish, but | Thou * shalt en- | dure:
 Yea, all of them shall wax | old | like a | garment;
8 As a vesture | shalt Thou | change them,
 And | they | shall be | chang'd.
9 But Thou | art the | same,
 And Thy | years shall | have no | end.
10 The children of Thy servants | shall con- | tinue,
 And their seed shall be es- | tab-lish'd be- | fore | Thee.

11 GLORY be to the Father, etc.

Prayer of the Day

ETERNAL Lord, God of our fathers — with whom a thousand years are as one day, and who hast been our Refuge from one generation to another: mercifully remember us sinners who are of yesterday, strangers and sojourners on the earth where Thy Son also tabernacled in the flesh:

72. NEW-YEAR EVE

And so receive us into the pardoning comfort and the strong keeping of Thy grace, that we come not into condemnation before Thee for any of our years that are past; but may be, now and in all ages, in Thy Son our Savior;

For His sake, who with the Father and the Spirit—one God—liveth and reigneth, the same, yesterday, to-day, and forever: AMEN.

Hymn of Praise

ISAAC WATTS, D.D., 1719. (Dox. added.)

OUR God! our help in ages past,
  Our hope for years to come;
Our shelter from the stormy blast,
  And our eternal home!
Under the shadow of Thy throne
  Thy saints have dwelt secure;
Sufficient is Thine arm alone,
  And our defense is sure.

2 Before the hills in order stood,
  Or earth received her frame,
From everlasting Thou art God,
  To endless years the same.

A thousand ages, in Thy sight,
  Are like an evening gone;
Short as the watch that ends the night,
  Before the rising sun.

3 Time, like an ever-rolling stream,
  Bears all its sons away;
They fly, forgotten, as a dream
  Dies at the opening day.

Our God! our help in ages past,
  Our hope for years to come!
Be Thou our guard while troubles last,
  And our eternal home.

4. Let all the pow'rs in heav'n give praise: Let earth, with glad ac-cord, Thy Name ex-alt to endless days, Who art the on-ly Lord! O Ho-ly, Bless-ed Mighty One!—Thou God whom we a-dore; To Thee be glo-ry—Father, Son, And Spir-it, ev-er-more. A-MEN.

EVAN. C. M. D.   WILLIAM HENRY HAVERGAL, 1849.

MONTHLY SONGS OF PRAISE

[For Songs for the "*Signal Days*" (Days on which the Monthly Order is set aside), see those Days in Offices for the Year]

I. LORD'S DAY FIRST IN THE MONTH
MORNING

Introductory Response

THE Mighty One, God Je- | hovah, hath | spoken,
And called the earth from the rising of the sun unto the | going | down there- | of.
Out of Zion, the per- | fection of | beauty,
God | hath | shi-ned | forth. [Ps. l, 1, 2]

WILLIAM SAVAGE, d. 1789.

Psalm Chant Ps. c, xciii.

WILLIAM CROTCH, Mus. Doc., d. 1847

MAKE a joyful noise unto Jehovah, | all ye | lands.
Serve Jehovah with gladness:
Come be- | fore His | presence with | singing.
2 Know ye that Jehovah, He is God:
It is He that hath made us, and | we are | His:
We are His people and the | sheep of | His | pasture.
3 Enter into His gates with thanksgiving,
And into His | courts with | praise:
Give thanks unto | Him, and | bless His | Name.
4 For Jehovah is good;
His lovingkindness en- | dureth for | ever,
And His faithfulness | unto | all gener- | ations.

316   I. LORD'S DAY FIRST IN THE MONTH — MORNING

5 JEHOVAH reigneth; He is | cloth'd with | majesty;
  Jehovah is cloth'd with strength;
  He hath | girded Him- | self there- | with.
6 The world also is establish'd, that it | cannot be | mov'd.
  Thy throne is establish'd of old:
  Thou | art from | ever- | lasting.
7 The floods have lifted up, O Jehovah,
  The floods have lifted | up their | voice;
  The floods | lift | up their | waves.
8 Above the voices of many waters,
  The mighty breakers of the sea,
  Jehovah on | high is | mighty.
    Thy testimonies are very sure:
    Holiness becometh Thine house, O Je- | hovah, for | ever- | more.
9 GLORY be to the Father | and • to the | Son
  And | to the | Ho-ly | Ghost:
10 As it was in the beginning, is now, and | ev-er | shall be,
  World | with-out | end: A- | men.

GEORGE COOPER, d. 1876.

Hymns of Praise

[One to be chosen from the following]

HYMN No. 1.   L. M.   ISAAC WATTS, D. D., 1719.   (Dox. added.)

BEFORE Jehovah's awful throne,
  Ye nations! bow with sacred joy:
Know that the Lord is God alone:
  He can create, and He destroy.

2 We are Thy people, we Thy care,—
  Our souls, and all our mortal frame:
What lasting honors shall we rear,
  Almighty Maker! to Thy Name?

3 We'll crowd Thy gates with thankful songs,
  High as the heavens our voices raise;
And earth, with her ten thousand tongues,
  Shall fill Thy courts with sounding praise.

4 Wide as the world is Thy command
  Vast as eternity, Thy love;
Firm as a rock Thy truth must stand,
  When rolling years shall cease to move.

I. LORD'S DAY FIRST IN THE MONTH — MORNING 317

5. O Father, Son, and Holy Ghost— Thou God Most High! Thee we adore: From earth and all the heav'nly host, To Thee, all glory evermore! A-MEN.

OLD HUNDREDTH. L. M. GUILLAUME FRANC, 1543.

HYMN No. 2. H. M. ANONYMOUS. (Dox. added.)

O HOLY, holy Lord,
　Creation's sovereign King,
Thy majesty adored,
　Let all Thy creatures sing:
Who wast, and art, | Nor time shall see
And art to be; | Thy sway depart.

2 Great are Thy works of praise,
　O God of boundless might!
All just and true Thy ways,
　Thou King of saints in light!
Let all above, | Conspire to show
And all below | Thy power and love.

3 Who shall not fear Thee, Lord!
　And magnify Thy Name?
Thy judgments sent abroad
　Thy holiness proclaim:
Nations shall throng | And Thee adore,
From every shore, | In holy song.

4. Thou God—the Father, Son, And Spirit—ever blest! To Thee, Most Glorious One, All worship be addressed! Let earth adore, While angels bow And worship now And evermore. A-MEN.

DARWALL. H. M. JOHN DARWALL, 1770.

I. LORD'S DAY FIRST IN THE MONTH — MORNING

HYMN No. 3. 7s, 6l.   HENRY FRANCIS LYTE, 1834. (Dox. added.)

GOD of mercy, God of grace!
Show the brightness of Thy face:
Shine upon us, Savior! shine;
Fill Thy Church with light divine;
And Thy saving health extend
Unto earth's remotest end.

2 Let the peoples praise Thee, Lord!
Be by all that live adored:
Let the nations shout and sing,
Glory to their Savior King;
At Thy feet their tribute pay,
And Thy holy will obey.

3 Let the peoples praise Thee, Lord!
Earth shall then her fruits afford;
God to man his blessings give;
Man to God devoted live;
All below, and all above,
One in joy and light and love.

NASSAU. 7s, 6l.   JOHANN ROSENMÜLLER, 1655.

HYMN No. 4. L. M.   ISAAC WATTS, D. D., 1719. (Dox. added.)

FROM all that dwell below the skies,
Let the Creator's praise arise:
Let the Redeemer's Name be sung,
Through every land, by every tongue.

2 Eternal are Thy mercies, Lord!
Eternal truth attends Thy word:
Thy praise shall sound from shore to shore,
Till suns shall rise and set no more.

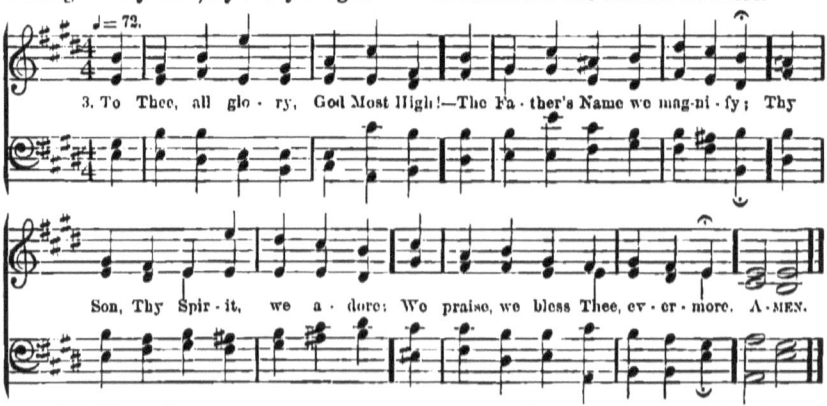

DENBIGH. L. M.   HENRY JOHN GAUNTLETT, Mus. Doc.

I. EVENING
LORD'S DAY FIRST IN THE MONTH

Introductory Response

LOOK unto Me, and | be ye | sav'd,
　All the | ends | of the | earth.
Unto Me every | knee shall | bow,
And every | tongue • shall con- | fess unto | God.
[Is. xlv, 22, 23 (Rom. xiv, 11)]

Sir Frederick Arthur Gore Ouseley, LL. D., Mus. Doc.

Psalm Chant
Ps. lxvii.

Richard Langdon, d. 1798.

GOD be merciful unto | us, and | bless us,
　And cause His | face to | shine up- | on us;
2 That Thy way may be | known upon | earth,
　Thy sal- | vation a- | mong all | nations.
3 Let the peoples praise | Thee, O | God;
　Let | all the | peo-ples | praise Thee.
4 O let the nations be glad and | sing for | joy:
　For Thou shalt judge the peoples with equity,
　And govern the | na-tions | up-on | earth.
5 Let the peoples praise | Thee, O | God;
　Let | all the | peo-ples | praise Thee.
6 The earth hath yielded her increase:
　God, even our own | God, shall | bless us.
　God shall bless us;
　And all the ends of the | earth shall | fear | Him.

7 Glory be to the Father | and • to the | Son
　And | to the | Ho-ly | Ghost:
8 As it was in the beginning, is now, and | ev-er | shall be,
　World | with-out | end: A- | men.

Joseph Barnby.

I. LORD'S DAY FIRST IN THE MONTH — EVENING

Hymns of Praise

HYMN No. 1. L. M.   ISAAC WATTS, D. D., 1719. (Dox. added.)

THE heavens declare Thy glory, Lord!
In every star Thy wisdom shines;
But, when our eyes behold Thy word,
We read Thy Name in fairer lines.

2 The rolling sun, the changing light,
And nights and days Thy power confess;
But the blest volume Thou hast writ
Reveals Thy justice and Thy grace.

3 Sun, moon, and stars convey Thy praise
Round the whole earth, and never stand;
So, when Thy truth began its race,
It touched and glanced on every land.

4 Nor shall Thy spreading gospel rest
Till through the world Thy truth has run,
Till Christ has all the nations blessed,
That see the light, or feel the sun.

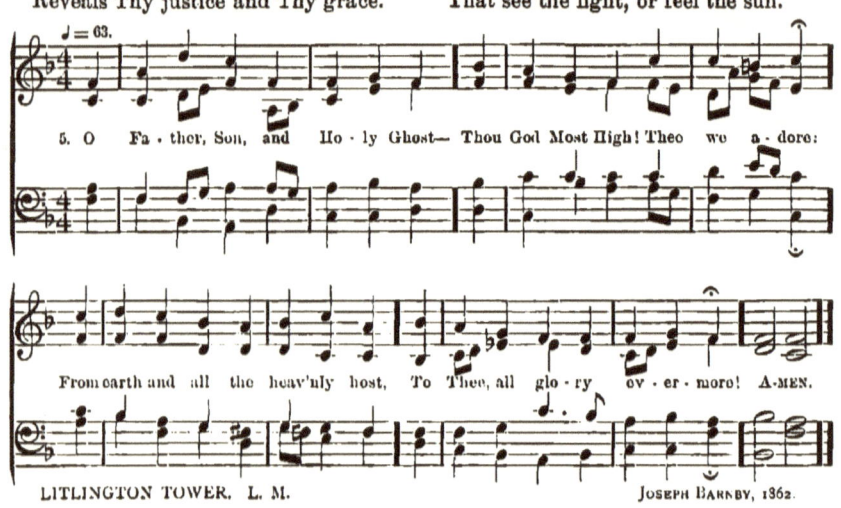

5. O Father, Son, and Holy Ghost— Thou God Most High! Thee we adore;
From earth and all the heav'nly host, To Thee, all glory evermore! A-MEN.

LITLINGTON TOWER. L. M.   JOSEPH BARNBY, 1862.

HYMN No. 2. 8787.   HENRY USTICK ONDERDONK, D. D., 1827. (Dox. added.)

BLEST be Thou, O God of Israel,
Thou, our Father, and our Lord!
Blest Thy majesty forever!
Ever be Thy Name adored.

2 Thine, O Lord, are power and greatness,
Glory, victory, are Thine own;
All is Thine in earth and heaven,
Over all Thy boundless throne.

3 Riches come of Thee, and honor,
Power and might to Thee belong;
Thine it is to make us prosper,
Only Thine to make us strong.

4 Lord, to Thee, Thou God of mercy,
Hymns of gratitude we raise;
To Thy Name, forever glorious,
Ever we address our praise!

I. LORD'S DAY FIRST IN THE MONTH — EVENING 321

5. Glo-ry in the high-est! Glo-ry Un-to God for ev-er-more—
Fa-ther, Son, and Ho-ly Spir-it! Thee let earth and heav'n a-dore. A-MEN.

ALL SAINTS. 8787. German, 1698.

HYMN No. 3. C. M. HENRY FRANCIS LYTE, 1834. (Dox. added.)

As BRIGHT and lasting as the sun,
As lofty as the sky,
From age to age Thy word shall run,
And chance and change defy.

2 The covenant of the King of kings
Shall stand forever sure;
Beneath the shadow of Thy wings
Thy saints repose secure.

3 In earth below, in heaven above,
Who, who is Lord like Thee?
O, spread the gospel of Thy love,
Till all Thy glories see!

4. O Ho-ly, Bless-ed, Might-y One! Thou God whom we a-dore;
To Thee be glo-ry— Fa-ther, Son, And Spir-it— ev-er-more! A-MEN.

ST. ANN'S. C. M. WILLIAM CROFT, Mus. Doc., 1708.

21

322   I. LORD'S DAY FIRST IN THE MONTH — EVENING

HYMN No. 4. S. M.   ISAAC WATTS, D. D., 1719.   (Dox. added.)

THY Name, Almighty Lord,
Shall sound through distant lands:
Great is Thy grace, and sure Thy word;
Thy truth forever stands.

2 Far be Thine honor spread,
And long Thy praise endure,
Till morning light, and evening shade,
Shall be exchanged no more.

3. We join the heav'n - ly --- host, Thy glo - rious Name to praise; Thou
Fa - ther, Son, and Ho - ly Ghost! — One God to end - less days. A - MEN.

ST. THOMAS. S. M.   GEORG FRIEDRICH HÄNDEL, d. 1759.

II. LORD'S DAY SECOND IN THE MONTH
MORNING

Introductory Response

JEHOVAH send thee help from the | sanc-tu- | ary,
And | strengthen | thee • out of | Zion!
Remember | all thine | offerings,
  And ac- | cept thy | sac-ri- | fice!   [Ps. xx, 1-3]

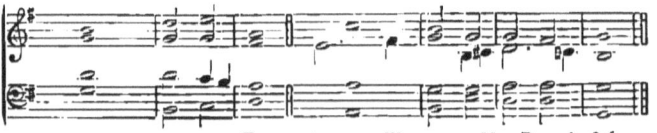

THOMAS ATTWOOD WALMISLEY, Mus. Doc., d 1856.

II. LORD'S DAY SECOND IN THE MONTH—MORNING 323

Psalm Chant From Ps. cxlv.

HENRY SMART, d. 1879.

1 I WILL extol Thee, my | God, O | King;
 And I will bless Thy | Name for | ever and | ever.
2 Every | day · will I | bless Thee;
 And I will praise Thy | Name for | ever and | ever.
3 Great is Jehovah and highly to be prais'd;
 And His greatness | is un- | searchable.
 One generation shall laud Thy works to another,
 And shall de- | clare Thy | might-y | acts.
4 They shall utter the memory of Thy great goodness,
 And shall sing of Thy | right-eous- | ness.
 Jehovah is gracious and merciful;
 Slow to anger, and of | great | lov-ing- | kindness.
5 Jehovah is good to all;
 And His tender mercies are over | all His | works.
 All Thy works shall give thanks unto Thee, O Jehovah,
 And Thy | saints shall | bless | Thee.
6 Thy Kingdom is an ever- | last-ing | Kingdom,
 And Thy dominion endureth through- | out all | gener- | ations.
7 The eyes of all wait upon Thee;
 And Thou givest them their | food · in due | season.
 Thou openest Thy hand,
 And satisfiest the desire of | ev-ery | liv-ing | thing.
8 Jehovah is righteous in all His ways,
 And gracious in | all His | works.
 Jehovah is nigh unto all them that call upon Him,
 To all that | call upon | Him in | truth.
9 Jehovah preserveth all | them that | love Him;
 But all the | wicked will | He de- | stroy.
10 My mouth shall speak the | praise · of Je- | hovah;
 And let all flesh bless His holy | Name for | ever and | ever.

11 GLORY be to the Father | and · to the | Son
 And | to the | Ho-ly | Ghost:
12 As it was in the beginning, is now, and | ev-er | shall be,
 World | with-out | end: A- | men.

WILLIAM BOYCE, Mus. Doc., d. 1779.

II. LORD'S DAY SECOND IN THE MONTH — MORNING

Hymns of Praise

HYMN No. 1. 11s, 10s.   FRANCES RIDLEY HAVERGAL, 1872. (Dox. added.)

HOLY and infinite! viewless! eternal!
Vailed in the glory that none can sustain,
None comprehendeth Thy being supernal,
Nor can the heaven of heavens contain.

2 Holy and infinite! limitless, boundless,
All Thy perfections and powers and praise:
Ocean of mystery! awful and soundless
All Thine unsearchable judgments and ways.

3 King of eternity! what revelation
Could the created and finite sustain,

But for Thy marvelous manifestation,
Godhead incarnate in weakness and pain!

4 Therefore archangels and angels adore [Thee,
Cherubim wonder, and seraphs admire;
Therefore we praise Thee, rejoicing before Thee,
Joining in rapture the heavenly choir.

5 Glorious in holiness, fearful in praises,
Who shall not fear Thee, and who shall not laud?
Anthems of glory Thy universe raises,
Holy and infinite! Father and God!

6. Mighty Jehovah! to Thee be all blessing; Lord over all! Thee we praise and adore:
Thee with Thy Son and Thy Spirit, confessing— Father of Glory, One God evermore. A-MEN.

LEILA. 11s, 10s.   Sir MICHAEL COSTA, d. 1884.

HYMN No. 2. L. M.   ANONYMOUS. From Latin Hymn "Te Deum," ascribed to Ambrose, Bishop of Milan, A. D. 390. (Dox. added.)

LORD God of Hosts, by all adored!
Thy Name we praise with one accord;
The earth and heavens are full of Thee,
Thy light, Thy love, Thy majesty.

2 Loud hallelujahs to Thy Name
Angels and seraphim proclaim;
Eternal praise to Thee is given
By all the powers and thrones in heaven.

3 The apostles join the glorious throng,
The prophets aid to swell the song,
The noble and triumphant host
Of martyrs make of Thee their boast.

4 The holy church in every place
Throughout the world exalts Thy praise;
Both heaven and earth do worship Thee,
Thou Father of eternity!

II. LORD'S DAY SECOND IN THE MONTH — MORNING

5. To Thee, all glo-ry, God Most High!— The Fa-ther's Name we mag-ni-fy; Thy Son, Thy Spir-it, we a-dore: We praise, we bless Thee, ev-er-more. A-MEN.

WINCHESTER NEW. L. M. German, 1690.

HYMN No. 3. 7s, 6l.   ANONYMOUS, 1863. (Dox. added.)

GLAD as when the glorious shout
Of the morning stars rang out,
Thee, Creator, will we praise,
And our hymns of triumph raise.
Sun and moon, your songs unite;
Praise Him, all ye stars of light!

2 Louder yet our strains be borne,
Mindful of that happy morn,
When the world's Redeemer rose,
Victor, from the grave's repose;
Who by death subdued the grave:
Mighty He our souls to save.

3 Looking for that rest above,
For the Sabbath of Thy love,
Here to-day by hope we rise
To our mansion in the skies:
Here by faith and love prepare
For our endless Sabbath there.

4 Praise a-bove all prais-es be, Lord Je-ho-vah! un-to Thee: Thee, E-ter-nal God, Most High— Thee we laud and magni-fy: Glorious o'er the heav'nly host—Father, Son, and Ho-ly Ghost. A-MEN.

KELSO. 7s, 6l. EDWARD JOHN HOPKINS, Mus. Doc., 1872.

II. LORD'S DAY SECOND IN THE MONTH — MORNING

HYMN No. 4. L. M. ISAAC WATTS, D. D., 1719. (Dox. added.)

JEHOVAH reigns! He dwells in light,
Girded with majesty and might;
The world, created by His hands,
Still on its firm foundation stands.

2 But ere this spacious world was made,
Or had its first foundation laid,
Thy throne eternal ages stood,
Thyself the ever-living God.

3 Like floods the angry nations rise,
And aim their rage against the skies:
Vain floods, that aim their rage so high!
At Thy rebuke the billows die.

4 Forever shall Thy throne endure:
Thy promise stand forever sure;
And everlasting holiness
Becomes the dwellings of Thy grace.

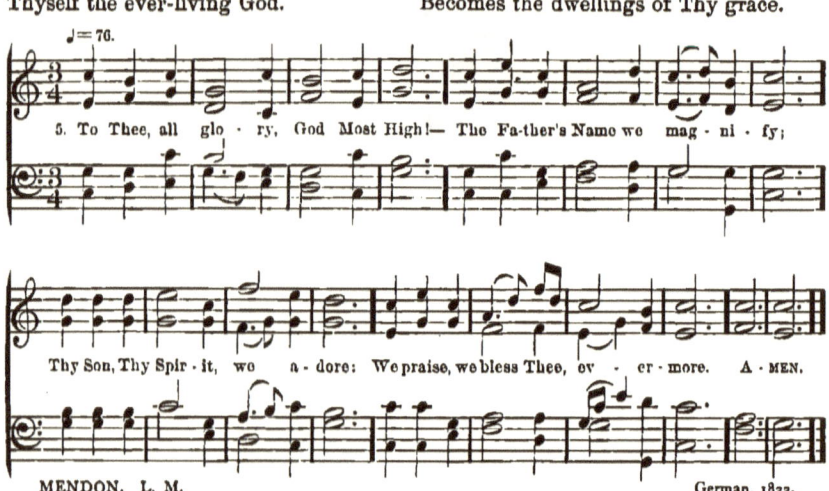

5. To Thee, all glo - ry, God Most High!— The Fa-ther's Name we mag - ni - fy;
Thy Son, Thy Spir - it, we a - dore: We praise, we bless Thee, ev - er - more. A - MEN.

MENDON. L. M. German, 1822.

II. EVENING
LORD'S DAY SECOND IN THE MONTH

Introductory Response

LIFT up your hands to the | sanc- | tu- | ary,
And | bless | ye Je- | hovah.
Jehovah bless Thee | out of | Zion!
Even He that | made | heaven and | earth. [Ps. cxxxiv. 2, 3]

WILLIAM HENRY HAVERGAL, d. 1870.

Psalm Chant

From Ps. xcii.

The EARL OF MORNINGTON, d. 1781.

IT is a good thing to give thanks | unto Je- | hovah,
And to sing praises unto | Thy Name, | O Most | High:
2 To show forth Thy lovingkindness | in the | morning,
And Thy | faithful-ness | ev-ery | night.
3 With an instrument of ten strings | and * with the | psaltery,
With a solemn | sound up- | on the | harp.
4 For Thou, Jehovah, hast made me | glad * through Thy | work:
I will triumph in the | works of | Thy | hands.
5 How great are Thy works, O Jehovah!
Thy thoughts are | ver-y | deep.
Thou, Jehovah, art on | high for | ev-er- | more.
6 For, lo, Thine enemies, O Jehovah,
For, lo, Thine enemies | shall | perish;
All the workers of in- | iqui-ty | shall be | scatter'd.
7 The righteous shall flourish | like the | palm tree:
He shall grow | like a | cedar in | Lebanon:
8 They are planted in the | house * of Je- | hovah;
They shall flourish in the | courts of | our | God.

9 GLORY be to the Father | and * to the | Son
And | to the | Ho-ly | Ghost:
10 As it was in the beginning, is now, and | ev-er | shall be,
World | with-out | end: A- | men.

JOHN LARKIN HOPKINS, Mus. Doc., d. 1873.

328 II. LORD'S DAY SECOND IN THE MONTH—EVENING

Hymns of Praise

HYMN No. 1. 10s, 11s.   Sir ROBERT GRANT, 1839. (Dox. added.)

O, WORSHIP the King, all-glorious above,
And gratefully sing His wonderful love;
Our Shield and Defender, the Ancient of days,
Pavilion'd in splendor, and girded with praise.

2 Thy bountiful care what tongue can recite?
It breathes in the air, it shines in the light,
It streams from the hills, it descends to the plain,
And sweetly distills in the dew and the rain.

3 Frail children of dust, and feeble as frail,
In Thee do we trust, nor find Thee to fail;
Thy mercies how tender! how firm to the end!
Our Maker, Defender, Redeemer, and Friend.

4 O Measureless Might! Ineffable Love!
While angels delight to hymn Thee above,
Thy humbler creation, though feeble their lays,
With true adoration shall join in Thy praise.

5. O Father and Son and Spirit, a-bove—Thou God on-ly One! to Thee be all love: From earth and from heaven, all glory to Thee, As ev-er was given and ev-er shall be. A-MEN.

HANOVER. 10s, 11s.   WILLIAM CROFT, Mus. Doc., 1708.

HYMN No. 2. C. M.   RIPPON'S COLLECTION, 1800. (Dox. added.)

AMID the splendors of Thy state,
O God! Thy love appears,
Soft as the radiance of the moon
Among a thousand stars.

2 In all Thy doctrines and commands,
Thy counsels and designs,
In every work Thy hands have framed
Thy love supremely shines.

3 Sinai, in clouds, and smoke, and fire,
Thunders Thine awful Name!
But Zion sings, in melting notes,
The honors of the Lamb.

4 Angels and men! the news proclaim
Through earth and heaven above;
And all, with holy transport, sing—
That God the Lord is love.

II. LORD'S DAY SECOND IN THE MONTH — EVENING 329

BELMONT. C. M.   Samuel Webbe, Jr., d. 1843.

HYMN No. 3. S. M.   Pratt's Collection. (Dox. added.)

Jehovah, God Most High!
We spread Thy praise abroad:
Thro' the whole world Thy fame shall fly,
O God, Thine Israel's God!

2 Wonders of grace and power
To Thee alone belong;
Thy church those wonders shall adore
In everlasting song.

3 Amen, our lips repeat—
Amen, we shout again:
Here all our wishes are complete,
Let God our Savior reign!

ARMES. S. M.   Philip Armes, Mus. Doc.

330 II. LORD'S DAY SECOND IN THE MONTH—EVENING

HYMN No. 4. 8787.   Edward Osler, M. D., 1836. (Dox. added)

WORSHIP, honor, glory, blessing,   2 As the hosts of heaven adore Thee,
  Lord, we offer to Thy Name;   We, too, bow before Thy throne;
Young and old, their thanks expressing,   As the angels serve before Thee,
  Join Thy goodness to proclaim.   So on earth Thy will be done.

CARTER. 8787.   Edmund S. Carter.

III. LORD'S DAY THIRD IN THE MONTH
MORNING

Introductory Response

THOU hast said, | Seek ye • My | face :
  My heart saith unto Thee,
    Thy face, O Je- | ho-vah, | will I | seek.   [Ps xxvii, 8]

RICHARD FARRANT, d. 1580.

III. LORD'S DAY THIRD IN THE MONTH—MORNING 331

Psalm Chant Ps. lxxxiv.

KNYVETT, from HANDEL.

HOW amiable are Thy tabernacles, O Je- | hovah of | hosts!
My soul longeth, yea, even fainteth for the courts of Jehovah;
My heart and my flesh cry out | unto the | liv-ing | God.
2 Yea, the sparrow hath found her a house,
And the swallow a nest for herself, where she may | lay her | young,
Even Thine altars, O Jehovah of | Hosts, my | King • and my | God.
3 Blessed are they that | dwell • in Thy | house:
They will be | still | prais-ing | Thee.
4 Blessed is the man whose | strength • is in | Thee;
In whose heart are the | high- | ways to | Zion.
5 Passing through the valley of Weeping, they make it a | place of | springs;
Yea, the early rain | cover- • eth | it with | blessings.
6 They go from | strength to | strength,
Every one of them appeareth be- | fore | God in | Zion.
7 O Jehovah, God of Hosts, hear my prayer:
Give ear, O | God of | Jacob.
Behold, O God our Shield,
And look upon the | face of | Thine an- | ointed.
8 For a day in Thy courts is better | than a | thousand.
I had rather stand at the threshold of the house of my God,
Than to | dwell • in the | tents of | wickedness.
9 For Jehovah, God, is a | sun • and a | shield:
Jehovah will | give | grace and | glory:
10 No good thing will He withhold from them that | walk up- | rightly.
O Jehovah of Hosts, blessed is the | man that | trust- • eth in | Thee.

11 GLORY be to the Father | and • to the | Son
And | to the | Ho-ly | Ghost:
12 As it was in the beginning, is now, and | ev-er | shall be,
World | with-out | end: A- | men.

JAMES TURLE.

III. LORD'S DAY THIRD IN THE MONTH — MORNING

Hymns of Praise No. 1. C. M.   Nahum Tate, 1703. From Latin "Te Deum," ascribed to Ambrose, Bishop of Milan, 390. (Dox. added.)

O God! we praise Thee, and confess
  That Thou the only Lord
And everlasting Father art,
  By all the earth adored.

2 To Thee all angels cry aloud;
  To Thee the powers on high,
Both cherubim and seraphim,
  Continually do cry:—

3 O holy, holy, holy Lord,
  Whom heavenly hosts obey,
The world is with the glory filled
  Of Thy majestic sway!

4 The apostles' glorious company,
  And prophets crowned with light,
With all the martyrs' noble host,
  Thy constant praise recite.

5 The holy church throughout the world,
  O Lord, confesses Thee,
That Thou the eternal Father art,
  Of boundless majesty.

LAUD. C. M.   John Bacchus Dykes, Mus. Doc.

Hymn No. 2.   H. M.   J. Young, pub. 1843. (Dox. added.)

O, for a shout of joy,
  Worthy the theme we sing;
  To this divine employ
    Our hearts and voices bring;
Sound, sound, thro' all the earth abroad,
The love, th' eternal love of God.

2 Unnumbered myriads stand,
  Of seraphs bright and fair,
  Or bow at Thy right hand,
    And pay their homage there;
But strive in vain with loudest chord,
To sound Thy wondrous love, O Lord.

3 Yet sinners saved by grace,
  In songs of lower key,
  In every age and place,
    Have sung the mystery —
Have told in strains of sweet accord,
Thy love, Thy sovereign love, O Lord.

4 Though earth and hell assail,
  And doubts and fears arise,
  The weakest shall prevail,
    And grasp the heavenly prize,
And through an endless age record
Thy love, Thy changeless love, O Lord.

III. LORD'S DAY THIRD IN THE MONTH — MORNING 333

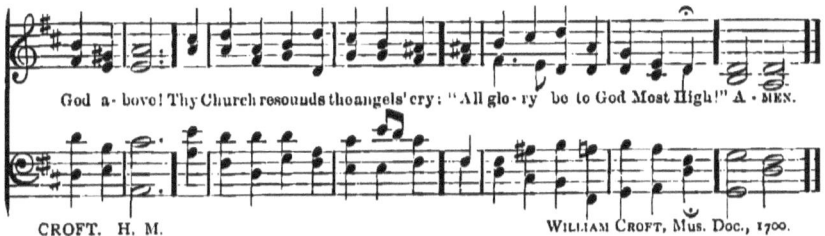

CROFT. H. M.   WILLIAM CROFT, Mus. Doc., 1700.

HYMN No. 3.   P. M.   REGINALD HEBER, D. D., pub. 1827. (Slightly alt.)

HOLY! holy! holy! Lord God Almighty!
Early in the morning our song shall rise to Thee;
Holy! holy! holy! merciful and mighty —
Father, Son, and Spirit — blessèd Trinity!

2 Holy! holy! holy! all the saints adore Thee,
Casting down their golden crowns around the glassy sea;
Cherubim and seraphim falling down before Thee,
Who wert and art and evermore shalt be.

3 Holy! holy! holy! though the darkness hide Thee,
Though the eye of sinful-man Thy glory may not see;
Only Thou art holy; there is none beside Thee,
Perfect in power, in love and purity.

4 Holy! holy! holy! Lord God Almighty!
All Thy works shall praise Thy Name, in earth and sky and sea;
Holy! holy! holy! merciful and mighty —
Father, Son, and Spirit, blessèd Trinity!

NICAEA. P. M.   JOHN BACCHUS DYKES, Mus. Doc., 1861.

334 III. LORD'S DAY THIRD IN THE MONTH — MORNING

HYMN NO. 4. L. M.   PHILIP DODDRIDGE, D. D., pub. 1775.   (Dox. added.)

TRIUMPHANT, Lord, Thy goodness reigns And grace erects our ruined frame,
Through all the wide celestial plains; A fairer temple to Thy Name.
And its full streams unceasing flow
Down to the abodes of men below. 3 O, give to every human heart
 To taste, and feel how good Thou art;
2 Through nature's work its glories shine; With grateful love and reverent fear,
The cares of providence are Thine; To know how blest Thy children are.

WAREHAM. L. M.   WILLIAM KNAPP, 1738.

III. EVENING

LORD'S DAY THIRD IN THE MONTH

Introductory Response

IT shall come to pass that at evening time there | shall be | light.
And it shall come to pass in that day,
That living waters shall go | out • from Je- | ru-sa- | lem.

[Zech. xiv, 7, 8]

EDWARD JOHN HOPKINS, Mus. Doc.

III. LORD'S DAY THIRD IN THE MONTH.—EVENING   335

Psalm Chant   Psalm viii.

WILLIAM RUSSELL, d. 1813.

O JEHOVAH our Lord, how excellent is Thy Name in | all the | earth!
　Who hast set Thy | glory up- | on the | heavens.
2 Out of the mouth of babes and sucklings hast Thou establish'd strength,
　Because of Thine | ad-ver- | saries,
　　That Thou mightest still the | ene-my | and · the a- | venger.
3 When I consider Thy heavens, the | work · of Thy | fingers,
　The moon and the | stars which | Thou · hast or- | dained;
4 What is man, that Thou art | mindful of | him?
　And the son of man, | that Thou | visit-est | him?
5 For Thou hast made him but little | lower than | God,
　And crownest him with | glo-ry | and | honor.
6 Thou madest him to have dominion over the | works · of Thy | hands;
　Thou hast put | all things | under his | feet:
7 All sheep and oxen,
　Yea, and the | beasts · of the | field;
　The fowl of the air, and the fish of the sea,
　Whatsoever passeth | through the | paths · of the | seas.
8 O Jehovah our Lord, how excellent | is Thy | Name!—
　How excellent is Thy | Name in | all the | earth!

9 GLORY be to the Father | and · to the | Son
　And | to the | Ho-ly | Ghost:
10 As it was in the beginning, is now, and | ev-er | shall be,
　World | with-out | end: A- | men.

HENRY LAWES.

336 III. LORD'S DAY THIRD IN THE MONTH — EVENING

Hymns of Praise

HYMN NO. 1. 7s, D.   JAMES MONTGOMERY. (Dox. added.)

HOLY, holy, holy Lord
  God of Hosts! when heaven and earth,
Out of darkness, at Thy word
  Issued into glorious birth,
All Thy works before Thee stood,
And Thine eye beheld them good,
While they sang with sweet accord,
  Holy! holy! holy! Lord!

2 Holy! holy! holy! all
  Heaven's triumphant choir shall sing,
While the ransomed nations fall
  At the footstool of their King:
Then shall saints and seraphim,
Harps and voices, swell one hymn,
Blending in sublime accord,
  Holy! holy! holy! Lord!

3. Ho-ly, Ho-ly, Ho-ly One! Blessing, hon-or, to Thy Name! While the end-less a-ges run, Praise shall swell with high acclaim: Thee, Eter-nal God, Most High—Thee we laud and mag-ni-fy; Glorious o'er the heav'nly host— Fa-ther, Son, and Ho-ly Ghost. A-MEN.

HONITON. 7s. D.   E. FLOOD.

HYMN NO. 2. 8s7s, D.   THOMAS WILLIAM BAXTER AVELING, D. D., 1844. (Dox. added.)

HAIL! Thou God of grace and glory!
  Who Thy Name hast magnified,
By redemption's wondrous story,
  By the Savior crucified:

2 Thanks to Thee for every blessing,
  Flowing from the Fount of love;
Thanks for present good unceasing,
  And for hopes of bliss above.

3 Hear us, as thus bending lowly,
  Near Thy bright and burning throne;

We invoke Thee, God most holy!
  Through Thy well-belovéd Son:

4 Send the baptism of Thy Spirit,
  Shed the pentecostal fire;
Let us all Thy grace inherit,
  Waken, crown each good desire.

5 Bind Thy people, Lord! in union,
  With the sevenfold cord of love;
Breathe a spirit of communion
  With the blesséd hosts above.

III. LORD'S DAY THIRD IN THE MONTH — EVENING 337

OSWALD. 8787. JOHN BACCHUS DYKES, Mus. Doc.

HYMN No. 3. L. M.   ISAAC WATTS, D.D. (Dox. added.)

THE praise of Zion waits for Thee,
Great God! and praise becomes Thy house;
There shall Thy saints Thy glory see,
And there perform their public vows.

2 O Thou whose mercy bends the skies,
To save when humble sinners pray!

All lands to Thee shall lift their eyes,
And grateful isles of every sea.

3 Soon shall the flocking nations run
To Zion's hill, and own their Lord;
The rising and the setting sun
Shall see the Savior's Name adored.

SEASONS. L. M. IGNAZ JOSEF PLEYEL, d. 1831.

338   III. LORD'S DAY THIRD IN THE MONTH — EVENING

HYMN No. 4.   L. M.   ISAAC WATTS, D.D., d. 1748. (Dox. added.)

BE Thou exalted, O my God!
  Above the heavens where angels dwell;
Thy power on earth be known abroad,
  And land to land Thy wonders tell!

2 High o'er the earth Thy mercy reigns,
  And reaches to the utmost sky;
Thy truth to endless years remains,
  When lower worlds dissolve and die.

3. O Father, Son, and Holy Ghost— Thou God Most High! Thee we adore:
From earth and all the heav'nly host, To Thee, all glory evermore! A-MEN.

CANONBURY. L. M.   ROBERT SCHUMANN, Ph. D., d. 1856.

IV. LORD'S DAY FOURTH IN THE MONTH
MORNING

Introductory Response

I HAVE set watchmen upon thy walls, O Je- | ru-sa- | lem;
They shall never hold their | peace | day nor | night:
Ye that are Jehovah's remembrancers, | keep not | silence,
  Till He make Jerusalem a | praise | in the | earth.   [Is. lxii, 6, 7]

Sir GEORGE JOB ELVEY, Mus. Doc.

Psalm Chant
Psalm xlviii, 1-3, 8-14.

JOHN RANDALL, Mus. Doc., d. 1799.

G REAT is Jehovah,
And highly | to be | prais'd,
In the city of our God,
| In His | ho-ly | mountain.
2 Beautiful in elevation,
The joy | of the * whole | earth,
Is Mount Zion, on the sides of the north,
The | city * of the | great | King.
3 God hath made Himself known in her palaces | for a | refuge.
As we have | heard, so | have we | seen
4 In the city of Jehovah of Hosts, in the | city * of our | God.
God will es- | tab-lish | it for | ever.
5 We have thought on Thy lovingkindness, O God,
In the | midst * of Thy | temple.
As is Thy Name, O God,
So is Thy praise unto the | ends | of the | earth:
6 Thy right hand is full of righteousness.
Let Mount | Zion be | glad,
Let the daughters of Judah rejoice,
Be- | cause of | Thy | judgments.
7 Walk about Zion, and go round about her:
Number the | towers there- | of;
Mark ye well her bulwarks,
Con- | sider her | pal-a- | ces:
8 That ye may tell it to the gener- | a-tion | following.
For this God is our God for ever and ever:
He will be our | guide ev'n | un-to | death.

9 GLORY be to the Father | and * to the | Son
And | to the | Ho-ly | Ghost;
10 As it was in the beginning, is now, and | ev-er | shall be,
World | with-out | end: A- | men.

HENRY SMART, d. 1879.

IV. LORD'S DAY FOURTH IN THE MONTH—MORNING

Hymns of Praise

HYMN No. 1. L. M.   ISAAC WATTS, D.D., 1719. (Dox. added.)

HIGH in the heavens, eternal God!
Thy goodness in full glory shines;
Thy truth shall break through every cloud
That veils and darkens Thy designs.

2 Forever firm Thy justice stands,
As mountains their foundations keep:
Wise are the wonders of Thy hands;
Thy judgments are a mighty deep.

3 From the provisions of Thy house
We shall be fed with sweet repast;
There, mercy like a river flows,
And brings salvation to our taste.

4 Life, like a fountain rich and free,
Springs from the presence of our Lord;
And in Thy light our souls shall see
The glories promised in Thy word.

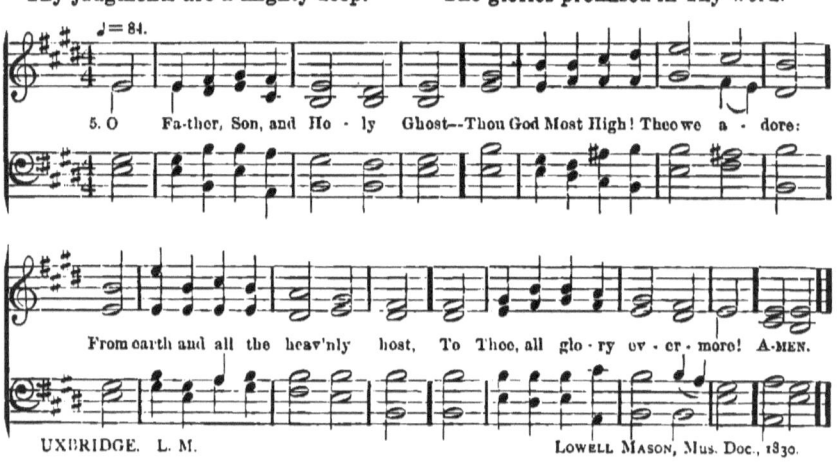

5. O Father, Son, and Holy Ghost—Thou God Most High! Thee we adore:
From earth and all the heav'nly host, To Thee, all glory evermore! A-MEN.

UXBRIDGE. L. M.   LOWELL MASON, Mus. Doc., 1830.

HYMN No. 2. 8787, D.   RICHARD MANT, D.D., pub. 1837. (Dox. added.)

LORD, Thy glory fills the heaven;
Earth is with its fullness stored;
Unto Thee be glory given,
Holy, holy, holy Lord!
Heaven is still with anthems ringing;
Earth takes up the angels' cry,
Holy! holy! holy! singing,
Lord of hosts, Thou Lord most high!

2 Ever thus in God's high praises,
Brethren, let our tongues unite,
While our thoughts His greatness raises,
And our love His gifts excite:

With His seraph train before Him,
With His holy church below,
Thus unite we to adore Him,
Bid we thus our anthem flow.

3 Lord, Thy glory fills the heaven,
Earth is with its fullness stored;
Unto Thee be glory given,
Holy, holy, holy Lord!
Thus Thy glorious Name confessing,
We adopt the angels' cry,
Holy! holy! holy! blessing
Thee, the Lord our God most high!

IV. LORD'S DAY FOURTH IN THE MONTH — MORNING 341

4. { God on High! let all adore Thee; Heav'n and earth Thy praises bring! } [spring.
   { We Thy people bend before Thee: (Omit........................) } Light doth from Thy presence
   D. C. To Thy Name, O God, victorious—(Omit .... Blessing, honor, love, and praise.

Father, Son, and Spirit— glorious!— Lord of all to endless days; A-MEN.

ST. CHAD. 8787, D.   RICHARD REDHEAD.

HYMN NO. 3. 7s.   JAMES EDWIN MILLARD, D.D., pub. 1848. (Dox. added.)

GOD eternal, Lord of all!
Lowly at Thy feet we fall:
All the world doth show Thy praise;
We our voices glad would raise.

2 All the holy angels cry,
Hail, thrice holy, God most high!
Lord of all the heavenly powers,
Be the same loud anthem ours.

3 Glorified apostles raise,
Night and day, continual praise:
With the prophet's goodly line
We in mystic bond combine.

4 All Thy church, in heaven and earth,
Jesus! hail Thy spotless birth; —
Seated on the judgment-throne,
Number us among Thine own!

5. Thee, Eternal God, Most High— Thee we laud and magnify:
Glorious o'er the heav'nly host— Father, Son, and Holy Ghost. A-MEN.

MONKLAND. 7s.   German.

IV. LORD'S DAY FOURTH IN THE MONTH—MORNING

HYMN NO. 4. S. P. M. ISAAC WATTS, D.D., 1719. (Dox. added.)

THE Lord Jehovah reigns,
And royal state maintains,
His head with awful glories crowned:
Arrayed in robes of light,
Begirt with sovereign might,
And rays of majesty around.

2 Upheld by Thy commands,
The world securely stands,
And skies and stars obey Thy word:
Thy throne was fixed on high
Ere stars adorned the sky:
Eternal is Thy kingdom, Lord.

3 Let floods and nations rage,
And all their powers engage;
Let swelling tides assault the sky:
The terrors of Thy frown
Shall beat their madness down:
Thy throne forever stands on high.

4 Thy promises are true,
Thy grace is ever new;
There fixed—Thy church shall ne'er re-
Thy saints with holy fear   [move:
Shall in Thy courts appear,
And sing Thine everlasting love.

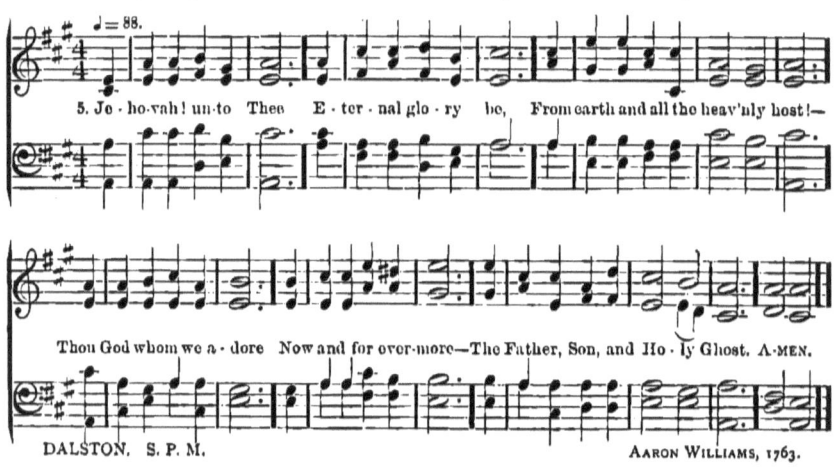

5. Je-ho-vah! un-to Thee E-ter-nal glo-ry be, From earth and all the heav'nly host!—
Thou God whom we a-dore Now and for ever-more—The Father, Son, and Ho-ly Ghost. A-MEN.

DALSTON. S. P. M.   AARON WILLIAMS, 1763.

IV. EVENING
LORD'S DAY FOURTH IN THE MONTH

Introductory Response

THERE is a river, the streams whereof make glad the | city of | God,
The holy place of the | taber-nacles | of the * Most | High.
Jehovah of | Hosts is | with us;
The God of | Ja-cob | is our | refuge. [Ps. xlvi, 4, 7]

HENRY ALDRICH, D. D., d. 1710.

Psalm Chant

Psalm xxiii.

F. WALKER.

JEHOVAH is my shepherd; | I * shall not | want.
    He maketh me to lie down in green pastures:
    He leadeth me be- | side the | still | waters.
2 He re- | storeth my | soul:
    He guideth me in the paths of righteousness | for His | Name's | sake.
3 Yea, though I walk through the valley of the | shadow of | death,
    I will fear no evil; for | Thou art | with | me:
4 Thy rod and Thy staff, they | com-fort | me.
    Thou preparest a table before me in the | pres-ence | of mine | enemies:
5 Thou hast anointed my | head with | oil;
    My | cup | run-neth | over.
6 Surely goodness and lovingkindness shall follow me all the | days * of my | life:
    And I will dwell in the | house * of Je- | hovah for- | ever.
7 GLORY be to the Father | and * to the | Son
    And | to the | Ho-ly | Ghost;
8 As it was in the beginning, is now, and | ev-er | shall be,
    World | with-out | end: A- | men.

JOHN CAMIDGE, Mus. Doc., d. 1859.

IV. LORD'S DAY FOURTH IN THE MONTH — EVENING

Hymns of Praise

HYMN NO. 1. L. M. ISAAC WATTS, D.D., 1719. (Dox. added.)

My God, my King, Thy various praise
Shall fill the remnant of my days:
Thy grace employ my humble tongue
Till death and glory raise the song.

2 The wings of every hour shall bear
Some thankful tribute to Thine ear;
And every setting sun shall see
New works of duty done for Thee.

3 Thy works with sovereign glory shine,
And speak Thy majesty divine:
Let Zion in her courts proclaim
The sound and honor of Thy Name.

4 But who can speak Thy wondrous deeds?
Thy greatness all our thoughts exceeds:
Vast and unsearchable Thy ways;
Vast and immortal be Thy praise.

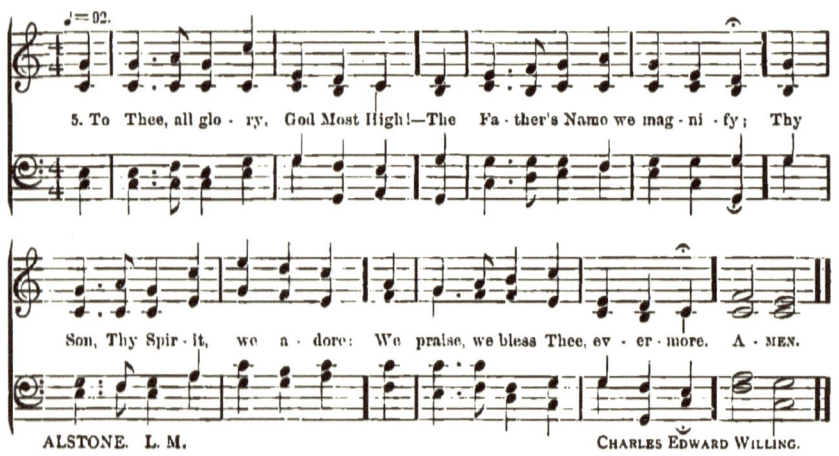

5. To Thee, all glo-ry, God Most High!—The Fa-ther's Name we mag-ni-fy; Thy Son, Thy Spir-it, we a-dore: We praise, we bless Thee, ev-er-more. A-MEN.

ALSTONE. L. M. CHARLES EDWARD WILLING.

HYMN NO. 2. P. M. ARTHUR TAPPAN PIERSON, D. D. (Dox. added.)

To THEE, O God, we raise
  Our voice in choral singing;
We come with prayer and praise,
  Our hearts' oblations bringing;
Thou art our fathers' God,
  And ever shalt be ours;
Our lips and lives shall laud
  Thy Name, with all our powers.

2 Thy goodness, like the dew
  On Hermon's hill descending,
Is every morning new,
  And tells of love unending.

We bless Thy tender care
  That led our wayward feet
Past every fatal snare
  To streams and pastures sweet.

3 We bless Thy Son, who bore
  The cross, for sinners dying;
Thy Spirit we adore,
  The precious blood applying.
Let work and worship send
  Their incense unto Thee;
Till song and service blend,
  Beside the crystal sea.

IV. LORD'S DAY FOURTH IN THE MONTH — EVENING 345

4. { O God—the Father, Son, And Spirit!—we adore Thee: } In grace enthroned art Thou;
   { Eternal, Glorious One! All heav'ns give praise before Thee: }
All blessing to Thy Name!—Who hast been, and art now, And e'er shalt be, the same. A-MEN.

ST. NICHOLAS. P. M.   JOHANN CRÜGER, 1648.

HYMN No. 3. 8787.

PRAISE to Thee, Thou great Creator!
Praise to Thee from every tongue;
Join, my soul, with every creature,
Join the universal song.

2 Father! source of all compassion!
Pure, unbounded grace is Thine:

JOHN FAWCETT, D. D., pub. 1782, alt. (Dox. added.)

Hail! Thou God of our salvation!
Praises for Thy love divine!

3 For Thy countless blessings given,
For our hope of future joy, [heaven,
Praise shall sound through earth and
Sound Jehovah's praise on high!

4. Father, Son, and Spirit — glorious! Lord of all to endless days;
To Thy Name, O God, victorious — Blessing, honor, love, and praise! A-MEN.

STUTTGARD. 8787.   JOHANN GEORG CHRISTIAN STÖRL, 1711.

IV. LORD'S DAY FOURTH IN THE MONTH — EVENING

HYMN No. 4. L. M.   ISAAC WATTS, D. D., d. 1738, alt.   (Dox. added.)

GREAT is the Lord! What tongue can frame
An honor equal to His Name?
How wonderful His glorious ways!
The Lord is awful in His praise!

2 Vast are Thy works, Almighty Lord!
All nature rests upon Thy word;
And clouds, and storms, and fire obey
Thy wise and all-controlling sway.

3 Thy glory, fearless of decline,
Thy glory, Lord, shall ever shine;
Thy praise shall still our breath employ
Till we shall rise to endless joy.

ADORATION. L. M.   SAMUEL SEBASTIAN WESLEY, MUS. DOC., 1872.

V. LORD'S DAY FIFTH IN THE MONTH
MORNING

Introductory Response

THEY that know Thy Name will put their | trust in | Thee;
For Thou, Jehovah, hast not forsaken | them that | seek | Thee.
[Ps. ix, 10]

BENJAMIN ST. JOHN BAPTIST JOULE.

V. LORD'S DAY FIFTH IN THE MONTH — MORNING 347

Psalm Chant
Psalm lxv, 1-8.

JAMES TURLE.

PRAISE waiteth for Thee, O | God, in | Zion:
 And unto Thee shall the | vow | be per- | form'd.
2 O Thou that hearest prayer,
 Unto Thee shall | all flesh | come.
  Iniquities prevail against me:
  As for our trans- | gres-sions, | Thou * shalt for- | give them.
3 Blessed is the man | whom Thou | choosest,
 And causest to approach unto Thee,
  That | he may | dwell * in Thy | courts.
4 We shall be satisfied with the goodness of Thy house,
 Thy | ho-ly | temple.
  By terrible things Thou wilt answer us in righteousness,
  O | God of | our sal- | vation;
5 Thou that art the confidence of all the | ends * of the | earth,
 And of them that are afar | off up- | on the | sea:
6 Who by His strength setteth | fast the | mountains;
 Being | gird-ed a- | bout with | might:
7 Who stilleth the roaring | of the | seas.
  The roaring of their waves,
  And the | tu-mult | of the | peoples.
8 They also that dwell in the uttermost parts are a- | fraid * at Thy | tokens:
  Thou makest the outgoings of the morning and | eve-ning | to re- | joice.

9 GLORY be to the Father | and * to the | Son
 And | to the | Ho-ly | Ghost;
10 As it was in the beginning, is now, and | ev-er | shall be,
 World | with-out | end : A- | men.

ROBERT COOKE, d. 1814.

V. LORD'S DAY FIFTH IN THE MONTH — MORNING

Hymns of Praise

HYMN NO. 1. L. M.   OLIVER WENDELL HOLMES, M. D., pub. 1859. (Dox. added.)

LORD of all being! throned afar,
Thy glory flames from sun and star;
Center and soul of every sphere,
Yet to each loving heart how near!

2 Sun of our life, Thy quickening ray
Sheds on our path the glow of day;
Star of our hope, Thy softened light
Cheers the long watches of the night.

3 Lord of all life, below, above,
Whose light is truth, whose warmth is love,
Before Thine ever-blazing throne
We ask no luster of our own.

4 Grant us Thy truth to make us free,
And kindling hearts that burn for Thee,
Till all Thy living altars claim
One holy light, one heavenly flame!

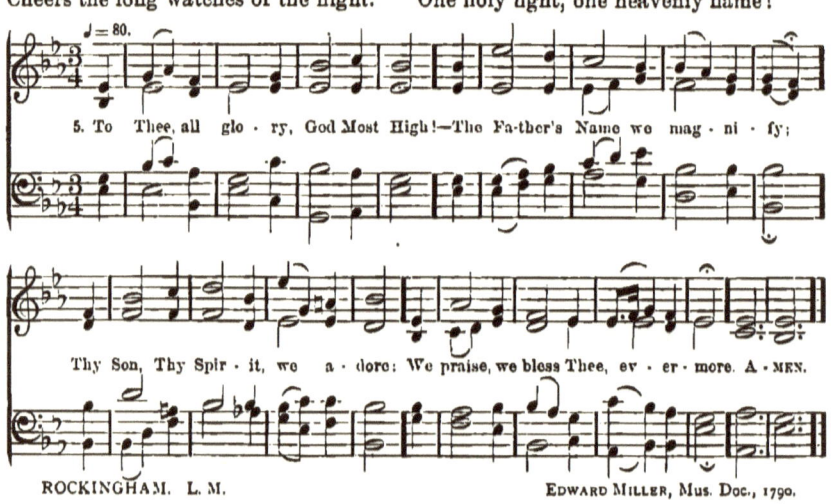

ROCKINGHAM. L. M.   EDWARD MILLER, Mus. Doc., 1790.

HYMN NO. 2. S. M.   JAMES MONTGOMERY. (Dox., author unknown.)

O THOU above all praise,
  Above all blessing high,
Who would not fear Thy holy Name,
  And laud, and magnify!

2 O for the living flame
  From Thine own altar brought,

To touch our lips, our souls inspire,
  And wing to heaven our thought!

3 God is our strength and song,
  And His salvation ours;
Then be His love in Christ proclaimed
  With all our ransomed powers.

EXALTATION. S. M.   ANON.

V. EVENING
LORD'S DAY FIFTH IN THE MONTH

Introductory Response

WITH Thee, O God, is the | fountain of | life:
In Thy | light shall | we see | light.   [Ps. xxxvi, 9]

Sir FREDERICK ARTHUR GORE OUSELEY, LL.D., Mus. Doc.

Psalm Chant
From Psalm cxix.

JOHN ROBINSON, d 1762.

FOREVER, O Jehovah, Thy word is | settled in | heaven.
   Thy faithfulness is | un-to | all gener- | ations.
2 I have seen an end of | all per- | fection ;
   But Thy commandment | is ex- | ceed-ing | broad.
3 Thy word is a lamp unto my feet,
   And light | unto my | path.
   Thy testimonies have I taken as a | her-i- | tage for- | ever.
4 Thou art my hiding-place and my shield :
   I | hope * in Thy | word.
   I love Thy commandments above gold,
   | Yea, a- | bove fine | gold.
5 The opening of Thy | words giveth | light ;
   It giveth under- | standing un- | to the | simple.
6 Order my footsteps | in Thy | word ;
   And let not any iniquity have do- | min-ion | o-ver | me.

350   V. LORD'S DAY FIFTH IN THE MONTH — EVENING

7 Thou art nigh, O Jehovah,
And all Thy com- | mand- ˙ ments are | truth.
I rejoice at Thy word, as one that | find-eth | great | spoil.

8 Let my lips utter praise,
For Thou teachest | me Thy | statutes.
Let my tongue sing of Thy word;
For all Thy com- | mand- ˙ ments are | right-cous- | ness.

9 GLORY be to the Father, etc.

HENRY JOHN GAUNTLETT, Mus. Doc., d. 1876.

Hymns of Praise

HYMN NO. 1.   8787.   RICHARD MANT, D. D.   (Dox. added.)

GOD, my King, Thy might confessing,
  Ever will I bless Thy Name;
Day by day Thy throne addressing,
  Still will I Thy praise proclaim.

2 Nor shall fail from memory's treasure,
  Works by love and mercy wrought—
Works of love surpassing measure,
  Works of mercy passing thought.

3 Full of kindness and compassion,
  Slow of anger, vast in love,
Thou art good to all creation;
  All Thy works Thy goodness prove.

4 All Thy works, O Lord, shall bless Thee,
  Thee shall all Thy saints adore;
King supreme shall they confess Thee,
  And proclaim Thy sovereign power.

TRUST.   8787.   FELIX MENDELSSOHN-BARTHOLDY, 1840.

V. LORD'S DAY FIFTH IN THE MONTH—EVENING 351

HYMN NO. 2. C. M. ISAAC WATTS, D. D., 1705. (Dox. added.)

ETERNAL Wisdom! Thee we praise,
Thee the creation sings;
With Thy loved Name, rocks, hills, and [seas,
And heaven's high palace rings.

2 How wide Thy hand hath spread the [sky!
How glorious to behold!
Tinged with a blue of heavenly dye,
And starred with sparkling gold.

3 Infinite strength and equal skill,
Shine through the worlds abroad,
Our souls with vast amazement fill,
And speak the builder, God.

4 But still the wonders of Thy grace
Our softer passions move;
Pity divine in Jesus' face
We see, adore, and love.

5. O Ho - ly, Bless-ed, Might - y One! Thou God whom we a - dore; To
Thee be glo - ry— Fa - ther, Son, And Spir - it— ev - er - more! A - MEN.

DUNDEE. C. M. GUILLAUME FRANC, 1615.

Ascriptions and Other Songs

Te Deum, Gloria in Excelsis, Gloria Patri, All Holy, Sanctus, Benedictus, Doxology of Israel, three *Doxologies in meter, Benedicite Omnia,* and *Song of Daniel,* are for use under "IX, Song of Ascription," in the Morning or Evening Service—one of these being chosen at each Service. If an Ascription may not conveniently be sung, it may be *said* in unison, by All.

No. 1   𝕿𝖊 𝕯𝖊𝖚𝖒 𝕷𝖆𝖚𝖉𝖆𝖒𝖚𝖘   (A Chief Song of the Church)

Author and date unknown: probably a compilation from a Morning Hymn of the early Church dating near the time of the apostles. It is traceable in some of its materials in the middle of the third century, or earlier; and is said to have been compiled in its present form by Ambrose, Bishop of Milan, for the baptism of Augustine, abt. 387. It is full of echoes of Holy Scripture; having for key-note, Is. vi, 3, with Rev. iv, 8; v, 13.

The Chants are from WILLIAM RUSSELL, d. 1813; Sir JOHN GOSS, Mus. Doc., d. 1880; PHOCION HENLEY, d. 1764.

PART I

WE praise Thee, O God;
   We acknowledge Thee to | be the | Lord.
     All the earth doth worship Thee, the | Fa-ther | ev-er- | lasting.
2 To Thee all angels cry aloud;
   The heav'ns and all the | powers there- | in:
     To Thee Cherubim and Seraphim con- | tin-ual- | ly do | cry—
3 "Holy! Holy! Holy! Lord | God of | Sabaoth;
   Heaven and earth are full of the | majes-ty | of Thy | glory."
4 The glorious company of the a- | pos-tles | praise Thee;
   The goodly fellowship of the | proph-ets | praise | Thee;
5 The noble army of | mar-tyrs | praise Thee;
   The holy Church throughout all the | world · doth ac- | knowl-edge | Thee—
6 The Father, of an infinite majesty;
   Thine adorable, true, and | on-ly | Son;
     Also the Holy | Ghost, the | Com-fort- | er.

PART II

7 Thou art the King of Glory, O Christ!
Thou art the everlasting | Son • of the | Father.
When Thou tookest upon Thee to deliver man,
Thou didst humble Thy- | self • to be | born • of a | virgin.
8 When Thou hadst overcome the | sharpness of | death
Thou didst open the kingdom of | Heav'n to | all be- | lievers.
9 Thou sittest at the right hand of God,
In the glory | of the | Father:
We believe that Thou shalt | come to | be our | Judge:
10 We therefore pray Thee, help Thy servants
Whom Thou hast redeem'd with Thy | pre-cious | blood;
Make them to be number'd with Thy saints
In | glo-ry | ev-er- | lasting.

PART III

11 O Lord, save Thy people, and | bless Thy | heritage;
Govern them and | lift them | up for- | ever.
12 Day by day we | magni-fy | Thee;
And we worship Thy Name, | ev-er, | world with- | out end.
13 Vouchsafe, O Lord, to keep us this | day without | sin:
O Lord, have mercy upon us, have | mer- | cy up- | on us;
14 O Lord, let Thy mercy be upon us, as our | trust • is in | Thee:
O Lord, in Thee have I trusted;
Let me | nev-er | be con- | founded. || A-MEN. ||

[For an Anthem form of "Te Deum," see next page]

In *Gloria in Excelsis* (on the following page), the repetition in the Book of Common Prayer ("Thou that takest away the sins of the world, have mercy upon us") is omitted. It is no part of the original hymn—not being found in any of the ancient Latin or Greek liturgies, or even in the earliest Prayer Book in English, 1549. For its appearance in the second Prayer Book of King Edward VI, 1552, no reason is known; an error in printing has been suggested. Also "*sins* of the world" is changed to "sin of the world," in accordance with John, 1, 29.

No. 2 Gloria in Excelsis Deo (The Great Doxology)

Author and date unknown. Based on Luke, ii, 14; John, i, 29; probably (with Te Deum) a compilation from a Morning Hymn of the early Church near the time of the apostles; traceable in the first half of the second century; present form supposed to date from the middle of the fourth century. See note on page preceding.

The Chants are from WILLIAM CROTCH, Mus. Doc., d. 1847; JOSEPH THOMAS COOPER, d. 1880.

PART I

G LORY be to | God on | high;
And on earth | peace, good- | will toward | men.
2 We praise Thee, we bless Thee, we | wor-ship | Thee,   [glory,
   We glorify Thee, we give thanks to | Thee for | Thy great |
3 O Lord God, | heav'n-ly | King,
   God the | Fa-ther | Al- | mighty.
4 O Lord, the only begotten Son, | Je-sus | Christ;
   O Lord God, Lamb of | God, Son | of the | Father;

PART II

5 That takest away the | sin • of the | world,
   Have | mer- | cy up- | on us:
6 Thou that takest away the | sin • of the | world,
   Re- | ceive | our | prayer:
7 Thou that sittest at the right hand of | God the | Father,
   Have | mer- | cy up- | on us.

PART III (Same Music as Part I)

8 For Thou | only art | holy;
   Thou | on-ly | art the | Lord;
9 Thou only, O Christ, with the | Ho-ly | Ghost,
   Art most high in the glory of | God the | Father. A- | men.

Gloria in Excelsis Deo   Another musical setting: author and date unknown.

PART I

G LORY be to | God on | high;
And on earth | peace, good- | will toward | men.

ASCRIPTIONS AND OTHER SONGS 359

2 We praise Thee, we bless Thee, we | wor-ship | Thee,
  We glorify Thee, we give thanks to | Thee for | Thy great | glory,

PART II

3 O Lord God, | heav'n-ly | King,
  God the | Fa-ther | Al- | mighty.
4 O Lord, the only begotten Son, | Je-sus | Christ;
  O Lord God, Lamb of | God, Son | of the | Father;

PART III

5 That takest away the | sin • of the | world,
  Have | mercy up- | on us:
6 Thou that takest away the | sin • of the | world,
  Re- | ceive our | prayer:
7 Thou that sittest at the right hand of | God the | Father,
  Have | mercy up- | on us.

PART IV (Same Music as Part I)

8 For Thou | only art | holy;
  Thou | on-ly | art the | Lord;
9 Thou only, O Christ, with the | Ho-ly | Ghost,
  Art most high in the | glory • of | God the | Father. ‖A-MEN.‖

No. 3 Gloria Patri (The Less Doxology)

Author and date unknown: traceable in the middle of the second century. See Matt. xxviii, 19, 20; II Cor. xiii, 14; Rev. v, 13, 14; xi, 17.

GLORY be to the Father | and • to the | Son
And | to the | Ho-ly | Ghost:
2 As it was in the beginning, is now, and | ev-er | shall be,
  World | with-out | end: A- | men.

HENRY LAWES, d. 1662.

ASCRIPTIONS AND OTHER SONGS

No. 4 **All Holy—** (An Ascription of the New Covenant)

[Instead of "Hallelujah of the Heavenly Host," at the Lord's Table — at discretion]

Based on Rev. xv, 4; Ps. xcix, 3; cxi, 9; 1 Chron. xvi, 8, 10, 35; Is. vi, 3; Rev. iv, 8-11; John, xvii, 11; Luke, i, 49; Matt. vi, 9; Acts, iv, 30; Luke, xi, 13; Eph. i, 13; 1 Thess. iv, 8; Matt. xxviii, 19; II Cor. xiii, 14; Ps. xcvii, 12; ciii, 1; cv, 3; cvi, 47; cxlv, 21.

ALL Holy Thy Name, Lord God, Thou | One Je- | hovah! —
Holy! Holy! Holy! the Name of the | Father • and the | Son • and the | Spirit:
2 All glory and blessing and love unto Thee, O God of | our sal- | vation! —
The Almighty, who art from everlasting to ever- | lasting:
A- | men • and A- | men.

Sir GEORGE JOB ELVEY, Mus. Doc.

No. 5 **Sanctus** [Isaiah, vi, 3; Rev. iv, 8] (The Seraphic Hymn)

HOLY! Holy! Holy! Je- | hovah • of | hosts!
The whole earth is | full of | Thy | glory.
2 Holy! Holy! Holy! Lord | God • the Al- | mighty,
Who wast and who | art • and who | art to | come. ‖A-MEN.‖

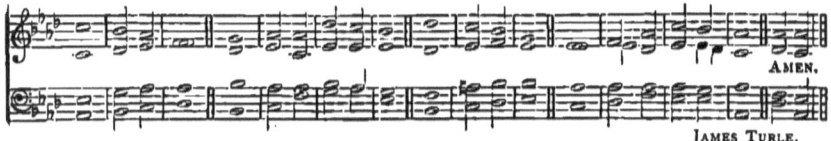

JAMES TURLE.

Sanctus Another musical setting.

ASCRIPTIONS AND OTHER SONGS   361

W. S. P., 1887.

No. 6 **Benedictus** [Luke, i, 68–79.]   (Song of Zacharias)

B LESSED be the Lord, the | God of | Israel;
  For He hath visited and wrought re- | demp-tion | for His | people,
2 And hath rais'd up a mighty sal- | vation for | us
  In the | house * of His | ser-vant | David:
3 As He spake by the mouth of His holy prophets that have | been of | old —
  Salvation from our enemies and from the | hand of | all that | hate us;
4 To show mercy | toward our | fathers,
  And to remember His | ho-ly | cov-en- | ant.

5 GLORY be to the Father, etc.

GEORGE MURSELL GARRETT, Mus. Doc.

[The remainder — in Advent, Days Nos. 65–68: *Gloria* above, omitted]

5 The oath which He sware unto Abra- | ham our | father,
  To grant unto us that we being deliver'd out of the | hand *
  of our | en-e- | mies
6 Should serve | Him without | fear,
  In holiness and righteousness be- | fore Him | all our | days.

7 Yea, and Thou, Child, shalt be called The Prophet | of the * Most | High:
  For Thou shalt go before the face of the | Lord * to make | ready His | ways;
8 To give knowledge of salvation | unto His | people
  In the re- | mis-sion | of their | sins,

9 Because of the tender mercy | of our | God,
  Whereby the Dayspring from on ' high shall | vis-it | us,
10 To shine upon them that sit in darkness and the | shadow of | death,
  To guide our feet | into the | way of | peace.

11 GLORY be to the Father, etc.

ASCRIPTIONS AND OTHER SONGS

No. 7 Doxology of Israel
Psalm lxxii, 18, 19

Blessed be Jehovah God, the | God of | Israel,
Who only | do-eth | won-drous | things:
2 And blessed be His glorious | Name for- | ever;
And let the whole earth be fill'd with His | glory: A- |
men • and A- | men.

THOMAS EDGERTON, EARL OF WILTON, d. 1882.

No. 8 Thou Father— (METRICAL)
TATE and BRADY, 1696 (alt.)

♩ = 80.

Thou Fa-ther, Son, and Ho-ly Ghost— Our God! whom Heav'n's triumphant host

And wait-ing saints on earth a-dore: To Thee all glo-ry, bless-ing, praise!—

Who wast from ev-er-last-ing days, Art now, and shalt be ev-er-more. A-MEN.

DRESDEN. 888,888.   "Swiss Tune."

ASCRIPTIONS AND OTHER SONGS 363

No. 9 **Ages unto Ages—** *(METRICAL)* (1877)

A-ges un-to a-ges sing, Prais-ing God with high ac-claim: We our glad Ho-
san-nas bring, Blessing Thine e-ter-nal Name: Glo-ry be to God on high! Praise from all th'an-
gel-ic host! Ev-er Thee we mag-ni-fy— Fa-ther, Son, and Ho-ly Ghost! A-MEN.

ST. GEORGE. 7s, D. Sir GEORGE JOB ELVEY, Mus. Doc., 1860.

No. 10 **Glory, Thanks—** *(METRICAL)* (1887)
[Instead of "Te Deum," at discretion — after Recognition of New Members]

GLORY, thanks, Thy Church doth render, Mighty Lord! to Thee alone: Girded with Thy ho-ly splendor,
Thou hast made Thy grace Thy throne; God Eternal, God Eternal—Father, Son, and Holy Ghost! A-MEN.

REGENT SQUARE. 878747. HENRY SMART, 1868.

364 ASCRIPTIONS AND OTHER SONGS

No. 11 Benedicite Omnia (Ancient Hebrew Canticle)

Modeled on Psalm cxlviii: adopted into Christian worship, fourth century. A portion is here given, with a few words from the Psalm.

HENRY WILSON, 1860.

O ALL, etc. | bless ye the Lord: PRAISE HIM, AND MAG-NI-FY HIM FOR EVER.

O ALL, etc. | bless ye the Lord: PRAISE HIM, AND MAG-NI-FY HIM FOR EVER. A-MEN.

O ALL ye Works of the Lord, | bless ye the Lord:
PRAISE HIM, AND MAGNIFY HIM FOR EVER.
2 O ye Angels of the Lord, | bless ye the Lord:
PRAISE HIM, AND MAGNIFY HIM FOR EVER.
3 O ye Heav'ns of Heav'ns, | bless ye the Lord:
PRAISE HIM, AND MAGNIFY HIM FOR EVER.
4 O ye Waters that be above the firmament, | bless ye the Lord:
PRAISE HIM, AND MAGNIFY HIM FOR EVER.
5 O ye Sun and Moon, | bless ye the Lord:
PRAISE HIM, AND MAGNIFY HIM FOR EVER.
6 O ye Stars of Heav'n, | bless ye the Lord:
PRAISE HIM, AND MAGNIFY HIM FOR EVER.
7 O ye Winter and Summer, | bless ye the Lord:
PRAISE HIM, AND MAGNIFY HIM FOR EVER.
8 O ye Nights and Days, | bless ye the Lord:
PRAISE HIM, AND MAGNIFY HIM FOR EVER.
9 O ye Mountains and all Hills, | bless ye the Lord:
PRAISE HIM, AND MAGNIFY HIM FOR EVER.
10 O ye Heights and Depths, | bless ye the Lord:
PRAISE HIM, AND MAGNIFY HIM FOR EVER.
11 O ye Seas and Floods, | bless ye the Lord:
PRAISE HIM, AND MAGNIFY HIM FOR EVER.
12 O ye Children of Men, | bless ye the Lord:
PRAISE HIM, AND MAGNIFY HIM FOR EVER.

ASCRIPTIONS AND OTHER SONGS 365

13 O ye Kings of the earth and all Peoples, | bless ye the Lord:
PRAISE HIM, AND MAGNIFY HIM FOR EVER.
14 O ye Servants of the Lord, | bless ye the Lord:
PRAISE HIM, AND MAGNIFY HIM FOR EVER.

15 O ye Spirits and Souls of the Righteous, | bless ye the Lord:
PRAISE HIM, AND MAGNIFY HIM FOR EVER.
16 O ye holy Men and humble of heart, | bless ye the Lord:
PRAISE HIM, AND MAGNIFY HIM FOR EVER. || A-MEN. ||

No. 12 &ong of Daniel   Daniel, ii, 20-23

[Appropriate on any National Day]

B LESSED be the Name of God for | ever and | ever:
For wisdom and | might | are | His:
2 And He changeth the | times • and the | seasons;
He removeth | kings, and | setteth up | kings:
3 He giveth wisdom | unto the | wise,
And knowledge to | them that | know under- | standing:
4 He revealeth the deep and | se-cret | things:
He knoweth what is in the darkness,
And the | light | dwelleth with | Him.
5 We thank Thee and praise Thee, O Thou | God • of our | fathers,
Who hast giv'n us | wisdom and | might. A- | men.

JOHN FRECKLETON BURROWES, d. 1852.

[The three following are Psalms, one of which may at discretion be added in the Service, after IV, or VII, or X]

Venite Exultemus Deo   Psalm xcv, 1-7

O COME, let us sing | unto Je- | hovah•
Let us make a joyful noise to the | rock of | our sal- | vation,
2 Let us come before His presence | with thanks- | giving,
Let us make a joyful noise | un-to | Him with | psalms.

3 For Jehovah is a | great | God
And a great | King a- | bove all | gods.
In His hand are the deep places | of the | earth;
The heights of the | mountains are | His | also.
4 The sea is His, | and He | made it:
And His hands | form'd the | dry | land.

5 O come, let us worship | and bow | down;
  Let us kneel before Je- | ho-vah | our | Maker:
6 For He | is our | God,
  And we are the people of His pasture
  And the | sheep of | His | hand. [A-MEN.]

Cantate Domino
Psalm xcviii

O SING unto Jehovah a | new | song;
  For He hath | done | marvelous | things:
2 His right hand, and His | ho-ly | arm,
  Hath wrought sal- | va-tion | for | Him.

3 Jehovah hath made known | His sal- | vation:
  His righteousness hath He openly | show'd • in the | sight •
    of the | nations.
4 He hath remember'd His lovingkindness and His faithfulness
    toward the | house of | Israel:
  All the ends of the earth have seen the sal- | va-tion | of our
    | God.
5 Make a joyful noise unto Jehovah, | all the | earth:
  Break forth and sing for | joy, yea, | sing | praises.
6 Sing praises unto Jehovah | with the | harp;
  With the harp and the | voice of | mel-o- | dy.

7 With trumpets and | sound of | cornet
  Make a joyful noise be- | fore the | King, Je- | hovah.
8 Let the sea roar, and the | fulness there- | of;
  The world, and | they that | dwell there- | in;

9 Let the floods | clap their | hands;
  Let the hills sing for joy to- | gether; be- | fore Je- | hovah:
10 For He cometh to | judge the | earth:
  He shall judge the world with righteousness,
  | And the | peoples with | equity. [A-MEN.]

Benedic Anima Mea
Psalm ciii, 1-4, 20-22

B LESS Jehovah, | O my | soul;
  And all that is within me, | bless His | ho-ly | Name.
2 Bless Jehovah, | O my | soul,
  And forget not | all His | ben-e- | fits:
3 Who forgiveth | all • thine in- | iquities,
  Who | heal-eth | all • thy dis- | eases;
4 Who redeemeth thy | life • from de- | struction;
  Who crowneth thee with loving- | kindness and | ten-der |
    mercies.
5 Bless Jehovah, ye angels of His; ye | mighty in | strength,
  That fulfill His word, hearkening unto the | voice of | His |
    word.

ASCRIPTIONS AND OTHER SONGS 367

6 Bless Jehovah, all | ye His | hosts;
   Ye ministers of | His, that | do His | pleasure.
7 Bless Jehovah, all ye His works, in all places of | His do- | minion:
   Bless Je- | ho-vah, | O my | soul. [A-MEN.]

[Additional to the foregoing, the following Scriptural songs, with music, may be found distributed among various Days in *Offices for the Year*, and among the *Monthly Psalms*]

JUBILATE DEO: Psalm c.   *Part of Psalm Chant, Monthly Lord's Day, I. M'rg.*
DEUS MISEREATUR: Psalm lxvii.   *Psalm Chant, Monthly Lord's Day, I. Ev'g.*
BONUM EST CONFITERI: Psalm xcii.   *Psalm Chant, Monthly Lord's Day, II. Ev'g.*
DE PROFUNDIS: Psalm cxxx.   *Psalm Chant, Day No. 19.*
PSALM OF THE NATION: From Psalm xliv. } For any National
DOXOLOGY OF DAVID: From I Chron. xxix. } Day   *Psalm Chant, Day No. 64.*
SONG OF THE ANGELS: Luke, ii, 14.   *Introductory Response, Days Nos. 69, 70, 71.*

[Also the following, without music]

MAGNIFICAT (Song of the Virgin Mary): Luke, i, 46-55. *Additional, after Scripture of the New Covenant, Days Nos. 69, 70, 71.*

NUNC DIMITTIS (Song of Simeon): Luke, ii, 29-32. *Additional, after Scripture of the New Covenant, Days Nos. 70, 71.*

[The following, with music, are in the various Usages in Church Fellowship]

Now unto Him that is able to do exceeding abundantly — Eph. iii, 20, 21:
    Ascription — Recognition of Members on Transfer

Now unto Him that is able to guard us — Jude, 24, 25:
    Ascription — Recognition of Members on Confession

Blessed be Thou, O Jehovah — From I Chron. xxix, 10, 11, 12, 14:
    Blessing — in the Offertory

HALLELUJAH OF THE HEAVENLY HOST — From Rev. iv, v, vii, xi, xv, xix:
    At the Lord's Table

Suffer the Little Children — Luke, xviii, 16: Is. xlv, 3: lxv, 23: Ps. cv, 8:
    Presentation Hymn — The Baptism of Little Children

One generation shall laud Thy works to another — Ps. cxlv, 4: lxxix, 13:
    Ascription — The Baptism of Little Children

THE CHURCH

ACTS AND USAGES IN THE CHURCH FELLOWSHIP

It is the teaching of Christ's inspired apostles and evangelists that, as the whole VISIBLE CHURCH on earth embodies the general Christian fellowship, so, in any place, A CHURCH embodies the Christian fellowship as local and stated.

Beyond this simple form, in which Churches appear in the New Testament — locally distinct, yet all in communion one with another through their common fellowship in Christ Jesus, and their common acceptance of the apostolic guidance — further organization in various directions has often been deemed desirable both within the Church and for constituting many Churches into a general Church. As such further organization, with its mode and extent, must necessarily be decided in each case by the judgment of those concerned, the Acts and Usages here provided confine themselves within the sphere of the simple Christian fellowship — in the following view.

1. A Church of Jesus Christ is created by no human act of organization; but in such act only recognizes the fact of its local fellowship as constituted by the Holy Spirit, and assigns through Him its stated ministries.

2. It devises no basis of membership for itself; but recognizes and welcomes as its members those who, consenting thereto and gathering statedly with it, confess Christ and show discipleship toward Him.

3. It observes the ordinances of the Lord Jesus.

4. It administers within itself the government of Christ through the indwelling of the Holy Spirit; and this according to the Word of God which is its only Law, and under the leadership which Christ assigned to His apostles.

5. It stands in the communion of Christ's whole Church — being in fellowship through Him with all His Churches and with all His people.

THE CHURCH
(ACT OF ORGANIZATION)

RECOGNITION OF THE CHURCH FELLOWSHIP
Through Common Confession of Christ,
and Covenant

This is an act (omitting the directions as to its form in a public Service) fitted for adoption by vote in a meeting called for the organization of a Church—the decisive act by which a company of disciples recognize themselves as becoming statedly a Church of Christ. It is taken as the basis of the Usages (which follow) in the Recognition of New Members on Transfer from other Churches, and on Confession of Christ.
After its more private adoption—which may be by a vote of Declaration (see such a form appended)—it will properly have place in the public Service in which the new Church receives recognition in the fellowship of the Churches.
In such public Service, unless the Minister be one of the members of the new Church, he observes to change the pronouns "we," etc., to "you," etc., throughout. In such public Service all the members of the new Church join aloud in the Responses printed in small capitals.

Invocation
IN the Name of the Lord Jesus! [All] AMEN.

Warrant
WE are here gathered together — a company of Christian disciples in [name of the place, town, etc.] — remembering this word of our Lord and Savior; Where two or three are gathered together in My Name, there am I in the midst of them; Verily I say unto you, What things soever ye shall bind on earth shall be bound in heaven: [Matt. xviii, 20, 18]

Also this that He saith; Every one who shall confess Me before men, him will I also confess before My Father who is in heaven: [Matt. x, 32]

Further, this teaching of Christ's apostle Paul; With the heart man believeth unto righteousness; and with the mouth confession is made unto salvation. [Rom. x, 10]

Wherefore as it is written by the prophet of old:
We are inquiring concerning Zion
WITH OUR FACES THITHERWARD,
Saying among ourselves — Come ye, and let us join ourselves to Jehovah
IN AN EVERLASTING COVENANT THAT SHALL NOT BE FORGOTTEN. [Jer. l, 5]

Forasmuch then as Almighty God in eternal grace through Christ, according to the sure testimony of His Word, offers unto sinful men salvation and life eternal, granting His Spirit to work in them repentance, and to unite them to His Son in the new life of faith and holy obedience:

And since all who believe on Christ Jesus are called in one Body, which is His Church, to confess Him before men:

Presentation

THEREFORE we — having received grace from God to believe on and follow His Son, and in His providence having our place together here — do now stand forth before the world and before unseen witnesses, to recognize and to declare ourselves in the communion of the whole Church of God, and in our local fellowship a Church of Jesus Christ, through our common confession of Him our Lord and Savior.

<small>In the public Service for Recognition of the new Church, the full names of those present to join in it are now called in two classes: first those on Transfer from other Churches, with their respective localities and Churches designated; then those on Confession of Christ; they all, as named, come forward and remain standing before the Minister. For convenience any unbaptized may be grouped separately at one side.</small>

Confession of Christ

<small>[All Christian disciples present rise, and stand through this Confession]</small>

WITH the Apostles, and the Church in all ages and throughout the world;
With the Heavenly Jerusalem, the joyful assembly of the redeemed on high;

<small>[The new members (and all Christian disciples present) join aloud —]</small>

WE CONFESS JESUS THE CHRIST,
THE SON OF THE LIVING GOD: AMEN.

<small>[All sit except Minister and the new Church]</small>

<small>[Matt. xvi, 13-19; iii, 16, 17; xvii, 5. Also: Rom. x. 9, 10; Matt. x, 32, 33; Lk. xii, 8, 9; Jn. xii, 42, 43; 1 Cor. xii, 3 (l. c. : 1 Jn. iv, 14, 15; v, 1-5, 9]</small>

Avowal of Covenant with God

THUS standing forth before the world to confess the Son of God, we openly avow our covenant with Jehovah — the Father and the Son and the Holy Spirit, One God — in the everlasting covenant of His grace:
Claiming Him as our God and Father, and our Portion for ever;
Trusting in Christ His Son for full forgiveness and eternal life;
Looking to His Spirit for all light and strength and sanctifying grace:
While, in repentance for all our sins,
  We turn from an ungodly world —
  We deny the lusts of the flesh —
  We renounce the works of the devil —
To be joined unto Christ Jesus, our Savior and Head;
To walk in all His ordinances in the Gospel, and make Him our Example;
To seek God in prayer with thanksgiving;
To submit lovingly to His will;
To hold our possessions as His trust;
To dwell in meekness, and follow charity with all men;
And to work for the upbuilding of Christ's Kingdom —
Looking for Him to come again in glory and take us unto Himself:

[All] AMEN.

The Seal—Baptism

ACCORDING as our Lord hath appointed BAPTISM, the seal of the Christian confession and covenant in His Church — a symbol of the putting on of Christ in our new life by the Holy Spirit — We are baptized (or otherwise we present ourselves for Baptism) into the Name of the Father and of the Son and of the Holy Spirit:

RECOGNITION OF THE CHURCH FELLOWSHIP 371

[And we who aforetime have been baptized do now severally confirm the act
and faith of our former Baptism:] [Assent] AMEN.

[Matt. xxviii, 18, 19: Mk. xvi, 16: Gal. iii, 27: also references in the "Usage for Recognition of
New Members on Confession of Christ"]

At a public Service, Baptism, if requisite, is immediately administered, and may be in the form
set forth in the Usage for "Recognition of New Members on Confession."

Covenant in Church Fellowship

AND now, standing forth and joining ourselves in one company to confess
Christ, we therein recognize our fellowship in especial as a Church — a local and
stated fellowship in the communion of the Church Universal, in liberty under
Christ's government alone:
    Wherein we covenant to walk together obediently to the Word of God;
    In the administration of Christ's fellowship, truth, and order, in His house,
    In a common worship and a concerted Christian work in the community,
    In the meekness of our Lord Jesus caring one for another unto edification,
    Keeping the unity of the Spirit in the bond of peace, with sympathy and
      brotherly love: [All] AMEN.

Greeting in the Church

WHEREFORE — seeking due recognition in the fellowship of all the Churches —
We salute one another in this Church of Christ:
    WE GREET ONE ANOTHER IN THE ETERNAL COVENANT OF OUR
    GOD.
    Into the communion of the whole Visible Church we enter with joy,
      THROUGH THESE GATES OF ZION WHICH THE LORD HIMSELF
      DOTH OPEN —
    Even the King, our Shepherd, the Master of Assemblies,
      WHO HOLDETH THE KEYS IN HIS RIGHT HAND.
We receive one another, as workers together in furthering Christ's gospel in
the earth,
    Pilgrims together unto the triumphant Church and glorious Kingdom of our
God on high: [All] AMEN.

Grace in the Church

THIS is the grace of God, in which, with His whole Church we stand.
Christ's apostle Paul thus declares: [Gal. iii, 26; Rom. viii, 14]
    Ye all are sons of God, through faith, in Christ Jesus:
      FOR AS MANY AS ARE LED BY THE SPIRIT OF GOD, THESE ARE
      SONS OF GOD.
    So we, who are many, are one body in Christ,
      AND SEVERALLY MEMBERS ONE OF ANOTHER. [Rom. xii, 5]

Benediction in the Church

AND this is the apostle's benediction upon those that receive the calling of God
to be in His Church: [Phil. iv, 7; Gal. vi, 18]
The peace of God, which passeth all understanding, guard your hearts and your
minds in Christ Jesus:
    Brethren, the grace of our Lord Jesus Christ be with your spirit: [All] AMEN.

Ascription in the Church [Eph. iii, 20, 21]

In a public service, to be said responsively; but if no other song be appointed to follow immediately, then this may be *sung*, or said in unison, by All standing; for tune, see Recognition of New Members on Transfer

Now unto Him that is able to do exceeding abundantly above all that we | ask or | think,
ACCORDING TO THE POWER THAT | WORK-ETH | IN | US —
Unto Him be the glory in the Church and | in Christ | Jesus,
UNTO ALL GENERATIONS FOR | EVER AND | EVER: A | MEN.

In a public service, the new Church resumes seats, after singing with the whole congregation standing, "Te Deum," or other Ascription.

CHURCH DECLARATION

SETTING FORTH THE FOREGOING ACT FOR ADMINISTRATION

THIS company of visible disciples of Jesus Christ statedly gathered together in His Name in [Town, etc. State, etc.],and known as [the designation of the church],declares its foregoing Recognition of the Church Fellowship to be its Act of Organization, having force in all Church procedure; yet only as serving to develop and administer the authority of Christ and His sole rule in His Church, according to the Word of God.

In the Recognition of New Members, the more private procedure and the public Usages are to represent the spirit and substance of the foregoing Act in any convenient forms; provided that such forms (with Baptism, or with the open confirming of a Baptism aforetime) shall enforce as the test of discipleship this that our Lord has ordained for fellowship in His Church — an open confession of Jesus Christ before men, with credible profession of a full purpose for a life of godly obedience through faith in Him as the only Savior.

The foregoing Act — as also this Declaration — is alterable no otherwise than as accords with the Word of God; and only by two successive votes, each of not less than four-fifths of all such members as are present respectively in two meetings of the Church — provided that the two votes be each the vote of a majority of all the resident members; notice that alteration is proposed having been given publicly in the congregation on the Lord's Day preceding each of the meetings; the two meetings being separated by not less than two months or more than six months.

FORM OF DOCTRINE

CHURCH DECLARATION

THIS Church of Jesus Christ sets forth principal facts and truths of Holy Scripture in the following Form of Doctrine, as a convenient summary for private study and for public testimony; which, for such uses, is to have the consent of the members as a *declarative rule*, as far as accords with the Word of God; yet is this Form not a *test* for membership, or for fellowship with other Churches, since only Christ Himself has authority to ordain the terms of fellowship in his Church

The Form of Doctrine — as also this Declaration — is alterable no otherwise than as may accord with the Word of God; and by a vote of not less than three-fourths of all such members as are present in a meeting of the Church — provided that the same vote be that of a majority of all the resident members; notice that alteration is proposed having been given publicly in the congregation on the Lord's Day preceding.

[Here is to follow the Form of Doctrine adopted by the Church]

EXECUTIVE RULES

CHURCH DECLARATION

This Church of Jesus Christ — providing only for administering Christ's Fellowship, Truth, and Order, according as these may be found in the Word of God — brings into effect its Recognition of the Church Fellowship and its Form of Doctrine by the following Executive Rules.

The Executive Rules — as also this Declaration — are alterable by a vote of not less than three-fourths of all such members as are present in a meeting of the Church, with such quorum as the Church in its rules may require; notice that alteration is proposed having been given publicly in the congregation on the Lord's Day preceding.

[Here are to follow the Executive Rules adopted by the Church]

RECOGNITION OF NEW MEMBERS ON TRANSFER FROM OTHER CHURCHES

[USAGE IN THE CHURCH FELLOWSHIP]

This may be at any time, but statedly occurs when the Church is gathered together for the Communion at the Lord's Table; taking the place of the usual Confession of Christian Faith VIII in the general Service. And before each such stated season, timely announcement and invitation are to be given in the congregation.

The Recognition of New Members on Confession of Christ follows this.

Words in brackets may be changed or omitted; and if the Service be private any appropriate changes are made. Responses printed in small capitals are for utterance by all the Church, including the Minister.

I. Presentation

ANNOUNCEMENT

BELOVED in the Lord:

The Great Head of the Church, in whose Name we are gathered together, giveth us the privilege at this time to recognize [a] new member[s] in our fellowship, on transfer from His Church elsewhere. [Matt. xviii, 20, 10]

God hath called — Gather My saints together unto Me;

THOSE THAT HAVE MADE A COVENANT WITH ME BY SACRIFICE.

Thy vows are upon me, O God:

IN THE MIDST OF THE CONGREGATION WILL I PRAISE THEE.

[Ps. l, 1, 5; lvi, 12; xxii, 12]

HYMN

Usually omitted; but if desirable (as when there are many new-comers, or for any reason) the following, announced by its first line, may be sung by the Church; or other Hymn may be used.

Tune, ORIENTE, S. M. See in Part V, below.

COME, ye that fear the Lord,
  And love Him while ye fear;
Come, and with heart and hand record
  Your vow and cov'nant here.

2 Here to His altar brought,
  Your holy vows renew,

To be, in word and deed and thought,
  Faithful to Him and true.

3 So shall His staff and rod
  Conduct you and defend:
God is a cov'nant-keeping God,
  And loves unto the end.

JAMES MONTGOMERY, d. 1854.

RECOGNITION OF NEW MEMBERS ON TRANSFER

CALL

You from Christ's Church elsewhere who are present to enter the special fellowship gathered here:

We salute you in the common faith; for as many as were baptized into Christ did put on Christ. [Gal. iii, 27]

Stand up amid our assembly —
IN THE NAME OF THE LORD JESUS!

Minister announces the place and name of every Church from which a member comes by transfer — calling the full names of all such members from each Church in its turn; the persons as named rise and remain standing till the end

II. Confession of Christ

BELOVED: Grace to you and peace be multiplied.

When, as we trust, it pleased God aforetime to grant His Spirit, working in you repentance and uniting you to His Son Jesus in the new life of faith and holy obedience, you then became joined unto Christ's Body, the Church, in the confession of His Name.

Now by God's providence having your place with us, you openly renew in this company of disciples your confession of our Lord and Savior:

[Assent by the new-comers] *Amen.*

III. Covenant

AVOWAL OF COVENANT WITH GOD

THUS confessing the Son of God, you thereby avow among us your covenant with Jehovah — the Father and the Son and the Holy Spirit, One God — in the everlasting covenant of His grace: [Assent by the new-comers] *Amen.*

COVENANT IN THE CHURCH

MOREOVER, renewing among us your confession of Christ, you therein recognize your fellowship in especial with this Church as a local and stated fellowship in the communion of the Church Universal, in liberty under Christ's government alone:

Wherein you covenant to walk together with us obediently to the Word of God;
In the administration of Christ's fellowship, truth, and order, in His house,
In a common worship and a concerted Christian work in the community,
In the meekness of our Lord Jesus caring one for another unto edification,
Keeping the unity of the Spirit in the bond of peace, with sympathy and brotherly love: [Assent by the new-comers] *Amen.*

IV. Welcome

The Church rise and stand, joining in Responses

BEHOLD therefore, Beloved:
This Church stands by your side in fellowship henceforth.
We greet you in the eternal covenant of our God:
WE WELCOME YOU INTO THIS COMPANY OF DISCIPLES.
These gates of Zion we open unto you with joy;
YEA, THE LORD HIMSELF DOTH OPEN THEM.

We receive you to work in company with us in furthering Christ's gospel in the earth,

And to go with us, pilgrims together, unto the triumphant Church and glorious Kingdom of our God on high: [Church] **AMEN.**

RECOGNITION OF NEW MEMBERS ON TRANSFER

V. Hymn of Fellowship

All still standing

Omitted at discretion; one of the following may be sung by All —

HYMN No. 1

DEAR Savior! we are Thine
By everlasting bands;
Our hearts, our souls we would resign
Entirely to Thy hands.

2 Thy Spirit shall unite
Our souls to Thee, our Head;
Shall form in us Thine image bright,
And teach Thy paths to tread.

3 Since Christ and we are one,
Why should we doubt or fear?
Since He in Heaven has fixed His throne,
He'll fix His members there.

PHILIP DODDRIDGE, D. D., d. 1751.

HYMN No. 2

PLANTED in Christ, the living Vine,
This day, with one accord,
Ourselves with humble faith and joy
We yield to Thee, O Lord.

2 Joined in one body may we be:
One inward life partake;

One be our heart, one heav'nly hope
In every bosom wake.

3 Then, when among the saints in light
Our joyful spirits shine,
Shall anthems of immortal praise,
O Lamb of God, be Thine!

SAMUEL FRANCIS SMITH, D.D., 1843.

All the remainder, except Ascription, may be omitted when Recognition of New Members on Confession of Christ is to follow.

VI. Grace

All still standing

Now let us all hear and declare the grace of God in His Church.
Christ's Apostle Paul thus declares:

Ye all are sons of God, through faith, in Christ Jesus:
FOR AS MANY AS ARE LED BY THE SPIRIT OF GOD, THESE ARE SONS OF GOD.
So we, who are many, are one body in Christ,
AND SEVERALLY MEMBERS ONE OF ANOTHER. [Rom. xii, 5]

376   RECOGNITION OF NEW MEMBERS ON CONFESSION OF CHRIST

Thus saith Jehovah : The mountains shall depart,
AND THE HILLS BE REMOVED;
But My kindness shall not depart from thee,
NEITHER SHALL THE COVENANT OF MY PEACE BE REMOVED.
[Is. liv, 10]

BENEDICTION   [Phil. iv. 7 ; Gal. vi, 18]
BELOVED : The peace of God, which passeth all understanding, guard your hearts and your minds in Christ Jesus :
The grace of our Lord Jesus Christ be with your spirit.   [All] AMEN.

VII. Ascription   [Eph. iii, 20, 21]   All still standing

To be said responsively ; but if there be no Recognition of New Members on Confession of Christ, nor any song to follow immediately in the general service, then this may be *sung*, or said in unison, by All —

Now unto Him that is able to do exceeding abundantly above all that we | ask or | think,
ACCORDING TO THE POWER THAT | WORK-ETH | IN | US —
Unto Him be the glory in the Church and | in Christ | Jesus,
UNTO ALL GENERATIONS FOR | EVER AND | EVER : A | MEN.

Sir GEORGE JOB ELVEY, Mus. Doc.

If there be no Recognition of New Members on Confession of Christ, to follow this, the congregation remains standing for the song of Ascription instantly following in the general service.

RECOGNITION OF NEW MEMBERS ON CONFESSION OF CHRIST
WITH BAPTISM
[USAGE IN THE CHURCH FELLOWSHIP]

This may be at any time, but statedly occurs when the Church is gathered together for the Communion at the Lord's Table; taking the place of the usual Confession of Christian Faith (VIII) in the general Service. And before each such stated season, timely announcement and invitation are to be given in the congregation. If there be Recognition of New Members on Transfer from Other Churches, it precedes this.
Words in brackets may be changed or omitted; and if the service be private any appropriate changes are made. Responses printed in small capitals are for utterance by all the Church including the Minister.

I. Presentation
ANNOUNCEMENT
BELOVED in the Lord :
The Great Head of the Church — who saith, Where two or three are gathered together in My Name, there am I in the midst of them — giveth us the privilege at

RECOGNITION OF NEW MEMBERS ON CONFESSION OF CHRIST 377

this time to recognize [a] new member [s] in our fellowship, on confession of Christ. [Matt. xviii, 20, 19]

Hear the word of our Lord Jesus: Every one who shall confess Me before men, him will I also confess before My Father who is in heaven.

Also, Christ's apostle Paul teacheth: With the heart man believeth unto righteousness; and with the mouth confession is made unto salvation.
[Matt. x. 31; Rom. x. 10]

Hymn omitted at discretion: one of the following may be sung by All—

HYMN No. 1. C. M.

THE promise of My Father's love
Shall stand forever good —
Christ said; and gave His soul to death,
And sealed the grace with blood.

2 To this dear covenant of Thy word,
I set my humble name;
I seal th' engagement of my Lord,
And make my filial claim.

ISAAC WATTS, D. D., 1707.

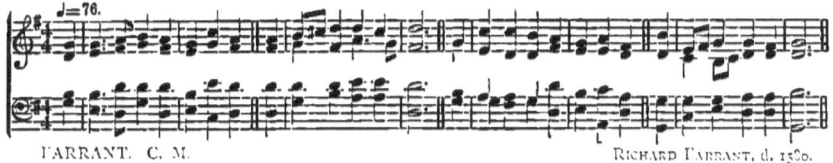

FARRANT. C. M.   RICHARD FARRANT, d. 1580.

HYMN No. 2. C. M.

WITNESS, ye men and angels now,
Before the Lord we speak;
To Him we make our solemn vow;
From Him our strength we seek.

2 Behold! to Christ, Redeemer, King,
Ourselves with joy we yield;

Our vows, for all life's fleeting years,
To Him, this day, are sealed.

3 Lord, guide our doubtful feet aright,
And keep us in Thy ways;
And while we turn our vows to prayers,
Turn Thou our prayers to praise.

BENJAMIN BEDDOME (alt.), 1730.

DEDHAM. C. M.   WILLIAM GARDINER, 1830.

HYMN No. 3. C. M.

I'M not ashamed to own my Lord,
Or to defend His cause;
Maintain the honor of His word,
The glory of His cross.

2 Firm as His throne His promise stands,
And He can well secure

What I've committed to His hands
Till the decisive hour.

3 Then will He own my humble name
Before His Father's face,
And in the New Jerusalem
Appoint my soul a place.

ISAAC WATTS, D. D., 1709.

378 RECOGNITION OF NEW MEMBERS ON CONFESSION OF CHRIST

CALL

You who are present to enter the visible Church of God:
Come ye and join yourselves to Jehovah   [Jer. 1, 5]
IN AN EVERLASTING COVENANT THAT SHALL NOT BE FORGOTTEN.
Come with us, and we will do you good;
FOR JEHOVAH HATH SPOKEN GOOD CONCERNING ISRAEL.
[Num. x, 29]
Come hither and stand forth —
IN THE NAME OF THE LORD JESUS!

Minister calls the full name of every candidate: the persons as named come forward and remain standing before Him till the end. Deacons may assist him, grouping separately at one side any who are to be baptized.

II. Confession of Christ

WARRANT

BELOVED: Peace be unto you:
We [who have awaited your coming in hope] greet you with blessing.

Forasmuch as Almighty God in eternal grace through Christ, according to the sure testimony of His Word, offers unto sinful men salvation and life eternal, granting His Spirit to work in them repentance, and to unite them to His Son Jesus in the new life of faith and holy obedience:

And since all who believe on Christ Jesus are called in one Body, which is His Church, to confess Him before men:

PROPOSITION

THEREFORE you — having received grace from God to believe on and follow His Son, and in His providence having your place [from childhood] among us — do now stand forth from the world before these witnesses and those unseen, to join with this company of disciples, and with the whole Church of God, in confessing our Lord and Savior.

CONFESSION OF CHRIST

[The Church (and all Christian disciples present) rise, and stand through this confession]
WITH the Apostles, and the Church in all ages and throughout the world;
With the Heavenly Jerusalem, the joyful assembly of the redeemed on high;

[The Church (with the other disciples) and the candidates, All, join aloud—]
WE CONFESS JESUS THE CHRIST,
THE SON OF THE LIVING GOD: AMEN.

[All sit except Minister and candidates]

[Matt. xvi, 15-19; iii, 16, 17; xvii, 5. Also: Rom. x, 9, 10; Matt. x, 32, 33; Lk. xii, 8, 9; Jn. xii, 42, 43; 1 Cor. xii, 3 l. c.; 1 Jn. iv, 14, 15; v, 1-5, 9].

III. Vows in Covenant

THUS standing forth from the world to confess the Son of God, you openly vow unto Jehovah — the Father and the Son and the Holy Spirit, One God — in the everlasting covenant of His grace:
Claiming Him as your God and Father, and your Portion for ever;
Trusting in Christ His Son for full forgiveness and eternal life;
Looking to His Spirit for all light and strength and sanctifying grace:
While in repentance for all your sins,

You turn from an ungodly world —
You deny the lusts of the flesh —
You renounce the works of the devil —
To be joined unto Christ Jesus, your Savior and Head;
To walk in all His ordinances in the gospel, and make Him your example;
To seek God in prayer with thanksgiving;
To submit lovingly to His will;
To hold your possessions as His trust;
To dwell in meekness, and follow charity with all men;
And to work for the upbuilding of Christ's Kingdom —
Looking for Him to come again in glory and take you unto Himself:

[Assent by candidates] *Amen.*

IV. Baptism — the Seal

INSTITUTION

ACCORDING as our Lord hath appointed in His Church, the seal of the Christian confession and covenant is BAPTISM — a symbol of the putting on of Christ in our new life by the Holy Spirit.

[All these Scripture portions following, as far as to "Confirmation," are omitted at discretion; especially if none are to be baptized]

For, even in the Old Covenant thus saith Jehovah by His prophet: [Ezki. xxxvi, 25-27]
I will sprinkle clean water upon you,
AND YE SHALL BE CLEAN:
A new heart also will I give you,
AND A NEW SPIRIT WILL I PUT WITHIN YOU;
And I will take away the stony heart out of your flesh,
AND I WILL GIVE YOU A HEART OF FLESH:
And I will put My Spirit within you,
AND CAUSE YOU TO WALK IN MY STATUTES.

HEAR our Lord's last command to His disciples before His ascension:
All authority hath been given unto Me in heaven and on earth:
Go ye therefore, and make disciples of all the nations, baptizing them into the Name of the Father and of the Son and of the Holy Spirit: [Matt. xxviii, 18, 19]
He that believeth and is baptized shall be saved. [Mk. xvi, 16]

Also, let this teaching of Christ's apostle Paul be pondered deeply in your hearts: As many of you as were baptized into Christ did put on Christ. [Gal. iii, 27]

[Also, it is profitable that these Scriptures be consulted privately: Matt. iii, 13-17; Mk. i, 9-11; Lk. iii, 21, 22; Jn. iii, 13-17; i, 31, 33; Acts, ii, 38-41; viii, 36-38; ix, 1-; xxii, 16; viii, 12; x. 44, 47, 48; xvi, 14, 15, 33; xviii, 8; xix, 1-5; Rom. vi, 3-5; I Cor. i, 13; xii, 13; Eph. iv, 4-6; Col. ii, 12; I Pet. iii, 21]

CONFIRMATION OF BAPTISM AFORETIME

[Omitted when no previous Baptism is to be confirmed.]
[Also in Churches in which the Laying on of Hands is accepted as a Scriptural Usage to follow Baptism, this Confirmation is omitted, and the form immediately following this is used instead]

YOU who aforetime have been baptized do now [severally] confirm the act and faith of your former Baptism: [Assent by all baptized candidates] *Amen.*

380 RECOGNITION OF NEW MEMBERS ON CONFESSION OF CHRIST

LAYING ON OF HANDS — upon any baptized aforetime

[Only when "Confirmation" above has not been used, and in Churches which accept this Usage: see Matt. xix, 13-15; Mk. x, 13-16; Acts, viii, 14-19; ix, 10-19; xix, 5, 6; Heb. vi, 1, 2]

Minister — having knowledge of any who have been baptized (who may be grouped separately at one side) — indicates to them one by one to come near, taking each in turn by the right hand, and demanding thus —

HAST thou been baptized into the faith and confession of Jesus Christ?
[Answer] *I have.* [or other form of assent]

DOST thou now confirm the act and faith of thy former Baptism?
[Answer] *I do.* [or other form of assent]

WHAT is thy name? [Answer — the Baptismal Name, without surname]

At the same time, the *full* name in writing should be given to the Minister

Minister then lays his hands on the person's head, praying thus, or to this purport —

[Heb. vi, 2; Also: Heb. xiii, 20; 1 Pet. v, 10]

**THOU God of the everlasting covenant:
Through the continual abiding of Thy Spirit, perfect, confirm, and strengthen this Thy child,
Whom Thou hast called in Christ Jesus, unto Thine eternal glory:**
[All] **AMEN.**

Thus with every one severally of the baptized: but any of such, conscientiously declining to confirm a former Baptism, may be omitted here, and assigned among those to be baptized, as below.

THE BAPTISM

Minister, now taking his place as for ministration of Baptism (if he have not already so done) indicates to any awaiting baptism, to come near one by one, taking each by the right hand (disposing the person near the Font as convenient), and demanding thus —

What is thy name? [Answer — the Baptismal Name, without surname]

At the same time, the *full* name in writing should be given to the Minister

Minister then baptizes the person with water — therewith pronouncing the Baptismal Name, and declaring the Baptism, according to Matt. xxviii, 19.

[*The Baptismal Name*] — **I BAPTIZE thee into the Name of the Father and of the Son and of the Holy Spirit:** [All] **AMEN.**

In instant response to this AMEN after each Baptism, All present may give praise to God, singing or saying in unison —

Adapted.

LAYING ON OF HANDS — upon any baptized at this time

Minister (in Churches in which the Laying on of Hands is accepted as a Scriptural Usage to follow Baptism) then lays his hands on the person's head, praying thus, or to this purport —

[Heb. vi, 2; Also: 1 Pet. v, 12; II Tim. i, 9; 1 Thess. ii, 12]

**THOU God of all grace;
Receive now this Thy child, whom Thou callest with a holy calling:
And through the continual abiding of Thy Spirit, perfect, confirm, and strengthen Thy child in Christ Jesus,
Unto life eternal in Thine own Kingdom and Glory:** [All] **AMEN.**

[Heb. vi, 1, 2; Gen. xlviii, 14-16; Matt. xix, 13-15; Mk. x, 13-16; Acts, ix, 10-19; viii, 14-19; xix 5, 6; Num. xxvii, 18, 23; Deut. xxxiv, 9; Mk. xvi, 18; viii, 23; Acts, xxviii, 8]

RECOGNITION OF NEW MEMBERS ON CONFESSION OF CHRIST

V. Covenant in the Church

AND now, standing forth to join with us in confessing Christ, you therein recognize your fellowship in especial with this Church as a local and stated fellowship in the communion of the Church Universal, in liberty under Christ's government alone:
> Wherein you covenant to walk together with us obediently to the Word of God;
> In the administration of Christ's fellowship, truth, and order, in His house,
> In a common worship and a concerted Christian work in the community,
> In the meekness of our Lord Jesus caring one for another unto edification,
> Keeping the unity of the Spirit in the bond of peace, with sympathy and brotherly love: *[Assent by candidates]* **Amen.**

VI. Welcome
The Church rise and stand, joining in Responses

BEHOLD therefore, Beloved:
This Church stands by your side in fellowship henceforth.
> We greet you in the eternal covenant of our God:
> WE WELCOME YOU INTO THIS COMPANY OF DISCIPLES.
> We receive you who now set forth to follow Christ with us,
> WE WILL HAVE YOU IN OUR CARE AND SEEK YOUR GOOD.
> These gates of Zion we open unto you with joy;
> YEA, THE LORD HIMSELF DOTH OPEN THEM;
> Even the King, our Shepherd, the Master of Assemblies,
> WHO HOLDETH THE KEYS IN HIS RIGHT HAND.

Into the communion of Christ's whole visible Church, by His authority we now receive you.
> We welcome you — turning from an ungodly world,
> Whose sorrows are without hope,
> Whose perils are without help,
> Whose joys flee away,
> Whose substance perishes with the using —
> We welcome you to God's great household of faith and love,
> The home of souls, the habitation of peace through God's Spirit,
> The blessed and immovable Kingdom of Christ His Son.

We receive you to work in company with us in furthering Christ's gospel in the earth,
And to go with us, pilgrims together, unto the triumphant Church and glorious Kingdom of our God on high: [Church] **AMEN.**

VII. Hymn of Fellowship
All still standing

Omitted at discretion: one of the following may be sung by All—

HYMN NO. 1. C. M.

COME in, Thou blessèd of the Lord,
  Stranger nor foe art thou:
We welcome thee with warm accord,
  Our friend, our brother, now.

2 Come with us — we will do thee good,
  As God to us hath done;

Stand but in Him as those have stood
  Whose faith the victory won.

3 And when, by turns we pass away,
  And star by star grows dim,
May each, translated into day,
  Be lost and found in Him.
  JAMES MONTGOMERY, d. 1854.

382 RECOGNITION OF NEW MEMBERS ON CONFESSION OF CHRIST

ST. AGNES. C. M.　　　　　John Bacchus Dykes, Vicar, Mus. Doc., 1853.

HYMN No. 2. C. M.

Happy the souls to Jesus joined,
And saved by grace alone;
Walking in all His ways, they find
Their heaven on earth begun.

2 The Church triumphant in Thy love—
Their mighty joys we know:
They sing the Lamb in hymns above,
And we in hymns below.

3 Thee in Thy glorious realm they praise,
And bow before Thy throne;
We in the kingdom of Thy grace:
The kingdoms are but one.

4 The holy to the holiest leads,
And thence our spirits rise;
For he that in Thy statutes treads,
Shall meet Thee in the skies.
　　　　　　Charles Wesley, 1745.

HYMN No. 3. L. M.　　*For Young Disciples.*

Come, ever-blesséd Spirit! come,
And make Thy servants' hearts Thy home;
Thus consecrated, Lord! to Thee,
May each a living temple be.

2 Arm these Thy youthful soldiers, Lord!
With shield of faith, and Spirit's sword:
Forth to the battle may they go,
And boldly fight against the foe.

3 With banner of the cross unfurled,
O, may they overcome the world,
And so, at last, receive from Thee
The palm and crown of victory!

4 O, grant us so to use Thy grace
That we may see Thy glorious face;
And ever with the heav'nly host,
Praise Father, Son, and Holy Ghost!
　　　　Christopher Wordsworth, D. D., 1865

ROSE HILL. L. M.　　　　　Joseph E. Sweetzer, 1849.

VIII. **Grace**　　　　　　　　　　　　All still standing

Now let us all hear and declare the grace of God in His Church:
Thus saith Jehovah:
　　I have blotted out as a thick cloud thy transgressions,
　　And as a cloud thy sins; for I have redeemed thee.
　　　　　　　　　　　　　　　　　　　　　　[Is. xliv, 22]
So then, as Christ's apostle Paul teacheth,
　　Ye are no more strangers and sojourners, but ye are fellow-citizens
　　　　with the saints,
　　And of the household of God,
　　Being built upon the foundation of the apostles and prophets,
　　Christ Jesus Himself being the chief corner-stone.
　　　　　　　　　　　　　　　　　　　　　　[Eph. ii, 19, 20]

BENEDICTION [1 Thess. v, 23; Gal. vi, 18]

BELOVED: The God of peace Himself sanctify you wholly; and may your spirit and soul and body be preserved entire, without blame at the coming of our Lord Jesus Christ.
The grace of our Lord Jesus Christ be with your spirit: [All] AMEN.

IX. Ascription [Jude, 24, 25] All still standing

To be said responsively: but if there be no song (*Te Deum*), etc., to follow immediately in the general service, then this may be *sung* or said in unison, by All; Tune, at end of Recognition of New Members on Transfer from other Churches.

Now unto Him that is able to | guard us * from | stumbling,
AND TO SET US BEFORE THE PRESENCE OF HIS GLORY WITHOUT BLEMISH | IN EX- | CEED-ING | JOY —
To the only God our Savior, through Jesus | Christ our | Lord —
GLORY, MAJESTY, DOMINION, AND POWER, BEFORE ALL TIME, AND NOW, AND FOR | EV-ER- | MORE : A- | MEN.

The new members now retire to their places in the congregation; and All remain standing for *Te Deum* or other song of Ascription instantly following in the general service.

The Communion at the Lord's Table

THIS Ordinance of Christ is observed at stated seasons appointed by the Church: special observance also may be had as the Church may appoint or allow. Among the seasons stated or special may be included the anniversaries of our Lord's Resurrection, and of the Gift of the Holy Spirit on the Day of Pentecost.

Announcement of each stated Communion season is given in the congregation on the Lord's Day preceding, besides earlier notice as requisite for any persons concerned.

When the Church is gathered together for the Lord's Supper — the general Service having proceeded as far as XIII, Sermon — announcement is then to be made that "The Lord's Table is here spread" — with any requisite Invitation and Exhortation to commune. The Communion Service proper then begins, taking the place of all that would follow in the general Service.

The connected Service as far as to the Sermon mainly observes the usual Order, but with variations as shown in THE SERVICE IN THE LORD'S HOUSE in early pages of this book (see also the Notes there given, and the shortened Order of Service). For convenience the special Order of the connected Service is here shown in outline; and the *Litany* and the *Offertory* are included.

Words in brackets are to be omitted at discretion: portions in small capitals are for utterance by All — congregation with Minister: portions in italics, by congregation alone.

The Communion at the Lord's Table

With the Order of the Service Connected
INCLUDING
The Recognition of New Members in the Church

ALSO AN ANCIENT CREED, LITANY, THE LORD'S PRAYER,
OFFERTORY, SCRIPTURE PREFACES AND SENTENCES,
HALLELUJAH OF THE HEAVENLY HOST

[See in first part of the book, THE SERVICE IN THE LORD'S HOUSE, with the Notes preceding it; also its alternatives and omissions.]

I Introductory
1 SENTENCE   From Minister
2 RESPONSE   Sung, or said, by All

II Christian Summary
Either CHRIST'S SUMMARY OF THE LAW: *Or* THE BEATITUDES OF THE GOSPEL

III Hymn

IV Scripture of the Old Covenant   FROM MINISTER
[Omitted at discretion, in this service]

V Responsive Lesson   OF MINISTER AND CONGREGATION

VI Psalm Chant   OF CONGREGATION
[Omitted at discretion, when new members are to be recognized in the Church]

VII Scripture of the New Covenant   FROM MINISTER
1 GOSPEL OF OUR LORD JESUS
2 APOSTOLIC WORD

[One of these Lessons, omitted at discretion in this service]

VIII Confession of Christ — in Fellowship
RECOGNITION OF NEW MEMBERS IN THE CHURCH
    1 ON TRANSFER FROM OTHER CHURCHES   See page 373
    2 ON CONFESSION OF CHRIST   See page 376

If no new Members be present for Recognition in the Church — then without announcement this ancient creed may be said in unison by all Christian disciples present, standing; or other brief form of Christian Confession appointed for the Church.

THE COMMUNION AT THE LORD'S TABLE 385

AN ANCIENT CREED

Of unknown origin; but probably a revision and enlargement, 362-373, of primitive formulas used at Baptism in the First Church of Christ, in Jerusalem.

[For Note as to the change in this creed at one point, see page vii]

I BELIEVE IN ONE GOD THE FATHER ALMIGHTY,
MAKER OF HEAVEN AND EARTH,
AND OF ALL THINGS VISIBLE AND INVISIBLE:

AND IN ONE LORD JESUS CHRIST, THE ONLY-BEGOTTEN SON OF GOD,
GLORIFIED WITH THE FATHER BEFORE THE WORLD WAS —
THE SAME WAS THE WORD THAT WAS IN THE BEGINNING WITH GOD, AND
    WAS GOD —
THROUGH WHOM ALL THINGS WERE MADE:
WHO FOR US MEN, AND FOR OUR SALVATION, CAME DOWN FROM HEAVEN,
AND WAS INCARNATE BY THE HOLY GHOST OF THE VIRGIN MARY,
AND WAS MADE MAN:
AND WAS CRUCIFIED ALSO FOR US UNDER PONTIUS PILATE;
HE SUFFERED AND WAS BURIED:
AND THE THIRD DAY HE ROSE AGAIN ACCORDING TO THE SCRIPTURES:
AND ASCENDED INTO HEAVEN,
AND SITTETH AT THE RIGHT HAND OF THE FATHER:
AND HE SHALL COME AGAIN WITH GLORY TO JUDGE BOTH THE QUICK
    AND THE DEAD;
WHOSE KINGDOM SHALL HAVE NO END.

AND I BELIEVE IN THE HOLY GHOST, THE LORD AND GIVER OF LIFE,
WHO PROCEEDETH FROM THE FATHER AND THE SON,
WHO WITH THE FATHER AND THE SON TOGETHER IS WORSHIPED AND
    GLORIFIED;
WHO SPAKE BY THE PROPHETS.

AND I BELIEVE ONE CATHOLIC AND APOSTOLIC CHURCH:
I ACKNOWLEDGE ONE BAPTISM FOR THE REMISSION OF SINS:
AND I LOOK FOR THE RESURRECTION OF THE DEAD:
AND THE LIFE OF THE WORLD TO COME. AMEN.

[*Alternative:* Instead may be the ancient creed set forth in THE SERVICE IN THE LORD'S HOUSE]

IX Song of Ascription BY CONGREGATION

One of the following ancient Doxologies — see ASCRIPTIONS AND OTHER SONGS

No. 1. TE DEUM LAUDAMUS: No. 4. ALL HOLY:
No. 2. GLORIA IN EXCELSIS DEO: No. 6. BENEDICTUS:
No. 3. GLORIA PATRI: No. 10. GLORY, THANKS (metrical)

When new Members have been recognized in the Church on Confession of Christ, *Te Deum* is the preferable Ascription, as an instant response of joy and praise at the end of the Recognition; if it may not be sung conveniently, then *Gloria in Excelsis* is appropriate: or No. 4, *All Holy;* or No. 10, *Glory, Thanks* (metrical)

25

THE COMMUNION AT THE LORD'S TABLE

X The Prayers

1 PRAYER FOR THE ESTATE OF CHRIST'S CHURCH GENERAL, AND IN THE LOCAL FELLOWSHIP — brief, and free in form.
2 After the above (or in its stead) the LITANY may be used, if acceptable to the Church — Congregation uttering the suffrages.

LITANY

[In main portions arranged from the Anglican Litany of Cranmer, with other reformers, set forth, 1545, 1549, 1552: on the basis of a compilation, probably from ancient forms, by Gregory the Great near the end of the sixth century]

O GOD, the Father in Heaven,
Be merciful to us sinners:
  God be merciful to us sinners.
O Lord God, our Father in Christ Jesus;
In His Name show Thy mercy upon us sinners:
  Lord God, in Christ Jesus show Thy mercy upon us sinners.
O Lord God, whose blessèd Spirit cleanseth us from our sins and helpeth our infirmities;
Show Thy mercy upon us sinners, and grant us Thy full salvation:
  Lord God, by Thy Spirit grant us sinners Thy full salvation.

Remember not, Lord, our offenses, nor the offenses of our forefathers;
Neither take Thou vengeance of our sins:
Spare us, O Lord; Spare Thy people whom Thou hast redeemed with the precious blood of the Lamb of God;
And be not angry with us forever:
  Spare us, O Lord.

Deliver us, O Lord:
From all evil and mischief,
From sin, from the crafts and assaults of the devil,
From Thy wrath and from everlasting perdition:
  Deliver us, O Lord.

From all blindness of heart,
From pride, vain glory, and hypocrisy,
From envy, hatred, and malice, and all uncharitableness:
  Deliver us, O Lord.

From all inordinate and sinful affections,
And from all the deceits of the world, the flesh, and the devil:
  Deliver us, O Lord.

From lightning and tempest, from fire and flood,
From plague, pestilence, and famine,
From battle and murder, and from violent death:
  Deliver us, O Lord.

From tumult and riot, from all sedition, conspiracy, and rebellion;
From all false doctrine, heresy, and schism;
From hardness of heart, and contempt of Thy word and commandment:
  Deliver us, O Lord.

By the mystery of Thy holy Incarnation and Nativity, O Thou Only-begotten Son of God;
By Thy baptism, fasting, and temptation:
  Deliver us, O Lord.

By Thine agony and bloody sweat,
By Thy cross and passion,
By Thy precious death and burial;
By Thy glorious resurrection and ascension;
And by the coming of the Holy Ghost: *Deliver us, O Lord.*
In all time of our tribulation, in all time of our prosperity;
In the hour of death and in the Day of Judgment:
Deliver us, O Lord.

Blessed Lord God: We Thy children through Christ Jesus do hope in Thy lovingkindness —
And we beseech Thee to hear us:
That it may please Thee to rule and guide Thy holy Church universal in the right way:
We beseech Thee to hear us, Blessed Lord.
That it may please Thee by Thy gracious Spirit to illuminate all ministers in Thy Church with true knowledge and understanding of Thy Word,
So that by both their preaching and their living they may show it and set it forth:
We beseech Thee to hear us, Blessed Lord.
That it may please Thee, the Lord of the harvest, to send forth laborers into Thy harvest:
We beseech Thee to hear us, Blessed Lord.
That it may please Thee to bless and guide Thy Servant the chief Magistrate of this Nation, and all whomsoever Thou hast clothed with authority in our civil State;
Enduing them with wisdom to govern us in the fear of God;
That they may bear rule as those that serve Thy Christ whom Thou hast exalted as Head over all:
We beseech Thee to hear us, Blessed Lord.
That it may please Thee to bless the rulers in all lands,
And to dispose their hearts and minds to the knowledge and obedience of Thy Son, the King of kings;
That in His Name they may execute justice and maintain truth, to the blessing of all the peoples:
We beseech Thee to hear us, Blessed Lord.
That it may please Thee to give to all nations, unity, peace, and concord:
We beseech Thee to hear us, Blessed Lord.
That it may please Thee to give and preserve to our use the kindly fruits of the earth, so that in due time we may enjoy them:
We beseech Thee to hear us, Blessed Lord.
That it may please Thee to give to all Thy people increase of grace to hear meekly Thy Word, and to receive it with pure affection, and to bring forth the fruits of the Spirit:
We beseech Thee to hear us, Blessed Lord.
That it may please Thee to bring into the way of truth all such as have erred and are deceived:
We beseech Thee to hear us, Blessed Lord.
That it may please Thee to strengthen such as do stand,
And to comfort and help the weak-hearted, and to raise up those who fall;
And finally to beat down Satan under our feet:
We beseech Thee to hear us, Blessed Lord.

That it may please Thee to succor, help, and comfort all who are in danger, necessity, and tribulation:
>*We beseech Thee to hear us, Blessed Lord.*

That it may please Thee to preserve all who journey, and those who go down to the sea in ships;
And to be with the sick and with all those in peril and pain, and to protect young children;
And to show Thy pity upon all exiles, prisoners, and captives:
>*We beseech Thee to hear us, Blessed Lord.*

That it may please Thee to defend and provide for the fatherless children and widows, and all who are desolate and oppressed:
>*We beseech Thee to hear us, Blessed Lord.*

That it may please Thee to have mercy upon all men:
>*We beseech Thee to hear us, Blessed Lord.*

That it may please Thee to forgive our enemies, persecutors, and slanderers; and to turn their hearts:
>*We beseech Thee to hear us, Blessed Lord.*

That it may please Thee to give us true repentance:
To forgive us all our sins, negligences, and ignorances;
And to endue us with the grace of Thy Holy Spirit to amend our lives according to Thy holy Word:
>*We beseech Thee to hear us, Blessed Lord.*

O Lord God, hear, and have mercy upon us and upon all men, through the Lamb of God who taketh away the sin of the world:
>*Lord God, hear; and have mercy upon all souls that Thou hast made.*

O Lord God, hear, and let Thy lovingkindness be for the comfort of all the meek and of every one that waiteth for Thee:
>*Lord God, hear; and let Thy light arise on all that seek Thee.*

O Lord God, hear us, and direct our hearts into the love of Thee;
And multiply unto us grace and peace, in the knowledge of God our Father and of Jesus Christ our Lord, through the power of Thy Holy Spirit:
>*Lord God, hear us with Thy whole household, and keep us unto Life eternal.*

O Lord our God, all glory now and ever be to Thee:
>AMEN.

[1 PRAYER FOR THE ESTATE OF CHRIST'S CHURCH — see above]
[2 THE LITANY — see above]
3 THE PRAYER OF THE DAY   [Omitted at discretion]
4 THE SILENT MOMENT OF PRAYER   [Omitted at discretion]

O THOU that seest the heart!
We lift up our hearts in silence unto Thee —

*   *   *   *   *   *

5 THE LORD'S PRAYER — by All

OUR FATHER WHO ART IN HEAVEN,
HALLOWED BE THY NAME.
THY KINGDOM COME.
THY WILL BE DONE ON EARTH, AS IT IS IN HEAVEN.

GIVE US THIS DAY OUR DAILY BREAD.
AND FORGIVE US OUR TRESPASSES,
AS WE FORGIVE THOSE WHO TRESPASS AGAINST US.
AND BRING US NOT INTO TEMPTATION,
BUT DELIVER US FROM EVIL.

FOR THINE IS THE KINGDOM, AND THE POWER AND THE GLORY,
FOR EVER AND EVER. AMEN.

XI 𝔒ffertory   *On any Day as appointed*

Preceded by requisite announcement of the object
Delayed till after sermon, if expedient
While the benevolent offerings of the congregation are being collected, Minister may utter appropriate sentences of Scripture; to each sentence there may be a very short musical response (on the organ, or sung); or a brief silence may separate the sentences
The arrangement below suggests Sentences proper to different objects
At the Communion Season the Offering is in behalf of the Church Fellowship: see below
In the beginning of every Offering — Sentences 1–4 are appropriate

1. REMEMBER the words of the Lord Jesus, how He Himself said — It is more blesséd to give than to receive. *Acts xx, 35*

2. LAY not up for yourselves treasures upon the earth, where moth and rust do consume, and where thieves break through and steal;
But lay up for yourselves treasures in heaven, where neither moth nor rust doth consume, and where thieves do not break through nor steal. *Matt. vi, 19-21*

3. YE know the grace of our Lord Jesus Christ —
That though He was rich, yet for your sakes He became poor,
That ye through His poverty might become rich. *II Cor. viii, 9*

4. THE Lord Jesus sat down in the temple over against the treasury,
And beheld how the multitude cast money into the treasury. *Mk*

FOR THE SPREAD OF THE GOSPEL

5. HONOR Jehovah with thy substance,
And with the first-fruits of all thine increase. *Pro*

6. FREELY ye have received; freely give. *M*

7. GOD loveth a cheerful giver:
And God is able to make all grace abound unto you. *II Cor*

8. LOOK not each of you to his own things, but each of you also to the things of others:
Have this mind in you which was also in Christ Jesus. *Phil. ii, 4, 5*

9. TO do good and to communicate, forget not:
For with such sacrifices God is well pleased. *Heb. xiii, 16*

10. CAST thy bread upon the waters;
For thou shalt find it after many days. *Eccl. xi, 1*

11 Every man shall give as he is able,
According to the blessing of Jehovah thy God, which He hath given thee.
Deut. xvi, 17

12 Bring ye the whole tithe into the treasury,
And prove Me now herewith, saith Jehovah of hosts,
Whether I will not open you the windows of heaven, and pour you out blessing.
Mal. iii, 10

13 If the readiness is there, it is acceptable according as a man hath, not according as he hath not.
II Cor. viii, 12

FOR THE FELLOWSHIP—IN THE CHURCH, OR WITH OTHER CHURCHES

14 God is not unrighteous to forget your work and the love which ye show toward His Name,
In that ye ministered unto the saints, and still do minister.
Heb. vi, 10

15 The ministration of this service not only filleth up the measure of the wants of the saints, but aboundeth also through many thanksgivings unto God.
II Cor. ix, 12

16 Charge them that are rich in this present world —
That they do good, that they be rich in good works,
That they be ready to distribute, willing to communicate;
Laying up in store for themselves a good foundation against the time to come,
That they may lay hold on the life which is life indeed.
I Tim. vi, 17

17 He that soweth sparingly shall reap also sparingly;
And he that soweth bountifully shall reap also bountifully.
II Cor. ix, 6

18 Thy prayer is heard,
And thine alms are had in remembrance in the sight of God.
Acts, x, 31

FOR THE POOR

19 The poor shall never cease out of the land:
Therefore, I command thee, saying — Thou shalt surely open thy hand unto thy brother,
To thy needy, and to thy poor, in thy land.
Deut. xv, 11

20 Whoso stoppeth his ears at the cry of the poor —
He also shall cry, but shall not be heard.
Prov. xxi, 13

21 Blessed is he that considereth the poor:
Jehovah will deliver him in the days of evil.
Ps. xli, 1

22 It is written — He hath scattered abroad, he hath given to the poor;
His righteousness abideth forever.
II Cor. ix, 9

23 He that giveth unto the poor shall not lack.
Prov. xxviii, 27

24 Whoso hath the world's goods, and beholdeth his brother in need, and shutteth up his compassions from him -
How doth the love of God abide in him?
I Jn. iii, 17

25 He that hath pity upon the poor lendeth unto Jehovah.
Prov. xix, 17

THE COMMUNION AT THE LORD'S TABLE 391

26 IF thou draw out thy soul to the hungry,
And satisfy the afflicted soul;
Then shall thy light rise in darkness,
And thine obscurity be as the noon-day. Is. lviii, 10

27 THE King shall answer and say unto them at His right hand —
Verily I say unto you, inasmuch as ye did it unto one of these My
brethren, even these least, ye did it unto Me. Matt. xxv, 40

GENERAL BENEFICENCE

28 TAKE ye from among you an offering unto Jehovah:
Whosoever is of a willing heart, let him bring it, Jehovah's offering.
Ex. xxxv, 5

29 UPON the first day of the week, let each one of you lay by him in store, as
he may prosper. 1 Cor. xvi, 2

30 GIVE, and it shall be given unto you:
Good measure, pressed down, shaken together, running over, shall they give
into your bosom. Lk. vi, 38

31 THE liberal soul shall be made fat;
And he that watereth shall be watered also himself. Prov. xi, 25

32 THE liberal deviseth liberal things,
And by liberal things shall he stand. Is. xxxii, 8

33 THERE is that maketh himself rich, yet hath nothing:
There is that maketh himself poor, yet hath great wealth. Prov. xiii. 7

34 THE merciful man doeth good to his own soul.
He that hath a bountiful eye shall be blesséd. Prov. xi, 7: xxii, 9

35 HEAR the word of the Lord Jesus:
Thou shalt be blesséd;
Because the poor, the maimed, the lame, the blind, have not wherewith to
recompense thee:
For thou shalt be recompensed in the resurrection of the just. Lk. xiv, 14

All the Offerings having been brought to the Minister are by him deposited before the Congregation (but those that collect them may deposit them if that usage be preferred)

[Minister]   Let us present this offering to God.

Immediately All rise, standing during the short Offertory Prayer and Blessing: The Prayer may be in these words, or to this purport —

LET this our humble offering, O God, be accepted in Thy grace, and made fruitful in blessings by Thy power:
And through Thine own Offering for us — even the most holy Sacrifice in Thy Son — bestow on us Thy Spirit;
That we, offering ourselves also unto Thee, may be accepted now and ever:
In the Name of the Lord Jesus: [All] AMEN.

392   THE COMMUNION AT THE LORD'S TABLE

All singing, or saying in unison, this Blessing — From 1 Chron. xxix. 10, 11, 12, 14

BLESSÉD BE THOU, O JEHOVAH, OUR GOD FOR | EVER AND | EVER!
BOTH RICHES AND | HON-OR | COME OF | THEE:
ALL THAT IS IN THE HEAVEN AND IN THE | EARTH IS | THINE;
FOR ALL THINGS COME OF THEE, AND OF THINE | OWN ' HAVE WE
| GIV-EN | THEE.

Sir GEORGE ALEXANDER MACFARREN, Mus. Doc.

[*Omissions :* either the Offertory Prayer or Blessing, or both, at discretion]

A contribution for the ordinary expenses of the Church (not announced), may be at the same time; but for such contribution alone the Offertory is not used

XII Hymn of Praise   OF CONGREGATION

Omitted at discretion when new Members have been recognized in the Church

---

—— NOTICES ——   [May be after Sermon, or may be omitted]

XIII Sermon

[May be omitted, or much shortened — particularly at Evening]

XIV The Communion at the Lord's Table
ON THE DAYS APPOINTED: CONCLUDING THE SERVICE

I Bidding to the Lord's Supper

Minister, announcing that "the Lord's Table is here spread," invites and exhorts all Christ's disciples present; using these words, or such other words relative to this Ordinance as are according to Holy Scripture :
[The portions in brackets are omitted at discretion]

IN the day when the Lord Jesus rose again from the dead, at eventide when His disciples were gathered together, Behold, He Himself stood in the midst of them — according to His promise — and saith unto them, Peace be unto you.

Since we also are gathered together in His Name, let the eyes of our faith be opened to behold Him present with us, that He may be known of us in the breaking of the bread.

For we are to consider in our hearts, Beloved in the Lord, that this Table here spread before us in our pilgrimage through this world, is the Table of our Savior and Master, Jesus Christ the Son of God, who loved us and gave Himself up for us — dying for our sins, according to the will of our God and Father. For on the night before our Lord Jesus was delivered to be crucified, He in His tender love and care ordained this Supper for His first friends who believed on Him, and for "them also who should believe on Him through their word."

Whatever we do at this table, therefore, we do it as His disciples; we do it, as He Himself said, "in remembrance of Him."

[Our Lord Jesus, who has now gone up above all heavens, and is exalted in the glory of the Father — and yet manifests Himself by the Holy Spirit in His Church through all days — declares this Supper to be the communion of all His disciples in His Body and His Blood; still further teaching through His apostle Paul, that all who sit in faith at His Table do so partake of Christ Jesus that they themselves become joined together in Him as One Body — dying unto sin in His death, living anew and nourished unto God from His Life. Yet that so great a mystery of eternal grace be not a cause of our stumbling, He gives us plainly to know that this our communion in Him is not a mere bodily partaking, but is of the spirit through the body; for He saith — "It is the spirit that quickeneth; the flesh profiteth nothing."]

Know then, all you who are Christ's disciples, that He gives you place at this Table — even every one, however weak, who believing with the heart on Him, stands in the confession of His Name before men. For, if we be sincere toward God, our comfort is this — that "His Spirit also helpeth our infirmity." [Know this moreover: that all you here are even made priests unto God; since all our Lord's disciples, even the least, are called "to be a holy priesthood, to offer up spiritual sacrifices, acceptable to God through Jesus Christ."]

Considering these things in our hearts, Beloved in the Lord, let us all now partake with faith — first receiving grace that we may now be stirred up within ourselves into love toward God our Father and unto charity with all men. Let our partaking at this Table be in self-recollection, penitence, and prayer; unto godly obedience; with thankfulness and praise, and with a joyful hope. "For as often as we eat this bread and drink the cup, we proclaim the Lord's death, *till He come.*" Behold! He is coming! in the fullness of the times He shall be revealed from the heavens in the glory of the Father, to take us unto Himself.

[Scriptures represented in the above: Matt. xviii, 20; Lk. xxiv, 30, 31, 35, 36; Eph. v, 2; Gal. i, 4; Rom. xv, 3; Jn. xiii, 1; xvii, 9, 20 (9-26); Lk. xiv, 15; I Pet. iii, 22; Heb. iv, 14; Matt. xxvi, 26-28; Mk. xiv, 22-24; Lk. xxii, 19, 20; Jn. vi, 51-63; 11 Cor. v, 16; I Cor. x, 16, 17; xi, 23-26; Rom. vi, 5-11; viii, 10, 11; I Cor. vi, 15; xii, 27; Eph. v, 30; Matt. x, 31; Rom. x, 10; viii, 26; I Pet. ii, 5, 9; Rev. i, 6; v, 10; Matt. xxii, 37-40; Mk. xii, 29-31; I Cor. xi, 26-31; I Pet. i, 14; II Cor. ix, 15; Heb. iii, 6; vi, 11; I Thess. iv, 13-19; Matt. xxvi, 29; Mk. xiv, 25; Lk. xxii, 16, 18]

|| Scripture Preface to the Lord's Supper

Minister reads slowly, without comment, one (or more) of the following or like portions of Holy Scripture

1 ISAIAH'S VISION OF MESSIAH.   Isaiah, lii, 14: His visage was so marred —
                                liii, 2-8: For He grew up before Him —
                                10-12: Yet it pleased Jehovah to bruise Him —

2 GOD'S GIFT OF HIS SON.   John, iii, 16-18: The word of our Lord Jesus:
                                God so loved the world —
                                    (ending in vs. 18) — is not judged.

3 CHRIST'S DISCIPLES GIVEN TO HIM OF THE
                    FATHER.   John, vi, 37-40: The word of our Lord Jesus:
                                All that which the Father giveth Me —

4 THE PARTAKING OF CHRIST'S FLESH AND BLOOD.
John, vi, 51-63: Our Lord Jesus said:
I am the living Bread —

5 THE GOOD SHEPHERD. John, x, 7: The word of our Lord Jesus:
Verily, verily —
9: I am the door —
11: I am the good Shepherd —
14-18: I am the good Shepherd —

6 THE SHEPHERD AND THE SHEEP. John, x, 27-30: The word of our Lord Jesus:
My sheep hear My voice —

7 COMFORT THROUGH FAITH: THE COMFORTER
ABIDING. John, xiv, 1-5: The word of our Lord Jesus:
Let not your heart be troubled —
6: I am the Way —
13-24: And whatsoever ye shall ask —

8 THE TRUE VINE. John, xv, 1-11: The word of our Lord Jesus:
I am the true vine —

9 CHRIST'S COMMANDMENT OF LOVE. John, xv,
12-17: The word of our Lord Jesus:
This is My commandment —

10 OUR LORD'S FAREWELL PRAYER. John, xvi, 33: The Lord Jesus said to the disciples:
These things have I spoken —
xvii, 1-5: These things spake Jesus —

11 OUR LORD'S FAREWELL PRAYER. John, xvii,
6-11: Our Lord Jesus prayed to the Father, and said:
I manifested Thy Name —
15-24: I pray not —

12 JUSTIFICATION AND LIFE THROUGH CHRIST'S
DEATH. Romans, v, 1-11: Being therefore justified by faith —

13 LIFE THROUGH CHRIST. Romans, viii, 11-17: If the Spirit of Him —

14 CONSUMMATE TRIUMPH THROUGH CHRIST JESUS.
Romans, viii, 31-39: What then shall we say to these things —

15 UNSEARCHABLE GRACE. Romans, xi, 33-36: O the depth of the riches —

16 CHRISTIAN MAGNANIMITY FOR CHRIST'S SAKE.
Romans, xv, 1-7: We that are strong —

17 DISCERNING THE LORD'S BODY. I Corinthians,
v, 7, 8: Our Passover also hath been sacrificed —
xi, 26-29: For as often as ye eat —
31: But if we discerned ourselves —

18 THE CHURCH ONE BODY IN CHRIST. I Corinthians, xii, 12-14: As the body is one —
26, 27: And whether one member suffereth —

19 THE GRACE OF SONSHIP THROUGH CHRIST.
Galatians, i, 3-5: Grace to you and peace —
iii, 26-29: For ye all are sons of God —

20 CHRIST THE HEAD OVER ALL. Ephesians, i,
2-7: Grace to you and peace —
19-23: According to that working —

21 RICHES OF GRACE. Ephesians, ii, 4-10: God, being rich in mercy —

22 WALKING IN LOVE, LIKE UNTO GOD. Ephesians, iv, 30-32: Grieve not the Holy Spirit of God —
v, 1, 2: Be ye therefore —
[ending in vs. 2] sacrifice to God.

23 CHRIST THE RECONCILIATION. Colossians, i,
12-23: Give thanks unto the Father —
[ending in vs. 23] — which ye heard.

THE COMMUNION AT THE LORD'S TABLE

24 IN CHRIST ALL FULLNESS AND ALL VICTORY.
   Colossians, ii, 9, 10: In Christ dwelleth all the fulness —
    13-15: And you, being dead —

25 THE BEGINNING OF THE RESURRECTION.
   Colossians, iii, 1-4: If then ye were raised —
    12-16: Put on therefore as God's elect —
    17: And whatsoever ye do —

26 GRACE AND HOPE.   Titus, ii, 11-14: The grace of God hath appeared —

27 THE SYMPATHETIC HIGH PRIEST. Hebrews,
    iv, 14-16: Having then a great High Priest —

28 UTTERMOST AND ETERNAL REDEMPTION.
   Hebrews, vii, 25, 26: Jesus Christ is able to save to the uttermost —
    ix, 11, 12: And Christ having come —

29 THE NEW AND LIVING WAY. Hebrews, x,
    19-23: Having therefore, Brethren, boldness —

30 COMING UNTO THE CITY OF THE LIVING GOD:
   Hebrews, xii, 1-3: Seeing we are compassed about with so great a
    cloud of witnesses, let us lay aside —
    18, 19: For ye are come not unto a mount —
    22-24: But ye are come unto Mount Zion —
    [ending in vs. 24] — blood of sprinkling.

31 THE LIVING HOPE.   I Peter, i, 2, 3-9: Grace to you and peace be multiplied —

32 THE NEW LIFE IN CHRIST JESUS. I Peter, i,
    13-21: Girding up the loins of your mind —

33 CHRIST THE CORNER-STONE. I Peter, ii, 4-9: Coming unto Christ, a Living Stone —

34 SONSHIP TOWARD GOD.   I John, iii, 1-3: Behold what manner of love —

35 LOVE FROM GOD: LOVE TO THE BRETHREN.
   I John, iv, 7-16: Beloved, let us love one another —
    19: We love, because He first loved us —

36 THE TESTIMONY OF GOD — LIFE IN HIS SON.
   I John, v, 3-5: This is the love of God —
    9-13: If we receive the witness of men —

37 FAITH, PRAYER, HOPE.   Jude, 20, 21: Ye, Beloved, building up yourselves —

38 HEAVENLY HALLELUJAHS TO THE LAMB OF
   GOD. Rev. v, 6-13: Behold, the Lion that is of the tribe of Judah —
    14: Amen.

—— Minister now stands at the Lord's Table
[Deacons standing near, in their place: congregation rise]

III Hallelujah of the Heavenly Host From Rev. iv, v, vii, xi, xv, xix

[Minister] **Let us lift up our hearts with the whole heavenly host:**
   WE LIFT THEM UP UNTO GOD.   [Lam. iii, 41]

This Hallelujah is sung, or said in unison, by All, standing: its rendering may be responsive if preferred. The *prefaces* are not intended for usual utterance. [Tune by JOSEPH BARNBY.]
The first part (Nos. 1-10) may usually suffice, but any smaller portion may be used: at the Ascension and the Advent the whole is suitable, if convenient.
Alternative: instead, at discretion, may be sung Ascription No. 4, *All Holy*, page 360.

THE COMMUNION AT THE LORD'S TABLE

[Behold, a throne set in heaven, and One sitting upon the throne; and round about the throne, four living creatures, that rest not day and night, saying—] [Rev. iv, 8, 9]

1 HOLY! Holy! Holy! The Lord | God • the Al- | mighty,
   Who was and who | is . and who | is to | come.
2 Glory and honor and thanks to Thee that sittest | on the | throne,
   To Thee that | livest for | ever and | ever.

[And the four and twenty elders sitting on thrones, with crowns of gold on their heads, fall down and worship, casting their crowns before the throne—] [Rev. iv, 11]

3 WORTHY art Thou, our Lord and our God, to re- | ceive the | glory,
   And the | hon-or | and the | power:
4 For Thou didst cre- | ate all | things,
   And because of Thy will they | were and | were cre- | ated.

[And in the midst of the throne and the living creatures and the elders, behold, a Lamb standing, as though it had been slain:
And He came; and He taketh the Book out of the right hand of Him that sitteth on the throne:
And the living creatures and the elders fall down before the Lamb, and they sing a new song—] [Rev. v, 9, 10]

5 WORTHY art Thou, the Lamb, to take the Book, and to open the
   seals thereof: for | Thou wast | slain,
   And didst purchase unto God with Thy blood men of every tribe
   and | tongue and | people and | nation,
6 And madest them to be unto our God a | Kingdom and | Priests;
   And they | reign up- | on the | earth.

[The voice of many angels round about the throne—ten thousand times ten thousand, and thousands of thousands—] [Rev. v, 12]

7 WORTHY is the Lamb that hath been slain to re- | ceive the | power,
   And riches and wisdom and might and | honor and | glory and |
   blessing.

[And every created thing that is in the heavens, and on the earth, and under the earth, and in the sea, and all things that are in them, are heard, saying—] [Rev. v, 13, 14]

8 UNTO Him that sitteth on the throne, and unto the Lamb, be the
   blessing | and the | honor
   And the glory and the dominion for | ever and | ever. A- | men.

[A great multitude, which no man could number, out of every nation, and of all tribes and peoples and tongues, white-robed, and with palms in their hands, crying with a great voice—] [Rev. vii, 9]

9 SALVATION unto our God who sitteth | on the | throne,
   And | un-to | the | Lamb.

[And all angels, falling on their faces before the throne, worshiping and saying—] [Rev. vii, 12]

10 AMEN: Blessing and glory and wisdom | and thanks- | giving
    And honor and power and might be unto our God for | ever and |
    ever: A- | men.

[The remainder usually omitted]

THE COMMUNION AT THE LORD'S TABLE

[At the sounding of the seventh angel, great voices in heaven, saying —] [Rev. xi, 15]

11 THE Kingdom of the world is become the Kingdom of our Lord and | of His | Christ:
And He shall | reign for | ever and | ever.

[And the elders, who sit on their thrones before God, falling upon their faces, worship Him —]
[Rev. xi, 17]

12 WE give Thee thanks, O Lord God, the Almighty, who | art * and who | wast;
Because Thou hast taken Thy great | pow-er | and hast | reigned.

[Those that stand on the glassy sea mingled with fire, victorious, having harps of God, sing the song of Moses and the song of the Lamb —] [Rev. xv, 3, 4]

13 GREAT and marvelous are Thy works, O Lord | God,* the Al- | mighty;
Righteous and true are Thy | ways, Thou | King * of the | ages.

14 Who shall not fear, O Lord, and glori- | fy Thy | Name?
For Thou | on-ly | art | holy;

15 For all the nations shall come and | worship be- | fore Thee;
For Thy righteous acts have | been made | man-i- | fest.

[An angel comes down out of heaven, crying with a mighty voice. "Fallen, fallen, is Babylon the Great": and a voice of a great multitude in heaven is heard —] [Rev. xix, 1-4]

16 HALLELUJAH! Salvation and glory and power be- | long * to our | God:
For true and righteous are His judgments; Hallelujah! | A-men : | Hal-le- | lujah!

[And as the voice of a great multitude, and as the voice of many waters, and as the voice of mighty thunders —] [Rev. xix, 6, 7]

17 HALLELUJAH! for the Lord our God, the Al- | migh-ty, | reigneth:
Let us rejoice and be exceeding glad, and let us give the | glo-ry | un-to | Him.

18 For the marriage of the | Lamb is | come.
And His Bride hath made herself ready. Halle- | lujah! | A- | men.

IV The Bread   Congregation sit: in prayers All kneel or bow down

[The Words of Institution are combined from Matt. xxvi, 26-30; Mk. xiv, 22-26; Lk xxii, 14-20; 1 Cor x. 16; xi, 23-26]

1 Minister may lift any of the plates, saying —
THE Lord Jesus, in the night in which He was betrayed, took Bread —
And blessed, giving thanks:
Likewise do we in His Name.

2 Still holding the Bread, he offers the Prayer of Blessing —

[All] AMEN.

3 He breaks the Bread, saying—
The Lord Jesus brake the Bread —

4 He gives the Bread into the hands of Dea-cons, who, draw-ing near, stand till he has thus said—
And gave it to the disciples, saying —
Take, eat:
This is My Body which is broken for you:
This do in remembrance of Me.

THE COMMUNION AT THE LORD'S TABLE

5 Deacons distribute, first to Minister, then to Congregation

6 During distribution, the Minister sitting at the Table, may utter slowly and solemnly at intervals appropriate Sentences of Holy Scripture, if he so choose: but much of the time should be in stillness

7 Any communicant omitted may signify it by rising

8 After distribution, the Deacons return the plates into the hands of the Minister standing, who replaces them on the Table

9 Then — the Deacons being seated in their places near — the Minister distributes to them

10 Afterward, Minister sitting at the Table, may thus say, if he so choose — [Lk. xxii, 29, 30]

 AFTER the Supper, the Lord Jesus said unto the disciples:
 I appoint unto you that ye may eat and drink at My Table in My Kingdom.

At discretion, during distribution of the Bread any of these, or like Sentences, may be recited

1 THE Bread which we break, is it not a communion of the Body of Christ?
                     1 Cor. x, 16

2 WE who are many, are one Bread, one Body; for we all partake of the one Bread.
                     1 Cor. x, 17

3 THE word of our Lord Jesus:
 I am the Living Bread which came down out of Heaven:
 Yea, and the Bread which I will give is My flesh, for the life of the world.
                     Jn. vi, 51

4 OUR Lord Jesus saith:
 As the Living Father sent Me, and I live because of the Father;
 So he that eateth Me, he also shall live because of Me.
                     Jn. vi, 57

5 THUS saith our Lord Jesus:
 My Father giveth you the true Bread out of Heaven:
 For the Bread of God is that which cometh down out of Heaven, and giveth life unto the world.
                     Jn. vi, 32, 33

6 CHRIST, His own self, bare our sins in His Body upon the tree;
 By whose stripes we were healed.
                     1 Pet. ii, 24

7 HEAR Christ's own word concerning Himself:
 The Son of Man came to give His life a ransom for many.
                     Matt. xx, 28

8 BEFORE our eyes Jesus Christ is openly set forth crucified.
                     Gal. iii, 1

9 BY the will of God we have been sanctified through the offering of the body of Jesus Christ once for all.
                     Heb. x, 10

10 CHRIST, when He had offered one sacrifice for sins forever, sat down at the right hand of God:
 For by one offering He hath perfected forever them that are sanctified.
                     Heb. x, 12, 14

V The Cup

1 Minister pours into the cups, saying— THE Lord Jesus in like manner took also the Cup.

2 Minister may lift any of the cups, saying— He took the Cup, and blessed, giving thanks: Likewise do we in His Name.

3 Still holding the cups, he offers the Prayer of Thanksgiving—
[All] AMEN.

4 He gives the cups into the hands of Deacons, who, drawing near, stand till he has thus said— The Lord Jesus gave the Cup to the disciples, saying— This is My Blood of the new Covenant which is shed for many unto remission of sins: This do, as oft as ye drink it, in remembrance of Me.

Omitted at discretion [Verily, I say unto you, I shall not drink henceforth of this fruit of the vine, until that day when I drink it new with you in My Father's Kingdom.]

5 Deacons distribute, first to Minister, then to Congregation.

6 During distribution, the Minister sitting at the Table, may utter slowly and solemnly at intervals appropriate Sentences of Holy Scripture, if he so choose: but much of the time should be in stillness.

7 Any communicant omitted may signify it by rising.

8 After distribution, the Deacons return the cups into the hands of the Minister standing, who replaces them on the Table.

9 Then—the Deacons being seated in their places near—the Minister distributes to them—

10 Afterward, Minister standing at the Table, may thus say, if he so choose— [Rev. xix, 9]

A VOICE from Heaven:
Write, Blessed are they who are bidden to the Marriage Supper of the Lamb: These are true words of God.

At discretion, during distribution of the Cup any of these, or like Sentences, may be recited

1 THE Cup of blessing which we bless, is it not a communion of the blood of Christ?   1 Cor. x, 16

2 PRECIOUS blood, as of a Lamb without blemish and without spot, Even the blood of Christ, slain from before the foundation of the world.
1 Pet. i, 19, 20; Rev. xiii, 8

3 THE blood of Christ, who through the eternal Spirit offered Himself without blemish unto God.   Heb. ix, 14

4 THUS saith Jehovah unto Moses:
The life of the flesh is in the blood:
It is the blood that maketh atonement for your souls by reason of the life.
Lev. xvii, 11

5 APART from shedding of blood there is no remission.   Heb. ix, 22

6 NOW in Christ Jesus we that once were far off are made nigh in the blood of Christ.   Eph. ii, 13

400 THE COMMUNION AT THE LORD'S TABLE

7 THE blood of Jesus, the Son of God, cleanseth us from all sin.   1 Ju. i, 7

8 CHRIST suffered for sins once, the righteous for the unrighteous,
That He might bring us to God.   1 Pet. iii, 18

9 FAITHFUL is the saying, and worthy of all acceptation,
That Christ Jesus came into the world to save sinners.   1 Tim. i, 15

10 OF God are we in Christ Jesus,
Who was made unto us wisdom from God, and righteousness and sanctification and redemption.   1 Cor. 1, 30

VI The Hymn of Thanksgiving   By All standing
Announced from the Hymnal used in the Church
(Minister)

When the Lord Jesus and the disciples had sung a Hymn, they went out unto the Mount of Olives:

In like manner do we, before going hence, sing a Hymn of Thanksgiving, in Christ's Name.

This Hymn, preferably in meter, but which may be in chant, or an anthem, should express the fellowship of Christ's redeemed Church, with thanksgiving and praise to God for His great salvation: it should either be, or end with, an Ascription to God — the Father and the Son and the Holy Spirit

VII Benediction   All still standing

The following; or one of the forms of Ascription with Benediction assigned in the usual Service
(II Pet. i, 2: also from II Cor. xiii, 14: from Heb. xiii, 20, 21).

BELOVED: Let your going forth be in the Name of the Lord.

Grace to you and peace be multiplied in the knowledge of God and of Jesus our Lord, with the communion of the Holy Spirit:

Now the God of peace, who brought again from the dead the great Shepherd of the sheep with the blood of an eternal covenant, even our Lord Jesus, make you perfect in every good thing to do His will, working in you that which is well pleasing in His sight, through Jesus Christ; and to Him be the glory for ever and ever: [All] AMEN.

Or this —   [Ps. cxxix, 8: from Eph. vi, 23: from I Cor. xiii, 14.]

THE blessing of Jehovah be upon you.

Peace be to you, Brethren, and love with faith, from God the Father and the Lord Jesus Christ, with the communion of the Holy Spirit, evermore:
[All] AMEN.

After the AMEN has been said, this may instantly be sung, at discretion:

W. S. P., 1897

Ministration

OF

The Baptism of Little Children

[USAGE IN THE CHURCH FELLOWSHIP]

This may be at any time; but certain days also are statedly assigned for it by the Church; and before each such stated season timely announcement and invitation are to be given in the congregation. The Minister should be notified during the week before a proposed Baptism. This Ministration takes the place of the usual Confession of Christian Faith in the general service.

Words in brackets may be changed or omitted; and if the service be private any appropriate changes are made. The Responses, printed in small capitals, are for utterance by all the Church, including the Minister.

I Presentation

ANNOUNCEMENT

BELOVED in the Lord:
It is the privilege of Christ's Church to receive little children in His Name.
Let any such now be brought hither in faith.

Immediately may be sung, or said responsively or otherwise, the following, or the first part thereof — while the Baptismal group (already in the congregation or else now to enter) coming forward without delay, stand before the Minister, who takes his place for the ministration of Baptism. Deacons may stand near to assist as requisite in ushering and placing the group

EDWIN GEORGE MONK, MUS. DOC.

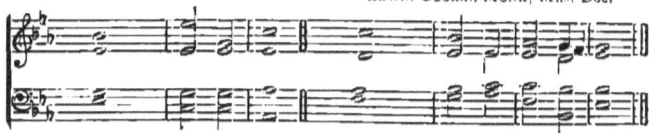

1 SUFFER the little children to come unto Me, and for- | bid them | not :
 For to such belongeth the | King-dom | of | God.
2 I will pour My Spirit up- | on thy | seed,
 And My | blessing up- | on thine | offspring.
3 For they are the seed of the blessèd | of Je- | hovah,
 And their | off-spring | with | them.
4 Our God hath remembered His cove- | nant for | ever,
 The word which he commanded to a | thou-sand | gen-er- | ations.
[Lk. xviii, 16: Is. xliv, 3: lxv, 23: Ps. cv, 8]

402   MINISTRATION OF THE BAPTISM OF LITTLE CHILDREN

—Or this Hymn may be sung—

CHERITH. C. M. LOUIS SPOHR, 1835

SEE Israel's gentle Shepherd stand,
With all inviting charms!
Hark! how He calls the tender lambs,
And folds them in His arms!

2 We bring them, Lord, with fervent
And yield them up to Thee; [prayer,
Joyful that we ourselves are Thine,
Thine let our offspring be!

PHILIP DODDRIDGE, D. D., 1740.

II **Warrant** [Matt. x, 32: Lk. ix, 48]

OUR Lord Jesus — who saith, Every one who shall confess Me before men, him will I also confess before My Father who is in heaven — saith also, Whosoever shall receive a little child in My Name receiveth Me.

Hear this record: [From Matt. xix, 13-15; Mk. x, 13-16; Lk. xviii, 15, 16]
They were bringing unto Him also their babes, that He should lay His hands on them, and pray: and the disciples rebuked them.
But when Jesus saw it, He was moved with indignation, and said, Suffer the little children to come unto Me, and forbid them not; for to such belongeth the Kingdom of God:
And He took them in His arms, and blessed them, laying His hands upon them.

[All the remainder of the Warrant may usually be omitted: if any part be used, the first section is preferable.]

Hear also this record of the most ancient Church of God:
God Almighty said to the patriarch Abraham: I will establish My covenant between Me and thee and thy seed after thee throughout their generations for an everlasting covenant, to be a God unto thee and to thy seed after thee.
And God gave him the covenant of circumcision.
For I have known him, saith Jehovah, to the end that he may command his children and his household after him, that they may keep the way of Jehovah.

[Gen. xvii, 7; xviii, 19; Acts, vii, 8]

Wherefore, after many generations, Jehovah by the mouth of His prophet reminds His wayward people — [Is. xli, 8]
    Thou, Israel, My servant,
    Jacob whom I have chosen,
      THE SEED OF ABRAHAM MY FRIEND.

Also the Psalmist bears witness,— [Ps. lxxviii, 5-7]
    Jehovah established a testimony in Jacob,
      AND APPOINTED A LAW IN ISRAEL,
    Which He commanded our fathers,
      THAT THEY SHOULD MAKE THEM KNOWN TO THEIR CHILDREN:
    That the generation to come might know them,
      EVEN THE CHILDREN WHO SHOULD BE BORN;
    Who should arise and declare them to their children,
      THAT THEY MIGHT SET THEIR HOPE IN GOD.

Consider that not less, nor less sure, are the promises and gifts of the New Covenant in the Son of God.

Thence, Christ's apostle Paul thus declares concerning the households of believers: The unbelieving husband is sanctified [*i. e.* outwardly] in the wife, and the unbelieving wife is sanctified [*i. e.* outwardly] in the brother [*i. e.* the believing husband]: else were your children unclean: but now are they holy [*i. e.* consecrated to God]. [1 Cor. vii, 12-14]

Also this is the word of Christ's apostle Peter: To you is the promise, and to your children. [Acts, ii, 39]

III Salutation

BELOVED: Grace and peace to you and to your household [s]:
IN THE NAME OF THE LORD JESUS.

IV Confession of Christ

WITH us, and with the Church in every age and in every place, you openly confess Jesus, the Christ, the Son of the Living God:
[Assent by the parents or guardians — joining with Minister] *Amen.*

V Baptismal Covenant

PROPOSITION

SEEING that Christ our Savior kindly receives little children, you would that yours also might now be received of Him:

And for a pledge of your faith that he receives your offspring you cause your little one [s] here to be sealed in Baptism; yet not trusting to this outward sign, but looking to the grace which it signifies.

COVENANT

If in the Baptismal group there be more than one household, the Minister prefaces the covenant with these words —

[SINCE here is a group of households, the Baptismal covenant now to be made is entered into in behalf of every several child by its respective parents] *or* [guardians].

AND now, in faith dedicating [this child] *or* [these, your children] [respectively] to the Lord your God, you covenant —

To bring up [this little one] *or* [these little ones] in the nurture and admonition of the Lord;

To instruct [this child] *or* [them] in the gospel of our Lord Jesus Christ;

And to pray and labor in faith that — through regeneration by the Holy Spirit — [this child] *or* [these children],

    Turning from an ungodly world —
    Denying the lusts of the flesh —
    Renouncing the works of the devil —

Be brought to believe on the Son of God and to confess His Name;
Be grafted into the Body of Christ, which is His Church;

And be evermore inclined and led of God to walk in the covenant of His grace and in the way of His commandments, whose end is everlasting life:
[Assent by the parents or guardians—joining with Minister]   *Amen.*

VI Baptism — The Seal

Minister thus demands, by households separately, and for every child as in its turn brought nearer to the font—

NAME this child in God's covenant—

[Answer — the Baptismal name without surname]
At the same time should be given to the Minister in writing the *full* name of the child and of the parents or guardians, with the place and date of the child's birth.
Minister, having disposed the child as may be convenient near the font, baptizes the child with water—therewith pronouncing the Baptismal name, and declaring the Baptism according to Matt. xxviii. 19—

I BAPTIZE this child [*the Baptismal name*] **into the Name of the Father and of the Son and of the Holy Spirit :**   [All]   AMEN.

BAPTISMAL PRAYER

After all the Baptisms — while the Baptismal group remain standing, and the congregation kneel or bow down — Minister offers a *short* prayer of the purport following—

1 Thanksgiving — to God who gathers His Church on earth :
— for the privilege of God's people to bring their offspring with them in the covenant.
2 Supplication — for all little children, that God may call them into the household of His Son :
— for [this child] *or* [these children] now dedicated :
That God's providence may spare, guide, bless :
That the parents may have grace to fulfill their vows :
That the Holy Spirit may early work renewal — and thence, personal faith and confession of Christ, union with Him in His visible Church, and share in His eternal Kingdom :
3 All in the Name of the Lord Jesus :   [All]   AMEN.

VII Church Accord

[All of this may be omitted when not appropriate] The Church rise and stand, joining in the Response.

BEHOLD therefore : the Church — the larger household — stands, testifying that it has place for little ones :

Because our Master, who hath gone up on high, saith that whosoever receiveth little ones in His Name, receiveth Him ; we receive [this child] *or* [these children] as embraced in the hope and care of Christ's Church —

NUMBERED WITH THE LAMBS IN THE FOLD OF THE GOOD SHEPHERD.

TOKEN

Usually postponed till some assigned anniversary : but if the Token be given at the Baptism, Minister thus addresses parents or guardians — All still standing —

FOR memorial of the covenant now made on behalf of your little one [s], and for token thereof through future years —

MINISTRATION OF THE BAPTISM OF LITTLE CHILDREN   405

Receive now [from the Church] for [your] *or* [each] child the Holy Scriptures, inscribed with the record of this day's act of faith:
For the Word of God herein is able to make wise unto salvation through faith which is in Christ Jesus—a light upon the path to lead the child to confirm this covenant, unto eternal life: [All] AMEN.

Minister gives the proper volume for each child respectively

VIII Baptismal Hymn   All still standing

Usually omitted: one of the two following, at discretion, may be sung by All

No. 1 PACKINGTON. S. M.   J. BLACK.

OUR children Thou dost claim,
  O Lord our God, as Thine:
Ten thousand blessings to Thy Name
  For goodness so divine.

2 How great Thy mercies, Lord!
  How plenteous is Thy grace!

Which, in the promise of Thy love,
  Includes our rising race.

3 Our offspring, still Thy care,
  Shall own their fathers' God!
To latest times Thy blessing share,
  And sound Thy praise abroad.

ANON. 1779.

No. 2 SHEPHERD. 8787, D.   HENRY SMART, d. 1879.

SAVIOR! who Thy flock art feeding
  With the shepherd's kindest care,
All the feeble gently leading,
  While the lambs Thy bosom share:
Now, our little ones receiving,
  Fold them in Thy gracious arm;
There, we know, Thy word believing,
  Only there, secure from harm.

2 Never, from Thy pasture roving,
  Let them be the lion's prey:
Let Thy tenderness, so loving,
  Keep them all life's dangerous way.
Then within Thy fold eternal,
  Let them find a resting-place,
Feed in pastures ever vernal,
  Blest with vision of Thy face.

WILLIAM AUGUSTUS MUHLENBERG, D. D. 1826.

MINISTRATION OF THE BAPTISM OF LITTLE CHILDREN

IX **Grace**   [Is. xl, 11: Ps. ciii, 17, 18]   All still standing

THE Lord Jehovah shall feed His flock like a shepherd:
He shall gather the lambs in His arm,
AND CARRY THEM IN HIS BOSOM.
The lovingkindness of Jehovah is from everlasting to everlasting
upon them that fear Him,
AND HIS RIGHTEOUSNESS UNTO CHILDREN'S CHILDREN —
To such as keep His covenant,
AND TO THOSE THAT REMEMBER HIS PRECEPTS TO DO THEM.

AN APOSTOLIC BENEDICTION   [From II Thess. iii, 17]
THE grace of our Lord Jesus Christ be with you all forever.   [All]   AMEN.

X **Ascription**   [Ps. cxlv, 4; lxxix, 13]   All still standing

To be said responsively; but if there be no song to follow immediately in resuming a general service, then this may be sung, or said in unison, by All.

ONE generation shall laud Thy works to another, | O Je- | hovah,
AND SHALL DE- | CLARE THY | MIGH-TY | ACTS.
We, Thy people, the sheep of Thy pasture, will give Thee | thanks for | ever:
WE WILL SHOW FORTH THY PRAISE TO ALL GENER- | A-TIONS. |
A- | MEN.

Sir GEORGE JOB ELVEY, Mus. Doc.

If the Baptism be a part of a general Service, that Service may now proceed with one of the brief songs of Ascription — All still standing, and at the end of such brief song the Baptismal group retire from before the Minister; but if the Ascription be long they may retire earlier.

INDEX OF THE PSALM CHANTS

[The INTRODUCTORY RESPONSES are not shown in this Index]

PSALM			PAGE
VIII	O Jehovah our Lord, how excellent	*Russell*	335
VIII	" " " "	*Lawes*	335
IX	I will give thanks unto Jehovah	*Norris*	277
XVIII	I love Thee, O Jehovah my Strength	*Hawes*	110
XXII	My God, my God, why hast Thou forsaken me?	*Joule*	86
XXIII	Jehovah is my Shepherd	*Walker*	343
"	" " " "	*Camidge*	343
XL	I waited patiently for Jehovah	*Bridge*	77
XLIV (with I Chron. We have heard with our ears, O God	*Dupuis*	272
XLV	xxix)My heart overfloweth with a goodly matter	*Wesley, Samuel*	136
XLVIII	Great is Jehovah	*Randall*	339
XLVIII	" " "	*Smart*	339
LXV	Praise waiteth for Thee, O God, in Zion	*Turle*	347
LXV	" " " " " "	*Cooke*	347
LXVII	God be merciful unto us, and bless us	*Langdon*	319
LXVII	" " " " " " " "	*Barnby*	319
LXVIII	Let God arise	*Jones, John*	142
LXXXIV	How amiable are Thy tabernacles	*Knyvett, from Händel*	331
"	" " " "	*Turle*	331
LXXXIX	I will sing of the lovingkindnesses	*Woodward*	307
XCII	It is a good thing to give thanks	*Mornington, Earl of.*	327
XCII	" " " " "	*Hopkins, J. L.*	327
XCIII (with c)	Jehovah reigneth; He is clothed with majesty	*Crotch*	315
"	" " " " " "	*Cooper*	316
c (with xciii)	Make a joyful noise unto Jehovah	*Crotch*	315
"	" " " " "	*Cooper*	316
CII	Hear my prayer, O Jehovah	*Havergal*	313
CIV	Bless Jehovah, O my soul	*Soaper*	5
CXVIII	O give thanks unto Jehovah	*Gladstone*	97
CXIX	Forever, O Jehovah, Thy Word	*Robinson*	349
"	" " " "	*Gauntlett*	350
CXXX	Out of the depths have I cried unto Thee	*Hopkins, E. J.*	70
CXXXVIII	I will give Thee thanks	*Barnby*	122
CXLV	I will extol Thee, my God, O King	*Smart*	323
"	" " " " "	*Boyce*	323
Habakkuk, iii	O Jehovah, I have heard the report of Thee	*Cooper*	289
(Combined Texts)	Holy! Holy! Holy! Thou Jehovah of Hosts	*Turle*	148

INDEX OF VARIOUS SCRIPTURE PORTIONS IN MUSIC

			PAGE
I Chron. xxix, 10, 11, 12, 14	{ Blessed be Thou, O Jehovah our God (Offertory) }	*Macfarren*	392
I Chron. xxix, 10-19	{ Blessed be Thou, O Jehovah, the God of our Fathers (Doxology of David — Thanksgiving Day) }	*Dupuis*	272
Psalm lxii, 18, 19	{ Blessed be Jehovah God, the God of Israel (Doxology of Israel) }	*Wilton, Earl of*	362

408 INDEX OF VARIOUS SCRIPTURE PORTIONS IN MUSIC

			PAGE
Psalm cxxxvi, 1, etc.	For His lovingkindness endureth forever (Thanksgiving Response)	*W. S. P.*	270
Psalm cxlv, 4; lxxix, 13	One generation shall laud Thy works to another (Baptism of Children)	*Elvey*	406
Isaiah, vi, 3; with Rev. iv, 8	Holy! Holy! Holy! Jehovah of hosts (Sanctus — Chant)	*Turle*	360
Isaiah, vi, 3; with Rev. iv, 8	Holy! Holy! Holy! Jehovah of hosts (Sanctus — Anthem)	*W. S. P.*	360
Daniel, ii, 20-23	Blessed be the Name of God forever (Song of Daniel)	*Burrowes*	365
Luke, i, 68-79	Blessed be the Lord, the God of Israel (Benedictus)	*Garrett*	361
Luke, xviii, 16; with Is. xliv, 3; lxv, 23; Ps. cv, 8	Suffer the little children to come (Baptism of Children)	*Monk*	401
Ephesians, iii, 20, 21	Now unto Him that is able to do (Recog. of New Members)	*Elvey*	376
From Rev. iv, v, vii, xi, xv, xix	Holy! Holy! Holy! the Lord God the Almighty (Hallelujah — The Communion)	*Barnby*	396

[For other notable Scriptural Songs occurring in various Services — see page 367]

INDEX OF COMPOSERS OF CHANTS

INCLUDING THE INTRODUCTORY RESPONSES

[For full names of composers, with dates, see the pages referred to]

	PAGE	
ALDRICH	343	*Introd. Response* ..... There is a river, the streams whereof
BARNBY	114	*Introd. Response* ..... Unto Him that loveth us
"	122	*Psalm cxxxviii* .... I will give Thee thanks
"	146	*Introd. Response* .... Holy! Holy! Holy! the Lord God, the Almighty
"	319	*Psalm lxvii* .... God be merciful unto us, and bless us
"	396	HALLELUJAH OF THE HEAVENLY HOST (From Rev. iv, v, vii, xi, xv, xix)
BATTISHILL	134	*Introd. Response* ..... Lift up your heads, O ye gates
"	275	*Introd. Response* ..... Behold, the Lord Jehovah will come
BOYCE	323	*Psalm cxlv* .... I will extol Thee, my God, O King
BRIDGE	77	*Psalm xl* .... I waited patiently for Jehovah
BURROWES	108	*Introd. Response* ..... Amen: Blessing and glory
"	365	SONG OF DANIEL (Ascription) Dan. ii, 20-23
CAMIDGE	343	*Psalm xxiii* .... Jehovah is my Shepherd
COOKE	347	*Psalm lxv* .... Praise waiteth for Thee, O God, in Zion
COOPER	289	(*For Psalm*) *Hab. iii* .. O Jehovah, I have heard the report of Thee
"	316	*Psalms, c, xciii* ...... Make a joyful noise unto Jehovah
"	358	GLORIA IN EXCELSIS (2d part) Ascription
CROTCH	270	*Introd. Response* ..... O praise Jehovah, all ye nations
"	303	*Introd. Response* ..... Glory to God in the highest
"	315	*Psalms, c, xciii* ...... Make a joyful noise unto Jehovah
"	358	GLORIA IN EXCELSIS (1st part) Ascription
DIXON	68	*Introd. Response* ..... The sacrifices of God are a broken spirit
DUPUIS	272	{ *Psalm xliv,* } .... We have heard with our ears, O God { *I Chr. xxix* }
EDWARDS	4	*Introd. Response* ..... Jehovah is good
ELVEY	338	*Introd. Response* ..... I have set watchmen upon thy walls
"	360	ALL HOLY (Ascription)
"	376	Now unto Him that is able to do (Closing Ascription)
"	406	One generation shall laud Thy works to another (Closing Ascription)

INDEX OF COMPOSERS OF CHANTS 409

	PAGE	
FARRANT	330 *Introd. Response*	Thou hast said, Seek ye My face
GARRETT	361 BENEDICTUS (Ascription) Lk. 1, 68-79	
GAUNTLETT	350 *Psalm cxix*	Forever, O Jehovah, Thy Word
GLADSTONE	97 *Psalm cxviii*	O give thanks unto Jehovah
GOSS	353 TE DEUM (2d part) Ascription	
HAVERGAL	313 *Psalm cii*	Hear my prayer, O Jehovah
"	327 *Introd. Response*	Lift up your hands to the sanctuary
HAWES	110 *Psalm xviii*	I love Thee, O Jehovah my Strength
HENLEY	353 TE DEUM (3d part) Ascription	
HILES	95 *Introd. Response*	Worthy is the Lamb that hath been slain
HOPKINS, E. J.	70 *Psalm cxxx*	Out of the depths have I cried unto Thee
"	83 *Introd. Response*	Worthy art Thou, the Lamb
"	334 *Introd. Response*	It shall come to pass that at evening time
HOPKINS, J. L.	327 *Psalm xcii*	It is a good thing to give thanks
JACKSON	287 *Introd. Response*	Jehovah cometh; He cometh
JONES, JOHN	142 *Psalm lxviii*	Let God arise
JOULE	86 *Psalm xxii*	My God, my God, why hast Thou forsaken me?
"	346 *Introd. Response*	They that know Thy Name
KELWAY	140 *Introd. Response*	Worthy art Thou, our Lord and our God
KNYVETT, from HÄNDEL	331 *Psalm lxxxiv*	How amiable are Thy tabernacles
LANGDON	319 *Psalm lxvii*	God be merciful unto us, and bless us
LAWES	335 *Psalm viii*	O Jehovah our Lord, how excellent
"	359 GLORIA PATRI (Ascription)	
LEE	293 *Introd. Response*	It shall come to pass in that day
MACFARREN	76 *Introd. Response*	Behold, I lay in Zion for a foundation
"	302 Blessed be Thou, O Jehovah our God (Blessing in the Offertory)	
MONK	401 Suffer the little children to come (Baptism of Children)	
MORNINGTON, Earl of	327 *Psalm xcii*	It is a good thing to give thanks
NORRIS	277 *Psalm ix*	I will give thanks unto Jehovah
OUSELEY	319 *Introd. Response*	Look unto Me, and be ye saved
"	349 *Introd. Response*	With Thee, O God, is the fountain of life
PYMAR	103 *Introd. Response*	Unto Him that sitteth on the throne
RANDALL	330 *Psalm xlviii*	Great is Jehovah
RIMBAULT	311 *Introd. Response*	A thousand years in Thy sight
ROBINSON	349 *Psalm cxix*	Forever, O Jehovah, Thy Word
RUSSELL	335 *Psalm viii*	O Jehovah our Lord, how excellent
"	352 TE DEUM (1st part) Ascription	
SAVAGE	315 *Introd. Response*	The Mighty One, God Jehovah, hath spoken
SMART	120 *Introd. Response*	Who shall not fear, O Lord
"	323 *Psalm cxlv*	I will extol Thee, my God, O King
"	330 *Psalm xlviii*	Great is Jehovah
SOAPER	5 *Psalm civ*	Bless Jehovah, O my soul
STAINER	126 *Introd. Response*	The kingdom of the world
STEGGALL	281 *Introd. Response*	Keep ye judgment, and do righteousness
(TRADITIONAL)	358 GLORIA IN EXCELSIS (1st part) Ascription	
	359 " " " (2d part) "	
	359 " " " (3d part) "	
TURLE	146 (For a *Psalm*)	Holy! Holy! Holy! Thou Jehovah of Hosts
"	331 *Psalm lxxxiv*	How amiable are Thy tabernacles
"	347 *Psalm lxv*	Praise waiteth for Thee, O God, in Zion
"	360 SANCTUS (Ascription) Is. vi, 3; Rev. iv, 8	
WALKER	343 *Psalm xxiii*	Jehovah is my Shepherd
WALMISLEY	322 *Introd. Response*	Jehovah send thee help from the sanctuary
WESLEY, SAMUEL	136 *Psalm xlv*	My heart overfloweth with a goodly matter
WILTON, Earl of	362 DOXOLOGY OF ISRAEL (Ascription) Ps. lxxii, 18, 19	
WOODWARD	307 *Psalm lxxix*	I will sing of the lovingkindnesses

Index of Composers of Music for Anthems, Short Responses, etc.

	PAGE	
(ADAPTED)	380	ALLELUIA! AMEN (Baptismal Response)
STEGGALL	354	TE DEUM (Anthem)
WILSON	364	BENEDICITE OMNIA (Ancient Canticle)
W. S. P.	xxv	AMEN (Closing Response — three forms)
"	270	For His lovingkindness endureth *(Thanksgiving Response)* Ps. cxxxvi
"	360	SANCTUS (Anthem) Is. vi, 3; Rev. iv, 8

Index of Meters

L. M.
	PAGE
Adoration	346
Alstone	344
Angels' Song	149
Calkin	119
Canonbury	338
Denbigh	318
Dryden	145
Duke Street	6
Germany	88
Grace Church	308
Hosanna	116
Kent	278
Litlington Tower	320
Meudon	326
Octavius	102
Old Hundredth	317
Park Street	105
Rockingham	348
Scepter	128
Seasons	337
Thanksgiving	8
Uxbridge	340
Wareham	334
Wimborne	275
Winchester New	325

L. M., 6 lines
Melita	90
St. Werbergh	78

C. M.
Beatitudo	375
Bedford	125
Belmont	329
Cherith	402
Dedham	377
Denfield	114
Dundee	351
Farrant	377
Laud	332
Loudon	143
Nottingham	111

	PAGE
Pilgrim Song	284
Rose Hill	382
St. Agnes	382
St. Ann's	321

C. M., D.
Evan	314

S. M.
Arnes	329
Exaltation	348
Ferguson	290
Olmutz	375
Packington	405
St. Thomas	322
Swabia	295
Thatcher	75

S. P. M.
Dalston	342

H. M.
Croft	332
Darwall	317
St. Godric	99

P. M.
Evermore	340
Holy Offerings	71
Nicaea	333
St. Nicholas	301, 345

6646664
Italian Hymn	137

6565, D.
Prague	98

7s
Monkland	341

7s, 6 lines
Dix	151
Kelso	325
Nassau	318

7s, D.
	PAGE
Coburg	292
Honiton	336
St. George	274, 363

7676. D.
Aurelia	310
Chenies	3
Day of Rest	107
Lancashire	82

8787
All Saints	321
Carter	330
Carthage	133
Lowe	123
Newton Ferns	296
Oswald	337
Shepherd	405
Stuttgard	345
Trust	350

8787, D.
Faben	131
Love Divine	72
Promise	139
St. Chad	341

878747
Madelay	280
Regent Square	286, 363

888,888
Dresden	362

10s
Toulon	94

10s, 11s
Hanover	328

11s, 10s
Lelin	324

INDEX OF METRICAL TUNES

[For full names of composers, with dates, see the pages referred to]

Adoration ....L. M... 346 ....S. S. *Wesley*	Litlington Tower.L. M ... 320 .... *Barnby*
All Saints..........8787.... 321 ...... *(German)*	London ....C. M ... 143 ....*(Scotch)*
Alstone............L. M.... 344 .... *Willing*	Love Divine.......8787, D. 72 ....*Zundel*
Angels' Song ......L. M. .. 149 ....*Gibbons*	Lowe ....8787.... 123 ....*Lowe*
Armes ....S. M.... 329 ....*Armes*	
Aurelia............ 7676, D. 310 .... *S. S. Wesley*	Madelay ....878747.. 280 ....*Reay*
	Melita ....L. M., 6 l 90 ....*Dykes*
Beatitudo ....C. M ... 375 ....*Dykes*	Mendon............L. M ... 326 ...... *(German)*
Bedford ....C. M ... 125 ....*Wheall*	Monkland ....7s...... 341 ...... *(German)*
Belmont...........C. M ... 329 ....*Webbe*	
	Nassau ....7s, 6 l.. 318 ......*Rosenmüller*
Calkin ....L. M ... 119 ....*Calkin*	Newton Ferns.....8787.... 298 .. *Samuel Smith*
Canonbury ....L. M ... 338 ......*Schumann*	Nicaea ....P. M ... 333 ....,.*Dykes*
Carter ....8787.... 330 .... *Carter*	Nottingham ....C. M ... 111 ....*Clarke*
Carthage ....8787.... 133 ....*Lvoff*	
Chenies ....7676, D. 3 ...... *Matthews*	Octavius...........L. M ... 102 .... *Sweetzer*
Cherith ....C. M ... 402 ....*Spohr*	Old Hundredth....L. M ... 317 ....*Franc*
Coburg.............7s, D .. 292 *Albert, Prince*	Olmutz ....S. M... 375 .. *Lowell Mason*
[Consort	Oswald ....8787.... 337 ....*Dykes*
Croft ....π. M ... 332 .... *Croft*	
	Packington.........S. M... 405 .... *J. Black*
Dalston............S. P. M.. 342 ...... *Williams*	Park Street........L. M ... 105 .... *Venua*
Darwall ....H. M ... 317 ..*John Darwall*	Pilgrim Song......C. M ... 284 .... *S. S. Wesley*
Day of Rest ....7676, D. 107 ...... *Elliott*	Prague ....6565, D. 98 ....*Calkin*
Dedham ....C. M ... 377 .... *Gardiner*	Promise ....8787, D. 139 ....*Smart*
Denbigh ....L. M ... 318 .... *Gauntlett*	
Denfield ....C. M ... 114 .... *Gläser*	Regent Square ....878747.. 286, 363.......*Smart*
Dix ....7s, 6 l.. 151 ....*Kocher*	Rockingham ......L. M ... 348 ....*Miller*
Dresden ....888,888. 362 ..*"Swiss Tune"*	Rose Hill..........C. M ... 382 .... *Sweetzer*
Dryden ....L. M ... 145 ....*Calkin*	
Duke Street ......L. M ... 6 ....*Hatton*	St. Agnes.........C. M ... 382 ....*Dykes*
Dundee ....C. M ... 351 ....*Franc*	St. Ann's ....C. M ... 321 .... *Croft*
	St. Chad ....8787, D. 341 .... *Redhead*
Evan..............C. M., D. 314 .... *Havergal*	St. George........7s, D ...274, 363 ....*Elvey*
Evermore.........P. M ... 304 ..... *J. S. Bach*	St. Godrie........II. M ... 99 ....*Dykes*
Exaltation........S. M ... 348 .. *(Anonymous)*	St. Nicholas ......P. M ... 301, 345.....*Crüger*
	St. Thomas ... ...S. M ... 322 .... *Händel*
Faben............8787, D. 131 .... *Willcox*	St. Werbergh.....L. M., 6 l 78 ....*Dykes*
Farrant...........C. M ... 377 .... *Farrant*	Scepter ....L. M ... 128 ....*Steggall*
Ferguson.........S. M ... 290 ....*Kingsley*	Seasons ....L. M ... 337 ....*Pleyel*
	Shepherd ....8787.... 405 .... *Smart*
Germany ....L. M ... 88 ....*Beethoven*	Stuttgard.........8787.... 345 ....*Störl*
Grace Church ....L. M ... 308 ....*Pleyel*	Swabia ....S. M ... 295 ....*(German)*
Hanover..........10s,11s. 328 .... *Croft*	Thanksgiving ....L. M ... 8 ....*Dykes*
Holy Offerings ....P. M ... 71 ....*Redhead*	Thatcher ....S. M... 75 .... *Händel*
Honiton ....7s, D .. 336 ....*Flood*	Toulon............10s .... 94 ......*Goudimel*
Hosanna ....L. M ... 116 ....*Dykes*	Trust ....8787.... 350 { *Mendelssohn-*
	Bartholdy }
Italian Hymn .....6646664. 137 .... *Giardini*	
	Uxbridge..........L. M ... 340 .. *Lowell Mason*
Kelso ....7s, 6 l.. 325 ..*E. J. Hopkins*	
Kent..............L. M ... 278 ....*Lampe*	Wareham.........L. M ... 334 ....*Knapp*
	Wimborne..... ...L. M ... 275 ....*Whittaker*
Lancashire ....7676, D. 82 .... *Smart*	Winchester New ..L. M ... 325 ...... *(German)*
Laud..............C. M ... 332 ....*Dykes*	
Leila..............11s,10s. 324 .... *Costa*	

Index of Metrical Hymns

FIRST LINES

[For full names of authors, with dates, see the pages referred to]

	PAGE	
Ages unto ages sing	363	[Ascription]
All Hail! Triumphant Lord	99	*Elizabeth Scott*
All praise to Thee, eternal Lord	308	*Martin Luther (Tr.)*
Amid the splendors of Thy state	328	*Rippon's Collection*
As bright and lasting as the sun	321	*Lyte*
Before Jehovah's awful throne	316	*Watts*
Behold the glories of the Lamb	125	*Watts*
Be Thou exalted, O my God	338	*Watts*
Blest be Thou, O God of Israel	320	*H. U. Onderdonk*
Christ, above all glory seated	133	*Woodford*
Christ is coming! let creation	280	*J. R. Macduff*
Come, ever-blessed Spirit! come	382	*Christopher Wordsworth*
Come in, thou blessed of the Lord! | Stranger	381	*Montgomery*
Come, let us join our cheerful songs	111	*Watts*
Come, let us sing the song of songs	119	*Montgomery*
Come, Thou long-expected Jesus	208	*Charles Wesley*
Come, ye that fear the Lord	373	*Montgomery*
Creator Spirit, by whose aid	145	*Dryden (from Latin)*
Dear Savior! we are Thine	375	*Doddridge*
Dread Jehovah! God of nations	72	*(Anonymous)*
Eternal God! Eternal King	278	*March*
Eternal Wisdom! Thee we praise	351	*Watts*
From all that dwell below the skies	318	*Watts*
Glad as when the glorious shout	325	*(Anonymous)*
Glory, thanks, Thy Church doth render	363	[Ascription]
God eternal, Lord of all	341	*J. E. Millard*
God, my King, Thy might confessing	350	*Mant*
God of mercy, God of grace	318	*Lyte*
Great God! we sing that mighty hand	8	*Doddridge*
Great is the Lord! what tongue can frame	346	*Watts*
Hail! Thou God of grace and glory	336	*Aveling*
Hail! Thou once despised Jesus	130	*Bakewell*
Happy the souls to Jesus joined	382	*Charles Wesley*
He comes in blood-stained garments	107	*Charitie L. Bancroft*
High in the heavens, Eternal God	340	*Watts*
Holy and infinite! viewless! eternal	324	*Frances R. Havergal*
Holy! holy! holy! Lord God Almighty	333	*Heber*
Holy! holy! holy! Lord! | God of hosts, eternal	151	*Christopher Wordsworth*
Holy, holy, holy Lord | God of hosts! When	336	*Montgomery*
Holy offerings, rich and rare	71	*Monsell*
Hosanna to the living Lord	128	*Heber*
I'm not ashamed to own my Lord	377	*Watts*
Jehovah, God Most High	329	*Pratt's Collection*
Jehovah reigns! He dwells in light	326	*Watts*
Let glory be to God on high	78	*(Anonymous, from Latin)*
Light of the lonely pilgrim's heart	284	*Denny*

INDEX OF METRICAL HYMNS 413

	PAGE	
Lo! He comes with clouds descending	286	Cennick
Lord God of hosts, by all adored	324	(Anonymous, from Latin)
Lord of all being! throned afar	348	O. W. Holmes
Lord of every land and nation	123	Robert Robinson
Lord, Thy glory fills the heaven	340	Mant
Mine eyes and my desire	75	Watts
My God, my King! Thy various praise	344	Watts
O Christ! our hope, our heart's desire	113	Chandler (from Latin)
O Christ! our King, Creator, Lord	88	Ray Palmer
O Christ, the Lord of heaven! to Thee	116	Ray Palmer
O for a shout of joy	332	J. Young
Of the Father's love begotten	304	Neale and Baker (from Latin)
O God, beneath Thy guiding hand	274	Leonard Bacon
O God, the Rock of Ages	3	E. H. Bickersteth
O God! we praise Thee, and confess	332	Tate (from Latin)
O Holy! holy! holy! Lord	148	J. W. Eastburn
O Holy, holy Lord!	Creation's	317	Anonymous
O Lord Most High, Eternal King	102	Neale (from Latin)
O Lord our God! arise	295	Wardlaw
O One with God the Father	310	How
O Savior, precious Savior	82	Frances R. Havergal
O Thou above all praise	348	Montgomery
O Thou essential Word	301	Catherine Winkworth (fr. Ger.)
O Thou whom we adore	290	Charles Wesley
Our children Thou dost claim	405	(Anonymous)
Our God! our help in ages past	314	Watts
Our Helper, God! we bless Thy Name	6	Doddridge
Our sins, our sorrows, Lord, were laid on Thee	94	Eddis
O worship the King, all-glorious above	328	Robert Grant
Planted in Christ, the living Vine	375	S. F. Smith
Praise to God, immortal praise	274	Anna L. Barbauld
Praise to Thee, Thou great Creator	345	John Fawcett
Rise, glorious Conqueror, rise	136	Bridges
Savior! who Thy flock art feeding	405	Muhlenberg
See Israel's gentle Shepherd stand	402	Doddridge
See, the Conqueror mounts in triumph	139	Christopher Wordsworth
See the ransomed millions stand	292	Conder
Spirit of power and might, behold	143	Montgomery
The heavens declare Thy glory, Lord	320	Watts
The Lord Jehovah reigns,	And royal state	342	Watts
The praise of Zion waits for Thee	337	Watts
The promise of My Father's love	377	Watts
Thou art the everlasting Son	90	(Anonymous, from Latin)
Thou Father, Son, and Holy Ghost	362	Tate and Brady
Thy Name, Almighty Lord	322	Watts
To Thee, O God, we raise	344	A. T. Pierson
Triumphant, Lord, Thy goodness reigns	334	Doddridge
Welcome, happy morning	98	Ellerton (from Latin)
Witness, ye men and angels now	377	Beddome
Worship, honor, glory, blessing	330	Osler
Worthy art Thou who once wast slain	105	Watts

www.ingramcontent.com/pod-product-compliance
Lightning Source LLC
Chambersburg PA
CBHW032137010526
44111CB00035B/594